FINANCIAL STATEMENT ANALYSIS

An Integrated Approach

PETER M. BERGEVIN

Valdosta State University

Upper Saddle River, New Jersey 07458

Library of Congress Cataloging-in-Publication Data

Bergevin, Peter M.
    Financial statement analysis : an integrated approach / Peter M. Bergevin.
        p. cm.
    Includes bibliographical references and index.
    ISBN 0-13-032534-1
        1. Financial statements. I. Title.

HF5681.B2 B447 2002
657'.3--dc21   2002031245
                                                                        CIP

Acquisitions Editor: Thomas Sigel
Editor-in-Chief: PJ Boardman
Assistant Editor: Kasey Sheehan
Editorial Assistant: Fran Toepfer
Media Project Manager: Nancy Welcher
Marketing Manager: Beth Toland
Marketing Assistant: Brian Rappelfeld
Managing Editor (Production): John Roberts
Production Editor: Renata Butera
Production Assistant: Diane Falcone
Permissions Coordinator: Suzanne Grappi
Associate Director, Manufacturing: Vinnie Scelta
Manufacturing Buyer: Arnold Vila
Design Manager: Pat Smythe
Designer: Kevin Kall
Interior Design: Karen Quigley
Cover Design: Blair Brown
Cover Illustration: Blair Brown
Cover Photo: Apple Computer, Inc.; A. Ramey/PhotoEdit; Union Pacific Railroad Museum; Michael Newman/PhotoEdit; Richard Megna/Fundamental Photographs; Fotopic/Omni-Photo Communications, Inc.
Illustrator (Interior): Karen Quigley
Manager, Print Production: Christy Mahon
Composition: Elm Street Publishing Services, Inc.
Full-Service Project Management: Elm Street Publishing Services, Inc.
Printer/Binder: Courier, Kendallville

Credits and acknowledgments borrowed from other sources and reproduced, with permission, in this textbook appear on appropriate page within text.

10 9 8 7 6 5 4 3 2 1
ISBN 0-13-032534-1 (Student)

Dedicated to Linda, Jillian, and Matthew

BRIEF CONTENTS

CONTENTS

CHAPTER 2

INFORMATION MANAGEMENT 23

CHAPTER 3

THE FINANCIAL STATEMENTS 61

CHAPTER 4

FINANCIAL STATEMENT COMPARABILITY 82

$\mathcal{C}$HAPTER 5

DATA DISCLOSURES 100

$\mathcal{C}$HAPTER 6

FINANCIAL STATEMENT INFLUENCES 118

$\mathcal{C}$HAPTER 7

REPORTING REQUIREMENTS 136

CHAPTER 8

INTRODUCTION TO SHORT-TERM LIQUIDITY ANALYSIS 157

$\mathscr{C}$HAPTER 9

ADVANCED SHORT-TERM LIQUIDITY ANALYSIS 182

$\mathscr{C}$HAPTER 10

INTRODUCTION TO CASH FLOW ANALYSIS 202

CHAPTER 11

ADVANCED CASH FLOW ANALYSIS 223

CHAPTER 12

OPERATING PERFORMANCE ANALYSIS 243

CHAPTER 13

ASSET UTILIZATION ANALYSIS 270

CHAPTER 14

CAPITAL STRUCTURE ANALYSIS 296

$\mathscr{C}$HAPTER 15

VALUATION AND FORECASTS 321

PREFACE

Welcome to the world of financial statement analysis! Financial statements contain numerous disclosures about business performance. Analysts convert that data into useful information. Why would anyone want to undertake such a job? The answer is simple: to improve decision making. *Financial Statement Analysis: An Integrated Approach* helps you make better economic choices and assist others in that task.

Corporate financial statements summarize business transactions in a relatively neutral manner. Analysts must tap into those unbiased reports and assign meaning to them. You learn how to mine rich veins of corporate disclosures and turn them into a mother lode of knowledge by using this text. It trains you to analyze historical results, interpret current operations, and forecast future performance.

I wrote this text for the beginning analyst. You only need to understand basic business principles and the workings of a personal computer to master its contents. It builds on those skills in a structured manner, instructing you how to thoroughly analyze financial statements. Moreover, this text teaches you how to supplement financial statements with other information sources, thereby providing the context necessary to produce valid analyses.

You will learn financial statement analysis in an exciting environment. This book's integrated nature, vivid examples, participatory format, and strong visual orientation actively engage you in a vibrant learning atmosphere.

DISTINCTIVE ATTRIBUTES

Financial Statement Analysis: An Integrated Approach contains a number of distinctive features that enable you to master this important business discipline. It emphasizes the art as well as the science of financial statement analysis. The book systematizes facts, principles, and methods, along with developing your perception, creativity, and resourcefulness. This text's unique approach to financial statement analysis strengthens comprehension of the subject matter, enlivens the material, and separates it from the competition. We now examine a number of its learning features.

PRACTICAL APPLICATION

This book favors practical application over theoretical discussion. It focuses on the "how to do it" and "what does it mean" aspects of analysis. As an important part of this philosophy, you become an active participant in the learning process. You analyze important issues and use the Internet to find information in every chapter. Real-life examples abound. An analysis of the personal computer (PC) industry, presented throughout the text, illustrates key learning points. End-of-chapter assignments pack a practical punch! Five integrated case studies complement the PC analysis. All of these case studies use existing industry and corporate data as inputs for analysis and decision making. In addition, the book guides you in updating your analysis via the Internet.

IN-CHAPTER FEATURES

Financial Statement Analysis: An Integrated Approach contains an array of exciting features that enliven analysis. Intriguing financial statement discussion items appear in every chapter. **What's Your Analysis?** sidebars require you to think about topical issues and answer stimulating questions about the subject matter. Shorter **vignettes** also appear throughout the book. The text's **Micro Analysis** segments briefly illustrate important financial statement considerations and provide additional links to the existing business world. **WEB exercises**, yet another in-chapter feature, capitalizes on the power of the Internet to sharpen your research skills and makes the subject matter timelier. Questions posed and tasks required in the **What's Your Analysis?, Micro Analysis,** and **WEB exercise** features help you learn the material in a refreshingly nontraditional manner.

COMPREHENSIVE ORIENTATION

Data drive analysis and information result from research. Numerous information sources amplify and clarify financial statement numbers. Analysts use a broad array of information to reach conclusions and make decisions. This text embraces this broad-based approach to financial statement analysis. In addition, it teaches you how to access needed information, rather than assuming you know how to find sources or letting you inefficiently discover them on your own. The conceptual research framework, presented in the second chapter of the book, explains the research process. Its accompanying appendix presents an extensive list of information sources and other reference material. These sources reflect life as we know it, emphasizing electronic data sources over their print medium counterparts.

This book teaches you much more than how to manipulate income statement and balance sheet numbers. We examine how political, regulatory, economic, financial, managerial, marketing, and accounting considerations influence financial statement disclosures to develop background needed to understand financial statement disclosures. By doing so, you learn to relate financial disclosures to their underlying commercial activities, the real stuff that makes business so exciting and dynamic.

The best analysts possess common sense, an inquisitive nature, an understanding of the world, broad business knowledge, and outstanding research abilities. These skills lend context to the content contained in a company's financial statements. This textbook stresses a holistic approach to financial statement analysis. It focuses on gathering and interpreting sufficient information to reach logical conclusions. Analysts must be able to make technical adjustments to financial statements, but they must also know how to conduct research and draw inferences from the data. *Financial Statement Analysis: An Integrated Approach* embraces the philosophy of favoring approximately correct analysis, rather than running the risk of being exactly incorrect. If you do not possess research skills and a logical mind, you can get a very precise and correct answer to the wrong question. You will achieve the ability to be approximately, and often times, exactly correct in your analysis by studying the material in this textbook.

FLEXIBLE APPEAL

Financial statements are scorecards of economic performance. All business majors and professionals must know how the commercial world keeps score and how to interpret those results. This book is written for individuals who want to know what every aspect of the financial scorecard means. It is an appropriate textbook for diverse groups of financial statement analysts. The text provides sufficient depth to challenge individuals well versed in finance and accounting, yet the text's user-friendly manner benefits individuals pursuing less quantitative careers in management and marketing. Your ability to make good economic decisions will improve, regardless of your career path, by studying the material in this text.

Information about numerous industries allows you to develop expertise in one or more areas of interest. The plentiful corporate disclosures in the appendixes offer you the opportunity to analyze past financial statements without unduly burdening you with the computational drudgery that often accompanies an introduction to financial statement analysis. Rest assured, however, that the book's discussions and assignments ensure your computational competency. In addition, the Internet industry assignments leverage knowledge obtained from the industry case studies and the numerical exercises to enhance your quantitative and analytical abilities.

INTEGRATED LEARNING SYSTEM

Financial Statement Analysis: An Integrated Approach tells an interrelated story. Its cohesive format facilitates comprehension and makes learning more enjoyable. Integration takes place on four levels throughout the text. Each integrated learning level builds on the previous ones to broaden and deepen your understanding of analysis.

eXTREMESTUFF.COM

The first level of interrelated material lays the groundwork for analysis. We examine a hypothetical Internet startup company to illustrate business formation, financial reporting, and analytical procedures. You will learn basic analysis by studying material presented about eXTREMESTUFF.com's first two years of business. Financial statements for additional years serve as the basis for Numerical Case assignments at the end of many chapters. Those assignments ensure computational competency and reinforce the basic objectives of analysis.

PERSONAL COMPUTER INDUSTRY

Personal computer (PC) companies' disclosures introduce you to realistic analysis. We devote specific attention throughout the text to four personal computer manufacturers. The financial statements of Apple Computer are benchmarked against three other prominent PC companies: Compaq, Dell, and Gateway. Analysis of Apple and the industry follows the eSTUFF discussions.

The integrated case approach analyzes the personal computer industry in a realistic but stable learning environment. Economic information and industry conditions supplement corporate financial statements in this integrated case approach. In other words, the case approach freezes economic activity over a discrete time period. Studying the events and results of PC industry from 1993 to 1998 strengthens your analytical abilities and enables you to continue evaluating this fascinating industry to the present day.

ANALYSIS OF OTHER INDUSTRIES

The integrated case approach is also the foundation for this text's third integrated learning activity. Airline, athletic footwear and apparel, discount retail, fast-food restaurants, and soft drink industry data appear in appendices to the book. Those disclosures provide inputs for Industry Case assignments, which parallel the PC industry's analysis. You will improve as an analyst by assessing one or more of these industries.

REAL-TIME LEARNING

The historical data of the Industry Cases enable you to develop your analytical skills; desktop technology empowers you to unleash your knowledge. You enhance the relevance of the case studies by accessing recent financial disclosures online. You can then incorporate that information into each industry's analysis. The Internet Industry Case assignments guide you in this task and round out the integrated learning approach.

TERMINOLOGY AND ADDITIONAL CONSIDERATIONS

The business world is complex and disorganized. Corporate financial statements reflect the less than orderly reality of commercial activities. This book clarifies and simplifies financial disclosures to facilitate learning. I standardized financial statements in certain instances to maintain comparability within industries. While numerically accurate, these disclosures do not precisely match the historical corporate disclosures in every example, and they could differ from the corporate disclosures that you will find as you explore the Internet.

This book assumes that fiscal years coincide with calendar years, except for the discount retail industry. Fiscal years end on January 31 for Kmart, Target, and Wal-Mart; therefore, Appendix D's yearly disclosures precede the fiscal year end by one month: 1998 disclosures represent the fiscal period ending January 31, 1999, 1997 financial statements equal a January 31, 1998 fiscal year end, and so on.

Inconsistent reporting periods skew analysis in three instances. Dell Computer's fiscal year ends in January, but its three competitors (Apple, Compaq, and Gateway) close their books at or towards the end of the calendar year. Nike ends it business year in May, but Reebok reports through December. Delta Air Lines' June 30 fiscal year does not match the December 31 business year-end of American or United. I did not adjust the disclosure periods for Dell, Nike, or Delta. Their 1998 financial statements, for example, represent reporting periods ending on January 31, 1998, May 31, 1998, and June 30, 1998, respectively.

American, Delta, and United are full-service air carriers. In addition, American owns and consolidates its travel technology segment, the Sabre Group, in its financial statements. Neither Delta nor United has a comparable segment. Data were available for American Airlines' Airline Group (its passenger and cargo services), and they are disclosed in Appendix B. Consequently, confusion could exist if you assign Internet Industry Cases because American's consolidated financial statements would not coincide with the Appendix material. One solution is to eliminate American from the analysis and have your students compare Delta with United.

We use a number of terms interchangeably throughout this book, although they have slightly different meanings. Many of them relate to financial items and knowledge constructs. Financial reporting, for example, usually refers to the financial statements. Financial disclosures represent the financial statements and other corporate data (e.g., management's discussion and analysis). Financial information connotes monetary data from all sources available for analysis. The distinction among financial reporting, disclosures, and information is somewhat arbitrary, and the book refers to them interchangeably.

Subtle knowledge distinctions also exist. Data are qualitative or quantitative disclosures, devoid of meaning. Information represents something of value to an analyst. Knowledge comes from understanding the information. In other words, information represents the meanings and interpretations attached to the data, and knowledge synthesizes the information. The lines between data, information, knowledge, and occasionally, wisdom blur. Consequently, this book treats these terms synonymously.

Public corporations' financial disclosures are available to everyone, but financial statements for privately held concerns are confidential. This book assumes data accessibility; consequently, it analyzes disclosures of companies whose stocks are publicly traded. In this text, all references to enterprises, entities, businesses, companies, and firms pertain to public corporations. Analytical techniques, however, are applicable to non-public entities.

ACKNOWLEDGMENTS

This first edition of *Financial Statement Analysis: An Integrated Approach* is truly a team effort. I am grateful to the many colleagues, students, Prentice Hall employees, and family members whose efforts, comments, and suggestions made this book possible.

I would like to thank the following faculty reviewers for their contributions:
Shyam B. Bhandari—*Bradley University*
John S. Bildersee—*New York University*
K. Michael Casey—*Henderson State University*
Charles Caliendo—*University of Minnesota*
Janet Kimbrell—*Oklahoma State University*
Robert Lin—*California State University–Hayward*
Brenda Mallouk—*University of Toronto*
Ida Robinson-Backmon—*North Carolina A&T State University*
Mike Ruble—*Central Washington University*
Vickie Ruble—*Lyndon, Washington*
John R. Simon—*Northern Illinois University*
John Theis—*The University of Texas of the Permian Basin*
Frank Tuzzolino—*Thunderbird–The American Graduate School of International Management*
Larry Wiggs—*Mesa Community College*

Numerous colleagues at Valdosta State University also helped with this book's publication. Dean Ken Stanley of the Langdale College of Business Administration supported the project from its inception. Accounting and Finance faculty members Bruce Caster, Leisa Marshall, and Karin Roland contributed material to the text. David Scott eagerly shared his extensive knowledge about book publishing with me. Bill Buchanan extensively reviewed the book and provided many useful suggestions. Becky Tracey, the department's senior secretary, helped with innumerable tasks, both large and small. Associate Dean Kent Moore and John Oliver, Head of the Management Department, provided non-accounting/finance perspectives. An eager and willing group of students at Valdosta State helped "crunch numbers." My thanks to Amy Bailey, Donna Deas, Jonathan Fuller, Carlton Greenway, Denise Hall, William Jones, Mary Kurtz, Jonathan Lewis, Melissa Rogers, Jennifer Suddeth, Kristy Thigpen, Rochelle Waldron, and Rebecca Wells. Ricanne Birchmore of Valdosta effectively prepared the book's charts.

I am very grateful to the wonderful people at Prentice Hall for all of their help. Editor-in-Chief P.J. Boardman provided me with the forum to write a new type of financial statement analysis text. Acquisitions Editor Thomas Sigel tirelessly guided me through every step of the journey and became a friend in the process. Many thanks to Renata Butera, Fran Toepfer, Kasey Sheehan, and Beth Toland for their assistance. Mei Lynn D'Alessandro deserves special thanks for introducing me to the many benefits of writing for Prentice Hall. I am also grateful for the help of Jenny Wood and Marilyn Stone at Elm Street Publishing Services, Inc.

In many ways, the Bergevin family wrote this book. My wife Linda provided technical assistance from the beginning along with constant support and motivation. My daughter Jillian supplied the inspiration, and my newborn son Matthew lent his sunny smile. In addition, my brother Glenn kept me grounded in the "real world" and audited the appendix material; my mother Dorothy served as my "unofficial editor;" and my dad Raymond taught me to do my best.

ABOUT THE AUTHOR

Peter M. Bergevin is a Professor and Head of the Department of Accounting and Finance at Valdosta State University's Langdale College of Business Administration where he teaches financial statement analysis, financial accounting, and international accounting. Prior to heading the department at one of Georgia's two regional universities, Pete was an Associate Professor of World Business at Thunderbird—The American Graduate School of International Management; Assistant Professor of Accounting at the University of Nevada, Las Vegas; and Assistant Professor of Business of Administration at Trinity University in Texas.

Dr. Bergevin received his Ph.D. in Accounting from Arizona State University. Since that time, he has authored numerous articles in the areas of statement analysis, financial accounting, and business education. His works have appeared in *The Journal of Lending & Credit Risk Management, The Journal of Commercial Bank Lending, The International Executive, and The Journal of Accounting and Finance Research.* In addition, the *Case Research Journal, Business Case Journal,* and the *Journal of Accounting Education* have published his cases on financial statement analysis.

Pete has taught and lectured in Mexico, New Zealand, and Europe. He enjoys traveling, renovating homes, reading about history and current events, and following sporting activities. Pete hopes his beloved Red Sox win a World Series before you finish reading this book, but he knows that won't happen. Despite his fascination with analyzing the personal computer industry, he struggles to get his PC to do what he wants it to do on a daily basis. Pete resides in Valdosta, Georgia with wife Linda, daughter Jillian, son Matthew, three dogs, and two horses.

1

INTRODUCTION TO FINANCIAL STATEMENT ANALYSIS

$\mathscr{C}$HAPTER LEARNING OBJECTIVES

Upon completion of this chapter, you should be able to:

◆ *Understand the decision emphasis of financial statement analysis and why a comprehensive approach is needed to meet this objective.*

◆ *Indicate who uses financial statements and how they use them to make decisions.*

◆ *Show the importance of generally accepted accounting principles (GAAP) to analysis, which organizations determine GAAP, why GAAP differs among countries, and the benefits of harmonizing GAAP.*

◆ *Determine the various concepts of capital maintenance and attributes of asset measurement.*

◆ *Articulate the benefits and limitations of the nominal dollar capital maintenance concept and historical cost valuation in financial reporting and analysis.*

◆ *Explain how inconsistent terminology, data volume, transaction complexity, information variability, and financial statement limitations can affect financial statement analysis.*

*A*nalysts separate something whole—an engine, a manufacturing process, a football team, a presidential election, or a financial statement—into its parts. They then examine the elements to find out their nature, proportion, function, and interrelationship. The analytical method provides insights about how the entirety operates, where it came from, and where it is going.

Financial statement analysis is the art and science of examining the components of a company's monetary disclosures, called **financial statements.** People form opinions about a firm's past, present, and future operations based on their analysis. These beliefs guide their own actions and influence others who rely on their recommendations. Decisions result: choices people make in allocating their financial resources.

OBJECTIVE

The objective of this book is to help you learn how to analyze financial statements.[1] It aims to help you develop your ability to critically evaluate corporate financial representations and related information. Chapter 1 begins this process by addressing four factors: The chapter begins by presenting the requirements for a comprehensive analysis. Next, we turn to analysts' objectives. The third section covers the standards that govern financial disclosures, and finally, we address disclosure challenges.

COMPREHENSIVE ANALYSIS

Financial statements communicate a firm's economic events to interested readers. They do so in aggregate form by summarizing an entity's dealings with people, organizations, processes, and things. In order to analyze this highly abstracted set of data, the analyst must understand the influences on financial statements and how to obtain information about those factors.

WEB **EXERCISE 1**

Go online to www.Apple.com and examine Apple Computer, Inc.'s financial statements. Click on "Hot News," locate "About Apple," and click on "Investor Information." Search "SEC Filings" for "Form10-K" and scroll through the most recent year's Form 10-K until you locate "Item 8, Financial Statements and Supplementary Data." Examine its contents.

BUSINESS ENVIRONMENT

Analysts must understand the overall economy, legal environment, political climate, and cultural context in which a company does business. They also have to consider a company's industry and its competition when judging financial performance. Such insights require knowledge of business strategies, managerial policies, information systems, productive capabilities, labor relations, distribution networks, and marketing channels, even though many of these factors exceed the scope of the financial statements. Analysts must answer such questions as these:

---

[1] This book views financial statement analysis from a broad perspective. Anyone who uses financial statement data to make decisions is considered a financial analyst or financial statement analyst for the purposes of this text. In a narrower sense, a financial analyst is an individual with expertise in evaluating financial investments with an emphasis on determining the risk and reward characteristics of stocks and bonds. See, for example, D. L. Scott, *Wall Street Words* (Boston: Houghton Mifflin, 1997), p. 145.

WEB
EXERCISE 2

Explore hoovers.com, zacks.com, and thomsoninvest.net for examples of Internet sites that can assist in your analysis.

◆ How sensitive are the company's activities to changes in economic conditions?
◆ Are there any legislative or regulatory initiatives pending that will affect business?
◆ Is the industry in which the company competes emerging, growing, or mature?
◆ Who are the firm's key competitors?
◆ Are management and the workforce well trained?
◆ Is the company planning any product introductions or market penetrations?

These questions cannot be answered by directly examining a company's financial statements; yet, such events have influenced previous corporate disclosures and affect their forecasts. Therefore, the analyst needs to develop a comprehensive perspective when analyzing financial statements, or risk making poor judgments and bad decisions.

DATA SOURCES

A broad-based approach to financial statement analysis requires a breadth of information. The analyst must locate and use a variety of current and historical data sources to supplement the financial data supplied by the company. Suppose, for example, you wanted to forecast earnings. Corporate income numbers are disclosed in the financial statements, so you might start with these data to construct an earnings trend line. Previous trends, however, do not guarantee future results. Economic conditions, market shifts, competitor initiatives, and managerial decisions also affect future earnings. You must consider these factors, and others like them, in a comprehensive earnings forecast.

WEB
EXERCISE 3

Examine "Item 7, Management's Discussion and Analysis of Financial Conditions and Results of Operations" for Apple Computer's most recent Form 10-K to read about management's thoughts on Apple's future.

Data come in many forms, are found in many places, contain various benefits, and have different costs. Moreover, information is fluid. One need only look to the Internet for evidence of the changing information landscape. Information can either be primarily numerical or verbal; it also contains various degrees of objectivity and subjectivity. Market share data gathered by an independent party, for example, are more reliable than those presented by someone with a vested interest in the company. Management's interpretation of those numbers is more subjective and qualitative than the market share data themselves. Analysts can find value in all of these information sources, provided they adjust for existing biases.

WHAT'S YOUR ANALYSIS

ANALYSTS' ETHICS

Financial analysts often release *research reports*, which provide potential investors with the analyst's opinion about a company. Relatively unknown firms crave research reports because they seek publicity. Other companies oppose these opinions; their managers fear that analysts may cast them in a negative light. Consider the ethical implications in the contrasting cases of Telesoft Corp. and First Union Bank.

Telesoft Corp. is a small telecommunications firm based in Phoenix, Arizona. It is not well known to investors. ComVest offered to provide a research report on Telesoft in exchange for ownership considerations.° The Dallas, Texas, securities firm speculated that its research report would add $15 per share to Telesoft's current $5 market price. In exchange for providing such a research report, ComVest proposed receiving stock warrants in Telesoft, which would enable the securities firm to purchase 100,000 shares of the company's common stock at $5.50 per share. Telesoft declined the offer. "Exchanging warrants for research was unequivocally the wrong way to go," according to Michael Zerbib, chief financial officer of Telesoft.[b]

A financial analyst's research reports affected First Union Bank of Charlotte, North Carolina, differently. First Union used the services of the investment-banking firm Bear Stearns to raise capital in the long-term debt market. The Wall Street investment bank earned over $10 million annually for its services to the North Carolina regional bank. Then a prominent analyst at Bear Stearns issued a critical assessment of First Union's operations and management. First Union responded by removing its bond-trading business from Bear Stearns, allegedly, because of the negative report.[c]

In Telesoft's case, the company lacked a credible favorable financial analysis; conversely, First Union was saddled with a negative one. ComVest proposed a financial analysis to solve Telesoft's dilemma, but Bear Stearns may have lost business due to its financial analysis of First Union.

Observations

As someone interested in financial analysis, how would you evaluate the ethical behavior of the parties involved in each of the two cases?

---

[a] C. Gaprarino, "Starved for Attention, Small Companies 'Buy' Wall Street Coverage," *Wall Street Journal*, July 14, 1999, pp. A1 and A10.
[b] Ibid, p. A10.
[c] R. Brooks, "Analyst's Silence on First Union Isn't Accidental," *Wall Street Journal*, August 17, 1999, pp. C1 and C4.

ANALYSTS' OBJECTIVES

People analyze corporate financial statements for various reasons. Seven groups of financial statement users exist: equity investors, credit granters, corporate managers, merger and acquisition specialists, internal and external auditors, regulators, and corporate employees. We now explore the objectives of each group.

The Coca-Cola Co.'s mission is "To maximize share-owner wealth over time." This mission statement embodies the orientation of all companies and their owners.

EQUITY INVESTORS

Equity investors are the ultimate risktakers. As business owners, their wealth increases when a company prospers, and it shrinks when the firm falters. They supply the risk capital that protects other stakeholders' investments in the firm. As such, they legally own the business, and the corporation is obligated to protect their interest. As shareholders, equity investors claim a *residual* interest in the assets of the company; they earn a return on their investment only after the other stakeholder claims have been satisfied.

Shareholders, like all people, try to improve their financial standing. They do so when corporations use their resources to the fullest extent possible in generating cash. Stock prices reflect the relative success of a company's cash-generating efforts.[2] The objective of equity investors, therefore, is to devise investment portfo-

---

[2] See, for example, A. C. Shapiro and S. D. Balbirer's discussion of wealth maximization in Chapter 5 of *Modern Corporate Finance: A Multidisciplinary Approach to Value Creation* (Upper Saddle River, NJ: Prentice Hall, 2000).

lios that maximize wealth, subject to an acceptable level of risk. They analyze financial statements to assist in that task.

The market in which investors purchase new, as opposed to existing, shares of stock are sold is called the *primary market.* In most instances, however, equity investors don't buy stock directly from a company; they purchase shares from other equity investors in *secondary markets.*[3] Regardless of where they acquire ownership, equity investors analyze financial statements and related information to build wealth. They evaluate corporate cash-generating abilities by using current and historical data. Equity investors seek answers to such questions as these:

◆ Will corporate actions increase the present value of future cash distributions?
◆ How much cash does the core business activity generate?
◆ What are the long-term earnings prospects of a company?
◆ Is a company financed primarily with equity investments or borrowed funds?
◆ How does a company being analyzed compare with its competitors?

Equity investors are influenced by theories that developed in the last half of the 20th century. In the 1950s, *portfolio theory* provided a framework for evaluating investment risks and rewards.[4] In the next decade, the *capital asset pricing model (CAPM)* extended portfolio theory.[5] The CAPM quantifies the price of risk and formally specifies the relationship between risk and reward. Following this, the *efficient market hypothesis* states that stock prices fully reflect all publicly available information.[6] According to this hypothesis, excessive rates of returns cannot be earned through financial analysis. This might lead one to ask, "Why should equity investors analyze financial statements?" Equity investors do so for the following reasons:

◆ Their efforts ensure market efficiency.
◆ They realize positive, if not excessive, rates of return, because companies create wealth over time.
◆ Some of them think they can beat the market.
◆ They need to value privately held enterprises.
◆ People often pay them for their opinions.

CREDIT GRANTERS

Creditors analyze financial statements to assess the probability of prompt and complete loan repayment. They make loans for both short and long periods of time. **Short-term creditors** finance current business operations. A manufacturer trading with a merchant, for example, establishes reasonable certainty of repayment before extending goods on credit to the retailer. Most vendors know their customers; consequently, they have little need for formal financial statement analysis for short-term trade credit arrangements.

---

[3] Financial intermediaries, such as the New York Stock Exchange, facilitate these *secondary* or *after* market transactions.
[4] See, for example, H. A. Markowitz, "Portfolio Selection," *Journal of Finance,* March 1952, pp. 77–91.
[5] One example of CAPM is W. F. Sharpe's, "Capital Asset Prices: A Theory of Market Equilibrium under Conditions of Risk," *Journal of Finance,* September 1964, pp. 425–442.
[6] A summary of this hypothesis is contained in E. F. Fama's "Efficient Capital Markets: A Review of Theory and Empirical Work," *Journal of Finance,* May 1970, pp. 383–417.

Long-term creditors finance major projects, such as building construction and machinery acquisitions. These lenders spend considerable resources analyzing an applicant's financial statement. Credit analysts evaluate the financial disclosures to determine a loan applicant's debt service capability. They investigate a number of factors in doing so, including credit history, outstanding obligations, and cash flow projections. Lenders protect their investment by formalizing loan contracts, collateralizing them, and establishing protective covenants.[7]

Capital structure, the relative proportion of an entity's liabilities and equity, influences lending decisions. Analysts attempt to determine whether additional debt will enable an entity to leverage borrowed funds into incremental cash flows or prove too great of a drain on corporate resources. Equity financing, therefore, represents a margin of safety to creditors. A credit analyst judges the adequacy of a company's safety margin before lending it money.

CORPORATE MANAGERS

Managers are business professionals who operate the firm for the owners' benefit. As corporate employees, their duty is to maximize corporate share price through the productive and prudent use of the entity's assets. Managers seek to add value to the enterprise through their efforts. Inefficient management creates a **value gap**, or the difference between the firm's worth if it were optimally managed and its actual value.

Managers use financial statement information to control and plan corporate activities. These disclosures help them formulate business strategies, product offerings, and marketing initiatives. Operating executives monitor resource utilization and seek ways to improve it using financial statement data. Corporate data also help managers identify, explain, and remedy differences between financial performance and budgeted expectations.

A potential problem exists because managers control the flow of a firm's financial information. They are charged with supplying relevant and reliable financial information to corporate outsiders, but as insiders, they have greater access to information. However, managers should not capitalize on their inherent information advantage. They have a **fiduciary duty**, or an obligation to protect equity investors' interests, in running the firm. Like shareholders (and most people, for that matter), managers want to maximize their wealth. Investors and managers contract to protect their respective self-interests. Financial statements can assist in these contracting arrangements.[8]

MERGERS AND ACQUISITION SPECIALISTS

Merger and acquisition (M&A) specialists attempt to increase shareholder value through corporate realignment. They benefit from the fees they receive for their services. These specialists continually search for undervalued companies—firms whose true worth exceeds their market price. In other words, they try to find

---

[7] Covenants protect the lender's claim by mandating that the borrower's financial position remain in approximately the same conditions that existed at the inception of the loan.

[8] The study of the field of contracting agreements between owners and managers is known as agency theory. For a discussion of this theory see H. I. Wolk and M. G. Tearney, *Accounting Theory: A Conceptual and Institutional Approach*, 4th Ed. (Cincinnati: South-Western, 1997), pp. 42–44.

value gaps in one or both parties to a prospective business consolidation. A successful merger or acquisition decreases gaps in value and helps maximize shareholder wealth. Financial statement analysis assists these analysts in determining whether the companies are worth combining. Data analysis, for instance, could reveal operating inefficiencies, product duplications, or overlapping markets. A business combination could reduce costs or increase revenues, thereby unlocking shareholder value.

Merger and acquisition specialists often make numerous adjustments to the financial statements when valuing a firm. They make these corrections to better account for market value; again, this indicates the limitations inherent in financial statement disclosures and the need for supplementary information. As other types of financial analysts do, M&A specialists seek the most relevant information possible when deciding whether to combine separate entities.

INTERNAL AND EXTERNAL AUDITORS

Internal auditors assess corporate operations, and external ones render an opinion about the accuracy of an entity's financial statements. Auditors employed by an entity ensure compliance with corporate policies, measure performance, and recommend operating improvements. Independent certified public accountants express an opinion about the fairness of a company's financial statements. Both auditing groups analyze financial statements in performing their jobs. For example, internal auditors use financial statement ratios to measure asset utilization. External auditors document those assets' existence and confirm their ownership in attesting to the accuracy of management's assertions about them.

Not only do auditors evaluate financial statements in doing their jobs, but their opinions also influence other analysts' judgments. Managers base many decisions on internal audit reports, and external stakeholders rely on independent audit opinions. Poor audits can cause incorrect and costly decisions. Consider a company that appears profitable, according to its financial statements, and as such, it continually receives clean audit opinions. The glowing financial statements, however, resulted from fraudulent financial reporting, and the audit failed to detect the deceit. In reality, the company is bankrupt! Precious resources could be squandered on a nonproductive enterprise.

REGULATORS

Many government agencies analyze financial statements as part of their regulatory duties. **The Securities and Exchange Commission (SEC)**, for example, administers U.S. securities laws. The commission's charge is to ensure that investors and creditors receive full and fair disclosure about corporate activities. Corporations file many forms with the SEC to that end, and commission analysts monitor the extent to which entities comply with securities laws.

The *Internal Revenue Service (IRS)* also uses financial information. This agency's analysts judge taxpayer compliance with the Internal Revenue Code. For example, the IRS's *net worth analysis* determines if a taxpayer's standard of living coincides with his or her reported net worth, as determined by an assessment of an individual's financial statements.

Government analysts help regulate specific industries. Bank regulators, for example, rely on financial statement information to ensure that financial institutions are adequately funded and customers' investments are protected. Analysts work for such agencies as the Federal Reserve System, the Office of the Comptroller of the Currency, and state banking commissions. Government analysts also help regulate other industries, such as insurance, communication, and transportation.

CORPORATE EMPLOYEES

MICRO NALYSIS 8

General Electric Co.'s American labor unions consist of 34,000 workers or 10 percent of its global labor force. The terms of the contracts these unions negotiated with the company in 2000, however, were extended to the other 163,000 American nonunion General Electric employees.

Employees analyze corporate disclosures to improve their bargaining position with management. Workers seek wage and benefit adjustments, often on the basis of financial data, when negotiating a contract. A labor union, for example, could cite record earnings, large management bonuses, and higher compensation packages at similar firms to justify salary demands. Financial disclosures that measure worker productivity, such as the amount of operating cash flow generated per employee, are also bargaining tools. Negotiating is a two-way street, however. Companies also use financial disclosures to buttress their position in contracting with employees.

As with the other categories of financial statement users, employee analysts benefit from accurate and timely representations of corporate performance. Although the specific content and procedures differ among analysts, they all use publicly disclosed data in order to make better decisions. Presenting a true and fair picture of corporate performance is the goal of financial reporting; making sense of those disclosures is the job of financial analysts.

REPORTING STANDARDS

Authoritative pronouncements and accepted conventions influence financial statement disclosures. Analysts must understand these **generally accepted accounting principles (GAAP)** in order to interpret financial statements. These standards provide a common ground for analysis. We discuss the key aspects for setting these standards in the following sections.[9]

WEB EXERCISE 5

Go to www.sec.gov to find out about the SEC and to www.fasb.org to learn about the FASB.

A COLLABORATIVE PARTNERSHIP

Financial statement principles provide a basis for measuring, valuing, and comparing economic activity. These standards ensure consistent disclosure over time and permit meaningful comparisons among companies. Commercial, economic, legal, cultural, social, political, and educational factors have all influenced their development. Some principles have haphazardly evolved; others were deliberately created. Moreover, reporting principles change over time, as business practices and the user needs shift. Analysts need to remember that financial reporting standards are human contrivances, not immutable laws of nature!

A working relationship between the public and private sectors determines the authoritative standards that constitute GAAP. The federal government's SEC has legal authority to set accounting standards, but it has generally ceded that task to a private organization, the **Financial Accounting Standards Board**

---

[9] This section of Chapter 1 discusses financial reporting orientation and the rule-making process. Chapters 6 and 7 address specific accounting principles.

MICRO ANALYSIS 9

High-tech firms opposed FASB's proposed revisions for reporting business consolidations because they viewed the proposal as harmful to their acquisitions strategies.

(FASB).[10] The SEC reviews GAAP as part of its regulatory responsibilities. The SEC often influences the FASB by taking a position on unresolved financial reporting issues. The collaborative effort between the SEC and FASB has produced many accounting principles that constitute the backbone of financial reporting.

Reporting standards affect corporate profitability and financial position; consequently, many of the principles are quite controversial. However, despite some dissatisfaction, the public/private partnership succeeds, for the most part, in producing timely and detailed financial reporting standards. These rules have contributed to efficient capital markets, the mechanism by which economic resources are allocated.

FINANCIAL REPORTING STANDARDS

The FASB succeeded the Accounting Principles Board as the private sector rule maker in 1973. The existing organization's membership is more diverse than its predecessor, which was dominated by public accountants. Businesspeople, financial executives, and educators have all served on the board. The FASB's standard-setting authority extends to corporate financial statements, accompanying notes, and supplementary disclosures. The board establishes GAAP primarily through its Statements of Financial Accounting Standards. It also interprets existing standards, issues technical bulletins, and addresses emerging business practices. Statements of Financial Accounting Concepts influence FASB's standards. Those conceptual guideposts provide the theoretical underpinnings for its decisions.

WEB EXERCISE 6

Nasdaq.com, nyse.com, and amex.com provide information about NASDAQ, the New York Stock Exchange, and the American Stock Exchange, respectively. Go to each Web site.

THE INTERNATIONAL DIMENSION

Throughout the world, GAAP varies, complicating financial statement analysis. Analysts must distinguish between substantive economic differences and ones that result merely from different disclosure methods—a challenging task. Multinational enterprises must conform to various interpretations of GAAP. A publicly traded company reports according to the standards where its stock is listed.[11] Firms traded on the New York Stock Exchange, for example, must adhere to the United States' GAAP, regardless of where they are headquartered.

In some instances, the differences in accounting treatments among nations are rather minor, but in other cases, they can be quite pronounced. Language, cultural, legal, and economic similarities account for comparable financial reporting disclosures. In the United States and the United Kingdom, for instance, GAAP are quite similar. And the reporting standards for many European countries are similar to one another but differ markedly from those of the United States and United Kingdom. For instance, German and French standards are part of the European Model of financial reporting.[12] Exhibit 1-1 differentiates the two financial reporting models.

Commerce has rapidly evolved into a global marketplace, and financial reporting must keep pace with the growth of multinational enterprises. One means of doing so is through the efforts of the **International Accounting**

---

[10] Accounting Series Release No. 150 of the SEC, *Statement of Policy on the Establishment and Improvement of Accounting Rules,* effectively yielded financial reporting standard setting to the FASB.

[11] In general, this statement is true, although some countries allow compliance with another nation's GAAP or international standards.

[12] See, for example, R.D. Nair and W. G. Frank, "The Impact of Disclosure and Measurement Practices on International Accounting Classification," *The Accounting Review,* July 1980, pp. 426–439.

CHARACTERISTIC	ANGLO-AMERICAN MODEL	EUROPEAN MODEL
Economic emphasis	Market based	Government influenced
Primary source of financing	Stock markets	Banks
Legal basis	Common law	Codified Roman law

WEB EXERCISE 7

Go to the IASC's Web site at www.iasc.org.uk/.

Standards Committee (IASC). The objective of this committee is to harmonize financial reporting standards. Unlike FASB and other national standard-setting bodies, the IASC cannot require use of its GAAP. Some countries accept International Accounting Standards and require companies to comply with them. The IASC tends to have the most influence on accounting standards in developing nations. It is unlikely that international body will replace the FASB as the primary U.S. financial reporting authority. The U.S. board views itself as the premier financial standard–setting body in the world, the one that has produced the best set of in-depth financial reporting standards.

Perhaps the greatest contribution of the IASC is its effort to reduce reporting differences among countries. This has led to more comparable financial statements, improved comparative financial analysis, and more efficient allocation of financial resources. Most agree that financial statement analysts would benefit from more uniformity among GAAP.

WHAT'S YOUR ANALYSIS

CORPORATE FINANCING

American corporations have broader ownership bases than companies domiciled in other parts of the world. The shares of stock in U.S. companies tend to be controlled by many different individuals and groups; equity investments in other countries, however, reside in the hands of fewer people and organizations. How do you analyze the differences?

Corporate ownership by banks in the two largest economies in the world demonstrates the difference. Japanese banks own 75 percent of the corporate equity of Japanese companies with whom they have a working relationship. But in the United States, only 25 percent of all equity is owned by financial institutions.[a] The type of debt carried by U.S. companies also differs from that of its global competitors. A World Bank study found that total bank loans made to U.S. companies equaled 50 percent of the nation's gross domestic product, but banknotes equaled 150 percent and 170 percent of the respective gross domestic products for Japan and Germany. The corporate bond market, in contrast, equaled 110 percent of American output, but only 75 percent and 50 percent of the gross domestic product for Germany and Japan, respectively.[b]

Such structural differences affect many aspects of financial reporting and analysis. For example, GAAP in the United States place a far greater emphasis on fully disclosing corporate activities in the financial statements than the financial reporting rules do in most European and Asian countries. Because of the diversity of debt and equity financiers in the United States, such protection is needed for those investors. In Germany and Japan, however, the disclosures are not as extensive due to the close working relationship between the companies and their banks. In other words, GAAP in a specific country reflect the business orientation of that country.

Bank financing is often referred to as *patient* financing and lending, whereas nonbank equity and debt is known as *impatient* financing. Because American firms tend to be financed with impatient capital, the companies and their analysts are usually very interested in short-term results. Analysts tend to place a great emphasis on the earnings per share of the current quarter and even more weight on the forecast of the next quarter's earnings. This short-term view is captured in the axiom that a management is only as good as its current and expected quarterly earnings. Consistent with their patient capital perspective, German and Japanese companies, and their analysts, consider a much longer time horizon when evaluating financial performance.

Observations
Discuss whether equity analysts would be as concerned about the current stock price of a German or Japanese company as they would be about the market value of a U.S. entity. How do you think the growth of multinational corporations will affect analysis?

---

[a] A. Murray, "New Economic Models Fail While America Inc. Keeps Rolling; Why?" *Wall Street Journal*, December 12, 1997, pp. A1 and A14.
[b] Ibid.

DISCLOSURE CHALLENGES

Diligent research yields powerful insights about present and future corporate performance, but less than perfect information complicates the task. There are constraints and biases inherent in any data set. The final section of this chapter addresses two concerns: capital maintenance selection and information complexities.

CAPITAL MAINTENANCE SELECTION

Two qualitative reporting characteristics influence financial disclosures. Analysts value **relevant information,** which helps them predict the future and provides feedback about the past. They also want **reliable information,** which consists of unbiased and verifiable data. These two qualities conflict at times; consequently, GAAP are not always effective in capturing both relevance and reliability in every financial statement disclosure.

The extent of relevant and reliable information depends on the financial reporting system's means of maintaining capital. Financial statements are reported on the basis of a specific type of investment assumption, called **capital maintenance.** This concept measures the amount of an investment that must be recovered through revenues before income is earned. At issue is what constitutes an investment. To illustrate, assume a merchant sold one computer during a reporting period. It cost $1,000 and was sold for $1,500. The cost of replacing the computer decreased to $800 during the reporting period. General price levels increased by 10 percent from the time the computer was purchased until it was sold. Is profit $500, $700, or $400?

The **nominal dollar concept of capital maintenance** underlies the U.S. system of financial reporting. Consequently, the merchant's income is $500 ($1,500 − $1,000) under current GAAP. The company, however, is a going concern, and it must replace its inventory on an ongoing basis. An argument could be made that the profit is $700, or the $1,500 selling price less the $800 replacement cost. This method of reporting maintains capital on the basis of physical units. Profit could also be $400, or $1,500 in sales revenue less the inflation-adjusted cost of the computer $1,100 (i.e., $1,000 * 1.10). This income reflects capital maintained in general purchasing power terms. Although theoretically sound, the physical units and general purchasing power concepts of capital maintenance violate GAAP.

Asset valuation methods are related to capital maintenance concepts. The **historical cost** principle governs resource measurement within the nominal dollar concept of capital maintenance. This value is only one of many measurable asset attributes; others are replacement cost, selling price, and liquidation value. These measures contain economic value, but GAAP do not require their disclosure.

Consider a company that owns $1,000 in cash. It discloses that amount of money as an asset on its balance sheet. You would probably agree the financial disclosure represents economic reality. It is both relevant and reliable; moreover, the dollar's historical, replacement, and liquidation values equal one another. Now assume the company uses a two-year-old computer in running its business. How should the firm measure this asset? GAAP dictate using historical cost less some adjustment for depreciation. The dollar value you arrive at, however, depends upon a number of assumptions: the expected life of the computer, the method used to calculate depreciation, and its scrap value.

MICRO
ANALYSIS 10

Many countries in South America have experienced hyperinflation, with general price levels increasing over 100 percent per year. Does adhering to the nominal dollar concept of capital maintenance make sense for South American companies?

MAJOR LEAGUE REPORTING

Generally accepted accounting principles favor reporting assets and liabilities on the basis of past exchange prices, or historical cost. Major League Baseball, however, differs from GAAP when it comes to a financial reporting basis. Baseball puts a different spin on the ball when it comes to valuing resources and obligations. How would you umpire baseball's pitch?

A 1982 guideline enacted by the franchises of America's pastime emphasizes market values over historical costs. The *60-40 rule* requires that each team maintain $60 of assets for every $40 of liabilities.[a] Assets and liabilities, however, are not defined in accordance with GAAP. A team's asset base equals its appraised market value, and its liabilities include total player payroll and all deferred salaries. For example, if the Boston Red Sox have a current and deferred payroll of $100 million and other obligations of $150 million, then the team must have a current market value of at least $375 million to comply with the 60-40 rule. Market values can and do change dramatically in a short period of time. For example, winning the World Series, announcing a new taxpayer-financed ballpark, securing a more lucrative television and radio broadcast contract, or signing a superstar could each serve to increase the market value of a team.

In general, appraised asset valuations are not permitted under GAAP. External financial reporting conventions consider market values harder to verify and more likely to be manipulated than historical exchange prices. Moreover, salaries incurred in the current reporting period are business expenses; as such they only become liabilities if they are unpaid. In GAAP's view, baseball strikes out!

Observations
Baseball's valuation of its assets and liabilities raises many analytical questions:

◆ Do you agree with GAAP's contention that market values are less reliable than historical costs?

- ◆ Does this view prevail in all instances?
- ◆ How could fair values be more relevant than historical exchange prices for decision-making purposes?
- ◆ How would allowing either historical costs or market values to serve as the basis for financial reporting affect financial statement analysis?

ᵃ "Getting Fiscal: 60-40 or Fight," *Sports Illustrated,* December 21, 1998, pp.119–120.

The historical cost valuation of the computer provides reliable data, but are they relevant? You might ask the following questions as you examine the reported value of the computer on the balance sheet: What if the computer's **book value** (i.e., historical cost minus depreciation) does not equal its

- ◆ market value?
- ◆ replacement cost?
- ◆ cash-generating ability?
- ◆ economic value, based on what you *think* it is worth?

Remember the statement earlier in the chapter that M&A specialists need to adjust financial statements to estimate the economic worth of a firm.

Answers are unimportant right now. They do illustrate, however, the difficulties analysts encounter when valuing assets.

The financial reporting system measures selective aspects of multidimensional economic events. An analyst must be aware that financial statements contain incomplete data and expand his or her information sources to compensate for this limitation.

INFORMATION COMPLEXITIES

Five obstacles inhibit a financial analyst's quest for complete understanding of corporate activities: inconsistent terminology and format, data volume, transaction complexity, information variability, and financial statement limitations.

Terminology and financial statement format vary among analysts and companies. These inconsistencies confuse and inhibit analysis. For instance, individuals who own a company can be referred to as stockholders, shareholders, equity investors, or owners. Similarly, terms such as fixed assets; long-term assets; plant and equipment; tangible assets; capital resources; productive assets; property, plant, and equipment; and land, buildings, and machinery all denote long-term economic resources.

Managing divergent terminology depends on grasping the common characteristics of a reported item, irrespective of its name. For instance, long-term productive resources meet the definition of that asset class. They have the following characteristics:

- ◆ Future economic benefits
- ◆ Currently controlled by the company
- ◆ A result of a past transaction
- ◆ Tangible
- ◆ Capable of producing revenues over multiple reporting periods

Generally accepted accounting principles remain silent with respect to the format of the financial statements. There isn't a single correct arrangement for the income statement or balance sheet. Some companies report detailed financial statements, but others provide only aggregate data.

Data volume concerns many fledgling analysts. At first, an analyst may wonder if enough information exists with which to conduct an analysis. The problem quickly takes an ironic twist. There are too much data! The problem is one of information overload. An analyst must filter information for relevance and reliability. The company being analyzed, their disclosures to the SEC, media stories and government reports about the entity provide a staggering array of information. And the Internet makes these disclosures, and other information, available with a few keystrokes and mouse clicks!

Analysts also have to contend with transaction complexities. Disclosure reflects business. As commerce becomes more complicated, so do corporate disclosures. Consider wages and salaries. Wages expense is not a complicated disclosure when a company pays all of its employees an hourly wage. However, many firms, especially in the high-tech industry, supplement employees' salaries with options to buy their company's stock at a set price. If the entity prospers, market prices rise, and employees increase their wealth by exercising their options. Reporting stock-based compensation is more difficult than reporting hourly salaries. Significant questions exist about the financial statement impact and disclosure requirements for stock options. In addition to acknowledging existing reporting complexities, analysts must realize that the world of commerce is fluid: New business methods emerge constantly.

Information sources vary in worth: Some are good, and some are bad. Misleading, untimely, and false information abounds. Bad information taints analysis; researchers must identify it and then ignore it. Sources, by their nature, are biased. For example, management reports corporate financial statements and makes other disclosures; consequently, these reports, although audited, lack a certain degree of objectivity. Analysts should not infer faulty or fraudulent reporting but rather take into account that, like all people, managers want to be viewed favorably.[13] Augmenting management information sources with independent data reduces management bias.

Financial statements are limited in their disclosure capabilities. Many items are hard to quantify. Human capital, for example, goes unreported as an asset. Companies cannot buy people; they can only compensate them for their services. People, however, do matter, and they produce revenues and cash flow. Bill Gates is an invaluable asset to Microsoft, and it doesn't take financial analysis to know that Michael Jordan's retirement hurt the Chicago Bulls! Management quality, intellectual capital, employee morale, reputation, and strategic positioning are also unreported or underreported, but items affect financial performance and must be considered in an analysis.

WEB

EXERCISE 8

Examine Apple Computer's "Stock-based Compensation" footnote following the financial statements in its most recent Form 10-K.

SUMMARY

Equity investors, credit granters, corporate managers, M&A specialists, internal and external auditors, regulators, and corporate employees analyze financial

---

[13] Such behavior is an example of agency conflict.

statements. Each group of analysts has specific reasons for doing so. Regardless of the objective, all analysts convert corporate, industry, and economic data into useful information. They make decisions on the basis of the information and their analysis of it.

Financial statements conform to GAAP. In the United States, these standards are set by the FASB in conjunction with the SEC. All financial statement data are limited and incomplete, due to information complexities, including the use of a single capital maintenance concept, inconsistent terminology, complex business transactions, reporting variability, and the lack of a way to quantify nonfinancial information such as human capital.

This chapter states that good data, diligent research, and creativity produce good financial statement analyses. Chapters 2 through 15 develop these themes. The discipline is as much an art as it is a science!

KEY TERMS

Book value
Capital maintenance
Capital structure
Equity investors
Fiduciary duty
Financial Accounting Standards Board (FASB)
Financial statement analysis
Financial statements
Generally accepted accounting principles (GAAP)
Historical cost
International Accounting Standards Committee (IASC)

Long-term creditors
Managers
Merger and acquisition (M&A) specialists
Nominal dollar concept of capital maintenance
Relevant information
Reliable information
Research reports
Short-term creditors
Securities and Exchange Commission (SEC)
Value gap

INTRODUCTORY NOTE TO END OF CHAPTER ASSIGNMENTS

Industry Cases (IC), Industry Internet Cases (IIC), Conceptual Cases (CC), and Numerical Cases (NC) constitute end-of-the-chapter assignments throughout this book. Industry Cases and Industry Internet Cases require analysis of six industries (listed following). Conceptual Cases cover a variety of topics, industries, and companies. Numerical Cases relate to eXTREMESTUFF.com, a hypothetical retailer used to demonstrate analytical procedures. This material is introduced in Chapter 3. Not all chapters contain all types of cases

Industry Cases require analysis of six industries from 1993 through 1998. Industry overviews and corporate financial statement data are contained in Appendixes A–F of this text. Industry Internet Cases require you to access current financial statement data for the companies listed at their Web sites. You can find Internet addresses in the *Resource Guide* that accompanies Chapter 2.

The industries and their companies are as follows:

Personal Computer Industry (Appendix A)
Apple Computer, Inc., Compaq Computer Corp., Dell Computer Corp., and Gateway, Inc. (The PC industry overview is presented in Chapter 5, along with a review of economic conditions from 1993 to 1998.)

Airline Industry (Appendix B)
American Airlines, Delta Air Lines, Inc., and United Air Lines, Inc.

Athletic Footwear and Apparel Industry (Appendix C)
Nike Corp. and Reebok International, Ltd.

Discount Retail Industry (Appendix D)
Kmart Corp., Target Corp., and Wal-Mart Stores Inc.

Fast-Food Restaurant Industry (Appendix E)
McDonald's Corp. and Wendy's International, Inc.

Soft Drink Industry (Appendix F)
The Coca-Cola Co. and PepsiCo.

INTERNET INDUSTRY CASES

Examine the most recent Form 10-K for each company within an industry and find the following items:

a. Complete name of the company
b. Address and telephone number
c. Date of the end of its fiscal period

1-1   *Personal Computer Industry*

1-2   *Airline Industry*

1-3   *Athletic Footwear and Apparel Industry*

1-4   *Discount Retail Industry*

1-5   *Fast-Food Restaurant Industry*

1-6   *Soft Drink Industry*

CONCEPTUAL CASES

1-1

Analysis of Financial Statements: Investors, Employees, and Employers

United Airlines became the largest employee-owned company in the world as a result of a corporate recapitalization in 1994. The shareholders of UAL Corp. (United's parent company) granted 55 percent ownership of the company to its pilots, machinists, salaried staff, and managers in exchange for wage and benefit concessions. To effect the recapitalization, the company purchased the old company stock and issued new ownership shares in their place to United's employees as well as to the previous owners.

United's salary structure motivated the recapitalization of the air carrier, according to many industry analysts. The air carrier's wages were formulated when the federal government regulated the industry. Such government involvement enabled airlines to recoup their operating costs through set ticket prices during that era. Industry deregulation in the late 1970s and early 1980s, however, resulted in market-based ticket prices and spurred formation of new airlines. These newer companies paid wages determined by the marketplace, which resulted in substantially lower salaries than those paid by United.

To compensate for the salary imbalance between United and its competitors, employees agreed to exchange wages for equity shares in the airline. After incurring net losses for three consecutive years, United returned to profitability in 1994, the year of its recapitalization.

a. Explain which group(s) of financial analysts United's employees belonged to before and after the recapitalization of the airline.
b. As a result of the recapitalization, did the employees' objectives in analyzing United's financial statements change?
c. Assume you are a nonemployee investor in United. Explain your motivation for allowing United's employees to become majority owners of the air carrier.
d. Assume you are an employee of United. Explain your motivation for accepting shares of stock in exchange for reductions in salary and benefits.
e. Is United's return to profitability attributable to its recapitalization?

1-2

Securities Analysts and Equity Investors

McDonald's Corp. experienced lackluster financial performance and a lagging stock price in the late 1990s. Part of the problem, in the opinion of some securities analysts, was substandard product quality. These analysts felt that the company's uninspired menu hindered corporate profitability. Consequently, those analysts were not recommending acquisition of the Golden Arches' stock to their clients.

The company introduced a new cooking technique in 1999 in an attempt to improve product quality. The fast-food giant's Just for You kitchen system involves cooking hamburgers to order, rather than making sandwiches prior to customer purchases. The company took a bold step to convince securities analysts of its commitment to improved product quality. Company management proposed that the analysts work a shift at a McDonald's restaurant. Over 100 financial analysts accepted McDonald's offer and experienced how the Just for You system operates. Many securities professionals cited the firsthand opportunity to experience the change in McDonald's as the reason they took the company's challenge.

a. Do you think the analysts-as-workers plan served any real purpose, or was it just a publicity stunt?
b. A company's products, prices, placement (location), and promotions influence their financial statement performance. Which one of the "Four P's" contributed to McDonald's poor performance, in the analysts' opinion?
c. List some information contained in financial statements that would indicate whether the Just for You system benefited McDonald's. Name another source, apart from the financial statements, that would reflect similar information.

Creditors and a Financial Statement Analysis Technique

Financial institutions increasingly evaluate applicants' ability to repay loans with credit-scoring models. Lenders construct statistical measures with financial and demographic inputs. The resulting credit-scoring model assists them in forecasting a loan applicant's debt-paying ability. Loans are awarded to applicants whose point totals meet or exceed a cutoff point and denied to those who fall below it.

Applicants provide the lender with economic and personal information when applying for a loan. Lenders then feed these data into the credit-scoring model, which awards points based upon the applicants' responses. For example, an individual with income stability receives more credit-scoring points than a loan candidate with earnings variability. Lenders then sum up points from each category to determine if the applicant achieves the needed point total.

a. Assess whether credit-scoring models make the lending process more objective, more efficient, and fairer.
b. Do you think such models eliminate the need for lender judgment in granting loans?
c. Discuss whether credit-scoring models lessen the need for lenders to analyze financial statements.

Business Liquidation

Hechinger Co. decided to go out of business to "maximize value for its creditors," according to a statement released by the company. The home-improvement retailer continually lost market share to bigger rivals, such as Home Depot and Lowe's, during the 1990s. Hechinger initially tried to reorganize its operations under federal bankruptcy protection laws, which would have allowed the company to rearrange loan terms with its creditors. Management eventually decided, however, that the company would be unable to continue as a going concern. The company cited "continued losses and stiff competition" as the reasons for shutting down operations.

Hechinger liquidated the business by selling the assets of its 117 stores. Cash from the sale was used to partially satisfy creditor claims against the company. Investors did not realize any cash from Hechinger's corporate liquidation.

a. Do you think Hechinger's creditors improperly analyzed the company's financial statements before extending credit to the firm?
b. Did Hechinger's shareholders improperly analyze the company's financial statements before investing in the firm?
c. Explain why cash generated from Hechinger's liquidation was used to retire debts rather than return the owners' investment in the company.
d. Discuss how financial statement analysis could have assisted management in determining that liquidation would "maximize creditor value."

Merger and Acquisition Financial Statement Analysis

The food industry annually sells $450 billion worth of merchandise to American supermarkets. The industry is going through a transition period, due to changes in operating conditions. These events have led some M&A specialists to speculate that certain food manufacturers will take over weaker firms.

Before changes began to occur in the industry, food companies realized healthy profits from increased product demand, constant price hikes, cost-cutting measures, and favorable sales terms with the fragmented supermarket industry.

Things began to change in the mid-1990s, however. Population shifts and consumption changes dampened overall demand for food industry products. Price-sensitive customers began buying store-labeled products instead of brand names. Food companies reduced costs to the extent possible, but significant additional reductions soon became unattainable. Supermarket chains acquired other grocers or merged with them. These business combinations enhanced the food retailers' bargaining power with food manufacturers.

Some M&A specialists believe consolidation of food makers is inevitable. The increased efficiencies of the larger companies, according to these analysts, will improve the remaining firms' financial performance. Takeovers, which tend to reduce jobs and combine management positions, however, are often not well received. Such is the case in the food industry. Bestfoods, for example, opposed consolidating its Skippy peanut butter and Hellman's mayonnaise brands with those of another food company. According to Bestfoods' chief executive officer, Dick Shoemate, "The best protection from a takeover is to be getting the maximum out of your assets."

a. Food industry consolidation could result in greater industry efficiency, according to some financial statement analysts. Cite three types of gains that could be realized by combined food companies.
b. List specific ways in which you think a merged entity's financial performance could be measured.
c. Explain the rationale underlying Mr. Shoemate's comment that using assets effectively could prevent a takeover.

1-6

Business Ethics and Financial Statement Disclosures

Varity Corp., a manufacturer of machinery and automotive parts, evolved from the Massey-Ferguson farm equipment company. Agricultural implements proved to be a drain on profitability during the early 1980s; therefore, the company decided to focus on the automotive segment of the business. As a result of this strategic decision, Varity created Massey Combines Corporation (MCC) as an independent entity. Many Varity workers were enticed to work for MCC. Workers received notice under the Project Sunshine campaign, which stated, "When you accept employment with Massey Combines Corporation (a Varity spin-off) . . . benefits programs will remained unchanged. . . . We are all optimistic that our new company has a bright future."

Five thousand Varity employees went to work for MCC. The combine company had net worth of negative $46 million (i.e., its liabilities exceeded assets by $46 million) when operations began in 1986. MCC declared bankruptcy by the end of 1988 and liquidated its assets shortly thereafter. Varity discontinued health care benefits to MCC employees upon dissolution of the company, citing a provision in its health plan that stated, "The company hereby reserves the right, by action of the board, to amend or terminate the (health) plan or trust at any time."

a. Assume you worked for Varity prior to the MCC spin-off. Explain how financial statement analysis could have influenced your decision to accept employment with MCC.
b. Do you think a negative net worth at the beginning of business operations destined MCC to failure?
c. Discuss whether Varity Corp. acted ethically in its Project Sunshine campaign and its treatment of MCC employees.

Management Compensation

American Airlines did not pay its executives any bonuses for the 1999 fiscal year. The parent company of American, AMR Corp., cited the air carrier's failure to meet financial goals as the reason for denying its managers additional pay beyond their salaries. American's substandard financial performance was evidenced by the company's decrease in profitability: It was down $325 million from 1998.

A primary reason for the decline in income was a ten-day pilot *sick-out*, which caused cancellation of thousands of flights. The work slowdown resulted from a labor dispute when American Airlines purchased regional Reno Air. The pilots at the smaller airline were paid less than their American Airlines counterparts at the time of acquisition. The Allied Pilots Union wanted pay increases for the new American employees. Management denied the request, and the sick-out ensued. Court decisions eventually forced the pilots back to work.

a. Give a reason why investors, who seek to maximize their wealth, would choose to reduce corporate profits by paying bonuses to corporate executives.
b. Discuss the importance of financial statements in determining management bonuses.
c. Explain how financial statement analysis could have helped management determine whether to give in to the pilots' demands or let them walk off the job.
d. How could financial statement analysis have assisted the pilots in determining whether to call for a sick-out?
e. Managers should use corporate resources productively and prudently in their capacity as agents of the owners. Were American's executives negligent in safeguarding the air carrier's assets by allowing the sick-out?

Market Efficiency and Financial Statement Analysis

An apparent paradox often exists when companies announce their quarterly earnings. Firms that report net income sometimes realize stock price decreases, but market values can increase for firms that report net losses during a three-month period.

Investors' expectations explain this seemingly inconsistent behavior. Financial statement analysts forecast quarterly earnings for publicly traded companies. Companies, such as First Call/Thompson Financial, compile these analysts' forecasts. Investors then incorporate the predictions forecasts into corporate stock prices, prior to the companies' release of earnings numbers. The release of earnings numbers do not move stock prices, but market values fluctuate to the extent that announced earnings deviate from expected ones. Stock prices tend to remain unchanged when actual corporate earnings meet forecasts, increase when they exceed them, and decrease when earnings fall short of analysts' expectations.

a. Assess the following statement: "There is no need to undertake financial statement analysis because earnings forecasts already exist."
b. What information besides previous quarters' financial statement disclosures influence analysts' quarterly forecasts?
c. Discuss whether the stock market's response to earnings forecasts and announcements makes sense in light of the efficient market hypothesis.

U.S. and Foreign Generally Accepted Accounting Principles

Foreign companies' corporate financial statements must comply with, or be reconciled to, the United States' GAAP in order for their stock to be traded on American stock exchanges. The FASB favors continuing this rule. Wall Street investment banking houses and the stock exchanges, however, back a movement that would allow foreign companies to list on American exchanges provided they comply with International Accounting Standards.

The FASB cites lack of clarity, detail, and completeness in international standards as reasons why it opposes compliance with foreign GAAP for foreign firms. They view those who favor international GAAP as promoting their interests ahead of good financial reporting. The FASB and its supporters contend stock exchanges and investment bankers want to generate more foreign businesses, regardless of whether it diminishes financial disclosure content.

a. Present an argument that proponents of international GAAP could use to rebut FASB's contentions.
b. What benefits would financial statement analysts realize if foreign companies were listed on U.S. stock exchanges?
c. Do you see a problem in comparing the financial statements of a domestic company, which complies with the United States' GAAP, and a foreign company, which complies with international GAAP?

1-10

Foreign Companies' Financial Statements

Philips N.V., an industrial conglomerate based in the Netherlands, manufactures products such as consumer electronics, communications equipment, domestic appliances, medical systems, and semiconductors. The company reported its financial statements in Dutch guilders, the Dutch national currency, until the late 1990s. Philips began reporting its financial statement in the new currency of the European Union at the turn of the century. This union of nations promotes European economic integration, and its European Monetary Unit (or euro) has been replacing the national currencies of member nations.

Befitting its home country, Philips' financial statements comply with Dutch GAAP. Some reporting variations exist between Dutch and U.S. GAAP. Apart from specific technical differences under the two methods, Dutch GAAP allows financial reporting under generally *acceptable* accounting principles, rather than the United States' generally *accepted* accounting principles. Given this reporting latitude, Philips made disclosures that maintained capital on the physical units basis, rather than in nominal dollars.

a. Assume you are comparing Philips's financial statements with those of an American company. What impact does Philips's reporting in guilders (or euros) have on your analysis?
b. Would the company's monetary change from guilders to euros affect your analysis?
c. Describe how Philips's compliance with Dutch GAAP would hinder comparative financial statement analysis with an American firm.
d. Explain how Philips's disclosures made on the basis of the physical units concept of capital maintenance would affect your comparative analysis.

1-11

Financial Reporting and Capital Maintenance

Capital maintenance theory influences financial statement disclosures, including reported profits. Most financial reporting systems, including the American one, assume an entity maintains its capital in nominal dollars. The difference between the historical cost of resources and their selling price determines income under this concept of capital maintenance. Changes in general price levels (inflation or deflation) and the cost of the specific items being sold are not considered in nominal dollar income determination. Adjusting financial statements for overall or specific price changes in goods and services produces different income levels than those resulting from the nominal dollar concept.

Prices for most goods and services increased throughout most of the 1980s and 1990s. In contrast, in the PC industry, which emerged during that time period, costs actually decreased: Technological innovations and intense competition reduced raw material, component, and finished product costs. Consistent with the nominal dollar concept of capital maintenance governing financial reporting, companies such as Apple, Compaq, Dell, and Gateway did not adjust their financial statements to account for changing prices.

a. Explain why the nominal dollar concept of capital maintenance prevails in financial reporting.
b. List the two alternatives to the nominal dollar concept of capital maintenance.
c. Discuss the premise underlying each of these two alternative capital maintenance theories.
d. Would each of those alternative concepts produce more or less profit for a PC company during the latter part of the 20th century?

1-12

Inconsistent Financial Statement Disclosures

Apple Computer, Inc.'s long-term economic resources appeared to double from 1994 to 1999: The company reported $159 million of property, plant, and equipment in the earlier period and $318 million five years later. However, the company's disclosure of these assets differed in those two reporting periods. The company made fuller financial statement disclosure in 1994 than in 1999. Apple reported four categories of fixed assets in 1994: land and buildings, machinery and equipment, office furniture and fixtures, and leasehold improvements. In 1999, the company reported a single category—titled property, plant, and equipment.

a. Which of the two fixed asset disclosures would a financial analyst find more informative?
b. Speculate on Apple Computer's motivation for reducing its fixed asset disclosure over time.
c. Assume an analyst found Apple Computer's 1999 financial statement disclosure of fixed asset disclosure inadequate. Discuss strategies for supplementing the disclosure.

2 INFORMATION MANAGEMENT

CHAPTER LEARNING OBJECTIVES

Upon completion of this chapter, you should be able to:

◆ *Find and use the information necessary to conduct a thorough financial statement analysis.*

◆ *Explain the benefits of categorizing information as economic, industry, or corporate type; rely on information experts; use a decision model; and construct information matrices.*

◆ *Describe why benchmarking a company's financial statements is vital to analysis.*

◆ *Indicate the importance of Securities and Exchange Commission disclosures to analysis and access them via the EDGAR database.*

$\mathcal{F}$inancial statement analysis is a learning process. Analysts gain perspective over time, through effort, and with information. This chapter can't help you with the first two parts of the process, but it can teach you about managing information. Financial statements are a necessary but insufficient data set from which to form opinions about corporate performance and wealth. You must complement them with other data sources. Analysts use a variety of information about a company, its competitors, their industry, and the economy when making decisions and recommendations.

Research methods, sources, and insights are interrelated knowledge builders, the necessary ingredients for good financial statement analysis. You must access data, convert them into information, and incorporate that knowledge into your analysis. In other words, research fuels information, which propels analysis. This chapter helps you meet your research and information needs in three ways. First, we present a framework for managing information. Next, we examine information categories. The final section evaluates innovations in knowledge dissemination. This chapter helps you learn how to manage data and information; you can find specific information sources in *Resource Guide,* the appendix to this chapter.

WHAT'S YOUR ANALYSIS

FIELD OF INQUIRY

Information for analysis comes from many sources. A primary one is intellectual curiosity. What message does the following story contain for analysts?

Noted physicist Richard Feynman tells a story in his autobiography about inspiration for his research.[a] One day Dr. Feynman saw some students tossing around a dinner plate like a Frisbee in the cafeteria. A Cornell medallion affixed to the plate wobbled at a different rate of speed than the plate itself. Feynman calculated the wobble ratio of the medallion to the dinner plate as two to one. When a colleague asked what the significance of the ratio was, he replied, "There's no importance whatsoever. I'm doing it for the fun of it."

Well, actually, the wobbling dinner plate did have significance. It was the start of field of inquiry and analysis that earned Dr. Feynman the Nobel Prize in physics!

Observations
Discuss why an open mind and intellectual curiosity may be of value to a financial statement analyst. How do these traits relate to the research process?

[a] R. A. Feynman, *Surely You're Joking Mr. Feynman!* (New York: Norton, 1985), pp. 157–158.

A FRAMEWORK FOR MANAGING INFORMATION

First, we examine techniques for planning, gathering, and controlling information. We then investigate information characteristics, a means of classifying data, a methodology for interacting with information experts, and a model for processing information.

INFORMATION CHARACTERISTICS

Sufficient resources exist to produce an analysis. Every good business library contains them. In addition, electronic media offer a wealth of information that is usually timelier than print sources' information. The problem is not finding enough information, but managing **information overload,** or the fact that too much data exist.[1] Moreover, much data are of dubious quality or unimportant to the task at hand. Skilled analysts use good and beneficial information and ignore the bad and irrelevant sources.

Successful forecasts and the assessment of past operations depend on valid data, which contain common information characteristics. Recall from Chapter 1 that financial disclosures should be relevant and reliable. These two qualitative characteristics also pertain to information sources. *Relevant information* contributes to and makes a difference in decisions. It helps to predict future events and provides feedback about past ones. *Reliable information* discloses events accurately. Facts are reported in an unbiased and neutral manner.

An analyst must evaluate every information source used in an analysis.[2] If a source does not improve decision-making capabilities for whatever reason, the analyst must discard it. Irrelevant and unreliable data detract from analysis and can lead to incorrect conclusions. Common sense is an analyst's best weapon. He or she should ask the following:

◆ Do I know the source?
◆ Is it reputable?
◆ Does the information contained in the source seem credible?
◆ Can I verify the information elsewhere?

If the answer is no to any of these questions, the analyst should not use the source. Ignore sources that are trying to sell a product or service or convince you of something! Information is not the intent of these outlets. After the credibility of information is established, the next step is to classify it.

CLASSIFYING DATA

The **information pyramid** is one means of categorizing data. Exhibit 2-1 shows a pyramid containing three tiers of information:

◆ *Foundation.* At the base of the pyramid, macroeconomic resources provide a context for the analysis.
◆ *Center.* In the middle section, industry data frame corporate disclosures.
◆ *Summit.* At the top level, corporate data contain company-specific information.

Economic conditions influence corporate disclosures. Information about the overall state of the economy provides context to the analysis. The middle tier of the pyramid limits data to the industry of interest. Specific conditions, characteristics, and events for a group of companies are identified at this stage of research. The pinnacle of the information pyramid represents company-specific

---

[1] The Financial Accounting Standards Board wrestles with the problem of information overload within the narrow context of the financial statements themselves. See, for example, *Statement of Financial Accounting Concepts No. 5,* "Recognition and Measurement in Financial Statements of Business Enterprises," (Stamford, CT: FASB, 1984).

[2] Gradations in relevance and reliability exist. For example, management's discussion and analysis in its Form 10-K are inherently biased, which limits their reliability; however, this section can still provide valuable information to an analyst.

EXHIBIT 2-1
Information Pyramid

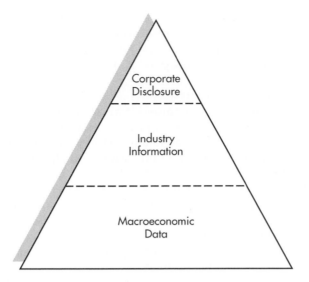

information. Corporate financial disclosures and data provided by independent sources constitute information at this level.

Note that dashed lines, rather than solid ones, separate levels in Exhibit 2-1. Information sources are not mutually exclusive. Like the economic activity they represent, data cross classification boundaries. For example, Apple Computer's business activities influence performance of the personal computer (PC) industry. Consequently, industry sources contain data about Apple, and corporate reports convey information about the PC industry. In addition, economic conditions affect the PC industries' performance, and vice versa. Macroeconomic and industry data sources report this interaction.

INTERACTING WITH DECISION EXPERTS

Basic analysis helps analysts define the industry and companies of interest. When this task has been completed, more detailed research is required. Time ultimately constrains everyone and everything; therefore, efficient research is important. Prudent analysts use all available resources to locate relevant and reliable data.

Sometimes emerging analysts neglect intellectual capital. Use people wisely. The next best thing to knowing something is knowing where to find it. The next best thing to knowing where find something is knowing whom to ask. To this end, an efficient analyst asks questions. A competent business reference librarian can provide additional information sources and expedite the research process. The flowchart presented in Exhibit 2-2 illustrates how an analyst works with a librarian to find answers.[3]

AN INFORMATION PROCESSING MODEL

Up to this point, we have examined information characteristics, classified data, and discussed research tactics. This portion of the chapter explains how to process

---

[3] Flowchart based on material from P. M. Bergevin and L. A. Miller, "Financial Statement Analysis: The Research Process in a Business Library," *Journal of Business & Finance Librarianship,* Volume 1, Number 4, 1993, pp. 49-59.

EXHIBIT 2-2
Research Inquiry Flowchart

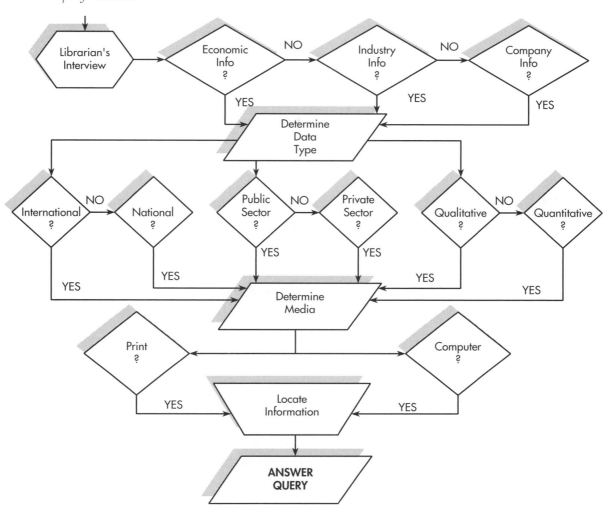

data after the information has been obtained. The **Financial Statement Analysis (FSA) Decision Model** is a systematic method for using information to make decisions. It is a repetitive, closed-looped procedure, as illustrated by Exhibit 2-3.

In the first cycle of the model (denoted by the solid lines), an analyst does the following:

◆ Gathers information related to the analysis (inputs)
◆ Analyzes the assembled set of information (process)
◆ Makes a decision or recommendation on the basis of the financial statement analysis (output)

An analysis improves by repeating the cycle as often as needed. In subsequent cycles, feedback adjusts inputs and processes (denoted by the dashed lines in Exhibit 2-3).

EXHIBIT 2-3
FSA Decision Model

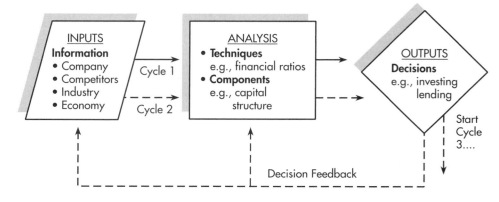

EXHIBIT 2-4
Inventory Decision Model

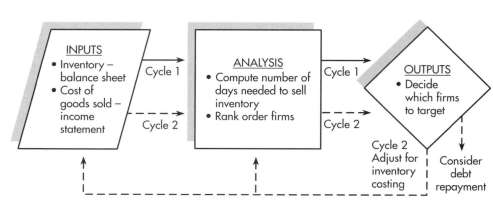

By the turn of the century, PC companies aimed to supply their resellers with about one month's worth of inventory.

Toward the end of 2000, PC resellers held an average of 11 weeks of inventory. The market prices of Apple and Compaq declined during that time. Do you think there was a connection?

Computer companies rewarded resellers with bonuses based on sales volume until the mid-1990s. So-called soft money *rewards became so great that many retailers sold PCs near cost in order increase unit sales and reap large manufacturers' bonuses.*

To illustrate the model's operation, assume you have begun to manufacture PCs.[4] You want to target merchants who can efficiently sell your PCs. You analyze a list of electronics retailers to see how quickly they move products. As a first step, financial statements are gathered and analyzed. Exhibit 2-4 presents the initial cycle of analysis.

Some companies that you eventually trade with disappoint you. They do not sell inventory as quickly as anticipated. This feedback propels the FSA Research Model. You take the following steps:

◆ *Assess feedback.* Determine that your decision needs improvement (start cycle 2).
◆ *Seek improvement.* Refine the informational inputs and analysis.
◆ *Improve your inputs.* Consider inventory-costing methods as a determinant of inventory turnover. You determine that most of your customers use the first-in-first-out (FIFO) method of valuing inventory, but some cost inventory on a last-in-first-out (LIFO) basis.
◆ *Improve your analysis.* Convert those companies reporting on a LIFO basis to FIFO-based disclosures. Recalculate the number of days data-adjusted firms need to sell inventory.

---

[4] The FSA Decision Model example is deliberately simple and somewhat unrealistic. It is presented to draw the readers' attention to the need for refining inputs, analysis, and decisions. The example is based on the concept of inventory conversion, which is presented in greater detail in Chapter 9.

◆ *Improve your output.* Select those companies that sell inventory within an acceptable time frame, based on a common method of financial reporting.

Your second decision is better than the first one, because you improved your information and analysis. It is not the end of the process, however. You certainly want to be paid for your sales. You have to evaluate debtor payment. You can further refine your decision by including this factor as a decision input and analyzing the results of the appropriate calculations.

DO THE MEANS JUSTIFY THE ENDS?

People sometimes make incorrect decisions, despite rigorous analysis. Is analysis more important than the decisions that result? Consider the timeless advice of a noted analyst of financial information, Alan Greenspan. The chairman of the Federal Reserve Board analyzes large amounts of quantitative and qualitative data in solving national and international economic problems. Greenspan's analyses command global respect. He addressed the importance of the analytical process by stating, "In analytical people, self-esteem relies on the analysis and not the conclusions."[a]

Observations
Analysts may be wrong for all the right reasons, or they could be right for all the wrong ones. Which do you think Chairman Greenspan would rather be? How about you? Discuss how meticulous research and rigorous analysis improve the odds of making good economic decisions.

_____

[a] "The Three Marketers," *Time Magazine,* February 15, 1999, p. 4.

INFORMATION SOURCES

Information about companies, industries, and the economy appears in both electronic and print media. Each type of data source and medium helps you analyze financial statements. This portion of the chapter examines the need for incorporating sources from each tier of the information pyramid into analysis, discusses organizing corporate data, and explains the need for using current information.

Branches of the federal government provide an array of macroeconomic data and links to other sources that provide them. Examine the Department of Commerce's site at *www.doc.gov* and the Department of Labor at *www.dol.gov.*

ECONOMIC CONDITIONS

Economies expand, prosper, contract, and recede on a recurring, but irregular, basis over time. These **business cycle** stages affect historic corporate performance and influence company projections. Consequently, analysts must include macroeconomic information when evaluating financial statements. An analyst should consider the following economic factors, and changes in them, when analyzing a company:[5]

_____

[5] These recommendations are based on a discussion presented by F. J. Fabozzi, F. Modigliani and M. G. Ferri in *Foundations of Financial Markets and Institutions,* (Upper Saddle River, NJ: Prentice Hall, 1998), pp. 103–111.

◆ General price levels (i.e., inflation or deflation)
◆ Unemployment rate
◆ Business cycle stage
◆ Interest rates
◆ Currency exchange rates (e.g., U.S. dollar versus the Japanese yen)

Overall price levels have increased slightly in the United States over the past two decades. During this same time period, however, the cost of PCs decreased markedly. When looking at the performance of PC manufacturers, analysts must take into account that the industry's cost structure does not reflect that of the general economy.

An efficient means of locating corporate information is to use the ticker symbol, which is the company's abbreviation for stock quotation purposes.

Go to www.hoovers.com/ to find information about the computer industry.

Look at Item 1 (Business) of Apple Computer's most recent Form 10-K at www.apple.com to determine if manufacturing and marketing PCs is a seasonal business.

An analyst frames corporate analysis with an understanding of the economy and an informed opinion of where it is headed. Business cycles do not, however, affect all industries and companies equally. Automobile revenues and income, for example, mirror business cycles. In periods of economic prosperity, such as when unemployment, inflation, and interest rates are low, car sales and profits soar. They falter in economic downturns.[6] The profits of companies in other industries do not vary to a great extent with changes in the economy. An electric utility company's earnings, for example, remain relatively stable, regardless of whether the economy is expanding or contracting.[7]

Financial statement analysis does not occur in vacuum! An analyst must understand how economic behavior influences a company and its industry. His or her efforts in this area provide context to the corporate analyses.

INDUSTRY CONSIDERATIONS

Industry research connects macroeconomic assessment to corporate analysis. An **industry** represents a specific portion or branch of economic activity. Firms within an industry offer similar products, pursue common markets, and trade with shared customers.[8] Industry knowledge provides an historical context, establishes operating conditions, and offers benchmarking data for the firms of interest. One way to understand an industry is to think of concentric circles representing shared attributes. At the outer layer is a mega-industry or an **economic sector.** Manufacturing and retail trade, for example, are traditional sectors of the economy. As the circles narrow, the common attributes increase, thereby eliminating more and more of the economic sector's firms. Ultimately, an industry emerges. Exhibit 2-5 demonstrates the circle approach to the PC industry—those companies that design, manufacture, and market PCs. Progressing toward the circle's center clarifies perception of which segment of the PC industry is being referred to, its companies, and where it fits within an economic context.

Every industry has a **life cycle** that progresses from inception, through growth, to maturity, and, ultimately, into decline. Life cycle stage influences analytical perceptions of all companies within that industry. Income and cash flows, for example, are larger in growing and mature industries than they are in newer ones. Within each life cycle stage, industries experience also relative degrees of prosperity (often correlated with macroeconomic conditions).

---

[6] The common stock of such firms is called *cyclical stocks* because corporate profits are so susceptible to changes in economic activity. Equity investors bid up (or down) the price of the stock in anticipation of the economy reaching a high (or low) level.

[7] Such stocks are countercyclical, not because the companies necessarily have their best performances in recessions, but because stock prices tend to peak during those times. They balance, or counter, cyclical stocks.

[8] Defining an industry is an inexact science. Standard industry classifications presented in the text's supplement offer the most thorough taxonomy of industries. The industries used for purposes of this text are less than strictly orthodox. We defined and selected them based on appeal to beginning analysts.

EXHIBIT 2-5
Industry Context Concentric Circle Representation

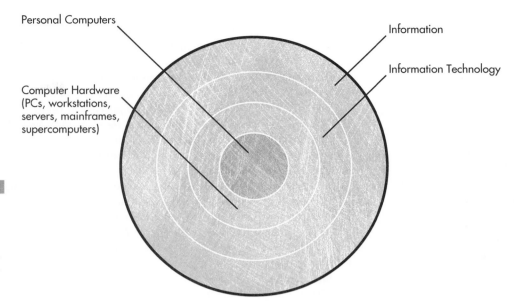

Personal Computers

Information

Information Technology

Computer Hardware
(PCs, workstations,
servers, mainframes,
supercomputers)

MICRO *A*NALYSIS 6

Some corporations cannot be classified into one industry. General Electric Co. is an example of a successful conglomerate; its diverse product line includes home appliances, jet engines, financial services, and many other goods and services.

MICRO *A*NALYSIS 7

Conglomerates such as GE are hard to benchmark. What do you compare them with? Because of their unique structure, industry norms and competitors with the same business lines do not exist. Regardless of such difficulties, conglomerates, like all companies, must be benchmarked. Creating composite industry data based on the conglomerate's business segments, or benchmarking it against an approximately similar company, provides points of comparison.

Industry information provides insight about its economic condition, which in turn affects analysis.

Industry data connect the upper and lower tiers of the information pyramid. As noted in the previous section, industry knowledge helps explain sensitivity to changes in the economic cycle. In addition, industry information helps an analyst understand the following:

◆ **Corporate trends**, such as the annual growth rate of a company's revenues
◆ **Corporate seasonality**, or the extent to which activities vary within a fiscal year
◆ **Corporate price changes**, which can mirror the overall shifts in purchasing power or be independent of the general inflation rate

Knowledge of industry and corporate performances facilitates comparisons and enriches analysis. To analyze a company, an analyst **benchmarks** it, or compares corporate performance measures against similar observations. Two common reference points are industry averages and competitors' results. Analysts create valid benchmarks by correctly defining the industry in which a company operates and identifying its competition.

WHAT'S YOUR ANALYSIS

INDUSTRY CLASSIFICATIONS

Defining industries is difficult. Here is how the federal government has dealt with the issue.

An **industry classification system** facilitates the collection, tabulation, presentation, and analysis of data relating to companies and industries. It is a logically determined system of numbering, based on various types of economic activity. Industry classification helps ensure data accuracy, uniformity, and comparability. Analysts find this system useful because many sources are referenced by industry classification code.

The United States formed the **Standard Industrial Classification (SIC)** system in 1937. The system underwent periodic changes thereafter; the last revision was in 1987. Ten major business sectors, such as manufacturing, transportation, and mining, compose the SIC. These sectors serve as the first digit in a four-digit code. The following three digits further narrow an industry. Now, however, the United States has a new industry classification system,[a] The **North American Industry Classification System (NAICS)** is in the process of replacing the U.S. SIC system.

The United States, Canada, and Mexico approved NAICS in 1997, and the system provides consistent data among these three countries. It also increases comparability with the *International Standard Industry Classification (ISIC)* system. The new six-digit code collects data on a single physical unit or establishment basis. The number of classification sectors increased from 10 to 20, more accurately reflecting changes in the economy and creation of new business types. For example, the new system identifies over 350 new industries and 9 new service sectors. Eventually, all information providers will adopt NAICS. Meanwhile, the older four-digit SIC codes are still used by many prominent information sources.

Observations

Discuss how industry classification systems assist benchmarking efforts. Explain how the eventual conversion to NAICS will help transnational financial statement analysis.

---

[a] *North American Industry Classification System* (Washington, D.C.: U.S. Department of Commerce, National Technical Information Service, 1997).

WEB *EXERCISE 4*

Find a listing of SIC codes at www.osha.gov/oshstats/sicser.html.

WEB *EXERCISE 5*

Go to www.quicken.com/, www.quote.com/, or www.quote-watch.com/. Confirm that Apple Computer's ticker symbol is AAPL.

WEB *EXERCISE 6*

Examine stock prices by going to www.dowjones.com/. Find Apple Computer's most recent stock price.

CORPORATE DISCLOSURES

Businesses engage in activities that their managers think the market values more than what the activities cost to produce. Successful efforts in this regard add **value** to the economy and increase a company's stock price. Shareholder wealth rises accordingly. Consequently, a firm that adds as much value as possible through its commercial endeavors maximizes its stock price and the wealth of its shareholders. **Shareholder wealth maximization** is the primary objective of every for-profit enterprise. All other corporate goals are less important than that of maximizing share price! A skilled analyst understands and accepts this underlying premise when evaluating a company's financial disclosures.

Companies add value to consumers through a variety of strategies, including product superiority, brand differences, pricing advantages, and distribution convenience. Their financial statements report the results of these tactics. Other corporate disclosures and noncorporate information supplement corporate financial statements. These data sources contribute to the body of information, which stock analysts and investors use to determine share price (and a company's worth).

The previous section addresses the need to benchmark corporate performance against specific competitors or the industry as a whole. For more insight on corporate performance, analysts also need to know how a company has performed over time. They use corporate data to benchmark a company against itself.

Each information source provides specific types of corporate information. Capturing those aspects in a **source and information matrix** allows an individual to quickly determine an appropriate source for a specific information requirement. Exhibit 2-6 presents an example of a source and information matrix for

EXHIBIT 2-6
Source and Information Matrix

COMPANY INFORMATION

INFORMATION SOURCE	Addresses	Directors, Officers	SIC Code/Business Type	History	Financial Statements	Financial Strength	Securities, Bonds	Subsidiaries	Market Share/Ranking	Stock Ownership	Industry
Encyclopedia of American Business									Good		
Everybody's Business				Good					Good		
Hoover's Handbooks	Good	Good	Good	Good				Good	Good		
International Directory of Company Histories				Good							
Moody's Handbook of Common Stocks		Some			Good	Good			Some		
Moody's Manuals	Good	Good	Good	Good	Good	Good	Good	Good			
S & P Corporate Records	Good	Good	Good		Good	Good	Good	Good			
S & P Stock Reports	Good				Good	Good	Good				
Industry & Trade Outlook											Good
Value Line	Good	Some			Good	Some	Good		Some		

■ Good Information   ▦ Some Information   ☐ Rarely Include

WEB EXERCISE 7

The SEC's Web site is www.sec.gov. You can access corporate disclosures through its EDGAR database. Visit the Web site to learn about the SEC and its EDGAR database.

WEB EXERCISE 8

Access Apple Computer's public disclosures through the SEC Web site. Go to www.sec.gov, click on "EDGAR Database," "Search the EDGAR Database," and "Search the EDGAR Archives." Type Apple Computer in the search box. Examine Apple's list of public disclosures. Click on Form 10-K for the most recent year. Does it contain the same information as disclosed by Apple Computer at apple.com?

some information sources listed in the chapter's appendix.[9] You are encouraged to develop your own matrices to facilitate your analyses.[10]

SECURITIES AND EXCHANGE COMMISSION FILINGS

One primary corporate information source deserves special attention: disclosures filed with the Securities and Exchange Commission (SEC). We now examine this important information source.

The Securities Exchange Act of 1934, subsequent laws, and assorted regulations require publicly traded companies to file specific reports with the SEC.[11] The most important of these reports are the following:

◆ **Form 10-K.** An annual report that contains audited financial statements, notes to the financial statements, and other financial, operational, managerial, and legal information.
◆ **Form 10-Q.** A quarterly (three-month) report similar to Form 10-K but less detailed and unaudited.
◆ **Form 8-K.** A report that provides information on material events affecting a corporation's financial condition.
◆ **Proxy Statement.** Information attached to a proxy solicitation (the written authority to act for another individual). It lists the items that a corporation will vote on, including candidates for the board of directors, salaries for officers, and the retention of an independent auditor.

[9] Adapted from "Business Information Sources," prepared by the Odum Library Staff at Valdosta State University, Valdosta, Georgia, 1999.
[10] Source and information matrices also can help classify industry and economic data sources.
[11] For a more complete discussion of the reports required by the SEC, see F. K. Skousen, *An Introduction to the SEC*, Sixth Edition, (Cincinnati: South-Western Publishing Co., 1994).

◆ **Form S-1.** A statement a company files before trading its securities on a national stock exchange. It lists the securities that will be traded as well as information about the business.

◆ **Form S-4.** A form that registers securities used to effect a business combination.

Analysts rely heavily on these publicly available forms and others required by the SEC. Form 10-K is especially informative. It contains a wealth of background information as well as a company's audited financial statements. Moreover, these reports are readily available through the **SEC's Electronic Data Gathering, Analysis, and Retrieval System (EDGAR)** database as well as at most companies' Web sites.

Corporations usually provide an annual report to their shareholders in addition to Form 10-K.[12] In fact, these glossy-covered shareholders' reports are probably the most familiar of all corporate disclosures. A **shareholders' annual report** contains the financial statements and general company information. Shareholders' annual reports lack the breadth of information contained in Form 10-Ks.[13] Moreover, the narrative sections in a shareholders' annual report tend to market the company, casting it in a favorable light.

A company closes its accounting records at the end of its fiscal year and then has its financial statements audited. Consequently, it files Form 10-Ks about three months after the end of the business year. A company's Form 10-K becomes public information sometime in late March, for example, if the firm's fiscal year coincides with the calendar year. Analysts trade on current information; therefore, companies must supplement annual disclosures periodically.

KEEPING CURRENT

Financial statement analysis requires continual commitment. Economic, industry, and corporate changes constantly occur. Alternative sources often provide timelier information, and a broader array of it, than those disclosed in the financial statements. The financial media, for example, inform people of significant corporate events on a daily basis. An analyst must remain current by continually monitoring diverse information sources about corporate activities. Ignoring these information sources diminishes the quality of analysis and can lead to bad decisions. The first step in keeping abreast of events is to read a daily financial newspaper. The next step is to find weekly and monthly periodicals to add perspective to economic, industry, and corporate events.

IDEAS AS INFORMATION SOURCES

Analysts are always looking for current information and ways to interpret information. But keeping current means more than reading a newspaper.

Ideas expand and deepen views about corporate disclosures. These intellectual resources are limited only by the analyst's imagination. One creative resource for improving analysis comes from managerial practice. There are many management

MICRO *A*NALYSIS 8

A good rule of thumb in financial statement analysis is to read a shareholders' annual report backward. The financial statements and their notes are contained at the back of the report, and the public relations material is in the front.

WEB *E*XERCISE 9

Access Apple Computer through www.sec.gov. Determine when Apple's fiscal year ended and when it filed its most recent Form 10-K.

WEB *E*XERCISE 10

Check out The Wall Street Journal's *Web site at www.wsj.com/.*

WHAT'S YOUR ANALYSIS

---

[12] The images and logos used on this book's cover are representative of the visually appealing displays found in shareholders' annual reports.

[13] Financial statements may not appear directly in Form 10-K but in the annual report or proxy statement. In such instances, these information pieces refer the reader to the location of the financial statements.

theories put forth to improve performance by measuring managers' compliance with recommended behavior. For example, one theory focuses on management's reflective capabilities.[a] This concept states that lack of reflection is the root cause of all corporate failure. Lack of reflection reveals itself in an organization's inability to do the following:

◆ Monitor the business environment
◆ Understand the customer
◆ Know the competition
◆ Assess performance
◆ Expand corporate intellectual capacity
◆ Break outdated assumptions

Although reflection theory targets managers, analysts can also evaluate how well the firm being analyzed addresses each one of the six categories.

Observations

Discuss how each one of the six factors pertaining to reflection influences financial statement analysis. Do you think Dr. Feynman would do more than following the press if he were a financial analyst?

---

[a] M. Hammer and S. A. Stanton advance this concept, described in "The Power of Reflection," *Fortune Magazine,* November 24, 1997, pp. 291–296.

TECHNOLOGICAL ADVANCES

The Internet, computerized databases, and other online sources greatly expand the amount of information available to an analyst. This section addresses both the advantages and disadvantages of these developing media.

ADVANTAGES

Electronic information enhances the speed and convenience of gathering data. Digitally transmitted data increasingly control the information landscape. The print medium, hindered by unfavorable production and distribution costs, is struggling to keep pace. Electronically transmitted material is more plentiful, convenient, flexible, integrated, and adaptable than the traditional print research option. This combination of speed and power makes online data invaluable for financial statement research. Apple Computer's Investor Relations home page, shown in Exhibit 2-7, exemplifies many of these features. (Notice the links to corporate information in the upper left-hand corner.)

Information is increasingly becoming available in **real-time**. Analysts can conduct more accurate analysis with real-time information, or data as they exist at the moment, than they can using older, less relevant data. Gateway Computer's stock information reflects both the power and real-time availability of Internet information. The charts in Exhibit 2-8 disclose a one-year trend in Gateway's stock prices and its current price (as of this book's printing date).

EXHIBIT 2-7

Apple Computer Investor Relations

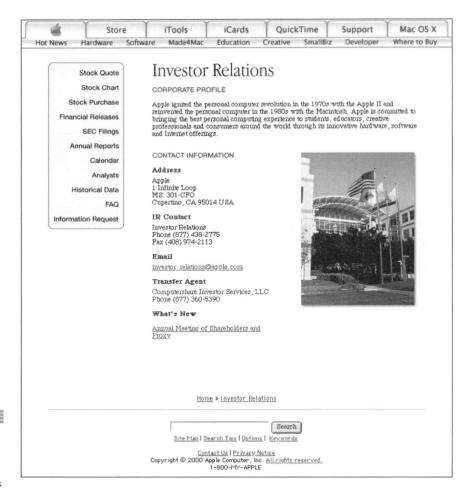

WEB EXERCISE 11

Locate the stock chart for Gateway, Inc. at gateway.com. Examine the trend of stock prices from 2001 to the present.

MICRO ANALYSIS 9

An axiom: You can't believe everything you read.

MICRO ANALYSIS 10

Another axiom: Garbage in, garbage out.

MICRO ANALYSIS 11

Two more axioms for analysts: I think; therefore, I am! (René Descartes, French philosopher and mathematician). IBM's motto: THINK!

DISADVANTAGES

Improvements in resource dissemination are both a blessing and a curse: They improve the information set, but they also facilitate misinformation. Computer-based information problems result from the same factors that create its value. Internet production costs are relatively inexpensive, and computer-generated information moves fluidly in and out of circulation. Printed information remains permanently on record; computer-generated data do not. Consequently, more print material is peer reviewed and professionally edited than are computer sources.

Vetting is the process of investigating, evaluating, and examining a subject in a thorough and expert way. Using material that has been completely reviewed before publication is a good way to begin vetting information. Data that have not been vetted stand a greater chance of providing the reader with misinformation or disinformation than do rigorously reviewed sources. Analysts who use unvetted sources risk contaminating their analyses and stand a greater likelihood of making bad economic decisions.

How do you know what constitutes good and bad information? No guarantees exist, but you should keep an open mind, exercise good judgment, and employ a healthy skepticism when reviewing all data sources. In short, use common sense!

EXHIBIT 2-8A

Gateway, Inc.
Current Stock Price

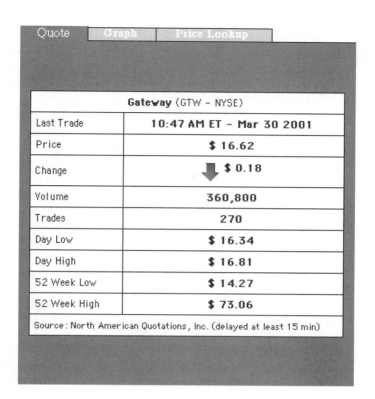

EXHIBIT 2-8B

Gateway, Inc.
One-Year Stock Trend

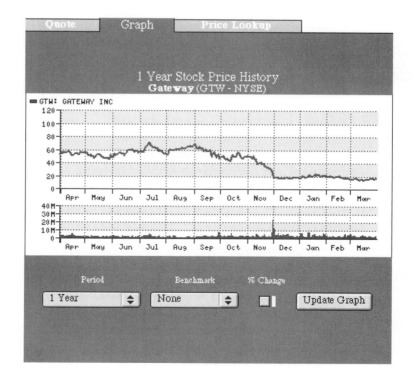

MASSIVE SUBSTITUTIONS CAN KILL AN ANALYSIS

Data do not always help analysis. How do you view the law of massive substitutions?

The availability of online data seemingly confirms the economic law of massive substitutions. This precept states that inexpensive goods replace more costly ones. Such an activity creates an illusion of value, but, in reality, substance is not increased, and it is often diminished as a result of the substitution.[a]

Virtually anyone can provide information on the World Wide Web. All it takes is a PC and a little expertise. The valueless goods, in other words, tend to reside alongside the good sources appearing on the Internet. Together, they are reducing the role of hard copy as the primary information provider. Analysts must be aware that the vetting process for print sources is often missing for online data. Much of what is available online is very good, but some of it is a waste of cyber ink!

Analysts should avoid the dangers of three other potential massive substitutions: Don't confuse analysis with words, computations, or format. Advances in word processing technology greatly reduce the cost of producing words, and spreadsheets help analysts to do numerous calculations in a short amount of time. Similarly, high-powered visual presentation software applications improve the appearance of financial statement analysis. But these technological advances add nothing to the rigors of the analysis or the conclusions drawn from the data.

Observations

Do software applications help you to think critically? Do they replace observation and reflection or assist those traits? How do you think Warren Buffet and Alan Greenspan feel about the bells and whistles approach to analysis?

---

[a] Based on an essay by A. Dixit, "My System of Work (Not!)," *American Economist,* Spring 1994, pp. 10–16.

SUMMARY

Research precedes analysis. The analytical process feeds on information and collapses without it. This chapter provides insights for gathering and managing information. It presents a framework for informational analysis; provides methods for accessing sources of economic, industry, and corporate data; and encourages analysts to use current data and to be prudent when evaluating information sources. (See the appendix to this chapter for an extensive list of specific electronic and print references.)

Finding the proper data for the required task continually challenges the analyst. In addition, the research aspect of analysis never ends, and it should continually provide better information over time. The availability of data staggers the imagination, but not all of the information is good or relevant. This chapter introduces you to some research methods and information categories. This material, however, does not contain all of the techniques, information sources, or ways to conduct research. Every analyst gathers and analyzes data in different ways. There is no one right way to do the job, nor is there one set of correct information. Analysts, however, conduct research. A thorough financial statement analysis demands it.

MICRO *A*NALYSIS 12

One final axiom: Nike's motto:
Just do it!

KEY TERMS

Benchmark
Business cycle
Economic sector
Electronic Gathering, Analysis, and
  Retrieval System (EDGAR)
Financial Statement Analysis (FSA)
  Decision Model
Form 8-K
Form S-1
Form S-4
Form 10-K
Form 10-Q
Industry
Industry classification system
Information overload

Information pyramid
Life cycle
North American Industry
  Classification System (NAICS)
Price changes
Proxy statement
Real time
Seasonality
Shareholder wealth maximization
Shareholders' annual report
Source and information matrix
Standard industrial classification (SIC)
Trends
Value
Vetting

INTERNET INDUSTRY CASES

Find the following information for the companies in Internet Industry Cases 2-1 through 2-6:

a. Corporate ticker symbol
b. Current share price of common stock
c. Aggregate market value of the company
d. Chief executive officer of the company
e. Principal products
f. Markets and distribution
g. Number of financial statements
h. Names of financial statements
i. Number of notes to the financial statements

2-1 *Personal Computers: Apple, Compaq, Dell, and Gateway*

2-2 *Airlines: American, Delta, and United*

2-3 *Athletic Footwear: Nike and Reebok*

2-4 *Discount Retailers: Kmart, Target, and Wal-Mart*

2-5 *Fast-Food Restaurants: McDonald's and Wendy's*

2-6 *Soft Drink Companies: Coca-Cola and PepsiCo.*

CONCEPTUAL CASES

2-1

Corporate Strategy and Financial Statement Analysis

Corporations engage in various strategies to maximize their stock prices. Many companies within the same industry use similar business models; in fact, this often helps define an industry. Fast-food restaurant companies, for example, employ a common revenue model. They earn revenue from two sources: selling their products and franchising their operations.

The franchising arrangement allows a company to grow rapidly with a relatively small capital investment from its owners. Such companies as McDonald's, Burger King, and Wendy's have successfully used the franchising model. Those firms and others allow independent operators, or franchisees, the right to use their name, concept, products, and soon in exchange for a fee. Thus, a partnership exists between a franchisor and its franchisees. Both parties believe that these arrangements are in the best interest of their respective shareholders. Franchisors attempt to profit by transferring their knowledge, technology, and brand recognition to their business partners. Franchisees try to leverage those advantages for their own benefit. If the business strategy is successful, both parties increase their shareholders' wealth.

In another business model, soft drink firms form partnerships with bottlers rather than bottling their product themselves. The Coca-Cola Co. and PepsiCo. have bottling arrangements throughout the world. Like franchising, bottling agreements are designed to maximize shareholder wealth.

a. List information strategies (not sources) that would increase your knowledge of franchising and bottling arrangements.
b. Examine a recent Form 10-K for either McDonald's or Wendy's to learn about its franchising arrangement and the percentage of stores that are company owned and independently controlled.
c. Find out about a Coca-Cola or PepsiCo. bottling partnership in either firm's Form 10-K.

2-2

Seasonality, Analysis, and Research

Sales in many industries have peak and slack periods throughout the year, but other types of businesses recognize relatively consistent revenues throughout the year. Quarterly sales data reflect the extent of seasonality within a business or industry. Analysts use quarterly reports to update annual financial statements and assist with forecasting future performance.

Seasonality may affect each of the industries analyzed in the Industry Cases: the PC, airline, athletic footwear, fast-food restaurant, discount retail, and soft drink industries. Three potential research sources exist for determining if seasonal factors influence financial performance of companies: industry, corporate, or a combination of industry and company data.

a. Would you initially examine economic, industry, or corporate data to begin to learn about the effects of seasonality on a company? Why?
b. Explain where you would find information about seasonality in a company's Form 10-K.
c. Discuss how an evaluation of sales revenues from a company's four most recent Form 10-Qs could provide insights about seasonality.

d. Based on your research, determine the extent of seasonality for the six industries used in the Industry Cases.

2-3

Profit Determinants and Research

The cost of jet aircraft fuel influences profitability in the airline industry. It is one of the largest recurring expenses for air carriers. Consequently, there is an inverse relationship between fuel costs and net income. As gas prices rise, profits fall. This is not a lockstep relationship, however. To a certain extent, airlines offset gas price hikes by passing the additional costs on to their customers; similarly, reductions in airfares decrease airlines' profits when gas is cheap.

Supply and demand determines oil prices, which result from many factors. A vibrant global economy, for instance, heightens petroleum demand, but a contracting economy has less need for fuel. Oil producers try to match supply with anticipated demand in a manner that maximizes their wealth. These supply and demand factors illustrate one reason why understanding economic conditions benefits industry and corporate analysis.

a. Discuss a research approach for determining the relationship between fuel prices and airline profits.
b. Examine a recent Form 10-K of United, Delta, or American to determine if corporate disclosures provide any specific information about their fuel costs. Cite where you found this information.
c. Does your airline present any strategies for offsetting oil price variability?

2-4

Benchmarking Against Competition

McDonald's Corp. sold more hamburgers than anyone else in the world did at the turn of the century. The second-largest hamburger fast-food chain was not, however, Wendy's International. That honor belongs to Burger King, which had 11,000 outlets and generated systemwide sales of $10.9 billion by the end of the 20th century. The Home of the Whopper commanded 19 percent of the U.S. hamburger market, trailing McDonald's industry-leading 43 percent share of the market.

McDonald's and Wendy's remained independent companies entering the 21st century; they focused strictly on fast-food sales and franchising their concepts. Burger King, on the other hand, was part of the Diageo PLC conglomerate. Founded in 1954, the U.S. company was acquired by Grand Metropolitan, PLC. This British concern, which also owned Pillsbury and many liquor concerns, merged with brewer Guinness Beer PLC to form Diageo.

a. List as many reasons as possible explaining the difficulty of benchmarking McDonald's Corp. against Burger King.
b. Present a research strategy to determine whether sufficient information about Burger King exists to compare it with McDonald's.

2-5

Benchmarking Over Time

PepsiCo. consisted of two major business segments at the end of the 20th century: soft drinks and snack foods. The company generated approximately $20 billion of annual revenues from selling its Pepsi-Cola and Frito-Lay products. The Coca-Cola Co., PepsiCo.'s primary competitor, derives all of its revenues from the manufacture and sale of soft drinks and noncarbonated beverages.

PepsiCo. had a third business segment, fast-food restaurants, until 1997. A separate, independent company was formed for its restaurants that year. PepsiCo. shareholders became owners of TRICON Global Restaurants, Inc., a publicly traded company, at that time. Pepsi's former Taco Bell, Kentucky Fried Chicken (now KFC), and Pizza Hut units make up TRICON. The combined sales of the three restaurant chains approximated $11 billion annually at the time of the spin-off.

a. Assume PepsiCo.'s financial statements reported results from all three segments through 1997 but only those of the remaining two segments thereafter. Discuss your ability to benchmark the performance of PepsiCo. throughout the 1990s.
b. Where would you find the information to determine whether PepsiCo.'s financial statements were adjusted to reflect ownership of only the soft drink and snack food segments before 1998?
c. Discuss the positive and negative aspects of benchmarking Pepsi against Coke in 1996 and 2001.
d. How comfortable are you in benchmarking these two companies against each other?
e. Name another source that you could benchmark PepsiCo. against.

2-6

Financial Statement Analysis Research Model

One means of measuring corporate profitability is by calculating the rate of return on common shareholders' equity. Return on equity (ROE) measures the amount of profitability earned by a company's common shareholders during a reporting period. Analysts compute ROE by dividing common shareholders' equity into net income.

Many companies' ownership structures contain preferred stock as well as common stock. Befitting its name, shareholders of this class of stock receive their dividends before common stock investors get a cash return on their investment. Consequently, dividends payable to preferred shareholders reduce earnings available for distribution to common stockholders.

Common stock constituted Apple Computer's ownership base until 1997. In that year the company issued $150 million of preferred stock to Microsoft. In 2000, Microsoft elected to convert its preferred stock into common stock. Assuming you were unaware of the issuance and conversion of preferred stock, you calculated a rate of return on common shareholders' equity from 1995 through 2000 using the ratio described in the first paragraph. Your research revealed the preferred stock information after computing those returns on common equity.

a. Explain why your research findings about the preferred stock issue affects input considerations of the financial statement analysis research model.
b. Describe how the preferred stock information influences the analytical process undertaken in the financial statement analysis research model.
c. Discuss how including preferred stock as an input and analytical factor could change the output of the FSA Decision Model.
d. Present an argument as to why you did not have to adjust the FSA Decision Model when the information about preferred stock became known.

2-7

Economic Conditions

Heavy machinery manufacturers, forestry products, and basic metals companies are mature cyclical industries, meaning there is usually a relationship between the profitability of well-established companies such as Caterpillar, International Paper, and Alcoa and the overall health of the economy. Income for companies in cyclical industries tends to surge in expanding economies but decline in contracting ones. Cyclical companies also boost income during inflationary periods. They increase their selling prices more than their operating costs when general price levels increase throughout the economy.

In the late 1990s the American economy experienced sustained growth. Gross domestic product (GDP), the total economic output of goods and services, grew at an annual rate of 4 percent. Price levels, however, were relatively stable during that time period. Monetary policy was aimed at controlling inflation. The effort of the Federal Reserve System, the independent central bank of the United States, was successful in this regard. In addition, productivity gains and intense competition put downward pressure on prices. Cyclical companies felt the effects of the low rates of inflation. Many cyclical companies' profits were flat or declined during the economic expansion of the late 1990s. Stock prices of mature cyclical companies lagged those of noncyclical firms and emerging industries during this time.

a. Would macroeconomic research focused solely on GDP growth correctly frame an analysis of a cyclical industry in the late 1990s?
b. Was GDP growth or price stability more important in determining the earnings of mature cyclical companies?
c. Explain why further research about mature cyclical industries is warranted when analyzing a company in one of these businesses.

2-8

Industry Classification

The World Wrestling Federation (WWF) became a publicly traded company in 1999. Its stock is now traded on the over-the-counter market alongside Microsoft, Intel, and Apple Computer. A different type of viewer, the financial analyst, now watches this sport.

Professional wrestling consisted of a number of regional operations until the 1980s. Vince McMahon consolidated many of these small businesses under the WWF umbrella during the 1980s. Coining the term *sports-entertainment*, the WWF dropped the pretense of unscripted competition and heightened the spectacle's soap opera aspect. The result proved successful: The WWF generated nearly $1 billion in annual revenue in the late 1990s. Turner Broadcasting, now merged with AOL Time-Warner, cloned the WWF formula with its World Championship Wrestling (WCW) business, which provides programming for the company-owned television stations of the media giant. The WWF also broadcasts its product on cable television. Wrestling shows were among the highest rated cable television programs in the later part of the 1990s.

a. Discuss the difficulty of classifying sports-entertainment as an industry.
b. Develop a research strategy for overcoming the classification obstacles.
c. Do you anticipate any problems benchmarking the WWF against the WCW?
d. List other potential benchmarks for the WWF.

RESOURCE GUIDE

Financial statement analysis requires comprehensive research. This appendix provides you with specific references for finding data and information. Its eight sections contain bibliographies of prominent information sources and a means to assess them.

Topic	Information	
Business Internet addresses	Web site references for Prentice Hall, government agencies,regulators, organizations, stock exchanges, and financial media	44
Corporate and industry Internet addresses	Web sites references for the companies and industries discussed in this text	48
Web site evaluation	Criteria for evaluating the value of a Web site	50
Search engines and words	Web site addresses used to search for information and useful words for conducting financial statement searches	50
Electronic databases	Brief descriptions of selected electronic databases	53
Print Resources	A list of financial newspapers and magazines that serves as economic and industry references.	54
Industry Classifications	Industry classifications according to the North American Industry Classification System (NAICS), Standard Industrial Classification (SIC), and Standard & Poor's Industry Surveys	55
Form 10-K	Parts and items contained in the Security and Exchange Commission's Form 10-K	59

BUSINESS INTERNET ADDRESSES

Prentice Hall's Learning on Internet Partnership (PHLIP)
http://www.prenhall.com/phlip/
The PHLIP Web site provides tools and links for conducting research. It also includes a place for students to interact with other students and professors.

Prentice Hall's Learning on Internet Partnership (PHLIP) for *Financial Statement Analysis: An Integrated Approach*
http://www.prenhall.com/phlip/bergevin/
This Web site is the Internet companion to the textbook.

The Prentice Hall Investment Challenge
http://www.ichallenge.net/prenticehall/
The stock market is turned into a game on this site, where players can use their own investment strategies to experience all of the major stock exchanges. Real-time updates are available as well as newsletters, e-mails, and telephone support.

GOVERNMENT AGENCIES AND REGULATORS

Bureau of Economic Analysis
http://www.bea.doc.gov/
This Web site contains national, international, and regional economic information. It includes information about production, purchases, prices, and personal income.

Bureau of Labor Statistics
http://www.bls.gov/
The Bureau of Labor Statistics, part of the United States Department of Labor, provides historical and current statistical information about all aspects of labor at this Web site.

Bureau of Transportation Statistics
http://www.bts.gov/
The Bureau of Transportation provides data for the rail, air, and land transportation industries at this Web site.

Department of Agriculture (USDA)
http://www.usda.gov/
The USDA Web site contains information about the rules, regulations, and operations of all aspects of the agricultural industry.

Department of Commerce (DOC)
http://www.doc.gov/
This Web site provides links to economic information, business development, and commercial growth as part of the DOC's mission to create jobs, grow the economy, and enhance economic development and living standards.

Department of Energy (DOE)
http://www.eia.doe.gov/
The DOE Web site presents information about the energy industries including rules, regulations, current events, historical data, and environmental issues.

Department of Labor (DOL)
http://www.dol.gov/
The DOL site contains information about industrial relations, employment practices, and the legal issues that pertain to them.

Department of Transportation (DOT)
http://www.dot.gov/
The DOT's Web site includes statistical data and government reports for the transportation industries and companies involved in those industries.

Department of Treasury
http://www.ustreas.gov/
This Web site provides historical and forecast economic data.

Federal Reserve Board
http://www.federalreserve.gov/
The Federal Reserve Board's Web site includes information on monetary policy, the banking system, and regulatory actions. It contains numerous research reports and data about these topics.

Internal Revenue Service
http://www.irs.ustreas.gov/
The Internal Revenue Service discloses tax rates and regulations at its Internet address.

International Trade Administration
http://www.ita.doc.gov/
This Web site contains import and export data such as trade statistics, tariffs, and balance of payments.

International Trade Commission
http://www.usitc.gov/
The International Trade Commission reports on current trade issues, industry competitiveness, and global and regional trade developments.

Occupational Health and Safety Administration (OSHA)
http://www.osha.gov/
As part of its responsibility for protecting America's workers, OSHA presents information on corporate compliance with workplace safety regulations at its Internet address.

Office of Management and Budget
http://www.whitehouse.gov/omb
This Web site contains the Federal government's financial management objectives. It includes the federal budget and forecasts of national income and disbursements.

Securities and Exchange Commission (SEC)
http://www.sec.gov/
The SEC's Web site provides information consistent with its mission of full and fair financial disclosures for investors. Its electronic data gathering, analysis, and retrieval system (EDGAR) allows access to corporate filings with the regulatory body.

ORGANIZATIONS

Pro2Net
http://www.pro2net.com/
Pro2Net provides information about financial reporting requirements. It also contains numerous links to legal, human resource, and financial planning resources.

American Institute of Certified Public Accountants
http://www.aicpa.org/
The accounting profession's Internet address includes current information on financial reporting issues and the profession's position on them

Financial Accounting Standards Board (FASB)
http://www.fasb.org/
The official site of the FASB contains information about official financial reporting pronouncements, current projects, and emerging issues.

International Accounting Standards Committee (IASC)
http://www.iasc.org.uk/
The global promulgator of financial reporting standards presents its standards, interpretations, and current projects at its Web site

National Association of State Boards of Accountancy (NASBA)
http://www.nasba.org/
The NASBA's Internet address includes information about continuing professional education courses related to financial reporting

STOCK EXCHANGES

Each stock exchange has a Web site that contains stock quotes and other market data for listed companies. The Internet addresses for the stock exchanges are as follows:

American Stock Exchange	http://www.amex.com/
Chicago Stock Exchange	http://www.chicagostockex.com/
NASDAQ	http://www.nasdaq.com/
New York Stock Exchange	http://www.nyse.com/
Pacific Exchange—Stock & Options	http://www.pacificex.com/
Philadelphia Stock Exchange	http://www.phlx.com/

FINANCIAL MEDIA

Media Web sites contain a vast amount of financial information. Each site has its own strengths and weaknesses. The same data are often contained in numerous Web sites, including industry information, corporate data, analytical reports, news articles, press releases, and stock quotes. The value of a particular address is a function of the information needed, reliability of the information source, and the analyst's familiarity with the Web address. Some of the more prominent media Web sites follow:

All Business Network	http://www.all-biz.com/
Barron's	http://www.barrons.com/
BigBook	http://www.bigbook.com/
BigCharts	http://www.bigcharts.com/
Bloomberg Personal On-line	http://www.bloomberg.com/
Business Week	http://www.businessweek.com/
Business Wire	http://www.businesswire.com/
CNBC	http://www.msnbc.com/news/com
CNNfn: The Financial Network	http://www.cnnfn.com/
CompaniesOnline	http://www.companiesonline.com/
Corporate Information	http://www.corporateinformation.com/
Dow Jones	http://www.dowjones.com/
Dow Jones Business Directory	http://www.businessdirectory.dowjones.com/
Dun & Bradstreet	http://www.dnb.com/
Economist	http://www.economist.com/
Financial Times	http://www.FT.com/
Forbes Digital Tool	http://www.forbes.com/
Fortune.com	http://www.fortune.com/
Hoover's Online	http://www.hoovers.com/
Industry Link	http://www.industrylink.com/
InfoUSA	http://www.infousa.com/
Investor's Business Daily	http://www.investors.com/
MarketWatch.com	http://www.marketwatch.com/
Motley Fool	http://www.fool.com/
MSNBC	http://www.msnbc.com/
NETworth's Equities Center	http://www.quotes.com/

New York Times	http://www.nytimes.com/
PR Newswire	http://www.prnewswire.com/
Quicken.com	http://www.quicken.com/
QuoteWatch.com	http://www.quotewatch.com/
Reuters News Service	http://www.reuters.com/
The Street.com	http://www.thestreet.com/
Value Line Publishing Co.	http://www.valueline.com/
The Wall Street Journal	http://www.wsj.com/
Thomson Financial	http://www.tfn.com/
Yahoo! Finance	http://www.finance.yahoo.com/
Zacks	http://www.zacks.com/

CORPORATE AND INDUSTRY INTERNET ADDRESSES

This book analyzes the financial data of 16 companies in six industries. Corporate and industry Web sites are as follows:

PERSONAL COMPUTERS

Companies
Apple Computer, Inc.	http://www.apple.com/
Compaq Computer Corp.	http://www.compaq.com/
Dell Computer Corp.	http://www.dell.com/
Gateway, Inc.	http://www.gateway.com/

Industry
BYTE	http://byte.com/
Dataquest	http://www.dataquest.com/
Electronic News	http://sumnet.com/enews/
Information Week	http://informationsweek.com/
InfoWorld	http://www.infoworld.com/
International Data Corp.	http://www.idcresearch.com/
META Group Inc.	http://metagroup.com/
PC Magazine	http://www.zdnet.com/pcmag/
PC Week	http://www.pcweek/

AIRLINES

Companies
American Airlines, Inc.	http://www.aa.com/
Delta Air Lines, Inc.	http://www.delta-air.com/
United Air Lines, Inc.	http://www.ual.com/

Industry
Air Bulletin	http://www.airconnex.com/
Air Carrier Financial Statistics	http://www.dot.gov/ost/aviation/
Airline Business	http://www.airlinebusiness.com/
Air Transport Association	http://www.air-transport.org/
Air Transport World	http://www.atwonline.com/
Plane Business	http://www.planebusiness.com/
Federal Aviation Administration	http:www.faa.gov/

ATHLETIC FOOTWEAR AND APPAREL

Companies
Nike Corp.	http://www.nike.com/
Reebok International Ltd.	http://www.reebok.com/

Industry
American Apparel Manufacturers Association	http://www.americanapparel.org/
Apparel Industry Magazine	http://www.aimagazine.com/
Apparel Network	http://www.apparel.net
The Apparel Strategist	http://www.appstrat.com/
Footwear Industries of America	http://www.fia.org/
Sporting Goods Manufacturers Association	http://www.sportlink.com/
Shoe Stats	http://www.fia.org/

DISCOUNT RETAILERS

Companies
Kmart Corp.	http://www.kmart.com/corp
Target Corp.	http://www.target.com/
Wal-Mart Stores, Inc.	http://www.walmart.com/

Industry
International Mass Retailers Association	http://www.imra.org
National Retail Federation Inc.	http://www.nfr.com

FAST FOOD RESTAURANTS

Companies
McDonald's Corp.	http://www.mcdonalds.com/
Wendy's International, Inc.	http://www.wendys.com/

Industry
Nation's Restaurant News	http://www.nrn.com/
Restaurant Business	http://www.restaurant.biz.com/
Restaurants USA	http://www.restaurant.org/
National Restaurant Association	http://www.restaurant.org/
International Franchise Association	http://www.franchise.org/

SOFT DRINKS

Companies
The Coca-Cola Company	http://www.thecoca-colacompany.com/
PepsiCo.	http://www.pepsico.com/

Industry
American Institute of Food Distribution Inc.	http://www.foodinstitute.com
Beverage World	http://www.beverageworld.com/
Prepared Food	http://www/preparedfoods.com/

WEB SITE EVALUATION

Analysts must assure themselves of the value of a Web site before using it. Follow these recommendations[1]:

Authority. Determine who has the authority for the Web site by looking for such items as

- Corporate trademarks
- Acknowledgment of Web site ownership
- List of corporate addresses and telephone numbers
- Links to the company (if it is not the company's site)

Accuracy. Check the accuracy of the site's financial statement data by establishing that it has been

- Clearly displayed
- Verified
- Filed with the SEC
- Professionally presented (e.g., free of grammatical and spelling mistakes)

Objectivity. Assess the objectivity of the site by determining the

- Motivation for the site
- Extent to which advertising appears on the site
- Degree of separation between advertisements and editorial content
- Reasonableness of disclosures and claims made by the company

Timeliness. Evaluate the timeliness of the site by checking the

- Date of the last update
- Length of time it has been in existence
- Dates of filings with regulatory agencies, such as the SEC
- Links to other Web sites

Coverage. Determine the degree of coverage offered by the site by reviewing

- That all items related to the company are disclosed and not just selective ones
- The manner in which product, market, and financial information are presented

SEARCH ENGINES AND WORDS

You can find significant information on the Internet by using search engines. Research your topic by typing in key words related to the company or topic of interest. Refine your search with additional key words. The more accessible search engines include:

---

[1] Based on recommendations by J. Alexander and M. A. Tate, *Web Site Evaluation*, Wolfgram Memorial Library, Widenar University.

AltaVista	http://www.altavista.com/
AOL Netfind	http://www.aol.com/netfind/
Excite	http://www.excite.com/
Go Network	http://www.go.com/
HotBot	http://www.hotbot.com/
Infoseek	http://www.infoseek.com/
LookSmart	http://www.looksmart.com/
Lycos	http://www.lycos.com/
MetaCrawler	http://www.metacrawler.com/
Netscape Netcenter	http://home.netscape.com/
Snap	http://home.snap.com/
WebCrawler	http://www.webcrawler.com/
Yahoo	http://www.yahoo.com/

SEARCH WORDS

Key words initialize computerized searches. An alphabetical listing of some financial statement analysis key words is as follows[2]:

Accounting standards
Accounting systems
Advertising
Advertising research
Alliances
Analysts' reports
Annual reports
Antitakeover strategy
Antitrust
Appraisals
Arbitration
Artificial intelligence
Asset management
Asset utilization
Assets
Associations
Auditors
Audit reports (opinions)
Automation
Bailouts
Balance sheet
Benchmarking
Benefits
Best practices
Beta
Board of directors
Bonus plans
Brand identity
Budgeting

Business combinations
(consolidations)
Business cycle
Business failure
Business interruptions
Business plans
Business strategies
Business to business
Buyouts
Campaigns
Capital investment
Capitalization
Capital structure
Cash flow(s)
Cash flows from operations
Cash management
Chairman of the board
Chief executive officer
(CEO)
Communications
Compensation
Competition
Competitive intelligence
Compliance
Computerization
Conglomerate
Contracts & agreements
Contributed capital

Corporate culture
Corporate mission
Corporate responsibilities
Cost control
Cost engineering
Cost of goods sold (cost of sales)
Cost reduction
Credit management
Creditors
Cultural Issues
Customer service
Database management
Debt management
Decision making
Deferred taxes
Demographics
Deregulation
Derivatives
Disclosure
Discounting
Disruptive technology
Distribution channels
Distributors
Diversification
Diversity
Divestiture
Dividends

---

[2] Many of these words were included based on the experience of the library staff at Valdosta State University and contained in its "Key Word Search" instructional material.

Downsizing
Earnings
Earnings per share (EPS)
Earnings quality
Economic contraction
Economic expansion
Economics
Effectiveness
Electronic commerce
Electronic media
Employee relations
Engineering
Entrepreneurship
Environmental issues
Employee stock option
  plan (ESOP)
Ethics
Expenses
Facilities design
Facilities management
Factory automation
Fiduciary responsibility
Financial Accounting
  Standards Board
  (FASB)
Financial flexibility
Financial instruments
Financial modeling
Financial planning
Financial ratios
Financial reporting
Financial statements
Fixed costs (expenses)
Forecasting
Foreign investment
Foreign operations
Form 8-K
Form 10-K
Form 10-Q
Form S-1
Franchises
Fraud
Fund raising
Generally Accepted
  Accounting
  Principles (GAAP)
Global integration
Going concern
Going public
Goodwill
Governance
Government

Gross profit (margin)
Growth strategies
Hostile takeover
Human capital
Human resources
Incentives
Income statement
Industry
Industry conditions
Information economy
Information manage-
  ment
Information processing
Information technology
Innovation
Insurance
Intellectual capital
Intellectual property
Interest rates
International
  Accounting
  Standards Committee
  (IASC)
Internships
Inventory management
Investment policy
Investor relations
Investors
Initial public offering
  (IPO)
Internal revenue service
  (IRS)
Joint venture
Labor relations
Layoffs
Leadership
Leases
Legal issues
Legislation
Liabilities
Liquidity
Litigation
Loans
Logistics
Long range planning
Management informa-
  tion systems
Management strategies
Management structure
Managers
Manufacturing
Market capitalization

Markets
Market share
Merger integration
Mergers & acquisitions
Monopolies
Motivation
Multinational
Multinational enterprises
Negotiating
New economy
Net income
Notes to the financial
  statements (footnotes)
Old economy
Operating performance
Operations
Organizational structure
Outlook
Outsourcing
Patents
Payables
Pension plans
Performance evaluation
Perquisites
Personal development
Plant relocation
Poison pill
Policies
Positioning
Pricing
Product development
Production control
Product mix
Product planning
Product strategy
Productivity
Profit margin
Profitability
Public relations
Purchasing
Quality control
Receivables
Reengineering
Regulation
Research and develop-
  ment (R&D)
Resignations
Resource allocation
Restructuring
Retained earnings
Return on investment
Revenues

Risk analysis	Start-up business	Technology development
Risk management	Statement of cash flows	Telecommunications
Safety	Statement of sharehold-	Termination
Seasonality	ers' equity	Trade
Securities and Exchange	Stock analysis	Trade agreement
Commission (SEC)	Stock buy-back (treasury	Trade secrets
Security	stock)	Transportation
Self-regulation	Stock options	Trends
Segment data	Stock price	Turnaround manage-
Shareholder relations	Strategic planning	ment
Shareholders	Succession planning	Unemployment
Shareholders' equity	Supplemental disclo-	Valuation
Short term planning	sures	Variable costs (expenses)
Social responsibilities	Systems management	Venture capital
Spin-offs	Taxation	Wages

ELECTRONIC DATABASES

Several business indexes reside online. These databases contain article abstracts and some full-text information from a variety of sources. These resources provide timely and specific research assistance. In addition, the analyst can usually rely on the quality of information available in the business indexes. The databases include the following:

ABI/Inform (University Microfilm International, 1971–Present)
ABI/Inform covers a variety of business and management topics including corporate histories, competitive intelligence, and product development. It provides information about advertising, banking, broadcasting, computers, economics, foreign investment, health care, insurance, international trade, management, marketing, public administration, real estate, taxation, telecommunications and transportation.

Business Dateline (University Microfilm International, 1985–Present)
Business Dateline specializes in company and executive profiles, corporate strategies, marketing, financial services, and regional business. It concentrates on the technology, manufacturing, and service industries.

Business and Industry (OCLC FirstSearch Database, 1994–Present)
Business & Industry contains a wealth of international data. It provides information on both public and private companies.

FINDEX: Directory of Market Research Reports, Studies and Surveys (OCLC FirstSearch Database, 1985–Present)
This database provides index research studies, surveys and audits for all major industries.

Lexis-Nexis UNIVerse (Lexis-Nexis Academic Universe, Various Dates–Present)
Lexis-Nexis UNIVerse contains trade journals, annual reports, company profiles, market share reports, tax laws, regional newspapers, country reports, government publications and many other business related information sources.

Wilson Business Abstracts (OCLC FirstSearch Database, 1986–Present)
Wilson Business Abstracts covers accounting, advertising, communications, computer, economics, finance, government regulation, mergers & acquisitions, personnel, and small business.

Worldscope GLOBAL (OCLC FirstSearch Database, Various Dates–Present)
Worldscope GLOBAL presents financial information on nearly 9,000 of the world's largest companies representing over 30 countries.

PRINT RESOURCES

Numerous print resources exist. These data sources often contain more historical information than their online counterparts. They can also be easier to read than electronic information. Some of the prominent print resources include the following:

ECONOMIC SOURCES

Business Conditions Digest (Washington, DC: U.S. Government Printing Office, monthly).
Economic Indicators (Washington, DC: U.S. Government Printing Office, monthly).
Handbook of U.S. Labor Statistics (Washington, DC: U.S. Department of Labor, annually).
Monthly Labor Review (Washington, DC: U.S. Department of Labor, monthly).
Survey of Current Business (Washington, DC: monthly).
U.S. Industry and Trade Outlook (Washington, DC: U.S. Department of Commerce, annually).
U.S. Statistical Abstract, Census Bureau (Washington, DC: U.S. Department of Labor, annually).

INDUSTRY SOURCES

Industry Norms and Key Business Ratios (New York: Dun & Bradstreet, annually).
Heil, S. and T. W. Peck (eds.), *Encyclopedia of American Industries* (Detroit: Gale Research, 1999).
Maurer, J. G., J. M. Shulman, and M. L. Rowe and R. C. Becherer, *Encyclopedia of Business* (New York: ITP, 1995).
North American Industry Classification System (Washington, DC: Office of Budget and Management, 1997).
RMA Annual Statement Studies (Philadelphia: RMA, annually).
Sawinski, D. M. (ed.), *U.S. Industry Profiles* (New York: Gale Research, 1995).
Standard & Poor's Industry Surveys (New York: McGraw Hill, annually).
Troy, L., *The Almanac of Business and Industry Ratios* (Paramus, NJ: Prentice Hall, annually).
Value Line (New York: Value Line, periodically).

CORPORATE DISCLOSURES

Dun & Bradstreet's Business Rankings (Bethlehem, PA: Dun & Bradstreet, annually).
Grant, T. (ed.), *International Directory of Company Histories* (Detroit: St. James Press, 1996).

Hoover's Handbook of American Companies (Austin, TX: Hoover's Business Press, annually).

Hoover's Handbook of Emerging Companies (Austin, TX: Hoover's Business Press, annually).

Hoover's Handbook of Private Companies (Austin, TX: Hoover's Business Press, annually).

Hoover's Handbook of World Business (Austin, TX: Hoover's Business Press, annually).

Moody's Banking and Finance Manual (New York: Moody's Investor Service, annually).

Moody's International Manual (New York: Moody's Investor Service, annually).

Moody's Handbook of Common Stock (New York: Moody's Investor Service, annually).

Moody's Industrial Manual (New York: Moody's Investor Service, annually).

Moody's Municipal and Government Manual (New York: Moody's Investor Service, annually).

Moody's OTC Industrial Manual (New York: Moody's Investor Service, annually).

Moody's Public Utility Manual (New York: Moody's Investor Service, annually).

Moody's Transportation Manual (New York: Moody's Investor Service, annually).

Moskowitz, M., R. Levering and M. Katz, *Everybody's Business* (New York: Doubleday, 1998).

Standard & Poor's 500 Guide (New York: McGraw Hill, annually).

Standard & Poor's Register of Corporations, Directors and Executives (New York: McGraw Hill, annually).

Standard & Poor's Stock Reports (New York: McGraw Hill, annually).

Value Line (New York: Value Line, periodically).

Warner, M. (ed.), *International Encyclopedia of Business & Management* (London: Routledge, 1996).

NEWSPAPERS AND PERIODICALS

Barron's (New York: Dow Jones & Co., weekly).
Business Week (New York: Time Inc., weekly).
Forbes (New York: Forbes, biweekly).
Fortune (New York: Time Inc., biweekly).
Investor's Daily News (Los Angeles: Investor's Daily News, business daily).
The Financial Times (London: The Financial Times, business daily).
Wall Street Journal (New York: Dow Jones & Co., business daily).

INDUSTRY CLASSIFICATIONS

NORTH AMERICAN INDUSTRY CLASSIFICATION SYSTEM (NAICS) STRUCTURE
TWO-DIGIT CODES (AS DEFINED BY NAICS)

11 Agriculture, Forestry, Fishing and Hunting   Activities of this sector are growing crops, raising animals, harvesting timber, and harvesting fish and other animals from farms, ranches, or the animals' natural habitats.

22 Utilities   Activities of this sector are generating, transmitting, and/or distributing electricity, gas, steam, and water and removing sewage through a permanent infrastructure of lines, mains and pipe.

23 Construction   Activities of this sector are erecting buildings and other structures (including additions); heavy construction other than buildings; and alterations, reconstruction, installation, and maintenance and repairs.

31–33 Manufacturing   Activities of this sector are the mechanical, physical, or chemical transformation of material, substances, or components into new products.

41–43 Wholesale Trade   Activities of this sector are selling or arranging for the purchase or sale of goods for resale; capital or durable nonconsumer goods; and raw and intermediate materials and supplies used in production, and providing services incidental to the sale of the merchandise.

44–46 Retail Trade   Activities of this sector are retailing merchandise generally in small quantities to the general public and providing services incidental to the sale of the merchandise.

48–49 Transportation and Warehousing   Activities of this sector are providing transportation of passengers and cargo, warehousing and storing goods, scenic and sightseeing transportation, and supporting these activities.

51 Information   Activities of this sector are distributing information and cultural products, providing the means to transmit or distribute these products as data or communications, and processing data.

52 Finance and Insurance   Activities of this sector involve the creation, liquidation, or change in ownership of financial assets (financial transactions) and/or facilitating financial transactions.

53 Real Estate and Rental and Leasing   Activities of this sector are renting, leasing, or otherwise allowing the use of tangible or intangible assets (except copyrighted works), and providing related services.

54 Professional, Scientific, and Technical Services   Activities of this sector are performing professional, scientific, and technical services for the operations of other organizations.

55 Management of Companies and Enterprises   Activities of this sector are the holding of securities of companies and enterprises, for the purpose of owning controlling interest or influencing their management decision, or administering, overseeing, and managing other establishments of the same company or enterprise and normally undertaking the strategic or organizational planning and decision making of the company or enterprise.

61 Educational Services   Activities of this sector are providing instruction and training in a wide variety of subjects.

62 Health Care and Social Assistance   Activities of this sector are providing health care and social assistance for individuals.

71 Arts, Entertainment, and Recreation   Activities of this sector are operating or providing services to meet varied cultural, entertainment, and recreational interests of their patrons.

72 Accommodation and Food Services   Activities of this sector are providing customers with lodging and/or preparing meals, snacks, and beverages for immediate consumption.

81 Other Services (except Public Administration)   Activities of this sector are providing services not elsewhere specified, including repairs, religious activities, grant making, advocacy, laundry, personal care, death care, and other personal services.

91–93 Public Administration   Activities of this sector are administration, management, and oversight of public programs by Federal, State, and local governments.

EXHIBIT 2-9

NAICS Sectors, Groups, and New Industry Classifications

SECTOR	NAME	SUB-SECTORS	INDUSTRY GROUPS	NEW INDUSTRIES
11	Agriculture, Forestry, Fishing and Hunting	5	19	20
21	Mining	3	5	—
22	Utilities	1	3	6
23	Construction	3	14	3
31–33	Manufacturing	21	84	79
42	Wholesale Trade	2	18	—
44–45	Retail Trade	12	27	17
48–49	Transportation and Warehousing	11	29	28
51	Information	4	9	20
52	Finance and Insurance	5	11	23
53	Real Estate and Rental and Leasing	3	8	15
54	Professional, Scientific, and Technical Services	1	9	28
55	Management of Companies and Enterprises	1	1	1
56	Administrative and support and Waste Management and Remediation Services	2	11	29
61	Educational Services	1	7	12
62	Health Care and Social Assistance	4	18	27
71	Arts, Entertainment, and Recreation	3	9	19
72	Accommodation and Food Services	2	7	10
81	Other Services (except Public Administration)	4	14	19
92	Public Administration	8	8	2
20	**Total**	**96**	**311**	**358**

EXHIBIT 2-10

Standard Industrial Classification (SIC) Structure (two-digit codes)

SIC	Agriculture		
01	Agricultural Production—Crops
02	Agriculture Production—Livestock
07	Agricultural Services
08	Forestry
09	Fishing, Hunting and Trapping
SIC	**Mining**
10	Metal Mining
12	Coal Mining
13	Oil and Gas Extraction
14	Nonmetallic Minerals, exc. Fuel
SIC	**Construction**
15	General Building Contractors
16	Heavy Construction Contractors
17	Special Trade Contractors
SIC	**Manufacturing**
20	Food and Kindred Products
21	Tobacco Products
22	Textile Mill Products
23	Apparel and Other Textile Products
24	Lumber and Wood Products, exc. Furniture
25	Furniture and Fixtures
26	Paper and Allied Products
27	Printing and Publishing
28	Chemicals and Allied Products
29	Petroleum Refining and Related Coal Industries
30	Rubber and Misc. Plastics Products
31	Leather and Leather Products
32	Stone, Clay, Glass, and Concrete Products
33	Primary Metal Industries
34	Fabricated Metal Products
35	Indus. And Comm. Machinery & Computer Equip.
36	Electronic and Electric Equipment
37	Transportation Equipment
38	Instruments and Related Products
39	Miscellaneous Manufactures
40	Railroad Transportation
41	Local and Interurban Passenger Transit
42	Trucking and Warehousing

EXHIBIT 2-10
Continued

SIC	Manufacturing	SIC	Finance, Insurance, and Real Estate
43	United States Postal Service	64	Insurance Agents, Brokers, and Service
44	Water Transportation	65	Real Estate
45	Transportation by Air	67	Holding and Other Investment Offices
46	Pipelines, exc. Natural Gas		
47	Transportation Services	SIC	Services
48	Communications	70	Hotels and Other Lodging Places
49	Electric, Gas, and Sanitary Services	72	Personal Services
		73	Business Services
SIC	Wholesale Trade	75	Automotive Repair, Services, and Parking
50	Wholesale Trade—Durable Goods	76	Miscellaneous Repair Services
51	Wholesale Trade— Nondurable Goods	78	Motion Pictures
		79	Amusement and Recreation Services
SIC	Retail Trade	80	Health Services
52	Building Materials, Hardware, and Garden Supplies	81	Legal Services
53	General Merchandise Stores	82	Educational Services
54	Food Stores	83	Social Services
55	Automotive Dealers and Service Stations	84	Museums, Botanical Gardens, etc.
56	Apparel and Accessory Stores	86	Membership Organizations
57	Home Furniture and Furnishings Stores	87	Engineering, Accounting, Mgmt., and Related Svcs.
58	Eating and Drinking Places	88	Private Households
59	Miscellaneous Retail	89	Miscellaneous Services
SIC	Finance, Insurance, and Real Estate	SIC	Public Administration
60	Depository Institutions	91–97	Administration
61	Nondepository Credit Institutions		
62	Security and Commodity Brokers	SIC	Nonclassified Establishments
63	Insurance Carriers	99	Nonclassified Establishments

EXHIBIT 2-11
Standard & Poor's Industry Surveys Classification Structure

	INDUSTRY	ABBREVIATION
1.	Aerospace & Defense	AD
2.	Agribusiness	AG
3.	Airlines	AIR
4.	Alcoholic Beverages & Tobacco	ABT
5.	Apparel & Footwear	AF
6.	Autos & Auto Parts	AAP
7.	Banking	BA
8.	Biotechnology	BT
9.	Broadcasting & Cable	BC
10.	Capital Goods	CG
11.	Chemicals: Basic	CB
12.	Chemicals: Specialty	CSP
13.	Communications Equipment	CE
14.	Computers: Commercial Services	CCS
15.	Computers: Consumer Services & Internet	CCSI
16.	Computers: Hardware	CH
17.	Computers: Networking	CN
18.	Computers: Software	CS

	INDUSTRY	ABBREVIATION
19.	Electric Utilities	EU
20.	Environmental & Waste Management	EWM
21.	Financial Services: Diversified	FSD
22.	Foods & Nonalcoholic Beverages	FNB
23.	Healthcare: Facilities	HF
24.	Healthcare: Managed Care	HMC
25.	Healthcare: Pharmaceuticals	HP
26.	Healthcare: Products & Supplies	HPS
27.	Homebuilding	HB
28.	Household Durables	HD
29.	Household Nondurables	HND
30.	Insurance: Life & Health	ILH
31.	Insurance: Property-Casualty	IPC
31.	Investment Services	IS
32.	Leisure Products	LP
33.	Lodging & Gaming	LG
34.	Metals: Industrial	MI
35.	Metals: Precious	MP
36.	Movies & Home Entertainment	MHE
37.	Natural Gas Distribution	NGD
38.	Oil & Gas: Equipment & Services	OGES
39.	Oil & Gas: Production & Marketing	OGPM
40.	Paper & Forest Products	PFP
41.	Publishing	PUB
42.	Restaurants	RES
43.	Retailing: General	RG
44.	Retailing: Specialty	RS
45.	Savings & Loans	SL
46.	Semiconductor Equipment	SCE
47.	Semiconductors	SC
48.	Supermarkets & Drugstores	SD
49.	Telecommunications: Wireless	TWLS
50.	Telecommunications: Wireline	TWLN
51.	Transportation: Commercial	TC

FORM 10-K

Form 10-K's format is as follows:

Cover Page

◆ Name, address and telephone number of the registrant (reporting company).
◆ Securities registered (e.g., common stock).
◆ Aggregate market value and number of shares issued and outstanding.

Part I. General disclosures provide information about a company and its scope of its operations.

◆ Item 1. Business disclosures about products, markets, materials, and other general information.

- ◆ Item 2. Properties that are controlled by the company.
- ◆ Item 3. Legal proceedings potentially affecting financial results.
- ◆ Item 4. Shareholder voting matters.

Part II. Financial data and management's discussion of its performance.

- ◆ Item 5. Market for the registrant's common equity.
- ◆ Item 6. Selected financial data.
- ◆ Item 7. Management's discussion and analysis (MD&A) reports the results of operations; provides an overview of the company; discusses net sales, profit margins, research and development, special charges, financial expenses, tax provisions, liquidity and capital resources and Y2K compliance; and addresses factors that may affect future performance.
- ◆ Item 7a. Disclosures about market risk.
- ◆ Item 8. Financial statements and supplementary data.
- ◆ Item 9. Changes in and disagreements with accountants on accounting and financial disclosures.

Part III. Information about the owners, directors and managers of the company.

- ◆ Item 10. Directors and executive officers of the registrant.
- ◆ Item 11. Executive compensation.
- ◆ Item 12. Security ownership of certain beneficial owners and management.
- ◆ Item 13. Arrangements with named executive officers.

Part IV. Additional exhibits and schedules.

- ◆ Item 14. Exhibits, financial statement schedules and reports on Form 8-K.

3 THE FINANCIAL STATEMENTS

Upon completion of this chapter, you should be able to:

◆ *Describe the composition and objectives of each of the four financial statements.*

◆ *Show how the economic entity, periodicity, monetary unit, stable dollar, and going concern assumptions, as well as the revenue recognition, matching, and historical cost principles influence financial statement disclosures.*

◆ *Distinguish between cash flow reporting and the accrual basis of accounting.*

◆ *Articulate the importance of cash flows from operating activities.*

◆ *Explain and give examples of financial statement articulation.*

$\mathcal{G}$enerally accepted accounting principles (GAAP) require disclosure of four specific **financial statements**:

◆ the balance sheet
◆ the income statement
◆ the statement of shareholders' equity
◆ the statement of cash flows

Analysts use the information contained in the statements of financial position, operating performance, ownership interest, and cash flows as primary inputs for economic decision making.

In Chapter 3 we define the objective, key terms, and format for each financial statement. This chapter paves the way for the analysis that follows. We present a hypothetical company, eXTREMESTUFF.com (eSTUFF), to facilitate financial statement understanding and technical analysis. This chapter consists of six topics. The first two sections present key concepts and an orientation to the financial statements. The remaining four sections examine each financial statement in greater detail, beginning with the income statement.

FINANCIAL STATEMENT CONCEPTS

We examine financial statement objectives, principles, assumptions, interrelationships, and additional financial statement information in the first section of the chapter. Numerical values are added to the conceptual discussion in the next section.

OBJECTIVES

Analysts more accurately refer to corporate disclosures as **general-purpose external financial reports.** These statements provide information to diverse user groups, who use them for making various decisions, as noted in Chapter 1. Every analyst seeks information about the following items, regardless of his or her specific decision objective. Analysts want to

◆ understand cash flows
◆ know the composition of a firm's resources
◆ distinguish between creditor and owner claims against those resources
◆ evaluate changes in wealth over time

A company seeks to increase shareholder wealth by maximizing share price. Cash flows determine an entity's degree of success in meeting that goal. Consequently, people primarily seek information about a firm's cash-generating abilities when assessing financial statements.

BROADENING FINANCIAL DISCLOSURES

Financial statements exist because the market values them. You would not be reading this book otherwise. What is your opinion on potential changes to financial statement reporting?

Financial disclosures are not static constructs. They change over time to meet the needs of information users. The marketplace continually seeks more and better information. Individuals and agencies meet that demand in a number of ways. Recent Financial Accounting Standards Board (FASB) considerations illustrate financial reporting flexibility. The FASB is studying whether it should play a significant role in providing nonfinancial information to analysts and other interested individuals.[a] An FASB steering committee investigated a comprehensive business-reporting model. Such a model could result in providing relevant information to investors, creditors, and other analysts. The committee is considering recommending voluntary disclosures of nonfinancial information, based on corporate best practices. Some of the areas considered for inclusions in the FASB's comprehensive business reporting model are

- ◆ corporate objectives and strategies
- ◆ scope of the business
- ◆ the impact of industry structure on the company
- ◆ performance measures
- ◆ management's analysis of changes in performance
- ◆ key trends
- ◆ forward-looking information

Observations

Do you think analysts would benefit from the development of a comprehensive business model? Is the FASB competent to oversee such disclosures, or are these beyond the FASB's expertise? Do alternative information sources provide such data more efficiently? Will companies voluntarily make such disclosures, especially about their strategies, objectives, and performance measures? Do you think companies should be required to make such disclosures?

---

[a]Information based on "FASB Looks at Non-Financial Disclosures," *Investor Relations Business*, May 24, 1999, pp.12–13.

MICRO ANALYSIS 1

Exhibit 21 of Apple Computer's 1999 Form 10-K lists seven subsidies of Apple Computer, Inc.

WEB EXERCISE 1

Access Apple Computer's most recent 10-K through the investor's information section at www.apple.com/. Examine Note 1—Summary of Significant Accounting Policies to determine if Apple's reporting of Financial Instruments *conforms to the historical cost principle.*

ASSUMPTIONS

The **economic entity assumption** means that the company is an independent, separate, and distinct entity from its owners. Consequently, only the economic activities of the firm are reported in its financial statements. The resources, obligations, and wealth of its owners are not commingled with those of the reporting entity. In addition, the firm reports on the basis of economic substance, rather than legal form. For example, a company reports one set of financial statements for legally distinct corporations when common ownership exists.

Financial statement reporting is also influenced by four other assumptions:

ASSUMPTION	DEFINITION
Periodicity	A company discloses its financial statements on regular, recurring basis.
Going concern	An entity will continue operating indefinitely into the future.
Monetary unit	A firm reports all financial statements in dollars (for U.S. firms).
Stable dollar	An enterprise does not adjust for changes in general price levels (inflation).

The last two premises contain the essence of the nominal dollar concept of capital maintenance, which is discussed in Chapter 1.

MICRO ANALYSIS 2

According to Apple Computer's Note 1—Summary of Significant Accounting Policies, "the Company recognizes revenues at the time products are shipped. Provisions are made currently for product returns, price protections, rebates and other sales programs."

PRINCIPLES

Transactions are recorded at historical exchange prices, and those **historical costs** tend to serve as the valuation basis on the financial statements.[1] Financial statements are also reported on the basis of **accrual accounting**, which consists of the **revenue realization principle** and **matching principle**. Under the revenue realization principle, revenues are recognized when products are exchanged for cash or claims to cash.[2] Its complement, the matching principle, deducts the costs of generating those revenues when they are earned. The costs matched against revenues are **expenses**. Accrual accounting differs from the cash basis of accounting. The latter method, which violates GAAP, recognizes revenues and expenses when cash is received and paid.

WHAT'S YOUR ANALYSIS

REVENUE RECOGNITION

Corporations comply with GAAP when recognizing revenue. The precise point at which revenue is realized, however, is sometimes subject to dispute.

Sears, Roebuck & Co. aggressively marketed its Sears credit card. Customers use the card for the majority of purchases at Sears.[a] In addition, financing charges from these cards accounted for over one-half of Sears' $2.2 billion 1998 operating profit. Sears earned more profit from financing customers' payments than it did from selling inventory. A raft of nonpayments on card balances, however, forced Sears to tighten its credit policies. This change resulted in decreased sales and financial revenues as well as an increase in bad debt expenses. Overall, net income declined.

Pressure from the Securities and Exchange Commission (SEC) forced discount-club retailers to recognize revenues more conservatively then they had been doing.[b] Consumers pay an up-front annual membership fee to shop at warehouse-type stores selling bulk items at deeply discounted prices. Companies such as BJs Wholesale Club, Costco, and Sam's Club recognized revenues when the members joined the club. Responding to SEC concerns, BJs changed its accounting practice to recognizing revenues over the life of the membership. The switch decreased BJs' earnings per share by approximately 3 percent. Costco and Sam's Club followed BJs' lead.

Financial giant Conseco Inc. recently changed revenue realization practices on certain loans sensitive to interest rate fluctuations.[c] Their previous policy recognized certain gains (revenues) immediately. These revenues, however, were often offset by losses (expenses) in future periods. The new method records revenues only after matching losses to gains. Operating profit decreased by 48% as a result of Conseco's change to a more conservative revenue realization policy.

Observations

Each of these three cases illustrated questionable revenue recognition practices that increased corporate revenues and income. They have been replaced with more con-

---

[1] Exceptions to this general statement are discussed later in the text.
[2] This definition presumes the reporting entity has *earned* the revenue (i.e., it did everything it has to do to earn the benefits resulting from the revenues). In addition, revenues can be *realizable,* rather than realized. In this instance, a company holds assets that can readily be sold for cash or claims to cash.

servative revenue recognition policies, ones that reduced earnings. These cases demonstrate that revenue realization is more easily grasped in theory than implemented in practice. How would you analyze the managements' initial judgment in each case? Suggest ways that analysts can learn about corporate revenue recognition policies and whether any controversial practices exist.

[a] J. B. Cahill, "Sears Is Tightening Accounting Methods in Credit Card Unit, Lifting Loan Losses," *Wall Street Journal*, January 29, 1999, p. A3.
[b] E. MacDonald and L. Johannes, "Discount-Club Retailers Shift Accounting," *Wall Street Journal*, October 20, 1998, p. A3.
[c] J. Bailey, "Conseco Halts Gain-on-Sale Accounting, Cutting Estimate for Operating Profit," *Wall Street Journal*, September 9, 1999, p. A4.

WEB EXERCISE 2

Use the Internet to locate the most recent Form 10-Ks for Compaq, Dell, and Gateway. Are the revenue recognition policies of these three companies comparable with Apple's revenue recognition policy?

INTERRELATIONSHIP OF FINANCIAL STATEMENTS

Each financial statement reports a specific type of economic activity (such as a firm's financial position or cash flows). The same underlying transactions, however, serve as the inputs for all of the financial statements. These disclosures, therefore, relate to one another through the process of **articulation**.

Analysts deepen their knowledge of economic relationships by understanding the articulation process. A balance sheet, for example, reports a cash amount at a specific time. Measuring the cash difference between two balance sheets yields the net change in cash over a period of time. The statement of cash flows reports that monetary change.[3] It explains how the beginning cash balance became the ending amount of cash. The cash flows statement explains the history of cash. The balance sheet conveys the end result of resource's history, its worth at one point in time.

WEB EXERCISE 3

Examine Apple Computer's Form 10-K. Find a supplemental schedule titled "Valuation and Qualifying Accounts and Reserves."

ADDITIONAL FINANCIAL STATEMENT DISCLOSURES

An additional financial statement component exists. **Notes to the financial statements** amplify and clarify the numerical disclosures contained in the four financial statements. These integral **footnotes** (**notes**) consist of words, numbers, and tables that provide additional information about the data contained in the statements themselves. **Supplementary information,** though not directly part of the basic financial statements, often appears in financial statement presentations. Many corporations present these schedules and narrative disclosures as an additional means of communicating economic information. Both the footnotes and supplementary information are governed by the FASB.

FINANCIAL STATEMENT ORIENTATION

The four financial statements constitute the backbone of the information set for any analysis. A basic set of financial statements is presented in this section of the chapter. The disclosures of a hypothetical Internet retailer, eSTUFF, are used to illustrate them.

[3] For purposes of discussion, a reporting period is one year. The terms *reporting period, period,* and *one year* are used interchangeably.

eXTREMESTUFF.COM

A group of recent college graduates decided to form their own business, rather than work for someone else. These aspiring entrepreneurs perceived a market niche for extreme sports equipment, especially those items not stocked by traditional sporting goods retailers. These budding businesspeople did not want to open a storefront because they lacked capital, desired a broader market penetration, and perceived a better retail distribution channel. As a result, they founded eXTREMESTUFF.com (eSTUFF), an Internet retailer.

The entrepreneurs supplemented their own corporate funding with bank financing and **venture capital**. The latter funds came from an investment firm that specialized in financing unproven, but potentially very profitable, businesses. The venture capitalists became part owners in eSTUFF, taking an equity position in the firm. The company began operations on January 1, 2000.

eSTUFF'S FINANCIAL STATEMENTS

A **balance sheet**, or statement of financial position, existed since the beginning of 2000 as a result of the corporate financing. The entity's initial **assets**, or economic resources, consisted of invested cash. The company, in turn, used that cash to acquire other assets, such as computer equipment and inventory. The entrepreneurs' and venture capitalists' interest in the resources constituted initial **shareholders' equity**, or owners' investment. The sole **liability**, or obligation to nonowners, was the money the company owed to the bank. An equation captures eSTUFF's financial position: *assets = liabilities + shareholders' equity*.[4]

The balance sheet changes with every business transaction. For example, eSTUFF's assets and liabilities increased when the business acquired inventory from a vendor on credit. Both sides of the balance sheet equation decreased when the Internet retailer paid for the products. Consequently, the balance sheet remains in equilibrium. An entity's resources always equals the claims against them by its owners and creditors at a specific point in time.

Like all profit-seeking businesses, the purpose of eSTUFF was to maximize owners' wealth. To that end, it sold its merchandise at historical cost plus markup. The statement that reports the results of a company's wealth-seeking activities over a period is the **income statement.** The equation *revenues – expenses = net income (or net loss)* reports the extent of the success of the wealth producing activities.

Assuming a company earns income, it can either keep the profit in the business or distribute it to the owners. The former concept is known as **retained earnings**, and the latter one is called **dividends**.[5] Income-related decisions capture the most important aspect of the **statement of shareholders' equity**. This statement, in essence, reports *beginning shareholders' equity + net income – dividends = ending shareholders' equity*. Another way to view the statement of shareholders' equity is as the linkage between the income statement and balance sheet. It connects the two statements because the income statement measures wealth changes over time, and the balance sheet brackets that income statement with the beginning and ending retained earnings.

---

[4]To stress the ownership interest in the business, the equation can be rearranged as *assets – liabilities = shareholders' equity*. Consequently, shareholders' equity equals *net* assets.

[5]A company must have sufficient cash as well as retained earnings in order to declare and pay a cash dividend.

WEB EXERCISE 5

Find Apple's most recent set of financial statements.

WEB EXERCISE 6

Note the similarities and differences between Apple's financial statements and those for eSTUFF.

All corporate stakeholders require information about cash. As noted earlier, however, revenues and expenses do not equal cash inflows and outflows. For example, eSTUFF made some sales in 2000 that went uncollected until the next year. The fourth financial statement compensates for this shortcoming. The **statement of cash flows** reports the net change in cash during a reporting period. Cash is provided or used by three distinct activities: *operating*, *investing*, and *financing* activities. The first section of this statement reports cash flows from the ongoing major activities of the business; the next portion discloses cash flows for the acquisition and disposal of long-term assets; and the final section details sources and uses of cash from owner and creditor financing.

FINANCIAL STATEMENT NUMBERS

eXTREMESTUFF.com's first two years of business are summarized in its comparative financial statements, contained in Exhibit 3-1.[6]

EXHIBIT 3-1

eXTREMESTUFF.com, Inc. (in thousands of dollars, except per share amounts and par values)

INCOME STATEMENTS
FOR THE YEARS ENDED DECEMBER 31

	2001	2000
Sales revenue	$1,200	$1,000
Cost of goods sold	660	600
Gross profit	540	400
Selling expenses	352	250
Administrative expenses	133	85
Income from continuing operations	55	65
Financial expenses	20	10
Pretax income	35	55
Income tax expense	14	22
Net income	$ 21	$ 33
Earnings per share	$ .42	$ .79

STATEMENT OF SHAREHOLDERS' EQUITY
FOR THE YEARS ENDED DECEMBER 31

	COMMON STOCK	ADDITIONAL PAID IN CAPITAL	RETAINED EARNINGS
Balance as of January 1, 2000	—	—	—
Common stock issued, $1 par value	$42	$378	
Net income	—	—	$33
Dividends declared and paid	—	—	(8)
Balance as of December 31, 2000	$42	$378	$25
Common stock issued, $1 par value	8	72	—
Net income	—	—	21
Dividends declared and paid	—	—	(2)
Balance as of December 31, 2001	$50	$450	$44

---

[6]Disclosures are usually presented in reverse chronology. Many companies present comparative balance sheets first. The income statements are presented first in this text to demonstrate how business operations of a reporting period affect financial position. In addition, most established companies report the two most recent balance sheets but disclose income statements, statements of shareholders' equity, and statements of cash flows for the past three years.

EXHIBIT 3-1
(*continued*)

BALANCE SHEETS
DECEMBER 31

	2001	2000
Assets		
Current assets:		
Cash	$ 45	$ 30
Accounts receivable, net	140	120
Inventory	250	200
Prepaid expenses	5	10
Total current assets	**440**	**360**
Property, plant, and equipment:		
Equipment, net	380	400
Intangible Assets:		
Trademark	15	20
Total assets	**$835**	**$780**
Liabilities and Shareholders' Equity		
Current liabilities:		
Accounts payable	$ 50	$160
Accrued liabilities	21	50
Taxes payable	0	5
Total current liabilities	**71**	**215**
Long-term liabilities:		
Notes payable	220	120
Total liabilities	**291**	**335**
Shareholders' equity:		
Contributed capital:		
Common stock, $1 par value	50	42
Additional paid in capital	450	378
Total contributed capital	**500**	**420**
Retained earnings	44	25
Total shareholders' equity	**544**	**445**
Total liabilities and shareholders' equity	**$835**	**$780**

INCOME STATEMENT

The income statement is also known as the *statement of earnings, statement of operating performance, profit and loss statement,* or *P&L statement*. Regardless of title, this financial statement reports corporate profitability (or loss). eSTUFF, for instance, earned $33,000 in its first business year and $21,000 in its second business year, or $.79 and $.42 per share of stock, respectively, in those two periods.

INCOME STATEMENT COMPONENTS

The income statement consists of four parts: revenues, expenses, income or loss, and earnings per share. Revenues are asset increases or liability settlements that result from delivering goods and rendering services. Sales or services constitute an entity's central business activity. *Gains* are like revenues, except they arise from

EXHIBIT 3-1
(continued)

**STATEMENT OF CASH FLOWS
FOR THE YEARS ENDED DECEMBER 31**

	2001	2000
Cash, beginning of the year	**$ 30**	**—**
Cash flows from operating activities:		
Net income	$ 21	$ 33
Depreciation expense, equipment	120	100
Amortization expense, trademark	5	5
Changes in current accounts:		
Accounts receivable	(20)	(120)
Inventory	(50)	(200)
Prepaid expenses	5	(10)
Accounts payable	(110)	160
Accrued liabilities	(29)	50
Taxes payable	(5)	5
Net cash provided (used) by operating activities	*(63)*	*23*
Cash flows from investing activities:		
Purchase of equipment	(100)	(500)
Acquisition of trademark	—	(25)
Net cash provided (used) by investing activities	*(100)*	*(525)*
Cash flows from financing activities:		
Issue notes payable	100	120
Issue common stock	80	420
Pay cash dividend	(2)	(8)
Net cash provided (used) by financing activities	*178*	*532*
Net change in cash	**$ 15**	**$ 30**
Cash, end of the year	**$ 45**	**$ 30**

peripheral or incidental transactions.[7] Selling products earned eSTUFF's revenues over the Internet; consequently, the company reported revenues but not gains.

Expenses are cost of doing business. Assets decrease and liabilities increase when revenues are sought. Our hypothetical Internet retailer had four types of expenses: cost of goods sold, selling and administrative expenses, financial expense, and tax expense.[8] *Losses* are similar to expenses, except they occur from peripheral or incidental transactions.

Revenues and gains less expenses and losses equal **net income**, or the change in wealth over a period of time. Many income categories exist, as evidenced by eSTUFF's income statements. Profit can be measured before or after taxes, and it can also be determined before or after operating and financial expenses.

Earnings per share (EPS) is a prorated income disclosure. It reports the amount of income earned by each share of stock during a reporting period.

---

[7] For a more complete discussion of all of the financial statement elements, refer to the FASB's *Statement of Financial Accounting Concepts No. 6*, "Elements of Financial Statements," (Stamford, CT: FASB, 1985).
[8] The first three expenses are costs of o*perating* eSTUFF. Financial expense is eSTUFF's annual cost of *financing* a portion of its assets through debt.

Shareholders held 42,000 and 50,000 shares of eSTUFF common stock in 2000 and 2001. eSTUFF's EPS were $.79 in 2000 and $.42 in 2001 ($33,000 / 42,000 shares and $21,000 / 50,000 shares).[9]

INTERNET REVENUES

Some dot-com companies have an interesting interpretation of the revenue realization principle. What do you make of it?

Internet intermediaries find product buyers on behalf of the sellers, who are often the manufacturers of the goods. The dot-com companies serve as distributors in the transactions and earn a commission on facilitating such sales. The reporting issue is that many of these electronic intermediaries record revenues for the full amount of the sale price, rather than recognizing revenue for just the amount of their commission. The FASB calls such a practice "grossing up revenues." The SEC also insists these companies should only be recognizing revenue to the extent of their commissions. Some analysts believe that such companies as Priceline.com, Healtheon/WebMD, and Ventro Corp. have overstated their revenues by using this practice.[a] Lynn Turner, chief accountant for the SEC, summarized the problem by stating that revenue recognition represents the biggest item on the financial statements, but it has the fewest rules governing it.[b]

Observations

How do you think dot-coms that arrange transactions between buyers and sellers should recognize revenues? The SEC and FASB are considering tightening rules on revenue recognition for dot-com companies. Do you think they should? Does this issue apply to eSTUFF?

A buy and hold scam is one way to fraudulently inflate revenues. The company records revenues earned from a customer who does not take possession of the goods.

[a]See, for example, R. McGough and E. MacDonald, "Healtheon Pushing Limits on Revenue?" *Wall Street Journal*, p. C1, February 7, 2000; and E. MacDonald "Plump from Web Sales, Some Dot-Coms Face Crash Diet of Restriction on Booking Revenue," *Wall Street Journal*, p. C4, February 28, 2000.
[b]E. MacDonald, "Concerns on Internet Firms' Accounting Prompt SEC to Seek Tighter Standards," *Wall Street Journal*, p. A2, December 18, 1999.

DISCLOSURE CONVENTIONS

eXTREMESTUFF.com discloses income in a *multiple-step* format. Various expense categories determine different concepts of profit (e.g., gross profit, income from continuing operations), ultimately yielding net income. eSTUFF's income statement illustrates a multiple-step format. Conversely, a *single-step* income statement reports all categories of revenues and gains and then subtracts all expenses and losses from them to determine pretax income. GAAP allow either method.

The income statement reports income on an **all-inclusive** basis. Revenues, gains, expenses, and losses, irrespective of how they occurred, affect current income. In other words, unusual events that do not result from normal business operations are also reported in the income statement.[10] eSTUFF did not have any

---

[9]It is assumed that the stock was issued at the beginning of each year.
[10]Certain specific exemptions to this all-inclusive concept of income exist. These exemptions have to be reported in the owners' equity section of the balance sheet as *other components of comprehensive income*. They are discussed in Chapters 7 and 12.

MICRO
ANALYSIS 8

Apple Computer changed from a single-step income statement to multiple-step format in the mid-1990s.

unusual economic events in its first two years of operations, but if it did, those revenues (gains) and expenses (expenses) would have been disclosed.

As noted in Chapter 1, the *nominal dollar concept of capital maintenance* determines income under GAAP. Investment recovery occurs when selling price exceeds the historical cost of the assets sold. No income adjustments are made for price changes in general or specific goods.[11] Price changes, however, distort reported disclosures. Assume an inflation rate of 10% during 2001. One might argue that eSTUFF's revenues did not increase by $200,000 ($1,200,000 − $1,000,000), but by $100,000 after restating the previous year's revenues to their 2001 equivalent amount of purchasing power ($1,000,000 × [1.10/1.00] = $1,100,000).

LINE ITEM DISCLOSURES

Cost of goods sold (cost of sales) is the difference between the retail and historical cost of inventory sold during a reporting period. Merchants and manufacturers deduct their cost of sales from sales revenues to determine **gross profit (gross margin)**. eSTUFF's gross profits were $400,000 in 2000 and $540,000 in 2001. Apart from its cost of goods sold, eSTUFF's **operating expenses** consist of *selling* and *administrative* expenses (sometimes called selling, general and administrative, or S,G&A, expenses) and other recurring business costs.[12] Deducting these expenses from gross profit determines income from operations. This income number represents earnings from core business activities. Our Internet merchant made a pretax profit of $55,000 from selling merchandise in its second year of business.

Operating income is adjusted upward or downward for other revenues (and gains) and expenses (and losses). The most prominent item in this category is interest on borrowed funds. eSTUFF incurred a $20,000 financial expense in 2001, which represented interest on borrowed funds (i.e., notes payable).[13] **Income tax expense** is based on a percentage of those earnings. eSTUFF's tax rate was 40% for each year reported.

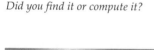

WEB
EXERCISE 7

What is Apple's tax rate for the most recent reporting period? Did you find it or compute it?

MATCHING EXPENSES

WHAT'S YOUR ANALYSIS

There is an old axiom in financial reporting: "Let the expenses follow the revenues." Did the following companies do so?

Expenses should be matched against revenues when the revenues are reported. They are reported when incurred, regardless of cash flows. Similar to revenues, theoretical understanding of expense recognition is easier than practical implementation. The following three cases provide evidence.

Sylvan Learning Systems was criticized for underreporting its operating expenses.º The company established not-for-profit entities, which were legally independent of Sylvan. These not-for-profits marketed Sylvan's products and provided services for the company. The costs of these activities were reported as expenses for the not-for-profit enterprises but not for Sylvan. When the information about these marketing expenses became public, Sylvan's stock dropped by $200 million.

---

[11]Such changes are the essence of the general-price-level and physical units concepts of capital maintenance.

[12]Depreciation expense, salaries expense, utilities expense and rent expense exemplify operating expenses. Most companies collapse these different types of expenses into just a few line items for disclosure purposes.

[13]It is assumed that borrowing took place at the beginning of each year. Interest rates were 8.33% in 2000 and 10% in 2001.

Rite-Aid Corp., the nation's third largest drugstore chain, held back up to 16% of accounts payable due to vendors. The company claimed the deductions were made for defective merchandise shipped to its stores. The amount of the holdbacks far exceeded industry norms and reduced Rite-Aid's reported expense for goods sold. In addition, the company recorded larger than expected expenses related to the cost of building new stores.[b] Eventually, the company adjusted its expense recognition policies. These changes reduced Rite-Aid's 1999 net income by $143 million.

The entertainment industry's matching of expenses to revenues is being changed due to pressure from the American Institute of Certified Public Accountants (AICPA).[c] Conventionally, film marketing and advertising costs were amortized over many years. As of 1999, they should be expensed immediately, often before the motion pictures are released. Similarly, film producers have begun to amortize production costs for a period of time not to exceed ten years. Before the AICPA directive, these costs were charged against revenues over the expected revenue producing periods of the film. Projected film revenues often stretched for many decades. In reality, very few films have the legs of *Gone with the Wind*![d] Multigeneration production cost amortization defied reporting logic. Hollywood's earnings are expected to drop about $1.5 billion annually, due to the adjustments for reporting expenses.

Observations

Discuss the propriety of the expense treatments of Sylvan, Rite-Aid, and the movie industry. Do you view their practices as aggressive accounting tactics or income manipulation? How would those practices affect your analyses?

---

[a]R. McGough, "A Controversy over Aggressive Accounting Sends Sylvan Learning Systems Stock Plunging," *Wall Street Journal*, January 4, 1998, p. C2.
[b]M. Maremont, "Rite-Aid Repays Some Disputed Deductions from Vendors' Bills," *Wall Street Journal*, September 9, 1999, p. B2 and R. Brenner and M. Maremont, "Rite Aid Restates Year Net Downward, Reversing Some Accounting Maneuvers," *Wall Street Journal*, pp. A4 and A8.
[c]E. MacDonald, "Rules to Change for Accounting in Hollywood," *Wall Street Journal*, September, 16, 1999, p. B12.
[d]*Legs* is show business jargon for an entertainment property that produces revenues over a protracted period of time.

STATEMENT OF SHAREHOLDERS' EQUITY

There are two primary components to shareholders' equity: *contributed capital* and *retained earnings*. This statement reports their beginning and ending amounts, as well as changes in them. Each component of shareholders' equity is discussed in turn.

CONTRIBUTED CAPITAL

Contributed capital reports the owners' investment in a business and is evidenced by the stock the entity issued.[14] Two primary stock classes exist: The most prevalent type issued is called **common stock**, and in some instances, companies also issue **preferred stock**. These shareholders receive dividends before common

---

[14]Cash is the primary means of financing an entity, but other consideration (assets) may be exchanged for stock.

WEB

EXERCISE 8

Did owners invest additional capital into Apple in the most recent reporting period? If so, explain.

shareholders but do not benefit to the extent common owners do when the company is profitable.[15] The selling price of the stock (fair value or market value) differs from its **par value** (or legal capital).[16] The difference between these amounts is defined as **additional paid in capital in excess of par.** Par value and additional paid in capital taken together equal total contributed capital. eSTUFF sold common stock worth $420,000 in 2000 and an additional $80,000 in cash the next year. The Internet retailer sold shares for $10 each in 2000 ($420,000 of contributed capital / 42,000 shares).[17]

RETAINED EARNINGS

Retained earnings are the cumulative amount of income kept within the business for all the years the business has been operating. Analysts need to remember that retained earnings are intangible: This concept does not have a physical substance! Inasmuch as revenues and expenses do not equal cash inflows and outflows, net income does not equal net cash. Consequently, retained earnings summarizes the total amount of income (another concept) invested in the enterprise's resources. eSTUFF did not have any earnings when it started business on January 1, 2000. It earned $33,000 in income its first year but declared and paid dividends of $8,000.[18] Retained earnings was $25,000 at the end of the year. That amount, in turn, became the beginning balance for 2001. Undistributed income of $19,000 in eSTUFF's second business year increased retained earnings to $44,000 by December 31, 2001.

BALANCE SHEET

The balance sheet, or statement of financial position, reports resources and claims against the resources at end of each reporting period. Assets, liabilities, and shareholders' equity are more prevalent terms for economic resources and claims to them. Each of these three elements is examined in the following sections.

ASSETS

Assets are revenue-producing resources. More specifically, assets are future economic benefits, which are controlled by the entity as the result of past transactions. They are classified as either current or long-term resources, based on their convertibility into cash. **Current assets** become cash within one year or one operating cycle, whichever is longer.[19] **Long-term assets** produce cash indirectly. They generate revenues that result in cash. Noncurrent assets exist for more than one

---

[15]Preferred stock is a safer, less risky investment than common stock. Preferred stock exhibits some of the characteristics of long-term debt rather than equity capital.

[16]Par value equals the minimum legal selling price for stock in most states.

[17]The same approach could be used for the 2001 stock issue, which generated $80,000 in cash.

[18]Cash dividends are the most prevalent form of investor compensation but not the only kind. Other types, such as stock and property (noncash asset) distributions, exist. In addition, a company needs retained earnings to *declare* a dividend, but it must have the cash (stock or property) to *pay* them.

[19]An *operating cycle* is the length of time it takes for a company to convert inventory into cash in the ordinary course of business. For most industries, the operating cycle is shorter than one year; consequently, this text assumes current asset conversion within one year.

WEB *Exercise 9*

Examine Apple's inventory disclosures. Did the company disclose raw materials, work-in-process, and finished goods inventories? Speculate on why a manufacturer's inventory is more complex than a retailer's goods.

WEB *Exercise 10*

Every company costs its inventory on a basis, such as first-in, first-out or last-in, first-out. Which method does Apple use to cost its inventory? How about Compaq, Dell, and Gateway?

MICRO *Analysis 9*

One of the great advantages to a click retailer versus a brick merchant is that traditional fixed asset costs for buildings and equipment is greatly reduced.

MICRO *Analysis 10*

Many intangible assets have tremendous value to a company but appear as relatively small amounts on the balance because they are reported on an historical cost basis.

reporting period—hence their long-term designation and distinction from current assets. The three major categories of long-term assets are financial investments; property, plant, and equipment; and intangible assets.

CURRENT ASSETS

Liquidity, or a resource's nearness to cash, determines the sequence of current asset disclosures. *Cash* is reported first because it is readily available to pay the maturing obligations (liabilities) of the firm.[20] *Accounts receivable* represent expected collections of unpaid customers' bills.[21] *Inventory* reports the historical cost of unsold products at the end of the reporting period. Other current assets, or prepaid expenses, represent advanced payment made for future expenses such as insurance, rent, and advertising. Unlike other current assets, these items will not be converted into cash. They will, however, be consumed in the normal course of business. For most firms, prepaid expenses are relatively insignificant current assets.

eSTUFF reported $45,000 of unencumbered cash by the end of its second year of business. The company had $140,000 of net accounts receivable at that time. Aggregate receivables exceeded that amount, but an allowance was made for estimated customer defaults (i.e., not everyone pays their bills). The company owned $250,000 of merchandise that it expected to sell at marked-up prices and had $5,000 worth of prepaid expenses at the end of 2001.

PROPERTY, PLANT, AND EQUIPMENT

Property, plant, and equipment represent a firm's productive, long-term tangible resources. The historical cost of these assets is charged to operating expenses over their productive (revenue-producing) life. The accumulation of these cost allocations reduces the value of an asset on the balance sheet to its *book*, *carrying*, or *net* amount. Our hypothetical retailer discloses $400,000 and $380,000 of net equipment at the end of 2000 and 2001, respectively.

INTANGIBLE ASSETS

Intangible assets mirror property, plant, and equipment, except for their lack of physical substance. A company controls a right, often a legal one, to do something with its intangible assets that helps it generate revenues. Patents, copyrights, franchises, leaseholds, trademarks, and trade names exemplify intangible assets. In eSTUFF's case, the company acquired a trademark at a cost of $25,000. The company has amortized this distinctive corporate symbol over a five-year period at $5,000 per year.

---

[20]Any restrictions placed on cash, that affect its liquidity must be disclosed. Moreover, cash dedicated to a long-term use, such as the retirement of a noncurrent note payable, is reported as a long-term investment. Disclosures about cash or reclassifying it as another asset illustrate the reporting concept of substance over form: A company reports the economic substance of its accounts, rather than their legal basis. In this case, cash is classified as such only if it is unencumbered.

[21]Investments in short-term securities are usually classified between cash and receivables. These investments in the stocks and bonds of other companies are very liquid and will be sold in the near term. Due to reporting complexities, these assets, along with their long-term counterparts, are discussed in Chapter 7.

LIABILITIES

Liabilities are future economic sacrifices arising from present obligations to transfer assets or provide services, which arose from past transactions. These obligations are categorized as either current (short-term) or long-term liabilities, depending on their payment date.

CURRENT LIABILITIES

Current liabilities, such as obligations to vendors, employees, landlords, advertisers, utility companies, and taxing authorities, require cash payment within the next year. Unlike current assets, which are listed in order of liquidity, current liabilities follow no strict disclosure pattern. eSTUFF reported $71,000 worth of current liabilities at the end of its second year of business. Its *accounts payable* represents vendor obligations for previously purchased inventory. The firm's *accrued liabilities* are the sum of the unpaid bills for other operating costs.

LONG-TERM LIABILITIES

Long-term (noncurrent) liabilities are existing obligations that will be paid beyond the next reporting period. *Bonds payable*, *notes payable*, and *mortgages payable* are examples of long-term obligations. Some noncurrent liabilities, such as a mortgage, require periodic payments. The debt, therefore, is partitioned between the current and long-term liability categories, based on payment date. In our case, eSTUFF owed money to its bank on two notes. The company borrowed $120,000 in 2000 and $100,000 in the following year. Neither obligation will be paid in 2002.

SHAREHOLDERS' EQUITY

Shareholders' equity represents the owners' claim to the assets of the firm. The balance sheet disclosures for contributed capital and retained earnings are also disclosed in the statement of shareholders' equity. Notice that common stock, additional paid in capital, and retained earnings on eSTUFF's balance sheet at the end of 2001 equal those on its statement of shareholders' equity. This relationship among equity disclosures is another example of how the financial statements interrelate or articulate.

DID THEY LIE?

Analysts rely on the integrity of financial statements when making decisions. Sometimes such reliance is unwarranted.

McKesson and HBO & Co. (HBOC), two health care companies, merged in January 1999. Within months of the merger, it became apparent that HBOC had booked nonexistent sales. The fallout claimed the jobs of the top executives at the newly combined firm, erased $9 billion of the company's market value, and required reducing 1999's net income by $153 million.[a] Financial fraud differs from aggressive financial reporting tactics. It is a deliberate action to deceive financial statement users. Many times companies committing fraud receive unqualified audit opinions, only to have the truth revealed at a later time.

STATEMENT OF CASH FLOWS

The statement of cash flows differs from the other three financial statements in that it reports cash information, rather than accrual-based disclosures. As noted earlier in the chapter, this statement reports three types of cash flows: operations, investments, and financing. The latter two sections *directly* report how much cash came into and went out of a business during a reporting period. Operating activities usually disclose cash activities *indirectly* by reconciling net income to operating cash flows.

CASH FLOWS FROM OPERATING ACTIVITIES

The most important section of this statement is **cash flows from operating activities**. It reports net cash provided or used by the core activity of a business, or its central wealth-creating endeavor. Operating cash flows are reported on either a *direct* or an *indirect* basis. The direct basis reports cash received from the sale of goods and services and cash paid to suppliers for inventory, to employees for services, and to others who have a claim against the company. The indirect method reconciles accrual-based net income to operating cash flows by reporting noncash items and changes in current balance sheet accounts. Direct cash flows provide more information to financial statement users, but most companies report on an indirect basis.[22]

Using the indirect basis, eSTUFF reported an increase in operating cash of $23,000 in 2000 and a $63,000 decrease in 2001. Depreciation of equipment and trademark amortization were added to net income because these expenses do not require cash payments. Net income was increased or decreased for *changes* in current assets (excluding cash) and current liabilities, based on how each account's change affected cash flows.

CASH FLOWS FROM INVESTING ACTIVITIES

The second section of the cash flow statement reports **cash flows from investing activities**. These disclosures inform financial statement users about the cash used (provided) by the acquisition (disposal) of long-term assets. As a business start-up, eSTUFF used cash to buy assets. Therefore, it had net cash outflows from

---

[22]Chapter 10 contains a procedure for converting indirect cash flows from operations to the direct method.

investing activities during its first two years of business. The cost of equipment ($500,000) and trademark ($25,000) in 2000, and the additional purchase of equipment in 2001 ($100,00), reduced the company's cash balance.

CASH FLOWS FROM FINANCING ACTIVITIES

The final portion of the cash flow statement reports **cash flows from financing activities**. This section of the statement contains information about cash received from investors and cash returned to them. As such, it measures changes in long-term liabilities and shareholders' equity for a reporting period. The Internet retailer generated cash from financing activities during its first two years of business. This reflects a normal pattern for a new business as investors inject cash into a company to get it started. Stock issues accounted for $420,000 and $80,000 of cash in 2000 and 2001, respectively. Bank financing in the form of long-term notes resulted in cash inflows of $220,000 ($120,000 in 2000 and $100,000 in 2001). Dividend payments, however, reduced these cash infusions by $8,000 and $2,000 in 2000 and 2001, respectively.

SUMMARY

This chapter examines the objectives and composition of the four financial statements that form the cornerstones of financial analysis. A discussion of the financial statements of eSTUFF, a hypothetical Internet retailer of extreme sports gear, facilitates much of the discussion. Financial statements tie together through the process of articulation. These disclosures represent an integrated summary of economic activity, rather than four separate pieces of information. Individuals who view them as such produce better analyses. The progression of net income, from its determination on the income statement through its adjustment of shareholders' equity to the balance sheet disclosure of the retained earnings, illustrates financial statement articulation.

This chapter introduces the financial statements. After studying it, you should be able to comprehend basic corporate disclosures. The business world, however, is complex; so too are corporate financial disclosures. More advanced disclosure aspects are presented throughout the remainder of this book.

KEY TERMS

Accrual accounting	Current assets
All-inclusive income	Current liabilities
Additional paid in capital in excess of par	Dividends
Articulation	Earnings per share (EPS)
Assets	Economic entity assumption
Balance sheet	Expenses
Cash flows from financing activities	Financial statements
Cash flows from investing activities	Footnotes (notes)
Cash flows from operating activities	General-purpose external financial reports
Common stock	Going concern
Contributed capital	Gross profit (gross margin)
Cost of goods sold (cost of sales)	Historical cost

Income
Income statement
Income tax expense
Liabilities
Liquidity
Long-term assets
Long-term (noncurrent) liabilities
Matching principle
Monetary unit
Notes to the financial statements
Operating expenses
Par value

Periodicity
Preferred stock
Retained earnings
Revenues
Revenue realization principle
Shareholders' equity
Stable dollar
Statement of cash flows
Statement of shareholders' equity
Supplementary information
Venture capital

NUMERICAL CASES

3-1

eXTREMESTUFF.com.

Chapter 3 presents background material and financial statements for the hypothetical Internet retailer, eSTUFF. Use that knowledge and data to do the following:

a. Explain how the net change in cash reported on its statements of cash flows articulates with cash reported on the balance sheets.
b. Explain how net income articulates among eSTUFF's income statement, statement of shareholders' equity, and balance sheet.
c. Use the information provided in the balance sheets and statement of cash flows to compute the historical cost of equipment and reconcile it to the equipment's net balance (book value) for 2000 and 2001.
d. Compute the interest rate for each note payable from the information contained in the income statements and balance sheets. (Assume each note was issued at the beginning of the year.)
e. State some probable reasons that eSTUFF does not own land or buildings.
f. Discuss the soundness of eSTUFF's dividend policy in light of the company's age and its financial condition.

3-2

eXTREMESTUFF.com.

Use the two-year extension of eSTUFF's financial statements to answer the questions below. (The financial statements for 2000 and 2001 are the same as those presented in Chapter 3.)

The equipment was purchased at the beginning of 2003, but short-term investments were made at the end of that year. The note payable was retired at the end of 2003.

a. Explain how net income (loss) affects the statement of shareholders' equity.
b. Explain how dividends affect the statement of shareholders' equity.
c. Why don't dividends appear on eSTUFF's income statement?
d. Examine the ending balances of the statement of shareholders' equity. On what other financial statement do those amounts appear?
e. How do you explain the changes in cash from one balance sheet to the next?

f. Discuss how the annual depreciation charges reported on the statement of cash flows were derived.

g. Discuss how the equipment's book values were determined for each year.

eXTREMESTUFF.com, Inc.

INCOME STATEMENTS
FOR THE YEARS ENDED DECEMBER 31
(IN THOUSANDS OF DOLLARS, EXCEPT PER SHARE AMOUNTS)

	2003	2002	2001	2000
Sales revenue	$1,310	$1,240	$1,200	$1,000
Cost of goods sold	800	719	660	600
Gross profit	510	521	540	400
Selling expenses	355	312	352	250
Administrative expenses	150	150	133	85
Income from continuing operations	5	59	55	65
Financial expenses	20	20	20	10
Pretax income	(15)	39	35	55
Income tax expense (benefit)	(6)	16	14	22
Net income	$ (9)	$ 23	$ 21	$ 33
Earnings per share	$ (.18)	$ .46	$ .42	$ .79

STATEMENT OF SHAREHOLDERS' EQUITY
FOR THE YEARS ENDED DECEMBER 31
(IN THOUSANDS OF DOLLARS, EXCEPT PAR VALUE)

	COMMON STOCK	ADD. CAPITAL	RET. EARNINGS
Balance as of January 1, 2000	—	—	—
Common stock issued, $1 par value	$42	$378	
Net income	—	—	$33
Dividends declared and paid			(8)
Balance as of December 31, 2000	$42	$378	$25
Common stock issued, $1 par value	8	72	—
Net income	—	—	21
Dividends declared and paid			(2)
Balance as of December 31, 2001	$50	$450	$44
Common stock issued, $1 par value	—	—	
Net income	—	—	23
Dividends declared and paid			(2)
Balance as of December 31, 2002	$50	$450	$65
Common stock issued, $1 par value	—	—	
Net income	—	—	(9)
Dividends declared and paid			
Balance as of December 31, 2003	$50	$450	$56

BALANCE SHEETS
DECEMBER 31
(IN THOUSANDS OF DOLLARS, EXCEPT PAR VALUE)

	2003	2002	2001	2000
Assets				
Current assets:				
Cash	$ 34	$187	$ 45	$ 30
Short-term investments	60	—	—	—
Accounts receivable, net	160	175	140	120
Inventory	335	270	250	200
Prepaid expenses	8	12	5	10
Total current assets	597	644	440	360
Property, plant and equipment:				
Equipment, net	204	260	380	400
Intangible Assets:				
Trademark	5	10	15	20
Total assets	$806	$914	$835	$780
Liabilities and Shareholders' Equity				
Current liabilities:				
Accounts payable	$110	$ 80	$ 50	$160
Accrued liabilities	40	43	21	50
Taxes payable	—	6	—	5
Total current liabilities	150	129	71	215
Long-term liabilities:				
Notes payable	100	220	220	120
Total liabilities	250	349	291	335
Shareholders' equity:				
Contributed capital:				
Common stock, $1 par value	50	50	50	42
Additional paid in capital	450	450	450	378
Total contributed capital	500	500	500	420
Retained earnings	56	65	44	25
Total shareholders' equity	556	565	544	445
Total liabilities and shareholders' equity	$806	$914	$835	$780

STATEMENT OF CASH FLOWS
FOR THE YEARS ENDED DECEMBER 31
(IN THOUSANDS OF DOLLARS)

	2003	2002	2001	2000
Cash, beginning of the year	$ 187	$ 45	$ 30	—
Cash flows from operating activities:				
Net income	$ (9)	$ 23	$ 21	$ 33
Depreciation expense, equipment	136	120	120	100
Amortization expense, trademark	5	5	5	5
Changes in current accounts:				
Accounts receivable	15	(35)	(20)	(120)
Inventory	(65)	(20)	(50)	(200)
Prepaid expenses	4	(7)	5	(10)
Accounts payable	30	30	(110)	160
Accrued liabilities	(3)	22	(29)	50
Taxes payable	(6)	6	(5)	5
Net cash provided (used) by operating activ.	107	144	(63)	23
Cash flows from investing activities:				
Purchase of equipment	(80)	—	(100)	(500)
Acquisition of trademark	—	—	—	(25)
Purchase of short-term investments	(60)	—	—	—
Net cash provided (used) by investing activ.	(140)	—	(100)	(525)
Cash flows from financing activities:				
Issue (retire) notes payable	(120)	—	100	120
Issue common stock	—	—	80	420
Pay cash dividend	—	(2)	(2)	(8)
Net cash provided (used) by financing activ.	(120)	(2)	178	532
Net change in cash	$(153)	$ 142	$ 15	$ 30
Cash, end of the year	$ 34	187	45	$ 30

INDUSTRY CASES

Examine the financial statements for each company listed in the following cases.

a. Determine if that firm's net change in cash as reported on the statements of cash flows articulates with the difference in cash between beginning and ending cash balances for each year.

b. Determine if that firm's net income reported on the income statements articulates with net income reported on the statements of cash flows.

3-1 *Personal Computers: Apple, Compaq, Dell, and Gateway*

3-2 *Airlines: American, Delta, and United*

3-3 *Athletic Footwear: Nike and Reebok*

3-4 *Discount Retailers: Kmart, Target, and Wal-Mart*

3-5 *Fast-Food Restaurants: McDonald's and Wendy's*

3-6 *Soft Drink Companies: Coca-Cola and PepsiCo.*

4

FINANCIAL STATEMENT COMPARABILITY

$\mathcal{C}$HAPTER LEARNING OBJECTIVES

Upon completion of this chapter, you should be able to:

◆ *Explain the advantage of common size financial statements over those disclosed on a monetary basis.*

◆ *Compute vertical and horizontal common size income statements and balance sheets.*

◆ *Calculate compound annual growth rates and indicate why this method provides better information than alternative methods of horizontal analysis.*

◆ *Determine financial statement vertical profiles and moving averages.*

◆ *Use good judgment when reconciling financial statement inconsistencies, rounding numbers, computing ratios, scaling numerical amounts, and making qualitative assessments.*

$\mathscr{C}$omparable financial statements simplify analysis, but dissimilar disclosures muddle it. Benchmarking economic results is an important part of analysis, but financial statement variability complicates the task. Firms differ in size and entities changes over time. Standardizing financial disclosures solves the problem. This chapter presents techniques for equating data sets over time and among companies.

This chapter is divided into three sections: The first section presents basic methods for converting monetary disclosures into their percentage equivalents. The middle portion extends and refines those basic techniques. The final part of the chapter discusses other reporting factors that could inhibit analysis. We use the financial statements of eSTUFF, the Internet retailer introduced in the previous chapter, to demonstrate these techniques and reporting data-related issues.

BASIC COMMON SIZE FINANCIAL STATEMENT CONSIDERATIONS

MICRO ANALYSIS 1

Industry sources, such as Dun & Bradstreet's Industry Norms and Key Business Ratios *(Bethlehem, PA: Dun & Bradstreet, Annually), present common size financial statement data for standard industry classifications.*

Common size financial statements report financial statement disclosures as a percentage of another account or as a proportion of their previous balance. You can restate the monetary value of cost of goods sold, for example, as a percentage of the same period's revenues. Similarly, the current cost of sales can be recast as a percentage of the previous year's cost of goods sold. Analyzing the percentage terms, instead of the dollar amounts, helps analysts evaluate financial statements, compare firms, and benchmark over time.[1]

You would gain little knowledge by comparing the absolute dollar amount of net income earned a decade ago with the past year's profit. The amount of revenues generating those two income streams was, in all likelihood, quite different. Comparing earnings as a percentage of revenues for those two years produces a more meaningful within company evaluation. The argument also applies to comparisons among companies. A large company's net income usually exceeds that of its smaller competitors. Rather than comparing dollar amounts of net income, you can enrich your analysis by comparing the earnings percentage, or *net profit margins,* for the companies.[2]

This section of the chapter demonstrates how to common size financial statements in two ways. We demonstrate vertical and horizontal common sizing using eSTUFF's income statement and balance sheet accounts.[3] We then discuss some alternative horizontal analysis disclosures and conclude by examining the mathematical properties of vertical and horizontal common size statements.

---

[1] *Comparability* and *consistency* are used interchangeably in this text. Strictly speaking, however, the qualitative characteristic of comparability means different entities report information in the same way, according to FASB. Consistency is strictly viewed as a single enterprise reporting data in the same manner over time.

[2] Net profit margin is determined by dividing net income by revenues. We discuss profit margins in depth in Chapter 12.

[3] Conventionally, income statements and balance sheets are common sized. The disclosures in these financial statements capture the common size elements of the statement of shareholders' equity. In contrast, the format of the statement of cash flows, which yields net cash amounts, makes interpreting common size information from this statement difficult and not very useful.

WEB **EXERCISE 1**

Locate the most recent Form 10-K for Apple and Dell Computer. Explain why comparing the monetary amounts of the two firms' cost of goods sold does not make sense.

VERTICAL COMMON SIZE FINANCIAL STATEMENTS

A **vertical common size financial statement** reports each financial statement account as a percentage of that statement's largest account balance. A common size income statement, for instance, presents each account as a percentage of revenues. To calculate this, divide every reported line item on the income statement by that period's net revenues.[4] You can use the same approach to produce a common size balance sheet, but use total assets, or total liabilities plus total shareholders' equity, instead of revenues as the denominator. Exhibit 4-1 presents eXTREMESTUFF.com's vertical common size financial statements for its first two years of operations. The exhibit's disclosures are reported as both a percentage of the base amount and in thousands of dollars.

EXHIBIT 4-1
*eXTREMESTUFF.com
Vertical Common Size
Financial Statements*

eXTREMESTUFF.com INCOME STATEMENTS VERTICAL COMMON SIZE	2001	2001	2000	2000
Sales Revenue	$1,200	100.00%	$1,000	100.00%
Cost of goods sold	$ 660	55.00%	$ 600	60.00%
Gross profit	$ 540	45.00%	$ 400	40.00%
Selling expenses	$ 352	29.33%	$ 250	25.00%
Administrative expenses	$ 133	11.08%	$ 85	8.50%
Income from continuing operations	$ 55	4.58%	$ 65	6.50%
Financial expenses	$ 20	1.67%	$ 10	1.00%
Pretax income	$ 35	2.92%	$ 55	5.50%
Income tax expenses	$ 14	1.17%	$ 22	2.20%
Net Income	**$ 21**	**1.75%**	**$ 33**	**3.30%**
Earnings per share	**$ 0.42**		**$ 0.79**	

eXTREMESTUFF.com BALANCE SHEETS VERTICAL COMMON SIZE	2001	2001	2000	2000
ASSETS				
Current Assets:				
Cash	$ 45	5.39%	$ 30	3.85%
Accounts receivable, net	$ 140	16.77%	$ 120	15.38%
Inventory	$ 250	29.94%	$ 200	25.64%
Prepaid expenses	$ 5	0.60%	$ 10	1.28%
Total current assets	$ 440	52.69%	$ 360	46.15%
Property, Plant and Equipment:				
Equipment, net	$ 380	45.51%	$ 400	51.28%
Intangible Assets:				
Trademark	$ 15	1.80%	$ 20	2.56%
Total Assets	**$ 835**	**100.00%**	**$ 780**	**100.00%**

---

[4] Use a computerized spreadsheet to do these cumbersome and repetitive tasks.

EXHIBIT 4-1
Continued

eXTREMESTUFF.com BALANCE SHEETS VERTICAL COMMON SIZE	2001	2001	2000	2000
Liabilities and Stockholders' Equity				
Current Liabilities:				
Accounts payable	$ 50	5.99%	$ 160	20.51%
Accrued liabilities	$ 21	2.51%	$ 50	6.41%
Taxes payable	$ —	0.00%	$ 5	0.64%
Total current liabilities	$ 71	8.50%	$ 215	27.56%
Long-term Liabilities:				
Notes Payable	$ 220	26.35%	$ 120	15.38%
Total liabilities	$ 291	34.85%	$ 335	42.95%
Shareholders' Equity:				
Contributed capital:				
Common stock, $1 par value	$ 50	5.99%	$ 42	5.38%
Additional paid in capital	$ 450	53.89%	$ 378	48.46%
Total contributed capital	$ 500	59.88%	$ 420	53.85%
Retained earnings	$ 44	5.27%	$ 25	3.21%
Total shareholders' equity	$ 544	65.15%	$ 445	57.05%
Total Liabilities and Stockholders' Equity	$ 835	100.00%	$ 780	100.00%

MICROSOFT'S SUCCESS

The market capitalization of Microsoft, Inc. exceeded that of every other company in the history of business at the turn of the century. Windows has made Microsoft's cofounder, Bill Gates, the richest person in the world. Does the company's common size data tell you something about economic changes?

An increasing number of firms create wealth through knowledge and information, rather than committing large amounts of fixed assets to manufacture or distribute products. Consider some of Microsoft's vertical common size income statement data. In 1988 Microsoft's cost of goods sold was 25 percent of revenues. Research

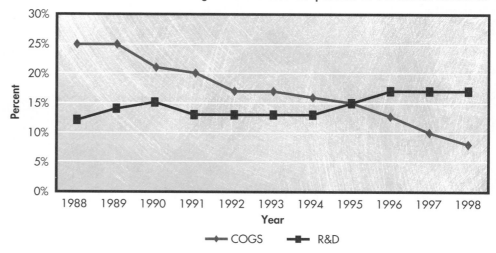

and development expenses that year equaled 12 percent of sales. A decade later, the cost of the sales had decreased to 8 percent of revenues, while 17 cents of every sales dollar went for research and development.[a] The graph on page 85 presents Microsoft's cost of goods sold and research and development expenses as a percentage of revenues from 1988 through 1998.

Observations

Do research and development and cost of goods sold trends reflect an increase or decrease in Microsoft's knowledge-based investments? Would you expect Microsoft's fixed assets to be a larger or smaller percentage of total assets than an industrial company, such as General Motors? Do you think the historical cost principle is more or less significant for information-based firms than for manufacturing concerns?

[a] Microsoft Inc.'s Annual Form 10-Ks.

HORIZONTAL COMMON SIZE FINANCIAL STATEMENTS

Horizontal common size financial statements measure account changes over time. One way to measure these changes is to establish a base period for every account equal to 100 percent. In succeeding years, each item is reported as a percentage of its base. Exhibit 4-2 presents the horizontal common size financial statements for eSTUFF.

eXTREMESTUFF.com INCOME STATEMENTS HORIZONTAL COMMON SIZE	2001	2001	2000	2000
Sales Revenue	$1,200[a]	120.00%	$1,000	100.00%
Cost of goods sold	$ 660	110.00%	$ 600	100.00%
Gross profit	$ 540	135.00%	$ 400	100.00%
Selling expenses	$ 352	140.80%	$ 250	100.00%
Administrative expenses	$ 133	156.47%	$ 85	100.00%
Income from cont. operations	$ 55	84.62%	$ 65	100.00%
Financial expenses	$ 20	200.00%	$ 10	100.00%
Pretax income	$ 35	63.64%	$ 55	100.00%
Income tax expenses	$ 14	63.64%	$ 22	100.00%
Net Income	$ 21	63.64%	$ 33	**100.00%**
	$ 0.42		$ 0.79	

eXTREMESTUFF.com BALANCE SHEETS HORIZONTAL COMMON SIZE	2001	2001	2000	2000
ASSETS				
Current Assets:				
Cash	$ 45	150.00%	$ 30	100.00%
Accounts receivable, net	$ 140	116.67%	$ 120	100.00%
Inventory	$ 250	125.00%	$ 200	100.00%

EXHIBIT 4-2
Continued

eXTREMESTUFF.com BALANCE SHEETS HORIZONTAL COMMON SIZE	2001	2001	2000	2000
Prepaid expenses	$ 5	50.00%	$ 10	100.00%
Total current assets	$ 440	122.22%	$ 360	100.00%
Property, Plant and Equipment:				
Equipment, net	$ 380	95.00%	$ 400	100.00%
Intangible Assets:				
Trademark	$ 15	75.00%	$ 20	100.00%
Total Assets	**$ 835**	**107.05%**	**$ 780**	**100.00%**
Liabilities and Stockholders' Equity				
Current Liabilities:				
Accounts payable	$ 50	31.25%	$ 160	100.00%
Accrued liabilities	$ 21	42.00%	$ 50	100.00%
Taxes payable	$ —	0.00%	$ 5	100.00%
Total current liabilities	**$ 71**	**33.02%**	**$ 215**	**100.00%**
Long-term Liabilities:				
Notes Payable	$ 220	183.33%	$ 120	100.00%
Total liabilities	**$ 291**	**86.87%**	**$ 335**	**100.00%**
Shareholders' Equity:				
Contributed capital:				
Common stock, $1 par value	$ 50	119.05%	$ 42	100.00%
Additional paid in capital	$ 450	119.05%	$ 378	100.00%
Total contributed capital	**$ 500**	**119.05%**	**$ 420**	**100.00%**
Retained earnings	$ 44	176.00%	$ 25	100.00%
Total shareholders' equity	**$ 544**	**122.25%**	**$ 445**	**100.00%**
Total Liabilities and Stockholders' Equity	**$ 835**	**107.05%**	**$ 780**	**100.00%**

[a] Amounts are in thousands of dollars.

MICRO ANALYSIS 2

Horizontal analysis reveals decreases in accounts as well as increases. Apple Computer's inventories in 1998 were only 5 percent of what they were in 1993!

ALTERNATIVE DISCLOSURES OF HORIZONTAL ANALYSIS

When setting the base year, accounts can either be *anchored* to the earliest period examined or *rolled forward* to the period preceding the year of interest.[5] To illustrate the two alternatives, assume eSTUFF's revenues were $1,240,000 in 2002. Exhibit 4-3 presents the differences between anchoring and rolling forward.

The amounts in the middle row of Exhibit 4-3 reflect data anchored to the year 2000. The final row of the exhibit, however, measures revenue change from the

---

[5] In this chapter's example of the horizontal common size statements of eSTUFF, anchoring and rolling forward the base year are identical because there are only two years of data.

EXHIBIT 4-3

*eXTREMESTUFF.com
Horizontal Common Size
Financial Statements—
Alternative Base Years*

YEAR	2002	2001	2000
Revenues	$1,240	$1,200	$1,000
2001 and 2002 as a percentage of 2000 revenues (anchoring)	124% ($1,240/$1,000)	120% ($1,200/$1,000)	100%
Annual percentage change in revenues (rolling forward)	103.3% ($1,240/$1,200)	120% ($1,200/$1,000)	100%

EXHIBIT 4-4

*eXTREMESTUFF.com
Alternative Horizontal
Common Size Percentage
Disclosures*

YEAR	2001	2000
Revenues (in thousands)	$1,200	$1,000
2001 as a percentage of the base year's (2000) revenues	120% ($1,200/$1,000)	100%
Change in revenues from 2000 to 2001	$200 ($1,200 – $1,000)	—
2001 as the percentage of change in the base year's (2000) revenues	20% ($200/$1,000)	100%

WEB EXERCISE 2

Examine Apple Computer's balance sheet disclosures in its most recent Form 10-K. Common size this year's total assets as a percentage of the previous year's resources. Is Apple's asset base expanding or contracting?

WEB EXERCISE 3

Examine Apple Computer's three income statement disclosures in its most recent Form 10-K. Compute current revenues using anchoring; then do so using the rolling forward approach.

preceding year. Sales in 2002 are reported as a percentage of 2001 revenues. In other words, we rolled forward the base year from 2000 to 2001.

The 2001 disclosures for eSTUFF in Exhibit 4-2 are listed as a percentage of the 2000 amounts. However, the percentage of increase or decrease is often more salient to an analyst. Therefore, you can express the percentage of change from the base period to the current period rather than disclose an account as a percentage of its base year amount. Exhibit 4-4 demonstrates the difference.

MATHEMATICAL PROPERTIES OF COMMON SIZE STATEMENTS

Vertical and horizontal common size statements measure different concepts; therefore, the arithmetic results of one technique do not apply to the other approach. Consider the current asset information contained in Exhibits 4-1 and 4-2. When these accounts are vertically common sized (Exhibit 4-1), their percentages add together, yielding the correct total percentage for current assets. However, the horizontal common size percentages for these four accounts do not sum vertically (Exhibit 4-2), as is illustrated in Exhibit 4-5.

Notice columns 2, 3, and 4. Adding down columns and subtracting across rows yield correct numbers. The amounts in rows 1 through 4 sum to row 5 in each of the three columns. Similarly, the difference between a row's second and third columns equals the dollar amount of the fourth column.

Now consider percentages. Adding the percentages of individual accounts (rows 1–4) in column 5 equals their total percentage (row 5, column 5). The percentages in the column 5 cells, however, do not reflect the percentage change across rows. That is, a column 4 cell divided by its corresponding column 3 cell does not equal the percentage in the corresponding column 5 cell. Row 5 illustrates this point: $80,000 / $360,000 ≠ 52.8%.

EXHIBIT 4-5

eXTREMESTUFF.com
Mathematical Properties of
Common Size Statements

1 ACCOUNT	2 $ AMOUNT 12/31/01 (000)	3 $ AMOUNT 12/31/00 (000)	4 $ AMOUNT OF CHANGE IN 2001 (000)	5 2001 VERTICAL COMMON SIZE (PERCENTAGE OF TOTAL ASSETS)	6 2001 HORIZONTAL COMMONSIZE (PERCENTAGE CHANGE)
1 Cash	$ 45	$ 30	$ 15	5.4%	50.0%
2 Accounts rec.	$140	$120	$ 20	16.8%	16.7%
3 Inventory	$250	$200	$ 50	30.0%	25.0%
4 Prepaid exp.	$ 5	$ 10	$(5)	.6%	(50.0%)
5 **Total**	**$440**	**$360**	**$ 80**	**52.8%**	**22.2%**

Next, look at column 6. Dividing an amount in column 4 by its base year value (column 3) results in the corresponding cell percentage of column 6. Row 5 data demonstrate this property: $80,000/ $360,000 = 22.2%. This is not the case, however, for summing the final column (i.e., 50% + 16.7% + 25% – 50% ≠ 22.2%).

You must be aware that horizontal and vertical common size financial statements contain related, yet different, information about the company being analyzed. The former method conveys account information across time periods (**interperiod** relationships). The latter method relates data about different accounts within the same (**intraperiod**) time frame.

COMMON SIZE FINANCIAL STATEMENT EXTENSIONS

Basic common size information is essential; extending these financial statement techniques provides additional insights. We now examine three ways of doing so: compound annual growth rates, data smoothing, and financial statement profiles.

WEB
EXERCISE 4

Look at Apple Computer's three income statement disclosures in its most recent Form 10-K again. Recall your computation of current revenues as a percentage of previous year's revenues from WEBexercise 3. Now calculate the percentage change in previous year's revenues and compare them.

COMPOUND ANNUAL GROWTH RATES

Anchoring and rolling forward the base year are simplistic horizontal common sizing techniques that lack important interperiod information. Neither report average rates of account changes: Anchoring merely relates each year's account to a single observation point, and rolling the data forward benchmarks an account against its previous period's balance. The **compound annual growth rate** method solves this problem. This analytical technique measures an account's average rate of change over a specified time period.

More than two years of data are needed to understand the compound annual growth method. Refer to eSTUFF's revenue data in Exhibit 4-3. Revenues in 2001 and 2002 were 20 percent and 24 percent larger than the 2000 base year revenues. They grew by 20 percent in the first year (from 2000 to 2001) and by 3.3 percent in the second year (from 2001 to 2002). An important question remains: How much did revenues grow annually? Did they increase by 12 percent per year (24% / 2 years) or by 11.65 percent ([20% +3.3%] / 2)?

Technology can help you quickly calculate compound growth changes. Use the internal rate of return (IRR) function command on your spreadsheet to compute compound annual growth rates.

An approximate answer is 12 percent, and 11.65 percent is somewhat more accurate. Actually, 11.4 percent is the annual revenue growth from 2000 to 2002. The inaccurate responses ignore the fundamental relationship between time and money. Specifically, 2002 revenue is a function of sales for 2000 and 2001, plus the effect of revenue growth from 2000 to 2001. In other words, annualized growth rates must explicitly consider the compounding effect of account changes in previous periods to be accurate.

It is easier to understand compound annual growth rates using several observations. For the sake of illustration, assume five additional years of revenues (2003–2007) for eSTUFF. As you study the next exhibit, keep the following points in mind:

◆ Alternative methods of horizontal analysis yield different percentage measures of growth over time.
◆ Anchoring and rolling forward approaches do not capture annual account changes.
◆ Simple annual growth rates only approximate actual growth.
◆ Simple growth rates overestimate annual account changes.
◆ Compound rates correctly measure annual growth.
◆ Cumulative growth rates capture annual change for the whole time period examined.
◆ Set period growth rates (e.g., five years) capture account changes for a specific period of time.

Exhibit 4-6 presents sales figures and related horizontal common size data. The second and third rows of Exhibit 4-6 contain percentages from the methods previ-

EXHIBIT 4-6

eXTREMESTUFF.com Compound Annual Growth Rates

	2007	2006	2005	2004	2003	2002	2001	2000
Sales revenues	$1,420[a]	$1,350	$1,330	$1,290	$1,310	$1,240	$1,200	$1,000
Base year	42%	35%	33%	29%	31%	24%	20%	—
Rolling forward	5.2%	1.5%	3.1%	–1.5%	5.6%	3.3%	20%	—
Total year-to-date simple annual growth rate	6.0%	5.8%	6.6%	7.3%	10.3%	12.0%	20%	—
Total year-to-date compound annual growth rate	5.1%	5.1%	5.9%	6.6%	9.4%	11.4%	20%	—
Five-year simple annual growth rate	2.9%	2.5%	6.6%	—	—	—	—	—
Five-year compound annual growth rate	2.7%	2.4%	5.9%	—	—	—	—	—

[a] in thousands of dollars.

ously discussed. Note how the percentages for the first three years mirror those in Exhibit 4-3.[6]

The fourth row of data discloses simple growth rate on a total year-to-date basis. We divided the percentage growth from the $1,000 sales in 2000 by the corresponding number of periods (e.g., 2003: 31% / 3 years = 10.3%, 2006: 35% / 6 years = 3.3%). Simple growth rates are inaccurate. For example, multiplying the base year amount by 10.3 percent annually does not equal 2003 revenues of $1,310 ($1,000 * 1.103*1.103*1.103 = $1,342).

Row 5 measures growth on a total year-to-date compound basis. We calculate the compound annual growth rate between a current period's monetary amount and the $1,000 base year revenues. Thus, the compound growth rate for 2003 includes revenue for four years (from 2000 through 2003), or three periods of compounding. The 2007 growth rate is a function of the revenue stream for all eight years reported (2000 through 2007), and seven periods of compounding. The compound annual growth rate is better than simple growth rates. It yields accurate results (e.g., 2003: $1,000 * 1.094 * 1.094 * 1.094 = $1,310).

The last two rows represent annual growth over a five-year period. Data in row 6 were computed on a simple five-year average basis (e.g., 2006: [($1,350 − $1,200) / $1,200] / 5 years = 2.5%). The exhibit's last row reports the compound growth rate on a five-year basis. For example, compound growth for 2005 employs revenues from 2000 through 2005 in its calculation, but compound growth for 2007 uses the last six years of sales data (2002 through 2007).

FINANCIAL STATEMENT PROFILES

You can condense vertical common size disclosures for ease of understanding. (See Exhibit 4-1.) Notice that we produced a vertical analysis for each of the two years. To collapse the years observed into a common size profile of eSTUFF's financial performance, follow these steps:

◆ Sum the monetary amounts for each account.
◆ Divide the account totals by the appropriate number of years (e.g., two in this case).
◆ Vertically common size the average account balances against revenues or assets.

This process smooths or averages the data over the periods analyzed. Exhibit 4-7 contains eSTUFF's two-year income statement profile.

EXHIBIT 4-7
eXTREMESTUFF.com Vertical Common Size Income Statement Profile (2000 and 2001, in thousands of dollars)

Sales revenue	$1,100	100.00%
Cost of goods sold	$ 630	57.27%
Gross profit	$ 470	42.73%
Selling expenses	$ 301	27.36%
Administrative expenses	$ 109	9.91%
Income from cont. operations	$ 60	5.45%
Financial expenses	$ 15	1.36%
Pretax income	$ 45	4.09%
Income tax expenses	$ 18	1.64%
Net Income	**$ 27**	**2.45%**

[6] The percentages contain annual change in the base amount, rather than a percentage of the base year amount.

WAL-MART IS WINNING

The fortunes of two discount retailers have changed dramatically in little more than a decade. During that time span, Wal-Mart overwhelmed Kmart as the country's largest discount retailer. The following compound annual growth rate chart captures the changing fortunes of the two companies:

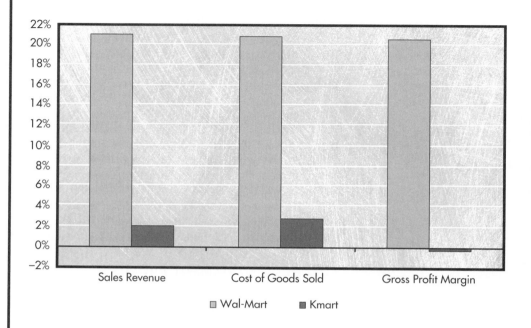

In 1989 Kmart earned $27 billion of revenue, which exceeded that of Wal-Mart by about $7 billion. For the 1999 fiscal year, the revenues of the company founded by Sam Walton were quadruple those of the besieged former industry leader: Wal-Mart's revenues were $138 billion compared with Kmart's $34 billion in sales. Anchored to 1989 amounts, Wal-Mart's sales increased by over 500 percent, but Kmart's grew by less than 25 percent, through 1999.[a] Not only has Wal-Mart's revenue increased substantially in that time period, but its gross profit has kept pace with sales growth. The company's operating profits have been a relatively consistent percentage of sales, whereas Kmart's have fluctuated from year to year. In addition, Wal-Mart has secured more favorable prices from vendors than its competitor as a result of its market dominance.

Observations

Do you think horizontal common size analysis would help you grasp the changes in Kmart and Wal-Mart? Discuss how additional compound annual growth rate information could provide information about the consistency of growth for Kmart and Wal-Mart. Which company would have more consistent compound annual growth rates in those areas? Securing lower prices from vendors enables a company to increase gross profit or lower its prices even further in hopes of increasing market share. Which strategy do you think Wal-Mart has adopted?

---

[a] Wal-Mart Stores, Inc. and Kmart, Inc. Annual Form 10-Ks.

EXHIBIT 4-8
*eXTREMESTUFF.com
Revenues and Cost of Goods
Sold*

YEAR	ANNUAL REVENUES	ANNUAL COST OF GOODS SOLD	3-YEAR MOVING AVERAGE OF REVENUES	3-YEAR MOVING AVERAGE OF COGS
2000	$1,000	$600	—	—
2001	$1,200	$660	—	—
2002	$1,240	$719	$1,147	$660
2003	$1,310	$800	$1,250	$726
2004	$1,290	$812	$1,280	$777
2005	$1,330	$815	$1,310	$809
2006	$1,350	$825	$1,323	$817
2007	$1,420	$855	$1,367	$832

WEB
EXERCISE 5

*Using the most recent Form 10-K
for Apple and Dell Computer,
compute each firm's income statement profiles through gross profit.
Do these numbers help answer
the question posed in the first
WEBexercise of this chapter?*

MICRO
ANALYSIS 6

*Constructing a four-quarter
moving average of a company's
revenues and comparing those
results with actual quarterly
sales indicate whether seasonality exists.*

MOVING AVERAGES

Vertical profiles average financial disclosures for all years in a data set. The strength of smoothing data for all periods analyzed, however, is also a limitation. Averaging financial statement data over numerous years can obscure trends within periods of interest. Annual disclosures, in contrast, reflect economic impact of a single reporting period. A middle ground exists: You can construct financial statements on a moving average basis. This common sizing technique captures more than one period of data but fewer than the complete data set.[7] Assume, for example, that you had an eight-year data set for eSTUFF and were interested in benchmarking the company's recent performance against its competitors. You might examine three-year common size moving averages of the firms of interest. Exhibit 4-8, based on Exhibit 4-6's revenues and assumed numbers for cost of goods sold, presents three-year moving averages.

After you average revenues, cost of goods sold, and other data, you can compute three-year vertical income statement profiles. You could then compare eSTUFF's recent operating performance against those of its competitors.

COMMON SIZING MUST ADDRESS THE ISSUE

The swoosh, golden arches, and the circle with the hyphenated script are among the most recognizable symbols in the world. The logos of Nike, Inc., McDonald's Corp., and The Coca-Cola Co. strike a chord with virtually everyone in the world. All three companies rely heavily on their image. Intangible resources such as these are of immense value to these firms, but analysts must tread carefully here.

Each firm's total assets grew annually, but only two companies' intangible assets increased on a compound annual basis.[a] Nike and McDonald's experienced double-digit growth in their intangible resources, but Coke's rate of growth in these assets stagnated.

---

[7] Moving averages are computed for an odd number of periods (usually three, five, or seven). For a three-year moving average, add the third oldest observation (e.g., 2002) to the first two periods' monetary values (e.g., 2000 and 2001) and divide by 3 to compute the average. Repeat the process by dropping the 2000 observation and adding the 2003 data. N–1 periods are lost to initialize the process (i.e., moving averages for 2000 and 2001 cannot be computed in this example).

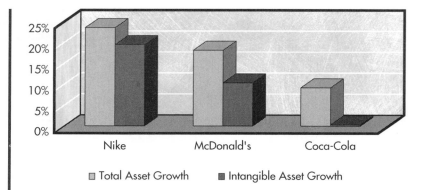

□ Total Asset Growth   ■ Intangible Asset Growth

Like most assets, intangible resources are reported at historical cost. Vertical common sizing reveals that intangible asset costs constitute a relatively small percentage of each firm's total assets.

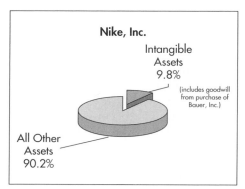

Nike, Inc.

Intangible Assets 9.8%
(includes goodwill from purchase of Bauer, Inc.)

All Other Assets 90.2%

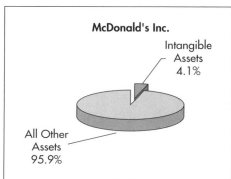

McDonald's Inc.

Intangible Assets 4.1%

All Other Assets 95.9%

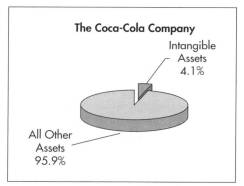

The Coca-Cola Company

Intangible Assets 4.1%

All Other Assets 95.9%

Observations

Discuss whether you could attribute Coke's relatively slow asset growth to its lack of intangible asset growth. So, as you lace up your Air Jordans, on your way to grab a Big Mac and a supersized Coke, what is the lesson you have learned about common size data?

Data are based on Form 10-Ks for Nike, Inc., McDonald's Inc., and The Coca-Cola Co.

DATA CONSIDERATIONS

Thus far we have focused on producing equivalent data sets. Carefully constructing and interpreting common size statements are the first steps in analysis; but you must consider other data factors. You must also account for observation quantity, financial statement inconsistencies, scaling disclosures, ratio computations, numerical rounding, and qualitative statements. The following sections examine these items in depth.

WEB EXERCISE 6

Locate investor relations for Apple Computer at apple.com. How many years of financial statements does the company provide?

WEB EXERCISE 7

Through 1997, Apple Computer reported income in a single-step format (revenues – expenses = net income). Examine the company's income statement in its most recent Form 10-K. Does Apple currently report income in a single- or multiple-step format? What does this tell you about the consistency of the company's financial disclosures?

MICRO ANALYSIS 7

Apple reported 1994 sales in thousands of dollars, but it disclosed 1998 revenues in millions. The company's 1994 revenues of $9.2 million, however, greatly exceeded the $5.9 million sales in 1998.

OBSERVATION QUANTITY

You must analyze a sufficient number of corporate disclosures to capture corporate and industry trends.[8] 10-K forms provide income statements, cash flows and shareholders for the past three years. They also disclose the current and previous years' balance sheets. But two or three years' worth of financial statements provides insufficient trend data. You need more financial statements, or what analysts call **observations**. Use common sense, though; trending a company back to its inception may provide historical perspective about the firm, but much of the earlier data are irrelevant to the analysis. Recall from Chapter 2 that information overload and misinformation can detract from the analysis. A good rule of thumb is to analyze a company's financial statements from the previous five to ten years.

FINANCIAL STATEMENT INCONSISTENCIES

Items and amounts disclosed on financial statements vary between reporting periods and among entities. Be aware of **financial statement inconsistencies**, and adjust them as needed. For example, eSTUFF's operating expenses are disclosed as two amounts: selling and administrative expenses. A competitor might combine them into a single selling, general, and administrative expense category. A third Internet retailer could simply disclose its operating expenses as a single amount. Moreover, eSTUFF could change its expense disclosure on subsequent income statements, reporting either more or less detail in the future.

So, how do you trend and common size financial statements when the accounts change over time and among competitors? Fortunately, most changes are insignificant. Formats change inconsequentially, and numerical values adjust immaterially. They do, however, complicate analysis. Convention dictates that you use the most recent information available.

SCALING DISCLOSURES

Scaling monetary values simplifies data presentation. eSTUFF, for instance, discloses monetary amounts in thousands of dollars. (e.g., revenues were $1,200,000 in 2001, not $1,200). Larger companies report in millions of dollars. Some firms might even report in billions. You must account for the scale of financial statements at the outset or risk grave errors. You must also verify the monetary unit

---

[8] For this discussion, we assume the reporting entity does not significantly change in the time period examined.

being reported. There is a significant difference between the value of one U.S. dollar and one Canadian dollar. The relative values of American greenbacks and Japanese yen are even greater.

RATIO COMPUTATIONS

WEB ℰXERCISE 8

Examine management's discussion and analysis in Apple's most recent Form 10-K. Does the company report any ratios?

A **ratio** is the quotient of one number divided by another numerical value. Expressed as a fraction, ratios describe the relationship between two (or more) financial statement disclosures. For example, the previously mentioned net profit margin (net income / net revenues) is a ratio. It explains the proportion of profit that existed for that period's level of revenue. As discussed in Chapter 8, ratios significantly contribute to the information set in analysis.

Balance sheet disclosures exist at specific dates (such as December 31, 2001). In contrast, income statement items represent revenues earned and expenses incurred over a period of time (e.g., for the year 2001). This difference influences ratio calculations. You should average balance sheet data when using them as a ratio input. Add the beginning amount of the balance sheet item with its ending amount and divide by two.[9] But organizations realize revenue and incur expenses throughout a reporting period; therefore, do not average these income statement disclosures.

Ratios are tools of analysis. Use them to generate information. You do not have to use every ratio in each analysis. And you can be creative: Make your own financial statement proportions if they help you gain insights about account relationships.

NUMERICAL ROUNDING

MICRO 𝒜NALYSIS 8

When considering whether to round a number, ask yourself, "Could rounding affect my decision?" If your answer is yes, do not round the number.

Analysts must also be aware of **numerical rounding**—whether numbers should be rounded and to what place they can be adjusted to avoid unnecessary clutter. Rounding is appropriate if it does not materially affect the information set or decisions stemming from that data. Obviously, such determinations require judgment. Round data to a whole number (or tenth of a whole number) for a completed process, but not for an intermediate step in a computation. For example, eSTUFF's net profit margin (net income / revenues) was 1.75 percent in 2001.[10] In discussing the company's operations, reference to a 1.7 percent or 1.8 percent profit margin would suffice. But given the relatively small percentage of revenues realized in profit, rounding the ratio up to 2 percent would not be judicious. Profit margin is also an input to another set of ratios—return on investment. You should use 1.75 percent when computing these ratios, rather than 1.7 percent or 1.8 percent.

Rounding numbers sometimes leads to slight mathematical inaccuracies. Refer to eSTUFF's vertical common size income statement for 2001 in Exhibit 4-1. Gross profit is 45 percent of revenues and operating expenses equal 40.41 percent. Income before taxes is more accurately 4.59 percent, rather than the reported 4.58

---

[9] Using only two observation points yields a broad estimate of the average balance sheet data. If data were available, adding the ending daily balance of a balance sheet account and dividing by 365 days in the year would result in a far superior average balance sheet ratio input.

[10] Profit margin equals net income as a percentage of sales revenue as disclosed on a vertical common size income statement. See eSTUFF's common size income statement in Exhibit 4-1.

percent. Extending the number of significant digits in the common sizing of the financial statements would eliminate most minor rounding errors, but at a cost of needlessly cluttering the statements and the analysis. Remember that minor math errors usually stem from rounding, but larger ones signify mistakes. Ignore the former, and correct the latter!

MICRO ANALYSIS 9

Apple Computer's 1998 net income was $309 million; it earned $310 million in 1994. The company's operating earnings were $522 million in 1994 and $261 million four years later. Was 1998's income as good as it was in 1994?

QUALITATIVE STATEMENTS

Analysts should use adjectives, such as *better* or *worse*, carefully. Haphazardly describing data biases analysis. Consider two corporations in the same industry. One company has a greater net profit margin than its competitor, but you cannot automatically conclude that the first company's net profit margin is better than that of the competition. The firm with the lower profit margin derived all of its earnings from its core business activities. The other company had a net operating loss, but it recorded large gains from selling fixed assets. Sustaining net earnings under these circumstances is impossible. The company is liquidating its productive base! Such a firm has a higher profit margin than its competitor, but not a better one.

SUMMARY

This chapter examines some preliminary financial statement topics. Common size techniques and other data considerations improve financial statement analysis. Vertical and horizontal common size financial statements express data in terms of percentage. Vertical common sizing converts each account's monetary value into a percentage of the aggregate amount reported: revenues on the income statement and assets on the balance sheet. Horizontal common sizing measures account changes over time. We present three methods of horizontal analysis: anchoring, rolling forward, and compound annual growth. Compound annual growth produces the most salient data.

You must analyze a sufficient number of reporting periods to benchmark a company over time and realize that data formats fluctuate from year to year and among firms. You must make data and formats consistent over time and comparable among companies. In addition, disclosures are often scaled; you need to consider numerical magnitude. Exercise care when computing ratios, rounding numbers, and making qualitative judgments about data.

Subsequent chapters use many of the preliminary procedures discussed here in a more realistic environment. They reinforce and extend the concepts of this chapter.

KEY TERMS

Common size financial statements	Numerical rounding
Compound annual growth rate	Observations
Financial statement inconsistencies	Ratio
Horizontal common size financial statements	Scaling
Interperiod analysis	Vertical common size financial statements
Intraperiod analysis	

NUMERICAL CASE

4-1

eXTREMESTUFF.com

Use eSTUFF's financial statements presented in NC 3-2 to compute the following information from 2000 to 2003:

a. Vertical and horizontal common size income statements and balance sheets
b. Compound annual growth rate income statement and balance sheet
c. Vertical profile of the income statement, balance sheet, and statement of cash flows
d. Three-year moving average income statement and balance sheet

INDUSTRY CASES

Use the income statement and balance sheet information presented for the text's six industries to note at least one interesting observation about each company's:

a. Vertical common size statements
b. Horizontal common size statements (either the anchored or rolling forward approach)
c. Compound annual growth rates

4-1 *Personal Computers: Apple, Compaq, Dell, and Gateway*

4-2 *Airlines: American, Delta, and United*

4-3 *Athletic Footwear: Nike and Reebok*

4-4 *Discount Retailers: Kmart, Target, and Wal-Mart*

4-5 *Fast-Food Restaurants: McDonald's and Wendy's*

4-6 *Soft Drink Companies: Coca-Cola and PepsiCo.*

INDUSTRY INTERNET CASES

Examine the most recent financial statements for the companies in the six industries listed in the appendixes. For each firm, identify the following:

a. Numerical reporting scale
b. Accounts listed within each financial statement element on the income statement (revenues and expenses) and balance sheet (assets, liabilities, and shareholders' equity)
c. Whether statement terminology is consistent from one company to another
d. Whether each firm discloses the same number of accounts
e. Any other reporting difference among the companies within an industry

4-1 *Personal Computers: Apple, Compaq, Dell, and Gateway.*

4-2 *Airlines: American, Delta, and United.*

5 DATA DISCLOSURES

CHAPTER LEARNING OBJECTIVES

Upon completion of this chapter, you should be able to:

◆ Understand why overall economic and industry conditions matter to financial statement analysis.

◆ Explain the state of the U.S. and international economy for 1993–1998.

◆ Discuss the background, environment, markets, and trends in the personal computer (PC) industry.

◆ Describe the performance of Apple Computer during the period analyzed.

◆ List some of Apple's competitors.

◆ Define the new, or information, economy and explain the role of the PC industry in it.

$\mathcal{A}$nalysis comes alive in Chapter 5! We now apply many of the concepts presented in the first four chapters to the PC industry, and we continue to use this industry throughout the remainder of the text. Evaluating existing data develops your analytical skills, familiarizes you with complexities and inconsistencies absent from contrived data, and relates people and events to the financial statements they create. The real world, however, is often untidy. Corporate disclosures lack the simplicity of eXTREMESTUFF.com. Moreover, the economy and industries change over time. You must include these factors in your analysis. A combination of technical knowledge, creative insights, and a realistic perspective about corporate disclosures allow you to analyze complex financial statements realistically.

The analysis of Apple Computer, Inc. and other PC firms covers the period from 1993 through 1998.[1] (You can find relevant financial statements in Appendix A.) Economic and PC industry data provide context for the analysis. The chapter is divided into four parts: The first section presents macroeconomic information for 1993–1998. Next, we examine PC industry data from those years. Third, we discuss 1993–1998 financial information about Apple Computer and its competitors. Finally, we describe the industry's role in moving the economy to the information age.

ECONOMIC CONDITIONS

The United States experienced sustained economic growth from 1993 through 1998. Productivity increased, unemployment declined, inflation decreased, and the stock market soared. The global economy coincided with the U.S. economy in the early years of analysis, but unsettling events occurred in some parts of the world during 1997 and continued in 1998. We now examine these economic conditions in greater detail.

MICRO ANALYSIS 1

Economic booms hurt some industries. The pawnshop industry, for example, suffered economic hardship during the 1990s. Do you have any thoughts as to why?

WEB EXERCISE 1

Use some of the Internet addresses listed in the supplement to Chapter 2 to update information about the U.S. economy from 1999 to the present year.

U.S. ECONOMY

The United States prospered economically from 1993 through 1998. Four exhibits illustrate the overall health of the American economy.

The **gross domestic product (GDP)** reports the annual output of goods and services produced by the economy. It is a primary measure of economic vitality and productivity. Exhibit 5-1 reports GDP in constant 1993 dollars. This means the effects of inflation have been factored out of the graphical representation of GDP.

The **unemployment rate** measures the percentage of employable Americans who were without jobs at a given time. Unemployment decreased during the period analyzed (Exhibit 5-2). The 4-percent 1998 unemployment rate approached an historic low for a peacetime economy.

Annual wholesale and retail price level changes report the amount of inflation (deflation) in the economy. The **producer price index (PPI)** measures price changes at the wholesale level, and the **consumer price index (CPI)** compares an average family's cost of living with a base year's amount. Exhibit 5-3 reveals that inflation was relatively low, and in some cases nonexistent, during the period analyzed.

---

[1] You can update the analysis by doing the Internet Industry cases.

EXHIBIT 5-1
Real Gross Domestic Product (billions of 1993 dollars) 1993–1998

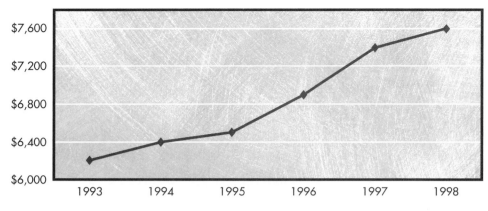

EXHIBIT 5-2
Unemployment Rate (annual percentage) 1993–1998

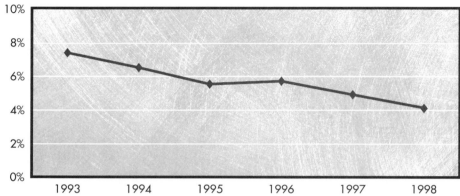

EXHIBIT 5-3
Inflation Rate (annual percentage change) 1993–1998

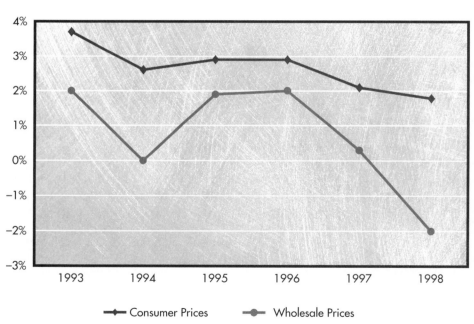

The stock prices of 500 major companies comprise **Standard & Poor's (S&P) 500** index. This weighted average index conveys the trend in market values of publicly traded companies. Investors placed an increasingly higher economic value on these firms as evidenced by Exhibit 5-4.

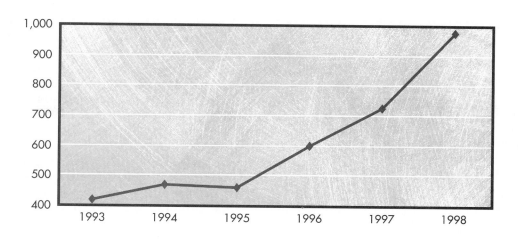

GLOBAL ECONOMY

Other industrialized countries' economies were healthy from 1993 to 1996, according to international statistical measures. Developing nations' economies also grew during those years. But weaknesses began to appear in certain regions during 1997. By the end of that year, most of Asia was in a recession. Russia and Latin America followed suit in 1998.

As a developing country, Thailand's economy depended on exporting goods to wealthier nations. An economic crisis erupted in mid-1997 when that country stopped attaching the value of its currency (the baht) to the U.S. dollar in an attempt to increase exports. The dollar had been strengthening against most of the world's major currencies up to that point. This made Thai exports, which were tied to the dollar's value, very expensive.

That policy shift set off a domino effect in Asia, referred to as the "Asian contagion."[2] Currencies fluctuated, interest rates rose, liquidity became scarce, and businesses failed in short order throughout Asia. The underlying causes of the Asian contagion were many, the Thai policy decision simply brought them to light. The reasons cited for the Asian economic crises included the following[3]:

◆ Out-of-control spending and borrowing on infeasible building projects
◆ Lax banking regulations
◆ Failure of businesses and banks to acknowledge existing bad debts
◆ Lack of accountability and openness (transparency) in Asian corporate reporting
◆ Business and political collusion and cronyism

The value of the ruble became so worthless that some Russian factories used the currency as roofing material.

Following closely on the heels of the downturn in Asia, Russia experienced economic difficulty. The fall of communism resulted in the breakup of the Soviet Union and a shift to market-based economies in Russia, its former Soviet Republics, and Eastern European countries. Some former Soviet bloc countries made a relatively smooth transition to capitalism. Russia did not. The nation defaulted on its debt. As a result, investors pulled out of Russia, credit dried up,

---

[2] J. Bowles, "The Asian Crises in Retrospect," *World Trade,* February 2000, pp. 56–57.
[3] Based on material from C. Patten, "Of Tigers, Bulls and Bears," *Time,* February 2, 1998. Mr. Patten was the last British governor of Hong Kong.

WEB EXERCISE 2

Visit the home page of the EU at http://www.europa.eu.int/.

MICRO ANALYSIS 3

Economic interdependency strengthens international relationships and reduces potential conflicts among countries. The formation of the EU is especially important to a region that experienced two devastating world wars in the 20th century.

WEB EXERCISE 3

Use the Internet addresses listed in the supplement to this text to update the status of the global economy from 1999 to the present year.

the stock market went into a tailspin, and government spending soared. The Russian economy had virtually collapsed by 1998.

Economic development in Latin America also slowed. Government debt, political instability, and the economic shock from the Asian contagion hurt the United States' economically emerging neighbors to the south. Many Asian, Central American, and South American economies began recovering by the end of 1998. Their currencies strengthened, stock values increased, public spending decreased, and bank reformation began.[4] The Russian economy, however, remained in disarray at the end of 1998.

These economic trouble spots did not affect economic conditions in the United States and Western Europe. Exhibits 5-1 through 5-4 demonstrate the strength of the U.S. economy. Western European countries were integrating their economies at that time into the **European Union (EU)**, which promotes common financial, legal, and tax rules among its member nations.

As a result of this integration, countries in the European Union changed in the following ways:

◆ They became more fiscally responsible.
◆ They reduced national trade barriers.
◆ They became more free market oriented.
◆ They relaxed many pro-labor employment laws.
◆ They allowed more corporate mergers and acquisitions.
◆ They standardized financial reporting.[5]
◆ They adopted a common currency, the European monetary unit or *euro*.

Partly as a result of the economic discipline demanded by the EU, Western European economies flourished in 1997 and 1998.

PERSONAL COMPUTER INDUSTRY

The **personal computer industry** consists of companies that design, manufacture, and market PCs and related devices to businesses and individuals. The industry originated in the 1970s, when technological innovations reduced computer size to the point where machines could fit on a desktop and process large quantities of data. Small businesses and individuals as well as large corporations began buying computers when prices decreased to affordable levels.

MOORE'S LAW

Gordon Moore was a founder and former CEO of Intel. He astutely observed a phenomenon in 1965 that has guided the strategies of many technology companies.

---

[4] See, for example, D. McDermott, "For Asia, Recovery Carries a Peril," *Wall Street Journal,* October 22, 1998, pp. A14 and A17.

[5] Technically, reporting alternatives have been reduced rather than eliminated. The process is one of harmonization, not standardization, accomplished through a series of European Directives.

Moore noticed a pronounced trend when he graphed data about memory-chip performance. He observed that each new type of computer chip was released within two years of its predecessor, and it was at least twice as powerful as the previous chip. Those observations have become known as *Moore's Law.* A corollary to Moore's Law states that computer costs decrease as rapidly as machine power increases. In effect, computing power grows and costs shrink over time.

Observations

Discuss the implications of Moore's Law on your analysis of the PC industry. Do you think it still holds? Will PCs continue to become more powerful and less expensive? Should you try to assess which firms successfully plan their operations around and control for Moore's Law?

DATA INPUTS

Dun & Bradstreet's (D&B's) annual publication *Industry Norms and Key Business Ratios* provides analysts with benchmarking data.[a] Do you think this source provides perfect benchmarking data?

Dun & Bradstreet bases industry information on four-digit SIC codes.[b] The publication discloses monetary income statements and balance sheets, common size financial statement information, and a variety of financial ratios. Analysts compute data for this industry source as follows:

◆ *Sample size.* Dun & Bradstreet analysts sample a number of firms within each industry every year. The number of companies sampled, however, varies from year to year.

◆ *Common size financial statements.* Analysts compute percentage statements for each firm in the sample. An unweighted average of those computations represents that industry's common size financial statements. This means that the smallest firm's data are considered equally as important as those of the largest company in the sample when computing common size data.

◆ *Monetary financial statements.* Analysts rank the total assets and revenues for each company in the sample from the highest to lowest dollar amounts. They then use the medians, or midpoints, in these rankings in conjunction with the unweighted common size data to produce typical financial statements. The income statement and balance sheet are inconsistent because the asset midpoint and revenue median usually stem from different companies. Moreover, using median asset and revenue values weights every firm's monetary values equally.

◆ *Ratios.* Next analysts rank-order each ratio computed (e.g., the current ratio) for the sampled companies. Three numerical disclosures result from this ranking: a median, upper quartile, and lower quartile ratio. The analysts then judge whether the highest of the three ratios computed is reported as the upper or lower quartile ratio.[c]

◆ *Alternative Reporting Methods.* Corporate disclosures of the sampled firms are unadjusted. For example, some firms may depreciate fixed assets on a straight-line basis, while others use an accelerated depreciation method. The analysts do not reconcile companies using accelerated depreciation to a straight-line method, or vice-versa.[d]

Observations
Discuss the imperfections in D&B's industry data. Do they invalidate the source as a valuable industry reference? Limit its usefulness? Why do you think the company would publish less than perfect reference material?

---

[a] Dun & Bradstreet, *Industry Norms and Key Business Ratios* (New York: Dun & Bradstreet), published annually.
[b] As defined by the 1987 U.S. Standard Industry Classification.
[c] Ratio judgments are discussed more thoroughly beginning with Chapter 8.
[d] As a practical matter, lack of corporate disclosures precludes such conversions. A better theoretical technique would be to only include firms in the sample that use the same depreciation method. This, too, is impossible because companies depreciating assets the same way use different methods to report other items (e.g., FIFO versus LIFO for inventory valuation).

MICRO $\mathscr{A}$NALYSIS 4

By 1997, PCs accounted for 71 percent of the $222 billion computer market, according to Dataquest.

INDUSTRY CHANGES

The PC industry changed during the period analyzed. A series of charts conveys these recent shifts. Exhibit 5-5 reports annual PC sales from 1993 through 1998, Exhibit 5-6 presents average PC prices during that time period, and

EXHIBIT 5-5
Annual Global Shipment of PCs (millions of units) 1993–1998

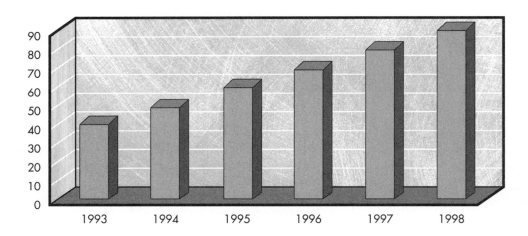

EXHIBIT 5-6
Average Wholesale Price of PCs (dollars) 1993–1998

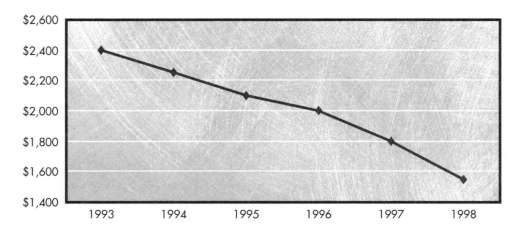

EXHIBIT 5-7
Composition of Global PC Market (percent) 1993 and 1998

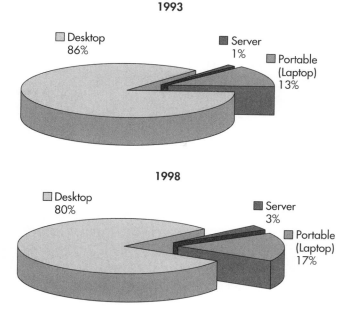

1993

Desktop 86%

Server 1%

Portable (Laptop) 13%

1998

Desktop 80%

Server 3%

Portable (Laptop) 17%

WEB EXERCISE 4

Find out more about the history of PCs at http://www.comput-ers.about.com.

MICRO ANALYSIS 5

Price decreases reduced profit per machine because companies could not reduce costs fast enough to offset the decline in sales prices.

Exhibit 5-7 discloses sales composition at the beginning and end of the period analyzed.[6]

These exhibits characterize an industry with increasing sales volume, decreasing product prices, and a movement away from desktop machines and toward laptops and network servers. The 90 million PCs sold in 1998 brought the total installed PC base to over 300 million units worldwide. Data from 1997 exemplify industry growth and decreasing computer prices. Unit shipments increased by 16 percent that year, but those sales boosted industry revenues by only 8 percent.[7] Percentage increases in laptops and servers indicate a trend toward product diversification, greater PC mobility, and more computing power.

MARKET SHARE

The PC industry was fragmented during the period analyzed. The top four companies in the industry accounted for approximately 36 percent of PC sales from 1993 through 1998. The composition of the leading companies, however, shifted dramatically during that time. Exhibit 5-8 shows the decline in the market share of IBM and Apple, coupled with the ascent of Compaq and Dell, indicates the changing fortunes of PC companies.

Worldwide, PCs became a standard business tool during the 1990s. The United States, however, continued to dominate the market for these devices. Exhibit 5-9 presents the 1998 composition of the global market for PCs.

---

[6] Data derived from Standard & Poor, *Industry Surveys Computers: Hardware 1993–1998* (New York: McGraw-Hill).
[7] *US Industry & Trade Outlook '99,* (New York: McGraw-Hill Companies and the U.S. Department of Commerce, 1999), p. 27-13.

EXHIBIT 5-8
PC Market Share (percent)
1993 and 1998

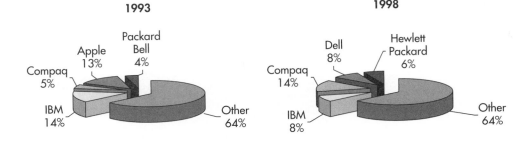

1993   1998

EXHIBIT 5-9
Geographical Purchases of PCs
1998

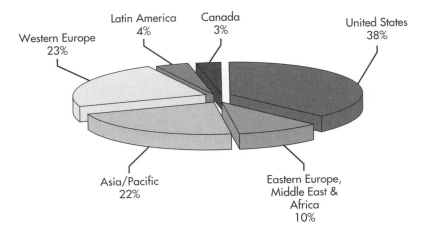

EXHIBIT 5-10
Annual Percentage Change in Sales 1998

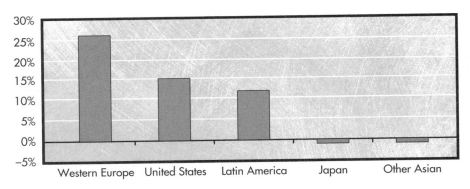

Exhibits 5-10 and 5-11 capture the industry's sensitivity to economic conditions. Exhibit 5-10 contrasts growth in the healthy Western geographical market segment with that of Asian countries in 1998, and Exhibit 5-11 presents changes in Asian purchases before and after the economic downturn in that region.

THE PC WAR

Apple Computer was once a PC industry leader. Do you think its architecture had anything to do with its loss of market share?

Seizing upon the growing trend in PCs, IBM entered the market in the early 1980s. In its rush to enter the fray, "Big Blue," as the computer giant is known,

EXHIBIT 5-11
*Annual Percentage Change in
Asian Sales 1996 and 1998*

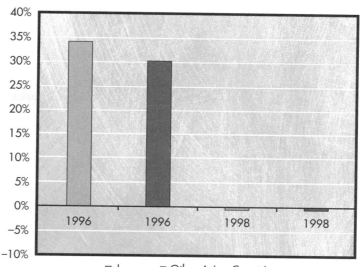

Japan   Other Asian Countries

elected to acquire key components from outside suppliers rather than develop them internally. IBM's decision had profound consequences for the PC industry. IBM selected Intel's computer chips and Microsoft's software to operate its PCs. The computer giant's decision meant IBM had no ownership claim on the composition of its type of PC. In other words, the architecture of the machine was *open,* or nonproprietary.

Other companies quickly entered the market. They manufactured and distributed IBM-like PCs. These "IBM clones" were often more powerful and less expensive than those of Big Blue. All of these computer makers used Microsoft's MS-DOS, and its Windows successor, as well as Intel CPUs. Companies that maintained proprietary systems, or *closed architecture,* were overwhelmed by the emerging industry standard. Apple Computer, for example, had its own operating system (Mac OS) and used Motorola microprocessors.[a] The creator of the Macintosh line of PCs experienced large decreases in its market share to less than 4 percent in 1998 as Wintel came to dominate the industry in the 1990s.

Observations

Discuss some of the advantages and disadvantages of Apple's unique PCs. Do you think not being an IBM clone was Apple's only reason for its poor financial performance in the mid-1990s?

---

[a] One of the many PC industry ironies is that Apple also uses IBM microprocessors in its machines.

WEB
EXERCISE 5

*Go to http://www.microsoft.com
and http://www.intel.com to find
out more about Microsoft and
Intel.*

INDUSTRY ENVIRONMENT

In the 1993–1998 time span, the industry was dominated by the **"Wintel" duopoly**: Microsoft's Windows operating system and Intel's Pentium microprocessors (central processing units, or CPUs). Ninety percent of PCs ran on a version of Windows, and Intel's CPUs powered 80 percent of the machines by 1996.[8] The

---

[8] Standard & Poor, *Industry Surveys Computers: Hardware 1993–1998* (New York: McGraw-Hill, annually).

standard design, high performance, and low prices of Intel's and Microsoft's products contributed to rapid industry growth.

MATURING MARKETS

The PC industry continued to mature from 1993 to 1998. It increasingly exhibited characteristics of an entrenched industry, such as the following:

◆ Intense competition
◆ Shrinking profit margins
◆ Increased emphasis on cost control
◆ Aggressive inventory management
◆ Broader product and service offerings
◆ Lack of core product differentiation among companies
◆ Fewer entrants into the industry and corporate consolidation
◆ Revamped distribution networks

Personal computing emerged as a major industry during the 1980s. Many firms' earnings and stock prices exceeded those in the more established sectors of the economy during that decade. Those conditions evaporated, for the most part, by the mid-1990s. Companies attempted to cut costs, increase sales, and offer more products (e.g., handheld devices) and services (e.g., Internet access) to gain competitive advantages in the maturing marketplace.

The product life cycle of a PC is short. Half of the profit earned from products introduced between 1993 and 1998 occurred within the first six months of product introduction, according to industry estimates.[9] The short **product duration**, or period of time that a product is economically viable, required PC companies to continually roll out new computers. Successful product launches resulted from effective research and development, efficient manufacturing, and successful distribution.

Because primary components of PCs were standardized, many consumers perceived the machines to be *commodities,* or indistinguishable boxes. Customers moved from brand loyalty (such as IBM) to value-based purchases during the period analyzed. Companies that failed to adopt to this changing environment ceased operations or were merged into more successful companies. Driven by lower component costs and intense competition, the average PC selling price kept declining. Companies had to reduce operating costs and efficiently manage inventories in order to survive.

Many key PC components were manufactured by a limited number of suppliers. Successful companies acquired raw materials as needed but did not maintain large inventory levels. Less successful PC companies either carried too much inventory or stocked out of the necessary components. Firms that failed to acquire components when needed had ordering backlogs and missed sales opportunities. Maintaining high inventory levels, on the other hand, unproductively tied up resources.

Distribution strategies shifted from 1993 to 1998. Companies conventionally sold computers to retailers, who sold them to the end users. Compaq and Apple

WEB EXERCISE 6

Examine Apple Computer's most recent Form 10-K. Does the company still use its own operating system and Motorola's microprocessors?

MICRO ANALYSIS 6

Remember Moore's Law!

MICRO ANALYSIS 7

Mother Nature rules! A typhoon reduced Taiwanese microprocessor production in the summer of 2000. Some PC firms experienced manufacturing delays, due to the parts shortage caused by the weather.

WEB EXERCISE 7

Examine the Web site of either Dell or Gateway and describe how easy it is to order a PC directly from the manufacturer.

MICRO ANALYSIS 8

The movement toward direct selling isn't the first change in industry selling practices. Apple Computer initially distributed its products exclusively through independent Apple resellers. It was only in the early 1990s that the company broadened its distribution channels and began selling to general merchandise stores, electronic superstores, and office product supercenters.

---

[9] Standard & Poor, *Computer Surveys: Computer Hardware,* June 3, 1999, p.3.

represented this traditional **indirect selling** approach. Dell and Gateway revolutionized PC distribution. These companies sold product directly to the end user. The power of the Internet and cost advantages inherent in **direct selling** motivated many indirect sellers to establish direct marketing channels. Increasingly, companies began selling on both a direct and indirect basis in an attempt to maximize sales.

PERSONAL COMPUTER COMPANIES

No one company or group of firms dominated the industry during the mid-1990s, as shown in Exhibit 5-8. The majority of the market (about 64 percent) consisted of firms other than the four industry leaders. The number of those other firms, however, dwindled from 1993 through 1998.[10] Consequently, the average market share per company increased during the time period analyzed. The four market leaders commanded about the same market share in 1998 as they did in 1993. Their composition and rank order of the top four firms, however, changed dramatically from 1993 to 1998 (Exhibit 5-8).

WHAT'S YOUR ANALYSIS

FIRST MOVERS

The *first mover concept* states that the company in a high-tech segment that gets its product to market first gains a powerful and virtually unassailable leadership position in that niche. This theory may not always work in practice.

The bandwagon mentality drives the first mover concept: A few technologically advanced consumers use the recently introduced product or service. If they find it beneficial, useful, or enjoyable, they spread the word. Other people quickly follow the "tekkies" lead. The first mover quickly becomes so large that it cannot be challenged.

While intuitively appealing, the first mover concept doesn't always hold water. Two examples illustrate. Xerox introduced the graphic user interface (GUI, pronounced "gooey") in its early Star computer. Apple soon adopted this point-and-click approach to personal computing. A relative latecomer, however, dominates the mouse and icon environment—you may be familiar with Microsoft's Windows application. Apple and another firm, Go, also made early moves in handheld computing devices. These computers failed in the marketplace. Of course, personal digital assistants that promise to read handwriting and then fail to do so tend not be big sellers. Palm Computing, a recent mover, has succeeded in the handheld computer category.

Observations

Discuss how financial statement analysis adds value to the assessment of the first mover theory. The first mover theory may explain financial success if other factors are equal. Do you think other things tend to be equal among companies? How important is it for financial statement analysts to be aware of those other matters?

---

[10] *US Industry & Trade Outlook '99,* (New York: McGraw-Hill Companies and the U.S. Department of Commerce, 1999), section 27, p. 2.

ACCOUNT	COMPOUND ANNUAL GROWTH RATE
Revenues	–5.7%
Cost of goods sold	–3.2%
Gross margin	–11.5%
Operating expenses	–14.2%
Operating income	18.2%
Net income	29.1%
Current assets	–3.1%
Property, plant and equipment	–12.0%
Total assets	–3.7%
Current liabilities	–9.5%
Total liabilities	–3.4%
Shareholders' equity	–4.1%
Total liabilities and S/E	–3.7%

WEB EXERCISE 8

*Examine Apple's recent EDGAR
filings with the SEC and indicate
whether its performance has
improved in recent years.*

MICRO ANALYSIS 9

*Apple's business model makes
benchmarking difficult. The company's proprietary systems
design requires it to develop software applications. Thus, Apple
has some elements of a software
company as well as those of a PC
manufacturer or computer hardware company.*

APPLE COMPUTER'S FINANCIAL PERFORMANCE

Apple Computer, Inc. (Apple) is the focal point of our PC analysis. Its economic performance fluctuated dramatically from 1993 through 1998. The company's market share decreased from 13 percent to about 4 percent during that time. Apple rivaled IBM as the industry leader in 1993 but slipped to a second-tier PC company by the end of that six-year interval. Note the compound annual growth rates for Apple Computer, shown in Exhibit 5-12, which mark the lack of growth in the company during the period analyzed.

COMPANY COMPARABILITY

We selected three competitors—Compaq Computer Corp. (Compaq), Dell Computer Corp. (Dell), and Gateway, Inc. (Gateway)—to benchmark Apple.[11] These four firms had comparable reporting methods. Exhibit 5-13 presets evi-

EXHIBIT 5-13

*Company Comparability
Significant Accounting
Policies of PC Companies*

COMPANY	REVENUE RECOGNITION	INVENTORY COSTING	EQUIPMENT: DEPRECIATION METHOD & LIFE	BUILDINGS: DEPRECIATION METHOD & LIFE
Apple	When shipped (with a provision for returns)	FIFO	St. line & acceler. (2–5 yrs)	St. line & acceler. (30 years)
Compaq	When shipped (with a provision for returns)	FIFO	Straight line (2–5 years)	Straight line (10–30 years)
Dell	When shipped (with a provision for returns)	FIFO	Straight line (2–10 years)	Straight line (10–30 years)
Gateway	When shipped (with a provision for returns)	FIFO	St. line & acceler. (2–5 yrs)	St. line & acceler. (10–30 yrs)

---

[11] We excluded one seemingly logical competitor, IBM. The breadth of computer products and services IBM offers extends far beyond PCs. Therefore, it is judged to be an inappropriate point of comparison for companies focused on PCs.

EXHIBIT 5-14

Sales Revenue of PC Companies (in billions) 1993–1998

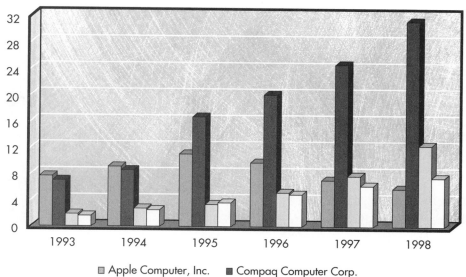

■ Apple Computer, Inc.   ■ Compaq Computer Corp.
□ Dell Computer Corp.   □ Gateway 2000 Inc.

EXHIBIT 5-15

Net Income of PC Companies (in millions) 1993–1998

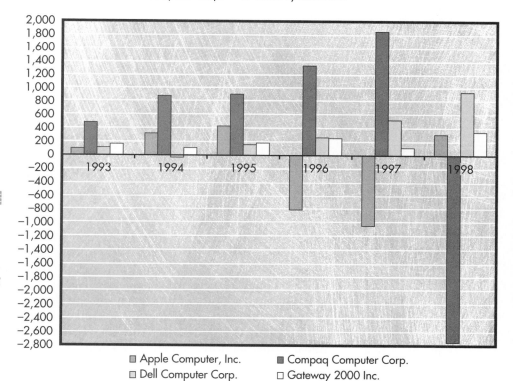

■ Apple Computer, Inc.   ■ Compaq Computer Corp.
□ Dell Computer Corp.   □ Gateway 2000 Inc.

WEB *E*XERCISE 9

Review Apple's notes to its financial statements in its most recent Form 10-K. Does the company still recognize revenues and cost inventory the same way it did from 1993 to 1998?

dence that all four PC companies employed similar accounting methods and exercised comparable judgment about resources.[12]

Exhibits 5-14 and 5-15 show the four companies' revenues and net income amounts, demonstrating the overall decline in Apple's performance and the

---

[12] Information taken from the respective companies' Form 10-K, in the section titled *Summary of Significant Accounting Policies.*

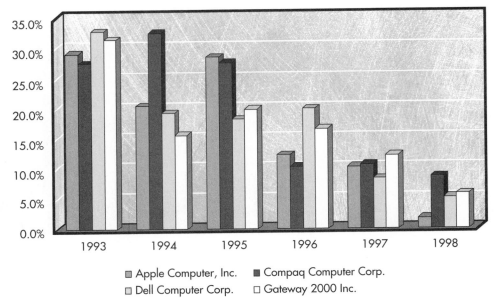

MICRO *A*NALYSIS 10

The North American Industry Classification System (NAICS) replaced the Standard Industrial Code (SIC) partly in response to the emergence of information-age industries. NAICS created nine new industry sectors to encompass the changes in technology. See Chapter 2 for more information.

MICRO *A*NALYSIS 11

The Internet offers an interesting contrast to the PC industry. Many Web-based companies have high stock prices, despite a lack of earnings. Investors value dot-com stocks more for their growth potential than their financial performance. Unlike the mature PC industry, the Internet industry is in its infancy.

■ Apple Computer, Inc. ■ Compaq Computer Corp.
□ Dell Computer Corp. □ Gateway 2000 Inc.

changing fortunes of the other PC firms.[13] Inventory levels reflected competitive pressures in the industry. Companies could no longer invest large amounts of resources in computer components and finished goods. Exhibit 5-16 presents each company's inventory as a percentage of total assets.

ECONOMIC CHANGE

The economy shifted from producing industrial goods to providing services during the latter part of the 20th century. A major component of the **service-based economy** is information. Knowledge that results from information has added immense value to the economy, individual firms, and people's lives. Personal computers were at the forefront of the information revolution. The PC is a **disruptive technology**, one that displaces entrenched ways of doing things. These landmark changes add value to the economy. Other examples of disruptive technologies include the printing press, steam engine, radio, automobile, and jet travel. In the case of the PC, it altered the quantity, quality, and cost of information. In addition, PCs spurred other information-related disruptive technologies, such as the Internet and electronic commerce (e-business).

Financial markets valued these **new economy** companies more than traditional industrial firms in many cases. Moreover, **old economy** firms altered many of the ways they did business as a result of the goods and services provided by new economy companies.

The PC industry was an early entrant into the information economy. Intellectual research played a crucial role in these companies' financial performance. Their proportion of property, plant, and equipment to total assets was less than that of old-line industrial firms. To a large extent, knowledge replaced things

---

[13] Corporate financial statements are analyzed for the calendar year, regardless of which month a company's fiscal year ends.

EXHIBIT 5-17
National and Computer Industry Productivity 1993–1998

MICRO $\mathcal{A}$NALYSIS 12

Although the Internet offers many opportunities for the PC industry, it also poses a threat. Users can now download from the Web many of the capabilities now embedded in (and priced as part of) the machines themselves. Personal Computer companies are now seeking to capitalize on the growth of the Internet industry. They have begun to offer a range of products and services that tie their machines to the Internet.

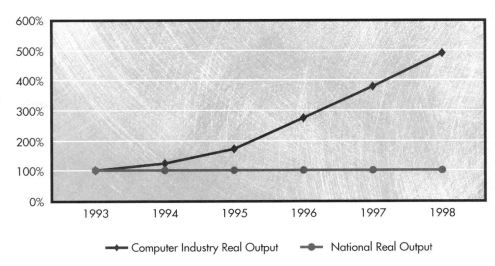

as the engine fueling revenues and profits in the PC industry. Exhibit 5-17 contrasts productivity gains made in the computer industry to those of overall economy during the period analyzed.

SUMMARY

Analysts gain insights about corporate performance by understanding economic conditions, industry peculiarities, and competitors' performance. This chapter introduces these factors for Apple Computer and the PC industry from 1993 to 1998. The U.S. economy expanded during that time, but some economies contracted during the latter years examined. The PC industry increasingly reflected a mature industry as competition intensified, profits shrank, product differentiation decreased, and companies attempted to control costs. Apple Computer lost market share, experienced sales declines, and saw profits vanish during the mid-1990s.

The analytical context outlined in this chapter applies to any company in any given industry. It serves as the basis for much of the material in the remainder of the book. The information in this chapter and Appendix A have more specific information about Apple Computer and the PC industry. Subsequent appendixes contain information about other industries. Many case study assignments in this and succeeding chapters are based on these data.

KEY TERMS

Consumer price index (CPI)
Direct selling
Disruptive technology
European Union (EU)
Gross domestic product (GDP)
Indirect selling
New economy
Old economy

Personal computer (PC) industry
Producer price index (PPI)
Product duration
Service based economy
Standard & Poor's (S&P) 500
Unemployment rate
"Wintel" duopoly

INDUSTRY CASES

Complete the following requirements as they applied from 1993 through 1998.

a. Chapter 2 states economies expand, prosper, contract, and recede. Describe the economies of the United States, Western Europe, Latin America, Russia, and Asia in those terms from 1993–1996 and 1997–1998.

b. Comment on the extent to which the economic performance of each industry listed in the text's appendixes is correlated with overall economic conditions.

c. An industry is a subset of an economic sector. Classify each one of the industries in the appendixes by economic sector. Classify each one of the industries in the appendixes by economic sector. Explain your rationale for each classification.

d. Refer to Chapter 2's *Resource Guide* appendix. Classify each industry according to its two-digit North American Industry Classification System code, four-digit Standard Industrial Classification system code, and two-digit Standard & Poor's Industry Survey classification structure.

e. Name a company that could have been included as part of the grouping for each industry contained in the appendixes.

f. Name an entity that could have served as a benchmark firm, despite sharing many of the characteristics of that appendix's industry.

5-1   *Personal Computers: Apple, Compaq, Dell, and Gateway*

5-2   *Airlines: American, Delta, and United*

5-3   *Athletic Footwear: Nike and Reebok*

5-4   *Discount Retailers: Kmart, Target, and Wal-Mart*

5-5   *Fast-Food Restaurants: McDonald's and Wendy's*

5-6   *Soft Drink Companies: Coca-Cola and PepsiCo.*

INDUSTRY INTERNET CASES

Examine each company's most recent disclosures for the industries in the appendixes. Address each of the following issues:

a. How does each company currently recognize revenue, cost inventory (if applicable), and depreciate fixed assets?

b. Compare each company's most recent income statement and balance sheet disclosures to the 1993 to 1998 statements contained in the appendix. Do the disclosures equal those in the appendix? If not, how do they differ?

c. Examine operating income, net income, and cash flows from operations for recent years. Are they greater than or less than the 1998 amounts?

d. Based on your perceptions, do you think each firm's has improved or regressed since 1998? (Do not make a lot of calculations.)

6

FINANCIAL STATEMENT INFLUENCES

$\mathscr{C}$HAPTER LEARNING OBJECTIVES

Upon completion of this chapter, you should be able to:

◆ *Indicate how judgment influences financial statement disclosures.*

◆ *Distinguish between revenue and capital expenditures; product and period costs; fixed and variable costs; and controllable and uncontrollable costs.*

◆ *Determine how various cost classifications affect financial statement analysis.*

◆ *Describe how managerial choices affect reported numbers and discuss ways to validate the integrity of those choices*

◆ *Articulate the value of a standard unqualified audit report to analysis. Understand why adverse reports, disclaimers of opinions, and going concern questions limit analysis.*

$\mathcal{T}$his chapter presents more factors that affect analysis of financial performance and position. Some of these items are divulged in corporate disclosures; others are reported elsewhere. Analysts must account for this information, regardless of disclosure format and location. Analysis of the PC industry, Apple Computer, or any reporting entity is incomplete, otherwise.

This chapter teaches you how to interpret certain financial statement items and make inferences about ones excluded from corporate reports. It can help you to make better judgments and reach more logical conclusions in analyzing financial disclosures, wherever they exist. This chapter begins with a discussion of analytical judgment. We then address basic cost considerations, other cost factors, managerial choices, and audit opinions, each of which influence financial statements analysis. Developing insights into these four topics can broaden your understanding of the financial reporting landscape and strengthen your ability to evaluate financial statements.

FINANCIAL REPORTING JUDGMENT

Analytical judgment is the ability to reach informed opinions about financial statements and related disclosures. The capacity to analyze disclosures depends, in part, on the ability to understand financial reporting inputs and techniques. Chapters 1–5 discuss some elements of judgment, either in financial statement preparation or interpretation. Various stakeholders make decisions that influence financial statement disclosures. Regulatory bodies, for example, influence financial reporting. Standard setters require nominal dollar income measurement and historical cost asset valuation. GAAP does not allow disclosure of other capital maintenance concepts or alternative asset attributes, even though they have merit.[1] Managers decide how to cost inventory (e.g., on a first-in, first-out or last-in, last-out basis) and depreciate fixed assets (e.g., straight-line or accelerated method).

WEB
$\mathcal{E}$XERCISE 1

Examine Apple Computer's most recent Form 10-K. Review its inventory costing and depreciation methods.

Analytical judgment extends beyond the realization that some financial reporting methods are acceptable but others violate GAAP and accounting principles allow multiple reporting methods for some economic events. Financial statement preparers make many other judgments, based on their interpretation of economic reality. Analysts, the users of financial statements, must understand their judgments. The remainder of this chapter addresses those issues. It presents an array of judgment-related economic considerations that influence the financial reporting process. Understanding these concepts can help you analyze financial statements and improve your analytical judgment.

BASIC COST CONSIDERATIONS

A **cost** is an economic sacrifice made to obtain something of value. A company acquires goods and services to conduct business operations. Maximizing stock price is the aim of these commercial activities. Business costs, therefore, are what an entity gives up to increase owners' wealth. Costs have many dimensions, thus

---

[1] Refer to the discussion of capital maintenance concepts and attribute valuation in the "Disclosure Challenges" section of Chapter 1.

complicating analysis. This section examines two basic cost considerations that affect financial statements: expenditure type and cost treatment. The next section addresses other cost factors.

MICRO ANALYSIS 1

Apple Computer's property, plant, and equipment are capital expenditures. Note how they declined as a percentage of total assets from 1993 to 1998.

MICRO ANALYSIS 2

All companies incur research and development costs not just high-tech ones. Burger King, for example, spent millions of dollars in the late 1990s to improve its french fries. Do you think they succeeded in overtaking McDonald's product, which analysts consider to be the gold standard of french fries?

WEB EXERCISE 2

What percentage of sales did Apple Computer spend for R&D in the most recent year reported?

MICRO ANALYSIS 3

Refer to Apple's income statements and balance sheets from 1993 to 1998. Where is R&D disclosed?

CAPITAL AND REVENUE EXPENDITURES

Subtracting costs from revenues affects income. Expense recognition is a matter of timing. An *expense* is that portion of an asset used to generate revenues within a specific reporting period.[2] Income statements report only those expenditures used to create current revenues. Costs, however, may benefit future periods as well as the current one. **Revenue expenditures** are costs that only produce revenues in the current period. A **capital (asset) expenditure**, on the other hand, contributes to revenues in future reporting periods, as well as the current one. The balance sheet initially reports capital expenditures. Income statements then disclose these costs over time in a rational and systematic manner.

Managerial decisions made by eXTREMESTUFF.com illustrate the difference between revenue and capital expenditures. The company does not own any land or buildings; the business start-up rents space to conduct business. Therefore, eSTUFF's rental costs help the e-tailer earn revenues in that period, but not in future ones. Conversely, the company purchased equipment for use in its operations. Its equipment will last five years and earn revenues in each one of those years.[3] The cost of equipment is a *capital expenditure,* but rent is a *revenue expenditure.* eSTUFF discloses rent expense and depreciation expense (for the equipment) as part of its selling and administrative expenses during a reporting period. The firm reports the remaining equipment cost as a fixed asset on its balance sheet.

The decision to classify cost as either capital or revenue expenditures is not as simple as you might conclude from the eSTUFF example. Distinguishing between revenue and capital expenditures is not always straightforward; sometimes judgment is required. Two complexities revolve around GAAP reporting requirements: First, practical considerations sometimes outweigh theoretical correctness when classifying costs; and second, economic complexities sometimes make expenditure classification difficult.

Research and development (R&D) costs illustrate the first complication. Companies incur costs attempting to create lasting knowledge. These expenditures can translate into a revenue stream over many reporting periods. For many firms, especially high-tech ones, these costs are critical in their wealth maximization efforts. These costs, however, are revenue expenditures, according to GAAP.[4] The FASB requires treating them as expenses because the success of individual R&D projects is uncertain.[5] In other words, because the value of R&D costs is difficult to measure, they are classified as revenue expenditures, rather than the more theoretically appropriate capital expenditures.

---

[2] See Chapter 3 for more formal definitions of all of the financial statement elements.

[3] You can compute the expected life from the company's statement of cash flows (see Chapter 3): equipment purchased in 2000 was $500,000 and depreciation expense was $100,000.

[4] "Accounting for Research and Development Costs," *Statement of Financial Accounting Standards No. 2* (Stamford, CT: FASB, 1974).

[5] The uncertainties extend beyond the probability of the success of R&D efforts. For instance, the amount of future revenues and cash flows generated from successful R&D efforts are difficult, if not impossible, to measure.

WEB

EXERCISE 3

Airlines lease aircraft as well as purchase them. Examine American, Delta, or United's most recent balance sheet to see if the company you selected capitalized leased aircraft.

Leasing demonstrates the economic complexity associated with classifying costs as either revenue or asset expenditures. A *lessee* pays for the right to use an asset legally controlled by another party (the *lessor*) in a **lease** arrangement. If the economic risks and rewards associated with that resource shift from the lessor to the lessee as a result of the contract, then the lessee capitalizes the asset and the lessor records a sale.[6] In substance, the lessee has purchased the asset from the lessor; its periodic lease payments merely represent a purchase on an installment basis.[7] If, however, the majority of risks and rewards remain with the lessor, the legal owner continues to capitalize the asset. The lessee has a revenue expenditure called rent expense, in this circumstance.

Determining precisely when ownership risks and rewards shift from the lessor to the lessee requires judgment. Many lease transactions are quite complex, and the transfer point is difficult to measure. The FASB's GAAP have specific criteria that state when the risks and rewards shift from lessor to lessee.[8] Sometimes GAAP compliance drives lease transactions, rather than the desire to distinguish between the economic differences of capital and revenue expenditures. Lessees, for example, usually structure leases so that they do not have to capitalize them. By treating leases as revenue expenditures, lessees avoid reporting a long-term liability (to offset the capitalized asset) and higher lease-related expenses in the early years of the lease.[9]

DISAPPEARING ASSETS

IBM's creative treatment for the computers it leased to other companies might lead one to ask, "Does anyone own these things?" What do you think?

IBM treated certain leases as sales-type leases, rather than operating leases in the 1980s and early 1990s.[a] By doing so, the computer manufacturer immediately recognized revenue (and income) on the transactions. The lessor would have merely generated rent revenue over time if it retained ownership of the computers. Companies that leased machines from IBM were motivated to treat the deals as operating leases, rather than capital leases. Lessees reduced their expenses and kept liabilities off their balance sheets by not capitalizing the computers.[b] The end result of these transactions was that IBM removed the leased computers from its balance sheet, but the lessees did not record them on theirs.

IBM initially did not meet the criteria for treating the leases as sales-type transactions. What did it do? Big Blue acquired an insurance policy from Merrill Lynch, which guaranteed that the computers would have a certain value when the leases were terminated.[c] This agreement enabled IBM to meet the criteria required to treat the leases as sales-type ones. The end result of IBM's arrangement with the financial intermediary was that neither the lessor nor the lessee capitalized these very real assets!

---

[6] This statement assumes a sales-type lease. The lessor profits from the immediate transfer of goods to the lessee as well as financing the lease in these arrangements. In the event that the lessor only earns revenue by financing the transaction (and not from selling the product) the lease is accounted for as a direct financing lease. The difference between the two methods usually does not affect analysis.

[7] Accounting for the transaction in this manner illustrates the concept of economic substance over legal form.

[8] "Accounting for Leases," *Statement of Financial Accounting Standards No. 13* (Stamford, CT: FASB, 1976).

[9] Expenses on a capitalized lease exceed rent expense on an operating lease in the early years of the lease term, due to the time value of money.

Observations

As an analyst, how would you react to IBM's tactic? Was it unethical behavior or merely aggressive accounting on the part of IBM? What was the impact of these transactions on the concept of capitalization? What type of footnote disclosure would you expect from IBM regarding the sales-type leases?

---

[a] Material based on M. W. Miller and L. Berton's "As IBM's Woes Grew, Its Accounting Tactics Got Less Conservative," *Wall Street Journal*, April 7, 1993, pp. A1 and A4.
[b] Recognizing the long-term liability increases firm leverage and reduces key performance indicators. (These concepts will be discussed in Chapters 13 and 14.) Expense reduction applies to the early years of a lease transaction. It results from the depreciation and interest expenses in the early years of capitalized leases, which, when taken together, exceed an operating lease's rent charge.
[c] Statement of Financial Accounting Standards No. 13 allows for sales-type leases when the present value of the minimum lease payments equals or exceeds 90 percent of the fair value of the leased asset. There must also be a dealer profit, assurance of collectibility of the lease payments, and no uncertainties surrounding the transaction for a sales-type lease to exist.

MICRO  NALYSIS 4

Apple Computer allocates property, plant, and equipment depreciation between period costs and product costs. P,P&E costs allocated to its administrative and selling operations appear in the income statement as part of S,G&A expenses. Fixed cost allocations devoted to the manufacturing process, however, become part of its inventory cost.

PRODUCT AND PERIOD COSTS

Product costs are inventory-related expenditures. Selling inventories, which are assets, creates cost of goods sold (an expense). **Period costs**, on the other hand, consist of noninventoried costs. The income statement reports the entire amount of these costs as expenses. In the terminology of the previous section, capital expenditures include product costs, but period costs are revenue expenditures.

Some costs are either period or product costs, depending on the circumstances. To understand what causes alternative costing for the same item, you must differentiate between merchandising and manufacturing concerns.[10] A *merchant* acquires completed goods from a manufacturer or wholesaler and markets those goods. A *manufacturer*, on the other hand, converts raw materials into completed products and then sells the finished goods.

The purchase price of inventory is a retailer's product cost.[11] Its period costs are the firm's selling and administrative expenses. The inventory eSTUFF purchases from manufacturers is its product cost, but the company's rent is one of its period costs. The firm's financial statements reflect the difference between the two cost treatments. eSTUFF's rent cost appears solely on the income statement as an expense, but inventory appears on the income statement as cost of goods sold (for the sold portion) and on the balance sheet as inventory (for the unsold portion).

Direct labor, indirect materials, indirect labor, and depreciation on the factory and machines assist a manufacturer in converting raw materials into finished goods. The costs of these inputs and processes attach to the cost of the raw materials. Taken together, they become the cost of the manufacturer's inventory. A manufacturer's wages, utilities, and depreciation are product costs if those costs are incurred in manufacturing the products. Its inventoried costs, therefore, consists of raw materials, labor used to make goods, utilities to run the factory, and depreciation on the factory building and machines. Cost of goods sold includes wages, utilities, and depreciation for sold products. Unsold goods, and the manufacturing costs attached to them, remain in inventory. Labor, depreciation, and utilities

---

[10] These differences affect various aspects of analysis, such as inventory turnover and estimating the age of assets. These topics are discussed in subsequent chapters.
[11] The purchase price includes transaction costs such as transportation.

EXHIBIT 6-1
*Inventory-Related Accounts
Merchants and Manufacturers*

ITEM	MERCHANT	MANUFACTURER
Inventory	One type: finished goods	Three types: raw materials, work in process, and completed (finished) goods
Costs of inventory (Product costs)	Purchase price	Direct materials, direct labor, and factory overhead (e.g., indirect materials, indirect labor, depreciation, rent, utilities)
Cost of goods sold	Historical cost of inventory items sold in a reporting period	Historical cost of completed (finished) goods sold in a period.
Period costs	All salaries, rent, depreciation, utilities, and so on.	Salaries, rent, depreciation, utilities, and so on, related to selling the inventory (but not in making it).

costs incurred in selling the manufactured products (as opposed to making them), however, are period costs for a manufacturing concern. A manufacturer's income statement reports the entire amount of these costs, just as a merchant would.

In short, certain costs incurred by manufacturers are divided between period and product costs, whereas merchants classify them strictly as period costs. Exhibit 6-1 contrasts the product and period costs for merchants and manufacturers. The financial statements of a manufacturer are far more complex than a merchandising concern, due to multiple inventory accounts and the costs that affect them. Analysts must take extra care when assessing a manufacturer's financial statements.

OTHER COST FACTORS

Financial statements disclose revenue and capital expenditures and product and period costs. The income statement (for expired costs) and the balance sheet (for unexpired ones) report these costs. Not all cost considerations, however, are disclosed in the financial statements. Understanding three other cost factors improves your decision-making capabilities: Cost control, cost behavior, and cost composition.

COST CONTROL

WEB *Exercise* 4

What is the trend of Apple Computer's R&D expenditures over the past three years?

A cost level that can be controlled or heavily influenced by managerial decisions is a **controllable cost**. On the other hand, an **uncontrollable cost** is unavoidable in running a business.[12] Controllable costs can be increased, decreased, or eliminated as the situation warrants, but uncontrollable costs cannot be changed (at least in

---

[12] Controllable and uncontrollable costs are not dichotomous concepts. Think of all costs on a continuum with the end points "controllable" and "uncontrollable."

the short run). In other words, management has discretion over controllable costs but not over uncontrollable ones.

Discretionary cost judgments affect financial statement disclosures. eSTUFF, for example, must pay for its inventory. Failure to do so would force the company out of business. Its inventory (and related cost of goods sold), therefore, is uncontrollable. Advertising costs, however, depend on management's willingness to promote the company and its products. Reducing controllable expenses increases profits in the short-run, and spending more on them decreases current earnings. The long-run implications, however, could produce just the opposite results: Heavy spending on controllable costs—such as advertising, R&D, and employee training—could increase future earnings. Conversely, failing to invest in these areas may boost current profits but could reduce corporate wealth in the long run.

Financial statements do not classify costs as controllable or uncontrollable. You need to know the company and industry to distinguish between these types of costs and closely monitor management's decisions regarding controllable costs. Thorough research enables you to get a sense of whether management is unduly influencing short-term earnings by reducing controllable costs to unacceptably low levels.

COST BEHAVIOR

Two cost behaviors exist. The total dollar amount of **fixed costs** remains constant, regardless of sales levels.[13] The unit cost for a fixed expenditure decreases as revenues increase. Conversely, **variable costs** remain constant per sales dollar. In other words, total variable costs increase and decrease in direct proportion to revenue changes.[14]

Total costs consist of fixed costs plus variable costs. The combination of these two costs defines industry characteristics and influence profitability. Variable costs dominate **labor-intensive** industries and companies. These businesses have a relatively low **breakeven point**, or that level of sales where revenues equal expenses. **Capital-intensive** operations have relatively high fixed costs and low variable costs. Their breakeven points are higher than labor-intensive industries. Capital-intensive industries, however, realize higher marginal profitability after the breakeven point has been surpassed.

Understanding cost behavior is beneficial when evaluating management's investment decisions. Assume eSTUFF considered automating its inventory retrieval and packaging functions. Such a capital expenditure would increase fixed costs and reduce the number of hourly inventory workers (a variable cost). This managerial decision would drive up the firm's breakeven point and expand its profit and loss margins. Exhibit 6-2 illustrates eSTUFF's change to automation.

Exhibit 6-2b demonstrates that fixed costs increase as a result of automation, but variable costs are reduced per sales dollar. (Notice that the slope of the variable cost line is flatter in Exhibit 6-2b than Exhibit 6-2a.) Two changes result if eSTUFF automates. First, the breakeven point requires more sales, because

---

[13] We use sales levels here because analysts evaluate external financial statements. Cost behavior in this environment relates to revenues. Sales level is really a subset of the cost behavior concept of activity level.

[14] Some costs are mixed—a combination of fixed and variable components. We assume costs are either fixed or variable to simplify the discussion.

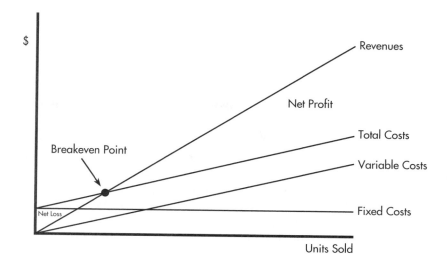

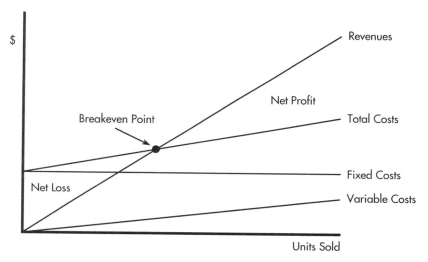

Ford Motor Co.'s Premier Auto Group (Lincoln, Jaguar, Volvo, Land Rover and Aston Martin) attempted to improve profitability in 2000. Management made plans to use joint parts for all five brands and share administrative costs among the nameplates. Ford anticipated reducing fixed costs through such strategies.

increased fixed costs drive up total costs initially. Second, greater profits result when eSTUFF exceeds the breakeven point, because variable cost per sales dollar is smaller. Successful capital investments contribute to increased profitability, but unsuccessful ones reduce earnings.

Information about specific cost behavior is usually unavailable in the financial statements. Expense classifications on the income statement combine fixed and variable costs. Thus, it is usually impossible for an external analyst to determine a firm's cost, volume, and profit activities. The analyst should try to understand, at least in broad terms, the cost behavior of a firm's expenses, likelihood of changes in them, and impact of such movements on profitability.

INDUSTRY-SPECIFIC MEASURES

Supplementary data in Form 10-K can provide cost-volume-profit data lacking in the financial statements themselves. Analysts can also sometimes find breakeven information from secondary sources. Corporate and other data source convey a wealth of information about performance efficiency. Insights generated from these sources are often worth the research effort. Seek it out!

Air carriers' SEC disclosures offer a case in point about breakeven information. Their profitability depends, to a large degree, on aircraft occupancy rates. Airlines' annual SEC disclosures indicate the following industry-specific cost-volume-profit disclosures:

◆ *Passenger load factor (load).* The percentage of available revenue passenger seat miles occupied during a reporting period. The load is computed by dividing the number of actual passenger seat miles flown by the number of available passenger seat miles.
◆ *Breakeven load factor.* The percentage at which revenues from actual passenger seat miles flown would equal operating expenses in a specific reporting period.
◆ *Passenger revenue per passenger mile.* The average revenue received for each mile a passenger is carried. This measure is determined by dividing operating passenger revenues by actual passenger seat miles.
◆ *Operating expenses per available seat mile.* The average operating expenses per passenger seat mile flown. It is determined by dividing the number of available seat miles into total operating expenses.

The following table contains data for United Air Lines' five most recent years of operations.[a]

ITEM	1998	1997	1996	1995	1994
Passenger load	71.6%	71.8%	71.7%	70.5%	71.2%
Breakeven load	64.9%	66.0%	66.0%	66.1%	68.2%
Passenger revenue per passenger mile (in cents)	12.4	12.6	12.4	11.8	11.3
Operating expenses per available seat mile (in cents)	9.2	9.5	9.3	8.9	8.8

Observations

Examine the data in the table in conjunction with United's financial statements in Appendix B. Explain why United earned an annual profit from 1994 to 1998. Assume United's passenger load was less than 71.6 percent in 1998. How would net income be affected? Assume United's breakeven load was less than 64.9 percent in 1998. How would net income be affected?

---

[a] Information taken from Form 10-K of UAL Corporation, the parent holding company of United Air Lines.

WEB EXERCISE 5

Examine United's passenger and breakeven load factors for the past reporting period. Do you think the company operated at a profit or loss? Verify your answer by referring to United's income statement.

COST COMPOSITION

Companies usually sell or provide more than one good or service. The proportion of each good sold or service rendered is a company's sales mix. Each product in the sales mix has a unique cost structure, which, when matched against that product's revenues, determines its profit margin.

Consider eSTUFF's business operations. It buys merchandising from an array of vendors. These goods are marked up to retail selling price, but markups differ among products. In addition, marketing strategies often dictate pricing. For exam-

WHAT'S YOUR ANALYSIS

ple, the e-tailer might sell some goods at or near cost to increase sales volume and entice shoppers to their Web site. Or the company might increase the selling price of high demand products but reduce those for slow-moving merchandise. eSTUFF's cost of goods sold percentage and gross profit margin in a given year represents an average cost of sales and profit before operating expenses. These percentages hold from period to period only if pricing strategies and sales quantity remain constant. To the extent that they differ, cost of goods sold and gross profit change as a percentage of sales revenue.

Companies do not disclose individual product costs or profit margins; analysts can only estimate them. Sometimes secondary sources provide approximate information about sales mix and product profit margins.[15] As noted in the discussion of cost behavior, however, an analyst can gain some perspective about financial performance by approximating some general factors about a company's product offerings. An analyst should estimate the following, to the extent possible:

- The current sales mix
- The profit margins of the products sold by the company
- Forecasts for any changes in the product mix
- Projections of shifting cost structures
- The expected sales volume and profit margin of any new products
- The sales mix and cost structures of the competitions' product offerings

These factors affect financial performance. Although you cannot corroborate such estimates with a company's financial statements, they can help you understand a company's reported results.

FORD'S PRODUCT MIX

Companies sometimes provide information about product mix. Do you think it can help analysis?

Ford Motor Co. identifies unit sales volume, product mix of vehicles, and the margin of profitability on each vehicle sold as important contributors to income in its Form 10-K.[a] Industry analysts distinguish between car and truck sales, but they do not disclose specific vehicle-type data. The company has recently lost market share in United States but increased profits. The following information, excerpted from its Form 10-K, provides the evidence:

ITEM	1998	1997	1996
Number of vehicles sold in the U.S. (in millions)	16	15.5	15.5
Ford's market share	24.6%	25.0%	25.2%
Cars sold in the U.S. (as a percentage of total vehicles sold)	51.0%	53.4%	55.3
Trucks sold in the U.S. (as a percentage of total vehicle sold)[b]	49.0%	46.6%	44.7%
Cars as a percentage of Ford's vehicle sales	39.7%	42.0%	44.9%
Trucks as a percentage of Ford's vehicle sales	60.3%	58.0%	55.1%
Income of Ford from vehicle sales (in billions)	$4.8	$4.7	$1.7

---

[15] *Secondary sources* are reliable noncompany sources.

MANAGERIAL JUDGMENT AND ESTIMATES

Management should produce financial statements that are **representationally faithful**, meaning that information disclosures should match economic reality, to the extent possible under GAAP. Financial reporting principles assist in this venture, but they are not the whole story. Managerial judgment and estimates influence financial statements in four ways: selection of accounting methods, estimation of future events, revenue recognition policies, and matching of expenses to revenues.

ACCOUNTING METHODS

Exercise 6

Examine Apple Computer's most recent Form 10-K for product information disclosures.

Exercise 7

Examine Ford's most recent Form 10-K to see how many vehicles it sold this past year, the proportion of cars to trucks, its market share, and net income.

Analysis 11

Apple Computer incurred a 1997 R&D change that lowered operating income by $375 million: its acquisition of NeXT Computer. Do you think this expense will recur?

Exercise 8

Examine the most recent Form 10-Ks for Apple, Compaq, Dell, and Gateway to see if their depreciation lives and methods are comparable.

Flexibility exists for reporting certain economic events. Alternative accounting treatments are allowed under GAAP for many economic activities. The amount of costs allocated to the income statement and balance sheet depend on management's reporting methods. Two examples are inventory costing and depreciation methods, mentioned earlier in the chapter. Analysis of eSTUFF's inventory and fixed assets depends on how it accounted for those transactions.[16]

Analysts value **consistency** and **comparability** when evaluating a company's selection of alternative reporting methods. The former characteristic indicates that a firm employs the same accounting method in each reporting period (e.g., eSTUFF used straight-line depreciation in 2000, 2001, 2002, 2003 and so on.). The latter quality means that a firm uses the same accounting method as its competition (e.g., the fixed assets of eSTUFF's competitors were depreciated on a straight-line basis).

Inconsistency and incomparability hinder analysis in two ways. First, benchmarking corporate performance over time and against competition becomes complex. Economic or methodological factors, or a combination of both, may cause numerical differences. Analysts must distinguish between economic (real) differences and accounting (alternative method) differences. The second problem exists when a firm changes its accounting method (e.g., from the accelerated to the straight-line depreciation method). These changes usually result in large adjustments to current income, they cannot be interpreted the same way as earnings from continuing operations because they do not arise from normal business operations.[17]

ESTIMATION OF FUTURE EVENTS

eSTUFF's equipment depreciation and trademark amortization illustrate the role managerial estimation plays in financial statement analysis. Consider the equip-

---

[16] Chapters 9 and 13 provide numerical examples.
[17] This issue is part of earnings quality, which is addressed in Chapter 12.

MICRO ANALYSIS 12

In the information economy, most fixed assets become economically obsolete long before they physically fail. Rapid technological innovations make estimating the productive lives for many assets extremely difficult.

WEB EXERCISE 9

Does Apple Computer make any current provisions for sales returns?

MICRO ANALYSIS 13

Some Internet companies serving as intermediaries between online buyers and sellers recognized revenue for the sales price of products, rather than just the commission earned for brokering the deals. The SEC cracked down on the practice, claiming it grossly overstated revenues. (See What's Your Analysis? on p. 70.)

ment that the company acquired in 2000. The company's perspective of the economic life and value shaped income measurement and asset valuation in the current and future reporting periods. Management had to estimate the expected life of the equipment and its residual (scrap or salvage) value, if any. Corporate officials made the same estimates for the intangible asset cost (trademark) in 2000 and the equipment purchased the following year. Those estimates determined annual depreciation (amortization) expense and each asset's book value at year-end. Understand that there is not necessarily a correct choice for these estimates. You should be confident, however, that the estimates are reasonable and conform to industry standards.

REVENUE RECOGNITION POLICY

Realization and *earned* are the two elements of **revenue recognition**. Revenues are realized when goods or services are exchanged for cash or claims to cash (accounts receivable). An entity that has fulfilled its obligation and is entitled to the benefits has earned revenue. Another way of understanding revenue recognition is to consider its cash implications in disclosing a sale for eSTUFF. The e-tailer recognizes cash only when it is reasonably certain to collect cash. The firm should not recognize revenue if substantial doubt exists as to its ability to collect cash from the sale.

Analysts judge if a company correctly recognizes revenues and does so in the correct reporting period. Recognizing revenues before they are earned violates GAAP. Such **premature revenue recognition**, or **front-end loading** revenues, is tempting, however, because it increases income. Often it is a matter of perception; gray areas exist. What one analyst may perceive as front-end loading others may regard as an acceptable, although aggressive, revenue realization policy.

Assume eSTUFF allows for estimated sales returns in determining net revenues. A sound estimate for merchandise returns results in an accurate recognition of annual revenue. An unrealistically low one, however, overstates net revenues and income. The problem is determining what constitutes a reasonable estimate of returns. eSTUFF's situation compounds the problem: The company is new and may lack enough information to make a good estimate.

Estimated sales returns and other revenue recognition items depend on managerial judgment. An analyst must carefully evaluate management's revenue recognition policy.[18] Some questions you can ask to determine whether a company is front-end loading revenues follow.

◆ Does the company have a revenue recognition policy that changes over time?
◆ Does it recognize revenues differently than the competition?
◆ Are there large numbers of product returns?
◆ Does it revise its estimates of product returns?
◆ Does it continually collect far less than 100 percent of its net revenues in cash?
◆ Does it replace its auditor regularly?
◆ Has it received negative financial media reports about its revenue practices?

MATCHING EXPENSES TO REVENUES

Improperly matching expenses to revenues is the opposite of prematurely recognizing revenues. A company can manipulate income through **improper expense**

---

[18] Subsequent chapters present many of the specific techniques to accomplish this task.

WEB **E**XERCISE 10

Refer to the most recent corporate disclosures for Apple and other PC firms. Is the current industry standard for costing inventory the same as it was from 1993 to 1998?

recognition by **back-end loading** them. Delaying expense recognition until a future period enhances current income, but it violates GAAP. Like revenue recognition, however, proper matching of expenses is sometimes a matter of opinion. For example, eSTUFF could improve current income by manipulating its judgments about equipment. The company could overestimate equipment life, continually extending its life, or overestimate residual values. These tactics are difficult to deduce. You should evaluate whether a company's expense practices conform to industry standards, are applied consistently over time, and have been subjected to media scrutiny.

AUDIT OPINIONS

MICRO **A**NALYSIS 14

KPMG LLP resigned as Rite Aid Corp.'s auditor in 1999, because it was "unable to continue to rely on management's representations."

MICRO **A**NALYSIS 15

PricewaterhouseCoopers LLP rendered an unqualified audit opinion for drkoop.com, Inc. for 1999, but the independent auditor's report stated, "the Company sustained losses and negative cash flows from operations since its inception. These matters raise substantial doubt about its ability to continue as a going concern."

WEB **E**XERCISE 11

Locate the 1999 audit opinions of CDNow.com, Inc., and EFAX.com to find out what their auditors thought of these companies' future prospects.

External auditors express an opinion about the fairness with which a company presents its balance sheet, income statement, statement of shareholders' equity, and statement of cash flows.[19] An unqualified opinion increases analysts' confidence that a firm's financial statements conform to GAAP. An opinion to the contrary, however, signals analysts to closely monitor certain items or steer clear of the company altogether.

Five types of audit reports exist:

◆ *Standard unqualified report.* The so-called *clean* audit opinion states that a company's financial statements are presented present fairly, in all material respects, in conformity with generally accepted accounting principles.

◆ *Qualified report—GAAP departure.* A company whose financial statements depart in some material aspect from GAAP earns this opinion. The opinion reads along the lines of "In our opinion, except for the GAAP departure, the financial statements present fairly . . . " The *overall* financial statements are presented fairly, despite the GAAP departure.

◆ *Adverse report.* If departures from GAAP are so pervasive that a company's financial statements do not conform to GAAP, then auditors issue an adverse opinion.

◆ *Qualified report—scope limitation.* Auditors render this type of opinion when they are unable to obtain sufficient evidence about certain financial statement disclosures. For example, if analysts are unable to examine a portion of the company's inventory, the company may receive a qualified opinion, based on the limited scope of the audit. Similar to a GAAP departure qualification, auditors believe the *overall* financial statements are presented fairly, despite the scope limitation.

◆ *Disclaimer report.* Auditors who cannot determine the fairness of financial statements do not express an opinion about them. They disclaim an opinion, due to severe limitations in conducting the audit.

Unqualified audit opinions buoy an analyst's confidence in the reliability of the financial statements. Analysts must seriously consider qualified audit reports. They must compensate for departures in GAAP and limitations of scope when analyzing a company. Financial statements that receive an adverse opinion or dis-

---

[19] The audit report appears immediately before or after the presentation of the financial statements in a company's Form 10-K.

claimer are unreliable sources of information. Analysts should not evaluate companies whose auditors have expressed such opinions. Auditor action also signals analysts: You should be wary of a company's financial statements if its auditors resign from the engagement.

Auditors add **explanatory language** to the report when a company receives anything but an unqualified opinion. These statements explain the matter of concern. Analysts need to pay close attention to the explanatory language in an audit opinion. In addition, analysts must be wary when auditors question a firm's ability to continue as a **going concern**. In such an instance, auditors express doubt as to whether the company can continue operations indefinitely into the future, due to significant economic problems. Auditors can express this concern even if a company's financial statements conform to GAAP. Like explanatory language for qualified audit opinions, analysts must closely evaluate the auditor's explanation of reported events.

A MATTER OF INDEPENDENCE

Business history provides ample evidence of companies that received clean audit opinions, only to have financial improprieties revealed at a later date. What is your reaction to some of the more prominent examples?

Sunbeam, HBOC/McKesson, Rite-Aid, Waste Management, and Cendant received unqualified audit opinions and then subsequently revealed significant accounting improprieties and adjusted their financial statements. Unfortunately, these examples do not even begin to approach the complete list of companies falling into this disreputable category. Many individuals question the thoroughness of the firms' auditors in theses situations.

Independent audit reports express an opinion about the fairness of the financial statements in conformity with GAAP. Auditors obtain reasonable assurance about whether the financial statements are free of material misstatement in rendering their opinion. To reach a conclusion, auditors gather evidence that supports, or refutes, management's representations presented in the financial statements. An analyst must remember that audit opinions do not guarantee accurate financial statements. Evidence gathered in an audit, for example, is often done on sample basis, because it may be impossible to audit every transaction.

Accountants are professionals who adhere to a code of ethics. Proper ethical conduct should negate potential conflicts of interest and result in auditors making morally correct choices. In the great majority of cases, auditors do act ethically, but challenges exist. Consider three areas of potential conflict. The audited company pays the auditor's fee; accounting firms sometimes provide managerial consulting for their clients as well as auditing them; and business consolidations have eliminated many audit clients.

Observations

Analysts gather additional information to provide insight about management's financial statements and the auditors' opinion of them. Why is it important to do the following?

- ◆ Assess the judgment and integrity of management
- ◆ Consider the financial reporting history of the company
- ◆ Investigate large and unusual changes in reported items

- ◆ Determine if any unusual pressures exist for management to attain certain levels of financial performance
- ◆ Verify auditor independence
- ◆ Constantly monitor the financial media for information about questionable reporting practices

FACTORS INFLUENCING APPLE COMPUTER AND THE PERSONAL COMPUTER INDUSTRY

MICRO

▼ **A**NALYSIS 16

KPMG Peat Marwick LLP replaced Ernst & Young LLP as Apple's auditors in 1997, the same year that the company replaced its CEO and most of its Board of Directors. Do think these two actions were related?

WEB

▼ **E**XERCISE 12

Who is Apple Computer's current auditor?

As discussed in Chapter 5, the PC industry matured during the 1990s: Competition increased, new industry entrants decreased, prices declined, and corporate restructurings occurred. We now evaluate how some financial statement influences discussed here apply to this industry.

Successful R&D activities are vital to PC companies. Revenue expenditures for R&D quantify management's commitment to developing knowledge. These costs are expensed in the period incurred, as noted earlier in the chapter. Apple Computer's R&D expenses exceeded industry averages during the period examined. The closed architecture of its machines may have necessitated higher R&D spending than the competition, which shared knowledge of the open architecture design. Apple reduced R&D on a percentage basis from 1993 to 1998. Fewer product offerings may have caused the spending decline. Then again, a desire to increase profits by reducing a discretionary cost could have been the motivation.

As manufacturing concerns, the PC industry's product-costing complexities might initially seem like a focal point of analysis. Closer examining the data, however, indicates this was not the case. Balance sheet data provided evidence. Befitting a knowledge industry, relatively little financing was invested in property, plant, and equipment (P,P&E). Percentage of investments in these assets declined over time for Compaq and Apple, remained stable for Dell, and increased for Gateway. Regardless of trend, P,P&E never amounted to more than one-fifth of each company's total assets. Consequently, allocation of depreciation between product costs (related to manufacturing costs) and period costs (for selling costs) was a minor part of the analysis. Moreover, firms drastically reduced their inventories during the period examined. Product costing issues became less important as inventories shrank.

One would suspect that rapid technological changes and decreasing prices altered the product mix and cost composition for PC firms. Moreover, strategic initiatives influenced corporate cost structure. Apple Computer, for example, drastically reduced product offerings when upper management changed in 1997.However, it is premature to judge the impact of cost adjustments on financial performance. Subsequent chapters consider these cost factors.

Accounting methods were comparable among firms over the period examined (Exhibit 5-13). In addition, companies consistently applied their accounting methods throughout the period studied. A search of the financial media did not reveal any financial reporting improprieties. Companies received standard unqualified reports from their auditors. Apple Computer switched external auditors in 1997. The company's 1997 Form 10-K cited no disagreements with its accountants.

APPLE COMPUTER'S AUDIT OPINION

KMPG LLP's opinion to Apple Computer's Board of Directors on October 11, 1999 read in part as follows:

> We have audited the accompanying consolidated balance sheets of Apple Computer, Inc. and subsidiaries as of September 25, 1999 and September 25, 1998, and the related consolidated statements of operations, shareholders' equity, and cash flows for each of the years in the three-year period ended September, 25, 1999. . . .
>
> In our opinion, the consolidated financial statements referred to above present fairly, in all material respects, the financial position of Apple Computer, Inc. and subsidiaries as of September 25, 1999 and September 25, 1998, and the results of their operations and their cash flows for each of the years in the three-year period ended September, 25, 1999 in conformity with generally accepted accounting principles.

Observations

What type of audit opinion did Apple receive? Do KMPG's representations guarantee that Apple's financial statements are 100 percent accurate? Discuss whether Apple's audit opinion adds to the credibility of its financial statements.

SUMMARY

This chapter addresses some important financial reporting considerations. It discusses the role judgment plays in financial statement preparation and interpretation. The chapter then relates judgment to basic cost items, other cost factors, managerial estimates, and audit reports. These items play a significant role in analysis. Financial statements sometimes report their impact. The analyst, however, often has to judge the effect of undisclosed factors.

The balance sheet initially reports capital expenditures, but income statement discloses revenue expenditures. Reporting these expenditures is sometimes based on practical considerations, as evidenced by R&D accounting. Another basic cost consideration is the inherent complexity of manufacturers' financial statements, due to inventory-related accounts. Certain costs that are expenses in the current reporting period for a merchant become revenue expenditures for a manufacturer. Selling products results in the expensing of these product costs.

Managerial judgment and estimation influence the numbers reported on financial statements. You should conduct research to assure yourself of management's integrity and their ability to recognize revenues and expenses in the correct reporting period. Audit reports express an independent opinion about the fairness of a company's financial statement. An unqualified opinion adds a level of assurance about the fairness of the financial statements, but it does not absolutely guarantee it. An adverse audit opinion or a disclaimer is a signal to discontinue your analysis. Analysts should cautiously assess disclosures when an auditor questions an entity's ability to continue as a going concern.

KEY TERMS

Adverse report
Analytical judgment
Breakeven point
Capital (asset) expenditure

Capital-intensive
Comparability
Consistency
Controllable costs

Cost
Disclaimer report
Explanatory language
Fixed costs
Going concern
Improper expense recognition (back-end loading)
Labor-intensive
Lease
Period costs

Premature revenue recognition (front-end loading)
Product costs
Qualified report—GAAP departure
Qualified report—Scope limitation
Representationally faithful
Revenue expenditures
Revenue recognition
Standard unqualified report
Uncontrollable costs
Variable costs

INDUSTRY CASES

Complete the following requirements for the industries presented in the appendixes at the end of the text.

a. Classify each industry as a manufacturing, merchandising, or service industry.
b. For manufacturing and merchandising industries, state whether inventory consists of only finished goods or raw materials, work in process, and finished goods.
c. For manufacturing and merchandising industries, state whether cost of goods sold consists of only finished goods or raw materials, work in process, and finished goods.
d. Identify one cost as a revenue expenditure and one that is a capital expenditure.
e. Classify depreciation on property, plant, and equipment as a period cost, product cost, or a combination of period and product costs.
f. Examine each expense category listed on the income statement. Do you think they can be classified as either fixed or variable?
g. Speculate on whether each expense category consists primarily of controllable or uncontrollable costs. Do the income statements allow you to draw definitive conclusions?
h. Determine whether R&D expenses are disclosed separately on the income statement. If they are not disclosed separately, do you think companies' in those industries incur R&D costs?

6-1   *Personal Computers: Apple, Compaq, Dell, and Gateway*

6-2   *Airlines: American, Delta, and United*

6-3   *Athletic Footwear: Nike and Reebok*

6-4   *Discount Retailers: Kmart, Target, and Wal-Mart*

6-5   *Fast-Food Restaurants: McDonald's and Wendy's*

6-6   *Soft Drink Companies: Coca-Cola and PepsiCo.*

INDUSTRY INTERNET CASES

Examine the most recent Form 10-K of each company within the industries listed in the book's appendixes. Address each of the following issues:

a. Identify one capital-intensive aspect and one labor-intensive aspect of the industry.

b. Examine the independent audit reports. Note and interpret any modifications to or departures from the standard unqualified report.

c. If available, locate cost-volume-profit analysis and market share information.

6-1 *Personal Computers: Apple, Compaq, Dell, and Gateway*

6-2 *Airlines: American, Delta, and United*

6-3 *Athletic Footwear: Nike and Reebok*

6-4 *Discount Retailers: Kmart, Target, and Wal-Mart*

6-5 *Fast-Food Restaurants: McDonald's and Wendy's*

6-6 *Soft Drink Companies: Coca-Cola and PepsiCo.*

7

REPORTING REQUIREMENTS

Upon completion of this chapter, you should be able to:

◆ *Identify the basic reporting requirements for business acquisitions, security investments, foreign investments, risk management, deferred compensation arrangements, and deferred taxes.*

◆ *Understand the primary analytical implications for each of the six topics addressed in this chapter.*

◆ *Indicate how certain disclosures deviate from historical cost reporting and the all-inclusive concept of net income.*

◆ *Relate this chapter's topics to the financial statements of Apple Computer, Inc., and other personal computer firms.*

◆ *Articulate how business maturation, industry factors, and the transition to the new economy influence reporting requirements and analytical considerations.*

*C*ommercial activities increase in complexity as a business matures. Companies also adopt new business practices as they emerge in the marketplace. Financial disclosures must reflect these increasingly sophisticated economic events. This chapter focuses on the reporting requirements for these topics. We address six reporting issues: business acquisitions, security investments, foreign investments, risk management, deferred compensation arrangements, and deferred taxes. For each economic event, we define it, present its essential reporting requirements, indicate its analytical implications, and give real-world examples using disclosures from Apple Computer and the personal computer (PC) industry.[1]

BUSINESS ACQUISITIONS

A **business acquisition** occurs when one firm (the **acquiring company**) purchases the productive assets of another entity (the **target company**). Companies make strategic decisions to integrate those acquired resources to increase firm value by enlarging market size, generating greater productivity, enhancing technology, and lowering costs. However, expected benefits from business acquisitions sometimes fail to materialize, possibly because the acquiring company paid too much or failed to integrate the businesses. These transactions reduce the acquiring company's shareholder wealth.

MICRO
▼ *A*NALYSIS 1

Acquisitions are high-risk business strategies because management must coordinate two large organizations, which consist of different resources, people, and corporate cultures.

There are three types of business acquisitions: The first type is when a company purchases a majority of the voting stock of the target. Thus, the acquiring or **parent company** controls the activities of the target or **subsidiary company**. Each company maintains its separate legal status in this business combination. The second category is a **merger**, whereby the acquiring company purchases all of the target's stock. The acquiring firm dissolves the acquired company and merges the target's business with its own operations. A **business consolidation**, the third kind of acquisition, takes place when a newly formed corporation acquires all the stock of combining companies and dissolves the original entities. Irrespective of acquisition type, the acquiring corporation uses cash, debt, its stock, or a combination of the three to finance the transaction.

FINANCIAL REPORTING REQUIREMENTS

Mergers and consolidations result in one company; therefore, the combined entity reports one set of financial statements. Parent-subsidiary disclosures are more complex. As legally separate firms, they keep their own accounting records. But only one economic entity exists, which is controlled by the parent company's shareholders. The parent combines the subsidiary's financial statements with its own and reports **consolidated financial statements**, which disclose the single economic entity's financial position and results of operations. The following discussion focuses on consolidated financial statements, but the principles of purchase accounting and goodwill apply to the financial statements of merged and consolidated entities as well.

WEB
▼ *E*XERCISE 1

Examine Apple Computer's most recent financial statements. Does the company report consolidated financial statements?

---

[1] We do not cover these topics in detail here. Some additional aspects are addressed in subsequent chapters. Other issues related to these topics are complex, however, and exceed the scope of this text. Refer to intermediate, advanced, and international accounting texts for more insights.

The **purchase method of accounting** governs financial reporting for business acquisitions.[2] This method

◆ Revalues the target's accounts from historical cost to fair value.
◆ Creates an intangible asset, called *goodwill*, when the purchase price exceeds the fair value of the acquired assets.
◆ Eliminates goodwill within a prescribed time period.

A parent firm essentially invests in the subsidiary's net assets (assets – liabilities). Like any asset's value, the fair market values of the assets acquired become their basis in the consolidated entity. In other words, the price the acquiring firm pays for the target's assets becomes the *historical cost* of those assets. The original historical cost of the target's assets ceases to exist for consolidated reporting purposes.[3]

An acquiring firm often pays an amount in excess of the fair market value of the target's net assets. A number of factors account for a premium purchase price: The target might have excellent management, talented workers, superior products, outstanding business locations, or favorable tax conditions. The difference between the purchase price of the target and the fair market value of the identifiable assets acquired is **goodwill**.[4] Capitalizing this intangible asset results in periodic charges against revenues in current and future reporting periods. It is eliminated within a prescribed time period.

A company cannot generate goodwill internally. It exists only as a result of a business acquisition.

Apple Computer put itself up for sale in January 1996. The company negotiated with Sun Microsystems for its takeover.

ANALYTICAL IMPLICATIONS

Consolidated financial statements reflect the economic entity assumption inherent in financial reporting. Regardless of legal structure, substantively one economic enterprise exists; therefore, consolidated financial statements convey information about this single entity. The strength of consolidated financial statements is also a weakness. Presenting consolidated financial statements obscures the economic results and position of each company in the combination. To offset this reporting deficiency, analysts should review management's discussion about its various businesses and examine financial statement footnotes that explain segment performance.[5]

Goodwill complicates analysis. It is the most intangible of all intangible assets. Patents, copyrights, trademarks, and other intangibles have a distinct identity

---

[2] At this writing, we assume the Financial Accounting Standards Board (FASB) will change the reporting requirements for business combinations. The new standard should reflect the changes outlined in the Board's existing Exposure Draft. Prior to the adoption of the new GAAP, Accounting Principles Board Opinion No. 16, "Business Combinations," governed consolidations. This opinion allowed for the use of the pooling-of-interests method in addition to the purchase method of accounting for business combinations. The pooling-of-interest method assumes shareholders of separate companies combined ownership interests for their mutual benefit. As such, one business was merged into, rather than acquired by, another entity.

[3] Accounts are not revalued to market when using the pooling-of-interest method. The historical cost of the resources on the target's balance sheet becomes the historical cost of the target's portion of assets on the consolidated balance sheet.

[4] The pooling-of-interest method does not use goodwill because historical costs are not revised to market values.

[5] Segment data comply with "Disclosure about Segments of an Enterprise and Related Information," *Statement of Financial Accounting Standard No. 131* (Norwalk, CT: FASB, 1997). Segments are disclosed along the lines of reportable business segments, geography (foreign versus domestic) and major customers. These classifications are determined by corporate operations. Note that the individual legal entities' financial statements do not have to be reported in compliance with FASB No. 131. Examining segmented data, however, provides some disaggregation information about the consolidated firm.

MICRO
ANALYSIS 4

Apple fired Michael Spindler as CEO and hired Gilbert Amelio as his replacement in February 1996. Within a week of the change, the company rejected Sun's overtures and announced it would not be taken over. Do you think the changes in management and strategy were related?

with a traceable historical cost. Goodwill does not have a separate identity, and its cost results from the excess of purchase price over the fair value of individual assets. Theoretically, goodwill has an infinite life. The value of the intangible asset could last forever! However, generally accepted accounting principles (GAAP) require analysts to look at it differently.[6] To determine periodic income, you must subtract goodwill expense from revenues. Goodwill amortization, like fixed asset depreciation, is a noncash expense.

When evaluating business acquisitions, analysts are concerned with the following:

- ◆ Type of business acquisition
- ◆ Organizational *fit* of the two companies
- ◆ Purchase price
- ◆ Value of goodwill
- ◆ Goodwill amortization period
- ◆ Effect of amortization on earnings

WHAT'S YOUR ANALYSIS

BUY HIGH, SELL LOW

How would you analyze the business acumen of the people who made the following acquisitions?[a]

- ◆ AT&T purchased NCR with stock valued at $7.4 billion in 1991. Ma Bell rang up only $3.4 billion when it sold NCR four years later.
- ◆ Quaker Oats snapped up Snapple for $1.7 billion in 1994. The company wasn't feeling its oats three years later when it unloaded Snapple for $300 million.
- ◆ Novel acquired WordPerfect in 1994 with stock valued at $1.4 billion. The company deleted nine-tenths of the word processor's purchase price when it was sold two years later.
- ◆ Eli Lilly purchased PCS Health Systems for $4 billion in 1994. The pharmaceutical company developed a giant headache when it sold PCS to Rite-Aid for $1.5 billion in 1998.
- ◆ Smithkline Beecham bought Diversified Pharmaceutical Services for $2.3 billion in 1994. The acquisition diversified Smithkline's earnings by $1.3 billion when it was sold for $1 billion in 1999.

Observations

None of these acquisitions worked out as expected. Why do you think they were made? Do you think the performance of the acquired companies increased or decreased the acquiring firms' share prices? Justify the sale of the acquired companies for an amount less than their purchase price.

---

[a] Based on an article by N. Deogun and S. Lipin, "Cautionary Tales: When Big Deals Go Bad," *Wall Street Journal,* December 8, 1999, p. C1.

---

[6] At this writing, current GAAP account for goodwill. The FASB proposed eliminating periodic goodwill amortization toward the end of 2000. In that case, companies would reduce capitalized goodwill only if it became impaired under that proposal.

Oracle Corp. attempted to acquire Apple Computer against the company's wishes in March 1997. Oracle gave up by the end of April. Apple fired Gilbert Amelio in July of that year.

Has Apple completely amortized goodwill resulting from its acquisition of NeXT Software? Look at its most recent Form 10-K to find out.

Steven Jobs became Apple Computer's interim chief executive officer in September 1997 at a salary of $1 per year.

REPORTING EXAMPLES AND OBSERVATIONS OF BUSINESS ACQUISITIONS

Industries tend to consolidate as they mature and the companies involved need greater operating efficiencies. The PC industry showed maturity during the mid-1990s: There were fewer total PC firms in the industry in 1998 than there were in 1993. Although one could still view the industry as fragmented by the end of the period examined, a few industry leaders, such as Compaq and Dell, emerged, increasing market share as firms consolidated. Computer companies also embraced various Internet strategies and added additional peripheral equipment during this time period. These actions also demonstrate the increasing maturity of the PC industry.

Apple Computer exchanged $427 million of cash and common stock to acquire NeXT Software, Inc. in 1997 and merged the company with Apple. NeXT developed and marketed Internet software, which Apple valued as a product enhancement. Steven Jobs, a cofounder of Apple Computer, was also a cofounder, chief executive officer (CEO), and president of NeXT. The Internet company had few tangible assets. The largest portion of Apple's purchase was $375 million for in-process research and development. Apple Computer expensed this cost in 1997, the year of acquisition. In addition, the acquisition created $52 million of goodwill for Apple. The company amortized the intangible asset over a three-year period.[7]

Apple acquired NeXT because its economic performance was faltering, industry conditions were good, and relationships among the companies' personnel already existed. The future will reveal whether the acquisition was wise and the purchase price justified. The company's stock price and financial performance will provide the evidence.

RESEARCH AND DEVELOPMENT WRITE-OFFS

One aspect of the information economy is that business acquisitions involve greater amounts of intangible assets. The most prevalent intangible asset acquired in high-tech industries is called *purchased* or *in-process research and development (R&D)*. Acquiring another entity's intellectual investigations has created a financial reporting controversy. What is your analysis of the situation?

Current GAAP treats purchased R&D acquired as revenue expenditure. But both the Securities and Exchange Commission (SEC) and FASB have become increasingly concerned with perceived abuses in this area of financial reporting. Over $11 billion of purchased R&D costs were expensed in 1998, compared with less than $1 billion in 1994.[8] Regulators and standard setters argue that acquiring companies overestimate the market value of in-process R&D so that they can immediately expense virtually all of their acquisition cost. Large purchased R&D values reduce goodwill, thereby lowering periodic amortization. This, in turn, curtails goodwill's drag on future earnings. High-tech companies counter SEC and FASB claims by stating that the purchased R&D valuations are legitimate because R&D represents the real value of the acquired firm.

---

[7] A small portion of the $52 million was attributable to nongoodwill intangible assets.

SECURITY INVESTMENTS

Companies often invest in other entities by purchasing securities of other entities. An **equity security** is an instrument that demonstrates ownership in a company such as a parent's acquisition of a subsidiary's stock. A **debt security** is one that indicates a creditor relationship with a firm or governmental agency. These assets employ otherwise idle cash productively; they earn revenues without reducing firm liquidity.[8]

FINANCIAL REPORTING REQUIREMENTS

WEB
EXERCISE 3

Go to the most recent financial disclosures of the PC companies discussed in this book. Do any of the four firms distinguish between debt and equity securities in the body of their balance sheets?

Corporations earn interest income on debt investments and dividend income from equity securities. The income statement reports these earnings as **financial revenues** or **income**.[9] **Realized gains (losses)** result when corporations sell security investments for more than (less than) they cost. The income statement also reports gains and losses on the sale of securities.

Complexities exist when a firm controls debt or equity securities at the end of a reporting period. How these investments are disclosed depends on their classification, which is a function of the extent of holdings and management's intentions. Exhibit 7-1 classifies securities and outlines their financial statement disclosures.

EXHIBIT 7-1
Debt and Equity Securities Categories and Disclosures

TYPE OF SECURITY	CATEGORY OF SECURITY	BALANCE SHEET VALUATION	UNREALIZED HOLDING GAIN OR LOSS
Debt	Trading	Fair value	Income statement
Debt	Available-for-sale	Fair value	Shareholders' equity
Debt	Held-to-maturity	Historical cost	Not applicable
Equity	Trading	Fair value	Income statement
Equity	Available-for-sale	Fair value	Shareholders' equity
Equity	Active minority interest—between a 20 percent and 50 percent ownership	Equity	Not applicable
Equity	Majority investment—greater than 50 percent ownership	Consolidation	Not applicable

[8] Security investments can be sold in the capital markets; therefore, these assets can revert into cash almost instantaneously.
[9] Technically, debt securities earn interest revenues, and equity investments earn dividend revenues. The exception is dividends earned from investments accounted for under the equity valuation method. This exception is discussed later in this section.

Securities can be passive or active investments. The first five categories listed in the exhibit are **passive investments**, or those securities in which the investor does not significantly influence the investee's operations. The last two categories indicate **active investments**, whereby an equity investor significantly influences the operations of its investee.

Trading securities are investments that will be sold in the near future. **Available-for-sale securities** might be sold in the short-term, or the company could retain them beyond the next reporting period. These two categories apply to both debt and equity investments. A company planning to hold debt until it matures classifies such investments as **held-to-maturity debt securities**. The final two investment categories in Exhibit 7-1 pertain to active equity investments. A company has an **active minority ownership** in another firm when it significantly influences, but does not control, its investee's decisions. **Majority ownership** equals control over an investee. In these instances, an investor owns the majority of an investee's voting stock.

Companies record debt and equity investments categorized as trading and available-for-sale securities at their market value on the balance sheet. The difference between trading and available-for-sale securities is in the treatment of the **unrealized gains** and **losses**. These gains and losses represent the difference between market value and historical cost (or the previous period's market value). They are unrealized because the securities have not been sold. Companies report unrealized gains and losses on trading securities in the "Current Income" section. Conversely, companies disclose unrealized gains and losses for available-for-sale securities in "Other Comprehensive Income" in the shareholders' equity section of the balance sheet. In other words, market-based adjustments for available-for-sale securities bypass the income statement and do not affect periodic income.

Held-to-maturity securities appear on the balance sheet at historical cost,[10] so there are no unrealized gains or losses associated with these debt investments. Active equity investments are not adjusted to market. An investor values active equity investments at historical cost plus their proportionate share of an investee's net income (loss).

ANALYTICAL IMPLICATIONS

Management might elect to forgo other uses of cash in order to generate returns from the debt and equity instruments of other entities. Prudent security investment strategies can increase profitability and share price. There are, however, risks to all investments. Moreover, security investments should not represent the core revenue-generating activity of the company.

Analysts must be aware of the following points for passive investment securities:

◆ Revenues (income) and realized gains (losses) are reported on the income statement after income from continuing operations.
◆ Unrealized gains (losses) appear on the income statement for trading securities but directly in shareholders' equity for available-for-sale securities.
◆ Market value adjustments for unrealized gains (losses) increase trading securities earnings volatility.

---

[10] Technically, they are reported at an *adjusted* historical cost basis. This modified cost method accounts for adjustments made to the discounts and premiums that attach to debt instruments.

◆ Adjustments to market values for unrealized gains (losses) change shareholders' equity for investors in available-for-sale securities without reflecting those changes in the income statement.

◆ Unrealized gains (losses) do not affect cash flows in the current reporting period.

Investors' accounting for active equity positions in other firms depends on ownership level. Active minority disclosures differ in form, rather than substance, from those of majority investments. A majority investor consolidates its financial statements with its investee because it controls that company (through a majority of voting stock). We examined these consolidated financial statements in the section on business acquisitions. An active minority owner influences, but does not control, an investee's actions, so it does not consolidate the investee's financial statements with its own.

An active minority owner adjusts the book value of its investment according to the investee's activities. Asset values increase for a proportionate share of the investee's income and decrease for a proportionate share of its dividends. To illustrate this concept, assume eSTUFF purchased 25 percent of On-Line.com for $100,000. If On-Line reported $60,000 in income and declared $20,000 total dividends, then the book value of eSTUFF's investment would be $110,000 ($100,000 + .25[$60,000] − .25[$20,000]).[11]

As noted, a parent company (investor) and subsidiary company (investee) relationship exists in majority ownership cases. Less than 100 percent ownership creates a minority ownership interest for the subsidiary. **Minority interest** represents the portion of a subsidiary not owned by the parent company. It affects consolidated financial statement disclosures and their analysis.

Assume eSTUFF purchased 75 percent of Real-Time.com. Consequently, non-eSTUFF investors own 25 percent of Real-Time. Put another way, minority shareholders of Real-Time have a claim to one-quarter of the subsidiary's assets and income. eSTUFF's consolidated financial statements, however, combine eSTUFF's financial statements with 100 percent of Real-Time's financial statements. The rationale for **full consolidation** is that eSTUFF controls all of Real-Time's operations by owning a majority (75 percent) of its voting stock. Minority ownership in its subsidiary exists and is reported on eSTUFF's consolidated financial statements. One-fourth of Real-Time's earnings are subtracted from eSTUFF's consolidated income. Minority interest is reflected on the consolidated balance sheet as part of eSTUFF's shareholders' equity. Although the subsidiary is listed as part of consolidated shareholders' equity, its minority interest does not entitle it to a claim to eSTUFF's assets.

REPORTING EXAMPLES AND OBSERVATIONS OF SECURITY INVESTMENTS

Apple Computer generated positive cash flows from operations from 1996 through 1998, despite massive losses in 1996 and 1997. A significant portion of this cash was invested in U.S. Treasury securities, U.S. corporate securities, and foreign securities. All of these investments matured in less than one year. Apple clas-

WEB EXERCISE 4

Does Apple Computer currently have any active equity investments?

MICRO ANALYSIS 10

Apple did not classify all of its investments as short-term investments (or marketable securities). In fact, Apple reported a majority of them as part of "Cash and Cash Equivalents" on the balance sheet. Low-risk investments with few restrictions on convertibility into cash are sometimes classified as cash equivalents *rather than short-term investments.*

---

[11] This transaction assumes fair market values equal book values and no goodwill was paid for On-Line.

sified its investments as available-for-sale securities. Consequently, Apple disclosed fair value adjustments to these securities were disclosed as an other component in the company's statement of shareholders' equity. Apple reported no gains or losses on these investments on the income statement.

The company had no long-term investments or any active ownership interests during the period of study. Other PC companies' investment strategies at that time tended to reflect Apple Computer's conservative short-term investment positions in the debt and equity of other entities.

FOREIGN INVESTMENTS

Multinational enterprises (MNEs) source materials, manufacture products and deliver services, and sell them worldwide. They engage in import/export activities, strategic alliances, and licensing arrangements with entities in other countries. They also establish subsidiaries through **foreign direct investments**. A foreign subsidiary usually reports its financial statements in local currency units, such as the Mexican peso, Japanese yen, or British pound. Just as they do for all other majority investments, GAAP require MNEs to consolidate subsidiaries' financial statements with their own. Complications arise because currency exchange rates vary over time. For example, the peso equivalent of a dollar at the beginning of the year probably differs from its value at year-end.

MICRO
ANALYSIS 11

Apple reports that most of the currency it receives from foreign subsidiaries is denominated in something other than dollars. Does it make sense that the PC maker translates its subsidiaries' activities on a current rate basis? Do you think a strong or weak dollar (relative to those foreign currencies) benefits Apple when the company converts those currencies into dollars?

FINANCIAL REPORTING REQUIREMENTS

There are two ways to consolidate a foreign subsidiary's financial statements: The current rate method or the temporal method.[12] The **current rate method** translates the foreign subsidiary's financial statements at the existing exchange rates.[13] The **temporal method** remeasures the foreign subsidiary's accounts at either the current exchange rate or an historical one, depending on whether the account is monetary or nonmonetary.

A *monetary* item is a contractual claim to receive or pay a fixed amount of money, such as accounts receivable and accounts payable. A *nonmonetary* account is not tied to a specific amount of funds, such as land and buildings. The temporal method remeasures monetary items at the current exchange rate and nonmonetary ones at their historical rates (i.e., the exchange rate that existed when an item was acquired).

Functional currency, or the monetary denomination of a subsidiary's primary economic events, determines whether a parent company uses the current rate or temporal method to consolidate a foreign investee's financial statements with its own. For example, if a Mexican subsidiary conducts most of its business in pesos, then the peso is its functional currency. The parent company would then use the current rate method to translate its subsidiaries' financial statements. Conversely, if most of the subsidiary's business is conducted in U.S. dollars, then the dollar is the functional currency, and the company would use temporal remeasurement.

---

[12] "Foreign Currency Translation," *Statement of Financial Accounting Standard No. 52* (Stamford CT, FASB, 1981).
[13] With this method, companies translate balance sheet accounts using the year-end exchange rate and flow statements using an average exchange rate.

WEB *E*XERCISE 5

Determine if Compaq, Dell, and Gateway adjust their income statements or balance sheets when converting their foreign subsidiaries' currencies. What does this tell you about the functional currency of each company's foreign subsidiaries? How about the translation method used?

ANALYTICAL IMPLICATIONS

The translation method used has implications for a parent company's financial disclosures. As with security investments, the method used affects the way foreign investments are reported. The temporal method treats remeasurement gains (losses) as income statement adjustments. The current rate method reports a cumulative adjustment to the consolidated statement of shareholders' equity. Similar to reporting available-for-sale securities, the income statement does not report the economic impact of current rate translations.

REPORTING EXAMPLES AND OBSERVATIONS OF FOREIGN INVESTMENTS

The four PC firms examined in this study were domiciled in the United States during 1993–1998. Each had a global presence by the 1990s. They all made foreign direct investments to better serve global markets, reduce manufacturing costs, and hedge against currency fluctuations. International operations, however, increased organization complexity and required greater control over productive resources.

Apple Computer had four foreign subsidiaries by the end of 1998—two in Ireland, one in the Netherlands, and one in Japan. The functional currencies of these subsidiaries were their local currencies (Irish punt, Dutch guilders, and Japanese yen). Apple accountants used the current rate method to translate the foreign subsidiaries' financial statements for consolidation purposes. There is an "Accumulated Translation Adjustments" section in Apple's statements of shareholders' equity to record these translations.

RISK MANAGEMENT

Business activities often create economic risks. The term **risk management** encompasses the numerous strategies and tactics used to reduce financial exposure resulting from the uncertainty inherent in such transactions. Many of these techniques are creative, complex, and somewhat risky themselves. This section examines them.

WEB *E*XERCISE 6

Visit the International Swaps and Derivatives Web site at www.isda.org.

MICRO *A*NALYSIS 12

The SEC estimated the notional amount of derivatives (the number of currency units or other goods specified in derivatives) at $70 trillion by the end of 1998.

FINANCIAL REPORTING REQUIREMENTS

Rapidly changing global markets increase risk management needs and lead to many financial innovations in this area. **Derivatives** are a primary tool that help companies manage risk. These instruments represent an exchange of promises between entities to do something in the future. The value of a derivative stems from the worth of another asset to which it is related. For example, eSTUFF might agree with a wholesaler to buy inventory next month. The purchase price could be set at the cost of today's inventory. This *forward contract* locks in eSTUFF's purchase price at the current cost of inventory. Therefore, eSTUFF is protected if the cost of inventory increases from now until next month, but it would pay a premium for the goods if inventory prices declined during that time. The value of eSTUFF's futures contract, therefore, is *derived* from the inventory costs.

Until recently GAAP did not require companies to report many derivative instruments in financial statement disclosures, because a promise to do something in the future (such as eSTUFF's agreement to buy inventory) did not create a

reportable event. In other words, the transacting parties did not exchange tangible consideration when making a derivative agreement. Thus, derivatives were often *off-balance sheet*, or unreported in the financial statements under previous GAAP. But derivatives do have economic value in the marketplace. Therefore, the FASB changed GAAP and now requires companies to report derivative assets and liabilities at fair value on their balance sheets.[14]

ANALYTICAL IMPLICATIONS

Like debt, equity, and foreign investments, some derivatives' adjustments to fair value are reported on the income statement. Others, however, bypass the income statement and are reported in the shareholders' equity section of the balance sheet. Thus, only certain derivative instruments are reported as part of the all-inclusive concept of net income. Also, earnings and shareholders' equity volatility can result from market value adjustments. If the fair value of the derivatives fluctuates from one reporting period to the next, then earnings and/or equity reflect these changes.

REPORTING EXAMPLES AND OBSERVATIONS OF RISK MANAGEMENT

Apple Computer engaged in some transactions to manage risk. The FASB standard that requires fair value financial statement disclosure of derivative interments did not become GAAP until after the period examined, so to a certain extent, Apple had off-balance-sheet risk. The company disclosed the risks associated with these transactions in Item 7-A of its Form 10-K.

A fundamental imbalance existed between the company's investing and financing activities, thereby exposing Apple to financial risk: The company issued long-term notes payable in 1994 and 1996 at fixed interest rates but held only short-term security investments that were susceptible to fluctuating interest rates. Thus, a decline in interest rates would reduce Apple's investment income but not its interest expense. So the firm entered into derivative transactions that effectively swapped its fixed-rate debt to floating-rate debt. This matched the interest expense on the notes with the interest earned by investments.

Apple reported minimal credit risk to its financial management strategies during the period examined. **Credit risk** is defined as a company's gross exposure to accounting losses if the counterparties to the risk management transactions fail to perform according to the agreement. Credit risk was low in the PC industry at this time, according to corporate disclosures.

DEFERRED COMPENSATION ARRANGEMENTS

A **deferred compensation arrangement** provides employees with future benefits for services rendered in the current reporting period, such as pensions, other retirement benefits (such as health and dental care), and matching corporate contributions to employee's savings plans. These business costs reduce current income as they are matched against current revenues. Other financial disclosures

---

[14] "Accounting for Derivative Instruments and Hedging Activities," *Statement of Financial Accounting Standard No.133* (Norwalk, CT, FASB, 1998).

depend on the type of deferred compensation arrangements that exists between a company and its employees.

FINANCIAL REPORTING REQUIREMENTS

Corporations compensate employees in the future for services currently rendered in one of two ways. **Defined contribution arrangements** are based on a predetermined formula. For example, eSTUFF may contribute 10 percent of each employee's salary to his or her individual employee retirement account. The company's periodic pension expense equals one-tenth of its salary expense. **Defined benefit arrangements**, in contrast, provide employees with set levels of benefits. eSTUFF, for example, could agree to pay employees $100 per month during retirement for each year worked.[15] In this case, eSTUFF must ensure that it has sufficient resources set aside to meet its commitment to retired employees. Expenses for defined benefit arrangements become a function of the current costs required to meet that obligation.

ANALYTICAL IMPLICATIONS

Defined contribution arrangements do not present any analytical difficulties. The income statement reports it as part of operating expenses.[16] The retirement benefit a person receives under this arrangement depends on two factors: how much money the company contributed to the fund on that person's behalf and how productively those funds were invested. Defined benefit arrangements, on the other hand, complicate analysis. Uncertainties abound. For example, a company has no way of knowing if an employee will work long enough to qualify for the benefits and how long he or she will live beyond retirement.

Various components affect defined benefit arrangements.[17] Exhibit 7-2 presents the three primary ones and defines them.[18]

Assume eSTUFF started a defined benefit pension plan on January 1, 2002. The entity that administers the company's pension plan, or **pension trustee**, computed the existing pension liability at that time.[19] The company contributed an

MICRO ANALYSIS 14

Many companies have converted their defined benefit plans to a cash balance plan to control costs and meet the needs of a more mobile workforce. A cash balance plan establishes allocations to individual participant accounts. The benefits of this plan can be rolled into another pension plan if the person changes companies.

EXHIBIT 7-2
Defined Benefit Pension Plan Primary Expense Components

COMPONENT	EXPLANATION
Service cost	Retirement benefits earned by employees in the current reporting period
Pension liability	Present value of obligation due to employees
Pension plan assets	Resources set aside to satisfy the pension liability

---

[15] This assumes an employee vests in the plan. *Vesting* entitles an employee to retirement benefits, regardless of whether he or she is employed by the firm.

[16] A portion of the defined contribution could be a product cost for a manufacturing concern. See Chapter 6 for a discussion of product and period costs.

[17] "Employers' Accounting for Pension Plans," *Statement of Financial Accounting Standard No. 87,* (Stamford, CT: FASB, 1985).

[18] Other factors affect pension expense, including adjustments for pension plan amendments and gains and losses resulting from changes in the market value of pension plan assets and assumptions underlying the pension obligation. These considerations exceed the scope of this discussion.

[19] This computation would be based on an array of actuarial assumptions (probabilities about future events such as employee service length, salaries, and life expectancies).

equal amount of cash to the pension fund (plan assets) to cover the obligation. The trustee invests those funds on eSTUFF's behalf. If the pension plan assets earn a rate of return equal to the growth in the pension liability, then pension expense equals current service cost.[20] Pension expense differs from the current service cost when plan assets and liabilities do not move in lockstep. For example, if the plan's obligations increased faster than fund earnings, the pension expense would exceed the annual service cost. The opposite condition would hold when plan assets earn a return on investment that is greater than the liability increase.

The income statement reports pension expense, but the balance sheet does not disclose pension plan assets and liabilities. In other words, defined benefit plan assets and liabilities are not capitalized. They are, for the most part, treated off-balance sheet.[21] The analyst must evaluate the pension footnote disclosure to determine the value of a plan's assets relative to its obligations. **Over-under funded deferred compensation arrangements** exist if assets (liabilities) exceed liabilities (assets). Analysts must examine notational disclosure to determine the extent of under- or overfunding. Companies must eventually use corporate resources to counteract underfunding.

OFF-BALANCE-SHEET ASSETS

The financial impact of deferred compensation arrangements differs from a decade ago. What do you think of the following situation?

The FASB promulgated a new reporting standard for defined benefit pensions when it found that a majority of plans were underfunded. In other words, a company's pension plan liabilities exceeded its plan assets, which were used to satisfy retirement obligations. Policy makers reasoned that adopting the new pension standard would ensure disclosure of such funding shortages. The economy boomed after the new rule became effective in the late 1980s, resulting in an unforeseen windfall for many firms: Their plans are now overfunded!

How did this happen? Companies fund defined benefit plans through an independent pension trustee. The trustee invests the cash contributions in other entities' securities, attempting to accrue enough resources to meet retirement claims. Pension funds frequently take ownership positions in other companies. Many equity investments generated large returns during the stock market run-up of the 1990s, and pension plan assets grew rapidly. Plan assets became so large in some instances that net periodic pension costs (pension expense) decreased below zero. In other words, pension expense became pension revenue!

The following table presents examples of the amount of overfunding of pension plans and the positive impact the overfunding had on corporate profitability for 1998 (in millions of dollars).°

COMPANY	TOTAL PENSION ASSETS	TOTAL PENSION LIABILITIES	PENSION SURPLUS	INCREASE TO PRETAX INCOME
General Electric	$43,477	$27,602	$15,875	$1,016
Bell Atlantic	37,022	28,936	8,886	627
Lucent Technologies	36,191	27,846	8,345	558
GTE	17,949	8,789	9,160	473
IBM	66,887	58,609	8,278	454

[20] Pension liabilities grow over time as well, due to the time value of money.
[21] Partial amounts of pension assets or liabilities are reported on the balance sheet in certain circumstances. These amounts are usually insignificant compared with the overall plan assets and obligation.

Observations

Do you think pension plan assets and liabilities should be reported on the balance sheet? Are overfunded pension plans assets? Should net periodic pension costs that increase revenues be reported as operating revenues? Do you think a decrease in stock prices would reduce overfunded pension plan assets?

° Data derived from E.E. Shultz's, "The Joy of Overfunding—Companies Reap a Gain off Fat Pension Plans," *Wall Street Journal,* June 15, 1999, pp. A1 and A6.

MICRO ANALYSIS 15

Stock options have made many high-tech employees millionaires in late 1999 and early 2000.

WEB EXERCISE 8

Examine Apple Computer's Employee Savings Plan footnote. How much did the company contribute to the plan in the most recent year reported?

REPORTING EXAMPLES AND OBSERVATIONS OF DEFERRED COMPENSATION ARRANGEMENTS

Employment arrangements in new economy industries often differ from those of industrial firms. Old-economy firms tend to have a stable workforce, a relatively large union presence, and defined benefit pension plans. In the new economy, employees tend to change jobs more frequently, are less likely to join a union, and receive compensation based on deferred contribution arrangements. The PC industry's post-employment compensation packages reflect its information age orientation.

Apple Computer's deferred salary arrangement, for example, was an employee savings plan during the period analyzed. It was approved under Section 401(k) of the Internal Revenue Code. Apple employees could defer a portion of their pretax earnings under this savings plan. The company, in turn, matched employee contributions to the savings plan up to a maximum of 6 percent of an employee's salary. In addition, Apple Computer and other PC firms provided **stock options** to many employees, which enabled them to purchase stock at predetermined prices. Employees benefited by exercising their options when market prices were greater than the exercise price.[22]

DEFERRED TAXES

Federal and state governments levy taxes on the earnings of corporations because they are distinct economic entities with an existence apart from their owners' personal lives. Companies report income as the periodic change in a firm's economic wealth as defined by GAAP. Governmental interpretation of taxable income sometimes differs from that of financial reporting. **Deferred taxes** result from these alternative views of income.

FINANCIAL REPORTING REQUIREMENTS

Whereas GAAP determine financial statement disclosures, laws regulate tax obligations to government agencies. Consequently, certain revenues and expenses are recognized in different reporting periods for financial and tax reporting purposes.[23] Alternative perspectives as to the proper timing of these revenues and expenses result in a **temporary difference**, the disparity between the book value

---

[22] We discuss stock options in detail in Chapter 12.
[23] Temporary differences usually exist because GAAP adhere to the accrual basis of reporting and tax laws favor the cash basis.

of an asset or liability (as determined by GAAP) and its tax basis. A temporary difference balances out over the life of the asset or liability, but it causes pretax financial income to differ from taxable income in specific reporting periods.[24]

Assume, for example, that eSTUFF depreciated its computer equipment on an accelerated basis for tax purposes but used straight-line depreciation for financial reporting disclosures. The book value of equipment per the financial statements would exceed its tax basis in the early years of the asset's life. In addition, eSTUFF's pretax financial income will be greater than its taxable income in those early reporting periods.[25] As a result of the temporary difference, eSTUFF would have a **deferred tax liability**. The balance sheet reports eSTUFF's future tax obligation resulting from the temporary difference. Viewed another way, a deferred tax liability exists because eSTUFF's future taxable earnings will eventually exceed its pretax financial income. In those future periods, eSTUFF's tax obligation will exceed its GAAP-based expense. A **deferred tax asset** would result if eSTUFF reversed its depreciation methods for tax and book purposes. The balance sheet would disclose a tax deferral, or the company's future tax savings as a result of the temporary difference.

ANALYTICAL IMPLICATIONS

The balance sheet reports one net *current* and one net *noncurrent* deferred tax amounts, depending on the asset (or liability) account to which the deferral relates. In the eSTUFF example, a noncurrent deferred tax liability exists because it stems from equipment, a noncurrent asset. In reality, companies have many current and noncurrent deferred tax assets and liabilities. Noncurrent deferred tax assets and liabilities are offset against each other, yielding a net noncurrent asset or liability. GAAP take the same approach for reporting current tax deferrals.

The behavior of deferred tax assets and liabilities differs from the majority of assets and liabilities. Most assets have a finite life, and virtually all liabilities have a predetermined payment date. This is not necessarily the case for tax deferrals. In the eSTUFF example, depreciation on the company's original computer equipment would eventually reverse (i.e., straight-line depreciation would become larger than accelerated depreciation). This would eliminate the original deferred tax liability. Now assume eSTUFF increased its equipment purchases annually and continued using accelerated depreciation for tax reporting purposes and the straight-line method for financial disclosures. Newly created deferred tax liabilities from the additional equipment purchases could more than offset the elimination of the first deferred tax liability. Consequently, the noncurrent deferred tax liability could increase over time.

Does Apple still report deferred tax current assets and deferred tax noncurrent liabilities?

REPORTING EXAMPLES AND OBSERVATIONS OF DEFERRED TAXES

Apple Computer reported deferred tax current assets and deferred tax noncurrent liabilities during the period analyzed. The amounts in the deferred tax current asset account remained relatively constant from 1993 through 1998. Temporary

---

[24] *Permanent* tax differences arise when one party considers something as a revenue or expense, but the other party does not. Permanent differences do not create deferred taxes or materially affect analysis.
[25] This condition exists because straight-line depreciation in those early years would be less than the accelerated expense. Eventually, straight-line depreciation will exceed accelerated method's annual expense. The total amount of asset depreciation is the same, regardless of depreciation method.

differences between the book value and tax basis for receivables and inventories accounted for a substantial portion of those current deferred tax assets.

The deferred tax long-term liability, however, was a different story. This non-current obligation was $629 million in 1993 and peaked at $702 million in 1995. A variety of strategies designed to lower taxable income created this substantial long-term obligation. One contributing factor was Apple's policy of investing foreign subsidiaries' earnings outside the United States. The company deferred taxes on the unremitted (to the United States) earnings of its overseas companies.

The deferred tax began to decline in 1996 and was reported at $173 million by 1998. Apple's net operating losses in 1996 and 1997 contributed to this reduction in long-term deferred tax liabilities. A **net operating loss** occurs when tax-deductible expenses exceed taxable revenues. The Internal Revenue Service allows these losses to offset previous income (loss carryback) or future income (loss carryforward). A company receives an income tax refund by carrying back losses and creates a deferred tax asset by carrying them forward. Apple's 1996 and 1997 net operating losses created carryforward benefits extending until 2012. These long-term deferred tax assets decreased the company's net long-term deferred tax liability from 1996 through 1998.

SUMMARY

This chapter examines important financial reporting topics and their analytical implications. We evaluate business acquisitions, security investments, risk management, foreign currency translation, deferred salary arrangements, and deferred taxes. We then relate each topic to the financial disclosures of Apple Computer and, to a lesser extent, the PC industry.

Be aware that changes in the marketplace and firm maturation increase reporting complexities. Also, many economic events specifically relate to new economy companies. Examples cited in this chapter include purchased R&D and compensation arrangements. This chapter also investigates market value reporting, instead of historical cost disclosures, for certain assets. Examples of current value reporting include trading securities, available-for-sale securities, and derivative instruments. Depending on the circumstances, companies report fair value adjustments for these financial instruments on either the income statement or shareholders' equity statement. Companies translate foreign subsidiaries' accounts similarly to security investments and derivatives: Consolidated financial statements report either an income statement or shareholders' equity statement adjustment, depending on conversion method. Finally, we discuss why governments' interpretation of taxable income sometimes differs from that of financial reporting.

KEY TERMS

Acquiring company	Current rate method
Active investment	Debt security
Active minority ownership	Deferred compensation arrangement
Available-for-sale securities	Deferred tax asset
Business acquisition	Deferred tax liability
Business consolidation	Deferred taxes
Consolidated financial statements	Defined benefit arrangements
Credit risk	Defined contribution arrangements

Derivatives	Passive investments
Equity security	Pension liability
Financial revenues	Pension plan assets
Foreign direct investments	Pension trustee
Full consolidation	Purchase method of accounting
Functional currency	Realized gains (losses)
Goodwill	Risk management
Held-to-maturity debt securities	Service cost
Majority ownership	Stock options
Merger	Subsidiary company
Minority interest	Target company
Multinational enterprise (MNE)	Temporal method
Net operating loss	Temporary difference
Over, or underfunded deferred com-	Trading securities
pensation arrangements	Unrealized gains (losses)
Parent company	

CONCEPTUAL CASES

7-1

Business Acquisitions

Businesses acquire other companies in an attempt to maximize shareholder value. Wealth maximization efforts lead to many interesting types of corporate acquisitions. Consider these recent acquisition strategies:

Roll-Ups. A company grows through its constant acquisition of small businesses in a fragmented industry. *Consolidators,* as roll-up firms prefer to be called, exist in such industries as waste management, funeral homes, dry cleaners, and rental equipment. They attempt to bring managerial efficiency and economies of scale to mom-and-pop operations.

Triple Plays. Three companies discuss combining operations. For example, Phelps Dodge bid on copper rivals Cyprus Amax and Asarco. Companies in old-line industries have favored triple plays. Weak sales prospects, global competition, productive overcapacity, and an inability to further reduce costs challenge these businesses. Three-way deals can offset those problems through efficient industry consolidation.

Carve Out Reacquisitions. An entity that sold off a company attempts to repurchase it. For example, Cendant Corp. reacquired Avis Group in 2000 after selling its automobile-rental firm in 1997. Viacom bid on Infinity Broadcasting in 2000, two years after it sold the broadcaster. Former parents try to acquire approximately 20 percent of the companies that they initially carved out.

a. Explain the primary reason why a company acquires another entity.
b. Will goodwill be created as a result of the acquisition strategies discussed in this case?
c. What evidence could you cite at the point of acquisition to determine if the stock market is in favor of an acquisition?
d. What evidence would you look for a few years after the consolidation when analyzing its success or failure?

7-2

Security Investments

The 1999 Coca-Cola Co. *Financial Review Incorporating Management's Discussion and Analysis* states the following:

Our Company has business relationships with three types of bottlers: (1) independently owned bottlers in which we have no interest; (2) bottlers in which we have invested and have a noncontrolling interest; and (3) bottlers in which we have invested and have a controlling interest. . . . We view certain bottling operations in which we have a noncontrolling ownership interest as key or anchor bottlers due to their level of responsibility and performance.

Bottlers in whom Coke has an active but noncontrolling interest produced and distributed 58 percent of The Coca-Cola Co.'s unit case volume. The Coca-Cola Company owned 40 percent of Coca-Cola Enterprises, which is the largest soft-drink bottler in the world. It also controlled 37 percent of Australian-based bottler, Coca-Cola Amatil. These two investments were valued at $1.9 billion at the end of 1999. Numerous other noncontrolling investments in bottlers throughout the world accounted for another $4.5 billion of the Coca-Cola Company's asset base.

a. Discuss whether the Coca-Cola investments described here are passive or active equity investments.
b. Would Coke consolidate the financial statements of Coca-Cola Enterprises or Coca-Cola Amatil with its own?
c. Discuss how you know that The Coca-Cola Co. consolidates the financial statements of some of its bottling subsidiaries.
d. The "Share-Owners' Equity" section of The Coca-Cola Co.'s balance sheet does not report any minority interest. What does this nondisclosure tell you about Coke's ownership levels in the bottlers that it controls?

7-3

Foreign Investments

Many U.S. companies announced lower-than-expected earnings for the second quarter of 2000 due to currency exchange rates fluctuations. McDonald's, Gillette, and Procter & Gamble were among the U.S. consumer firms that cited weakness in the euro as a primary reason for diminished earnings. The common currency of the European Union decreased in value by 30 percent from 1999 to the middle of 2000. American firms doing business in Europe found their products were more expensive than European competitors' as a result of the strengthening dollar. In addition, converting euros into dollars for consolidation purposes reduced the U.S. parents' profitability.

a. Do you think the euro or the dollar was the functional currency of the American companies' European subsidiaries?
b. Were the European subsidiaries' financial statements translated at the current euro to dollar exchange rate or was the temporal method?
c. Discuss the validity of management's assertions that earnings declines were due to softening of the euro.

7-4

Risk Management

Wal-Mart's 2000 Form 10-K contains the following footnote disclosure: "The Company routinely enters into forward currency exchange contracts in the regular course of business to manage its exposure against foreign currency fluctuations on cross-border purchases of inventory. These contracts are generally for short durations of six months or less."

A forward currency exchange contract commits Wal-Mart, or any entity, to exchange currencies with another entity in the future. The currency exchange rate is set today. Although the amount of the transaction, currency rate, and maturity date are set in advance, no money is exchanged until the settlement (payment) date.

a. Why does Wal-Mart enter into forward currency exchange contracts?
b. What risk would Wal-Mart have if it did not enter into these contracts?
c. Can you identify any risk associated with the contracts?
d. Assume Wal-Mart entered into an agreement with a Japanese vendor to purchase goods manufactured in Thailand. The transaction was denominated in dollars. Should Wal-Mart enter into a foreign currency exchange contract in yen (Japanese currency), bahts (Thai currency), or neither?

7-5

Deferred Compensation Arrangements

The following information is excerpted from Delta Airlines' footnotes to its 1999 Form 10-K:

Note 9. Employee Benefit Plans
DEFINED BENEFIT PENSION PLANS
The retirement plans we sponsor include defined benefit pension plans. The qualified defined benefit plans are currently funded to meet the minimum ERISA funding requirements.
The following table shows the change in projected benefit obligation for our defined benefit pension plans for the year ended June 30, 1999:

IN MILLIONS	1999
Projected benefit obligation at beginning of year	$8,342
Service cost	240
Interest cost and actuarial adjustments	746
Benefits paid	(456)
Projected benefit obligation at end of year	**$8,872**

The following table shows the change in the fair value of defined benefit pension plan assets for the year ended June 30, 1999.

IN MILLIONS	1999
Fair value of plan assets at beginning of year	$9,121
Actual return on plan assets	310
Employer cash contributions	45
Benefits paid	(456)
Fair value of plan assets at end of year	**$9,020**

a. Was Delta's defined benefit pension plan overfunded or underfunded at the end of 1999?
b. Did the amount of over- or underfunding increase or decrease from the beginning to the end of the fiscal year?
c. Indicate why the benefits Delta paid on its 1999 defined benefit plan decreased the projected pension plan and the plan assets.
d. Examine Delta's service cost, interest cost, and actual return on plan assets. Explain whether net periodic pension cost (pension expense) was greater

than or less than its 1999 service cost, based on the amounts disclosed in those three items.

7-6

Deferred Taxes

A bank commercial loan officer was reviewing financial statements as part of a customer's application for a line of credit. The commercial nursery wanted approval of the credit line, which would guarantee it funding up to a specified limit, to pay for maturing obligations. Something in the current liability section of the balance sheet, however, struck the analyst as odd.

The nursery grew plants that it sold to retail garden centers and landscaping contractors. It took four years from seeding a plant until it reached maturity. Consequently, the company carried four years worth of inventory in various growth stages. The analyst noticed a large current liability, captioned "Deferred Income Taxes." The tax deferral was the nursery's largest liability; it equaled total stockholders' equity! The magnitude of the current tax deferral resulted in negative working capital (current liabilities exceeded current assets). The nursery had already violated an existing covenant on a previous loan from the bank because of its working capital situation. That provision required the nursery to maintain positive working capital. The bank's policy was not to extend a line of credit to a company with inadequate working capital and to investigate, and possibly call in, loans that violated their protective covenants.

The loan officer's review of the "Liability for Deferred Income Taxes—Current" financial statement footnote revealed that the deferral resulted from alternative treatment of inventory costs. Agricultural concerns immediately deduct inventory planting, spraying, watering, and other maintenance costs from revenues in determining taxable income. Those costs are capitalized as part of the historical cost of inventory, however, for financial reporting purposes.

a. Explain why the tax deferral is a liability instead of an asset.
b. Why is the tax deferral classified as a current obligation rather than a noncurrent liability?
c. Discuss whether the deferred tax liability should be considered in the loan officer's working capital and credit analysis.

INDUSTRY INTERNET CASES

Examine the most recent Form 10-K for the companies in the six industries listed in the appendixes. Provide the following information (if applicable) for each reporting issue discussed in this chapter:

Business Acquisitions

a. List the company's recent business acquisitions.
b. Does any goodwill appear on the balance sheet?
c. What is the length of time taken to amortize goodwill?
d. Discuss any transactions accounted for as pooling of interests instead of as purchases.

Security Investments

a. Determine if the company has any passive debt or equity investments.
b. Are these securities disclosed as current or long-term assets?

c. Are unrealized gains (losses) on passive investments included in income or reported as adjustments to shareholders' equity?

d. Determine if the company has any active equity investments.

e. Are these securities majority or minority owned, or a combination of both?

f. Does the company report any minority interest?

g. What are the origins of minority interest?

Foreign Investments

a. List the foreign subsidiaries owned by the company (or the number of them if the list is extensive).

b. What are the functional currencies of the foreign subsidiaries?

c. Are the foreign subsidiaries' financial statements converted by the current rate or temporal method?

d. Are gains and losses on conversion reported in the income statement or as translation adjustments made to shareholders' equity?

Risk Management

a. Explain why the company needs to manage financial risk. (Read management's discussion and analysis in addition to the footnote disclosure.)

b. Do derivative instruments play a role in the company's attempts to manage risk?

c. Are derivatives reported at fair value on the balance sheet?

Deferred Compensation Arrangements

a. Does the company provide defined benefits or defined contributions to its employees?

b. Does it have a 401(k), or similar type, plan?

c. Briefly describe each deferred compensation plan.

d. Does the company have any off-balance-sheet assets or liabilities as a result of these plans?

Deferred Taxes

a. Does the company report a current deferred tax asset or liability?

b. Does the company report a long-term deferred tax asset or liability?

c. Do the tax deferrals constitute a significant portion of assets (liabilities)?

7-1 *Personal Computers: Apple, Compaq, Dell, and Gateway*

7-2 *Airlines: American, Delta, and United*

7-3 *Athletic Footwear: Nike and Reebok*

7-4 *Discount Retailers: Kmart, Target, and Wal-Mart*

7-5 *Fast-Food Restaurants: McDonald's and Wendy's*

7-6 *Soft Drink Companies: Coca-Cola and PepsiCo.*

INTRODUCTION TO SHORT-TERM LIQUIDITY ANALYSIS

CHAPTER LEARNING OBJECTIVES

Upon completion of this chapter, you should be able to:

◆ *Define liquidity and explain its role in financial statement analysis.*

◆ *Relate financing and investing decisions to the elements of the balance sheet.*

◆ *Distinguish between short-term and long-term financing and investing activities.*

◆ *Identify, calculate, and interpret liquidity measures for working capital, current account activity, and inventory-related conversion cycles.*

◆ *Conduct a preliminary short-term liquidity analysis of a company or industry.*

*T*horoughly understanding the individual financial statements and their components improves an analyst's decisions. Your comprehension of the corporate financial whole, in other words, depends on your grasp of its parts. To this end, Chapters 8–14 evaluate five specific areas of analysis: short-term liquidity, cash flows, operating performance, asset utilization, and capital structure. This chapter introduces short-term liquidity analysis. Chapter 9 continues this evaluation with advanced liquidity analysis. Chapters 10 and 11 examine cash flows in a similar fashion. Chapters 12, 13, and 14 present operating performance (income statement), asset utilization (balance sheet) analysis, and resource financing (balance sheet), respectively.[1] We shift from historical analysis to future-oriented analysis in Chapter 15. The chapter covers market valuation and financial statement projections.

THE OBJECTIVE OF SHORT-TERM LIQUIDITY ANALYSIS

Casper the Ghost was not his usual friendly self when his company, Harvey Entertainment, Inc., could not meet maturing obligations in 2000, due to insufficient liquid resources.

Identify Apple Computer's views on its liquidity by evaluating the company's "Item 7—Management's Discussion and Analysis" in the company's most recent Form 10-K.

Liquidity refers to an entity's ability to pay its debts. Analysts use the term in the context of meeting obligations without disrupting productive capabilities (e.g., selling fixed assets). Liquidity analysis, therefore, centers on current assets and current liabilities. **Short-term liquidity analysis** specifically measures a firm's ability to pay current obligations with cash generated from current assets. We discuss the procedures and techniques used to measure cash conversion and payment activities in this chapter and Chapter 9.

A company produces cash in the ordinary course of business by selling inventory or providing services to its customers. Creditors who contribute goods and services to those revenue-producing activities have a claim on a portion of the cash realized from sales and services. Short-term liquidity analysis determines whether an enterprise can reimburse the people and companies who contributed to the earning process in a timely manner. Refining liquidity analysis helps analysts to evaluate management's effectiveness in achieving that task.

This chapter consists of four sections. First, corporate financing and investing activities provide a context for analyzing liquidity. Next, we define key liquidity terms. We then present short-term liquidity measures using eXTREMESTUFF.com's data to illustrate those concepts. We conclude with a preliminary liquidity analysis of the personal computer (PC) industry.

FINANCING AND INVESTING ACTIVITIES

A statement of financial position reports a company's resources and claims against those resources at one point in time. The balance sheet equation (assets = liabilities + shareholders' equity) embodies that relationship. It reports lender (liabilities) and owner (shareholders' equity) contributions to the financing of the economic resources (assets). Asset accounts (e.g., inventory, equipment, buildings) report how management elected to allocate invested funds. These three interrelated bal-

---

[1] There are a variety of ways to analyze financial statements. For example, another approach to financial statement analysis divides the topic into liquidity, activity, profitability, and coverage segments. Because this text is an introduction to the discipline, however, focusing on the financial statements themselves, or specific portions thereof, is the only approach discussed here.

ance sheet elements represent the basic business model and enable a company to build wealth if managed correctly. Analysts must grasp resource financing and allocation to fully appreciate liquidity analysis, other areas of financial statement analysis, and wealth maximization efforts.

WEB EXERCISE 2

Are most of Apple's assets currently financed with debt or equity?

PRIMARY BUSINESS MODEL

Exhibit 8-1 presents the fundamental relationship between corporate financing and investor compensation. In this model, fund acquisition (1) creates (2a and 2b) corporate obligations. Those financing activities allow management to acquire assets (3).

Financing decisions represent a company's choices about the amount and types of debt and equity financing it will use to obtain resources. Management weighs the costs and benefits associated with each funding source in financing the firm. Cash constitutes the majority of investors' contributions at the firm's inception, regardless of funding source. These cash infusions provide the firm with liquidity. Management makes **investment decisions** by deciding how to allocate the cash among many resource alternatives. In effect, eSTUFF made those decisions at the beginning of 2000.

EXHIBIT 8-1
Primary Business Model Financing and Investing Activities

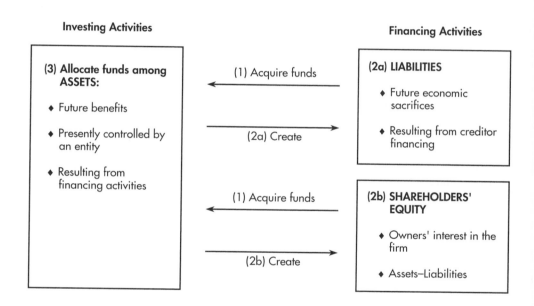

OPERATING BUSINESS MODEL

MICRO ANALYSIS 2

Ford Motor Co. leveraged long-term financing arrangements into a liquidity advantage. The company required its investment bankers, who benefit from handling Ford's stock and bond offerings, to provide low-cost short-term credit to the company.

Corporate owners and certain lenders make long-term commitments to the firm. The company converts a large part of its investments into illiquid resources, or long-term productive assets. Those resources, in turn, produce goods and services that generate additional liquidity. An entity's long-term assets, in other words, are essential but illiquid wealth builders. Short-term creditors provide goods and services to the firm in return for the promise of payment in the near term. An enterprise also needs those contributions to get its product to market. Both long- and short-term commitments to the firm, therefore, work together to provide liquidity to the firm.

Exhibit 8-2 extends the general balance sheet model of Exhibit 8-1 by separat-
ing assets and liabilities into their current and noncurrent segments.[2] Long-term
debt and owners' investments (1) finance long-term assets (2). Those assets work
in conjunction with short-term liabilities (3) to create short-term assets. Cash produced by the current assets is used to pay obligations (4).

eSTUFF paid vendors for goods, satisfied other short-term creditors, paid
interest on its notes, and distributed dividends to its shareholders during 2000
and 2001. For example, the hypothetical Internet company acquired inventories
(current assets) from suppliers (creating current liabilities) in order to sell them
(realize revenues). To the extent that eSTUFF has unpaid purchases as of the balance sheet date, a current liability exists. Our e-tailer would use available cash,
future cash collections from previous sales (accounts receivable), or cash receipts
from future sales (inventory) to meet those obligations as they become due. Cash,
accounts receivable, and inventory are current, and liquid, assets. Current liabilities are claims against those assets that require cash payment within the operating
cycle. Short-term liquidity analysis, in essence, examines the relationship between
current assets and current liabilities (denoted by the thinner horizontal arrows in
the upper portion of Exhibit 8-2).

Long-term resources complement liquid assets. eSTUFF needs its computer
equipment (a long-term asset) to process customer orders, control inventory,
and govern other aspects of running the business. eSTUFF's equipment adds
value to its wealth-producing activities. Without it, the business would fail. A
portion of the cash generated from operations, therefore, is used to pay obligations to long-term lenders (notes payable in eSTUFF's case) and compensate
owners (in the form of dividends). The thicker arrows in the lower portion of

EXHIBIT 8-2
*Operating Business Model
Financing, Investing, and
Operating Activities*

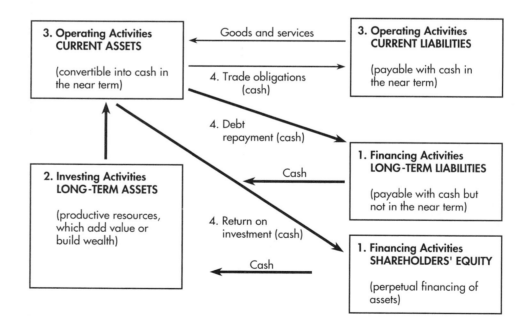

---

[2]This dichotomy is a simplification of the classified balance sheet discussed in Chapter 3.

Exhibit 8-2 denote the relationship between long-term financing and investing decisions. Chapters 13 and 14 examine the merits of asset utilization and capital structure analysis.

In summary, remember these things:

◆ Current assets are liquid. They exist as cash or will become cash within a short period of time.
◆ Long-term assets are illiquid. They will not be sold to generate cash in the ordinary course of business. Their productive capabilities, however, help create liquidity.
◆ All liabilities must be satisfied (usually with cash), but only current ones require payment in the near future.
◆ Shareholders' equity represents a corporation's source of perpetual funding. Owners' investments are not repaid. (There is no return *of* their investment.)[3] Returns to owners on corporate earnings (dividends, or return *on* investment) are discretionary payments.

We not elaborate on the notion that short-term liquidity focuses on cash conversion activities. The next section discusses liquidity terms, some of which are also described in Chapter 3, and concepts.

UNBALANCED BALANCE SHEETS

Short-term creditors usually finance current assets and long-term lenders and owners fund fixed assets. Asset acquisitions, however, sometimes do not match financing activities. The experience of savings and loan associations (S&Ls) illustrates that departure from normal asset financing can have severe consequences. What is your analysis of the S&L debacle?

Until the early 1980s, S&Ls used depositors' funds to finance home mortgages.[a] The liabilities were current obligations (accounts payable) because depositors could withdraw their cash at any time. However, 20- and 30-year home loans (in essence, notes receivable) resulted in long-term assets for the S&Ls. In other words, these institutions were borrowing short-term but lending long-term. This arrangement worked fine so long as interest rates were consistent and S&Ls made safe home mortgage loans.

Inflation increased the cost of money in the early 1980s. S&Ls had to increase interest rates in order to retain depositors and attract new funds. Consequently, S&Ls' cost of money (interest expense) increased, but the revenue stream, generated from long-term mortgages, remained fairly constant. Net losses ensued. The federal government attempted to assist S&Ls by deregulating the industry in 1982, allowing S&Ls to depart from their traditional mortgage-based roots.[b] Many S&Ls, however, lacked discretion; they engaged in speculative, risky, and sometimes fraudulent lending practices. Those loans were often uncollectible, which left many S&Ls insolvent. The

---

[3] The corporation, by definition, has an unlimited life. Individual shareholders can liquidate their investment through stock sales in secondary markets (covered in Chapter 1), but the capital contributed to the business remains. Management may contract ownership by paying dividends and repurchasing some of the company's own shares of stock activities, called treasury stock. Dividends and treasury stock reduce, but do not eliminate, the owners' investment in a going concern.

federal government bailed out the industry in order to prevent a widespread panic among the public.[c]

Observations

Explain whether the S&Ls industry's asset financing model corresponds with the conventional business model outlined in Exhibit 8-2. Do you suspect that conforming to the basic business model was an important investment consideration for S&Ls making speculative non–home mortgage loans? Do you think those S&Ls realistically reported their net receivables after making high-risk loans? How could their receivables disclosures hinder analysis?

---

[a] For a more detailed analysis see Chapter 16 of G. Smith, *Financial Markets, Assets and Institutions* (Lexington, MA: D. C. Heath, 1993).

[b] Garn–St. Germain Depository Institutions Act of 1982. This act also deregulated aspects of the banking industry as well as S&Ls.

[c] Financial Institutions Reform, Recovery and Enforcement Act of 1989. The cost of the bailout exceeded $200 billion, according to an estimate by William Seidman, chairman of the Resolution Trust Corporation, which oversaw the industry's restructuring.

TERM AND CONCEPTS

Current assets consist of cash and other assets expected to be sold, consumed, or converted into cash within one year, or one *operating cycle*, whichever is longer. Likewise, *current liabilities* are obligations expected to be liquidated within the longer of one year or one operating cycle. Understanding current account classification, therefore, is contingent on understanding the operating cycle concept.[4]

OPERATING CYCLE

An **operating cycle** is the length of time a company requires to convert goods or services into cash through its revenue producing activities. Simply put, the operating cycle reflects the time needed to convert tangible products or human activities back into cash. Exhibit 8-3 presents the operating cycles for service, merchandising, and manufacturing concerns.

The operating cycle for most businesses is less than one year.[5] Short-term liquidity, therefore, analyzes accounts that will become or use cash within one year of the balance sheet date.

CURRENT ACCOUNTS

The balance sheet lists current assets in **order of liquidity**, or their nearness to cash. Consider the current asset disclosures for eXTREMESTUFF.com (in thousands of dollars), initially presented and discussed in Chapter 3:

---

[4] We use the terms *current, short-term,* and *near-term,* as they pertain to assets and liabilities, interchangeably.

[5] Exceptions exist in complex manufacturing environments and production of specialty goods, as in building large ships and distilling fine liquors. Analyses of such companies and industries exceed the scope of this book.

EXHIBIT 8-3
*Operating Cycles
Three Types of Business
Operations*

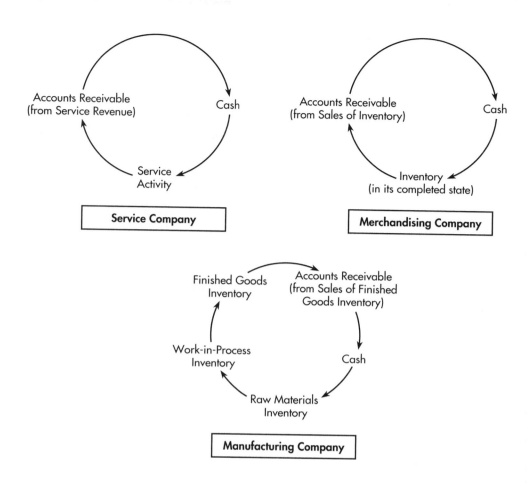

Cash disclosures often contain cash equivalents, such as certificates of deposit (CDs) and money market accounts.[6] If eSTUFF owned debt and equity securities, then these investments would be disclosed after cash, due to their liquidity in the capital markets.[7] Accounts receivable (or trade receivables) are reported after security investments, net of an estimate for uncollectible accounts. Inventory is the least liquid of current assets and is disclosed after receivables. Prepaid expenses, such as rent or insurance paid in advance, differ from other current assets because they will not be converted into cash. They are classified as liquid assets because they will be consumed within the year.[8]

---

[6] Certificates of deposit and money market accounts are more precisely classified as short-term investments because they earn interest and financial institutions place restrictions on their withdrawal. Many companies classify them as cash equivalents, however, because of their cash-like appearance, short maturity durations, and relatively small transaction costs for conversion into cash.

[7] Security investments are discussed in Chapter 7.

[8] Prepaid expenses may be considered like other current assets in a roundabout way: Paying cash in advance of the expense creates these assets. Consequently, eSTUFF will not pay cash in the upcoming reporting period when those expenses are incurred. Prepaid expense amounts are often relatively small and usually do not materially affect short-term liquidity analysis.

	2001	2000
Current assets:		
Cash	$45	$30
Accounts receivable, net	140	120
Inventory	250	200
Prepaid expenses	5	10
Total current assets	**$440**	**$360**

Current liabilities are neither disclosed in order of liquidity nor consistently classified by companies. eXTREMESTUFF.com, for example, discloses three current liabilities (in thousands of dollars):

	2001	2000
Current liabilities:		
Accounts payable	$50	$160
Accrued liabilities	21	50
Taxes payable	0	5
Total current liabilities	**$71**	**$215**

Conventionally, accounts payable are the first current liability disclosed. Accrued liabilities summarize numerous other current liabilities created in ordinary course of business. Obligations to pay salaries, rent, utilities, and similar accounts compose eSTUFF's current accruals. Other firms may elect to disclose these accounts separately or group them differently. The final short-term obligation discloses eSTUFF's outstanding obligations to tax agencies.

WEB EXERCISE 4

Compute Apple Computer's working capital at its most recent fiscal year-end.

WORKING CAPITAL

Working capital is the difference between a company's current assets and its current liabilities. Analysts consider it a primary indicator of liquidity, and they usually calculate it first when analyzing liquidity. A company whose current assets exceed its current liabilities has working capital, or is liquid. An entity is illiquid, or has negative working capital, when current liabilities surpass current assets.[9]

eXTREMESTUFF.com's working capital (in thousands of dollars) at the end of 2001 is as follows:

---

[9] This is a general statement that may not always be true. It depends on the industry, specific circumstances of the company, and timing of cash flows. These topics are explored in subsequent chapters.

	YEAR-END 2001
Total current assets	$440
Total current liabilities	71
Working capital	**$369**

The company's working capital increased by $224,000 in its second year of operations [2001 year-end ($369,000) – 2000 year-end ($145,000)].

Alternatively, average working capital (in thousands of dollars) could be reported for 2001 as follows:

	AVERAGE 2001
Total current assets [($360,000 + $440,000)/2]	$400
Total current liabilities [($215,000 + $71,000)/2]	143
Working capital	**$257**

In other words, eSTUFF had approximately $257,000 of working capital throughout 2001.

LIQUIDITY MEASURES

Liquidity ratios extend working capital analysis. As noted in Chapter 4, a *ratio* measures the proportion between one financial statement disclosure (or one group of disclosures) and another financial statement disclosure (or group of disclosures). In the case of liquidity ratios, the relative amounts of current accounts and their income statement counterparts provide analysts with information about the amount, timing, and certainty of corporate liquidity. They help people determine if a company can meet its maturing obligations and how effectively it can do so.

CURRENT RATIO

Analysts usually compute the **current (or working capital) ratio** when determining liquidity. This relationship measures the amount of current assets for each dollar in current liabilities. It is calculated as follows:

$$\text{Current (working capital) ratio} = \frac{\text{average current assets}}{\text{average current liabilities}}$$

A large current ratio indicates significant short-term liquidity or a *conservative* liquidity position. In general, a ratio exceeding one provides evidence that a company will be able to meet its maturing obligations. A ratio below one usually signifies short-term liquidity problems. Liquidity, however, is also a function of the following:

◆ Particular industry circumstances and trend within the company
◆ Entity's ability to sell inventory and collect receivables

◆ Timing of the cash inflows from those current asset conversions
◆ Payment dates of the current liabilities
◆ Amount of noncash current assets, such as prepaid expenses

The current ratio for eXTREMESTUFF.com in its second business year is computed as follows:[10]

CALCULATIONS FOR 2001 (IN THOUSANDS OF DOLLARS)	WORKING CAPITAL RATIO FOR 2001
$\dfrac{(\$360 + \$440) \,/\, 2}{(\$215 + \$71) \,/\, 2} = \dfrac{\$800\,/2}{\$286\,/2} = \dfrac{\$400}{\$143}$	2.80:1 or 2.80

Note the following points about eSTUFF's working capital ratio:

◆ A ratio's denominator is always one. Therefore, ratio discussions usually ignore it (e.g., the current ratio is 2.80).
◆ eSTUFF's current assets equaled an average of $2.80 for each dollar of current obligations during 2001 (or approximately $2.80 will be converted into cash in 2002 to pay for each dollar of maturing obligations).
◆ Balance sheet (financial position) data are averaged by taking the balance at the beginning of the year, adding it to the ending balance, and dividing by 2 (e.g., current assets for 2001 equal $360,000 + $440,000 / 2). This adjustment approximates annual balance sheet data.[11]

MICRO ANALYSIS 5

Apple Computer reduced the historical cost of its inventory to market value by reporting an additional $616 million cost of goods sold expense in 1996 for obsolete computers and components.

WEB EXERCISE 5

Read Factors that May Affect Future Results and Financial Condition in Apple's most recent Management Discussion and Analysis. How does the company account for obsolete components and products?

QUICK RATIO

A cautious measure of working capital is the **quick (or acid-test) ratio**. This ratio modifies the current ratio by eliminating inventory and prepaid expenses from its numerator. In other words, the quick ratio reduces current assets by noncash accounts (prepaid expenses) and current assets that would not generate cash if they could not be sold (inventory). Its formula looks like this:

$$\text{Quick (acid-test) ratio} = \frac{(\text{cash} + \text{short-term investments} + \text{accounts receivable})}{\text{current liabilities}}$$

eXTREMESTUFF.com's acid-test ratio for its second year of operations is computed as follows:

CALCULATIONS FOR 2001 (IN THOUSANDS OF DOLLARS)	QUICK RATIO FOR 2001
$\dfrac{(\$30 + \$120 + \$45 + \$140) \,/\, 2}{(\$215 + \$71) \,/\, 2} = \dfrac{\$335\,/\,2}{\$286\,/\,2} = \dfrac{\$167.5}{\$143}$	1.17:1 or 1.17

---

[10] Analysts need to exercise judgment when computing ratios. For example, eSTUFF began its business on January 1, 2000. The first year of business, therefore, does not represent normal operations. (Most current accounts did not exist on that date.) Consequently, averaging the data in 2000 is biased because zero would be used as beginning amounts for many current assets and liabilities. We use only 2001 ratios for eSTUFF to simplify the discussion.

[11] See the "Data Considerations" section of Chapter 4 for a more detailed explanation of averaging balance sheet data.

Averaged for the year, eSTUFF had $1.17 of highly liquid assets for each dollar of current debt. The acid-test ratio connotes a worst-case scenario with respect to current asset cash collections. It measures liquidity if eSTUFF sells none of the inventory.

Many analysts regard the acid-test ratio as too conservative because it ignores reality. Generally accepted accounting principles (GAAP) direct companies to report inventory at the lower of historical cost or prevailing market value. Market value is the current purchase or reproduction price of an item. If this net **replacement cost** exceeds **net realizable value** (an item's estimated selling price), the company should disclose the product at selling price. The balance sheet, in other words, reports inventory at a minimum of expected cash receipts. If inventory had no value in the marketplace, then it would not be reported on the balance sheet. Consequently, the quick ratio, which ignores cash flows from existing inventory, may be too stringent a measure of liquidity.

ACTIVITY MEASURES

We now turn our attention to three activity ratios and their corresponding time-related measures. A current **activity ratio**, or **turnover ratio**, quantifies the number of times a liquid account turns over annually in the normal course of business. The number of days the account is outstanding before it is sold, received, or paid in cash complements turnover activity. The following sections indicate how inventory, accounts receivable, and accounts payable activity provides liquidity insights.

MICRO ANALYSIS 6

Inventory turns over only if a company has the right products in the right location. Kmart knows. It recorded a $450 million loss in the second quarter of 2000. "We clearly had some of the wrong product in the wrong location," according to Kmart's chief executive officer.

INVENTORY ACTIVITY MEASURES

Inventory turnover is the number of times inventory is sold during a reporting period. This ratio is computed as follows:

$$\text{Inventory turnover} = \frac{\text{cost of goods sold}}{\text{average inventory}}$$

The denominator measures inventory items at their historical cost. Therefore,, you should use sales costs rather than revenue as the ratio's numerator. Using cost of goods sold maintains the consistency of historical cost values in the ratio. Substituting sales revenues for cost of goods sold overstates inventory turnover because it uses two different cost measures: historical (acquisition) cost in the denominator and retail cost (or selling price) in the numerator.[12] The resulting inventory turnover value creates the impression that the entity sold its inventory more frequently than it actually did.

A more meaningful inventory activity measure than the turnover ratio is the **number of days in inventory**. It reports the average number of days required to sell inventory and is calculated as follows:

$$\text{Number of days in inventory} = \frac{365 \text{ days}}{\text{inventory turnover}}$$

---

[12] Revenues are sometimes used to maintain comparability with published industry sources, which often use sales as the numerator in their inventory turnover ratios.

Analysts interpret the quotient of this ratio as the elapsed time from the date of inventory acquisition to its sale.[13] An inverse relationship exists between inventory turnover and the number of days in inventory: The higher the inventory turnover, the fewer days needed to sell inventory, and vice-versa.

The following computations and results present eSTUFF's inventory turnover and number of days in inventory:

CALCULATIONS FOR 2001 (IN THOUSANDS OF DOLLARS)	INVENTORY ACTIVITY MEASURES FOR 2001
$660 / [($200 + $250) / 2] = $660 / $225	Inventory turnover: 2.93 times
365 days / 2.93	Number of days in inventory: 124.4 days

The hypothetical e-tailer sold its inventory 2.93 times during 2001.[14] Put another way, it took eSTUFF an average of 124 days to sell an inventory item. For example, if the company bought an average inventory item on January 1, 2001, then it would have sold that average item on May 4, 2001.

WHAT'S YOUR ANALYSIS

CATEGORY KILLER KILLED: JUST FOR FEET STOPPED DEAD IN ITS TRACKS

The retail industry witnessed the emergence of *category killers* in the 1980s. These superstores threatened smaller specialty establishments and mass merchandisers by selling a single inventory item in volume. Some category killers, however, encountered liquidity problems due to the size and scope of their operations. How would you assess the performance of Just for Feet?

The Alabama-based mega-seller of athletic shoes went bankrupt in 2000. Its remaining assets were auctioned off piecemeal to the highest bidders during that year.[a] Poor inventory management contributed to the company's demise. Just for Feet was unable to pay for $70 million of inventory when it ran out of cash in 1999.[b] Ironically, the inventory wasn't even needed. These excess shoe purchases stemmed from Just for Feet's inability to merge two recently purchased athletic shoe retailers into its own operations. The acquiring firm lacked the capability to coordinate inventory purchases among the combined companies, so the parent firm bought unneeded shoes.

These surplus purchases compounded another inventory problem. Just for Feet was having trouble turning over its existing inventory. Like all category killers, the company maintained more diverse inventories than its smaller competitors. Just for Feet maintained 2,500 styles of footwear, compared with the usual 400 types of athletic shoes stocked by mall stores. Many of the styles were just not selling. The company masked some of its mounting liquidity problems in the late 1990s by rapidly opening new stores. New stores absorbed some of the company's stock of inventory. These newer outlets experienced brisk initial sales before revenues leveled off. Unfortunately, the firm could not continually grow its way out of its problems. The market, after all, can only absorb so many sneaker superstores. Lack of liquidity and high operating costs ultimately forced the company into bankruptcy.

---

[13] 360 days is often used in the numerator of the days in inventory ratio, based on historical precedent and mathematical simplicity. Differences between the quotients derived from 360 and 365 days are immaterial to an analysis.

[14] Numbers are rounded. A more accurate inventory turnover ratio is 2.93333 . . . , which, when divided into 365 days, yields 124.43 days. Dividing 2.93 into 365 days results in 124.57, which rounds up to 125 days. A one-day difference would be immaterial to an analysis.

Observations

Would you have expected an increase or decrease in Just for Feet's inventory turnover during 1999 and 2000? What about the number of days the company needed to sell inventory? Do you think information on same store inventory turnover would have helped analyze inventory? Explain how the company's quarterly filings with the SEC, Form 10-Q, could have benefited the analysis in addition to the annual Form 10-K filings.

---

[a] W. F. Bulkeley, "Category Killers Go from Lethal to Lame in the Space of a Decade," *Wall Street Journal*, pp. A1 and A8, March 9, 2000.

[b] C. Mollencamp and K. Greene, "How Just for Feet Wound a Path from Supremacy to Financial Peril," *Wall Street Journal*, pp. S1 and S2, November 3, 1999.

MICRO ANALYSIS 7

Heilig-Meyers declared bankruptcy in August 2000 when significant receivables failed to materialize into cash. A reduction in credit standards created additional customers for the furniture retailer, but many of those customers failed to pay for their purchases.

ACCOUNTS RECEIVABLE ACTIVITY MEASURES

Accounts receivable activity measures parallel those computations made for inventory. **Accounts receivable turnover** determine the number of times receivables are collected in cash during the year. The **number of days in accounts receivables** reports the average length of time between a credit sale and its cash collection. These two measures are computed as follows:

$$\text{Accounts receivable turnover} = \frac{\text{net credit revenues}}{\text{average net accounts receivable}}$$

$$\text{Number of days in accounts receivable} = \frac{365 \text{ days}}{\text{accounts receivable turnover}}$$

The accounts receivable activity ratios for eSTUFF in 2001 illustrate these activity measures.

CALCULATIONS FOR 2001 (IN THOUSANDS OF DOLLARS)	ACCOUNTS RECEIVABLE ACTIVITY MEASURES FOR 2001
$1,200 / [($120 +$140) / 2] = $1,200 / $130 365 days / 9.23	Accounts rec. turnover: 9.23 times Number of days in receivables: 39.5 days

eXTREMESTUFF.com collected cash on its outstanding accounts slightly more than nine times during 2001. In other words, an average credit sale was outstanding for nearly 40 days before it was realized in cash.

MICRO ANALYSIS 8

Powerful retailers, such as Wal-Mart, improve their inventory conversion cycles by requiring manufacturers to assume greater responsibility in supplying inventory on a just-in-time basis. The warehouse retailer Costco calls this strategy vendor-managed inventory.

INVENTORY CONVERSION CYCLE

Extending inventory and receivable activity measures adds perspective to short-term liquidity analysis. The **inventory conversion cycle** quantifies the operating cycle. This measure sums the number of days needed to sell inventory and the number of days required to collect on the resulting receivables:

Number of days in inventory
+ Number of days in accounts receivable
= Inventory conversion cycle

The inventory conversion cycle enables an analyst to track the average length of time it takes to convert inventory into cash. To illustrate, refer to eXTREMESTUFF.com's 2001 data for its inventory and receivable activity ratios.

Number of days in inventory	124.4 days
+ Number of days in accounts receivable	39.5 days
= Inventory conversion cycle	163.9 days

eSTUFF needs, on average, 164 days to convert an inventory purchase into cash. To put this amount of time into perspective, refer to the assumed average inventory purchase on January 1, 2001. That item would have been sold on May 4 of that year. The e-tailer collects customer payments 40 days after the sale, on June 13.

CONVERTING INVENTORY INTO CASH

Companies attempt to reduce the length of time required to convert inventory into cash. They try to spin the operating cycle faster to improve liquidity and boost profits. Analysts must weight these strategies designed to accelerate inventory conversion and improve liquidity. American Greeting Corp. is a case in point. How would you react to its plan to increase the speed at which it converts inventory into cash?

The nation's second-largest greeting card manufacturer changed strategies in an effort to improve profits and close the gap on Hallmark, the industry leader.[a] This industry experiences short, recurring periods of high sales volume. Special occasions, such as Valentine's Day and Mother's Day, drive the industry. Moreover, the public's taste in cards changes quickly. Manufacturers must constantly anticipate and meet the needs of a fickle marketplace. Managing customer *take-away* at the retail level, therefore, is vital to success. Card manufacturers and retailers profit from fast-selling cards; neither party benefits from slow-moving or stagnant inventory. American Greeting elected to manufacture and distribute cards much closer to specific holidays and other special occasions than it had done in the past. Management believed this approach would allow the firm to produce more marketable cards and improve customer take-away. American Greeting, in essence, planned to accelerate its operating cycle.

Observations

Assume American Greeting Corp.'s strategy is successful. Would the number of days in inventory increase or decrease? Would you anticipate any significant changes in accounts receivable turnover or the number of days to collect accounts receivable as a result of the policy change? Discuss why management might feel additional pressure by contracting its operating cycle.

---

[a] Material based on J. P. Mill's "Stock of American Greeting Plunges on Inventory Plan," *Wall Street Journal*, February 25, 1999, p. A4.

ACCOUNTS PAYABLE ACTIVITY MEASURES

Inventory acquisitions require cash payment. Merchants and manufacturers obtain finished goods and raw materials from their vendors in the ordinary course of business. Suppliers extend credit based on customer needs, credit history, and standard industry practices. **Accounts payable turnover** measures the annual number of vendor payments, and the **number of days in accounts**

payable computes the average time required to pay for purchases. These ratios look like this:

$$\text{Accounts payable turnover} = \frac{\text{cost of goods sold}}{\text{average accounts payable}}$$

$$\text{Number of days in accounts payable} = \frac{365 \text{ days}}{\text{accounts payable turnover}}$$

The following table contains eXTREMESTUFF.com's accounts payable activity ratios for 2001:

CALCULATIONS FOR 2001 (IN THOUSANDS OF DOLLARS)	ACCOUNTS PAYABLE ACTIVITY MEASURES FOR 2001
$660 / [($160 +$50) / 2] = $660 / $105 365 days / 6.29	Accounts payable turnover: 6.29 times Number of days in receivables: 58.1 days

eSTUFF took, on average, about 58 days to pay its suppliers.[15] For an item purchased on January 1, 2001, the company paid for it about February 27. In the next section we pair days in accounts payable with the other activity data discussed thus far to produce the final introductory measure of short-term liquidity analysis.

Is Dell's net cash conversion cycle positive or negative for its most recent year? What does a negative net cash conversion cycle mean?

NET CASH CONVERSION CYCLE

The **net cash conversion cycle** is the difference between the inventory conversion cycle and the number of days in accounts payable. This cycle is computed as follows:

Number of days in inventory
+ Number of days in accounts receivable
− Number of days in accounts payable
_____
= Net cash conversion cycle

Net cyclical activity provides information about liquidity financing. It represents the average length of time a company needs to fund its operating activities. The need for short-term financing is directly correlated with the number of days in this cycle; in other words, financing operations become costlier as the net cash conversion cycle lengthens. A negative net cash conversion cycle, on the other hand, means vendors finance working capital.

To better illustrate this contrast, we compute eSTUFF's net cash conversion data and adapt it for 2001. Its net cash conversion cycle is as follows:

Number of days needed to sell inventory	124.4 days
+ Number of days required to collect customers' accounts	39.5 days
− Number of days used to pay suppliers' accounts	58.1 days
= Net cash conversion cycle	105.8 days

---

[15] A more accurate measure of accounts payable activity uses purchases as the numerator of the turnover ratio. This refinement is discussed in the next chapter.

EXHIBIT 8-4

*eXTREMESTUFF.com
Alternative Net Cash
Conversion Cycles*

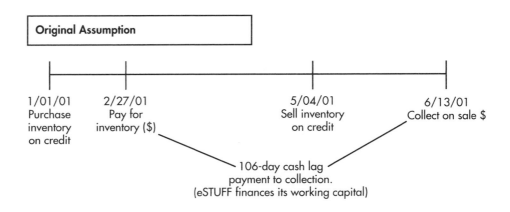

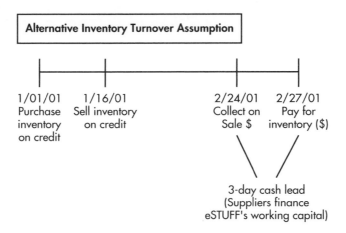

There are 106 days between when eSTUFF pays for its inventory and when it collects the sale. The company, therefore, must constantly finance three and a half months of inventory purchases.

Assume, for the moment, that eSTUFF sells inventory every 15.6 days, instead of 124.4 days. Its net cash conversion cycle would be reduced to –3 days under these circumstances (i.e., 15.6 days + 39.5 days – 58.1 days). eSTUFF would collect cash from inventory it purchased 55 days ago under this assumption, but eSTUFF would not pay for the inventory item until day 58. In other words, eXTREMESTUFF.com's vendors are financing its working capital. The company actually has the use of vendor cash for three days.

Exhibit 8-4 illustrates both net cash conversion cycle scenarios for 2001. It presents the company's investment in working capital and working capital financed by eSTUFF's suppliers.[16]

---

[16] Exhibit 8-4 makes a number of simplifying assumptions, including the following: eSTUFF reorders inventory when it pays for the previous purchase, we ignore the impact of sales-related transactions in 2000, and inventory costing (e.g., FIFO) does not affect analysis.

LIQUID COMPANIES PAY THEIR BILLS

Distributors supply products from manufacturers to retail establishments. These types of companies tend to have small profit margins. Success hinges on a firm's ability to efficiently acquire inventory, distribute it, collect on receivables, and pay for the goods. Failing in one aspect of the net cash conversion cycle creates a ripple effect in the other areas. What is your analysis of AmeriServe Food Distribution Inc.?

AmeriServe expanded rapidly by purchasing another food distributor. But there were problems: The company had trouble integrating the acquisition's operations into its own, and AmeriServe had large debt repayment requirements as a result of the purchase. These factors caused a liquidity crisis for the firm. The company compensated by skipping vendor payments. Suppliers retaliated by cutting off credit and forcing AmeriServe to pay cash.

The company, however, lacked cash; otherwise, it wouldn't have skipped vendor payments. Therefore, it could not supply its restaurants with inventory. AmeriServe's customers, in turn, found other suppliers. Burger King, for instance, canceled its 5,800-store account with the food distributor. AmeriServe lost over $2.2 billion in credit sales, or over a third of its sales and receivable base. The Dallas, Texas, food purveyor filed Chapter 11 bankruptcy protection in 1999 as a result of its liquidity problems.°

Observations

Did AmeriServe increase or decrease its accounts payable turnover as a result of its cash crunch? Do you think AmeriServe's inability to provide inventory to restaurants motivated restaurateurs to make timely payments on their accounts? Discuss the implication on the net cash conversion cycle if restaurants did, in fact, delay payments to AmeriServe. AmeriServe could not make credit or cash purchases; therefore, its inventory levels were low. Discuss how this result could confuse analysis of inventory activity measures (at least in the short term).

° Chapter 11 is a bankruptcy option that allows a firm to continuing operating while it reorganizes its business. In many instances, the reorganization results in reducing creditor claims against the company or replacing them with different claims. Both the owners and its creditors must agree to the corporate reorganization for it to become binding.

LIQUIDITY ANALYSIS OF THE PERSONAL COMPUTER INDUSTRY

This final section presents an introductory analysis of the PC industry's liquidity. As in other chapters, we center our analysis on Apple Computer and use Compaq, Dell, and Gateway to provide comparative data and industry perspective. We use liquidity measures for 1994 through 1998; we did not incorporate 1993 ratios because we used averaged balance sheet data (i.e., 1992 disclosures were not presented). Data are presented in Appendix A.

Recall from Chapter 4 that analysts must exercise caution when interpreting ratios. Be prudent in describing measures as good (bad), favorable (unfavorable), or acceptable (unacceptable). Such conclusions are reached in light of the surrounding circumstances and based on a substantive body of evidence. Informed people can and do reach different conclusions when analyzing companies. You may disagree with some of the PC industry analysis in this book; that's fine so long as your opinions are based on valid inputs and thorough analysis.

WORKING CAPITAL ANALYSIS

Working capital accounts dominated PC companies' balance sheets during the period analyzed. This is not surprising. Information-oriented firms require relatively few fixed resources to produce products and services. The composition of current accounts also changed from 1993 to 1998. Most notably, current assets became more liquid. The pie charts presented for Apple Computer in Exhibit 8-5 bear out these facts.

Short-term creditors financed more corporate assets than long-term obligations. This stands to reason, because PC firms tend to maintain high levels of current assets and use equity financing.[17] Also note that current liabilities increased at a faster rate than current assets did during the period analyzed. Exhibit 8-6 presents the working capital declines that resulted from this trend.

You could infer that the decrease in the industry's working capital during the period examined is bad because firms were less liquid, but consider this: Although companies do have to meet maturing obligations, too much liquidity can prove counterproductive. Capital is invested in relatively nonproductive

EXHIBIT 8-5
Composition of Apple Computer's Assets 1993 and 1998

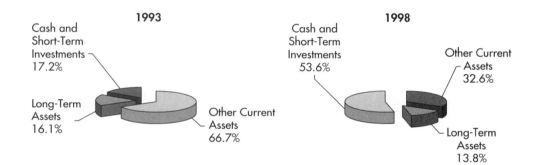

EXHIBIT 8-6
Current Ratios in the PC Industry 1994–1998

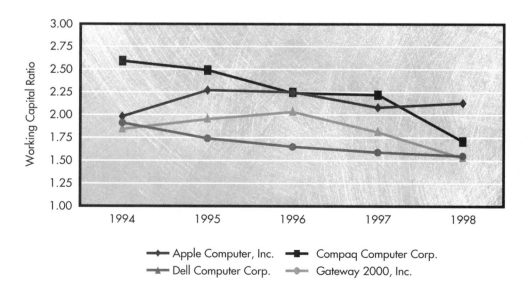

---

[17] Recall the discussion in the "Financing and Investing Activities" section of this chapter.

MICRO $\mathcal{A}$NALYSIS 10

Much of the long-term financing of new economy industries consists of equity investments made by venture capitalists.

WEB $\mathcal{E}$XERCISE 8

Compare Apple Computer's current and quick ratios for the current year with 1994's ratios. How have the relative amounts of the two ratios changed? What does this tell you about the degree of liquidity in Apple's current accounts over time?

MICRO $\mathcal{A}$NALYSIS 11

Apple began selling PCs directly to customers in November 1997 (the start of fiscal 1998).

assets in these instances. The PC industry's maturation accounted for at least part of the working capital reductions. Personal computers became a standard business tool and a larger part of people's personal lives during the 1990s. The open architecture of IBM-compatible machines altered consumer preferences from brand loyalty to product value. Because consumers started to view PCs as commodities, PC firms needed greater operating efficiencies to differentiate themselves. Better working capital management was one such strategy.

Industry conditions forced firms to reduce working capital as a means of remaining competitive and improving shareholder wealth. The hidden cost of financing high levels of current assets became unacceptable throughout the industry. Activity measures and conversion cycles specify where the working capital changes occurred. In the next sections, we analyze these measures.

INVENTORY ACTIVITY MEASURES

Inventory reduction was pronounced during the period analyzed. All the PC firms analyzed here increased inventory turnover from 1993 to 1998. The decrease in the number of days in inventories, shown in Exhibit 8-7, captures this trend.[18]

Rapidly changing technology (remember Moore's Law), greater competition, and declining prices all increased the cost of holding inventory. Companies responded by slashing inventories. Although all four of the companies reduced inventories during the years analyzed, data indicate that Dell and Gateway had fewer days in inventory than Apple or Compaq. The gap was smaller at the end of the period analyzed.

Inventory disparities may be partly attributable to the firms' different selling approaches. Dell and Gateway pioneered direct PC sales. Apple and Compaq, on the other hand, maintained a more traditional distribution channel: They sold computers to resellers, who in turn sold them to end users. Dell and Gateway needed far fewer PCs in inventory than resellers did. So long as the direct sellers had adequate components on hand, they could build the machines to order for the end users. Resellers, in contrast, had to stock sufficient finished goods to meet the

EXHIBIT 8-7
Days in Inventory for the PC Industry
1994–1998

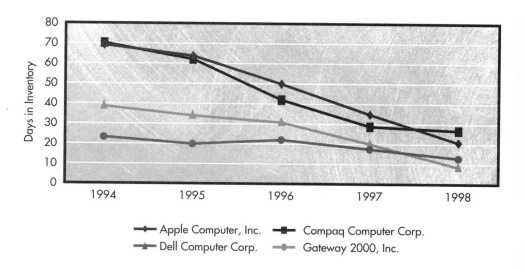

---

[18] There is an inverse relationship between turnover and the days in an account.

needs of its distributors. Apple and Compaq had to maintain excessive inventories whenever they misjudged retail sales trends. Thus, the resellers incurred inventory holding costs avoided by Gateway and Dell.

Direct selling is not the whole story, however; operational effectiveness must complement strategic decisions. Dell and Gateway's alternative distribution channel would have been meaningless unless they secured components on a timely basis, properly managed raw materials and work in process, efficiently built machines to order, and rapidly shipped them to customers. Moreover, low inventory levels and advantageous working capital positions do not necessarily equal success. It is possible that PC resellers, even with higher inventory levels, financially outperformed direct sellers. Future analysis explores that possibility.

Apple Computer's data, shown in Exhibit 8-8, illustrate inventory reductions. Its inventories declined from $1.4 billion in 1993 to $78 million in 1998, shown as a percentage of assets in the exhibit. Apple virtually eliminated its inventory by 1998. The company streamlined parts procurement, improved manufacturing processes, and increased direct computer sales. In fact, one could question whether Apple's inventory policy was too lean by 1998. Excessive order backlogs, increasing customer complaints, and declining revenues could indicate that Apple maintained insufficient inventories in the late 1990s. This issue warrants further investigation.

OTHER ACTIVITY MEASURES

As shown in Exhibits 8-9 and 8-10, receivables turnover remained relatively stable, and turnover of payables decreased during the period analyzed. These changes were neither as pronounced as those for inventory nor as consistent over time or among companies.

Exhibit 8-9 indicates that the industry's number of days needed to collect cash from customers remained fairly constant. On the whole, Dell and Gateway collected receivables faster than Apple and Compaq did. However, note that the direct computer sellers did become slightly more efficient in collecting receivables than the indirect sellers over time. (Their number of days needed to collect decreased.) Exhibit 8-10 demonstrates that all four firms took progressively longer to pay vendors in the later years of the study than the earlier ones. (Notice the increasing slopes of the trend lines.) On the whole, Gateway consistently met its obligations and collected on them faster than the competition did.

Apple Computer's receivables decreased and payables increased as a percentage of total assets from 1993 to 1998. Exhibit 8-11 reports the relative percentage of

When Apple was an industry leader in the early 1990s, it aggressively dealt with retailers. The company's rigid sales rules and quotas strained relations with many Apple resellers.

Apple can still play hardball with retailers. It discontinued selling iMacs to Best Buy Co. in April 1999 because the electronics chain refused to stock all five iMac designer colors.

How much inventory did Apple carry at the end of its most recent fiscal reporting period?

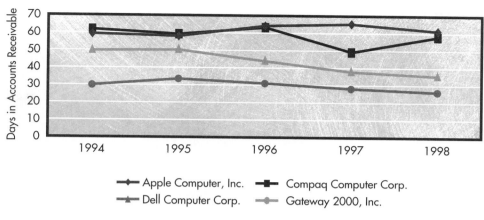

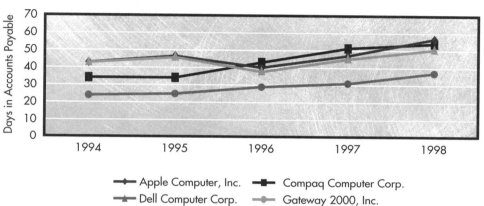

these two accounts to total assets in 1993 and 1998. These data provide further evidence that Apple (and the industry as a whole) decreased working capital as the industry matured.

WEB EXERCISE 10

Examine the four PC companies'
most recent financial statements.
Which firm has the lowest net
cash conversion cycle?

WEB EXERCISE 11

Have Apple Computer's conver-
sion cycles increased or decreased
since 1998?

CONVERSION CYCLES

Propelled by inventory reductions and supplemented by changes in receivables and payables, the PC industry's conversion cycles decreased over the period of analysis. Exhibits 8-12 and 8-13 present industry data and Exhibit 8-14 focuses on the inventory and net cash conversion cycles of Apple Computer.

Exhibit 8-12 demonstrates the industry's contracting inventory conversion cycle from 1993 to 1998. Another way to conceptualize this decline is that firms increased their manufacturing operating cycle velocity (Exhibit 8-3) over time. In addition, the firms complemented their faster operating cycles by extending payments to suppliers. Consequently, the decline in the firms' net cash conversion cycles (Exhibit 8-13) was even more pronounced than inventory conversion (Exhibit 8-12). Cycle reductions meant companies made fewer investments in working capital from 1994 to 1998. These two graphs reaffirm what becomes evident from the individual activity measures: Direct sellers were more efficient in managing working capital than the indirect sellers.

EXHIBIT 8-11

*Receivables and Payables
Percentages of Balance Sheet
Totals
Apple Computer
1993 and 1998*

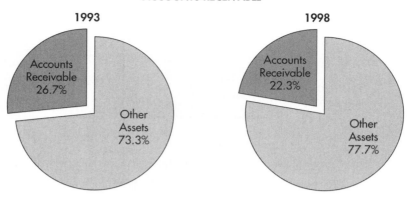

ACCOUNTS RECEIVABLE

1993

Accounts Receivable 26.7%

Other Assets 73.3%

1998

Accounts Receivable 22.3%

Other Assets 77.7%

ACCOUNTS PAYABLE

1993

Accounts Payable 14.4%

Other Liabilities & Shareholders' Equity 85.6%

1998

Accounts Payable 16.8%

Other Liabilities & Shareholders' Equity 83.2%

EXHIBIT 8-12

*Inventory Conversion Cycles
for the PC Industry
1994–1998*

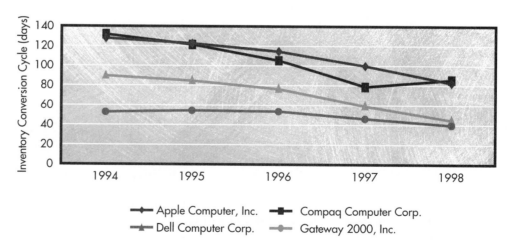

Apple Computer, Inc.   Compaq Computer Corp.
Dell Computer Corp.   Gateway 2000, Inc.

Gateway virtually eliminated the need for financing its working capital by 1998 (2 days for net cash conversion), and Dell actually had the use of its vendors' funds for a short period of time (a net cash conversion cycle of –6 days). By 1998, Gateway's aggressive supplier payment schedule and slightly slower inventory turnover had more than offset its ability to collect receivables faster than Dell. Consequently, its net cash conversion cycle was longer than Dell's in that year.

EXHIBIT 8-13

*Net Cash Conversion Cycles
for the PC Industry
1994–1998*

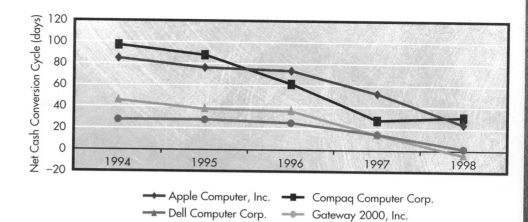

EXHIBIT 8-14

*Conversion Cycles for Apple
Computer
1994–1998*

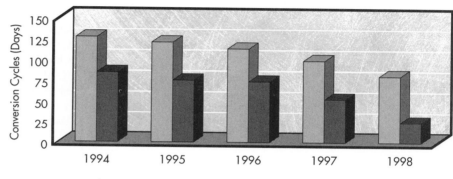

Apple Computer reduced its conversion cycles in two ways. The company decreased days in inventory (Exhibit 8-7) and lengthened payments to suppliers (Exhibit 8-10). Apple's constant receivable collections did not affect working capital analysis (Exhibit 8-9). The combined impact of inventory reductions and trade payable extensions altered the company's liquidity profile. The company transferred much of the cost of financing current assets from itself to its suppliers (Exhibit 8-14).

SUMMARY

This chapter introduces short-term liquidity analysis. This area of analysis focuses on an entity's ability to pay current liabilities with cash generated from current assets. Basic business models indicate the relationship between resource acquisitions and allocations. Analysts who understand these corporate financing and investing interrelationships are better able to analyze short-term liquidity. We introduce key liquidity terms and demonstrate how these terms serve as inputs to the liquidity analysis. There are three interrelated aspects of liquidity: working capital, activity measures, and cycle analysis. We use current account information from eSTUFF to illustrate liquidity measures for each of these aspects.

The chapter concludes with a liquidity analysis of the PC industry from 1993 through 1998. (The financial data of Appendix A provides inputs for the analysis.)

Data demonstrate working capital decreases and liquidity reductions during that time period. Substantial inventory reductions fueled the working capital decline. The PC companies also decreased accounts payable turnover—in other words, they increased the number of days to pay suppliers. Inventory and the net cash conversion cycles decreased as a result of changes in inventory and payables. Smaller corporate investments in working capital resulted. The trend toward less liquidity in the industry reflects greater working capital efficiencies, rather than an inability to satisfy maturing obligations.

KEY TERMS

Accounts payable turnover
Accounts receivable turnover
Activity ratio
Current (or working capital) ratio
Financing decisions
Inventory turnover
Inventory conversion cycle
Investment decisions
Liquidity
Net cash conversion cycle
Net realizable value

Number of days in accounts payable
Number of days in accounts receivable
Number of days in inventory
Operating cycle
Order of liquidity
Quick (or acid-test) ratio
Replacement cost
Short-term liquidity analysis
Turnover ratio
Working capital

NUMERICAL CASE

8-1

eXTREMESTUFF.com

Numerical case 3-2 at the end of Chapter 3 extends eSTUFF's financial statements through 2003. Use those data to compute the following short-term liquidity measures for 2002 and 2003. (Be sure to average balance sheet data.)

a. Working capital
b. Current ratio
c. Quick ratio
d. Inventory turnover
e. Number of days in inventory
f. Accounts receivable turnover
g. Number of days in accounts receivable
h. Inventory conversion cycle
i. Accounts payable turnover
j. Number of days in accounts payable
k. Net cash conversion cycle

INDUSTRY CASES

Examine the industry information and corporate financial statements presented in the appendixes. Prepare a short-term liquidity analysis from 1993 through 1998.

Compute liquidity measures and graph the results to assist in each analysis. (As noted in the chapter, your analysis of the PC industry may differ from the one presented here.)

8-1   *Personal Computers: Apple, Compaq, Dell, and Gateway*

8-2   *Airlines: American, Delta, and United*

8-3   *Athletic Footwear: Nike and Reebok*

8-4   *Discount Retailers: Kmart, Target, and Wal-Mart*

8-5   *Fast-Food Restaurants: McDonald's and Wendy's*

8-6   *Soft Drink Companies: Coca-Cola and PepsiCo.*

INDUSTRY INTERNET CASES

Extend your short-term liquidity industry case analyses by incorporating financial statement disclosures from 1999 through the most recent year. Research and note any substantial changes in the economy and industry that could affect liquidity. Incorporate those changes into your analyses. (Financial statement disclosures may not be the same as those presented in the appendixes. Use your judgment to make the necessary modifications.)

8-1   *Personal Computers: Apple, Compaq, Dell, and Gateway*

8-2   *Airlines: American, Delta, and United*

8-3   *Athletic Footwear: Nike and Reebok*

8-4   *Discount Retailers: Kmart, Target, and Wal-Mart*

8-5   *Fast-Food Restaurants: McDonald's and Wendy's*

8-6   *Soft Drink Companies: Coca-Cola and PepsiCo.*

9

ADVANCED SHORT-TERM LIQUIDITY ANALYSIS

$\mathcal{C}$HAPTER LEARNING OBJECTIVES

Upon completion of this chapter, you should be able to:

◆ *Compute and interpret an entity's liquidity index.*

◆ *Explain how inventory cost-flow assumptions, LIFO reserves, and LIFO liquidations affect inventory analysis.*

◆ *Indicate how cash sales and uncollectible accounts influence analysis of accounts receivable.*

◆ *Articulate why converting expenses to related cash-based amounts benefits analysis of current liabilities.*

◆ *Discuss the importance of financial flexibility in liquidity analysis.*

◆ *Describe why some technical adjustments to liquidity measures are sometimes impossible to compute or unnecessary to analyze.*

◆ *Provide a detailed liquidity analysis of a company or industry.*

*T*his chapter continues the discussion of how to assess a firm's ability to pay maturing obligations, refining the concept of analyzing liquidity. The first item quantifies current asset liquidity. The next three sections examine factors that influence inventory, accounts receivable, and accounts payable activity measures. Next we evaluate financial flexibility. To conclude, we further analyze Apple Computer's liquidity.

CURRENT ASSET LIQUIDITY

MICRO *A*NALYSIS 1

In some industries, firms have begun forming online business-to-business marketplaces to reduce inventory costs and streamline procurement. These e-business consortiums lessen dependence on distributors and enhance negotiating positions with suppliers. Examples of online marketplaces include automobile and tire manufacturers, aerospace companies, agricultural concerns, and health care providers.

WEB *E*XERCISE 1

Examine online business-to-business marketplaces in the aerospace industry by going to MyAircraft.com and in the agriculture industry by going to XSAg.com.

Chapter 8 presents numerous liquidity measures. The working capital ratio, for example, reports the amount of current assets per dollar of current liabilities. Other measures disclose the length of time needed to convert a current asset into cash. The number of days in inventory and accounts receivable are the most prominent of these activity measures. Linking such measures yields even greater liquidity information. The inventory conversion cycle provides operating cycle information by combining days in receivable with the time needed to sell inventory.

Missing from those Chapter 8 calculations, however, was an overall measure of a company's current asset liquidity. The inventory conversion cycle, for example, ignores the most liquid current assets in its calculation—cash and short-term security investments. The **liquidity index** compensates for that deficiency. It quantifies a company's overall degree of current asset liquidity.[1] The first step in calculating the index is to compute **product-dollar days**: a current asset's account balance multiplied by its number of days outstanding (e.g., the number of days in inventory).[2] Then sum product-dollar days for all current assets. To find the liquidity index, divide total product-dollar days by the amount of current assets:

$$\text{Liquidity index} = \frac{\text{total product dollar days}}{\text{current assets}}$$

Liquidity and the magnitude of the index are inversely related: A relatively small index indicates a high degree of liquidity, and a large one connotes illiquidity.

Consider the following inputs for eSTUFF's liquidity index for 2001 (in thousands of dollars)[3]:

CURRENT ASSET ACCOUNT	AMOUNT	DAYS REMOVED FROM CASH[4]	PRODUCT-DOLLAR DAYS
Cash	$ 45	1 day	$ 45
Short-term investments	0	1 day	0
Accounts receivable	$140	40 days	5,600
Inventory	250	124 days	31,000
Total	**$435**	—	**$36,645**

---

[1] Proposed by A. H. Finney, as reported by Chapter 16 of L. Bernstein, *Financial Statement Analysis, Theory, Application and Interpretation,* 5th ed. (Homewood, IL: Irwin, 1993).

[2] The liquidity index excludes prepaid expenses because these accounts are not converted into cash.

[3] This specific approach to calculating the liquidity index uses year-end current account data and an average number of days removed from cash. There are procedures, such as using all year-end data, but differences tend to be immaterial.

[4] These numbers are taken from Chapter 8 computations and rounded to nearest day.

The liquidity index for eSTUFF is 84.2 ($36,645,000 / $435,000). The company's relatively high index results from the majority of its working capital assets being tied up in slow-moving inventory.[5] Recall the computations from Chapter 8: If inventory took 16 days to sell instead of 124 days, then the company's liquidity index would be 22.2 ([$45,000 + $5,600,000 + $4,000,000] / $435,000). A lower index, therefore, indicates greater current asset liquidity.

As with all analytic measures, data quality influences the calculation of the liquidity index. Significant input factors affect purchasing, selling, and payment activities. The next three sections of this chapter examine inventory, accounts receivable, and accounts payable activity complexities.

WHAT'S YOUR ANALYSIS

JUST-IN-TIME INVENTORY AND THEN SOME

Pillowtex Corp. manufactures and markets blankets, sheets, and other bedding products. It introduced a new computerized management system to reduce inventories and speed its turnover. How do you think the company fared?

Pillowtex management believed a just-in-time (JIT) production system would increase profits. In a JIT system, raw materials are purchased and parts produced on an as-needed basis at each stage of production,[a] the reverse of traditional inventory management. Sales key JIT. In essence, a sale triggers a signal to the warehouse that more finished goods are needed. The warehouse, in turn, signals the last production stage of the demand, which then relays the information up the ladder to earlier stages of production. Ultimately, the message reaches the purchasing department, which buys more raw materials.

Coordinating each step in the just-in-time inventory process is crucial. In its first six months of JIT operations, Pillowtex had flat sales but managed to increase finished goods inventory by $75 million. Ballooning inventories resulted in expense recognition for obsolete inventory and idling of production plants to reduce levels of finished goods.[b] In addition, failure to efficiently turn over its inventory jeopardized Pillowtex's ability to pay liabilities as they came due.

Observations

Analysts must be aware that the success of changes in business strategies depends on proper implementation. Assess the following statement: The liquidity problems of Pillowtex attest to the fact that it is more difficult to execute strategies than to create them. Do you think Pillowtex's product days for inventory increased or decreased? How about the company's liquidity index?

---

[a] Explanation of just-in-time inventory adapted from R. W. Hilton, *Managerial Accounting*, 3rd ed. (New York: McGraw-Hill, 1997).
[b] J. C. Conklin, "Pillowtex Tries to Put Inventory, Debt Problems to Bed," *Wall Street Journal*, December 23, 1999, p. B4.

INVENTORY ACTIVITY MEASURES

A number of inventory-related factors influence financial disclosures and analysis. Three primary ones are inventory costing methods, last-in, first-out (LIFO)

---

[5] As with all measures, benchmarking over time and against competition yields insights as to whether a liquidity index is favorable or unfavorable.

MICRO ANALYSIS 2

The "Asian contagion" (see Chapter 5) benefited some companies. General Motors, for example, slashed up to 25 percent from material costs in 1999 by negotiating contracts with financially strapped Asian part suppliers.

MICRO ANALYSIS 3

General Motors estimates it saves between $3 billion and $4 billion annually by globally coordinating purchases of raw materials and components.

EXHIBIT 9-1
Inventory Costing Alternatives Financial Statement Implications

reserves, and LIFO liquidation. We discuss these items first in a retailing context and then in a manufacturing one.[6]

INVENTORY COST FLOW METHODS

Inventory costs change over time. An entity selects a logical means of allocating those historical costs between expenses (cost of goods sold for the sold items) and assets (inventory for the unsold ones).[7] This selection, to the exclusion of other acceptable methods, affects a company's profitability and financial position.

The two primary inventory valuation methods assume that either the earliest purchased goods or the last items acquired are sold first.[8] These cost flows, introduced in Chapter 3, are **first-in, first-out (FIFO)** and **last-in, first-out (LIFO)**. FIFO's complement is **last-in, still-here (LISH)** because the most recent purchases constitute ending inventory. The obverse of LIFO is **first-in, still-here (FISH)** because the first units available for sale remain in inventory under this cost flow assumption.

Exhibit 9-1 presents the primary financial statement implications of the FIFO and LIFO costing methods. (Phrases, such as *higher* and *lower,* contrast one costing method to its alternative.)

	FIRST-IN, FIRST-OUT (FIFO)	**LAST-IN, FIRST-OUT (LIFO)**
Price Increases		
Income statement	◆ Lower cost of goods sold (COGS) ◆ Higher income ◆ Worse matching	◆ Higher COGS ◆ Lower income ◆ Better matching
Balance sheet	◆ Higher inventory values ◆ Better approximation of historical cost to current value	◆ Lower inventory values ◆ Worse approximation of historical cost to current value
Price Decreases		
Income statement	◆ Higher COGS ◆ Lower income ◆ Worse matching	◆ Lower COGS ◆ Higher income ◆ Better matching
Balance sheet	◆ Lower inventory values ◆ Better approximation of historical cost to current value	◆ Higher inventory values ◆ Worse approximation of historical cost to current value

---

[6] Service entities do not manufacture or carry inventory. Companies such as airlines earn revenue by providing services rather than selling tangible goods. Inventory considerations, therefore, are irrelevant in the financial statement analysis of a service entity. Any property these firms have supports their service functions. An air carrier, for example, carries spare aircraft parts and food and beverages for its passengers. Such items obviously do not fit the definition of inventory, which consists of goods manufactured or held for sale in the ordinary course of business.

[7] The financial reporting for inventory costs does not have to match the physical movement of goods. Also, many companies use more than one inventory costing method.

[8] See, for example, G. Yarnell and R. Rikert (eds.), *Accounting Trends and Techniques 1999* (Jersey City, NJ: American Institute of Certified Public Accountants, 1999).

WEB
EXERCISE 2

Does IBM cost inventory on a FIFO basis like the four PC firms being analyzed in this text? Check its "Summary of Significant Accounting Policies" in its most recent Form 10-K.

WEB
EXERCISE 3

Do you think inventory is a significant item in the liquidity analysis of heavy machinery manufacturer Caterpillar Inc.? Examine how the company costs inventory at caterpillar.com.

Note that matching on income statements is better under LIFO than with FIFO, regardless of whether prices are increasing or decreasing, because LIFO matches the most recent costs (purchased this year) against this year's revenues. For balance sheet disclosures, FIFO inventory valuations more closely approximate current cost of goods than those reported under LIFO. With FIFO, companies report the most recent purchases as year-end assets, but with LIFO they usually disclose costs from previous years' acquisitions as part of inventory (remember LISH versus FISH).

The relative amounts of inventory and cost of goods sold reported on the balance sheet and income statement depend on price movements. Disclosures for eSTUFF demonstrate the relationship between price movement and financial statement disclosures. Assume the company reports on a LIFO cost flow basis, and a note to its financial statements amplifies inventory disclosures. The footnote states that inventory would have been $220,000 and $300,000 at the end of 2000 and 2001, respectively, if costed on a FIFO basis.[9] Exhibit 9-2 presents comparative calculations of cost of goods sold under the LIFO and FIFO costing assumptions for 2001. Note the following points made in converting LIFO costs of goods sold to a FIFO-based expense:

◆ Adding LIFO cost of goods sold ($660,000) to ending inventory ($250,000) determines LIFO goods available for sale ($910,000).
◆ Rearranging the initial portion of the LIFO cost of goods sold section determines purchases under this method. (Goods available for sale less beginning inventory equals purchases, or $910,000 – $200,000 = $710,000.)
◆ The amount of purchases is independent of inventory costing methods. Consequently, FIFO purchases equal those of LIFO ($710,000).
◆ eSTUFF computed FIFO cost of goods sold ($630,000) by adding 2000's ending inventory on a FIFO basis ($220,000) to purchases ($710,000) and subtracting FIFO-based inventory at December 31, 2001 ($300,000).

Inventory costs increased for eSTUFF during 2001. Note that beginning and ending inventories under FIFO exceeded those of LIFO in Exhibit 9-2. In addition, the $80,000 net increase in FIFO inventory ($300,000 – $220,000) was $30,000 greater than the incremental increase under LIFO ($250,000 – $200,000). These inventory amounts and net changes in their balances indicate a period of rising prices. Exhibit 9-2 data support the price dependency of the inventory and cost of

EXHIBIT 9-2
eXTREMESTUFF.com, Inc. Cost of Goods Sold—LIFO and FIFO

	LIFO (AS REPORTED)	FIFO (ALTERNATIVE)
Beginning inventory (December 31, 2000)	$200[a]	$220
+ Purchases during 2001	710	710
Goods available for sale	910	930
– Ending inventory (December 31, 2001)	250	300
Cost of goods sold for 2001	$660	$630

[a] All amounts are in thousands of dollars.

[9] For simplicity's sake, we ignore the implications of the inventory difference at the end of 2000 under the alternative reporting methods and focus strictly on 2001.

ACTIVITY MEASURE	LIFO (AS COMPUTED IN CHAPTER 8)	FIFO (ALTERNATIVE METHOD)
Inventory turnover: COGS / Average inventory	$660 / $225[a] 2.933 times	$630 / $260 2.423 times
Number of days in inventory: 365 / Inventory turnover	365 / 2.933 124.43 days	365 / 2.423 150.63 days

[a] All amounts are in thousands of dollars.

goods sold contentions of Exhibit 9-1: LIFO cost of goods sold ($660,000) exceed those of FIFO ($630,000) when inventory costs increase. eSTUFF can report higher income (gross margin) under FIFO ($570,000) than by the LIFO method ($540,000). Decreasing prices would have resulted in a reversal of the relative amounts of cost of goods sold and inventory.

Exhibit 9-2 numerically demonstrates that inventory-related valuations are a function of inventory costing method. So, too, are inventory activity measures.[10] Exhibit 9-3 presents inventory turnover and number of days in inventory for eSTUFF under the alternative costing approaches. This exhibit proves that inventory activity measures are a function of inventory costing method. Inventory would have turned less often under FIFO because the lower, older costs comprise cost of goods sold (the numerator) and the higher, more recent costs remain in inventory (the denominator).

In general, analysts can accurately compare inventory activity only when firms use the same cost flow assumptions. Benchmarking inventory turnover and days in inventory against firms that use different costing methods reduces analytic validity and can lead to incorrect conclusions.

WEB EXERCISE 4

Did Caterpillar disclose LIFO reserves in its 1999 financial statements?

MICRO ANALYSIS 4

Heavy machinery construction slowed in 2000, inventories swelled, and manufacturing costs increased. Would you expect an increase or decrease in Caterpillar's LIFO reserves?

LIFO RESERVES

Exhibit 9-2 presents a simplified version of the LIFO reserve concept. **LIFO reserve** is the difference between LIFO and FIFO costs when LIFO is used to report inventory. The Securities and Exchange Commission (SEC) mandates such a disclosure because LIFO inventory amounts often contain very old and irrelevant costs.[11] eSTUFF would, for example, disclose inventory (in thousands of dollars) on its balance sheets as follows:

	2001	2000
Inventory, less LIFO reserves of $50 and $20 in 2001 and 2000, respectively	$250	$200

---

[10] All ratios that include inventory in their calculations, such as the current ratio, are a function of the inventory costing method.

[11] See Regulation S-X, Rule 5-02. Technically, LIFO reserves disclose differences between the replacement cost of inventory at its LIFO valuation. In most instances, FIFO approximates the cost of replacing inventory (see Exhibit 9-1). As discussed in this chapter, FIFO = LISH; consequently, the most recent purchases of inventory under FIFO equal the current replacement cost of inventory.

	FIFO
Beginning inventory (LIFO $200 + LIFO reserve $20)	$220
+ Purchases (as derived from LIFO inventory costing)	710
Goods available for sale	930
Ending inventory (LIFO $250 + LIFO reserve $50)	300
Cost of goods sold under FIFO	$630

An analyst can use these LIFO disclosures to compute inventory under a FIFO basis. Exhibit 9-4 presents such a conversion. Numbers in this exhibit equal the FIFO inventory costing disclosures of Exhibit 9-2.

A more efficient means of computing FIFO cost of goods sold exists. In 2001, LIFO reserves increased from the beginning ($20,000) to the end of that year ($50,000). In other words, using FIFO increases the amount of unsold inventory by $30,000 compared with the unsold LIFO inventory. If the unsold FIFO inventory increased by $30,000, then its sold portion must have decreased by $30,000, relative to LIFO's cost of sales. Therefore, FIFO cost of goods sold was $30,000 less than the LIFO amount, or $630,000 ($660,000 − $30,000 = $630,000).

LIFO LIQUIDATION

In general, LIFO inventory valuations are not representationally faithful because they do not report the current cost of merchandise held for resale. This cost flow assumption's superior matching of expenses to revenues, however, usually compensates for its balance sheet deficiency. So long as inventories are stable or increasing over time, proper matching occurs because current inventory costs are deducted from the same period's revenues. However, a problem arises when a company reduces inventory levels. Previous period's inventory costs are matched against revenues earned in the current year. **LIFO liquidation**, as this concept is known, complicates analysis.

Liquidation of LIFO inventory overstates income in a period of rising prices, because less expensive goods purchased in earlier years become part of the current period's cost of goods sold. This distorts the perception of sustainable earnings. Continual depletion of older, less expensive inventory, in other words, cannot continue; therefore, future earnings will revert to matching current, more expensive costs against current revenues. When LIFO reverts to its customary cost-flow behavior, a company would have to report lower earnings. Fortunately, when a company liquidates inventory under LIFO costing, it includes a note to the financial statements disclosing its income implications.

MICRO *A*NALYSIS 5

Apple has disclosed raw materials, work in process, and finished goods inventories on both the face of the balance sheet and in its footnotes in previous reporting periods.

MANUFACTURING CONSIDERATIONS

Manufacturing companies maintain three inventories: raw materials, work in process, and finished goods. These distinct inventory categories complicate inventory activity analysis. Consider inventory turnover. Manufacturers sell only finished goods; therefore, including total inventory overstates the inventory turnover's denominator or understates the resulting ratio. An understated ratio, in turn, overstates the number of days a manufacturer needs to sell inventory.

WEB

EXERCISE 5

How did Caterpillar disclose raw materials, work in process, and finished goods inventories in its most recent Form 10-K?

We could use an alternative turnover ratio with only finished goods inventory in the denominator. However, this would involve ignoring raw materials and work in process. These two inventory amounts represent resources committed in the current period to the revenue-generating process. But excluding them has the opposite effect on inventory turnover: It overstates the ratio. The obvious solution would be to measure turnover activity for each inventory category. But this is infeasible because generally accepted accounting principles do not require companies to provide the information necessary to measure turnover of raw materials, work in process, and finished goods inventories.[12]

Convention dictates using total inventory to compute manufacturers' inventory turnover. It is also prudent to examine a firm's raw materials, work in process, and finished goods inventories, which are usually disclosed in the notes to the financial statements. You should ensure that a manufacturer's relative amounts of these inventories are consistent from year to year and that these percentages approximate those of its competitors. Large differences over time or against competition hinder benchmarking efforts. The analyst should investigate situations when a manufacturer's three inventories are inconsistent.

ACCOUNTS RECEIVABLE ACTIVITY MEASURES

We address two accounts receivable considerations in this section: type of sales revenue and bad debts.

SALES TYPE

Corporate assets increase when goods are sold or services provided. Revenues also increase as a result of selling goods or providing services. The entity receives either cash or a promise of cash (from a credit sale) when it earns revenue. Only credit sales create accounts receivable; therefore, you should use only these sales to compute receivable activity. However, GAAP do not require companies to distinguish between cash and credit sales in their financial disclosures, so analysts must make a practical adjustment: They use combined cash and credit revenues for the numerator of the accounts receivable turnover ratio. This accommodation overstates the numerator of the receivable turnover ratio, thereby overstating turnover and understating days in receivable.

Let us return to eSTUFF to illustrate what happens. Assume that our hypothetical e-tailer makes a third of its sales in cash.[13] eSTUFF overstates the previously computed 2001 accounts receivable turnover ratio at 9.23 times ($1,200,000 / $130,000). Its correct accounts receivable turnover is 6.15 times ($800,000 / $130,000), and the number of days actually required to collect accounts receivable is 59.3 days (365 / 6.15) rather than 39.5 (365 / 9.23).

Similar to limited information about manufacturers' inventories, lack of credit and cash sales data challenge analysts. They must use cash and credit revenues with the understanding that such disclosures misstate trade receivable activity. This error usually does not present a problem because the magnitude of the overstatement

---

[12] Management has access to such data, which enables them to compute individual inventory component activity measures.

[13] A customer using a debit card instead of a credit card is a cash sale for an e-tailer.

tends to be consistent over time and among companies within a specific industry. The percentage of cash sales, however, differs greatly among industries. Cash sales correlate with ultimate product consumption; in other words, retail merchants tend to make more cash sales than manufacturers and distributors do. The difference between computed and correct receivable activity, therefore, is greater for retailers than for other types of businesses.

LARGE, SMALL, AND MISSING RECEIVABLES

Kmart Corporation generates over $35 billion a year in revenues on an asset base of $15 billion. Yet, the discount retailer does not report any accounts receivable among its $8 billion in current assets. The company's primary competitors, Wal-Mart and Target, report accounts receivable, and the latter company's percentage of receivables exceeds that of the former firm. Can you explain why?

Target stores are the largest segment of the Target Corporation. This company also owns Mervyns and a department store division. In fact, the company formed when the Dayton and Hudson department stores merged. It was named Dayton Hudson until early 2000, when it adopted the name of its largest division. Department stores traditionally offer their own credit cards to customers. Dayton Hudson extended this practice with the Target charge card. Receivables currently constitute approximately 11 percent and 27 percent of Target's current and total assets, respectively.

Wal-Mart and Kmart accept cash, checks, debit cards, and credit cards. Credit cards behave like checks or debit cards from the retailer's perspective: A merchant deposits credit card receipts daily with its bank. The bank increases the retailer's account, net of the bank's fee. In essence, Kmart and Wal-Mart make only cash sales. So why does Wal-Mart report receivables of 6 percent and 2 percent of current and total assets, respectively? Because Wal-Mart also owns Sam's Club. The wholesale club division of the world's largest retailer offers Business Revolving Credit and Sam's Direct commercial financing programs to its corporate customers.

Observations

Discuss how corporate origins, strategies, and segments affect financial statement disclosures related to receivables. Which of the three discount retailers is most likely to have the largest discrepancy between sales revenues and credit sales revenues? Which one has the smallest difference between the two revenue streams? Would you be more concerned about one discount retailer's bad debts and net accounts receivable than the others? Which one? Why?

MICRO ANALYSIS 6

Regulators estimate that the largest 19 Japanese banks wrote off over $500 billion of receivables as uncollectible during the 1990s.

BAD DEBTS

Companies extend credit to increase sales. A cost of doing business is that some customers will not pay for their credit purchases. Firms acknowledge this business cost by estimating **bad debts** and matching that expense against revenues.[14] Bad debt expense is included in an income statement's selling expense category. A company reports accounts receivable on the balance sheet at net realizable basis (the expected amount of cash collections), rather than the amount it has the legal

---

[14] You can estimate bad debts as either a percentage of revenues or through an aging of accounts receivable.

EXHIBIT 9-5
eSTUFF
Doubtful Account Information

ALLOWANCE FOR UNCOLLECTIBLE ACCOUNTS	BEGINNING BALANCE	CHARGED TO EXPENSES	REDUCTIONS TO ALLOWANCE	ENDING BALANCE
Year ended 12/31/01	$3[a]	$4	$5	$2
Year ended 12/31/00	$0	$3	$0	$3

[a]All amounts are in thousands of dollars.

MICRO ANALYSIS 7

Xerox recognized an unusually high bad debt expense in the second quarter of 2000, reducing earnings by six cents per share. The firm cited an inability to collect on credit sales made by its Mexican subsidiary.

right to collect (gross accounts receivable). An allowance for uncollectible (doubtful) accounts reconciles gross receivables to its net balance.

A doubtful accounts schedule sheds additional light on trade receivable activity. This supplementary schedule informs analysts of a company's bad debt expense and the estimated amount of uncollectible accounts receivables, which are not disclosed on the financial statements themselves. It can be used in conjunction with cash flow analysis (covered in Chapters 10 and 11) to help analyze management's credit policies.

Assume eSTUFF provided the supplement shown in Exhibit 9-5 to its 2001 financial statements. Read this schedule from the earliest year to the latest year (or from bottom to top). At the inception of the business on January 1, 2000, there were no sales; hence, no bad debts existed. eSTUFF estimated $3,000 bad debts expense (a selling expense) in 2000. The company did not write off any customer's account as uncollectible during that year ($0, the third number on the schedule's bottom line). The balance in the allowance for doubtful accounts at year-end equaled the bad debt expense for 2000. In other words, the company had $123,000 of gross receivables at December 31, 2000 ($120,000 of net receivables + $3,000 in the allowance account.)

Data interpretation for 2001 is the same as 2000, except that eSTUFF wrote off $5,000 of accounts receivable as uncollectible during the year. The ending balance of uncollectible accounts equals $2,000 (the beginning balance plus the increase in the expense minus the write-offs, or $3,000 + $4,000 – $5,000). Gross accounts receivable for eSTUFF totaled $142,000 at the end of the second year of business ($140,000 of net receivables + $2,000 in the allowance account).

SEARS, ROEBUCK & REALLY BIG RECEIVABLES

Sears, Roebuck & Co.'s current asset composition differs from those of many other retailers, especially discount stores like Wal-Mart. Sears has a relatively large amount of accounts receivable. How would Sears' credit sales affect your analysis?

Receivables account for over half of Sears' $38 billion in assets. Twenty-six million customers actively use their Sears Charge Card and have an average outstanding balance of over $1,000.[a] To grasp the enormity of Sears' accounts receivable operation, consider the following fact: Wal-Mart realizes four times the revenues that Sears does; yet, Sears' allowance for doubtful accounts exceeds Wal-Mart's total accounts receivable!

Sears' credit sales influence its profitability. For example, analysts forecast quarterly earnings for companies before they file their Form 10-Qs with the SEC. These forecasts are influenced by management's representations of corporate performance. Sears provides analysts with detailed sales information, but it does not provide data about quarterly bad debt expense.[b]

[a] Sear. Roebuck & Co. 1998 Form 10-K.
[b] J. P. Miller, "Sears Profit to Exceed Forecasts, Aided by Credit-Card, Retail Areas," *Wall Street Journal*, April 6, 2000, p. B13.

ACCOUNTS PAYABLE ACTIVITY MEASURES

Accounts payable activity conveys information about supplier payments. Analysts combine this activity measure with those for inventory and receivables to investigate operating cycle activity and liquidity financing, as noted in Chapter 8. Accounts payable activity, however, measures debt repayment for only one type of current obligation. This section expands the payable activity concept, encompassing measures that appraise corporate capacity to meet all maturing obligations. We also address a conceptual consideration, similar to those evaluated for inventory and receivable activity, for liability activity measures.

ACCRUED LIABILITY ACTIVITY MEASURES

Other current liabilities exist besides accounts payable. Computing the length of time taken to pay them is similar to the approach used for trade obligations. **Accrued liability turnover** measures the number of times a company pays these obligations in a reporting period, and the **number of days in accrued liabilities** computes the average length of time the company takes to pay them. These ratios look like this:

$$\text{Accrued liability turnover} = \frac{\text{operating expenses}}{\text{average accrued liabilities}}$$

$$\text{Number of days in accrued liabilities} = \frac{365 \text{ days}}{\text{accrued liability turnover}}$$

Consider eSTUFF's 2001 operating (selling and administrative) expenses and accrued liabilities:

CALCULATIONS FOR 2001 (IN THOUSANDS OF DOLLARS)	ACCRUED LIABILITY ACTIVITY MEASURES
($352 + $133) / [($21 + $50)/2] = $485 / $35.5 365 days / 13.67	Accrued liability turnover: 13.67 times Number of days in accruals: 26.7

eSTUFF pays for its accruals almost 14 times per year; in other words, it takes an average of 27 days to pay nonvendor short-term financing for such items as salaries, rent, and advertising. We could compute tax turnover for eSTUFF similarly, using the company's taxes payable and income tax expense disclosures.

EXHIBIT 9-6
eSTUFF
*Comparative Analysis of
Liability Activity Measures*

ACTIVITY MEASURE	CONVENTIONAL COMPUTATION	ADJUSTED COMPUTATION
Accrued liability turnover	$485[a] / $35.5 = 13.67 times	$360 / $35.5 = 10.14 times
Days in accrued liabilities	365 days / 13.67 = 26.7 days	365 days / 10.14 = 36.0 days
Accounts payable turnover	$660 / $105 = 6.29 times	$710 / $105 = 6.76 times
Days in accounts payable	365 days / 6.29 = 58.1 days	365 days / 6.76 = 54.0 days

[a] All dollar amounts are in thousands of dollars.

MICRO **ANALYSIS 8**

*Tricon Global Restaurants was
food distributor AmeriServe's
biggest customer. The parent
company of Taco Bell, KFC, and
Pizza Hut restaurants provided
the troubled food distributor with
short-term liquidity when
AmeriServe was unable to pay
its bills.*

CONCEPTUAL CONSIDERATION FOR CURRENT LIABILITY MEASURES

Liability activity measures need refinement. The numerator in the accrued liability turnover ratio includes depreciation expense and other noncash charges. You need to subtract these accrual expenses from the ratio's numerator, because these expenses will not be paid with cash. You can make a similar adjustment for accounts payable activity measures. Cost of goods sold is the conventional numerator for the accounts payable turnover ratio. The flaw with this approach is that the accrual expense does not create accounts payable liabilities. Accounts payable result from inventory *purchases*, not from cost of goods sold.

eSTUFF had $125,000 of noncash operating expenses in 2001 ($120,000 depreciation expense and $5,000 amortization expense, as presented in Chapter 3's statement of cash flows). Purchases were $710,000 (Exhibit 9-2). Exhibit 9-6 contains the comparative liability measures using accrual expenses and cash obligations in the numerators of the turnover ratios. This exhibit contrasts previously computed current liability measures with more precise ones for eSTUFF. Accounts turnover slowed (to 10.14 times from 13.67 times) and the number of days in accruals increased (to 36.0 days from 26.7 days) when we factored noncash expense items out of the accrued liability activity measures. Purchases exceeded cost of goods sold, due to eSTUFF's 2001 inventory increase. Consequently, accounts payable turnover accelerated (to 6.76 times from 6.29 times) and the number of days in payables decreased (to 54.0 days from 58.1 days).

FINANCIAL FLEXIBILITY

MICRO **ANALYSIS 9**

*Sometimes companies need
short-term flexibility to facilitate
long-term financing. They can
secure bridge loans to make
long-term investments and
acquisitions. They quickly repay
these loans by issuing debt and
equity securities.*

Financial flexibility enables an organization to take advantage of unexpected opportunities and meet unforeseen obligations. Although this characteristic can be applied to both current and long-term analysis, it is conventionally used to evaluate current debt paying ability.[15] Analysts assess a firm's capacity to meet maturing obligations if cash flows are interrupted.

A number of events can reduce or eliminate operating cash inflows or accelerate their outflows. For example, a company could have slow moving inventory, high levels of nonperforming receivables, or more restrictive purchase terms.[16]

---

[15] Capital structure and asset utilization analysis evaluate long-term financial flexibility. We address this topic in subsequent chapters.

[16] In one respect, the quick ratio, discussed in Chapter 8, is a measure of financial flexibility.

You can begin to assess financial flexibility by creating "what if" scenarios for such possibilities, like the following:

◆ What if sales slow down?
◆ What if receivable turnover slows to a fraction of its historic levels?
◆ What if vendors change credit terms?

Analysts need to use their judgment at this juncture. Many scenarios are only remote possibilities and should be ignored. You should focus your attention on only those situations that might significantly affect financial flexibility.

You must make qualitative assessments about current operating conditions and the probability of future events when assessing financial flexibility. Knowledge of the economy, industry, and company can help you here. Analysts must evaluate all of the environmental factors affecting liquidity. Consider collection of accounts receivables. The probability of customer default is greater in a depressed economy than a prosperous one. Companies in mature industries will probably have fewer unexpected bad debts than those in emerging industries. An entity with a diverse client base will realize greater consistency of cash collections than a company with a concentrated group of customers.

You must also evaluate probable cash curtailments. You should determine if a firm can alleviate potential liquidity problems, how it will do so, and at what cost. Usually, companies use short-term financing to ensure financial flexibility. Two types of liquidity financing are credit lines and commercial paper. A **line of credit** is a prearranged loan from a financial institution, guaranteeing a specified maximum amount of short-term financing. An entity can also issue **commercial paper**. These promissory notes are unsecured short-term obligations requiring repayment within nine months.

Each method has its advantages and disadvantages. Commercial paper is usually available only to large established firms, because the loan is unsecured.[17] Interest rates on commercial paper tend to be lower than those on credit lines, but firms incur underwriting costs to issue these liabilities. More firms have access to credit lines than to commercial paper, but restrictive covenants on credit lines reduce financial flexibility and increase these loans' costs.[18] In addition, loans obtained from credit lines are payable upon demand: Financial institutions can *call them at any time.*

CAR SELLERS' FINANCIAL FLEXIBILITY

Business terms affect financial flexibility. What's your analysis of the purchase terms affecting automobile dealers? How do you think it influences their behavior?

The total invoice cost of an automobile is due to the manufacturer when a dealer buys a car, not when the retailer sells it. Consequently, dealerships must finance their inventory. Manufacturers help in this regard by remitting quarterly payments to dealerships. These *holdbacks* cover financing for the first 90 days.[a] After three months, dealers must finance their own vehicle holding costs.

Here is how the system works: The manufacturer's suggested retail price (MSRP) represents its recommended retail-selling price. The invoice price is the wholesale

---

[17] Firms issuing commercial paper do not have pledge specific assets as collateral for the loans.
[18] One such covenant requires the debtor to maintain a compensating cash balance with the lender. These balances reduce the available cash from the loan, thereby increasing the cost of borrowing.

cost to the dealer. An automobile's invoice price (wholesale price) includes about a 3 percent holdback. Consider a car with a $23,000 MSRP and a $20,000 invoice. The true cost to the dealer is $19,400 ($20,000 * .97, or invoice less a $600 holdback). The dealer's breakeven point for the car's first day on the lot is $19,400.[b] It increases slightly from day 2 through day 90 as the dealer incurs the cost of financing the automobile. After three months elapse, the holdback is effectively used up, and the dealer is on his or her own to fund the vehicle.

Observations
Discuss the implications of excess inventory on a car dealer's liquidity. Do liquidity considerations influence an auto dealer's willingness to sell below MSRP? Discuss why lines of credit would be vital to an automobile dealer's financial flexibility.

[a] See www.edmunds.com/edweb/holdback.
[b] For simplicity, we ignore dealer overhead here.

WEB EXERCISE 6

Visit a commercial paper Web site at cpmarket.com.

APPLE COMPUTER AND THE PERSONAL COMPUTER INDUSTRY

The trend of PC companies' liquidity indices reflected the industry's increasingly aggressive working capital profile. Exhibit 9-7 presents these indices from 1994 through 1998.[19] (Recall that a low index connotes high liquidity.)

Cash and marketable securities increased as a percentage of current assets during the period analyzed. Lower liquidity indices in the later years of the analysis indicate sufficient financial flexibility, despite contractions in overall working capital. Firms became more financially flexible as fewer resources were tied up in the less-liquid current assets of inventory and receivables. Gateway and Dell's indices indicate greater liquidity than Apple and Compaq throughout most of the period. This result supports the evidence produced by Chapter 8's individual activity measures.

EXHIBIT 9-7
PC Companies' Liquidity Indices 1994–1998

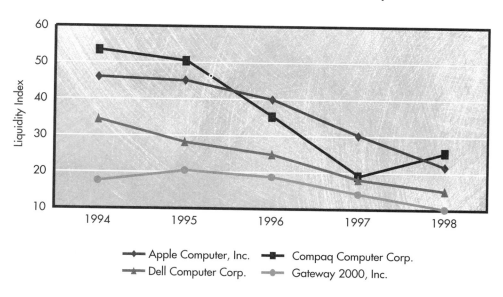

[19] We assume short-term investments to be immediately convertible into cash; therefore, their product dollar-days equal their account balances.

MICRO
ANALYSIS 13

Discuss whether Apple Computer's inventory composition of raw materials, work in process, and finished goods in 1998 would require significant analysis.

WEB
EXERCISE 7

What is Apple Computer's inventory at the end of its most recent annual reporting period? How is it allocated among materials, work in process, and finished goods?

INVENTORY ANALYSIS

The four PC companies used comparable inventory accounting; they all cost inventories on a FIFO basis, as noted in Chapter 5. Consequently, we do not have to adjust inventory data to render valid comparisons among these firms, because LIFO reserve and liquidation issues are irrelevant.[20]

Material and component costs decreased in the PC industry over time, despite the slight inflationary trend of the mid-1990s (see Exhibit 5-3). Financial statement data provide evidence of this decrease. Firms maintained their gross profit margins over the six years analyzed, except for Apple. Exhibit 9-8 reports the compound annual growth rates for sales, cost of goods sold, and gross profit for each firm analyzed.

Retail computer prices declined from 1993 to 1998. (This result is not surprising considering Moore's Law.) The first sub-$1,000 PCs were sold toward the end of 1997, and low-end machines sold for $600 by the next year. Twenty percent of the PC market consisted of sub-$600 machines by the end of 1998.[21] If selling prices declined while companies maintained their gross profit margins, then it stands to reason that PC firms' input costs must have decreased as well.

Apple Computer reported direct evidence of decreasing sales prices and input costs in Form 10-K. Exhibit 9-9 presents Apple's average selling price and cost of goods sold for its Macintosh computers in 1996 through 1998.[22]

Firms conservatively measured income as a result of costing inventory on a FIFO basis. Recall from a previous section that FIFO reports lower income than LIFO when prices decline. The industry's cost of goods sold reflected earlier, more expensive PCs. Thus, the companies matched older costs against more recent revenues. In addition, the companies reported the less expensive, more recently acquired components on corporate balance sheets. Drastic reductions in inventories, however, rendered any income distinctions between FIFO and LIFO immaterial by the end of the period analyzed. In effect, smaller inventories and increasing turnover minimized disclosure differences between the two methods.[23]

EXHIBIT 9-8

PC Companies' Compound Annual Growth Rates 1993–1998

	APPLE	COMPAQ	DELL	GATEWAY
Revenues	–5.7%	34.1%	43.7%	34.0%
Cost of goods sold	–3.2%	34.3%	43.8%	32.3%
Gross profit	–11.5%	33.5%	43.4%	41.7%

---

[20] Massive inventory reductions in the industry would have created a significant analytical issue if inventory were costed on a LIFO basis.

[21] Standard & Poor, *Computers: Hardware Industry Surveys,* June 3, 1999, p.4 (New York: McGraw-Hill, annually).

[22] Apple Computer, Inc. 1998 Form 10-K, "Management's Discussion and Analysis of Financial Condition and Results of Operations." The company did not disclose such data before 1996.

[23] The differences in reported numbers generated by FIFO and LIFO costing were greater in the earlier periods of analysis.

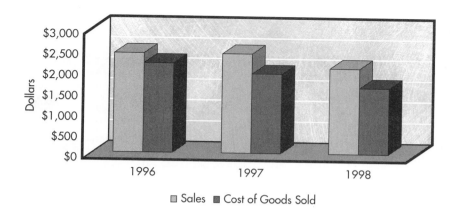

E-COMMERCE ALTERS INVENTORY ANALYSIS

Internet shopping offers a convenient way to purchase many items. You may have already purchased numerous goods online. Retail electronic commerce, however, represents just the tip of the cyber iceberg. Business-to-business e-commerce is reshaping the manufacturing landscape. How will this change affect financial statement analysis?

The digital age is transforming the commercial world from a make-to-stock economy to a make-to-order one. Dell Computer pioneered this approach in the PC industry by rapidly making PCs to customers' specifications. Other PC makers felt compelled to follow suit. Other industries are heading this way as well: Toyota and General Motors, for example, plan to make cars to order within one week's time.[a] If companies can process orders quickly, greater customer satisfaction ensues.

Manufacturing to order requires companies to procure raw materials and parts efficiently. Online purchases and sales cut costs and streamline the process by reducing paperwork and expediting orders. Business collaborations are also forming to drive down inventory prices:[b] Companies in the same industry are banding together to create online purchasing sites for parts and supplies. These electronic exchanges enhance buyers' bargaining power, reduce manufacturers' inventory holding costs, and further speed their inventory turnovers.

Observations

Discuss whether manufacturers' operating cycles will expand or contract as a result of increased e-commerce. Do you think working capital will increase or decrease if the promise of the Internet for business-to-business commerce is achieved? Do you think making automobiles to order would be more or less difficult than making PCs to order? Why?

---

[a] R. L. Simison, "GM Retools to Sell Cars Online," *Wall Street Journal*, February 22, 2000, p. B3.
[b] R. L. Rundle, "E-Commerce Coming to Health Care Industry," *Wall Street Journal*, February 28, 2000, p. B4.

RECEIVABLE ANALYSIS

Exhibit 9-10 presents the compound annual growth rate for accounts receivable and sales revenues for each of the four companies examined. Liquidity leaders Dell

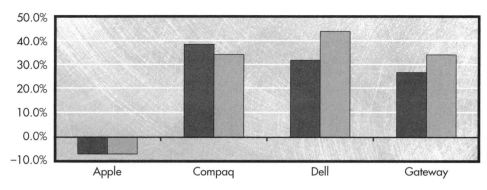

WEB
*E*XERCISE 8

*Examine Apple Computer's most
recent Form 10-K. Does the computer maker still disclose bad
debt information?*

and Gateway increased sales faster than receivables. Apple's two negative percent-ages equaled each other, and Compaq's revenues lagged receivable growth. Dell and Gateway's direct selling approach might have contributed to their lower receivable levels. These manufacturers sold to more end users than Apple and Compaq did. Cash sales in this segment of the market could have exceeded those for reselling arrangements with more traditional trade credit terms.

However, none of these differences between these companies' revenues and receivables differed dramatically. A reasonable inference is that each company's proportion of credit and cash sales remained fairly constant over time. The bias of including cash sales in receivable turnover measures, therefore, was inconsequen-tial to the analysis.

Bad debts also influence accounts receivable. Analysis of doubtful accounts provides additional liquidity insights in this area. Apple Computer disclosed bad debt data in supplementary schedules to its 10-K forms, as shown in Exhibit 9-11.

Apple Computer's total bad debt expense ($142 million) virtually equaled those specific accounts eliminated as uncollectible ($144 million) for the six-year period ana-lyzed. Consequently, the beginning balance of the allowance for doubtful accounts in 1993 ($83 million) is nearly identical to its 1998 ending balance ($81 million).[24]

EXHIBIT 9-11

*Apple Computer, Inc.
Valuation and Qualifying
Accounts*

ALLOWANCE FOR DOUBTFUL ACCOUNTS	BEGINNING BALANCE	CHARGED TO EXPENSES	DEDUCTIONS[b]	ENDING BALANCE
1998	$99[a]	$11	$29	$81
1997	91	35	27	99
1996	87	28	24	91
1995	91	17	21	87
1994	84	25	18	91
1993	83	26	25	84
Totals		**$142**	**$144**	

[a] in millions of dollars
[b] "Deductions" here is the same as "Reductions to Allowance" in Exhibit 9-5.

[24] Writing off an individual account (deductions) reduces gross receivables and the allowance account, but it does not reduce net accounts receivable. The expense recognition, an entirely separate transac-tion, reduces net receivables because it increases the allowance for doubtful accounts.

Apple Computer appears to have made adequate provisions for uncollectible credit sales. The existing balance in the allowance account exceeds annual debt expense and receivables write-offs. At the end of 1998, the company has the legal right to collect $1.036 billion in cash ($955 million net receivables plus $81 million in the allowance account). Apple Computer could write off substantially more customers' accounts in 1999 than it did in any previous year analyzed and still collect cash equivalent to its net receivables. The possibility exists, of course, that the doubtful account balances are so large because Apple delayed eliminating many uncollectible receivables from its records. Analysis of operating cash flows in Chapters 10 and 11 sheds further light on the adequacy of Apple's bad debt accounting.

EXERCISE 9

Do you think it is necessary to factor out depreciation when computing Apple's accrued liability turnover ratio? Check the firm's most recent Form 10-K to see if depreciation expense has increased significantly since 1998.

CURRENT LIABILITY ANALYSIS

The increasing liquidity of the industry from 1993 through 1998 did not require adjusting current liability measures. The enhanced liquidity of PC firms meant they could meet maturing obligations, regardless of how those liabilities were computed. It should be noted, however, that inventory reductions decreased purchases. Substituting purchases for cost of goods sold would have decreased accounts payable turnover (by lowering the numerator in the ratio) and increased the number of days taken to pay them.[25] This effect is just the opposite of what occurred for eSTUFF (Exhibit 9-6). Analysis of accrued liability turnover would not require an adjustment to cash paid for expenses. The industry has relatively few fixed assets; therefore, depreciation is relatively insignificant. Eliminating depreciation, a noncash expense, from the accrued liability turnover ratio would have an immaterial impact on that activity measure.

EXERCISE 10

What are management's most recent views regarding Apple's liquidity?

FINANCIAL FLEXIBILITY

The four PC firms analyzed increased their financial flexibility from 1993 to 1998. Substantial inventory reductions, combined with growing amounts of cash and marketable securities, support this contention. By the end of 1998, Apple, Compaq, Dell, and Gateway were able to pay near-term obligations, even in the event of unforeseen circumstances. Moreover, these firms had sufficient liquidity to take advantage of unexpected opportunities in the marketplace.

"Management's Discussion and Analysis," Item 7 of Form 10-K, addresses a company's perspective on liquidity and financial flexibility. It provides additional insight about these topics, but always consider the source of this information. Apple Computer, for example, expressed the opinion in its 1998 Form 10-K that it could meet maturing obligations. But the company also acknowledged that short-term borrowing, in the event it was needed, would be relatively costly due to poor recent financial performances.

SUMMARY

This chapter extends the previous chapter's discussion of short-term liquidity analysis. We present additional liquidity measures and factors along with a further analysis of the PC industry's liquidity in this chapter. We first examine the liquidity

---

[25] Manufacturers purchase only raw materials inventory. We would need internal cost accounting data to compute material acquisition costs.

index, which quantifies current asset liquidity through the concept of product days. This index provides additional liquidity insights beyond those produced by individual working capital measures. Using the PC industry as an example, we show that corporate liquidity can increase, despite working capital reductions.

This chapter also continues analysis of current activity measures. We explain the impact of inventory cost flow assumptions, LIFO reserves, and LIFO liquidation on inventory activity measures. We then indicate the relationship between accounts receivable turnover and confounding factors, such as credit sales and bad debts. This chapter also introduces the merits of using cash-based numbers as inputs for current liability ratios. Examples from eSTUFF demonstrate these adjustments. We use PC industry data to investigate some aspects of activity, such as bad debts; argue against the need for other adjustments (using purchases to compute accounts payable turnover); and point out the irrelevance of certain issues (LIFO reserves and liquidation).

Financial flexibility is an integral part of liquidity assessment. Analysts judge whether an entity can pay maturing obligations if its operating cash flows are interrupted. These assessments depend on forecasts of the amount, timing, and probability of cash flows. A firm's short-term borrowing capacity supplements financial flexibility. Established credit lines and commercial paper issues can enhance liquidity positions.

KEY TERMS

Accrued liability turnover	Last-in, still-here (LISH)
Commercial paper	LIFO liquidation
Bad debts	LIFO reserve
Financial flexibility	Line of credit
First-in, first-out (FIFO)	Liquidity index
First-in, still-here (FISH)	Product-dollar days
Last-in, first-out (LIFO)	Number of days in accrued liabilities

NUMERICAL CASE

9-1

eXTREMESTUFF.com

Numerical case 3-2 in Chapter 3 extends eSTUFF's financial statements through 2003. Use those data to complete the following liquidity requirements for 2002 and 2003.

a. Liquidity index.
b. Cost of goods sold on a FIFO basis. (Assume LIFO reserves of $60,000 at the end of 2002 and $75,000 at the end of 2003.)
c. Accounts receivable turnover and number of days in accounts receivable. (Assume eSTUFF made one-third of sales in cash.)
d. Bad debt expense and gross accounts receivable. (Assume the ending balance in the allowance for uncollectible accounts is $4,000 at the end of 2002 and $5,000 at the end of 2003; eSTUFF wrote off $3,000 of customer's accounts during 2002 and $6,000 in 2003.)
e. Accounts payable turnover and days in accounts payable. (Use purchases instead of cost of goods sold to compute these measures.)

INDUSTRY CASES

Examine the industry information and corporate financial statements presented in the appendixes. Compute liquidity indexes from 1994 through 1998. Adjust your short-term liquidity analysis made at the end of Chapter 8 based on the liquidity indexes or any other information you deem relevant. (As noted at the end of Chapter 8, your analysis of the PC industry may differ from than the one presented in the chapter.)

9-1 *Personal Computers: Apple, Compaq, Dell, and Gateway*

9-2 *Airlines: American, Delta, and United*

9-3 *Athletic Footwear: Nike and Reebok*

9-4 *Discount Retailers: Kmart, Target, and Wal-Mart*

9-5 *Fast-Food Restaurants: McDonald's and Wendy's*

9-6 *Soft Drink Companies: Coca-Cola and PepsiCo.*

INDUSTRY INTERNET CASES

Examine corporate financial statements from 1999 through the most recent year. Identify the following, where applicable and as data permit, for each company listed following:

a. Existing lines of credit
b. Management's assessment of liquidity
c. Inventory cost-flow assumption
d. LIFO reserves and LIFO liquidation
e. Proportion of raw materials, work in process, and finished goods inventories
f. Bad debt and allowance for uncollectible accounts information

Discuss how your findings would influence your short-term liquidity analysis presented for the Industry Internet Cases at the end of Chapter 8.

9-1 *Personal Computers: Apple, Compaq, Dell, and Gateway*

9-2 *Airlines: American, Delta, and United*

9-3 *Athletic Footwear: Nike and Reebok*

9-4 *Discount Retailers: Kmart, Target, and Wal-Mart*

9-5 *Fast-Food Restaurants: McDonald's and Wendy's*

9-6 *Soft Drink Companies: Coca-Cola and PepsiCo.*

10 INTRODUCTION TO CASH FLOW ANALYSIS

CHAPTER LEARNING OBJECTIVES

Upon completion of this chapter, you should be able to:

◆ *Explain the relationships among operating, investing, and financing cash flows and stages in the business life cycle.*

◆ *Convert indirect cash flows from operating activities to direct cash flows from operating activities.*

◆ *Describe the significance of cash received as a percentage of revenues and paid as percentage of cost of goods sold to business operations.*

◆ *Discern stability, efficiency, and inefficiency in an entity's operating cash flows and liquidity measures.*

◆ *Analyze a company or industry's cash flows from operating activities.*

$\mathcal{C}$ash ultimately determines business success or failure: In order for an entity to survive and prosper, it must take in more cash than it pays out over time. Accrual accounting complicates analysis in some ways. Financial statements primarily reflect business events as they occurred, regardless of the timing of cash receipts and payments. Corporate disclosures, in other words, emphasize wealth changes, rather than cash flows. This emphasis is not surprising considering the overriding corporate objective of wealth maximization. To truly comprehend wealth and changes in it, however, one must thoroughly understand cash.

Analysts must clearly distinguish between cash and wealth. Cash flow does not equal income, nor do cash balances coincide with accumulated profits. Cash is a tangible asset used to pay obligations and acquire other economic resources. Net income is a wealth-related construct, representing the change in net assets during a reporting period. Retained earnings symbolize undistributed entity (or owners') profits. A firm's assets intrinsically reflect the value of those accumulated earnings.

This chapter introduces cash flow analysis. It defines the objective of this area of analysis, relates cash flows to business decisions, identifies cash flow components, and examines operating cash flows. We conclude with an analysis of the personal computer (PC) industry's operating cash flows. Chapter 11 continues analyzing cash receipts and disbursements, focusing on longer-term investing and financing activities and relating them to operating cash flows. Cash flow analysis complements the liquidity material presented in Chapters 8 and 9. Subsequent chapters integrate cash flows and liquidity analysis with wealth and changes in it.

WHAT'S YOUR ANALYSIS

UNDERSTAND THE MONEY!

The catchphrase from the 1996 movie *Jerry Maguire* resonates throughout the business world: "Show me the money!" applies to everyone who has a vested interest in a company. Investors, lenders, managers, and others want money, or cash, from their association with a corporation. Unfortunately, the ultimate measure of liquidity is desired by all yet understood by few. Consider the following points and discuss why this knowledge gap exists.

Analysts can usually draw a sound inference from changes in the income statement, statement of shareholders' equity, and balance sheet: Increases in net income and net assets (owners' equity) are preferable to reductions in those areas. However, this logic does not hold for cash. The statement of cash flows resembles the other financial statements in some ways but differs from them in others. The income statement, shareholders' equity statement, and cash flows statement, for example, report change over time. The income and equity statements report wealth changes, but the statement of cash flows measures the net change in one asset. Cash is one of many productive corporate resources. Taken together, corporations use these assets to increase shareholder wealth. A critical factor in analyzing cash is determining how effectively the organization used it to create value, not how much exists at any point in time. Analysts must determine where the cash comes from, what it is used for, and how it will affect future revenue, income, and cash flows. A tall order, indeed. Showing the money is not enough. Although it probably wouldn't play in Hollywood, analysts need to "understand the money!"

Observations

Is positive cash flow always preferable to negative cash flow? Do you think a net decrease in cash for a reporting period is cause for alarm? Can you think of any other reasons why it is important to "understand the money"?

THE OBJECTIVE OF CASH FLOW ANALYSIS

People who conduct **cash flow analysis** evaluate past events and present conditions to forecast the amount, timing, and probability of future cash receipts and disbursements. They answer questions about such historical events as the following:

◆ How much cash came into and went out of the business?
◆ What were the primary sources and uses of cash?
◆ Were cash flow patterns consistent from year to year?

Analysts respond to those questions and ask more questions about the future, such as the following:

◆ Will the firm take in more cash than it pays out in future reporting periods?
◆ Will cash from recurring business operations allow the firm to prosper?
◆ How much cash will the business need to acquire long-term productive assets?
◆ Where will it come from?
◆ How much cash will the business require to compensate long-term creditors and owners for their investments?
◆ How confident am I regarding my cash forecasts?

BUSINESS DECISIONS AND CASH FLOWS

MICRO ANALYSIS 1

The bargaining position of parties sometimes determines the direction of cash flow. Historically, television networks such as NBC, ABC, and CBS paid local affiliates in exchange for airtime. Networks used the acquired airtime to broadcast national programming and commercials. These cash payments have been reduced in recent years, and some affiliates now must pay their networks for the right to broadcast national programs.

Recall from Chapter 8 the discussion of investing and financing decisions. As noted in that chapter, debt and equity capital acquired from creditors and shareholders result from corporate financing decisions. Management invests those funds in a variety of revenue-producing assets, trying to align corporate resources with the enterprise's objectives. In other words, those investment decisions reflect management's attempts to generate cash from business operations. Such operating activity behavior lies at the heart of cash flow analysis. Wealth maximization requires positive cash flows from recurring business operations. Financing and investing cash flows complement operations because those activities enable an entity to sell products and provide services. Your ability to forecast cash flows improves by understanding each of these three activities.

The Financial Accounting Standards Board (FASB) indicates the importance of cash-related activities by making them a central component of the standard setting body's conceptual framework. The FASB states that financial information must be useful in assessing future cash flows.[1] The Board further declares that providing information about the **amount**, **timing**, and **uncertainty of future cash flows** is the primary objective of financial reporting.[2] These three reporting goals help financial statement users predict how much cash will come into and go out of a business, when those cash flows will happen, and the probability with which they will occur.

---

[1] Financial Accounting Standards Board, "Objectives of Reporting by Business Enterprises," *Statement of Financial Reporting Concepts No. 1* (Stamford, CT: FASB, November 1978).
[2] Ibid, par. 37.

WEB
EXERCISE 1

Locate www.lycos.com/busi-
ness/cch/guidebook and click on
"cost of setting up the business."
Examine the list of required cash
expenditures needed to establish
a business.

MICRO
ANALYSIS 2

Many emerging Internet firms
continually seek cash infusions
from investors to keep their
fledgling businesses operating.
Such behavior is commonplace
for business start-ups.

The FASB asserts, "People engage in investing, lending, and similar activities to increase their cash resources. The ultimate test of success (or failure) of those activities in the extent to which they return more (or less) cash than they cost."[3] These statements echo what analysts have always understood: Cash is king! Analysts devote significant resources to understanding and forecasting cash flows.

CASH FLOWS AND CORPORATE LIFE

Cash acquisitions and allocations are influenced by an entity's stage in life. The **business life cycle** encompasses all phases of an organization's existence:[4] emergence, growth, maturity, and decline.[5] Characteristics for each life cycle stage are presented in Exhibit 10-1.

Each stage of the cycle exhibits specific cash-related behaviors. These phases differ with respect to their cash needs for operating, investing, and financing activities. Exhibit 10-2 graphs those cash flows.

Exhibits 10-1 and 10-2 define and display general cash flow behavior. The cash flows of eSTUFF typify certain cash flow traits of an emerging business. The nascent e-tailer raised significant cash to finance operations and used it for productive resources: eSTUFF acquired cash by selling stock and issuing notes, and it used this cash to purchase equipment and its trademark. These start-up activities decreased eSTUFF's net cash balance during its first two years of operations.[6]

EXHIBIT 10-1
*Business Life Cycle Stages
and Their Characteristics*

WEB
EXERCISE 2

Revisit the lycos.com site and
view "cost of running the business" to see a list of necessary
cash expenditures required for an
established firm.

STAGE IN LIFE	CHARACTERISTICS
Emergence	◆ Establish business ◆ Acquire funds from equity and credit investors ◆ Purchase assets ◆ Start operations
Growth	◆ Expand markets and products ◆ Increase asset base and revenue streams ◆ Experience rising costs
Maturity	◆ Achieve market, product, and revenue stability ◆ Experience heightened competition ◆ Restructure business activities to curtail costs and increase profitability
Decline	◆ Experience market contraction and reduced product demand ◆ Report revenue and profit declines ◆ Return investments to owners

---

[3] Ibid, par. 38.

[4] Previous chapters informally discuss many of these life cycle stages.

[5] The life cycle concept applies to products and industries as well as companies. It can also be used to evaluate revenues and profits.

[6] The hypothetical retailer had a positive cash flow from operating activities in 2000 and negative cash flow in 2001. Analysts must realize that individual firms can exhibit cash flows that differ from the norm in specific years, but the general patterns presented in the exhibits tend to hold. Moreover, cash flow behavior is indicative for stages of corporate life, rather than particular years.

EXHIBIT 10-2
Business Life Cycle
Schematic Representation of
Cash Flows

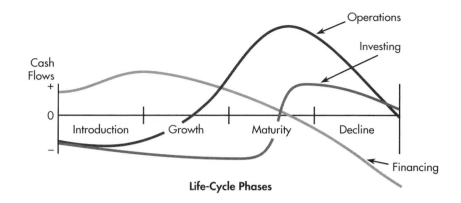

Life-Cycle Phases

WEB

EXERCISE 3

Read a summary of the
"Statement of Cash Flows"
(Statement of Financial
Accounting Standard No. 95) by
accessing the FASB's home page
at www.fasb.org.

WEB

EXERCISE 4

Is a cash flow statement required
under international accounting
standards? Go to
www.iasc.uk.org to find out.

STATEMENT OF CASH FLOWS

Generally accepted accounting principles (GAAP) require companies to report a statement of cash flows.[7] The statement discloses the overall change in cash during a reporting period and reconciles beginning and ending cash balances with it. The body of the statement consists of cash flows from operating, investing, and financing activities. Analysts use historic cash flow data in conjunction with accrual accounting disclosures to forecast future cash behavior and predict corporate cash balances.

Cash flows from operating activities is the most important section of the statement of cash flows. It discloses cash that came into and went out of a business from selling products and providing services. Investing activities focus on cash flows related to changes in a firm's productive capacity, such as property, plant, and equipment acquisitions. The third section of the statement, cash flows from financing activities, involves how the company funded those means of production. Financing activities include such events as issuing stock shares and bonds.

CASH FLOWS FROM OPERATING ACTIVITIES

MICRO

ANALYSIS 3

Central business activities
change over time. Hollywood
studios, for example, once existed
to make movies. Today, indepen-
dent firms produce most feature
films, and the large Hollywood
companies advertise and distrib-
ute them. Thus, established film
studios have shifted core activity
from production to marketing.

Operating activities are the lifeblood of a company. These cash flows are a barometer of corporate financial health; no business can survive for long without them. You need to check an entity's cash pulse frequently.

As noted in Chapter 3, cash flows from operating activities (CFOs) report the net cash provided by the core activity of a business, such as selling goods or providing services. The operating activities section of the statement reports the amounts of cash flowing into and out of a company from normal business activities. Analysts seek information about recurrent business patterns and trends from this section of the statement.[8] They evaluate operating cash flows to provide evidence of a company's ability, or inability, to generate sufficient cash from business

---

[7] Financial Accounting Standards Board, "Statement of Cash Flows," *Statement of Financial Accounting Standard No. 95* (Stanford, CT: FASB, 1987).

[8] "Net cash provided by" and "net cash used by" are the preferred phrases used to describe the net increase and decrease in cash from operating activities. "Cash flows," "net cash flow" and the preferred phrases are used interchangeably in this book.

operations over time. Analysts also use historical operating cash flow information and other data sources to forecast cash receipts and payments.

In certain respects, CFOs are less subjective than income. Operating income depends on accruals, deferrals, allocations, and estimates.[9] These managerial and accounting judgments affect the timing of revenues and expenses. On the other hand, CFOs simply report the amount cash provided and used by continual operations. Of course, companies can influence the amount and timing of their cash flows through such practices as product pricing, billing practices, and vendor payments. For example, significant price increases can enhance cash in the near term but might reduce sustainable cash flows by alienating present and future customers. Analysts must differentiate between long-term business practices that produce operating cash and short-term cash manipulations.

WEB EXERCISE 5

Does Apple Computer still report its CFOs on an indirect basis? Examine the company's statement of cash flows in its most recent Form 10-K.

WEB EXERCISE 6

For an example of direct CFO disclosure, go to www.compaq.com and examine Compaq's 1995 cash flow statement.

OPERATING CASH FLOW REPORTING METHODS

Companies disclose operating cash flows in one of two ways: The **direct method of operating cash flows** (or income statement approach) reports cash collected from revenues and paid for expenses, and the **indirect method of operating cash flows** (or reconciliation approach) discloses operating cash flows on an income-adjusted basis. Noncash expenses and current accounts changes adjust net income to determine cash flows from operations under the indirect method.

Befitting its name, the direct method presents more understandable and better information than its indirect counterpart. Most companies, however, report on an indirect basis.[10] The difference is strictly one of format; both methods report equivalent amounts of *net* cash from operations during a reporting period. Also, the other two sections of the cash flow statement are unaffected by the reporting basis of operating activities: Companies report investing and financing activities directly, irrespective of the operating section reporting method.

CONVERTING INDIRECT OPERATING CASH FLOWS TO DIRECT OPERATING CASH FLOWS

The income-adjusted approach of reporting CFOs obscures analysis. You cannot readily determine the amount of cash collected on sales, for example, using the indirect method. This and other direct information helps analysts to identify trends, benchmark companies, and relate cash flows to liquidity analysis. It makes sense, therefore, to convert indirect operating cash flows to a direct basis so that you can determine how much cash a company collected from customers and how much of it went to pay for operations.

The conversion process classifies the income statement's operating section into its major components and determines cash collections or payments for each of them.[11] Accrual-based revenues (expenses) are adjusted for changes in their

---

[9] Refer to the discussions in Chapters 3 and 6.

[10] Companies tend to report cash flows from operations on an indirect basis because it is relatively easy to adjust net income to determine cash flows from operations. In addition, entities are creatures of habit. The predecessor to the "Statement of Cash Flows," "Reporting Changes in Financial Position," used income as a starting point for its disclosures.

[11] More complex cash flow statements, such as those reported by most large corporations, require sophisticated adjustments and, sometimes, assumptions about the data. Such adjustments exceed the scope of this text.

EXHIBIT 10-3

eXTREMESTUFF.com
Cash Flows from Operating
Activities

Cash Flows from Operations—Indirect Basis		
	2001	**2000**
Cash flows from operating activities:		
Net income	$21[a]	$33
Depreciation expense, equipment	120	100
Amortization expense, trademark	5	5
Changes in current accounts:		
Accounts receivable	(20)	(120)
Inventory	(50)	(200)
Prepaid expenses	5	(10)
Accounts payable	(110)	160
Accrued liabilities	(29)	50
Taxes payable	(5)	5
Net cash provided by operating activities	**$(63)**	**$23**

Conversion to the Direct Basis		
	2001	**2000**
Sales revenue	$1,200	$1,000
Change in accounts receivable	(20)	(120)
Cash received from customers	$1,180	$880
Cost of goods sold	$660	$600
Change in inventory	50	200
Change in accounts payable	110	(160)
Cash paid to suppliers	$820	$640
Selling and administrative expenses	$485	$335
Change in prepaid expenses	(5)	10
Change in accrued liabilities	29	(50)
Less: depreciation and amortization	(125)	(105)
Cash paid for operating expenses	$384	$190
Tax expense	$14	$22
Change in taxes payable	5	(5)
Cash paid for taxes	$19	$17
Financial expense	$20	$10
Change in interest expense	0	0
Cash paid for interest	$20	$10

related balance sheet current accounts to determine cash flows.[12] eSTUFF's cash flow statement illustrates the conversion process. Exhibit 10-3 reconciles indirect CFOs to direct ones. This exhibit presents indirect CFOs (as disclosed in Chapter 3), the conversion process, and direct CFOs.

---

[12] You can measure these changes in two ways: You can take the difference in account balances between the beginning and ending balance sheets, or you can use the reported account changes disclosed by the indirect method on the statement of cash flows.

EXHIBIT 10-3
Continued

Cash Flows from Operations—Direct Basis				
		2001		2000
Cash flows from operating activities:				
Cash received from customers		$1,180		$880
Cash paid:				
To suppliers	$820		$640	
For operations	384		190	
For taxes	19		17	
For interest	20	1,243	10	857
Net cash provided by operating activities		$(63)		$23

° Amounts are in thousands of dollars

MICRO ANALYSIS 4

Depreciation is a noncash expense of the current reporting period. You must add it back to income for indirect CFOs reporting purposes or subtract it from expenses when reporting on a direct basis. It is not a source of cash and should not be considered one.

Net cash provided (used) by operating activities is the same for both the indirect and direct methods. eSTUFF's operating cash flows were $23,000 and $(63,000) in 2000 and 2001, respectively. As evidenced by the data in Exhibit 10-3, the direct basis provides a clearer picture of where the company's operating cash came from and went to during each business year. The conversion involves adding or subtracting changes in the balance sheets' current accounts during the reporting period to or from income statement disclosures. Consider the following adjustments in Exhibit 10-3:

◆ Accounts receivable represents uncollected revenues. An increase in receivables during a reporting period means revenues exceeded cash collected from customers. If receivables decrease, however, then cash inflows were greater than revenues. Consequently, we subtract an increase in receivables from revenues, and add a decrease to them. The accounts receivable of eSTUFF increased by $120,000 in 2000 (from $0 to $120,000) and $20,000 in 2001 (from $120,000 to $140,000). Those increases resulted in less cash collected ($880,000 and $1,180,000) than revenues realized ($1,000,000 and $1,200,000) in those years.

◆ We adjusted cost of goods sold for both inventory and accounts payable changes. Inventory acquisitions require cash payments, but accounts payable represent deferred merchandise payments. Therefore, we add an inventory increase to cost of goods sold but subtract an increase in accounts payable from it. We make the opposite adjustments when inventory and accounts payable decrease. eSTUFF's inventory increased during both years, but its accounts payable decreased in 2001 after increasing during the first year. Acquisitions from and payments to suppliers reflected those changes.

◆ We adjusted other expenses in a manner similar to cost of goods sold. These adjustments are illustrated in eSTUFF's cash payments for operations, taxes, and borrowing.

◆ We subtracted depreciation and amortization from operating expenses because they are noncash expenses. We reported the amounts of eSTUFF's depreciation ($100,000 in 2000 and $120,000 in 2001) and amortization ($5,000 each year) expenses in its indirect CFOs.[13]

---

[13] Acquisitions and disposals of long-term assets preclude computing depreciation and amortization expenses from changes in these assets' carrying values on the balance sheets.

INTERPRETING OPERATING CASH FLOWS

Merchants and manufacturers acquire inventory, prepare it for sale, sell it, collect from their customers, and pay their vendors. Analysts must understand how well a firm performs these tasks because they represent the central activities for retailers and industrialists. Therefore, they must compute and analyze direct cash flows from operating cycle activities, even if they don't recast the entire operating cash flow section on a direct basis.

ALTERNATIVE OUTCOMES

Analysts can improve their understanding of operating cycle activity by contrasting core events' actual cash performance with alternative outcomes. Modified data from eSTUFF demonstrate this comparative analysis. The second data column of Exhibit 10-4 reports eSTUFF's actual cash flows from buying and selling merchandise in 2001 (as presented in Exhibit 10-3). The next three data columns represent potential cash flows from alternative assumptions.

eSTUFF initially reported its annual percentage growth in revenues (20 percent) and cost of goods sold (10 percent) from 2000 to 2001 in Chapter 4 when we discussed common size statements. **Operating cycle stability** (the third data column) results when the annual compounding of a balance sheet account equals that of its corresponding income statement item. **Operating cycle efficiency** (data column 4) occurs when balance sheet accounts are compounded in such ways as to provide more (or use less) cash than stable operations. **Operating cycle inefficiency** has just the opposite effect on cash flows.

Exhibit 10-4 compounds receivables at 20 percent (equal to that of revenues) and 10 percent for inventory and payables (matching the increase in cost of goods

EXHIBIT 10-4
*eXTREMESTUFF.com
Alternative Operating Cycle
Outcomes*

	2000—BASE YR.	2001—AS REPORTED	STABLE CYCLE	EFFICIENT CYCLE	INEFFICIENT CYCLE
Sales revenues (20% increase)	$1,000[a]	$1,200	$1,200	$1,200	$1,200
Change in accounts rec.	120	(20)	(24)	(12)	(48)
Cash received from customers		$1,180	$1,176	$1,188	$1,152
Cash collected as a percentage of revenue		98.3%	98.0%	99.0%	96.0%
Cost of goods sold (10% increase)	$600	$660	$660	$660	$660
Change in inventory	200	50	20	10	40
Change in accounts payable	160	110	(16)	(32)	(8)
Cash paid to suppliers		$820	$664	$638	$692
Cash paid as a percentage of cost of goods sold		124.2%	100.6%	96.7%	104.8%

[a] Amounts are in thousands of dollars.

sold) for stable operations. A 10 percent receivable increase, a 5 percent inventory increase, and a 20 percent payable increase illustrate efficient operations. We demonstrate inefficient operations by a 40 percent receivable increase, a 20 percent inventory increase, and a 5 percent payable increase.[14]

eSTUFF would have collected 98 percent of revenues in cash if the receivables moved lock-step with sales (a 20 percent increase). If the company had been operating efficiently (a receivables increase of 10 percent, then a greater percentage of sales would have been realized in cash than for stable operations (99 percent versus 98 percent . The last column of cash collections in the exhibit demonstrates how larger increases in receivables (40 percent in this case) reduce cash receipts (96 percent versus 98 percent). The same logic prevails for assessing the percentage of cost of goods sold paid in cash. We present those results in the lower portion of Exhibit 10-4.

Significant differences between cash flows and accrual amounts are cause for alarm. In eSTUFF's case, for example, the amount of cash collected from customers during 2001 seems reasonable. Cash paid to suppliers, however, defies logic. The company paid more cash to suppliers than would have been expected than even under the inefficient operating scenario. Good analysts seek an explanation when such results occur for existing companies.

CONTROLLING CASH FLOWS

Companies such as Wal-Mart and Home Depot dominate their segments of the retail industry. Consider the effects of their business operations on cash flows.

Retailing has changed dramatically in the past few decades. Large companies have squeezed many smaller merchants out of business. These retail giants have been able to improve their negotiating clout with their suppliers, due to their ever-increasing market share. These merchants demand the following:

◆ *Better terms.* They drive hard bargains for deep discounts, and sometimes even free goods, from suppliers.
◆ *Cost sharing.* Retailers conserve cash by forcing suppliers to bear the burden for such business costs as advertising and resetting store displays.
◆ *Retroactive cash payments from vendors.* Smaller firms often pay higher prices for merchandise than do larger companies. When large retailers purchase smaller ones, they often seek retroactive pricing. Under this arrangement, the supplier applies the lower price to the purchases made by the smaller retailer before the business consolidation took place: The supplier actually rebates cash to the combined company.

Observations

Discuss the implications of the large retailers' tactics on cash flows. Do you think these business practices are illegal? Are they unethical? Can smaller merchants survive? How?

---

[14] We assume these percentages for the sake of illustration; they are not logically derived. Percentages of different magnitude would result in greater (or less) variability between efficient and inefficient operations.

OPERATING CASH FLOW TRENDS

One year's data provide insufficient information with which to assess operating cycle performance. Trends provide more information than do individual observations. Exhibit 10-5 extends the data from Exhibit 10-4 four years to demonstrate stability, efficiency, and inefficiency of cash receipts over time. (2000 base year data are excluded.)

Exhibit 10-5 demonstrates stable, increasing, and decreasing trends in cash collected from sales.[15] Stability helps project future cash flows. Analysts generally value efficient receivables collections because they improve corporate liquidity over time. The last data set of Exhibit 10-5 demonstrates the problem with ineffi-

EXHIBIT 10-5
eXTREMESTUFF.com
Operating Cash Inflow Trends

WEB
*E*XERCISE 7

Exhibit 10-5 presents revenue and receivable increases over time. Examine Apple Computer's Form 10-Ks from 1995 to 1998. Notice the change in revenues and receivables. Do you think account decreases affect the ability to analyze trends?

	2001	2002	2003	2004	2005
Operating Cycle Stability:					
Increase in sales revenues (20%)	$1,200.00[a]	$1,440.00	$1,728.00	$2,073.60	$2,488.32
Increase in accounts receivable (20%)	(24.00)	(28.80)	(34.56)	(41.47)	(49.77)
Cash received from customers	$1,176.00	$1,411.20	$1,693.44	$2,032.13	$2,438.55
Cash collected as a percentage of revenue	98.0%	98.0%	98.0%	98.0%	98.0%
Operating Cycle Efficiency:					
Increase in sales revenues (20%)	$1,200.00	$1,440.00	$1,728.00	$2,073.60	$2,488.32
Increase in accounts receivable (10%)	(12.00)	(13.20)	(14.52)	(15.97)	(17.57)
Cash received from customers	$1,188.00	$1,426.80	$1,713.48	$2,057.63	$2,470.75
Cash collected as a percentage of revenue	99.0%	99.1%	99.2%	99.2%	99.3%
Operating Cycle Inefficiency:					
Increase in sales revenues (20%)	$1,200.00	$1,440.00	$1,728.00	$2,073.60	$2,488.32
Increase in accounts receivable (40%)	(48.00)	(67.20)	(94.08)	(131.71)	(184.40)
Cash received from customers	$1,152.00	$1,372.80	$1,633.92	$1,941.89	$2,303.92
Cash collected as a percentage of revenue	96.0%	95.3%	94.6%	93.6%	92.6%

[a] Amounts are in thousands of dollars.

---

[15] Cash received as a percentage of revenues will equal precisely 98 percent when the annual percentage change for both accounts equals 20 percent. Varying that percentage from year to year (but maintaining the same percentage for revenues and receivables) will result in slight departures from 98 percent. These differences would not alter the conclusion of operating cycle stability.

cient cash collections. Liquidity suffers as eSTUFF collects fewer receivables in later years than in earlier years. The efficient and inefficient trend lines are reversed when analyzing cash paid for expenses. The percentage of expenses paid in cash decreases over time for efficient operations and increases for inefficient ones.

Analysts must understand the underlying corporate activities that produce cash flows. A firm may not be maximizing wealth, for example, if it is *too* efficient in collecting cash. A positive trend could result from an increasingly cautious credit policy. Such firms may be forgoing significant sales if they tighten credit terms over time. The competitive business climate usually precludes establishing overly conservative credit policies. A far more likely problem is an excessively aggressive credit policy, which decreases cash collections over time. The data in the lower third of Exhibit 10-5, for example, could represent eSTUFF's increasing failure to accrue realistic levels of bad debts. Such a trend reveals an even more distressing possibility: eSTUFF could have increasingly booked uncollectible sales. In this situation, the company has, at best, prematurely realized revenues or, at worst, fictitiously recorded sales. Neither prospect is very appealing.

OPERATING CASH FLOW AND LIQUIDITY

Exhibit 10-6 summarizes the liquidity (see Chapter 8) trend directions for stable, efficient, and inefficient operating cycle activity. (The behavior of cash received as a percentage of revenues (the top row of information) is covered in the discussion of Exhibit 10-5.)

Stable operations equate to consistency over time as cash and liquidity measures remain unchanged. Corporate liquidity and financial flexibility remain constant. Efficiently operating firms have increasing financial flexibility. An entity in this situation continually improves its ability to invest in unanticipated opportunities and finance unexpected problems without resorting to external funding. The trends in the inefficient operation column, however, do not bode well for a company. Sources of operating cash are decreasing but their uses are increasing in this circumstance. Liquidity and financial flexibility have, or will soon be, reduced to unacceptable levels.

EXHIBIT 10-6
Cash Flow and Liquidity Trends

MEASURE	STABLE OPERATIONS	EFFICIENT OPERATIONS	INEFFICIENT OPERATIONS
Cash received as a percentage of revenues	None	Increasing	Decreasing
Accounts receivable turnover	None	Increasing	Decreasing
Days in receivables	None	Decreasing	Increasing
Cash paid as a percentage of cost of goods sold	None	Decreasing	Increasing
Inventory turnover	None	Increasing	Decreasing
Days in inventory	None	Decreasing	Increasing
Accounts payable turnover	None	Decreasing	Increasing
Days in payables	None	Increasing	Decreasing
Inventory conversion cycle	None	Decreasing	Increasing
Net cash conversion cycle	None	Decreasing	Increasing

FORECASTING OPERATING CASH FLOWS

The preceding discussion of trends is overly simplified. Existing companies' CFOs do not move in the rigid patterns of Exhibit 10-5 or behave in the continuous manner implied by Exhibit 10-6. Assessing trends, however, can help you gauge the amount, timing, and probability of future cash flows. You can also use the information to assess a firm's ability to pay maturing obligations and need for future financing.

When forecasting, you should consider past cash flow trends, alternative future scenarios, and probable outcomes. The next step is to ask the right questions. The two most prominent ones are these:

◆ Will operating revenues and expenses increase, decrease, or remain constant?
◆ Will changes in current accounts equal those of their income statement counterparts?

Answers are difficult because many factors affect the future. You must forecast selling prices, component costs, consumer demand, market growth, and product introductions. At this point in the text, forecasting CFOs is premature because many of those items are addressed in subsequent chapters. The objective of cash forecasting at this point is to begin focusing on alternative outcomes and the probability that they will occur.

WHAT'S YOUR ANALYSIS

CASHING IN ON A HOME RUN

Biogen, Inc., became the second largest U.S. biotechnology firm in 1999, based on its market capitalization.ᵃ How confident would you be forecasting the company's future cash flows?

The meteoric rise of the company is attributable to the success of one medication: Avonex, a multiple sclerosis (MS) drug, accounted for 80 percent of the company's operating cash flows and revenues. Biogen's market value tripled in three years to $10.8 billion in 1999.ᵇ Its financial performance (in millions of dollars) illustrates why the market values Biogen so highly:

	1998	1997	1996
Sales revenues	$557	$411	$259
Net income	138	89	40
Cash flows from operations	167	97	42
Total assets	924	813	634

In essence, operating cash flows and income more than tripled on a doubling of revenues and a 50 percent increase in assets. This financial performance attests to the success of one blockbuster product. Biogen's exclusive right to sell the medication, or *orphan status* as granted by the Food and Drug Administration, expires in 2003. Competitors are waiting in the wings with copycat drugs. Analysts might contend that forecasting Biogen's future cash flows may be nearly as complex as the company's bioengineering feats, due to the uncertainty of future operations.

Observations

Discuss why you would have to consider the following factors in forecasting Biogen's cash flows:

- How well the Avonex market is protected
- Whether Biogen has penetrated the MS market further with complementary products
- Whether Biogen has developed a diversified revenue base
- If Biogen has created other blockbuster products

---

[a] Market capitalization equals the number of shares of stock outstanding multiplied by the stock's market price per share.

[b] Johanes, L., "Biogen Searches for Another Blockbuster Medication," *Wall Street Journal*, August 13, 1999, p. B4.

APPLE COMPUTER AND THE PERSONAL COMPUTER INDUSTRY

We now present an introductory analysis of the PC industry's cash flows. The discussion centers on the four firms' operating cash flows. We present operating, investing, and financing cash flow activities along with the industry's net cash flows as background information. These disclosures provide evidence of the industry's life cycle stage. We then examine operating cash flows in greater detail. Next, we convert Apple Computer's indirect CFOs to the direct method of reporting. We conclude by examining the industry's ability to collect cash and pay for components from selling PCs.

INDUSTRY CASH FLOWS

Exhibits 10-7A and 10-7B present annual aggregate cash flows of the four PC companies analyzed here. Exhibit 10-7A presents their accumulated cash flows from operating, investing, and financing activities. Exhibit 10-7B summarizes those activities by disclosing annual net cash flows for the four firms.

Exhibits 10-7A and 10-7B amply demonstrate the lack of clearly defined cash trends. The data graphed in Exhibits 10-7A and 10-7B, however, indicate that the PC industry was neither emerging nor declining from 1993 to 1998. One might argue whether the industry was growing, maturing, or transitioning from growth to maturity during the period analyzed, but such classifications are somewhat arbitrary and irrelevant. What is important to realize is that the industry was in midlife; its firms were facing opportunities and challenges associated with established entities.

Operating cash flows for the four PC firms became increasingly positive, on the whole, during the period of analysis. Cash flows from investing activities, on the other hand, declined markedly. Greater amounts of cash were used for financing activities over time, although the trend was inconsistent. Cash among the four companies increased during the period analyzed. This growth was partially offset by the four firms' $1.3 billion 1998 net cash loss.

Exhibits 10-7A and 10-7B merely provides a context for analyzing cash flows. Its graphs do not provide many significant insights. For purposes of this introductory cash analysis, note the following:

- Cash flows were inconsistent.
- The industry matured, despite cash flow variability (refer to Exhibit 10-1).
- We need to analyze cash flow and its relation to liquidity directly to improve our understanding of the industry's operating activities.

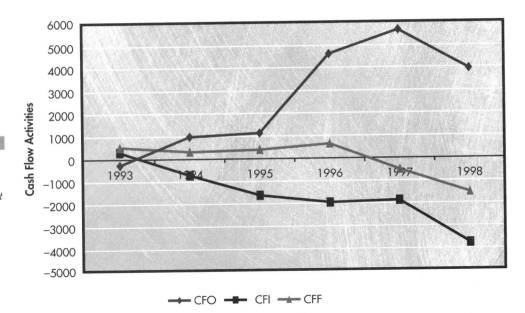

*Compaq Computer generated
$3.7 billion in CFOs in 1997 but
only $650 million the next year.
This dramatic decrease in the
largest PC company's cash performance accounted for the
decline in 1998 industry CFOs
and negative net cash flows.*

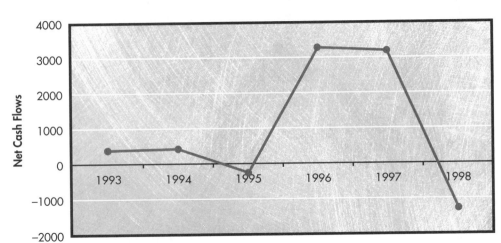

*Apple Computer's indirect CFOs
reported a decrease of $72 million
in accounts receivable during
1998; yet it reported receivables
on the balance sheet at $1.035
billion at the beginning of the
year and $955 million at fiscal
year-end (a difference of $80 mil-
lion). Discuss whether the $8
million discrepancy in receivables matters to your analysis.*

APPLE COMPUTER'S DIRECT OPERATING CASH FLOWS

All four firms disclosed cash flows from operations on an indirect basis. We convert Apple Computer's CFOs to a direct basis to illustrate that method's information content. Exhibit 10-8 presents Apple's 1998 cash receipts and disbursements for individual items and the net CFOs provided by manufacturing and
selling PCs.[16]

---

[16] We took account changes from Apple's indirect CFOs as reported in its 1998 Form 10-K. A few of the
Form 10-K disclosures differ slightly from those presented in Apple's statement of cash flows in
Appendix A. In addition, a few current accounts changes per the statement of cash flows differed
slightly from balance sheet account changes. These differences are usually immaterial and should not
concern the analyst.

		TOTALS
Cash Inflows:		
Sales revenue	$5,941[a]	
Decrease in accounts receivable	72	$6,013
Other revenue	68	
Gains arising from equity investments	(40)	28
Cash Outflows:		
Cost of goods sold	4,462	
Decrease in inventory	(359)	
Increase in accounts payable	(34)	4,069
Operating expenses	1,218	
Depreciation	(111)	
Decrease in other current assets	(31)	
Decrease in other assets	(83)	
Decrease in other current liabilities	85	
Decrease in restructuring cost	107	
Increase in in-process research and development	(7)	1,178
Tax expense	20	
Decrease in deferred taxes	(1)	19
Cash Flows from Operating Activities		
Cash received from:		
Customers	$6,013	
Other sources	28	
Total cash provided by operations		6,041
Cash Paid:		
To suppliers	4,069	
For operating expenses	1,178	
For taxes	19	
Total cash used in operations		5,266
Net Cash Flows from Operating Activities		**$775**

[a] All amounts are in millions of dollars.

WEB *EXERCISE 8*

Examine Apple Computer's most recent cash flow statement. Identify any CFO disclosures that differ from those in Exhibit 10-8. Discuss how you would account for them when converting to a direct CFO basis.

OPERATING CYCLE CASH FLOWS

Apple's CFOs reported on a direct basis equal that of the indirect method ($775 million). As mentioned previously, however, operating cash flows should be converted when the benefits of doing so outweigh the costs. Conversion can be a timely and complicated endeavor, especially if a company has engaged in numerous complex transactions. The process of converting the entire first section of the cash flow statement, therefore, may not be in the analyst's best interest.

A compromise does exist. Industry factors and liquidity data indicate that meeting market demands for PCs was a major determinant in corporate success during the period analyzed. Rapid technological change, price decreases, and cost-conscious consumers mandated manufacturing and distribution effectiveness. To a great extent, efficient inventory and receivable turnover, or operating cycle management, drove the industry. Therefore, cash collected from customers and paid to suppliers provides insights about performance in the PC industry. Information gathered from the background of the industry (Chapter 5) and the analysis of the liquidity (Chapters 8 and 9) support this contention. We can compute the direct cash flows from these informative activities to assist analysis.

EXHIBIT 10-9A
Operating Cash Received and Paid
1994–1998

	1998	1997	1996	1995	1994	WEIGHTED AVERAGE
Apple Computer						
Cash received from customers	$6,021[a]	$7,542	$10,268	$10,712	$8,988	
Cash received as a percentage of revenues[b]	101.3%	106.5%	104.4%	96.8%	97.8%	101.0%
Cash paid to suppliers	4,069	5,594	8,126	8,607	6,287	
Cash paid as a percentage of COGS[c]	91.2	97.9	91.7	104.9	91.9	95.9%
Compaq						
Cash received from customers	27,070	25,411	19,432	15,821	9,956	
Cash received as a percentage of revenues	86.8	103.4	97.1	94.9	91.6	94.6%
Cash paid to suppliers	23,015	17,397	13,247	11,951	8,770	
Cash paid as a percentage of COGS	96.0	97.6	89.2	97.2	107.8	96.5%
Dell						
Cash received from customers	11,744	7,582	5,108	3,347	2,837	
Cash received as a percentage	95.5	97.7	96.5	96.3	98.8	96.5%
Cash paid to suppliers	8,984	5,341	4,302	2,689	2,370	
Cash paid as a percentage of COGS	93.3	87.7	101.7	98.3	97.1	94.4%
Gateway						
Cash received from customers	7,419	6,232	4,992	3,523	2,618	
Cash received as a percentage of revenues	99.4	99.0	99.2	95.8	96.9	98.5%
Cash paid to suppliers	5,609	5,111	3,978	3,122	2,228	
Cash paid as a percentage of COGS	94.7	98.0	97.0	101.7	95.1	97.1%

[a] All dollar amounts are in millions, and current account changes are derived from balance sheets.
[b] Cash received from customers/sales revenue.
[c] Cash paid to suppliers/cost of goods sold.

WEB EXERCISE 9

Update Apple's cash received as a percentage of revenues from 1999 until the most recent year disclosed. Do you detect a trend?

EXHIBIT 10-9B

Cash Received as a Percentage of Revenues 1994–1998

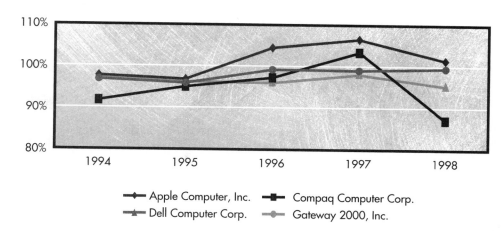

EXHIBIT 10-9C

Cash Paid as Percentage of Cost of Goods Sold 1994–1998

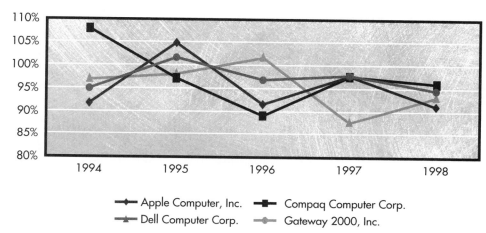

Exhibits 10-9A, 10-9B, and 10-9C present data from the PC manufacturers for the last five years reported.[17] Exhibit 10-9A reports the dollar and percentage amounts, as well as 5-year weighted average percentages, in tabular form, and Exhibits 10-9B and 10-9C graphically present cash inflows and outflows.

MICRO ANALYSIS 11

Gateway sells its computers at its Gateway Country Stores as well as on the Internet. The company uses these retail centers to sell extended warranties, provide repair services, and instruct its customers about Gateway PCs. The additional distribution channel and product extensions illustrate corporate behavior in a maturing market.

ANALYSIS OF OPERATING CYCLE CASH FLOWS

Competitive pressures required better management of corporate resources as the industry matured. Companies could no longer afford to tie up large amounts of cash in inventories and receivables, so PC manufacturers aggressively sought to minimize inventories and receivables during that time period. Those current account changes, in turn, affected operating cash flows. Note, for example, that

[17] We computed cash received and paid by adjusting accrual accounts with changes in current accounts as reported on corporate balance sheets. In some instances, these amounts differed slightly from those reported on statements of cash flows. Note, for example, Apple's 1998 cash received from customers is listed as $6,021,000 in Exhibit 10-9A but $6,013,000 in Exhibit 10-8. The difference results because accounts receivable decreased by $80 million per the balance sheet disclosures ($1.035 billion in 1997 and $955 million in 1998), and by $72 million per the 1998 statement of cash flows. Such discrepancies usually are immaterial.

cash paid as a percentage of cost of goods sold was relatively low in 1997 and 1998 throughout the industry. Every company paid less for sales costs in those years than they reported as cost of goods sold. Inventory reductions accounted for much of the low cash payments. That trend, however, could not continue indefinitely, because inventories cannot fall below zero! In subsequent years cash paid for supplies throughout the industry should become more closely correlated with cost of goods sold.

The data indicate that Dell and Gateway collected cash and paid suppliers more consistently than Apple and Compaq did. The annual percentages for Dell and Gateway clustered around their five-year weighted averages. Such was not the case for Apple and Compaq. The graphs in Exhibits 10-9B and 10-9C reinforce the numerical disclosures of Exhibit 10-9A. These three exhibits present results similar to liquidity analysis (Chapters 8 and 9). Exhibit 9-7, for example, reported greater liquidity levels and stability for Gateway and Dell than the other two PC firms. Consequently, forecasting cash received from customers and paid to vendors for Gateway and Dell is easier than doing so for Apple and Compaq, after revenues and cost of sales have been projected.

The data reveal peculiar results for Compaq and Apple. Compaq Computer, for example, had a relatively weak cash position. Compaq ranked last in percentage of cash collected from sales but second (behind Gateway) in percentage of cash paid for inventory. The largest of the four companies (in terms of revenues) was the only firm whose cash payments percentage (96.5 percent) exceeded its cash receipts percentage (94.6 percent). Moreover, the greatest discrepancy between these two percentages occurred in 1998 (cash paid was 107.8 percent and cash received was 91.6 percent). Those unfavorable cash flow numbers reinforce Compaq's poor liquidity index (Exhibit 9-7) and lagging activity measures (Chapter 8).[18] They also signal potential financial problems in the future.

Apple Computer's 1996-1998 levels of cash receipts were unsustainable. No company can collect more than 100 percent of its receivables in cash in the long run! Apple's cash collections, coupled with its bad debt disclosures (discussed in Chapter 9), however, indicate the firm's ability to collect its credit sales. One could infer from the data that Apple Computer's revenue and bad debt expense recognition policies were adequate. The company did not prematurely book revenues, and it made adequate provisions for uncollectible accounts.

Apple Computer conserved cash by reducing inventory (from $1.8 billion in 1995 to $78 million in 1998) during the period analyzed. This practice had also virtually run its course by the end of 1998. To a great extent, inventory and receivable reductions, rather than profitable computer sales, drove Apple CFOs. Its future operating cash flow will not benefit from such practices.

SUMMARY

This chapter introduces cash flow analysis. We begin by discussing the concept of business life cycles and relating cash flows to each stage in a firm's existence. We then review cash acquisition and allocation in the context of financing and investing decisions, and discuss the critical role of operating cash flows. We note that a

---

[18] A high liquidity index equals low (poor) liquidity, as discussed in Chapter 9.

firm must generate sufficient cash from core activities, such as selling products and providing services, to prosper. Converting indirect CFOs to the direct basis is one means of increasing CFO information content. Data from eSTUFF illustrate the conversion process. We modify eSTUFF's CFOs to indicate stable, efficient, and inefficient cash flow trends. These trends result from the interaction between accrual income statement accounts, such as revenues and cost of goods sold, and changes in current balance sheet accounts, such as accounts receivable, inventory, and accounts payable.

The last section presents an introductory analysis of the PC industry's cash flows. Evidence from the four firms' composite cash flows indicate a maturing industry. Their cash flows from operations, financing, and investing activities, however, lack the clearly delineated trends of the theoretical model presented in Exhibit 10-2. Data indicate that Dell and Gateway produced cash more consistently than Compaq and Apple did. Compaq lagged its counterparts with respect to cash collections and payments. Apple Computer's positive CFOs resulted, to a great extent, from inventory and receivable reductions.

KEY TERMS

Amount of future cash flows	Indirect method of operating cash flows
Business life cycle	Maturity (life cycle stage)
Cash flow analysis	Operating cycle efficiency
Decline (life cycle stage)	Operating cycle inefficiency
Direct method of operating cash flows	Operating cycle stability
Emergence (life cycle stage)	Timing of future cash flows
Growth (life cycle stage)	Uncertainty of future cash flows

NUMERICAL CASE

10-1

eXTREMESTUFF.com

Numerical case 3-2 at the end of Chapter 3 extends eSTUFF's financial statements through 2003. Use that data to do the following:

a. Provide evidence that eSTUFF is in the emerging stage of its business life cycle.
b. Convert CFOs reported on the indirect method to the direct basis for 2002 and 2003.
c. Evaluate cash received as a percentage of revenues and cash paid as a percentage of cost of goods sold from 2000 to 2003. Do you detect any trends in these cash flows? If so, has eSTUFF demonstrated stability, efficiency, or inefficiency in its operations?

INDUSTRY CASES

Use the industry information and corporate financial statements presented in the appendixes to answer the following:

a. Determine the business life cycle stage of the industry based on the abbreviated statements of cash flows for the firms within the industry.

b. Compute and analyze cash received as a percentage of revenues from 1994 to 1998 for each company.

c. Compute and analyze cash paid as a percentage of cost of goods sold from 1994 to 1998 for each company.

d. Identify any operating cycle cash flow trends.

e. Prepare an analysis of operating cash flow analysis for the industry. Compare and contrast the CFOs of the firms in each industry.

10-1 *Personal Computers: Apple, Compaq, Dell, and Gateway*

10-2 *Airlines: American, Delta, and United*

10-3 *Athletic Footwear: Nike and Reebok*

10-4 *Discount Retailers: Kmart, Target, and Wal-Mart*

10-5 *Fast-Food Restaurants: McDonald's and Wendy's*

10-6 *Soft Drink Companies: Coca-Cola and PepsiCo.*

INDUSTRY INTERNET CASES

Extend your operating cash flow industry case analyses by incorporating financial statement disclosures from 1999 through the most recent year. Research and note any substantial changes in the economy and industry that could affect cash flows. Incorporate those changes into your analyses. (Financial statement disclosures may not be the same as those presented in the appendixes. Use your judgment to make the necessary modifications.)

10-1 *Personal Computers: Apple, Compaq, Dell, and Gateway*

10-2 *Airlines: American, Delta, and United*

10-3 *Athletic Footwear: Nike and Reebok*

10-4 *Discount Retailers: Kmart, Target, and Wal-Mart*

10-5 *Fast-Food Restaurants: McDonald's and Wendy's*

10-6 *Soft Drink Companies: Coca-Cola and PepsiCo.*

11

ADVANCED CASH FLOW ANALYSIS

CHAPTER LEARNING OBJECTIVES

Upon completion of this chapter, you should be able to:

◆ *Explain the importance of investing and financing cash flows.*

◆ *Relate cash flows from investing and financing activities to those from operations.*

◆ *Describe an entity's need for sufficient and efficient cash flows.*

◆ *List and compute measures of cash sufficiency and efficiency.*

◆ *Provide an in-depth analysis of corporate and industry cash flows.*

S uccessful companies collect more cash than they pay out from business operations. Financing and investing decisions make those cash flows possible. Financing activities provide funds for asset acquisitions. Those resources generate cash when judiciously invested. Some of the cash produced by operations, in turn, compensates creditors and owners for their investments. This chapter continues cash analysis by examining the relationship among operating, investing, and financing cash flows. The first section discusses investing and financing activities. The next portion integrates financing and investing activities with those from operations, using cash performance measures to evaluate data from eSTUFF. The final section extends cash flow analysis of the personal computer (PC) industry.

CASH FLOWS FROM INVESTING AND FINANCING ACTIVITIES

Investing and financing disclosures summarize long-term sources and uses of cash. The second and third sections of the cash flow statement report investing and financing history. (Recall that the first section reports operating cash flows.) Analysts judge how well past cash acquisitions and allocations created value and project their role in future wealth maximization efforts.

INTERNET RETAILING AND THE NEED FOR CASH

Internet retailers presented attractive investment opportunities at the end of the 20th century, according to many investors. The financial performance of some new economy merchants quickly changed that opinion. Cash flows did not meet either the investors' or the e-tailers' expectations. What is your analysis of the situation?

Internet retailers' inherent advantage over traditional store-based retailers is that large amounts of cash do not have to be invested in costly fixed assets. *Brick* businesses were outdated, and Internet *clicks* constituted the new retailing business model, according to many entrepreneurs and investors. The majority of retailing would be conducted over the Internet, or so they thought. By 2000 some things had changed. Consider the fate of these e-tailers:

Examine Overstock.com's home page to find out more about how a liquidator of Internet retail business operates.

◆ Pets.com, a retailer of pet supplies, went out of business. It was the first publicly traded Internet company to fail.
◆ Eve.com, a beauty products concern, ceased operations.
◆ Living.com could not sell enough furniture to remain in business.
◆ Kibu.com, an Internet site selling merchandise to teenage girls, closed its doors.
◆ Mortgage.com, dedicated to lending money to homeowners, went out of business.
◆ Toysmart.com experienced a similar fate trying to peddle toys.

Each doomed Internet retailer frantically sought additional cash from investors as it neared bankruptcy. These merchants claimed additional cash from financing activities was needed to continue operations until their businesses became successful. Investors, however, began questioning the wisdom of providing additional funding to firms that were failing to generate operating cash. Analysts raised concerns about the viability of many e-tailers' business models. Each company that went out of business cited an inability to secure sufficient financing as a key reason for its demise.

Observations

How do you think cash flows from investing activities differ between an Internet retailer and a traditional retail store merchant? What is the life-cycle stage of Internet retailers? Given that life-cycle stage, was it unusual for the firms to need cash from financing activities?

Do you think using cash from financing activities to fund business operations is a viable long-run strategy? Why do you think investors were reluctant to provide further cash to those e-tailers? How do you think Internet retailers would use the cash, assuming they were able to get it?

CASH FLOWS FROM INVESTING ACTIVITIES

Property, plant, and equipment constitute the tangible productive base of an entity. These resources help build wealth through product creation, development, and distribution. The entity uses cash to acquire fixed assets, and sometimes it receives cash when those resources are sold. Intangible assets also produce cash by granting companies exclusive rights to make, use, or do something. Companies spend cash to obtain those entitlements. Financial investments, both current and long term, offer an earning alternative to otherwise idle cash. Companies use cash to purchase other entities' debt and equity securities. They receive cash in the form of interest and dividends and from securities' sales.[1]

Cash flows from investing activities (CFIs) are reported after operating cash flows.[2] This section of the cash flow statement discloses the acquisition, replenishment, and retirement of a firm's productive resources during a reporting period. Analysts examine this portion of the statement to gain perspective about whether the following are true:

◆ The company acquired property, plant, and equipment in a timely manner.
◆ Production upgrades and expansion improved the entity's competitive position.
◆ The benefits derived from intangible resources outweighed their cost.
◆ Security investments employed cash productively but prudently.
◆ Future investments will mirror past ones.

In short, analysts begin to assess asset productivity with information provided by the middle section of the cash flow statement.[3] They judge whether past asset acquisitions and disposals were warranted and forecast future cash disbursements and receipts in these areas.

An entity's age influences cash flows from investing activities, as noted in Chapter 10. Emerging firms and industries use cash to invest heavily in productive resources. That trend reverses itself as the entity matures. Established firms

---

[1] As noted in Chapter 7, equity investments generate dividend income and debt securities produce interest income.

[2] Arguably, cash flow statements should address cash flows from financing activities before investing activities. Initial financing precedes initial investments, as discussed in the business modeling section of Chapter 8 (Exhibits 8-1 and 8-2). This text examines cash flows from investment first because going concerns generate and use cash from both their investing and financing activities. Moreover, cash flow statements disclose investing activities before financing ones.

[3] We extend the discussion of asset productivity analysis in Chapter 13.

usually receive more cash than they use from their investments (refer to Exhibits 10-1 and 10-2). In addition, resource acquisition and disposal can dramatically affect cash flows for a specific reporting period. These transactions often involve significant amounts of money. Buying buildings and selling an ownership position in another firm, for example, create large changes in cash flows. Moreover, those purchases might not be repeated in the next year. Like operating cash flows, CFIs may exhibit instability from one reporting period to the next, but their behavior tends to relate to life-cycle phase.

Data from eSTUFF provide an example of how CFIs exhibit life-cycle behavior. The e-tailer spent substantial amounts of cash in its first two years of operations buying long-term assets: $525,000 in 2000 and $100,000 in the next year. Large cash expenditures are normal for a business start-up. As a new firm, eSTUFF had to establish productive capabilities; failure to do so would have resulted in few, if any, revenues and operating cash flows. Our hypothetical retailer had to acquire the assets that enabled it to sell inventory. The relatively large expenditures for tangible and intangible resources, in other words, allowed eSTUFF to compete in the marketplace.

A critical factor in CFI analysis is assessing value produced from those expenditures. Success depends on revenues realized, income earned, and operating cash generated compared with those assets' cost. Analysts must judge whether the sacrifices made to acquire the means of production were worth it and what future expenditures will be needed to run the business.

CASH FLOWS FROM FINANCING ACTIVITIES

The third major section of the cash flow statement reports a company's financing activities. *Cash flows from financing activities (CFFs)* disclose cash generated from debt and equity issues, and the cash used to retire them. It also reports cash distributions to shareholders as compensation for their investments. Analysts determine whether the amounts and trends of an entity's financing activities seem reasonable in light of the surrounding circumstances. They also project the amount and timing of future cash flows to and from investors.

Similar to investing activities, CFFs correlate to a life-cycle stage. New businesses, for example, require extensive **external financing**. Shareholders and creditors contribute cash to acquire assets and launch business operations in these instances. An established entity, on the other hand, has fewer needs for external financing than an emerging enterprise. Mature firms usually generate significant cash flows by selling goods and providing services. These activities are sources of **internal financing**. Established companies sometimes use these funds to reduce external financing by retiring debt and purchasing **treasury stock**. Debt retirement reduces a firm's obligations to long-term creditors. In treasury stock arrangements, a company acquires previously issued shares of its own stock. It can either retire those shares or reissue them at a later date. Treasury shares held for reissue temporarily reduce owners' equity, but retired shares permanently contract business capitalization.

Dividends reduce corporate cash balances and retained earnings.[4] These cash distributions are a return to the shareholders on their investment. Analysts assess whether cash transfers to owners were justified and then try to forecast future div-

WEB EXERCISE 3

Compare the CFIs of booksellers Amazon.com and Barnes & Noble by locating investor relations at the companies' Web sites at amazon.com and bn.com. Do you think the firms are at comparable life-cycle stages?

MICRO ANALYSIS 3

Venture capitalists provided over $50 billion of financing to Internet start-ups in 2000, according to research firm VentureOne.

WEB EXERCISE 4

Examine the CFFs for Amazon.com and Barnes & Noble. Do these cash flows support your conclusion about their respective life-cycle stages?

MICRO ANALYSIS 4

Xerox reduced its dividend from 20 cents to 5 cents a share when it decided to sell some of its assets. The dividend reduction conserved $400 million in cash per year. Do you think the company's plans to alter business strategies influenced dividend policy? What was the implication of the dividend reduction on cash flows from financing activities?

---

[4] A *declaration* of dividends reduces retained earnings, but their *payment* decreases cash. A short period of time exists between these two dates, during which the shareholders entitled to receive the dividend (owners as of the date of record) are established.

WEB EXERCISE 5

Find out what Xerox's current dividend is by going to xerox.com.

idend prospects. A firm with ample cash, and without many alternative uses for it, is well positioned to pay dividends. Conversely, less-liquid companies are better served by finding other uses for their scarce resource. An entity's life stage correlates to dividend payments. Mature firms, on the whole, distribute more cash to shareholders than do fledgling enterprises.

eSTUFF generated $532,000 of cash from financing activities in 2000 and $178,000 in 2001. Those large CFIs are not surprising. The new business needed significant cash infusions from shareholders and lenders to buy fixed assets and begin operations. One could question, however, the logic of eSTUFF's dividend payments, despite the relatively small amounts. On one hand, the company is securing financing to launch the business, but on the other, it is distributing a portion of earnings back to shareholders. Cash generated from business activities, arguably, could be better used to reduce external financing or as an additional funding source.

CASH EARNING PER SHARE

WHAT'S YOUR ANALYSIS

Earnings per share (EPS) are computed by dividing net income by shares of common stock, according to generally accepted accounting principles (GAAP). An alternative practice has emerged to GAAP-based EPS. What is your interpretation of its value?

Cash EPS is gaining acceptance from companies and analysts as a useful alternative to accrual-based EPS calculations.[a] Merger activity has pushed cash EPS to the forefront of the financial reporting vanguard. Premium purchase prices have created enormous amounts of goodwill on many consolidated companies' balance sheets. Amortization of these costs reduces current and future earnings. To compensate, some individuals think companies should add noncash expenses to income when computing EPS. They would then use the resulting *earnings before depreciation and amortization (EBDA)* as the numerator for cash-based EPS. Some advocates of cash-based EPS also add back taxes when approximating cash flows, thereby yielding earnings before taxes, depreciation, and amortization (EBTDA). Earnings before interest, taxes, depreciation, and amortization—EBITDA—is yet another measure.

Proponents claim cash-based EPS provides a more accurate representation of a firm's performance and reduces questionable accounting techniques that affect earnings. Opponents contend that cash EPS disclosures are not generally accepted and lack standardization. They argue that some cash EPS numbers result from EBDA, others from EBTDA, and yet others from EBITDA.

Observations

Do you think financial statement measures have to conform with GAAP to be useful to analysts? Assume that only amortization and depreciation expenses are added to net income to determine an approximation of operating cash flows. Do the results equal cash flows from operations in all cases? What is the fundamental difference in cash flows related to depreciation and amortization expenses and those for interest and taxes? Why do you think some advocates of cash EPS want to include interest and taxes in the cash EPS computation?

---

[a] "Pooling Method Dries up but Mergers May Go On," *Wall Street Journal*, September 23, 1999, pp. C2 and C3.

CASH FLOW RELATIONSHIPS

Established entities continually generate and use cash for investing and financing purposes. Notes to the financial statements, under captions such as "long-term debt" and "shareholders' equity," assist analysts in relating cash flows from financing and investing activities. Management's discussion and analysis of the firm's financial condition also provides information under captions such as "liquidity and capital resources" and "disclosures about market risk." Companies often disclose significant financing and investing activities before the transactions take place. The financial media report those impending economic events. These information sources provide the analyst with future sources and uses of cash, as opposed to the historic ones contained in Form 10-K.

Cash provided by financing activities often corresponds to that used by emerging enterprises for investment purposes. eSTUFF, for instance, issued $420,000 of common stock and borrowed $120,000 in 2000. The company purchased $525,000 of tangible and intangible assets in that year. A reasonable inference is that the equity and debt issues financed those acquisitions. Lack of internally generated cash (cash flows from operations) supports the contention that eSTUFF needed and used external financing to acquire long-term assets. Causal relationship between financing sources and investment uses becomes more difficult to detect as firms mature. For example, it is impossible to determine from Exhibit 3-1 the funding source for eSTUFF's $100,000 equipment purchase in 2000.

You should not be overly concerned with attributing a specific cash source to an explicit use for it. What ultimately matters is that an enterprise produces acceptable operating cash flows to sustain operations, ensure productivity, and compensate investors. Therefore, analysts need to understand the relationship between operating cash flows and those from investing and financing activities. The next section examines those links and introduces a series of financial statement measures that help relate the three aspects of cash flow.

CASH FLOW MEASURES

Analysts are concerned with the overall sufficiency and efficiency of cash flows. We can measure these two characteristics numerically. Although not as numerous or well known as their liquidity counterparts, cash flow ratios exist.[5] They relate CFOs with either another section of the cash flow statement or an income statement or balance sheet disclosure. This section uses data from eSTUFF to demonstrate the primary cash sufficiency ratio and its components, additional cash sufficiency measures, and cash efficiency ratios.

PRIMARY CASH SUFFICIENCY MEASURES

An entity must produce enough cash to compensate investors and maintain its productive capacity. **Cash sufficiency measures** quantify this ability. Analysts combine relative amounts of cash with other data to judge a firm's ability to meet

---

[5] Based on D.E. Giacomino and D.E. Mielke, "Cash Flows: Another Approach to Ratio Analysis," *Journal of Accountancy,* March 1993, pp. 55–58.

MICRO *A*NALYSIS 8

Companies often adjust operations to generate sufficient cash flow. Troubled automobile manufacturers Nissan and Mazda, for example, revamped purchasing procedures in the late 1990s to lower costs and conserve cash.

MICRO *A*NALYSIS 9

Nissan and Mazda, citing an overcapacity in the auto market, did not reinvest in manufacturing facilities. They made these decisions as part of the overall strategy that also altered materials acquisitions. Management curtailed reinvestment as another means of increasing cash flow.

its needs. **Cash flow adequacy** is the primary measure of an enterprise's ability to establish or replenish its productive base, pay long-term debt, and make distributions to owners. We compute this ratio as follows:

$$\text{Cash flow adequacy} = \frac{\text{Cash flow from operations}}{\text{Fixed assets purchased} + \text{long-term debt paid} + \text{cash dividends distributed}}$$

A ratio of one or more provides evidence that a firm's operating cash flows were sufficient to replace obsolete resources, meet contractual obligations to creditors, and compensate owners for their investment. A ratio of less than one has the opposite meaning. Viewed another way, if the numerator of the cash flow adequacy ratio exceeds its denominator, the company produced excess cash from business operations in a reporting period. The incremental cash flows produced by ongoing business activities are referred to as **discretionary cash flows**. They add liquidity to the firm and increase its financial flexibility. A company's liquidity and flexibility is diminished, in contrast, when the measure's denominator exceeds its numerator.

The components of cash flow adequacy provide further insight into an entity's ability to produce adequate cash flows. The **reinvestment ratio** measures the amount of operating cash used to replenish the productive base of an enterprise.[6] The **long-term debt payment ratio** computes the percentage of cash needed to pay long-term debt maturities. The **dividend payout ratio** reports the proportion of operating cash flows distributed to shareholders. We calculate these cash adequacy ratios as follows:

$$\text{Reinvestment ratio} = \frac{\text{fixed assets purchased}}{\text{cash flow from operations}}$$

$$\text{Long-term debt repayment ratio} = \frac{\text{long-term debt paid}}{\text{cash flow from operations}}$$

$$\text{Dividend payout ratio} = \frac{\text{cash dividends paid}}{\text{cash flow from operations}}$$

Unlike the overall cash flow adequacy measure, analysts favor small results when evaluating component ratios.[7]

Exhibit 11-1 shows the cash flow adequacy ratio and its components for eSTUFF. (Remember that the business is in the emerging life-cycle stage.[8]) The data from the exhibit indicate insufficient cash generated from operations during

---

[6] This book defines fixed assets as both tangible and intangible resources. Other sources measure reinvestment more narrowly (e.g., property, plant, and equipment / cash from operations). We use the broader ratio because intangible assets increasingly represent productive resources, especially as the economy shifts from an industrial to information base.

[7] This statement holds because the numerator and denominator in component measures are reversed from that of the overall sufficiency ratio. They are inverted to prevent mathematical confusion. In many reporting periods, one or more of the components of cash flow adequacy are zero. It is easier to understand the result of a measure when zero appears in the numerator rather than the denominator.

[8] We include ratios for 2000 because negative CFOs in 2001 could hinder analysis.

EXHIBIT 11-1

RATIO	2001	2000
Cash flow adequacy	−$63[a] / ($100 + $0 + $2) = -61.8%	$23 / ($525 + 0 + $8) = 4.3%
Reinvestment	$100 / −$63 = −158.7%	$525 / $23 = 2,283%
Long-term debt payment	$0 / −$63 = 0%	$0 / $23 = 0%
Dividend payout	$2 / −$63 = -3.2%	$8 / $23 = 34.8%

[a] Dollar amounts in thousands.

the first two years of business—not surprising, given eSTUFF's status as a new entity. The start-up's cash was inadequate for all measures in 2001, due to net operating cash outflows in that year. The e-tailer's ability to generate sufficient cash to purchase fixed assets and pay dividends was not much better in the previous reporting period. The cash flow adequacy ratio of 4.3 percent means that eSTUFF produced only four cents of cash from operations for every dollar needed to cover legal and economic obligations. The extremely large reinvestment ratio (2,283 percent) is the primary cause of cash insufficiency in 2000. In the early years of business, we would expect this ratio to be quite high as companies invest heavily in fixed assets. In fact, the ratio is an *investment* ratio, rather than a *reinvestment* ratio, for an emerging enterprise.

OTHER CASH SUFFICIENCY MEASURES

There are three other cash sufficiency measures. One is an alternative to the cash flow adequacy ratio and the other two measure the significance of noncash expenses on operating cash flows.

Free cash flows represent net operating cash available to a company after it has maintained its productive capacity and met its financing obligations to shareholders. Its formula follows:

$$\text{Free cash flows} = \text{Cash flows from operations}$$
$$- (\text{capital expenditures for capital maintenance} + \text{dividends})$$

Free cash flows provide an analyst with another means of measuring an entity's ability to grow internally and increase its financial flexibility.[9] It is a firm's ability to take advantage of unanticipated opportunities and meet unexpected challenges quantified in dollars. This measure conventionally does not include long-term debt payment, unlike the cash flow adequacy ratio.[10] eSTUFF's free cash flows typify

---

[9] The free cash flow formula is somewhat difficult to implement because information about capital maintenance expenditures are difficult to obtain. Analysts use expenditures for property, plant, and equipment in their place. This measure, however, yields a more stringent estimation of free cash flows because it represents capital expansion as well as capital maintenance. (i.e., A portion of the cash is expended to increase productivity, rather than to maintain it.)

[10] Experts debate as to whether debt repayment should be part of cash sufficiency analysis. Companies often establish *sinking funds* to pay long-term debt. These long-term assets provide the necessary cash to retire debt, precluding the need to use current operating cash flows to do so. Free cash flow computations conventionally exclude debt payment, but cash flow adequacy ratios include it.

those for a start-up firm and reinforce the results produced by the cash flow adequacy ratio. The firm's free cash flows were –$510,000 ($23,000 –[$525,000 + $8,000]) in 2000 and –$165,000 (–$63,000 –[$100,000 + $2,000]) a year later.

Depreciation and amortization are noncash expenses. Recall that we add them to income when computing indirect CFOs and subtract them from operating expenses in calculating direct CFOs. The **depreciation impact ratio** measures the percentage of operating cash flows derived from the periodic cost allocation of long-term assets. It is computed as follows:

$$\text{Depreciation impact ratio} = \frac{\text{depreciation} + \text{amortization expense}}{\text{cash flow from operations}}$$

A small proportion of depreciation to operating cash indicates financial strength. Operating cash flows correlate with income numbers in these cases because the cash flow statement adjustment for noncash expenses is relatively small.[11] A disproportionately large depreciation impact ratio means there are significant differences between income and CFOs. Operating cash flow may appear healthy, but a wealth increase (as evidenced by the income numbers) has not occurred.

Analysts evaluate depreciation impact in conjunction with reinvestment. They expect to see a reinvestment ratio that exceeds that for depreciation impact. A **recapitalization index** compares these two ratios:

$$\text{Recapitalization index} = \frac{\text{reinvestment ratio}}{\text{depreciation impact ratio}}$$

MICRO ANALYSIS 10

The reinvestment ratio should usually exceed that of depreciation impact. Industry conditions, however, influence the numbers. When overcapacity exists, such as in the automobile industry, this condition does not necessarily hold. A sign of financial health for Nissan and Mazda, for example, could be that their respective depreciation impacts were greater than reinvestment during restructuring.

When the recapitalization index exceeds one, a company is investing more cash in plant and equipment than it is allocating for the past costs of productive assets. If depreciation impact is the larger of the two ratios, it signals that the organization is not maintaining and expanding long-term resources. This problem is compounded by the fact that buildings and machinery costs increase over time. Thus, the reinvestment ratio must not only equal the dividend impact ratio, it must be larger than the dividend impact ratio to compensate for inflation and firm expansion.

The depreciation impact ratios for eSTUFF's first two years of business are 457 percent ($105,000 / $23,000) in 2000 and –198 percent ($125,000 / –$63,000) in 2001. Its large positive ratio in 2000 and negative measure for the succeeding year mean the company had more depreciation and amortization expenses than CFOs. These results clearly indicate eSTUFF did not contribute sufficient cash from operations to replace fixed assets. Again, however, consider that eSTUFF is in the emerging life-cycle phase. Its capitalization index demonstrates the overstatement of its depreciation impact ratio. This index is 5.00 for 2000 (2283 percent / 457 percent), which means the company invested five times as much cash in the business as it allocated for the use of fixed assets.

CASH EFFICIENCY MEASURES

Companies acquire assets and make sales to produce cash. **Cash efficiency measures** provide data about the extent to which that desired effect has been achieved.

---

[11] This discussion assumes changes in current assets and liability accounts approximate changes in related income statement accounts.

There are three measures of cash efficiency: The **cash flow return on asset ratio** is the percentage of operating cash produced per invested dollar; the **cash flow return on sales ratio** reports CFOs generated from selling goods and providing services; and an **operations index** relates cash from operations to income from continuing operations. These ratios are calculated as follows:

$$\text{Cash flow return on assets} = \frac{\text{cash flow from operations}}{\text{total assets}}$$

$$\text{Cash flow return on sales} = \frac{\text{cash flow from operations}}{\text{revenues}}$$

$$\text{Operations index} = \frac{\text{cash flow from operations}}{\text{income from continuing operations}}$$

Large returns on assets and revenues indicate successful operations. The third efficiency measure, the operations index, compares cash flows generated from continual business operations with wealth changes produced by the same activity. Its denominator excludes aspects of comprehensive income produced by unusual and infrequent economic events. A high degree of correlation between the two operating measures provides evidence of cash efficiency and stable earnings.[12]

Exhibit 11-2 presents eSTUFF's cash efficiency measures for its first two years of business.[13] It is difficult to evaluate eSTUFF's cash efficiency without the benefit of either a significant time period or other companies to benchmark its measures. However, we do know that negative operating cash flows such as eSTUFF's 2001 CFOs, produce inefficient cash. The positive CFOs in 2000 resulted in better cash efficiency measures than those in the next year.

The conclusions reached from cash sufficiency measures help an analyst make inferences about cash efficiency. *Sufficiency* means an entity produced enough operating cash for its intended purposes. *Efficiency* is defined as achieving a desired result with a minimum of waste. Therefore, cash flow sufficiency is a necessary condition for efficient cash flows. Based on Exhibit 11-1, we would judge that eSTUFF generated insufficient cash flows from its 2000 and 2001 operations. Consequently, we would conclude that the company's cash measures were inefficient.

EXHIBIT 11-2
eSTUFF's Cash Efficiency Measures 2000 and 2001

RATIO	2001	2000
Cash flow return on assets	–$63[a] / $835 = –7.5%	$23 / $780 = 2.9%
Cash flow return on sales	–$63 / $1,200 = –5.3%	$23 / $1,000 = 2.3%
Operations index	–$63 / $55 = -1.15%	$23 / $65 = 35%

[a] Dollar amounts are in thousands.

---

[12] This material touches on the important concept of earnings quality, which is discussed extensively in Chapter 12.
[13] We used year-end assets to compute the cash flow return on asset ratios. Alternatively, we could have averaged asset amounts for the year.

FUTURE CASH FLOWS AND THE VALUE TRAP

The airline industry is cyclical: More people fly in good times than in bad. Business expansions produce healthy cash flows, but economic contractions reduce them. Air carriers' stock prices, however, sometimes don't reflect recent cash flows. How do you analyze the following situation, which has been referred to as a *value trap?*

Air carriers were flying high at the end of the 20th century. The commercial airline industry was reporting record cash flows. The air carriers' stock prices, however, were relatively low. Many analysts viewed this apparent paradox as an example of the classic value trap.[a] According to this theory, stocks of certain industries, such as airlines, are not as good an investment as they appear. Their low market prices reflected anticipated problems. Many investors believed air carriers' future cash flows would not match recent levels, due to a number of circumstances, such as the following:

◆ Rising fuel costs
◆ Expected increases for labor
◆ Antiquated air fleets

Some analysts were especially concerned about the airlines' purchase of new aircraft. Airlines had placed plane orders that would not only maintain but also expand their fleets. When the seating glut hit the market, according to analysts' reasoning, ticket price reductions would follow. Ensuing fare wars, combined with increases in operating costs, would reduce operating cash flows. In short, proponents of the value trap theory believed future cash flows would not match present levels. Airline stocks, in their view, correctly priced the value of the airlines' future cash flows.

Observations

Assume that analysts correctly anticipated higher fuel costs and wages. How would these events affect CFOs? What changes would you expect in cash sufficiency and efficiency measures? Would the purchase of new aircraft affect CFOs? Assume an airline bought aircraft in its next business year. How would those transactions affect its cash adequacy ratio and free cash flow? Explain how to use the depreciation impact and reinvestment ratios to analyze aircraft investment. If investors place value on future cash flows, then do past cash flows help analysis?

---

[a] McGough, R., "Airline Stocks Look Like Tantalizing Buys, But Earnings Descent May Cause Turbulence," *Wall Street Journal,* August 20, 1999, p. C2.

APPLE COMPUTER AND THE PERSONAL COMPUTER INDUSTRY

The PC industry's cash flows from 1993 through 1998 indicated a maturing industry (refer to Exhibits 10-1 and 10-2). Operating cash flows increased, investing cash flows remained negative, and financing cash flows fluctuated around near zero during the period examined (Exhibit 10-7A). Cumulative industry cash flows for all activities were positive, except for 1995 and 1998 (Exhibit 10-7B). This final section elaborates on those results. We first investigate the PC industry's investing and financing activities. Then, using cash sufficiency and efficiency graphs, we relate those activities to operating cash flows.

WEB EXERCISE 7

Locate Apple's most recent Form 10-K. Identify management's views on significant financing activities by reading the company's long-term debt and stockholders' equity footnotes that accompany the financial statements.

MICRO ANALYSIS 12

The operations index can be considered an extension of the relationship between the depreciation impact and reinvestment ratios.

WEB EXERCISE 8

Find a copy of Compaq Computer's 1998 Form 10-K and see how changes in the industry affected the company's cash flow performance from 1997 to 1998. Contrast Compaq's cash use for its Digital and Tandem acquisitions.

WEB EXERCISE 9

Compare the most recent revenues for Dell and Compaq. Which company has grown faster from 1998 to the present reporting year? Does Compaq's free cash flow still exceed that of its competitor? Are Dell's cash flow returns on assets and revenues still greater than those for Compaq?

INVESTING AND FINANCING ACTIVITIES

The PC industry's financial statements reflected rapidly evolving business practices. Rapid technological changes, accelerated operating cycles, and the need for lower costs required better inventory management. Reduced inventory balances during the latter periods of analysis, for example, indicate greater management commitment to these business factors. Industry maturation triggered lower component costs and selling prices. Significant product demand and manufacturing efficiencies produced CFOs. The companies analyzed sold more PC units in 1998 than in 1993, but the amount of cash generated and used per machine decreased during that time period.

Investing and financing activities played a critical role in supporting industry change. Analysis of these cash flows raises some interesting issues. For example, one might expect reduced cash investments for a maturing information-oriented industry. Yet, the companies invested more cash in 1998 than in previous years. Cash flows from financing activities hovered near zero. Did PC firms raise additional capital to offset investor payments, or were they relatively dormant in both areas of financing?

Individual firms negotiated business evolution with varying degrees of success, which are reflected in their operating cash flows. All companies, however, demonstrated certain behavioral patterns with respect to investing activities. Unlike industrial-based firms, tangible fixed asset acquisitions and disposals were not the primary investing events for these knowledge-based entities. Companies invested significant cash amounts in other entities' securities and technology. Apple, for example, made large investments in these areas in 1997 and 1998, resulting in larger cash outflows in those years than for earlier years of the analysis.

Cash flows from financing activities varied among firms: Apple Computer acquired long-term debt financing and issued preferred stock, Dell contracted invested capital through treasury stock acquisitions, Compaq repaid debt, and Gateway's changes in capital were insignificant. In addition, companies retained cash within their firms. None of the four firms consistently paid dividends to shareholders.

Individual corporate cash flows did not mirror the industry profile or the theoretical model (Exhibit 10-2). Ratio analysis illustrates this disparity. The next two parts of this section examine cash sufficiency and efficiency measures, providing further evidence that some companies outperformed others.

CASH SUFFICIENCY MEASURES

Cash flow adequacy ratios demonstrated industry volatility. Exhibit 11-3A reports yearly cash adequacy for Apple, Compaq, Dell, and Gateway. As noted earlier in the chapter, cash sufficiency is indicated by a relatively high ratio of operating cash to economic commitments. All four firms exhibited instability, but Apple Computer's performance clearly lagged that of its competitors. The firm had inadequate cash flows in 1993 and 1995. Moreover, its cash flow adequacy ratios varied more than its competitors. Exhibit 11-3B presents a weighted six-year average of cash flow adequacy for the industry. It demonstrates Apple's inability to generate sufficient cash from operations during the period analyzed.

Recall that we can also use free cash flows to measure cash sufficiency. Exhibit 11-4 presents each entity's total free cash flow for the six-year period. The results contained in Exhibit 11-4 differ from those of the previous exhibit. Compaq produced more free cash than its competition, including Dell, which had the highest

EXHIBIT 11-3A

*PC Industry
Annual Cash Flow Adequacy
1993–1998*

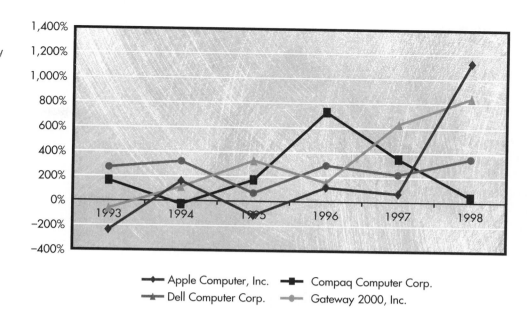

EXHIBIT 11-3B

*PC Industry
Weighted Average Cash Flow
Adequacy
1993–1998*

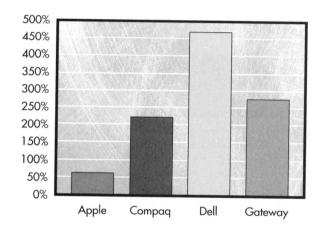

EXHIBIT 11-4

*PC Industry
Cumulative Free Cash Flows
1993–1998 (in millions)*

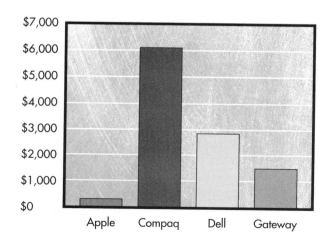

EXHIBIT 11-5

Apple Computer, Inc.
Cash Flow Adequacy
Components
1983–1998

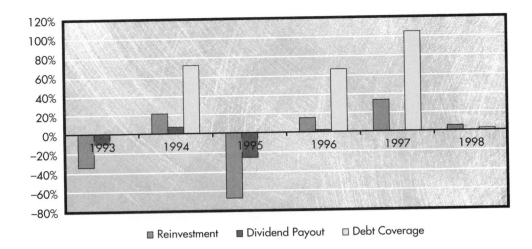

EXHIBIT 11-6A

PC Industry
Weighted Average
Depreciation Impact Ratio
1993–1998

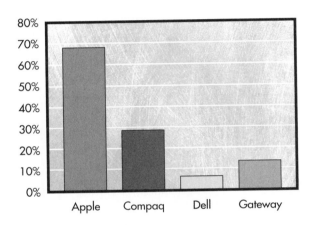

MICRO

***A**NALYSIS 13*

Do you think Gateway's cash
flow adequacy components were
more stable than Apple's?

cash adequacy ratio. These results are inherently biased, however, because free cash flows depend on firm size. Compaq's $6.1 billion free cash flows were produced from an average asset base of $11.4 billion and mean sales of $18.4 billion. Dell produced free cash flows of $2.9 billion with annual assets and revenues equaling $2.2 billion and $5.6, respectively.

We can examine cash adequacy for fixed asset purchases, long-term debt payment, and cash dividend distribution individually. Exhibit 11-5 shows Apple's cash flow adequacy components. This chart demonstrates Apple's inability to generate consistently sufficient cash to reinvest in fixed assets, pay debt, and distribute dividends. These results are not surprising, given Exhibits 11-3A and 11-3B. Negative operating cash flows resulted in inadequate cash flows in 1993 and 1995. The large positive component measures in 1997 also meant cash flows were insufficient in that year.[14]

Data in Exhibit 11-6A reveal that Apple and Compaq's depreciation constituted a much larger percentage of annual operating cash flows than its competitors'. Apple's depreciation impact ratio was 68 percent ($806 million / $1.183 billion). It

---

[14] Unlike the overall cash flow adequacy ratio, a smaller, positive percentage indicates sufficient cash flows for each component. (Remember, CFOs are in the denominator for component measures but appear in the numerator for overall cash flow adequacy.)

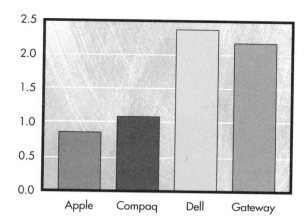

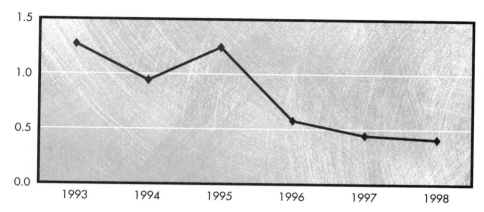

MICRO ANALYSIS 14

In defense of Apple, shrinking sales indicate corporate contraction. It may be that a recapitalization ratio of less than one is warranted for the smaller firm.

WEB EXERCISE 10

Does Apple's depreciation impact ratio exceed its reinvestment ratio for the most recent year reported?

clearly lagged the competition. Even more distressing was that its high depreciation impact ratio signaled weakness in asset refinancing. To fully understand Apple's problem in this area, we need to relate depreciation impact ratio to the reinvestment ratio. Over time, reinvestment in productive resources should exceed depreciation on them. Yet Apple's recapitalization index was less than one, while its competitors' indexes exceeded one. Exhibit 11-6B presents the weighted average recapitalization index for the four firms analyzed, and Exhibit 11-6C demonstrates Apple's decreasing commitment to replenish its productive capabilities.

Increased property, plant, and equipment costs compounded Apple's reinvestment problem. Future asset costs will, in all likelihood, exceed the amounts paid for assets that were depreciated in the time period analyzed.[15] Consequently, even if Apple's reinvestment ratio equaled its depreciation impact measure, the company would still have generated inadequate cash flows to replace fixed assets.

CASH EFFICIENCY MEASURES

Cash efficiency measures reinforce the dominant position with respect to Dell and Gateway in generating operating cash from its business activities. Exhibit 11-7 reports the weighted average cash flow return on assets for the four PC firms. This

---

[15] Moderate inflation in the construction and equipment manufacturing industries virtually assure higher costs for fixed assets.

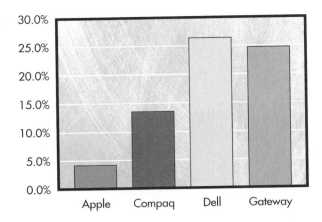

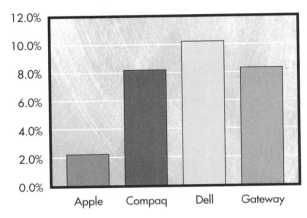

exhibit provides evidence of the superiority of the cash flow adequacy ratio over the free cash flows computation. Refer to Exhibits 11-3B and 11-4. Dell produced the most cash flow according to the adequacy ratio (Exhibit 11-3B) but trailed Compaq when measured in terms of free cash flows (Exhibit 11-4). Exhibit 11-7 supports the contention that Dell had superior operating cash flows. Each dollar Dell invested in resources produced 26.4 cents of operating cash, while Compaq generated half that amount. Compaq's larger free cash amounts were a function of its size rather than superior operating performance. Exhibit 11-8 provides further evidence of Dell's ability to surpass the competition with respect to generating cash from operations.

Exhibits 11-7 and 11-8 indicate Apple's inability to keep pace with the industry from 1993 to 1998. The company produced the lowest cash returns on its assets and sales. This result is not surprising; Apple demonstrated an inability to produce sufficient cash flows from operations (Exhibits 11-3 to 11-6). It is no wonder the company's cash flows were inefficient.

The final two exhibits in this chapter provide further evidence of variable cash flow performance within the industry. The average operations index (Exhibit 11-9A) and the indices for the six-year period for the four firms support cash flow differences. Gateway, Dell, and Compaq demonstrated a strong correlation between CFOs and operating income over the six-year period (Exhibit 11-9A). Apple, however, showed a negative relationship between two measures that should be correlated. Exhibit 11-9B reinforces Apple Computer's erratic operating index.

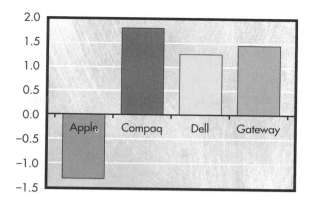

EXHIBIT 11-9A
PC Industry
Average Operations Index
1993–1998

EXHIBIT 11-9B
Apple Computer, Inc.
Annual Operations Index
1993–1998

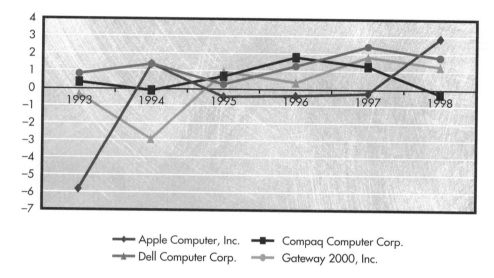

—◆— Apple Computer, Inc.   —■— Compaq Computer Corp.
—▲— Dell Computer Corp.   —●— Gateway 2000, Inc.

CASH FORECAST

Cash flow performance in the PC industry varied among companies during the period analyzed. Each firm's operating cash flows benefited to some extent from inventory reductions. But that ability to increase operating cash flows all but disappeared by the end of 1998. Evidence suggests Apple's operating cash flows were more inflated than the competitions', due to its greater inventory reductions. This result is troublesome because the company lagged its rivals' cash flow measures, even with those inventory decreases. Apple Computer's ability to increase market share and profit margin per machine will determine the success of future operating cash flows. The company's performance from 1993 to 1998, however, provides little evidence of its ability to generate strong operating cash flows.

The industry should continue to use operating cash flows to purchase securities and technology. The former investing activity provides income-producing assets and the latter adds to the knowledge base of a firm. With respect to technology acquisitions, companies could establish parent subsidiary relationships or merge entire entities into their operations in order to gain competitive advantages in a maturing industry. Cash flows related to tangible fixed assets will remain inconsequential, due to the small property, plant, and equipment base in this industry.

Dell and Gateway may repurchase their own stock, due to their strong cash positions. These treasury stock transactions would reduce the ownership base of the company and increase EPS. Apple and Compaq need to use cash to improve operations. These PC companies will also pay few, if any, dividends. Future financing activities should mirror past behavior in that respect.

The ability to buy companies and technology, make debt and equity investments, and purchase outstanding stock will depend on generating operating cash. The PC companies will need efficient computer manufacturing, marketing, and distribution to generate those cash flows. Dell and Gateway appear to better poised to meet the challenge than Apple or Compaq, based on performance during the period analyzed. The analysis of operating performance in Chapter 12 will help confirm or refute this judgment.

SUMMARY

This chapter extends the cash flow and liquidity analysis of the past three chapters. It examines cash flows from investing and financing activities and relates them to cash flows from operating activities. Investing activities consist of cash expenditures and receipts on fixed tangible assets, intangible assets, and investments in securities. Financing activities report cash that was collected from and distributed to shareholders and long-term creditors.

Cash sufficiency and efficiency measures report relationships between investing and financing cash flows and those from operations. Cash sufficiency measures gauge an entity's ability to generate adequate operating cash to pay maturing obligations. Cash flow adequacy, its components, the depreciation impact ratio, and recapitalization index produce data used to judge the sufficiency of operating cash flows. Efficiency ratios are the next step in cash evaluation. Cash returns on sales and assets, as well as the operations index, disclose cash produced by key business activities.

The cash analysis of the PC industry from 1993 through 1998 provides additional evidence that the firms had varying degrees of financial performances. After eliminating the size of the firms from the analysis, data indicate that Dell and Gateway's cash flows were superior to Compaq and Apple. Compaq's decreased cash flows in 1998 reduced the four firms' overall cash flow performance. Apple Computer lagged the other three firms throughout the period of analysis. Its future cash flows will depend on efficiently conducting core business operations.

KEY TERMS

Cash efficiency measures	External financing
Cash flow adequacy	Free cash flows
Cash flow return on asset ratio	Internal financing
Cash flow return on sale ratio	Long-term debt payment ratio
Cash sufficiency measures	Operations index
Depreciation impact ratio	Recapitalization index
Discretionary cash flows	Reinvestment ratio
Dividend payout ratio	Treasury stock

NUMERICAL CASE

11-1

eXTREMESTUFF.com

Numerical case 3-2 at the end of Chapter 3 extends eSTUFF's financial statements through 2003. Use that annual data to do the following:

a. Graph eSTUFF's cash flows from operating, investing, and financing activities from 2000 through 2003. Comment on the company's life-cycle phase.
b. Compute the cash sufficiency measures for 2002 and 2003.
c. Calculate the cash efficiency measures for 2002 and 2003. (Use average-year asset numbers when computing cash flow returns on assets.)
d. Graph the operations indexes from 2000 to 2003. Analyze the extent to which CFOs correlate with income from operations.

INDUSTRY CASES

Examine the industry information and corporate financial statements presented in the appendixes of the text. Confirm and analyze the following measures on an annual basis for the 1994 to 1998 period:

a. Compute the cash flow adequacy ratios and its components (reinvestment, long-term dividend payment, and dividend payout ratios).
b. Calculate free cash flows.
c. Compute the depreciation impact ratio.
d. Figure out the recapitalization index.
e. Assess the cash efficiency measures (cash flow return on sales ratio, cash flow return on asset ratio, and operations index).
f. Compare cash flow adequacy to free cash flows. Comment on any differences between the two measures.
g. Extend your Chapter 10 analysis of cash flows

11-1 *Personal Computers: Apple, Compaq, Dell, and Gateway*

11-2 *Airlines: American, Delta, and United*

11-3 *Athletic Footwear: Nike and Reebok*

11-4 *Discount Retailers: Kmart, Target, and Wal-Mart*

11-5 *Fast-Food Restaurants: McDonald's and Wendy's*

11-6 *Soft Drink Companies: Coca-Cola and PepsiCo.*

INDUSTRY INTERNET CASES

Extend your cash flow industry case analyses by incorporating financial statement disclosures from 1999 through the most recent year.

a. Research and note any substantial changes in the economy and industry that affected investing and financing cash flows. Incorporate those changes into your analyses.
b. Comment on recent cash flows from investing and financing activities.
c. Compute cash sufficiency and efficiency measures as necessary to enhance your analyses.
d. Update your cash analysis through the present year.

11-1 *Personal Computers: Apple, Compaq, Dell, and Gateway*

11-2 *Airlines: American, Delta, and United*

11-3 *Athletic Footwear: Nike and Reebok*

11-4 *Discount Retailers: Kmart, Target, and Wal-Mart*

11-5 *Fast-Food Restaurants: McDonald's and Wendy's*

11-6 *Soft Drink Companies: Coca-Cola and PepsiCo.*

12

OPERATING PERFORMANCE ANALYSIS

CHAPTER LEARNING OBJECTIVES

Upon completion of this chapter, you should be able to:

◆ *Explain the objectives for analyzing operating performance.*

◆ *Describe the importance of earnings quality in operating performance analysis.*

◆ *Identify characteristics of sustainable earnings.*

◆ *Distinguish between recurring and nonrecurring earnings and explain why they produce different earnings quality.*

◆ *Discuss how managerial decisions affect reported income.*

◆ *Present a preliminary analysis of a company or industry's operating performance.*

$\mathscr{C}$ ommercial activities produce cash. Most of a going concern's resources at any given moment, however, lack liquidity. Those assets and changes in them convey information about a firm's prosperity. People use these wealth-related disclosures in conjunction with cash flow information to make economic decisions. Corporate income statements and balance sheets provide analysts with the necessary inputs in this area of analysis. This chapter focuses on the income statement, which reports wealth changes during a reporting period. The next two chapters relate earnings to existing stores of wealth, information that is contained in the statement of financial position.

First, this chapter presents the objectives for analyzing the results of operations. Next, it addresses income composition and the theoretical considerations that influence operating performance. The third section examines the concept of earnings quality. Data from eSTUFF illustrate income and earnings quality factors. The final section analyzes the personal computer (PC) industry's operating performance.

OBJECTIVES FOR ANALYZING OPERATING PERFORMANCE

Operating performance analysis focuses on the sufficiency and sustainability of an entity's earnings. Analysts judge the effect of reported earnings on firm value and the implications of future income levels on shareholder wealth. Their conclusions result largely from the types of earnings an entity produces. A history of wealth creation from central business activities bodes well for a firm. On the other hand, lack of achievement in this area raises questions about corporate vitality and, perhaps, viability. Income derived from noncore transactions also affects analysis but differently than earnings generated from central business operations. Analysts evaluate income statements to determine the relative wealth enhancements from these income components. They assign values to core wealth-building activities and peripheral earnings.

INCOME AND WEALTH

Analysts must understand wealth and its related concepts to interpret income statement and balance sheet disclosures. **Wealth** is discrete: It is the amount of goods and services that an entity can consume at a given point in time.[1] **Wealth changes** report the extent to which those consumption levels change over a period of time. Those variations occur because firms develop, produce, and distribute economically valuable products. Operating performance focuses on wealth changes and how they affect an entity's affluence at specific points in time.

A firm's wealth-building activities affect existing cash balances and people's expectations of future cash flows. Shareholder value is a function of a firm's cash-generating prospects; stock prices reflect investors' expectations. Those anticipated cash receipts, in turn, result from the firm's ability to create sustainable wealth. eSTUFF, for example, does not receive cash from sales unless it has

---

[1] Analysts should always bear in mind that *reported* wealth in the financial statements is a function of the financial reporting system. Alternative capital maintenance concepts produce different wealth measurements.

acquired products, advertised them, contacted customers, processed orders, and shipped merchandise.

Cash receipts and disbursements related to business activities occur at discrete moments in time. The wealth-creating activities, however, often fail to coincide with the cash flows. Selling goods and providing services generate revenues, and matching the costs of producing them creates expenses.[2] The settling of accounts in cash, therefore, fails to accurately measure changes in wealth. eSTUFF, for example, earns revenue when it sells a product, regardless of whether it is a cash or credit transaction. The income statement supplements the cash flow statement by periodically reporting changes in wealth.[3] You must understand income theory, composition, and its value on a per-share basis to fully appreciate reported wealth changes.

INCOME THEORY

Income is the extent to which a company could consume products over time and be as well off at the end of the period as it was at the beginning, according to economic theory.[4] Financial reporting uses that premise as a guide for income measurement. Capital invested at the beginning of a reporting period less net assets owned at the end of that time equals income from a financial reporting perspective.

Income measurement depends on how the financial reporting system defines *capital maintenance* and *asset valuation*. As noted in Chapter 1, invested capital and net assets are determined by the nominal dollar concept of capital maintenance and modified historical cost principle. Reported income excludes adjustments for overall price level changes or those for specific items under this reporting system.[5] Thus, reported income equals annual wealth change as measured by the difference between the actual dollars invested at the beginning of the year and their historical cost at year-end. Defining income as the change in wealth between two points in time is not very informative. The **transaction approach** compensates by summarizing economic events (revenue and expense activities) that produce wealth changes during a reporting period.

INCOME COMPOSITION

Companies must report virtually all transactions affecting wealth on the income statement, under the all-inclusive income concept. The income statement classifies earnings into various components.[6] These amounts initially can be divided into operating income and nonoperating sections. Items in the latter category result from nonoperating activities and irregular items. Transactions that create those

---

[2] Theoretically, wealth is created at every step of business activity. Each of eSTUFF's business activities (e.g., acquiring inventory) adds value to the firm. Measuring wealth creation prior to a transaction between seller and buyer, however, is impossible. Therefore, entities only measure wealth when goods are sold or services provided.

[3] We discuss wealth changes in the context of the historical cost accounting system and nominal dollar concept of capital maintenance.

[4] See, for example, J. R. Hicks, *Value and Capital* (Oxford: Clarendon Press, 1946).

[5] There are exceptions to the historical cost principle, as noted in previous chapters. Asset valuation involves using *modified* historical cost.

[6] This discussion assumes the company is using the multiple-step income statement format. Review the income statement basics presented in Chapter 3.

EXHIBIT 12-1
Income Statement Activities

OPERATING SECTION	NONOPERATING SECTION	IRREGULAR ITEMS (A CONTINUATION OF THE NONOPERATING SECTION)
Revenues	Income from operations	Net income before irregular items
– Cost of goods sold	+ Other revenues (gains)	+/– Discontinued operations, net of tax
= Gross profit	– Other expenses (losses)	+/– Extraordinary items, net of tax
– S, G & A expenses	= Income from continuing operations before tax	+/– Change in accounting principles, net of tax
= Income from operations (assuming no other revenues and expenses)	– Income tax expense	
– Income tax expense		
= Net income	= Net income (assuming no irregular items)	= Net income
Earnings per share	Earnings per share	Earnings per share

WEB *EXERCISE 2*

The Financial Accounting Standards Board's (FASB's) Cases on Recognition and Measurement *present numerous one- and two-page cases related to income and earnings quality issues. Preview it at fasb.org. (You can order it online as well.)*

MICRO *ANALYSIS 4*

Union Carbide Corp.'s 1984 income statements exemplify the earnings implications of an extraordinary event. That year, a catastrophic chemical spill at the company's Bhopal, India, plant killed 3,000 people and injured many thousand others. The company reported extraordinary losses. The tragedy spurred environmental and safety reforms in the chemical industry.

two income streams differ from the recurring business operations that produce operating income. Exhibit 12-1 shows the income statement format for each income type.

The **operating section** reports the difference between a company's primary sources of revenues and the costs required to produce them.[7] The **nonoperating section** reports secondary economic events that changed wealth during the period reported. Nonoperating events are often denoted as **other revenues and gains** and **other expenses and losses.** Income earned on security investments is the most common other revenue and gain item. Interest on borrowed funds usually constitutes the largest portion of other expenses and losses.

Although other revenues and expenses are technically part of the nonoperating section of the income statement, firms often combine this category with operating income and report **income from continuing operations before tax.** Firms do so because wealth-related investing and financing activities occur continuously and are recurring transactions. In that case, a firm would deduct income tax expense from pretax operating income tax as the conventional final step in determining **net income.**

eSTUFF's income statements for 2000 and 2001 are consistent with the line items presented in the first two columns of Exhibit 12-1. The majority of the e-tailer's income resulted from operating activities. Financial expense was the sole nonoperating adjustment to income, and it reflects the annual cost of borrowing money from the bank. Interest expense is not an unusual item for a business, although it is tech-

---

[7] This section presents generalized income statement classifications. Account titles and classifications differ among companies.

WEB **EXERCISE 3**

Investigate Dow Chemical's acquisition of Union Carbide in 2001 at dow.com.

nically not part of the company's retail operation. Consequently, one could infer that all of eSTUFF's expenses originated from recurring operating events. In other words, all of its net income resulted from its principal business operations.

Three significant nonrecurring items sometimes affect net income. These **irregular items** produce gains or losses that companies must report separately. The income statement reports **discontinued operations** when an entity disposes of separate line of business. **Extraordinary items** result from unusual and infrequent events, such as uninsured property losses from natural disasters.[8] A **change in accounting principle** is the switch from one generally accepted accounting principle to another—for example, changing to the straight-line method of depreciation from an accelerated method for financial reporting purposes.

Irregular items require special care in the analysis of income. Their infrequent occurrence and special circumstances distinguish these gains and losses from the revenues and expenses produced by continuing operations. In addition, tax disclosures differ for irregular items. Whereas income from continuing operations is reported as one amount and taxed accordingly, each irregular item is reported on a net (or after-tax) basis.

Comprehensive income includes all changes in equity during a period of time. The all-inclusive income statement format reports almost all wealth changes, except in a few instances. These adjustments are listed in shareholders' equity as **other comprehensive income** items.[9] In other words, these disclosures bypass the income statement and are reported directly as adjustments to shareholders' equity. Items reported as part of other comprehensive income include market-value adjustments for available-for-sale securities and wealth modifications for foreign subsidiaries' currency translations.[10]

EARNINGS PER SHARE

MICRO **ANALYSIS 5**

Many technology companies compensate employees for services rendered with stock options. Some of these firms then purchase stock on the open market when employees exercise their options in order to limit EPS dilution. Do you think such practices are an unreported labor cost?

Aggregate income numbers contain biased information. Net income is positively correlated with firm size; large entities tend to earn more income than their smaller rivals. Earnings per share (EPS) provide analysts with a common measure of operating performance.[11] It quantifies the amount of income earned by each share of *common* stock, and must be disclosed on the face of the income statement. The computation for **basic EPS** is as follows:

$$EPS = \frac{(\text{Net income} - \text{preferred stock dividends})}{\text{Weighted number of outstanding shares of common stock}}$$

The ratio's denominator adjusts common stock to its full-period equivalence. For example, assume eSTUFF issued 8,000 shares of its common stock on July 1, 2001, rather than on January 1 of that year (as presumed in Chapter 3). Those shares

---

[8] GAAP require disclosure of a few events as extraordinary, although they do not meet the definition of unusual and infrequent.

[9] Firms can also add comprehensive income to net income in a *combined* statement of income. As a practical matter, most companies report other comprehensive items as part of the statement of shareholders' equity.

[10] See Chapter 7 for a review of these reporting requirements.

[11] To facilitate this discussion, this section makes some simplifications to *Financial Accounting Standard Statement No. 128,* "Earnings Per Share," (Norwalk, CT: FASB, 1997).

would have been outstanding for only half a year (July 1–December 31). In that case, EPS would be $.46 ($21,000 / [42,000 shares + 4,000 shares]), instead of the $.42 reported in Chapter 3 ($21,000 / [42,000 shares + 8,000 shares]).

Earnings per share disclosures depend on a company's capital structure.[12] A firm could have a **simple capital structure,** which consists of common stock and, possibly, preferred stock, or a **complex capital structure,** which contains outstanding stock and potential shares of common stock. Stock options and convertible securities complicate a simple capital structure. **Stock options** allow specific employees to purchase common stock at a set price within a specified time period. **Convertible securities** consist of long-term debt and preferred stock that can be converted into common stock at predetermined exchange rates.

When a firm has a simple capital structure, GAAP require disclosure of a single EPS number. Companies with a complex capital structure disclose **dual EPS** amounts: In addition to basic EPS, they must report **diluted EPS.** This disclosure assumes options were exercised and convertible securities exchanged during the reporting period. The effect of exercising options and converting securities reduces, or dilutes, EPS.[13]

We know that eSTUFF used simple capital structure because it disclosed a single EPS number. The company had no options or convertible securities during its first two years of business. Assume for the moment that the company's notes payable ($120,000 in 2000 and $220,000 in 2001) could have been converted into common stock.[14] In that case, eSTUFF would have used dual EPS presentation. The company would have disclosed a second EPS number each year to account for those conversions. The amounts reported for diluted EPS would have been lower than the reported basic EPS amounts of $.79 (2000) and $.42 (2001).

EARNINGS QUALITY

MICRO ANALYSIS 6

Many companies derived substantial earnings from equity investments in technology companies in the late 1990s when market prices of those stocks increased rapidly. A steep decline in their market value, beginning in mid-2000, reduced many investors' earnings.

Aggregate and per-share earnings data provide introductory information about earnings adequacy. All things being equal, more earnings are preferred to less. Unfortunately, things are not equal. Income produced from primary business operations are more valuable than those resulting from nonrecurring events. The probability that central business activities will recur in the future greatly exceeds that of nonoperating activities. Moreover, the amount of core earnings will deviate less than noncore activities from one period to the next. The repetition and stability of earnings produced by central business operations, in other words, are the essential wealth building activity of an enterprise.

Equivalent bottom-line earnings disclosures may not represent equal increments of wealth depending on the relative amounts of operating and nonoperating income. **Earnings quality** assesses the extent to which reported income disclosures change an entity's wealth. Analysts must make value judgments of various corporate earnings profit disclosures, a considerable challenge. They must thoroughly understand the sources of revenues and expenses that produced income

---

[12] We discuss EPS at this time to make the reader aware of EPS disclosures that appear on the income statement. Chapters 13 and 14 cover the analytical implications of EPS and capital structure complexities.

[13] Options and convertible securities that increase basic EPS are *antidilutive.* They are excluded from EPS calculations.

[14] Convertible debt securities are *bonds* payable, rather than *notes* payable. We use eSTUFF's existing debt to convey the essence of earnings dilution.

during the reporting period. Analysts must also take into account the assumptions, estimations, selections, conventions, and principles companies used in reporting income as they judge earnings quality.

Earnings quality can be rated on a continuum ranging from low to high quality. Companies whose earnings numbers represent true economic value, as opposed to the appearance of it, have a higher earnings quality than those whose reported profits do not represent recurring income. Interrelated characteristics help analysts' judge earnings quality: earnings sustainability, measurement, and management.

WHAT'S YOUR ANALYSIS

GETTING TO THE CORE OF THE MATTER

Continual business operations produce quality earnings. Income generated from ongoing business activities is sustainable in future periods, but earnings from nonrecurring transactions are not. Core activities define business operations and determine recurring earnings. Analysts must determine what constitutes a business core, which is not as easy as you might think. How do you assess core business activities?

A *core* is defined as the essence of something. In business it represents the integral commercial activities: those that drive profits. One might simplistically think of the business core as a product, either a good or service sold to customers. The changing economic landscape, however, has challenged companies to rethink that approach to core activities.[a] Analysts must also be aware of these changes.

One could argue that business processes, business designs, and control of intellectual property are more important wealth creators than tangible products. Consider an example of each of these three alternatives. Celestica, Inc., makes thousands of technology-related products for numerous companies. The firm bids on contracts with the understanding that it will have to rapidly change its manufacturing processes to meet the needs of its customers. Amazon.com views itself as bringing customers and products together over the Internet, rather than functioning as an online bookstore. E-commerce, according to Amazon, is a way of doing business as opposed to selling products. Disney creates entertainment. Mickey Mouse and friends become focal points for the company's theme park operations. The company also licenses the rights to reproduce its creations to other firms in exchange for royalty revenues.

Observations

Explain how a careful reading of "Item 1. Business" in a firm's Form 10-K helps analysts understand an entity's core operation. Discuss how recognizing a company's core business assists in analyzing earnings and operating cash flows. Do you think core business activities remain constant over time?

---

[a] Material based on B. Wysoki, Jr.'s "Corporate America Confronts the Meaning of a Core Business," *Wall Street Journal*, November 11, 1999, PP. A1 and A12.

EARNINGS SUSTAINABILITY

Earnings sustainability represents the capacity of an enterprise to produce income on a recurring basis. Sustainable earnings are permanent: They persist from one period to the next. Nonrecurring income is unsustainable and either temporarily affects wealth or has no impact on it at all. Revenues from ongoing operations, for example, produce sustainable earnings, but those realized extraordinary gains do not. Analysts place a greater value on recurring items than transitory ones. They have a far greater impact on a company's stock price.[15]

Sustainable revenues and expenses contain few, if any, earnings surprises. They make it relative easy to project future income and cash flow levels. Infrequently reported events, however, alter reported earnings and complicate income projections. Analysts have a difficult time predicting if, and when, such items will occur in the future and projecting their related cash flows. Recall that the three irregular items contained in Exhibit 12-1 do not represent sustainable earnings.[16] Those gains and losses, which significantly affect one period's net income, probably will not occur again. The value of irregular items reduces reported income quality. Net income, in these circumstances, consists of both permanent and transitory earnings. Analysts discount the impact of unsustainable income on stock prices because these items are one-time events.

More difficult than measuring the impact of irregular items is determining the sustainability of other revenues and expenses. Gains and losses in these categories occur both frequently and sporadically. For example, investment income from securities and interest expenses on borrowed funds are recurring events. Although not technically part of operating income, these investing and financing activities behave in a manner similar to operating revenues and expenses. Certain events in this other income statement category, however, do not occur often. Assume eSTUFF, for example, realized a large gain from an equipment sale and reported it as part of other revenues. The company could not sustain income earned from the disposal of that piece of equipment.

The greatest challenge is to analyze whether earnings sustainability exists within continuing operations. The title of this income statement section implies earnings sustainability, but this is not always the case. Revenues generated from special sales and infrequently occurring expenses can be reported as part of operating income. Analysts must determine whether any unusual operating events have occurred and assess their impact on sustained earnings.

Corporate restructurings are sometimes reported as part of continuing operations and pose a special problem for analysts. These events significantly alter a firm's net resources through a major realignment of corporate goals. They are reported infrequently but produce expenses that substantially reduce reported operating income. Analysts tend to discount the impact that restructurings have on earnings because they are one-time charges against revenues. In that respect, they are similar to nonoperating expenses.

Restructuring a business is, to a certain degree, an acknowledgment of past strategic failures. Such poor management decisions have affected past financial statements and will misstate future ones if left uncorrected. In one sense, the costs of strategic missteps were not reported as part of previous reporting periods' earnings. Consequently, restructuring expenses reported on the current income

MICRO ANALYSIS 7

Intel, the largest manufacturer of semiconductors for the PC industry, reduced its expected gains on high-tech equity investments from $950 million to $675 million in the fourth quarter of 2000, due to the decline in those investments' market value. Are Intel's investment earnings of the same quality as those produced by the sale of computer chips?

WEB EXERCISE 5

Intel.com is the home page for Intel. Look into the company's investment performance by examining the disclosures of its Intel Capital division.

MICRO ANALYSIS 8

The "big bath" theory motivates many corporations to restructure. According to this logic, a company recognizes a large one-time expense in order to "clean up" its balance sheet. Analysts will then look past the unusual loss and value the firm's future earnings growth.

---

[15] A significant body of research provides evidence that shareholders assign different values to recurring and nonrecurring earnings. See, for example, B. Lev, "On the Usefulness of Earnings and Earnings Research: Lessons and Directions from Two Decades of Empirical Research," *Journal of Accounting Research* (Supplement, 1989), pp. 153-192.

[16] An extraordinary gain, for example, increases wealth in the current reporting period. Wealth adjustments of this nature are referred to as *transitory* earnings. Earnings from changes in accounting principles are usually considered irrelevant because they report the cumulative effect of past events that do not affect future cash flows.

statement can be viewed as a catch-up disclosure for previously unrecorded business costs. Viewed from a forward-looking perspective, restructurings acknowledge that the earnings capabilities of certain corporate resources have been impaired and must be expensed immediately. Compounding the dilemma of corporate realignment is that expenses from one restructuring are often charged against operating revenues in more than one reporting period.

Even more difficult to analyze are cases of **multiple restructurings**. Some firms circumvent the intent of restructuring a business by reporting frequent restructurings. A single restructuring charge usually does not reduce the perception of sustainable earnings; operating expenses can be modified for the effect of the restructuring. However, continual restructurings muddle the analysis of earnings sustainability. At best, multiple restructurings call into question management's ability to make sound strategic decisions. At worst, they connote management attempts to hide recurring expenses so that analysts will discount the impact of restructuring on sustainable earnings. Multiple restructurings often indicate management's attempt to *manage* earnings, which is part of the next portion of the earnings quality issue.

Go to americanstandard.com and determine if the company has continued to restructure in recent years.

RESTRUCTURING CHARGES AND EARNINGS MANAGEMENT

Corporate behavior has led regulators and analysts to question whether some restructurings actually represent corporate reorganizations. Some companies have turned costs associated with corporate reorientation into an annual expense. How do you interpret multiple restructurings and the Securities and Exchange Commission's (SEC's) position on them?

Restructurings were designed to be one-time charges against revenues. Some companies, however, report them frequently. American Standard Cos., for example, restructured nine times from 1988 to 1998.[a] Regulators have become concerned over perceived abuses of these types of charges against revenues,[b] identifying two areas of concern. The first one, discussed in this chapter, is that multiple restructurings may be a means of hiding recurring business costs by burying them within the restructuring charge. The SEC fears that financial statement users will discount restructuring expense, including the recurring elements within it, because of the infrequent nature of restructurings.

The second questionable earnings management tactic consists of creating reserves and adjusting them to create earnings. A restructuring company creates reserve accounts when it expects future costs related to the restructuring. For example, a company that restructures in the current year matches that expense against current revenues. That firm may, however, make severance payments to fired employees in future periods, so it creates a reserve in the amount of the expected cash disbursements to offset the current expense.

The SEC contends that some companies overstate restructuring expenses and related reserves. In future periods, then, these firms can reduce the reserves and offset those reductions by recording revenues. In effect, the companies manage their earnings by dipping into unrealistically large reserve accounts.

Observations

What would be your initial impression about management if you were analyzing a company that continually reported restructuring charges? Comment on the ethical behavior of companies that aggressively report restructuring reserves. Explain why such companies do not seem to mind the fact that in order to create excessive reserves, they must match an overstated restructuring expense against revenues in the current period.

ᵃ Some of those disclosures were reported as one-time charges, rather than restructurings.
ᵇ The SEC instituted an earnings-management campaign in 1998. Part of the commission's thrust was to curb restructuring abuses.

MICRO ANALYSIS 9

Wal-Mart Store Inc. changed the way it recognized revenue for layaway sales in 2000. The company began recording revenues when customers completely paid for the merchandise, rather than when the layaway was made. Wal-Mart's earnings decreased by 2 cents per share in the second quarter of 2000 as a result of management's decision.

MICRO ANALYSIS 10

South Korean car manufacturer Hyundai more than doubled its commitment to R&D spending in 2000 as a means of becoming a global automaker

EARNINGS MEASUREMENT AND MANAGEMENT

The policies and procedures used by an entity to determine income define **earnings measurement.** If management systematically select accounting principles that favorably report earnings, they are engaging in **earnings management.** Every firm measures earnings, but you must evaluate if executives are managing them.

Managers make many choices that affect income. They make *business decisions* with the objective of adding economic value to the firm. Management elects to report those business activities through its *accounting decisions.* The relationship between business and accounting decisions results in reported income. Management's business decisions capture the essence of *what* must be measured, and their accounting choices reflect *how* they are reported.[17]

Consider eSTUFF's operations. The company purchased equipment to control its merchandising activities. That investment decision broadly defined what must be measured from an accounting perspective. For example, GAAP mandate capitalizing the asset's cost over its productive life. Management decides how to comply with GAAP, and those decisions affect income. Many of those decisions are discussed in previous chapters, such as eSTUFF's depreciation method and estimated life for its equipment.

Management makes other choices that affect earnings. Executives decide when long-term assets are repaired, impaired, obsolete, sold, or replaced. Internal decision makers influence perceptions about earnings sufficiency. For example, if eSTUFF was overly optimistic about the longevity of its equipment, then the unrealistically low annual depreciation expense overstates operating income. The reported earnings could mislead financial statement users. That income level, however, is unsustainable because it contains an insufficient allocation of historical cost in the current reporting period.

Management also affects reported earnings through discretionary spending decisions. Chapter 6 notes that some costs are more controllable than others. Management decides the level of spending for controllable items, like research and development (R&D) costs and advertising expenses. These expenditures result from internal decisions rather than external requirements, such as the need to purchase inventory at market prices from suppliers. Analysts must use their judgment when evaluating the effect of discretionary spending on earnings quality. For example, reducing spending for R&D and advertising in the current period increases reported earnings, but those decisions may be detrimental to future earnings. Imagine if eSTUFF neglected to advertise its business. Short-

---

[17] The constraints of the accounting system used to measure economic value also affect earnings and are addressed in this chapter and previous ones. See, for example, the discussion in Chapter 1 about the capital maintenance concepts.

term earnings would be enhanced, but the lack of promotion would diminish long-term wealth.

The earnings measurement issues related to eSTUFF's fixed assets and discretionary costs could be extended to other aspects of the e-tailer's business. Addressing every item that affects earnings quality, therefore, is a daunting, if not impossible, task. Although there is no definitive way to assess all the aspects of earnings quality, there are some considerations that can enhance analytical judgment and help develop a sense of earnings quality.[18] The following sections discuss these considerations.

IN-PROCESS RESEARCH AND DEVELOPMENT: HIGH TECH'S WAY TO MANAGE EARNINGS?

A large number of acquisitions have taken place in the high-tech sector of the economy. Many firms in these maturing industries seek external growth as a means to increase shareholder value. Companies targeted for takeover are often very expensive. Purchasing highly valued targets usually creates large amounts of goodwill, but high-tech firms often do not record substantial amounts of that intangible asset. How do you assess their current practice of reporting intangible assets?

Goodwill is the difference between the purchase price for a company and the fair value of its net assets. Subsequent amortization of goodwill reduces reported income. Managers generally do not like recognizing goodwill expense; they consider it a drag on earnings. Technology firms often avoid reporting substantial amounts of goodwill by treating a portion of the excess purchase price as *in-process R&D*, because GAAP allow acquiring companies to charge the cost of the target's R&D acquired against revenues in the year of purchase. Goodwill, in essence, is reduced by the amount in-process R&D recognized (and immediately written off) by the acquiring firm.

The SEC has moved to curb perceived abuse of reporting in-process R&D. Federal regulators contend that many high-tech companies overstate the one-time charge, thereby understating goodwill. The SEC argues that some firms use in-process R&D to manage earnings. According to the commission, companies do so because they believe analysts will discount the one-time reduction, but they would not ignore goodwill amortization.

Observations

Is GAAP's treatment of in-process R&D consistent with its general reporting requirements for R&D? Do you think it would be easy for an acquiring firm to estimate in-process R&D? Do you think analysts should consider goodwill amortization and in-process R&D charges when evaluating earnings quality?

BENCHMARKING

Comparative analysis facilitates earnings quality assessment. Analysts judge earnings numbers by benchmarking them, noting similarities and differences in

---

[18] The discussion on earnings quality analysis is an introduction to this complex subject. The American Accounting Association's *Earnings Quality Project* exemplifies a detailed investigation into this topic. This continual examination of earnings quality is funded by an SEC grant.

reported earnings components over time and against competition. Common sizing income statements help analysts eliminate interfirm and interperiod size differentials.

A preliminary step in benchmarking earnings quality is to determine the extent of financial reporting consistency and comparability. *Consistency* means a company uses the same accounting methods over time, and *comparability* denotes similar accounting methods among firms.[19] Earnings quality analysis is only meaningful when these reporting characteristics exist. Inconsistency or incomparability can introduce confounding variables in the analysis: in these situations, it may be difficult to tell if differences should be attributable to economic changes, alternative accounting methods, or a combination of both factors.

Income statement comparability and consistency extend beyond the use of the same accounting methods over time and among companies. Firms must also use acceptable revenue realization and matching principles. Analysts may question earnings quality when an enterprise uses aggressive accounting methods, those reporting techniques that produce relatively large earnings numbers by recognizing as much revenue and deferring as many expenses as possible in the current reporting period.[20] These practices exaggerate the amount of cash likely to be collected from revenues and minimize impending cash payments for expenses.

Many firms seek to increase their profit margin by reorienting their businesses. Many brand-name manufacturers, for example, now outsource the actual manufacture of their products. These companies focus on research, marketing, and distribution. Branded companies foster close working relations with the actual producers through careful attention to supply-chain management, which ensures timely delivery of high quality products.

EARNINGS SUFFICIENCY

Analysts should examine the following common size income measures to benchmark earnings quality after consistency and comparability have been confirmed or established:

◆ Gross profit
◆ Income from operations (before other revenues and expenses)
◆ Income from operations (after other revenues and expenses)
◆ Net income

Each of these common size income measures is referred to as a **profit margin,** which is the ratio of a reported income level to revenue. **Gross profit margin,** for example, is the proportion of gross profit to revenues. **Net profit margin** is computed by dividing net income by sales. Each profit margin can be used separately or in combination with others to develop a sense of earnings quality. Exhibits 12-2 and 12-3 contain data that illustrate these techniques.

Exhibit 12-2 presents the actual gross profit margin for eSTUFF in 2001 (as reported in Chapters 3 and 4) and assumes a gross profit increase or decrease by one percentage point from 2002 to 2004. If eSTUFF increased its gross profit mar-

EXHIBIT 12-2
eXTREMESTUFF.com
Gross Profit Alternatives

CASE	2001	2002	2003	2004
Case 1. Increasing Gross Profit	45%	46%	47%	48%
Case 2. Decreasing Gross Profit	45%	44%	43%	42%

---

[19] These terms are defined in Chapter 6.
[20] Chapter 6 discusses front-end loading of revenues and back-end loading of expenses.

gin (Case 1), then the company would have realized an increasing level of profit to cover expenses over time. Conversely, a declining gross profit margin (Case 2) shrinks the amount of revenues available to offset business expenses. eSTUFF would have 6 more percentage points of gross profit in Case 1 (48 percent) than in Case 2 (42 percent) by 2004 with which to meet selling, administrative, and financing expenses as well as absorb the shock of nonrecurring expenses.

The ability of revenues to cover expenses and produce acceptable profit margins is referred to as **earnings sufficiency.** It is a preliminary component of earnings sustainability. To explain why the *amount* of earnings is a necessary condition for earnings quality, we examine eSTUFF's other expenses. The e-tailer's non–cost of goods sold expenses were 42.1 percent of 2001 sales (selling expenses of 29.3 percent + administrative expenses of 11.1 percent + financial expenses of 1.7 percent). Data from Case 2 indicate that if those expense levels remained constant, then eSTUFF's profit would have been eliminated by 2004 (gross profit of 42 percent less expenses of 42.1 percent). Declining gross profit would have eliminated the company's ability to build wealth through its continual operations. Analysts must determine that sufficient earnings exist before they can focus on more complex earnings quality issues. Any income increases in Case 2 from nonrecurring events would have only boosted reported earnings temporarily. Such transitory earnings would not have solved the company's problem of its inability to create sustainable earnings.

RECURRING AND NONRECURRING EARNINGS

Two alternative scenarios of Case 1 in Exhibit 12-2 are presented in Exhibit 12-3. Case 1A assumes business costs after gross profits are constant from 2001 through 2004. They do not contain any nonrecurring gains or losses. Case 1B, however, contains a nonrecurring event in each year from 2002 to 2004 (bold cells in the table). These unique events alter profit margins.

Notice that the profit margins of income from operations (both before and after financial expenses) increased by one percentage point per year in Case 1A. The result occurs only if selling (29.3 percent), administrative (11.1 percent), and financial expense (1.7 percent) remain a constant proportion of revenues. Net profit margin in each year is 60 percent of pretax income, based on an annual income tax rate of 40 percent.

Case 1B's results are more varied than those in the first case. These differences are highlighted in Exhibit 12-3. Examine income from operations (before other expenses) in 2002. It is only 3.1 percent, instead of the expected 5.6 percent.

EXHIBIT 12-3
*eXTREMESTUFF.com
Case 1 Profit Margin
Alternatives*

	2001	2002	2003	2004
Case 1A				
Operating profit margin (before other expenses)	4.6%	5.6%	6.6%	7.6%
Operating profit margin (after other expenses)	2.9%	3.9%	4.9%	5.9%
Net profit margin	1.7%	2.3%	2.9%	3.5%
Case 1B				
Operating profit margin (before other expenses)	4.6%	**3.1%**	6.6%	7.6%
Operating profit margin (after other expenses)	2.9%	1.4%	**2.4%**	5.9%
Net profit margin	1.7%	0.8%	1.4%	**9.1%**

eSTUFF must have reported a nonrecurring operating expense in that year. Income from operations returns to the expected 6.6 percent in 2003. That profit margin decreases to 2.4 percent after other expenses were included in income. The expected profit margin was 4.9 percent (as reported in Case 1A). Another nonrecurring expense besides the 1.7 percent financial expenses must have reduced that profit margin in 2003. A nonrecurring item altered net profit margin in 2004. Net profit margin is 9.1 percent in 2004 of Case 1B, rather than the expected 3.5 percent, due to an irregular gain.[21]

Data of Exhibit 12-3 are graphically presented in Exhibits 12-4A and 12-4B. Exhibit 12-4A depicts a relatively high quality of earnings, based on two characteristics in the graphs: The trend of each earnings component increases over time, indicating growing cash sufficiency, and the consistent relationship among the three profitability measures in each year suggests that nonrecurring items are nonexistent. Profit margin variability over time in Exhibit 12-4B signifies lower earnings quality than that presented in Exhibit 12-4A. Analysts would have more confidence predicting 2005 profit margins in Case 1A than in Case 1B.

EXHIBIT 12-4A

eXTREMESTUFF.com
High Earnings Quality-
Case 1A

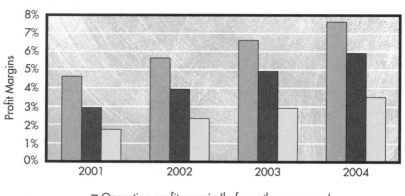

EXHIBIT 12-4B

eXTREMESTUFF.com
Low Earnings Quality-
Case 1B

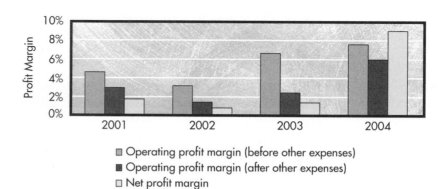

---

[21] This statement assumes a consistent income tax rate.

SOFT DOLLARS, REBATES, AND EARNINGS QUALITY

Shifting distribution channels have affected many PC firms, as noted in previous chapters. These changes affected computer dealers as well as PC manufacturers. Emerging business practices altered many distributors' earnings quality. What is your analysis of their earnings sustainability?

Computer dealers purchase PCs and related equipment from manufacturers and sell them to endusers.[a] Many PC makers were highly motivated to increase sales to increase market share and reduce costs for components. Manufacturers induced dealers to assist in their expansion efforts by offering bonuses for meeting sales targets, referred to as *soft dollars*. Industry leader Inacom Corp. disclosed in its 1997 Form 10-K, "The Company's primary vendors provide various incentives for promoting and marketing their products which typically range from 1% to 5% of purchases."

Many dealers started selling computers at or near cost in order to increase soft dollar revenue. This business practice produced earnings and growth for many distributors for a number of years. The advent of direct PC sales, however, altered the distribution landscape. Companies such as Dell and Gateway sold at lower prices to endusers, due to their cost-effective manufacturing and distribution techniques. Computer dealers were at a competitive disadvantage. To compensate, manufacturers selling through the traditional indirect dealer channels negotiated lower sales prices with their larger customers and provided dealers with *rebates* so that these brokers could profit from the negotiated sales.

The increasing popularity of direct distribution doomed many dealers by the turn of the century as manufacturers eliminated soft dollar bonuses, reduced rebates, and became direct distributors themselves. Inacom, for example, was liquidated in 2000.

Observations

Soft dollars and dealer rebates produced sufficient earnings for a period of time, but they eventually proved unsustainable. What does this tell you about the earnings quality of PC dealers? Discuss how industry analysis would have assisted you in assessing earnings quality when PC dealers were reporting profits from their operations.

---

[a] Background material from G. McWilliam's, "How Shifting Forces in PC Business Undid Top Dealer Inacom," *Wall Street Journal*, November 8, 2000, pp. A1 and A10.

INCOME AND CASH FLOW CORRESPONDENCE

Firms ultimately collect revenues in cash and pay most expenses with cash. Therefore, one would expect to see a degree of correspondence between income and cash flows. This relationship should be greatest between operating income and operating cash flows. Conceptually, these two amounts should virtually parallel each other over time. Exhibit 12-5 charts operating earnings and cash flows over the various life cycle states. Cash collected on sales and paid for expenses slightly lags the timing of revenue and expense recognition, according to Exhibit 12-5. High earnings quality, therefore, should reflect similar amounts of operating income and operating cash flows within reporting periods and over time. Low earnings quality, on the other hand, is generally characterized by greater variability between the two amounts.

EXHIBIT 12-5
*Operating Income
and Cash Flows
Life Cycle Stages*

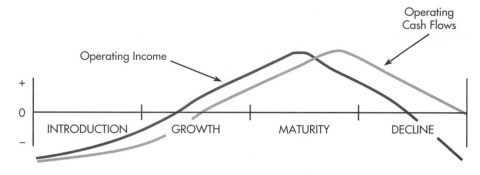

	2005	2006	2007	2008	2009	TOTAL
Operating income	$72[a]	$89	$83	$98	$119	$461
Operating cash flows	$78	$94	$89	$107	$117	$485

[a] Amounts in thousands of dollars.

	2005	2006	2007	2008	2009	TOTAL
Operating income	$72[a]	$89	$83	$98	$119	$461
Operating cash flows	$9	$125	$(3)	$129	$16	$276

[a] Amounts in thousands of dollars.

*Compare operating income and
cash flow for the dot-com company you examined in the previous two WEBexercises.*

Differences between the two measures exist. Depreciation reduces operating
income, but it has no impact on cash flows from operations.[22] Cash paid for interest on borrowed funds and for taxes reduce cash flows from operating activity
(CFOs) but is not included in computing operating income. An analyst can either
adjust for depreciation, interest, and tax differences, or acknowledge that CFOs
and operating income are highly correlated but not identical. The decision
whether to reconcile the two amounts is of secondary importance. It is more vital
to understand that operating income and cash flows correspond to each other
when earnings quality is high. Interperiod variability and significant aggregate
discrepancies between the two numbers indicate poor earnings quality.

Exhibits 12-6A and 12-6B present numerical examples of high and low earnings quality, based on the relationship between eSTUFF's assumed operating
income and assumed cash flows from operations. Assumed data were initiated in
2005, rather than 2000, because net losses and negative CFOs usually exist during
the introductory phase of the business life cycle (see Exhibit 12-5).[23]

The high degree of correlation between operating income and CFOs in Exhibit
12-6A indicates stability between income and cash flows. Earnings have substan-

---

[22] Cash expenditures made for fixed assets are investing activities.
[23] Using negative numbers that might have appeared in the introductory phase of operations would
have detracted from the analytical point being illustrated.

	2005	2006	2007	2008	2009	TOTAL
Operating income	$72[a]	$89	$83	$98	$119	$461
Net income	$43	$54	$50	$60	$71	$278
Operating cash flows	$78	$94	$89	$107	$117	$485

[a] Amounts in thousands of dollars.

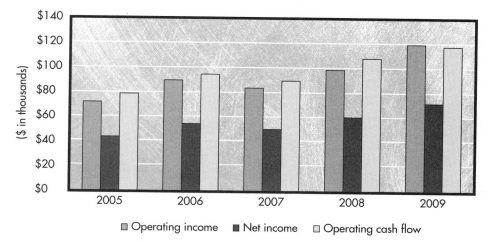

	2005	2006	2007	2008	2009	TOTAL
Operating income	$72[a]	$89	$83	$98	$119	$461
Net income	$22	$116	$55	$94	$(118)	$169
Operating cash flows	$9	$125	$(3)	$129	$16	$276

[a] Amounts in thousands of dollars.

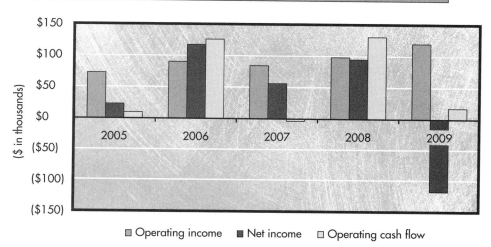

tial quality because they are realized in cash on a timely basis. Exhibit 12-6B is an example of a lower earnings quality, due to the lack of timing between reported incomes and net cash receipts.

Examining the relationship between operating cash flow and net income extends earnings quality analysis. Net income is comparable to operating income when other gains (losses) and irregular items are unreported or immaterial in amount. Net income, in these cases, differs from operating income only by the amount of income tax expense. Significant disclosures of other gains (losses) and irregular items result in larger differences between operating income and net income. (Refer to Exhibit 12-4B.) The transitory nature of those nonrecurring events lowers earnings quality. Thus, a high degree of correlation between net income and CFOs also provides evidence of a high earnings quality.

Consider Exhibits 12-7A and 12-7B, which extend Exhibits 12-6A and 12-6B with assumed net income data. The two income streams are comparable in Exhibit 12-7A, except for the taxes that affected net income. Both operating income and net income correlate to CFOs. Such is not the case in Exhibit 12-7B. Net income does not move in a pattern similar to operating income or cash flows. These discrepancies indicate the existence of various nonrecurring items through the years, which diminishes earnings quality.

ANALYSIS OF THE PERSONAL COMPUTER INDUSTRY

The final portion of this chapter continues the analysis of the PC industry, with an emphasis on Apple Computer. This section presents market share data, examines profit margins, and relates earnings numbers to cash flows. It is orientated toward assessing the firm's earnings quality.

MICRO $\mathscr{A}$NALYSIS 14

IBM's PC division returned to profitability after three years of losses, despite losing market share. The company's global market share decreased to 6.8 percent in 2001 from 7.9 percent the year before. The company attributed its success to its focus on direct sales to end users and the elimination of indirect selling practices.

MARKET SHARE

Personal computer companies design, manufacture, and distribute PCs and related equipment. A PC company's ability to create wealth results from its ability to sell products profitably. Market share data provide evidence of the public's acceptance of a company's PCs. The market share controlled by Apple, Compaq, Dell, and Gateway changed substantially from 1993 to 1998. These sales shifts provide context for understanding each firm's operating performance. Exhibit 12-8A presents each company's sales as a percentage of the cumulative revenues of the four firms from 1993 through 1998.[24] Exhibit 12-8B contrasts market share among the four firms at the beginning and end of the period analyzed.

Compaq was the market leader in sales from 1993 through 1998, as evidenced by the chart in Exhibit 12-8A. It accounted for nearly one-half ($110.4 billion) of the $222 billion sales made by the four firms analyzed. However, evidence of a market realignment among the four companies comes to light in Exhibit 12-8B. Compaq increased its 38 percent market share in 1993 to 54.8 percent within five years, while Apple Computer suffered a reversal of fortune. Apple's market share decreased from a dominant 42.2 percent in 1993 to 10.4 percent in 1998. Apple's revenues also reflected this loss in market share. In a period of sustained industry growth, Apple's 1998 revenues were only 54 percent ($5.9 billion) of their 1995 level ($11.1 billion). In contrast to Apple's performance, Dell more than doubled its market share and increased revenues six-fold.

---

[24] The PC market includes other firms besides the ones used in this discussion, as noted in Chapter 5. The four firms being analyzed constitute about 35 percent of the fragmented PC industry. For example, Apple's 1998 *overall* market share was 3 percent.

EXHIBIT 12-8A

Personal Computer Industry Relative Market Share 1993–1998

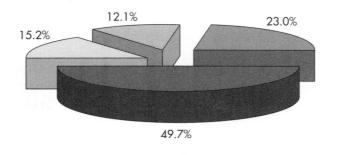

15.2% 12.1% 23.0%

49.7%

■ Apple ■ Compaq □ Dell ■ Gateway

EXHIBIT 12-8B

Personal Computer Industry Relative Market Share 1993 and 1998

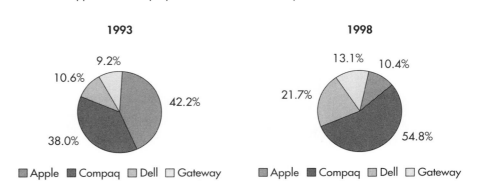

1993

9.2%
10.6%
42.2%
38.0%

■ Apple ■ Compaq □ Dell □ Gateway

1998

13.1% 10.4%
21.7%
54.8%

■ Apple ■ Compaq □ Dell □ Gateway

WEB *Exercise 10*

▼

Go to Apple Computer's homepage. Has the company reported net income or a net loss for its most recent annual reporting period?

EARNINGS SUFFICIENCY

The easy-to-use features of Apple's products provided the company with a competitive advantage and enabled Apple to charge a premium for its products during the infancy of the PC industry. The company's higher-than-average gross margins in the earlier years of the study resulted, in part, from its technological prowess. However, software mimicking Apple's technology eroded Apple's technological superiority. Competitors installed Microsoft's Windows, which is similar to but incompatible with the Mac operating system, on their machines during the period analyzed. Apple lost market share and revenues as Windows became the industry standard.[25] Consumers began to view PCs as interchangeable commodities and based purchases on prices rather than brand names.

Apple Computer's declining revenues and gross margins diminished its chances of generating sufficient earnings. Fewer dollars existed to absorb costs. Apple's fixed expense per PC, in other words, increased as its market share decreased. The other three firms experienced a more favorable result: Their fixed costs were spread over more PCs as their sales increased. The earnings sufficiency issue is reflected in Apple's gross profit margin. Exhibit 12-9A presents the average combined gross profit margins of the four firms in 1993 and 1998. Exhibit 12-9B graphs each firm's annual gross profit margin. Apple's superior gross margin had been eliminated by 1994.

---

[25] This discussion is not meant to imply that Apple's loss of a competitive advantage in operating systems was the only reason for the company's reduced market share and revenues. It was one contributing factor. It is only discussed to illustrate a company's inability to generate sufficient earnings when environmental factors erode gross margins.

1993

27.2% / 72.8%

☐ Cost of Goods Sold   ■ Gross Profit

1998

22.7% / 77.3%

☐ Cost of Goods Sold   ■ Gross Profit

EXHIBIT 12-9B
Personal Computer Industry
Gross Profit Margin
1993–1998

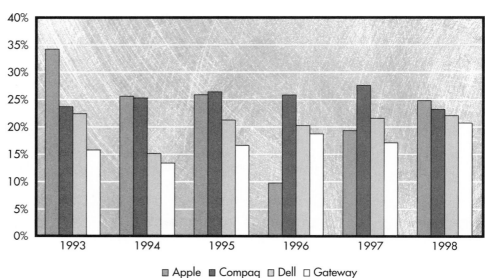

☐ Apple   ■ Compaq   ☐ Dell   ☐ Gateway

WEB

ℰXERCISE 11

Have any of the four PC firms
reported any significant nonre-
curring gains or losses in their
most recent Form 10-Ks?
Discuss their impact on earnings
sustainability, if any unusual or
infrequent transactions were
reported.

EARNINGS SUSTAINABILITY

Data underlying three sets of exhibits provide evidence of the industry's earnings sustainability. The graphs in Exhibits 12-10A and 12-10B report each firm's operating profits and expenses as a percentage of revenues. Exhibits 12-11A and 12-11B contain the relative amounts of spending on R&D. The series of graphs in Exhibit 12-12 depicts the relationship between operating income and operating cash flows for each firm.

Gross profit less operating expenses equals operating profit. Margins for operating profits and expenses, therefore, are the two sides of the gross margin coin. These complementary margins provide evidence of earnings sustainability. Exhibits 12-10A and 12-10B display operating profits and expenses as a percentage of sales.

None of the firms analyzed demonstrated overwhelming stability in their operating profit margins during the period. This result is not surprising, given the industry's lack of maturity. Various differences did exist, however, among firms. Dell's operating profits and expenses were relatively stable. Gateway's expense profile changed from 1993 to 1998. The company's increases in gross profit margins (Exhibit 12-9B) offset its growth in operating expenses (Exhibit 12-10B). These changes resulted in a relatively stable operating profit margin (Exhibit 12-10A). Gateway Country Stores, opened toward the end of the period analyzed, helped alter the company's expense structure. Gateway realized higher margins from

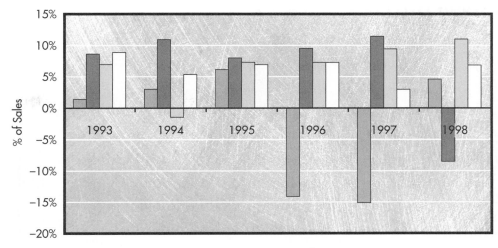

☐ Apple ■ Compaq ☐ Dell ☐ Gateway

EXHIBIT 12-10B
*Personal Computer Industry
Operating Expense Margin
1993–1998*

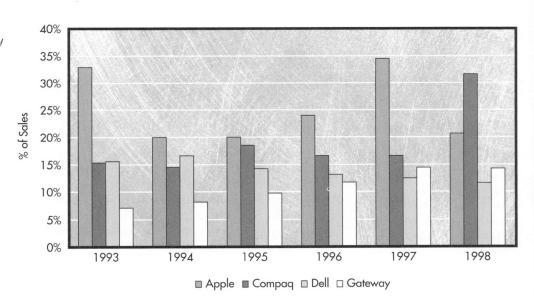

☐ Apple ■ Compaq ☐ Dell ☐ Gateway

WEB *E*XERCISE 12

*Contrast R&D expenses for
Apple and Compaq in the most
recent year reported. Does
Apple's knowledge-based expense
as a percentage of revenues still
exceed Compaq's spending for
R&D?*

goods and services sold from its stores than it did from direct PC sales. In-store sales and services fueled gross profit but increased selling and administrative expenses.[26]

Compaq and Apple demonstrated less sustainable earnings than the two direct computer sellers did. Compaq's profit margin was fairly stable until 1998. The substantive charge for in-process R&D costs that year (10.3 percent of revenues) accounts for the decline in profitability. That expense is nonrecurring and would not influence Compaq's ability to sustain earnings. The company's increased operating expenses (Exhibit 12-10B), however, indicates a growing inability to control costs and sustain earnings.

---

[26] Computer storefronts are discussed in Chapter 10.

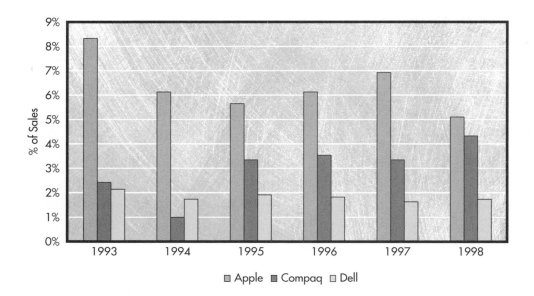

Apple Computer's profit margins and operating expenses were more erratic over the period analyzed than its competitors. The company reported restructuring charges in four of six years. Restructuring charges, increased selling, general, and administrative expenses, and shrinking gross profit margins produced net operating losses in 1996 and 1997. Continual restructuring raised questions about Apple's strategic vision and whether the company buried some recurring operating expenses within corporate restructurings.

Research and development costs varied among the direct and indirect computer resellers. Exhibit 12-11A presents R&D expenses over time. As evidenced from the graph, Apple and Compaq's R&D expenses significantly exceeded those of Dell.[27] Apple's knowledge-based costs exceeded Compaq's, although the gap between the two companies closed over time. The closed architecture of Apple's computers required greater development expenditures than those for the IBM clones. The company had to develop its own operating systems, for example, but open architecture firms used Microsoft's Windows system. In essence, Microsoft's costs for developing the industry's standard operating system were spread among the IBM clones. Apple, in contrast, bore its operating system cost alone.

The ability to produce revenues from knowledge-based endeavors also differed among firms, as is evidenced by the compound annual growth rates in Exhibit 12-11B. Dell's revenues grew faster than its R&D costs, indicating that the company sustained earnings from its intellectual activities. Compaq, however, spent relatively more on R&D than it realized in revenues. The company did not realize an increase in revenues commensurate with its growth in R&D spending.

Apple's R&D costs declined faster than its revenues fell. On the face of it, these data appear favorable because the drastic reduction in knowledge development is not matched by an equivalent decrease in revenues. The analyst must consider, however, that decreasing revenues raises earnings sufficiency concerns. Apple realized fewer dollars with which to cover fixed expenses from 1993 to 1998. In addition, Apple's levels of R&D spending indicate an earnings quality issue. If Apple spent as much on R&D in 1998 ($303 million) as it did in 1993 ($664 million), its

---

[27] Gateway did not disclose R&D expenses.

EXHIBIT 12-11B

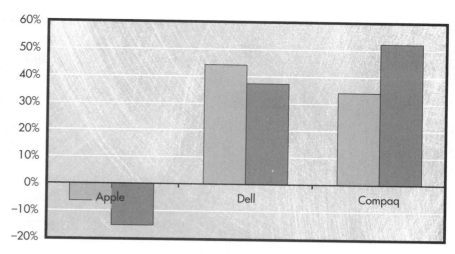

□ Revenues ■ Research and development expense

operating income of $329 million would have been a $32 million operating loss. Analysts could question whether reduced knowledge-based spending would produce fewer dollars of profit and cash flows in the future. Despite massive reductions in that discretionary account, Apple's R&D spending still exceeded that of its competitors in 1998 (Exhibit 12-11A). Apple had to spend more on knowledge development than its competitors but lacked the ability to absorb those additional costs as its gross margins declined over the period analyzed.

The PC industry reported immaterial amounts of other revenues and expenses and irregular items during the period analyzed. Transitory items reported after operations, in other words, were irrelevant to earnings sustainability analysis. Firms' operating profit margins were substantially the same as net profit margins, except for the effect of income taxes. Analysis would have produced similar results between operating cash flows and either net or operating profit margins.

Exhibits 12-12A through 12-12D relate each firm's operating income to its operating cash flow. This series of exhibits reinforce the superiority of the direct

WEB EXERCISE 13

*Has the correlation between
Apple Computer's operating
income and cash flows improved
since 1998?*

EXHIBIT 12-12A

*Apple Computer
Operating Income
and Cash Flows
1993–1998*

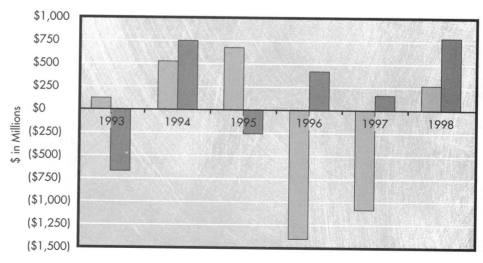

□ Operating income ■ Operating cash flow

EXHIBIT 12-12B

Dell, Inc.
Operating Income
and Cash Flows
1993–1998

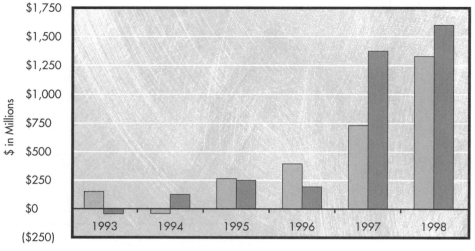

EXHIBIT 12-12C

Gateway, Inc.
Operating Income
and Cash Flows
1993–1998

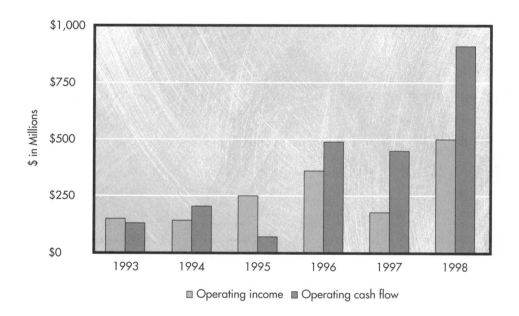

PC sellers' earnings quality. Both Dell and Gateway demonstrated a close correlation between operating income and cash flows. The two indirect PC sellers produced less pronounced relationships. Apple's earnings quality was especially troublesome when measured by the relationship between cash flow and profits. Exhibit 12-12A depicts negative correlation between Apple's earnings and CFOs. Analysts would have a more difficult task forecasting operating earnings (and cash flows) for Apple than either Dell or Gateway.

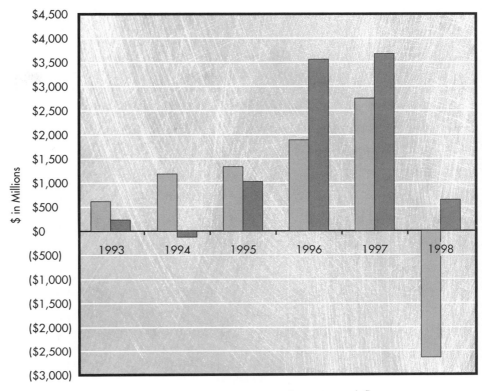

□ Operating income ■ Operating cash flow

SUMMARY

Chapter 12 describes analyzing operating performance with an emphasis on earnings quality. It focuses the analyst's attention on the sufficiency and sustainability of earnings. The types of earnings that a firm generates primarily determine these characteristics. Earnings produced from recurring transactions that stem from continual operations are superior to those generated by nonrecurring events. The chapter also distinguishes between income and cash flow as background for understanding operating performance.

The analyst must determine the inherent value in reported income numbers. This task is one of determining earnings quality, which in turn is a function of sustainability. Sustainable earnings can be reproduced in the future; they are the result of ongoing business operations. Other types of revenues and expenses occur infrequently and in varying amounts, and replication is unlikely. Consequently, stakeholders do not place as much value in them as they do recurring earnings. Management choices also affect reported income and the appearance of sustainability. Analysts must understand their selections and impute economic value to reported numbers.

The final portion of the chapter analyzes the operating performance of the PC industry. Many of the findings parallel those reported in the analyses of short-term liquidity and cash flows. Dell and Gateway's earnings quality exceeded those of Apple and Compaq from 1993 to 1998. The direct PC sellers' earnings were more highly correlated with cash flows than were their indirect selling counterparts'. Dell and Gateway exhibited greater stability of revenues and expenses. Much of the variance in Apple and Compaq's operating performance is attributable to such factors as restructuring charges, erratic R&D expenses, and write-offs for in-process R&D acquisitions. Those factors indicate less sustainability in the indirect sellers' reported income numbers.

KEY TERMS

Basic EPS
Change in accounting principle
Complex capital structure
Comprehensive income
Convertible securities
Corporate restructurings
Diluted EPS
Discontinued operations
Dual EPS
Earnings management
Earnings measurement
Earnings quality
Earnings sufficiency
Earnings sustainability
Extraordinary items
Gross profit margin
Income

Income from continuing operations (before tax)
Irregular items
Multiple restructurings
Net income
Net profit margin
Nonoperating section
Operating performance analysis
Operating section
Other comprehensive income items
Other expenses and losses
Other revenues and gains
Profit margin
Simple capital structure
Stock options
Transaction approach
Wealth
Wealth changes

NUMERICAL CASES

12-1

eXTREMESTUFF.com.

Numerical case 3-2 at the end of Chapter 3 extends eSTUFF's financial statements through 2003. Use these data to compute the following measures. (Note: NC 4-1 also required some of these computations as part of the common size financial statement assignment in NC 4-1.)

a. Gross profit margin
b. Operating profit margin (before other revenues and expenses)
c. Operating profit margin (after other revenues and expenses)
d. Net profit margin
e. Compound annual growth rate
f. Earnings per share

12-2

eXTREMESTUFF.com.

Graph the amounts of operating income, net income, and cash flows from operations. Analyze the degree of correspondence among them and the company's earnings quality.

INDUSTRY CASES

Examine the industry information, corporate financial statements, and related data presented in the text's appendixes. Prepare an operating performance analysis from 1993 through 1998. Use profit margin data and correspondence among cash flows and income as necessary. Identify any nonrecurring items or other income-related disclosures that might have affected your analysis. (As noted previously, your analysis of the PC industry may differ from that presented here.)

12-1   *Personal Computers: Apple, Compaq, Dell, and Gateway*

12-2   *Airlines: American, Delta, and United*

12-3   *Athletic Footwear: Nike and Reebok*

12-4   *Discount Retailers: Kmart, Target, and Wal-Mart*

12-5   *Fast-Food Restaurants: McDonald's and Wendy's*

12-6   *Soft Drink Companies: Coca-Cola and PepsiCo.*

INDUSTRY INTERNET CASES

Extend your operating performance case analyses by incorporating financial statement disclosures from 1999 through the most recent year. Research and note any substantially unusual or infrequent items that could have affected earnings quality during those years. (Financial statement disclosures may not be the same as those presented in the appendixes. Use your judgment to make the necessary modifications.)

12-1   *Personal Computers: Apple, Compaq, Dell, and Gateway*

12-2   *Airlines: American, Delta, and United*

12-3   *Athletic Footwear: Nike and Reebok*

12-4   *Discount Retailers: Kmart, Target, and Wal-Mart*

12-5   *Fast-Food Restaurants: McDonald's and Wendy's*

12-6   *Soft Drink Companies: Coca-Cola and PepsiCo.*

13 ASSET UTILIZATION ANALYSIS

CHAPTER LEARNING OBJECTIVES

Upon completion of this chapter, you should be able to:

◆ *Explain how the definitions of investment, capital, and assets affect asset utilization analysis.*

◆ *Indicate the significance of return on investment measures in the analysis of asset productivity.*

◆ *Compute return on assets and equity measures and their components.*

◆ *Discuss the need for technical adjustments to return on investment measures.*

◆ *Present a preliminary asset utilization analysis for a company or industry.*

$\mathcal{C}$ompanies control resources to build wealth. They invest in various types of productive assets in an attempt to create shareholder value. Prudent allocation of corporate funding helps an entity generate cash flow, earn income, and increase share price. Previous chapters examine the amounts, composition, and quality of cash flows and earnings. This chapter relates those financial performance indicators to the investments that produced them.

This chapter begins by explaining the reason for analyzing asset productivity. Next, it discusses capital and investment concepts, which are integral to understanding asset utilization measures. The third section presents a primary indicator of asset utilization—return on assets. Then we discuss return on equity, which extends the asset return concept. The fifth section addresses additional considerations that assist in analyzing assets and their productivity. Data from eSTUFF.com illustrate asset utilization measures. The sixth part analyzes the personal computer (PC) industry's use of its assets.

OBJECTIVE FOR ANALYZING ASSET UTILIZATION

MICRO ANALYSIS 1

Sara Lee began selling its manufacturing asset in the late 1990s. It may be that "nobody doesn't like Sara Lee," but another company is baking its cakes. The company decided to dedicate its resources to brand-name management and distribution networks. Executives believed that strategy would provide a better investment return than using capital for manufacturing facilities.

WEB EXERCISE 1

Examine Sara Lee's recent Form 10-Ks at saralee.com to determine if the composition of its fixed assets changed over time.

Asset utilization analysis links earnings to invested capital. It measures the relationship between a firm's inputs (assets) and its output (income). Analysts evaluate a firm's managerial effectiveness, determine rates of return to investors, benchmark performance over time and against competition, and forecast future operating performance and financial position by analyzing asset utilization.

Recall that Chapter 8 examines external investment, the initial step in beginning business operations. Analysts must differentiate between debt and equity financing as well as short- and long-term investment orientations. As noted in that chapter, the statement of financial position captures the essence of financing and investing decisions. Chapters 8, 9, 10, and 11 investigate liquidity issues arising from the interaction of those two activities. Chapter 12 broadens the analysis by examining wealth-building constructs, as opposed to the more narrowly defined cash considerations. The wealth-building activities addressed in that chapter, however, do not include analysis of the investments needed to produce them. This chapter compensates for that deficiency by examining firm capital and its relationship to income.

Management allocates funds among various assets. eSTUFF, for example, invested owners' money in inventory, equipment, and an intangible asset. External funding as well as income retained in the business financed additional operations. A fundamental question is how well eSTUFF, or any enterprise, created value with the resources at its disposal. Analysts examine the degree to which management effectively used its assets. Viewed from the owners' perspective, the issue becomes one of assessing whether the wealth created by the firm sufficiently compensated them for their investment. To make those judgments, an analyst must have a firm grasp of the concepts of investment, capital, and assets.

INVESTMENT ACTIVITIES

Return on investment is used to measure asset utilization. The term *investment*, however, has more than one meaning, depending on the context in which it is used. Analysts should also be aware that generally accepted accounting principles

(GAAP) greatly influence reported investment, regardless of how it is defined. This section discusses investment connotations and the related concepts of assets and capital.

ASSET VALUATION

An entity reports economic resources that it currently controls as assets.[1] In aggregate, assets are the resources that a firm relies on to earn income. They are reported on the balance sheet on a modified historical cost basis. In other words, the primary attribute measured by the financial reporting system is the historical amount of cash exchanged for that resource.[2] Exceptions to the historical cost principal do exist, however. Moreover, measurement limitations affect the reporting of assets on the balance sheet.

Recent Financial Accounting Standards Board (FASB) promulgations favor reporting assets at current value instead of their historical cost. Recall the discussion of securities investments in Chapter 7. The balance sheet discloses trading and available-for-sale securities at fair value. Similarly, it reports derivative instruments at their current worth or market value. The current GAAP favor disclosing relevant market value information when it is readily determinable.

The statement of financial position reports fixed assets at historical cost, net of depreciation. In this case, GAAP adhere to the historical cost principal because of the imprecision inherent in determining a fixed asset's fair value. eSTUFF, for example, would find it difficult to determine the current value of its partially depreciated equipment. In addition, it will not dispose of the equipment in the ordinary course of business. They will use it as part of the corporate going concern.[3]

The FASB has tried to maintain consistency in asset valuation. Its reporting requirements hinge on expected cash flows. Consider debt investments, for example. Companies sell trading and available-for-sale securities in the ordinary course of business. Therefore, their market values approximate expected cash receipts and provide relevant information to financial statement users. In contrast, companies will not their sell held-to-maturity investments; consequently, market values do not reflect expected cash flows and are irrelevant to their balance sheet valuation. These investments are reported at historical cost.

Two other aspects of asset valuation affect analysis. The first is the underreported value of certain assets, due to measurement difficulties. Reporting research and development (R&D) costs as an expense is a notable example. Another difficult-to-measure asset is human capital. The balance sheet does not report the value of managerial effectiveness, employee capabilities, corporate culture, and institutional knowledge; yet, wealth maximization requires them. The second issue affecting net asset valuation is a behavioral one: Management has a tendency to report events in their most favorable light. Lease capitalization is an example. Some companies structure lease terms so that the leased resources do not appear as an asset on the balance sheet.[4]

British Airways has made plans to lease aircraft by the month and engines by the hour.

Go to British Airways' financial statements (britishairways.com) and see if the company's short-term leasing plans became a reality. Indicate how the company reports leased aircraft.

---

[1] Review Chapters 3 and 8 for a more detailed definition of assets and their classifications.
[2] Chapter 1 introduces asset valuation and capital maintenance concepts.
[3] Chapter 3 defines the going concern concept.
[4] Chapter 6 notes that lessees favor reporting operating leases because capitalizing leases requires long-term liability recognition as well as long-term asset disclosure.

UNREPORTED KNOWLEDGE ASSETS

Bill Gates, Microsoft's founder, stated, "Our primary assets, which are our software and our software-development skills, do not show up on the balance sheet at all."[a] Does Mr. Gates' observation have implications for asset utilization analysis?

Research and development costs are expensed because the financial reporting system cannot measure their future benefits with any degree of certainty. The disclosure requirements for R&D costs are symptomatic of a more pervasive challenge facing compilers and users of financial statements: The existing system fails to measure human capital. For example, R&D is a by-product of intelligence and creativity. It does not result from some discrete unit of labor in the current reporting period but from the cumulative total of the knowledge in the organization and its employees. That knowledge base creates the current periods' intellectual investigations. Those inquiries, in turn, result in products that earn revenues and generate cash flows. Financial statements, however, are only proficient at summarizing an array of individual, identifiable business transactions.

Consider the challenges facing pharmaceutical companies. Eli Lilly & Co. realizes a quarter of its revenue from Prozac, an antidepressant medicine. The drug's patent, which grants Lilly the exclusive right to make and sell Prozac, was set to expire at the end of 2001. After its patent protection ends, generic drug manufacturers can introduce Prozac clones. These generic substitutes will drastically reduce Lilly's sales. Merck & Co. faced a similar situation. That company's U. S. patents for ulcers, hypertension, and high cholesterol medications were set to expire in 2001 as well. Merck realized $4.4 billion in U.S. sales from those drugs, or one quarter of its domestic revenues.

Observations

Do you think Lilly and Merck had to utilize human capital to produce its patented medications? If you responded yes, do you think the corporate financial statements appropriately valued those contributions? What indications would you look for as an analyst to determine if pharmaceutical companies are capable of maintaining revenues after blockbuster drugs' patents expire?

Discuss strategies for analyzing human capital's productivity and value to an enterprise.

---

[a] "Business: A Price on the Priceless," *The Economist,* June 12, 1999, p. 61.

CAPITAL CONCEPTS

An understanding of assets and investment depends on the definition of **capital.** Any form of wealth used to produce additional wealth is the starting point for defining capital. It equals an enterprise's sources of financing in the broadest sense of the definition. In balance sheet terminology, it is the sum of liabilities plus shareholders' equity. As such, capital equals total assets (total assets = total liabilities + shareholders' equity). A narrower definition of capital excludes short-term financing of current assets.[5]

---

[5] Corporate financiers view capital this way.

An even more restrictive definition of capital centers on the owners' investment in the entity. This narrower view equates capital to total shareholders' equity.[6] It excludes all liabilities from the definition. In other words, capital equals *net* assets in this limited context (total assets – total liabilities, shareholders' equity, or net assets). *Legal* capital is even more restrictive than the net asset perspective. This alternative considers capital as the investment required by statute, which is usually the par value of the stock outstanding.

Asset analysis depends on understanding the alternative perspectives on capital. Resource analysis focuses on interpreting **return on investment (ROI)** data. These measures consist of aggregate ratios and their components. The general model for ROI divides income by investment. Defining each item, therefore, determines the rate of return on investment. Chapter 12 addresses various interpretations of income, the numerator of the ratio. The definition of capital determines investment, the ratio's denominator. Defining capital as either total assets or net assets affects the ROI computation. In addition, asset interpretation influences the ROI calculation. Analysts may elect to depart from the modified historical cost basis mandated by GAAP to obtain more relevant information, so they can adjust for unreported and underreported assets.

Various interpretations of assets and capital can produce a vast array of potential ROI inputs. Therefore, the analyst's objective helps define assets and capital. The primary objectives are the topics for the next two sections of this chapter.[7]

MICRO

$\mathscr{A}$NALYSIS 3

Charles Conaway, who became Kmart's chief executive officer in 2000, announced his intention to raise the rate of return earned on investment by 2 percent.

RETURN ON ASSETS

The rate of **return on assets (ROA)** reports the percentage of income earned for each dollar invested in an entity's resources.[8] This measure provides financial statement users with the rate of return produced by the business's assets. The general ratio is computed as follows:

$$\text{ROA} = \text{Net Income} / \frac{(\text{beginning total assets} + \text{ending total assets})}{2}$$

eSTUFF's 2001 return on asset is calculated as follows (amounts in thousands of dollars):

CALCULATION FOR 2001	RETURN ON ASSETS
$21 / \dfrac{(\$780 + \$835)}{2}$ = $21 / $807.5	2.6%

---

[6] Accountants tend to view capital this way.

[7] The third and fourth sections of this chapter introduce asset and capital selections, depending on the particular ROI objective. However, GAAP modifications of assets are, for the most part, beyond the scope of this text.

[8] Most sources abbreviate return on assets as ROA, which is the convention used here. You might also encounter it as *ROTA,* return on *total* assets. ROTA measures investment return in the broadest sense of investment and capital.

WEB
EXERCISE 3

Find the inputs needed for computing Kmart's most recent rate of ROA at kmart.com.

MICRO
ANALYSIS 4

A traditional view of asset management centered on acquiring and maintaining resources that earned acceptable rates of return. An alternative perspective that is increasing in popularity calls for selling assets whenever a better opportunity for the money arises.

The company returned 2.6 cents for each dollar invested in resources during 2001.

MANAGERIAL ORIENTATION

Using ROA enables eSTUFF, or any firm, to assess managerial performance. Managers operate corporations on behalf of the owners. They use debt, equity, and internal financing to acquire resources in their efforts to maximize shareholder wealth. Management's ability to create wealth is determined, to a great extent, by how effectively they engage the firm's resources. Rates of ROA provide concrete measures of their success in this endeavor.

Various financial statement user groups have a vested interest in determining how well managers use assets. Executives use ROA data to benchmark their performance over time and against competition. Shareholders are interested in the overall rates of return produced by the managers they employ. Creditors want to evaluate the track record of their loan applicants.[9] Employees consider effective asset utilization as an indicator of corporate stability, job security, and compensation.

COMPONENTS OF RETURN ON ASSETS

Analysts gather more information about ROA by examining its components. Asset returns result from interaction between profit margins and asset turnover. Profit margins are the proportion of income to revenues, as noted in Chapter 12. Analysts compute **asset turnover** by dividing revenues by total assets. This measure reports the amount of sales each asset dollar generated in a given time period. ROA in component form is defined as follows:

$$\text{Return on assets} = \text{net profit margin} * \text{asset turnover}$$

or

$$\frac{\text{net income}}{\text{average total assets}} = \frac{\text{net income}}{\text{revenues}} * \frac{\text{revenues}}{\text{average total assets}}$$

The revenue terms in the profit margin's denominator and asset turnover's numerator cancel out, yielding the computation of an overall asset return as net income divided by total assets. eSTUFF's overall ROA and its component amounts for 2001 are computed as follows (amounts in thousands of dollars):

RETURN ON ASSETS		NET PROFIT MARGIN		ASSET TURNOVER
$\dfrac{\$21 / ([\$780 + \$835])}{2}$	=	$\$21 / \$1,200$	*	$\dfrac{\$1,200 / ([\$780 + \$835])}{2}$
2.60%	=	1.75%	*	1.486 times

In earning a 2.6 percent overall rate of ROA, eSTUFF had a 1.75 percent net profit margin and managed to produce almost $1.49 in sales for every dollar invested in resources.

---

[9] An analysis of capital structure is also very important to lenders. Chapter 14 addresses this matter.

An infinite number of profit margins and asset turnover combinations can produce equivalent ROAs. Data in Exhibit 13-1A present some alternative combinations of net profit margins and asset turnovers that would result in a 2.6 percent ROA for eSTUFF. The concave line in Exhibit 13-1B represents a graph of the data in Exhibit 13-1A, where all combinations of net profit margin and asset turnover on that line equal a 2.6 percent ROA. The parallel concave lines presented in Exhibit 13-1C represent a combination of net profit margins and asset turnovers that produce either a higher or lower rate of return than 2.6 percent. eSTUFF could improve its ROA beyond 2.6 percent by moving to the outermost line (or any point beyond the original 2.6 percent ROA line). To improve ROA, the company could increase profit margin more than it reduces asset turnover, or vice versa. The innermost concave line represents a combination of profit margins and asset turnovers that produced a rate of return less than 2.6 percent. Profit margin or asset turnover decreased faster than its complement increased in these situations.

EXHIBIT 13-1A

eSTUFF.com
2.6 Percent Profit Margin and Asset Turnover Combinations

RETURN ON ASSETS	NET PROFIT MARGIN	ASSET TURNOVER
2.60%	.5%	5.20 times
2.60%	1.0%	2.60 times
2.60%	1.5%	1.73 times
2.60%	2.0%	1.30 times
2.60%	2.5%	1.04 times
2.60%	3.0%	.87 times
2.60%	3.5%	.74 times

EXHIBIT 13-1B

eStuff.com
2.6% Return on Assets

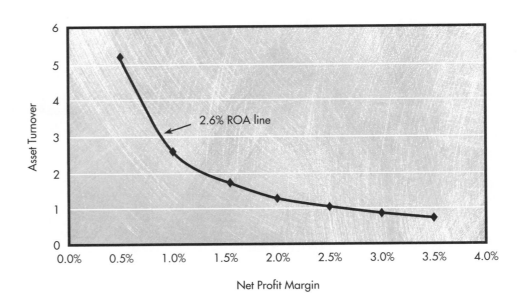

EXHIBIT 13-1C
eSTUFF.com
Alternative Returns on Assets

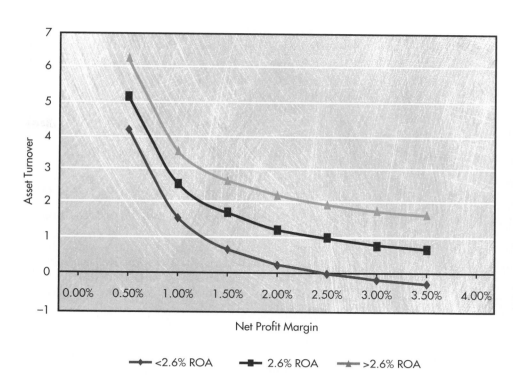

RETAILERS SEEK ADEQUATE RETURNS

Retailers invest heavily in property, plant, and equipment in order to sell merchandise. They must efficiently use those long-term assets in order to remain competitive. How do you interpret recent business decisions by merchants trying to increase their investment returns?

L. Daniel Jorndt, chief executive officer of Walgreen Co.s, describes his company's new strategy as a "7-Eleven on steroids."[a] The drugstore giant now builds stand-alone stores, instead of renting space in strip malls. Freestanding locations cost more to build and operate than Walgreen's traditional retail outlets, but evidence shows they increase customer count and generate additional sales.

Kmart closed 72 stores in 2000. The majority of locations were profitable, but their rates of return were unacceptable to new management. The company decided to direct its capital to other areas of the business and invest it in more profitable stores. They felt these efforts would improve asset returns.

Circuit City discontinued selling major appliances in 2000. The company opted to focus on electronic goods, which earned a higher profit margin than washers and dryers. Circuit City freed up 10,000 square feet of selling and warehouse space per store as a result of the decision. The firm increased floor space for electronic goods to 23,000 feet from 13,000 feet by dropping refrigerators and related items from its inventory.

Home Depot began selling home appliances at the beginning of the new century. Management viewed the additional product line as a natural extension for the home improvement giant's operations. The company anticipated increasing profit margins and sales per square foot by selling appliances.

WHAT'S YOUR ANALYSIS

MICRO *A*NALYSIS 5

Nordstrom Inc.'s department stores averaged sales revenues of $350 per square foot of selling space in 1999. That amount exceeded industry averages by over $100 per foot. High operating expenses, however, prevented the company from meeting average industry returns on assets.

WEB *E*XERCISE 4

What are the sales per square foot at the Neiman Marcus Group? Access Nordstrom's competitor at neimanmarcus.com.

Observations

Discuss how each company's shift in strategy could produce greater returns on assets. Consider both income and investment factors in your response. What risks do you see associated with each decision? How would you measure the success of these policy changes?

° D. Spurgeon, "Walgreen Takes Aim at Discount Chains, Supermarkets," *Wall Street Journal*, June 29, 2000, p. B4.

TECHNICAL ADJUSTMENTS TO RETURN ON ASSETS

Financial leverage substitutes fixed-charged financing (debt and preferred stock) for common equity financing. Leveraging influences ROA computations. To understand why, it is necessary to understand the difference between the tax treatments for debt and equity financing. Interest expense on borrowed funds is deductible for tax purposes, but dividends paid to shareholders are not. Assume two companies have equivalent operations, except for their financing methods. The firm that used debt financing would have less taxable income than an equity-financed company.[10] Interest expense, in other words, shields a portion of revenues from being taxed.

The tax-deductibility of interest expenses biases ROA analysis: ROA measures the earnings generated by assets; the proportion of the two financing methods, however, influences reported net income. Data from eSTUFF illustrate the problem. The company reported net income of $21,000 in 2001, the result of deducting $20,000 in interest expense from operating income. Consider two financing alternatives. First, assume the company had no debt; therefore, interest expense was zero. Second, assume the company had a relatively large amount of debt, and interest expense equaled $50,000. Data in Exhibit 13-2 present the impact of these alternatives, along with the excerpted 2001 income statement. Interest expense directly affects net income, as the data in the table indicate. Under each alternative, ROA would differ, because the measure's numerator (net income) changed depending on the assumption. Management's operating earnings, however, is the same in each case; it was merely the degree of debt financing that altered net income.

Net income is adjusted in the ROA computation to compensate for the debt financing bias. Analysts add **net interest expense**, which is interest expense multiplied by one minus the tax rate, to net income to determine profit earned. The aggregate ROA measure is computed as follows:

EXHIBIT 13-2
2001 Interest Expense and Net Income

INCOME STATEMENTS	AS REPORTED	ASSUMPTION 1	ASSUMPTION 2
Income from continuing operations	$55[a]	$55	$55
Financial (interest) expense	20	0	50
Pretax income	35	55	5
Income tax expense (40%)	14	22	2
Net income	**$21**	**$33**	**$ 3**

° Amount in thousands of dollars.

---

[10] Chapter 14 develops the financial leverage topic in greater detail. Chapter 15 investigates firm value.

EXHIBIT 13-3
Adjusted Return on Assets

ADJUSTMENTS	ORIGINAL DATA	ASSUMPTION 1	ASSUMPTION 2
Net income	$21[a] + ($20 * 6) = $33	$33 + $0 = $33	$3 + ($50 * .6) = $33
Return on assets	$\dfrac{\$33}{\$807.5} = 4.09$	$\dfrac{\$33}{\$807.5} = 4.09$	$\dfrac{\$33}{\$807.5} = 4.09$
Profit margin	$\dfrac{\$33}{\$1,200} = 2.75\%$	$\dfrac{\$33}{\$1,200} = 2.75\%$	$\dfrac{\$33}{\$1,200} = 2.75\%$
Asset turnover	$\dfrac{\$1,200}{\$807.5} = 1.49$	$\dfrac{\$1,200}{\$807.5} = 1.49$	$\dfrac{\$1,200}{\$807.5} = 1.49$

[a] Amounts in thousands of dollars.

$$\text{Return on assets} = \frac{\text{Net income + interest expense} * (1 - \text{tax rate})}{\text{Average total assets}}$$

Exhibit 13-3 demonstrates the adjustments for the data presented in Exhibit 13-2.[11] This exhibit also shows that after income is adjusted for interest expense, the ROAs are equivalent in each case. The adjusted data indicate management produced a 4.09 percent on return on the resources in place during 2001, exceeding the original 2.60 percent return reported in Exhibit 13-1A. Profit margin increased to a corrected amount of 2.75 percent as opposed to the previously computed 1.75 percent. Asset turnover did not change because income does not influence that ratio.

RETURN ON EQUITY

Return on equity (ROE) measures an entity's earnings on the capital invested by common shareholders.[12] This ratio excludes creditor and preferred shareholder financing. Only those funds provided by common shareholders are used to calculate ROE. The first part of this section explains this orientation and succeeding segments expand on it.

COMMON SHAREHOLDER ORIENTATION

Common shareholders provide an entity's risk capital; they accrue investment returns after the claims of the creditors and preferred shareholders have been satisfied. This shareholder group earns large rates of return when a business succeeds, but it does not receive a return on its investment if the business fails.[13] Due to their unique role in corporate finance, common shareholders are often regarded as providing the corporate financing cushion, as their funds act as shock absorbers for other investors.

Analysts must differentiate between a corporation's ROE and the rate earned by individual shareholders. The contributed capital section of the balance sheet

---

[11] Total assets would differ slightly under each alternative. Chapter 14 addresses that factor.

[12] Here we refer to return on equity as *ROE*, which is one conventional reference. You could also think of it as *ROCSE*, return on *common shareholders'* equity, or *ROCE*, return on *common* equity, as a reminder that preferred stock is excluded from the calculation.

[13] Common shareholders often do not receive a return *of* their investment, in addition to not earning one *on* their investment, when a business fails.

represents *direct* investments in the company by shareholders. Shareholders made these investments to start the business or provide it with additional capital once it was operating. Return on equity measures those rates of return. Keep in mind, however, that most equity investors purchase stock in the secondary market.[14] These individual rates of return are a function of corporate earnings and the share price paid in the secondary market.[15] They do not affect the company's ROE.

Retained earnings report an entity's accumulated undistributed income. These earnings, in effect, are the property of the common shareholders.[16] They represent a portion of the shareholders' overall claim to the company's net assets. Consequently, reported retained earnings are added to common shareholders' contributed capital when calculating ROE.

RATE OF RETURN ON EQUITY (ROE) RATIO

The general formula for computing return on equity is computed as follows:

$$\text{Return on equity} = \frac{\text{net income}}{\text{average common shareholders' equity}}$$

For example, eSTUFF's return on equity for 2001 is 4.25 percent (amounts in thousands of dollars):

CALCULATION FOR 2001	RETURN ON EQUITY
$\dfrac{\$21}{(\$445 + \$544)/2} = \dfrac{\$21}{\$494.5}$	4.25%

As with the ROA measure, this ratio can be better understood by disaggregating it and studying the components. Prior to doing that, however, it is necessary to introduce the financial structure leverage ratio.

FINANCIAL STRUCTURE LEVERAGE RATIO

The **financial structure leverage ratio** is a component of the ROE calculation. It measures the degree to which common shareholders provide asset financing. This ratio is computed as follows:

$$\text{Financial structure leverage ratio} = \frac{\text{average total assets}}{\text{average common shareholders' equity}}$$

Defining the financial structure leverage ratio enables us to disaggregate ROE.

COMPONENTS OF RETURN ON EQUITY

Common shareholders' equity serves as the investment base, instead of total assets, when computing ROE. That orientation means that the financial structure leverage ratio becomes part of equity return calculation. The general formula for computing ROE is as follows:

---

[14] Chapter 1 distinguishes between primary and secondary markets.
[15] Chapter 15 explores the price-earnings ratio.
[16] This statement assumes the firm gives no dividends to preferred shareholders.

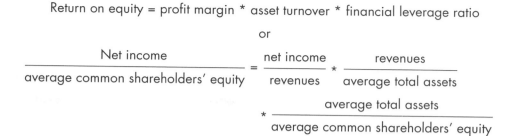

$$\text{Return on equity} = \text{profit margin} * \text{asset turnover} * \text{financial leverage ratio}$$

or

$$\frac{\text{Net income}}{\text{average common shareholders' equity}} = \frac{\text{net income}}{\text{revenues}} * \frac{\text{revenues}}{\text{average total assets}}$$
$$* \frac{\text{average total assets}}{\text{average common shareholders' equity}}$$

Similar to the ROA calculation, revenues (in the first and second term) and total assets (in the second and third term) on the component side of the equation cancel out, resulting in an overall return determined by dividing income by common equity. eSTUFF's 2001 ROE and its components are as follows (amounts in thousands of dollars):

RETURN ON EQUITY	PROFIT MARGIN	ASSET TURNOVER	FINANCIAL STRUCTURE LEVERAGE
$\dfrac{\$21}{\$494.5} = 4.25\%$	$\dfrac{\$21}{\$1{,}200} = 1.75\%$	$\dfrac{\$1{,}200}{\$807.5} = 1{:}486$	$\dfrac{\$807.5}{494.5} = 1.633$

The multiplicative effect of eSTUFF's financial structure leverage ratio increased the rate of return on equity to 4.25 percent from the 2.6 percent unadjusted return on total assets. Similar to the concept underlying Exhibit 13-1A, an infinite number profit margin, asset turnover, and financial structure leverage ratios could have produced a 4.25 percent ROE.[17]

The difference between the company's adjusted ROA (4.09 percent), however, was much closer to its 4.25 percent ROE. The interaction between the interest expense adjustment and financial leverage caused the difference between the two ratios to decrease. Chapter 14 will discuss that topic further.

TECHNICAL ADJUSTMENTS TO RETURN ON EQUITY

Analysts must adjust ROE computations if preferred shareholders provided significant equity financing. Preferred dividends reduce the amount of distributable earnings to common shareholders. Firms must subtract the amount of the current year's preferred dividends, whether paid or not, from net income in computing common equity returns.[18] Consequently,

$$\text{ROE} = \frac{(\text{Net income} - \text{preferred dividends})}{\text{average common shareholders' equity}}$$

and

$$\text{Profit margin} = \frac{(\text{Net income} - \text{preferred dividends})}{\text{revenues}}$$

---

[17] Equivalent ROEs are represented in a three-dimensional plane, rather than a two-dimensional line.
[18] Preferred dividends are considered a financial obligation of the firm, despite the fact that they are not statutorily required obligations. This view permits analysis of the investments' economic substance, rather than their legal form.

If a firm did not pay preferred dividends in previous years, then it must also subtract these accrued **dividends in arrears** from retained earnings. The adjustment made to ROE and the financial structure leverage in these instances looks like this:

$$ROE = \frac{(\text{Net income} - \text{current preferred dividends})}{(\text{average common shareholders' equity} = \text{preferred dividends in arrears})}$$

and

$$FSL = \frac{\text{average total assets}}{(\text{average common shareholders' equity} - \text{preferred dividends in arrears})}$$

eSTUFF did not need to adjust ROE because the company did not issue preferred stock.

Return on equity is *not* adjusted for interest expense, unlike the ROA computation. If an entity (i.e., common shareholders) elects to finance assets with debt, then the cost associated with that type of financing reduces the amount of income available to common shareholders. In other words, distributions to creditors are unavailable to corporate owners.

ADDITIONAL ASSET UTILIZATION CONSIDERATIONS

Fixed asset turnover, asset impairment, segment returns, and the shift toward an information economy provide additional challenges when analyzing the utilization of assets. The following sections briefly discuss these items.

MICRO ANALYSIS 6

Airlines have found an interesting way to get more mileage out of their fixed assets: Fly more people in smaller planes. American, Delta, and other air carriers began flying the Boeing 737-800 on transcontinental trips in the 1990s. The original 737 aircraft was designed a generation earlier for short hops and, as such, had very narrow seats. The seats in the newer version of the 737 maintained the cozy atmosphere of the original plane, despite the fact that they now fly long hauls.

FIXED ASSET TURNOVER

Fixed asset turnover is a subset of total asset turnover ratio, which, in turn, is a component of the ROA and ROE measures. It gauges the amount of revenue produced for every dollar invested in fixed assets. It is computed as follows:

$$\text{Fixed asset turnover} = \frac{\text{revenues}}{\text{average fixed assets}}$$

For example, eSTUFF's fixed asset turnover in 2001 is as follows (with dollar amounts in thousands):

CALCULATION FOR 2001		FIXED ASSET TURNOVER
$\dfrac{\$1,200}{(\$400 + \$380)/2} = \dfrac{\$1,200}{\$390}$		3.08 times

The hypothetical e-tailer recognized $3.08 in revenue for every dollar invested in property, plant, and equipment.

The denominator in this ratio can include intangible assets as well as tangible ones. This adjustment is intuitively appealing for firms that report substantial amounts of intangibles, such as knowledge-based companies. In eSTUFF's case, the adjusted fixed asset turnover ratio is computed as follows (amounts in thousands of dollars):

CALCULATION FOR 2001	PRODUCTIVE ASSET TURNOVER	
$\dfrac{\$1,200}{(\$420 + \$395) / 2} = \dfrac{\$1,200}{\$407.5}$		2.94 times

This long-term productive asset turnover ratio is lower than fixed asset turnover, but it provides a better measure of eSTUFF's utilization of all of its long-term assets.

Use caution when analyzing productive asset ratio trends. This measure exhibits more instability than short-term asset utilization ratios, such as inventory turnover.[19] Unlike current assets, fixed assets are acquired infrequently but in large increments. Therefore, their rate of turnover may differ dramatically from one period to the next.

WHAT'S YOUR ANALYSIS

SLOTLESS IN SEATTLE: AIRLINES SEEK TAKEOFF AND LANDING RIGHTS

Some airlines control scarce resources, and other air carriers struggle to obtain these assets. How do you think command of those limited assets affect air carriers' investment returns?

Airports have a limited number of gates from which aircraft can take off and land. They sell or lease those gates on a long-term basis to the airlines. Major airlines control most of the gates. A combination of their long-established business operations, strong financial position, and the aftereffects of former airline regulation contributed to this current state of affairs. Air carriers that control gates can sublease or rent unused gates, or slots, to other airlines. Gate-rich airlines can also swap their gates at one airport with carriers who control slots at other airports.

Industry practice for controlling these limited resources has affected corporate returns. Two issues exist. First, the major airlines that control the slots earn rental revenues from other, usually smaller, airlines that require space to serve a particular market. These smaller competitors contend rental rates are excessive. Second, major airlines monopolize certain key, or hub, airports through gate swapping arrangements. Smaller air carriers argue this practice creates an oligopoly, whereby the major airlines control certain markets and prevent competition.

Observations

Discuss the investment return implications for the airlines that control airport gates and for those that have to rent or lease them. Do you think the ability of an air carrier to utilize its gate resources is adequately reflected on its balance sheet?

MICRO **ANALYSIS 7**

Apple Computer reported in its 1997 Form 10-K that "the only such impairment losses identified by the Company...were those recorded in connection with the restructuring of operations."

ASSET IMPAIRMENT

Asset impairment exists when a resource's expected future cash flow is less than its reported book value. In such cases, the going concern principle is violated. The historical cost principle is the key to understanding why: As noted at the beginning of this chapter, GAAP mandate that fixed assets be reported at historical cost, because they will not be disposed of in the ordinary course of business; therefore, reporting them at fair value is considered irrelevant. Operating the asset in the normal course of business will recover historical cost invested in the resource. The inability to recover the cash invested in a fixed asset, however, invalidates the intent of historical

---

[19] Chapters 8 and 9 examine inventory turnover in the context of short-term liquidity analysis.

cost reporting. The asset, or a portion of it, is no longer economically viable. In effect, companies must report the impaired amount as an expense.[20]

Impaired asset losses are disclosed as part of other expenses and losses. Analysts must be aware of two potential disclosure problems. First, determining when an asset is impaired requires a great deal of judgment. Companies employing aggressive accounting policies are more reluctant to acknowledge impaired assets than their more conservative counterparts. Second, it is difficult to distinguish an individual asset's impairment from overall corporate impairment. Impaired assets are often treated as part of a corporate restructuring. This accounting treatment buries the losses from impaired assets as an undisclosed component of the larger restructuring expense.

SEGMENT RETURNS

Companies must disclose information about business divisions and the economic environments in which they operate.[21] Such **segment disclosures** add to the information set reported by consolidated financial statements. GAAP permit individual entities to determine how they report segment information. Every firm with multiple business lines defines its segments according to how it makes operating decisions. This self-selection process is termed the **management approach** to segment disclosures. Companies must report the revenues, income, and assets of their segments, regardless of how they categorize them.

Segment disclosures provide analysts with insight about the various business activities of a conglomerate. Analysts can compute the segments' ROA with such data. Sufficient disclosures exist that allow financial statement users to compute profit margins and asset turnover.[22] Shareholders' equity represents the owners' interest in the underlying net assets of an entity; therefore, equity cannot be segmented and ROE cannot be computed.

Analysts use segment analysis to gain insight into the relative performance of each business area of a company. Using these data, analysts can pinpoint particularly profitable or troubled portions of the enterprise. Consolidated financial statements, on the other hand, obscure individual business unit returns by aggregating the assets and earnings of all business segments.

KNOWLEDGE-BASED ASSET RETURNS

The emerging information-oriented economy has altered the resource composition of many firms. Traditionally, service providers, merchants, and manufacturers owned substantial amounts of fixed assets, which they used to generate revenues. Many businesses in the new economy have fewer dollars invested in land and buildings. They direct greater amounts of corporate financing toward R&D, intellectual capital, and the legal protection of information (e.g., patents, copyrights). These types of assets are less amenable to utilization analysis than fixed assets of the old economy. Many information-based assets go unreported (e.g., R&D) or underreported (e.g., intangible assets at historical cost).

---

[20] "Accounting for the Impairment of Long-Lived Assets," *Statement of Financial Accounting Standards No. 121* (Norwalk, CT: FASB, 1995).

[21] "Disclosures about Segments of an Enterprise and Related Information," *Statement of Financial Accounting Standards No. 131* (Norwalk, CT: FASB, 1997).

[22] *Statement of Financial Accounting Standards No.131* requires disclosures of interest expense applicable to each segment, thereby enabling the technical adjustment to the ROA computation.

Analysts are challenged by this fundamental shift in asset structure. The reported investment base for many new economy firms is less relevant than that for old economy companies. This makes interpreting investment returns more difficult. Although ROA and ROE remain useful tools for asset utilization analysis, analysts must supplement them with astute judgment. The analysis of the PC industry addresses some of these concerns.

KNOWLEDGE ASSETS MELD THE OLD AND NEW ECONOMIES

Technological advances influence asset productivity. Oil companies and machine-tool manufacturers are old-line industries that have benefited from changes in the new economy. How do you view the incorporation of knowledge-based resources by traditional industrialists?

In 1980, economic forecasters predicted $98-a-barrel oil in 1997. The actual price that year was $21, which was less expensive than an equivalent amount of bottled water.[a] Technology accounted for much of the change. It helped companies locate oil reserves. In addition, experiments on supercomputers allow petroleum engineers to determine how to extract the greatest amount of natural resources at the lowest possible cost from those fields. As a result, petroleum location, extraction, and production costs have substantially decreased in the past two decades.

Machine-tool companies shape, cut, and grind metal to produce tools for other industries, such as engine makers and automobile manufacturers. Inexpensive and powerful semiconductors embedded in many of these tools have broadened capabilities and improved their accuracy. These and other advances in the machine-tool industry have spurred manufacturing efficiency and slowed the increase in the cost of durable goods.[b] As a result, overall manufacturing productivity has exceeded growth in the rest of the economy during the past decade.

[a] G. McWilliams, "The New Economics of Oil," *Business Week*, November 3, 1997.
[b] S. Liesman, "Better Machine Tools Give Manufacturers Newfound Resilience," *Wall Street Journal*, February 15, 2001, pp. A1 and A8.

ANALYSIS OF THE PERSONAL COMPUTER INDUSTRY

This final section of the chapter presents an analysis of the PC industry's asset utilization and investment returns, focusing on investment returns earned by a knowledge-based industry. The first part examines issues surrounding an information-based investment structure. The remaining two sections analyze rates of return for PC firms from 1993 through 1998.

INTELLECTUAL ASSET FACTORS

The investment base of the PC industry differs from that of many other manufacturing concerns. Tangible fixed assets do not constitute a significant portion of the PC companies' total resources. The charts in Exhibit 13-4 disclose the industry's asset proportions during the period examined. Current assets made up the great majority of the industry's resources.[23] Fixed assets, by contrast, were only about 13

[23] Chapter 8 initially makes this point. Compaq, the largest of the four firms analyzed, reported two significant events in 1998, reducing the industry's percentage of current assets that year: The company's net operating loss created a long-term deferred tax asset and goodwill resulting from the acquisition of Digital. These events increased the percentage in the other assets category for the four-firm total in that year.

EXHIBIT 13-4
*Personal Computer Industry
Weighted Average Asset
Composition*

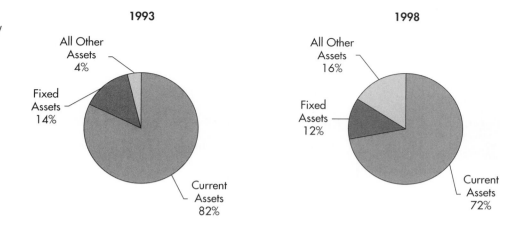

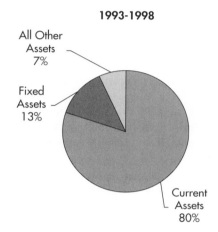

percent of the investment base for Apple, Compaq, Dell, and Gateway. A number of reasons accounted for this balance sheet profile.

First, PC companies purchased many components from other manufacturers during the period analyzed. Subcontracting in this manner reduced their plant and equipment needs. Second, PC companies outsourced much of the actual computer assembly to other firms. Those **manufacturers for hire** invested in production facilities and allocated those costs among their numerous customers. Consequently, the finished goods inventory of PC companies included manufacturing overhead costs. Their balance sheets, however, did not reflect the fixed asset costs because they were borne by the manufacturers they hired to assemble the PCs. Rapid inventory turnover and the trend toward direct computer selling also reduced the need to warehouse components and completed goods which in turn reduced investment in property storage and equipment.

The industry was oriented toward developing, marketing, and distributing PCs. The firms analyzed identified greater value in these activities than in assembling every PC and manufacturing each of its components. One could regard PC firms as coordinators of product creation, as opposed to old economy industrialists, which made virtually all parts of the finished goods. To a certain extent, the

EXHIBIT 13-5
*Compound Annual
Growth Rates
1993–1998*

COMPANY	PROPERTY, PLANT, AND EQUIPMENT	TOTAL ASSETS
Apple	−12.0%	−3.7%
Compaq	30.1%	41.4%
Dell	36.9%	35.7%
Gateway	54.6%	38.7%

WEB EXERCISE 9

*Go to sec.gov and examine the
filings for LSI Logic Corp.
Determine how the company
revalued its in-process R&D
costs when it purchased
Symbios, Inc.*

MICRO ANALYSIS 12

*Compaq's $9.1 billion purchase
of Digital in 1998 included over
$3 billion in in-process R&D,
which was immediately
expensed, and capitalized goodwill in excess of $2 billion.*

WEB EXERCISE 10

*Access the current financial dis-
closures of one of the PC companies analyzed here and compute
its compound growth rates for
total assets and property, plant,
and equipment since 1998.*

industry orchestrated, rather than manufactured, PCs. Tangible long-term assets consumed relatively few investment dollars as a result of this strategy.

Financial reporting requirements also influenced asset composition. As previously noted, R&D costs were expensed, rather than capitalized as intangible assets. These costs were a significant expenditure, as each company endeavored to roll out more powerful, less expensive machines before the competition. The firms' treatment of business acquisition costs also mitigated the amount of long-term balance sheet disclosures. Companies generally recognize the excess purchase price incurred in business acquisitions as goodwill. However, the PC firms treated in-process R&D, or the cost of the target's R&D, differently: They immediately charged it against revenues. They recognized the majority of their intangible costs as in-process R&D. That accounting treatment greatly reduced the amount of goodwill they capitalized.

Property, plant, and equipment growth was less than that for total assets for two of the four companies analyzed.[24] These compound annual growth rates for each firm are presented in Exhibit 13-5. Gateway's rapid fixed asset growth was attributable, in part, to its Gateway Country Store concept. The company attempted to increase profit margins by selling computer upgrades and services through retail outlets. That strategy increased plant and equipment expenditures, which could have slowed asset turnover.

Venture capitalists met most of the PC industry's early financing needs. Those investors became equity partners with technology-oriented entrepreneurs. That financing arrangement, coupled with the industry's small fixed asset requirements, reduced industry demand for debt and preferred shareholder financing. Consequently, adjusting investment returns for interest expense and preferred dividends was not an important factor in this asset utilization analysis.

RETURN ON ASSETS

Annual total asset returns are presented in Exhibit 13-6 for each PC firm. Evidence from the data indicate that the return trend for Dell improved through the years. Those for Apple declined. Gateway and Compaq's were fairly stable, except for a marked decline in one year (Gateway in 1997 and Compaq in 1998). The data provide some evidence that the direct sales strategy employed by Dell and Gateway utilized assets more efficiently than the indirect distribution channels used by Apple and Compaq.

Component analysis provides additional insight about asset returns. Exhibits 13-7A and 13-7B present each firm's annual profit margin and asset turnover. Data underlying Dell Computer's net profit margin trend indicate the company earned

---

[24] Apple's fixed assets decreased faster than its total assets. We construe this result in the same manner that we interpret the increase in the accounts of Dell and Compaq.

EXHIBIT 13-6
*Personal Computer Industry
Annual Return on Assets*

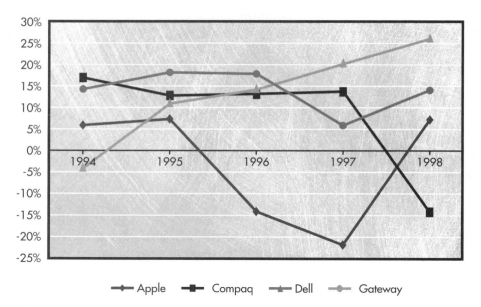

EXHIBIT 13-7A
*Personal Computer Industry
Annual Net Profit Margin*

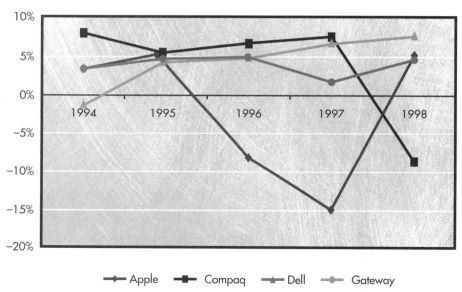

substantially more net profit per sales dollar than its competitors. Compaq's profit margin declined drastically in 1998, resulting from a $3.2 billion in-process R&D expense. Apple's poor operating performance throughout the period accounted for its net profit margin. Gateway's profit margin rebounded in 1998 after decreasing substantially in 1997. Market acceptance of its retail operations in the last year analyzed may have contributed to its improved profit margin.

The demarcation between direct and indirect computer sellers was most evident in asset turnover. Dell and Compaq generated over three dollars of sales for each dollar invested in assets, but Apple and Compaq earned less than two revenue dollars per asset dollar in the later years of the study. Even if the firms earned equivalent net profit margins, the direct sellers' higher asset turnovers would have produced greater returns than those for the indirect sellers. Gateway's asset turnover slowed during the period. That decrease could have

EXHIBIT 13-7B

*Personal Computer Industry
Annual Asset Turnover*

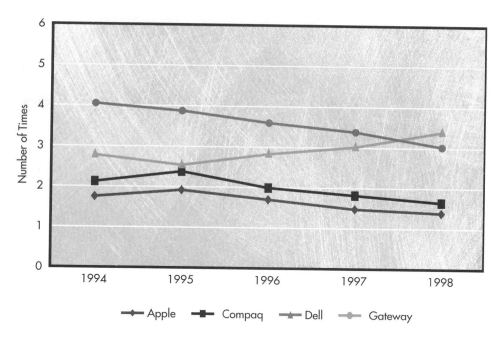

been attributable, in part, to the higher fixed asset costs incurred in opening its Gateway Country Stores.

Exhibit 13-8 summarizes asset returns from 1994 through 1998.[25] Dell appeared to utilize its total assets more efficiently than its competitors did toward the end of the period analyzed. Gateway's performance was fairly stable, except for the decline in 1997. A significantly lower profit margin caused that year's over-all rate of return to decrease. Rates of return on the assets of Compaq and Apple lagged those of the industry leaders.

Data from Apple Computer in Exhibit 13-9 support the contention made previously that interest expense insignificantly altered PC companies' returns on assets.[26] Apple Computer's adjusted net income increased net profit margins and ROA by

EXHIBIT 13-8

*Personal Computer Industry
Weighted Average Annual
Return on Assets
1994–1998*

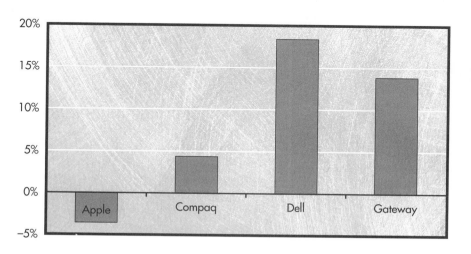

---

[25] Data are not available for 1993, due to balance sheet averaging.

[26] Apple disclosed interest expense and effective tax rates in its 1994–1998 Form 10-K notational disclosures.

EXHIBIT 13-9
*Apple Computer
Annual Unadjusted and
Adjusted Returns on Assets
and Components
1994–1998*

	1994	1995	1996	1997	1998
Unadjusted (as reported)					
Profit margin	3.4%	3.8%	−8.3%	−14.8%	5.2%
Asset turnover	1.75	1.92	1.70	1.48	1.39
Return on assets	5.9%	7.4%	−14.1%	−21.8%	7.3%
Adjusted					
Net interest expense (in millions of dollars)	$27	$30	$60	$71	$58
Profit margin	3.7%	4.1%	−7.7%	−13.8%	6.2%
Asset turnover	1.75	1.92	1.70	1.48	1.39
Return on Assets	6.5%	7.9%	−13.1%	−20.4%	8.6%

approximately one percentage point per year. These adjustments would not have altered Apple's ranking among the four firms analyzed. The other three PC firms carried significantly less long-term debt than Apple reported. Their ROA measures would have changed even less than those for Apple if the adjustments were made.

In-process R&D costs significantly reduced Apple's net income in 1997 and Compaq's earnings in 1998. It could be argued that these companies' net income amounts should have excluded those nonrecurring charges. Making those adjustments would have increased their respective net profit margins and ROA in those years.

At issue is whether those adjustments would have materially affected an analyst's perceptions. In Apple's case, the result would have been to decrease its 1997 net loss. Its ROA and profit margin would still have been negative and substantially lagged the industry's performance in that year. Compaq's 1998 charge for Digital's in-process R&D would have changed a $2.66 billion pretax operating loss to a $543 million pretax income. Assuming an optimistic scenario in which annual tax expense remained constant at $81 million, net income would have been $462 million ($543 − $81). These adjustments yield a net profit margin of 1.5 percent ($462 million / $31.2 billion in revenues) and a return on assets of 2.5 percent ($462 million / $18.8 billion in average assets).[27] As with Apple, Compaq's adjusted earnings yielded insufficient returns on the investments made to generate them.

MICRO NALYSIS 13

Do you think adjusting Apple's ROE for its $4.5 million preferred dividend would have materially affected the analysis of the company's asset utilization?

RETURN ON EQUITY

Financial structure leverage ratios differed among the four firms. Exhibit 13-10 reports the annual financial structure leverage measures from 1994 through 1998. Dell was more highly leveraged than Compaq and Gateway. Apple Computer increased its degree of leverage throughout the period examined. Its financial leverage structure ratio rivaled that of Dell by 1998.[28] Apple's poor financial performances in 1996 and 1997 may have forced the company to borrow long term. The company substantially increased its debt in 1996–1998, compared to 1993–1995.

---

[27] This adjusted ratio, like the adjusted profit margin, is understated. Ignoring the in-process R&D charge implies that the R&D cost has future measurable value, which would require capitalization, thus increasing total assets.

[28] Apple's increased financial leverage is reflected in Exhibit 13-9. Note how the adjustments to ROA and profit margin are greater in 1997 and 1998 than they were in 1994–1996.

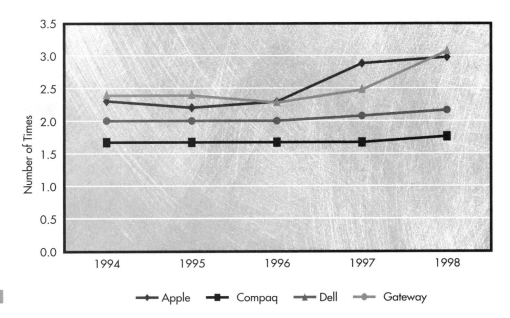

*The returns on investment for
Dell and Gateway far surpass
those for Apple and Compaq. The
industry leaders directly sell PCs
to end users, meaning they act as
retail merchants in addition to
computer makers. Could it be
that selling PCs adds greater
economic value to an entity and
increases its wealth to a far
greater extent than manufacturing the machines?*

Rates of return on shareholders' equity were similar to those earned on total assets, despite the differences in financial structure leverage ratios. Dell was the industry leader in the later years of the study, Gateway's returns remained relatively constant, Compaq's performance decreased over time, and Apple's ROE lagged the industry. Exhibits 13-11A (annual returns) and 13-11B (average returns) present each company's return on common equity.

Apple Computer's net losses in 1996 and 1997 illustrate the dual nature of financial leverage. It can hurt a firm's equity investors as well as help them. Apple's net losses in 1996 and 1997 produced negative asset returns. The company's financial structure leverage ratio amplified the extent of the negative returns on shareholders' investments. Chapter 14 examines the advantages and disadvantages of financial leverage in greater detail.

EXHIBIT 13-11A

*Personal Computer Industry
Annual Returns on Equity*

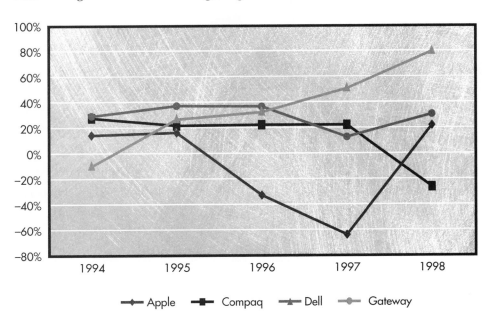

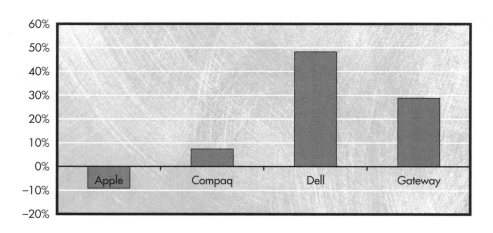

WEB

EXERCISE 11

*Has Compaq Computer become
comparable with its rivals by
reporting geographical segment
data? Go to compaq.com and
find out.*

SEGMENT RETURNS

The final set of exhibits graphically present the industry's ROAs by geographical segments for 1998.[29] Dell and Gateway earned strong returns domestically in 1998, but Apple's foreign investments produced higher returns than those earned by its U.S. segment. These results produced mixed signals. Data indicate that Apple efficiently utilized assets overseas but failed to do so domestically. That result was alarming because the United States was the largest market for Apple and its competitors during the period analyzed.

EXHIBIT 13-12A

*1998 Net Profit by
Geographical Segment*

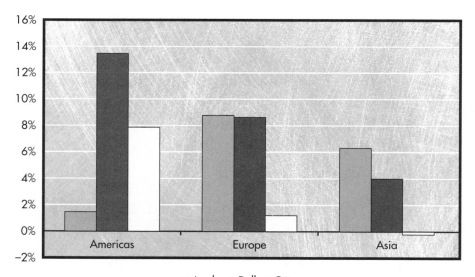

---

[29] Compaq did not disclose geographical segment data. Returns are based on segment operating income and net identifiable assets.

EXHIBIT 13-12B
*1998 Asset Turnover by
Geographical Segment*

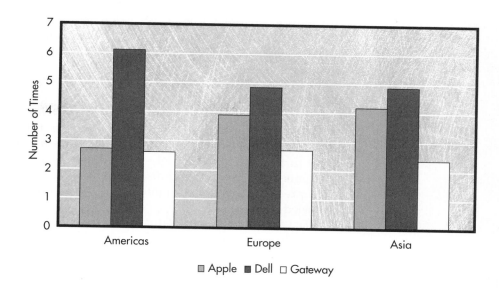

EXHIBIT 13-12C
*1998 Return on Assets by
Geographical Segment*

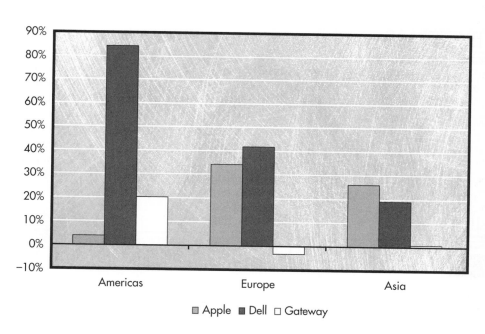

SUMMARY

This chapter examines how well an entity uses its economic resources. Investment returns are the primary vehicle for analyzing asset utilization. The rates of return on assets and equity are the two means for measuring capital productivity. These ratios' components add further insight into asset utilization.

This chapter also discusses the concept of investment. It points out that investment, like capital, has more than one meaning. In it broadest sense, investment (or capital) equals an entity's total assets. A narrower perspective equates investment (capital) to the net assets of the firm's owners. Analysts use ROA to measure resource utilization from a broad investment perspective and ROE to examine it in the narrower sense of the term. A company's ability to generate net profit margins and produce sales from its assets (asset turnover) is combined to calculate its ROA. A firm's ROE is computed by its financial structure leverage ratio with the two ROA components.

Debt and preferred equity considerations affect return on investment measures. An enterprise must adjust rates of return if those financing arrangements are material to its asset funding. Segment returns, asset impairment, and fixed asset turnover also add insight about an entity's ability to utilize assets if their amounts are significant and disclosed by the company. In addition, this chapter presents the challenges encountered when analyzing the investment returns of a knowledge-based industry.

The analysis of the PC industry's ability to use its assets produces results similar to those detected for liquidity and cash flows. Dell and Gateway appeared to utilize its assets more efficiently than Apple and Compaq did from 1993 to 1998. The relative rankings of the firms did not change when the data were adjusted for financing arrangements or examined on a segmented basis.

KEY TERMS

Asset impairment	Manufacturers for hire
Asset turnover	Net interest expense
Asset utilization analysis	Return on assets (ROA)
Dividends in arrears	Return on equity (ROE)
Financial leverage	Return on investment (ROI)
Financial structure leverage ratio	Segment disclosures
Fixed asset turnover	Segment returns
Management approach	

NUMERICAL CASE

13-1

eXTREMESTUFF.com.

Numerical case 3-2 at the end of Chapter 3 extends eSTUFF's financial statements through 2003. Use these data to compute the following measures for 2002 and 2003.

a. Net profit margin (adjusted for interest expense)
b. Return on assets
c. Return on assets (adjusted for interest expense)
d. Financial structure leverage ratio
e. Return on common shareholders' equity

INDUSTRY CASES

Examine the industry information and corporate financial data presented in the text's appendixes. Prepare an asset utilization analysis from 1993 through 1998. Make technical adjustments for interest expense and preferred dividends if the data permit; otherwise, assume those adjustments are immaterial to the analysis. Construct graphs, as needed, to help you interpret the data. Comment on the extent to which you think more information about such items as human capital, R&D, intangible assets, and segment reporting would assist in your analysis of asset utilization.

13-1   *Personal Computers: Apple, Compaq, Dell, and Gateway*

13-2   *Airlines: American, Delta, and United*

13-3   *Athletic Footwear: Nike and Reebok*

13-4   *Discount Retailers: Kmart, Target, and Wal-Mart*

13-5   *Fast-Food Restaurants: McDonald's and Wendy's*

13-6   *Soft Drink Companies: Coca-Cola and PepsiCo.*

INDUSTRY INTERNET CASES

Extend your operating performance case analyses by incorporating financial statement disclosures from 1999 through the most recent year. Research and note any disclosures about interest expense, preferred dividends, segment disclosures, impaired assets, and any other factors that would improve your analysis. (Financial statement disclosures may not be the same as those presented in the appendices. Use your judgment to make the necessary modifications.)

13-1   *Personal Computers: Apple, Compaq, Dell, and Gateway*

13-2   *Airlines: American, Delta, and United*

13-3   *Athletic Footwear: Nike and Reebok*

13-4   *Discount Retailers: Kmart, Target, and Wal-Mart*

13-5   *Fast-Food Restaurants: McDonald's and Wendy's*

13-6   *Soft Drink Companies: Coca-Cola and PepsiCo.*

14. CAPITAL STRUCTURE ANALYSIS

CHAPTER LEARNING OBJECTIVES

Upon completion of this chapter, you should be able to:

◆ *Describe the advantages and disadvantages of financial leverage.*

◆ *Compute the financial leverage index, debt to capital ratio, and debt to equity ratio, and use other techniques for analyzing capital structure.*

◆ *Relate capital structure composition to owner and creditor investment objectives.*

◆ *Discuss the various types of risks and their role in capital structure analysis.*

◆ *Present a preliminary capital structure analysis for a company or industry.*

$\mathcal{E}$conomic and industry conditions as well as corporate policies and practices affect financial performance. Actual results, therefore, sometimes fail to meet expectations. Wealth creation, in other words, entails risk. We have discussed certain factors that potentially affect earnings and cash flows throughout the text. Chapter 13 introduces a specific type of risk, one that substitutes debt for equity financing. That concept of financial risk serves as a focal point in understanding the relationship between debt and equity financing. This chapter addresses this topic, known as capital structure analysis.

This chapter first states the objective for analyzing capital structure. Next, we discuss debt and equity measurement issues. Third, we examine financial leverage's role in producing investment returns. The fourth section defines risk factors associated with resource financing and leverage. Fifth, this chapter presents an array of capital structure measures used to compare debt with equity. Data from eSTUFF.com illustrate many of the points made in the first five sections. The final section analyzes the personal computer (PC) industry's capital structure.

OBJECTIVE FOR ANALYZING CAPITAL STRUCTURE

Capital structure relates to the amount and types of long-term debt and equity used to finance assets. The primary components of capital structure are bonds payable, preferred stock, common stock, and retained earnings. Assets acquired with those funds are engaged in revenue-producing activities. Those central business activities produce sufficient cash flows, provided financing is properly structured and assets are effectively utilized. The proportion of debt to equity plays a critical role when analyzing asset financing. **Capital structure analysis** determines if an entity's combination of debt and equity enables wealth creation without unduly jeopardizing long-term solvency or financial flexibility.

Effective capital structure provides a firm with financial strength and stability. The proportion of debt to equity must compensate creditors for the use of their funds, provide equity investors with acceptable investment returns for the risks they incur, allow the company to take advantage of unforeseen investment opportunities, and insulate the firm from economic adversity. Analysts must judge whether a firm has the right mix of long-term debt and equity financing to meet these objectives. They need an in-depth understanding of financing leverage to do so.

FINANCING ACTIVITIES

The balance sheet reports how funds are acquired and allocated. Recall the fundamental relationship between these financing and investing activities, discussed in Chapter 8. Those activities are classified into short- and long-term components. Analysis initially focuses on near-term activities. Liquidity and operating cash flow analysis, covered in Chapters 8–11, involves the relationship between current accounts and short-term activities. Operating performance analysis (see Chapter 12) focuses on sustainable earnings, thus transitioning from current to long-term analysis. Chapter 13 relates earnings to the resources needed to produce them. This chapter discusses the long-term methods of financing those assets. To begin, we examine two important concepts underlying long-term financing arrangements.

CAPITAL STRUCTURE VALUATION

The financial reporting system applies to liability valuation as well as asset measurement. The historical cost system underlies generally accepted accounting procedures (GAAP), but modifications affect liability disclosures.[1] For example, eSTUFF's balance sheet reports accrued liabilities at an amount of cash equal to the goods or services received. This type of disclosure is an application of historical cost. Accounts payable, however, are reported at their **expected exit value.** That means those obligations are valued at the cash amount eSTUFF will pay vendors to eliminate their claims against the firm. The balance sheet discloses long-term notes and bonds payable at the **present value of expected cash flows,**[2] meaning that firms discount the future cash payments for these liabilities to their present value.[3]

The payment time horizon influences the valuation methods used to measure current and long-term liabilities. Accounts payable will be paid within a short period of time; therefore, their expected exit value is immaterially different than the present value of expected cash outflows. The present value of the cash required to eliminate the liability, in other words, equals the future value of the cash needed to pay the obligation. The length of time between the date of the balance and payment date for long-term debt, however, is much longer. Consequently, a firm would discount those obligations to their present value at an appropriate interest rate. The financial position statement, in other words, reports long-term financing arrangements at the amount of cash required to satisfy the obligation as of the balance sheet date.

The valuation of equity financing is more abstract than that for debt financing. The balance sheet reports shareholders' equity as the difference between assets and liabilities. However, there is no single valuation method that captures the owners' interest because assets and liabilities are a combination of measured attributes (e.g., historical cost and expected exit value). Contributed capital, the first section of shareholders' equity, is valued at the **historical proceeds,** or the amount of cash received when stock was issued.[4] Retained earnings, the second component of equity, defy valuation. The sum of undistributed earnings results from the interaction between balance sheet valuation methods and the nominal dollar concept of capital maintenance.[5]

DEBT AND EQUITY INVESTORS

Alternative attribute measurements for debt and equity accounts underscore the different objectives for their respective investor groups. We examine some owner

---

[1] We do not use the more conventional term, *historical cost principle*, because cost relates to asset valuation but not to liability valuation.

[2] We use eSTUFF's notes payable to increase financial statement understandability. Bonds payable more realistically reflect long-term debt financing.

[3] This concept also applies to certain assets. Chapter 7, for example, indicates that organizations should report held-to-maturity securities at modified historical cost. It is the time value of money adjustment (expected exit value from an asset perspective) that governs financial reporting in that instance.

[4] Firms do not always issue stock for cash; sometimes, they exchange it for goods and services. In those instances, contributed capital reflects the equivalent cash value of the goods and services received.

[5] Refer to Chapter 1 for a discussion of capital maintenance concepts. Retained earnings report a summary of periodic income that is undistributed to shareholders. One way to view a single period's income is as the difference between net assets at the end of a reporting period and the nominal amount of invested capital at the beginning of that period. Each asset is a function of the specific attribute measured in accordance with GAAP.

MICRO ANALYSIS 2

Many firms split their stock by issuing two or three shares for every share held by an investor. These splits increase the number of equity shares outstanding and reduce par value per share. Stock splits do not affect capital structure disclosures because they do not change the book value of shareholders' equity.

WEB EXERCISE 3

Examine Biofiltration Systems Corp.'s stock split in 2000. View its Form 10-K at biofiltrationsystems.com. Do you find the stock split unusual?

MICRO ANALYSIS 3

Investors bailed out nearly bankrupt drkoop.com, Inc., with a loan that allows them to convert the debt to common stock. The conversion rate was lower than the prevailing share price of the company's stock.

and creditor objectives in previous chapters, especially Chapters 1, 3, 8, and 13. We now review some of those objectives and the firm's need for capital.

Equity investors provide an entity's permanent financing. As such, they are patient investors. These corporate owners insulate the enterprise from the random business shocks that affect business operations and reduce profitability. They are entitled to an investment return only after the other claimants have been satisfied. Owners' funds afford a measure of security to creditors by acting as a financial cushion in times of economic adversity. In other words, equity contributors buffer debt investors from the possibility of nonpayment when current income and cash flow are insufficient to meet maturing obligations. Owners' investments are inextricably tied to the organization as a result of their role in corporate financing. Consequently, the balance sheet values their investment as the difference between asset and liability valuations.

Long-term creditors provide fixed-source financing for a specified period of time to an enterprise. From an investors' perspective, bonds and mortgages are safer investments than equity positions because they have a priority claim on the entity's assets. Conversely, the enterprise views them as a riskier means of financing because they entail predetermined cash payments at specified dates. Short-term funding arrangements are less formal than long-term contracts, but analysts consider them riskier for two reasons. First, an enterprise must pay for goods and services in the near term or risk losing access to them;[6] and, a firm can only acquire short-term credit if it demonstrates adequate long-term financing.[7]

Analysts consider three factors when assessing debt financing and capital structure analysis. First, as noted previously, current and noncurrent liabilities differ with respect to their origins, amounts, repayment schedules, and other characteristics. Conceptually, both are part of an entity's capital structure. Business operations, however, dictate excluding short-term obligations from capital structure analysis. Analysis reflects business practice by analyzing current liabilities as a component of short-term liquidity. Second, analysts usually exclude long-term deferred tax obligations from capital structure analysis because the cash required to satisfy these obligations does not exist with the degree of certainty it does for conventional long-term liabilities.[8] Third, preferred stock and bonds that can be converted into common stock are potential sources of common equity financing.[9] The analyst, however, should not reclassify them as such, unless it is apparent that those securities will be converted into common stock.

FINANCIAL LEVERAGE

WEB EXERCISE 4

Search the Internet for drkoop.com. Did you locate the company? Is it still in business?

Recall from Chapter 13 that financial leverage is the substitution of fixed-charge debt financing for variable-cost (dividend) equity financing.[10] That chapter introduces the topic as the financial structure leverage ratio, a component of return on equity (ROE). The analysis of Apple Computer demonstrates that

---

[6] Employees, for example, would quit working in a relatively short period of time if they were not paid for their services at the prescribed time.

[7] Vendors, for example, will only extend credit to going concerns. A certain amount of long-term financing is needed to establish business operations. The business model in Chapter 8 addresses business formation and supplier relations.

[8] Chapter 7 addresses this topic.

[9] See chapter 12 for more on this topic.

[10] Preferred stock is another means of substituting fixed-charge financing for variable cost financing.

financial leverage could either increase or decrease common shareholders' returns as compared with the rate of return on assets (ROA). This section builds on that discussion and provides a more detailed analysis of financial leverage.

CRUSHED BY DEBT

The Federal Reserve System reported the 1999 outstanding debt of nonfinancial U.S. corporations at $4 trillion.[a] Some companies can manage their debt, but others have difficulty doing so. How do you assess the following firms' debt management skills?

Filene's Basement Corp., a discount clothing retailer, experienced declining sales throughout the 1990s. Vendors eventually refused to extend credit for inventory. Finally, the company managed to secure credit from outside finance companies in order to pay cash to its suppliers.

Loewen Group Inc. is a consolidator of funeral homes. The company purchases independently owned mortuaries and centrally administers them. As part of the acquisition agreement, the funeral homes' names remain in place and the previous owners manage them for the Loewen Group.[b] This arrangement maintains the continuity and community relations vital to success in the funeral home industry. Loewen borrowed heavily to finance its funeral home acquisitions. Debt service requirements became so severe that the company substantially increased its prices.

Planet Hollywood rearranged its capital structure in 1999. Initially, the public received the company's concept of "eatertainment" well, but the market soon tired of paying higher prices for the movie-related concept. Cash flow problems ensued, and the company had trouble meeting its debt load. Planet Hollywood and its creditors arranged to transfer the company's existing equity to its bondholders in order to stay in business.

Observations

Discuss whether Filene's Basement Corp. inventory financing plan is a viable long-run solution. Do you think the Loewen Group's solution of substantially increasing prices for funeral services is a sound strategy for solving its debt service crises? What do you think motivated Planet Hollywood's creditors to become shareholders? Discuss how that reorientation affected their perspective on debt financing.

[a] As reported by G. Zuckerman, "U.S. Debt Boom: Living on Borrowed Dime?," *Wall Street Journal,* December 31, 1999, p. C1.
[b] Material based on D. Morse and M. Heinzl, "Funeral Home-Owners Discover the Downside of Sale to Consolidator," *Wall Street Journal,* September 17, 1999, pp. A1 and A6.

FINANCIAL LEVERAGE CONCEPTS

Most companies' capital structure consists of both long-term debt and equity. A point of contention in corporate finance is whether the proportion of debt and equity financing affects firm value. The answer could be both yes and no, depending on how strictly one subscribes to economic theory. The analytical implication is that the method of financing matters. Alternative tax treatments for distributions to debt and equity investors affect rates of return.

Conventional wisdom holds that every firm should have an optimal mix of debt and equity, that which would maximize firm value. This traditional financial view maintains that a certain degree of financial leverage benefits firms: They should substitute less expensive debt for more expensive equity capital. Too much debt, however, increases the cost of equity capital, according to this line of reasoning.[11] Adding debt over the optimal amount, therefore, becomes counterproductive as it increases the overall cost of financing the firm. Consequently, an entity should attempt to acquire the proper proportion of debt to equity so that it minimizes the cost of its debt and equity capital.

Research has demonstrated the fallacy of the traditional view.[12] The theory that has replaced the traditional perspective states that corporate cash flows are fixed in amount and have the same degree of risk, regardless of whether the firm is financed with debt or with equity. Consequently, the financing method is irrelevant; the value of the firm is independent of capital structure. This theory holds—in a world without corporate taxes. Introducing corporate income taxes alters the cash flows produced by debt and equity financing[13] because interest expense on borrowed funds is tax deductible, but dividends paid to shareholders are not. Therefore, net income and the cash that it produces depend on the proportion of debt and equity used to finance corporate assets.

DEBT FINANCING IMPLICATIONS

A firm increases ROE when the rate of ROA exceeds the cost of debt. When debt financing costs more than an entity earns on its assets, however, ROE is lowered. A firm with a significant amount of debt financing, therefore, can earn higher or lower equity returns than an equity-financed firm. Without financial leverage, an entity's ROE equals its ROA.[14] The introduction of financial leverage, however, alters the rates of return on assets and to shareholders. Exhibit 14-1 depicts the

EXHIBIT 14-1
Financial Leverage and Return on Equity

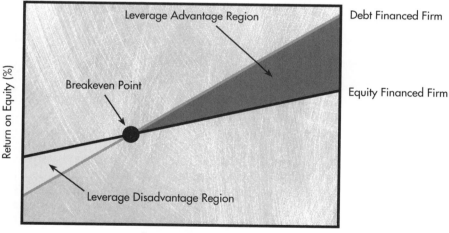

---

[11] This view holds that each firm had an optimal debt to equity ratio, which produces the lowest weighted average cost of capital.

[12] Modigliani, F. and M. H. Miller, "The Cost of Capital, Corporation Finance and the Theory of Investment," *American Economic Review*, June 1958, pp. 261–297.

[13] Here we assume that corporate taxes alter cash flows, due to the tax deductibility of interest expense; some research indicates otherwise. We also assume that costs associated with debt financing partially offset its tax advantage. Consequently, firms should not be completely financed with borrowed funds. A discussion of those offsetting costs exceeds the scope of this book.

[14] This statement assumes only debt and common equity financing. An unleveraged firm's ROA does not equal ROE when preferred stock financing exists.

EXHIBIT 14-2A
eSTUFF.com
2001 Interest Expense
and Net Income

INCOME STATEMENTS	AS REPORTED	ALTERNATIVE 1	ALTERNATIVE 2
Income from continuing operations	$55[a]	$55	$55
Financial (interest) expense	20	10	30
Pretax income	35	45	25
Income tax expense (40 percent)	14	18	10
Net income	21	27	15

[a] Amounts in thousands of dollars.

EXHIBIT 14-2B
eSTUFF.com
Rates of Return on
Assets and Equity

	AS REPORTED	ALTERNATIVE 1	ALTERNATIVE 2
Beginning retained earnings	$ 25[a]	$ 25	$ 25
Ending retained earnings	44	50	38
Beginning shareholders' equity	445	445	445
Ending shareholders' equity	544	550	538
Beginning total assets	780	780	780
Ending total assets	835	841	829
Return on assets	$\dfrac{(\$21 + \$12)}{\$807.5} = 4.09\%$	$\dfrac{(\$27 + \$6)}{\$810.5} = 4.07\%$	$\dfrac{(\$15 + \$18)}{\$804.5} = 4.10\%$
Return on equity	$21 / $494.5 = 4.25%	$27 / $497.5 = 5.43%	$15 / $491.5 = 3.05%

[a] Amounts in thousands of dollars.

relationship between ROE and financial leverage. The graph demonstrates both the potential advantage and disadvantage of debt financing. The value of financial leverage hinges on the cost of debt and the entity's rate of ROA.

Consider eSTUFF.com's investment return data for 2001. Exhibit 14-2A presents these figures along with two alternative scenarios about the cost of borrowed funds: The first assumes interest expense was $10,000, and the second assumes debt financing cost $30,000 in 2001. Data in Exhibit 14-2B present the balance sheet impact of those earnings and the rates of return on investment (ROI) for the three cases.

The beginning amounts of retained earnings, shareholders' equity, and total assets for 2001 are equivalent in all three cases. eSTUFF reported those amounts at the end of fiscal year 2000. The 2001 year-end amounts shift slightly, due to the amount of net income (reported in Exhibit 14-2A) carried to the balance sheet. The second column of Exhibit 14-2B shows the amounts reported for eSTUFF in Chapter 3. The first alternative scenario (column 3) reports an increase of $6,000 for retained earnings, shareholders' equity, and assets. The second alternative produces just the opposite result, lowering each account balance by $6,000. Consequently, equity and assets averaged for 2001 differ by $3,000 ($6,000 / 2) from the reported amount.

eSTUFF's asset returns are not materially different for the alternatives (4.09 percent, 4.07 percent, and 4.10 percent). Adding the net of tax interest expense in the numerator results in a constant income of $33,000. The slightly different common shareholders' denominators result from the different amounts of income affecting retained earnings in each case.[15]

The ROEs produced vastly different results, depending on the assumed cost of debt. As noted in Chapter 13, ROE computations use only net income in the numerator of this investment return measure, ignoring the after-tax interest adjustment. Consequently, the three income levels vary significantly ($21,000, $27,000, and $15,000). The total equity in each denominator differ slightly, due to the amount of income carried to retained earnings.[16] The ROE presented in Chapter 13 (column 2 of Exhibit 14-2B) is 4.25 percent when debt costs $20,000, the same percentage reported in Chapter 13. The ROE increases to 5.43 percent when debt is $10,000, and it decreases to 3.05 percent when the cost of debt financing is set at $30,000.

The rates of returns reported for eSTUFF in Chapter 13 (and in the second column of Exhibit 14-2B) indicate that the company had a slight degree of positive leverage. The company's 2001 ROE is 4.25 percent and its ROA is 4.09 percent. Its ROA, in other words, exceeds its debt cost, increasing the shareholders' rate of return. The first alternative scenario (debt cost = $10,000) illustrates how debt financing can enhance ROE under the right circumstances. The second alternative scenario demonstrates the risk of financial leverage. By increasing the assumed borrowing cost significantly ($30,000), the cost of debt financing becomes greater than eSTUFF's ability to earn an adequate return on its resources. In this case, ROE is less than ROA.

FINANCIAL LEVERAGE MEASURES

The financial structure leverage ratio, introduced in Chapter 13, is one method of calculating the extent of financial leverage. It is an adequate measure of an entity's financial leverage when used as a component ratio in ROE computations. The financial structure leverage ratio, however, is always greater than one.[17] Moreover, the ratio is in direct proportion to the amount of debt an entity carries. Therefore, the financial structure leverage ratio implies that debt financing is always preferred to equity financing. Exhibit 14-2B demonstrates, however, that the cost of debt could become too expensive in relation to the earnings produced by the assets. A more precise tool exists for analyzing debt.

The **financial leverage index** contrasts the rate of ROE to the rate of ROA. It is computed as follows:

$$\text{Financial leverage index} = \frac{\text{return on equity}}{\text{return on assets}}$$

---

[15] The method of financing is relevant in determining net income, but once that net income is reported, the net income (and not the financing method) becomes the relevant variable for changing retained earnings.

[16] Total assets must increase (decrease) by $6,000 at the end of 2001 because total equity increased (decreased) by that amount.

[17] This statement is true because total assets exceed common shareholders' equity, unless the firm is bankrupt (e.g., liabilities are greater than assets). For purposes of this discussion, we assume an entity is a going concern: we are analyzing viable (nonbankrupt) enterprises.

EXHIBIT 14-3

ESTUFF.com
2001 Financial Leverage
Ratio and Index

	AS REPORTED	ASSUMPTION 1	ASSUMPTION 2
Financial leverage index	$\dfrac{4.25\%}{4.09\%} = 1.04$	$\dfrac{5.43\%}{4.07\%} = 1.33$	$\dfrac{3.05\%}{4.10\%} = .74$
Financial structure leverage ratio	$\dfrac{\$807.5^a}{\$494.5} = 1.63$	$\dfrac{\$810.5}{\$497.5} = 1.63$	$\dfrac{\$804.5}{\$491.5} = 1.64$

ᵃ Dollar amounts are in thousands.

MICRO ANALYSIS 4

The income statement does not report the value of stock options as an expense. The difference between the market price of the stock and the exercise price of the options, however, is deductible for tax purposes. Bear, Stearns & Co. found that many high-tech firms increased their operating cash flows as a result of this beneficial tax treatment for options.

An index in excess of 1 provides evidence of positive financial leverage. An index equal to 1 means a firm realizes no advantage or disadvantage from debt financing. When the index is less than 1, a firm experiences negative effects from debt financing. Data in Exhibit 14-3 present eSTUFF's financial leverage ratios and financial leverage indexes for 2001. Note that the two alternative financial leverage measures provide conflicting signals about the value of eSTUFF's debt financing. The analyst should use the financial leverage index when the objective is to determine the effectiveness of debt financing. The financial structure leverage ratio is acceptable only when interest expense is immaterial to analysis or computing the ROE in component form (profit margin * asset turnover * financial structure leverage ratio). As a measure of debt financing, the financial structure leverage ratio overstates the economic value of financing assets with borrowed funds. The only time the financial structure ratio will yield a lower ROE than ROA is when an entity has a negative net profit margin, resulting from a net loss for the reporting period.[18]

WHAT'S YOUR ANALYSIS

STOCK REPURCHASES ALTER CAPITAL STRUCTURE

Companies purchase their own stock for a number of reasons. These equity transactions affect an entity's capital structure and sometimes alter its corporate leadership. What do you make of the following equity buybacks?

A company usually repurchases its own stock to boost share price. By reducing the number of shares outstanding, a company increases earnings per share (EPS). Stock acquisitions also signal investors that management thought the stock was undervalued. Investors then bid up the price of stock as a result of higher EPS and management's perception, according to this line of reasoning.

Corporate managers sometimes purchase their company's stock as a means of converting the publicly held entity to a private concern under their ownership. Management buyouts (MBOs) usually occur when managers think their company's stock is severely undervalued. Commercial banks provide financing to managers to effect an MBO. The transactions have occurred more frequently in traditional lines of business than in those considered part of the new economy. The relatively high share prices of information-oriented companies makes MBOs very expensive.

The exercise of executive stock options increases an entity's outstanding common stock. Companies sometimes purchase stock options from their corporate executives as part of a larger stock repurchase plan. MGM Grand, Inc., for example, introduced a 6 million share repurchase plan in 1999. Some of its executives exer-

---

[18] Chapter 13 illustrates this occurrence with data from Apple Computer in 1996 and 1997.

cised hundreds of thousands of options and sold them to the company at MGM's buy-back price of $50 a share. The market price of shares was $43 when the executives sold their shares to the company.

Observations

Discuss how stock repurchase plans contract capital and increase EPS. Do you agree with management's reasoning that these repurchase plans increase a stock's market price? How does a stock repurchase plan affect the proportion of debt to equity?

Assume an MBO takes place. Discuss the capital structure of the privatized firm. What role does the commercial bank play in it?

Could MGM have become a privately owned firm if the company repurchased enough of its own shares? Do you think MGM executives acted ethically or unethically by selling their stock to the company for $50 a share when it had a market value of $43?

RISK ANALYSIS

An enterprise's risk, or the possibility of losing something of value, is related to capital structure. The analyst must understand the various connotations of risk when analyzing an entity's proportion of debt and equity financing. In fact, the discussion to this point centers on the concept of **financing risk**, or the additional burden borne by shareholders' when debt is substituted for equity financing. This section examines other risk classifications and their relationship to financing risk.

WEB *EXERCISE 5*

One type of business risk in the PC industry is product obsolescence. Visit a PC firm's Web site and examine management's view on this type of risk.

WEB *EXERCISE 6*

Political instability is a business risk for multinational firms. Visit ntu.edu.sg to learn about the political risk of doing business in various countries.

CREDIT RISK

Credit risk is the possibility that a firm will not be able to make interest and principal payments of borrowed funds on time. Operating performance and financial structure determine the probability of default on contractual obligations. A firm that earns a high-quality income, has strong operating cash flows, and generates healthy returns on investment is less of a credit risk than an enterprise that has not produced those types of results. In addition, an entity's debt load influences credit risk. A firm with a **conservative capital structure**, or one with a disproportionately small amount of debt financing, is less of a credit risk than a highly leveraged firm, all other factors being equal.

Every company is subject to **business risk**, or the fluctuations in earnings and operating cash flows attributable to overall economic and industry-specific conditions. A company with a conservative capital structure is less of a business risk than one that finances its assets with debt. The more conservatively structured firm has fewer fixed costs than the highly leveraged firm that must continually service its debt obligations. The equity-financed firm, therefore, is better positioned to weather the random shocks that adversely affect every business than its debt-financed counterpart. Moreover, a company with a conservative capital structure has financial flexibility.[19] It can borrow funds in the event of an economic slowdown, whereas a leveraged firm might not be able to do so.

---

[19] Firms such as Moody's and Standard & Poor's rate entities' debt securities. Their ratings reflect judgment about the creditworthiness of the issuer and the type of security being issued.

BANKRUPTCY RISK

Analysts judge the **long-term solvency** of an entity as part of their capital structure assessment. They determine if a firm can generate sufficient cash flows to maintain productive capacity and meet debt and principal obligations. A company having difficulty meeting its obligations is said to be in **financial distress**. As with the less severe case of credit risk, highly leveraged firms are more susceptible to bankruptcy risk than companies with a more conservative capital structure. Many firms in financial distress petition the courts for bankruptcy protection. Under this arrangement, the courts suspend creditors' claims while a court-appointed trustee reorganizes the firm or liquidates it if the entity is not worth reorganizing.[20] **Bankruptcy risk**, therefore, is an extreme case of credit risk. It is highly likely that the judicial system will rearrange, reduce, or eliminate the claims of a bankrupt firm's creditors. A bankrupt firm loses autonomy when operating under a court-appointed trustee. The company also faces increased challenges at securing debt financing at acceptable costs if it emerges from the legal protection that bankruptcy affords.

Financial leverage is only one variable in determining risk. The analyst must include information about the other aspects of an entity's performance as well as economic and industry factors when analyzing long-term solvency and risk. The next section presents a risk measure that includes risk factors.

COMPREHENSIVE RISK

Common shareholders' expected ROIs are related to differences in perceived risk, according to financial economic theory. The equity market approach for assessing risk classifies it into two components: systematic and unsystematic risk. Owners eliminate a substantial portion of their risk by diversifying their investments. That strategy eliminates some of the risk inherent in investing, called **unsystematic risk**. Some risk, referred to as **systematic** or **market risk**, cannot be eliminated through diversification. It relates to an individual stock's risk, measured by the **beta coefficient**. Beta, in other words, captures the systematic risk of a stock.

Beta comprehensively measures the extent to which a stock moves with the overall market. A stock with a beta in excess of 1.0 is perceived as more volatile than the market as a whole. Conversely, a beta below 1.0 connotes greater stock stability than the overall market. Expressed another way, firms with a beta of more than 1.0 have greater variability in their equity returns than the overall stock market's returns. The opposite condition exists for firms with a beta of less than 1.0.

Published betas provide feedback on how the marketplace views an entity's risk. However, analysts should not use beta coefficients to replace individual assessment of risk. Beta coefficients provide risk information that analysts can use to confirm or reassess their views on corporate risk. An analyst should infer that a company's beta is how the equity market perceives a company's systematic risk in relation to the overall stock market's risk. He or she should not infer that a company with a beta below 1.0 is good and one with a beta above 1.0 is bad.

---

[20] Chapter 11 of the National Bankruptcy Code governs debt reorganization, and Chapter 7 codifies liquidation proceedings.

MARKET FINANCING: THE NEW LENDERS

Capital markets continue to alter debt financing, and information-based industries have assisted in the transformation.° What's your analysis of the change in corporate lending sources and practices?

Banks have long been the primary source of business lending. Financial institutions finance corporate activities in return for interest revenues and principal repayment. These somewhat static transactions present certain risks to borrowers and lenders: Banks absorb the entire risk associated with potential default, and corporations are locked into fairly restrictive contractual terms.

The emergence of capital markets as lending sources have alleviated the disadvantages of traditional bank financing. This market, where long-term debt is traded as well as shares of stock, efficiently gathers funds from those who have them and loans them to those in need. Advanced computing technology enables these low-transaction costs to occur seamlessly. Technological advances also allow companies to reduce financial risks by exchanging securities with other entities in mutually beneficial exchanges. Capital markets have also benefited banks. Financial institutions now reduce their lending risk through asset-backed securities. Banks package their loan portfolios in these arrangements and sell them to investors throughout the world.

Observations

The cost of financing is of far greater concern to companies and analysts than its source. Discuss how the emergence of capital markets as a lending alternative to banks could affect the cost of debt capital.

All transactions have risks associated with them. Can you think of any problems a company might have if it attempted to reduce its risk by engaging in swaps with other entities? How have financial reporting rule makers responded to the risks inherent in exchanges of financial instruments?

° Based on material from J. M. Schlesinger, "Why the Long-Boom? It Owes a Big Debt to the Capital Markets," *Wall Street Journal*, February 1, 2000, pp. A1 and A6.

CAPITAL STRUCTURE MEASURES

There are several ways to measure capital structure, some of which are covered in the financial leverage discussion. This section introduces additional methods for analyzing the proportion of debt to equity.

CAPITAL STRUCTURE COMPOSITION

An entity's proportion of short- and long-term financing sources should correspond to its investing activities. This means that current liabilities finance current assets, and long-term debt and equity fund plant, equipment, and intangible assets. Viewed from a liquidity perspective, operating cash flows satisfy accounts payable and accrued liabilities. From a long-term vantage point, solvent firms generate sufficient additional operating cash flows to pay the interest and principal on long-term debt and provide adequate rates of return to shareholders.

eSTUFF, for example, issued stock and borrowed cash on a long-term basis and purchased fixed assets. The company's statement of cash flows reports those financing and investing activities, and its balance sheet discloses those resources and claims against them. The e-tailer's business operations also created short-term claims against the company's assets. The company paid those current obligations when it converted inventory and receivables into cash.

Disproportionate levels of investing and financing activities signal financial distress. Assume for the moment that eSTUFF had to continually issue bonds or stock to pay for current liabilities. In effect, the firm needed long-term financing to finance ordinary business operations. It could not continue operating in this manner for very long, because our e-tailer would eventually need to compensate long-term investors for the use of their funds but would lack the cash flow to do so. eSTUFF would have a disproportionately large amount of long-term debt compared with its long-term asset base. The company's asymmetrical balance sheet would indicate poor capital structure and potential solvency problems.

COMMON SIZE STATEMENTS

Common size balance sheets contain information about capital structure composition. Analysts must take care in evaluating those data and carefully consider the information in light of the surrounding circumstances. We return to an analysis of eSTUFF to demonstrate this point.

Exhibit 14-4 shows data contained in eSTUFF's vertical common size balance sheet.[21] A brief interpretation of the data indicates that eSTUFF's current and non-current accounts apparently lack balance. In fact, data in Exhibit 14-4 display the disproportionate balance sheet characteristic described in the section "Capital Structure Composition." The e-tailer's proportion of current and long-term investments differs from that of its financing sources.

The analyst might conclude that eSTUFF is financially distressed. Two factors, however, should temper such a conclusion. First, the company is in its introductory life cycle stage. Financing activities are at their peak when a business begins operations.[22] The firm needs cash to begin operations as well as acquire fixed assets. Examining eSTUFF's statement of cash flows confirms that it used cash from financing activities for those purposes.

The second point the analyst needs to consider is the business environment in which the company operates. Unlike traditional storefront retailers, eSTUFF did not have to acquire retail space in order to conduct operations, thus reducing its demand for property and plant. A greater percentage of long-term cash commit-

EXHIBIT 14-4
eSTUFF.com
Common Size Balance
Sheet Data

	2000	2001
Current assets	46.2%[a]	52.7%
Long-term assets	53.8%	47.3%
Current liabilities	27.6%	8.5%
Long-term debt and shareholders' equity	72.4%	91.5%

[a] Accounts listed as a percentage of total assets.

[21] See Chapter 4 for eSTUFF's complete vertical common size balance sheet.
[22] See Chapter 10 for a discussion of life cycle phases and cash flows.

ments could have been directed toward noncapitalized expenditures, such as market research and advertising. Benchmarking the proportion of assets, liabilities, and shareholders' equity over time and against competition would provide evidence as to whether eSTUFF's capital structure adequately financed assets and compensated investors without jeopardizing the firm's solvency or financial flexibility.

THWARTING TAKEOVERS WITH POISON PILLS

WHAT'S YOUR ANALYSIS

MICRO *A*NALYSIS 8

Once in place, poison pills are hard to eliminate. Management at Sealed Air Co. did not believe poison pills were in its shareholders' best interest. The packing materials concern inherited one, however, when it purchased W.R. Grace's cryovac business in 1998. Sealed Air was unable to garner the 80 percent of shareholder votes required to eliminate the plan.

Many corporations have legal devices designed to prevent unwarranted takeovers, known as *poison pills.* How do you think they affect capital structure?

Poison pill plans make corporate takeovers very expensive by triggering massive stock issues when an uninvited overture is made for a firm. Existing shareholders receive the right to purchase additional stock at below-market prices. These plans provide a measure of security to an entity's directors and managers because hostile suitors cannot gain control of the firm and replace them.

Detractors of poison pills contend that many plans are not in the shareholders' best interest. These plans reward inefficient management, according to some shareholder advocates. Companies that have performed poorly usually have depressed stock prices, making them attractive takeover candidates. New ownership could mean an increase in profitability, but a poison pill plan often prevents this from happening.

Observations

Assume a takeover attempt activated a poison pill. What would be the effect on corporate structure? Present an argument defending the existence of a poison pill plan. Discuss how some shareholders might consider a poison pill plan to be a business risk for an entity.

DEBT TO CAPITAL RATIOS

WEB *E*XERCISE 7

Visx Inc. adopted a poison pill in 2000. Go to the company's Web site at visx.com and find information about the antitakeover measure.

WEB *E*XERCISE 8

Revisit coned.com and compute its most recent debt to equity ratio.

To better understand the proportion of debt to equity contained in common size balance sheets, we should examine ratios. These measures compare creditor financing with total asset or owner investments. The first measure is the **total debt to total capital ratio**, computed as follows:

$$\text{Total debt to total capital} = \frac{\text{average total debt}}{\text{average total assets}}$$

This is the most comprehensive ratio for measuring debt as a percentage of total financing activities.

The next ratio compares **total debt to total equity**, and it is calculated as follows:

$$\text{Total debt to total equity} = \frac{\text{average total debt}}{\text{average total shareholders' equity}}$$

We can adjust the numerator in the first two ratios to reflect a capital structure reality. Business operations require short-term creditor financing. Those claims are satisfied with cash collected on receivables and inventory sales. Therefore,

EXHIBIT 14-5
*eSTUFF.com
Debt to Capital and
Equity Ratios*

RATIO	COMPUTATION*
Total debt to total capital	$\dfrac{(\$335 + \$291)/2}{(\$780 + \$835)/2} = 38.8\%$
Total debt to total equity	$\dfrac{(\$335 + \$291)/2}{(\$445 + \$544)/2} = 63.3\%$
Long-term debt to total capital	$\dfrac{(\$120 + \$220)/2}{(\$780 + \$835)/2} = 21.1\%$
Long-term debt to total equity	$\dfrac{(\$120 + \$220)/2}{(\$445 + \$544)/2} = 34.4\%$

* Dollar amounts are in thousands.

we can factor those obligations out of the debt to equity ratios. This adjustment results in the **long-term debt to total capital** and **long-term debt to total equity ratios**:

$$\text{Long-term debt to total capital} = \frac{\text{average long-term debt}}{\text{average total assets}}$$

$$\text{Long-term debt to total equity} = \frac{\text{average long-term debt}}{\text{average total shareholders' equity}}$$

Exhibit 14-5 presents eSTUFF's 2001 debt to capital and equity ratios. Financial leverage is correlated to these ratios. A large proportion of debt connotes a high degree of leverage, whereas small percentages of debt indicate a conservative capital structure.

An analyst can gain insight about debt to investment ratios by reducing them to a dollar basis. For example, eSTUFF's total debt to total capital ratio means that the company owes almost 39 cents for every dollar used to acquire assets. Viewed another way, the e-tailer financed slightly more than 61 cents of every dollar invested with the owners' money. Long-term debt measures are interpreted in the same manner, except that liabilities include only noncurrent obligations.

EARNINGS COVERAGE RATIO

The **earnings coverage ratio** measures the extent to which operating income is able to meet the fixed charges on borrowed funds. A simplified version of the earnings coverage ratio is referred to as the **times interest earned ratio** because it reports operating earnings as a multiple of interest expense. The earnings coverage (times interest earned) ratio is computed as follows:

$$\text{Earnings coverage ratio} = \frac{\text{operating income before interest and taxes}}{\text{interest expense}}$$

A high earnings coverage ratio means that the entity had little trouble paying its contractual obligations on borrowed funds. A low ratio, however, indicates difficulty in meeting those financial commitments. When the ratio is less than one, an entity has generated insufficient earnings to meet its financing charges.

Earnings coverage for eSTUFF in 2001 is computed (in thousands of dollars) as follows:

$$\frac{\$55}{\$20} = 2.75$$

eSTUFF's earnings were sufficient to meet its interest obligation by 2.75 times. The company, in other words, produced $2.75 of earnings for each dollar it was obligated to pay on borrowed funds.

Numerous factors affect the earnings coverage ratio. First, the analyst might have to adjust operating income. He or she should ignore unusual or nonrecurring charges because they are unsustainable income elements. Second, the denominator of the ratio can be increased if an entity repaid principal as well as interest during the reporting period. This adjustment lowers the earnings coverage ratio. Third, the analyst might have to alter the reporting basis. Earnings coverage ratios measure an entity's ability to pay fixed costs, which require cash payments. The ratio, however, uses accrual income in the place of operating cash flow. This substitution is acceptable so long as operating income corresponds to operating cash flow. If these two measures vary greatly, then the analyst should use operating cash flows in the numerator. The fourth point also pertains to the cash and accrual issue. The earnings coverage ratio conventionally uses interest expense in the computation, an accrual-based number. In most instances, this is an adequate substitute for interest payments. If it is not, and the cash payments are disclosed, the analyst should replace interest expense with the actual amount of cash payments.[23]

BANKRUPTCY PREDICTION

A company in financial distress faces the possibility of bankruptcy and liquidation. The analytical measures discussed so far provide evidence about potential bankruptcy but do not directly measure its potential. There are several models of bankruptcy prediction; let us explore the most popular one.

The **Z-score** uses a statistically derived combination of weighted ratios to predict the likelihood of bankruptcy.[24] It is computed as follows:

$$\text{Z-score} = 1.2 \left(\frac{\text{net working capital}}{\text{total assets}} \right) + 1.4 \left(\frac{\text{retained earnings}}{\text{total assets}} \right)$$
$$+ 3.3 \left(\frac{\text{earnings before interest and taxes}}{\text{total assets}} \right) + 1.0 \left(\frac{\text{sales}}{\text{total assets}} \right)$$
$$+ .6 \left(\frac{\text{market value of equity}}{\text{book value of liabilities}} \right)$$

---

[23] There are numerous other technical adjustments to the earnings coverage ratio, but they exceed the scope of this text.

[24] Derived by E. Altman, "Financial Ratios, Discriminant Analysis and the Prediction of Corporate Bankruptcy," *Journal of Finance,* September 1968, pp. 589–609.

EXHIBIT 14-6
ESTUFF.com
Z-Score

RATIO	FACTOR	DATA[a]	COMPUTED AMOUNT	PARTIAL Z-SCORE
Net working capital / total assets	1.2	$257 / $807.5	.318	.382
Retained earnings / total assets	1.4	$34.5 / $807.5	.043	.060
Earnings before interest and taxes / total assets	3.3	$55 / $807.5	.068	.224
Sales / total assets	1.0	$1,200 / $807.5	1.486	1.486
Market value of equity / book value of liabilities	.6	$494.5 / $313	1.579	.947
eSTUFF's Z-score				**3.099**

[a] Dollar amounts in thousands.

The numerical Z-score is compared against benchmark numbers to gauge the probability of bankruptcy. A score in excess of 3.0 indicates a low probability of bankruptcy, but a score of less than 1.81 signifies a strong possibility of bankruptcy. A Z-score between those two numbers provides inconclusive evidence about bankruptcy probability.

Exhibit 14-6 shows eSTUFF's Z-score for 2001.[25] The partial Z-scores in the last column of the table result from multiplying the factor (column 2) by the computed amount of the data (column 4). eSTUFF's Z-score is 3.099, which we determined by summing the partial Z-scores in column 5. Based on that Z-score, our hypothetical e-tailer would be a low bankruptcy risk.

CAPITAL STRUCTURE ANALYSIS AND THE PERSONAL COMPUTER INDUSTRY

The proportion of debt and equity financing differed among PC firms from 1993 through 1998. Liability type was consistent among firms, however, regardless of overall debt level: Current obligations dominated debt financing and none of the firms reported any substantial long-term debt during the period examined.[26] We now turn our attention to why PC firms exhibited that type of debt structure and the bases for equity investments. We then examine the companies' capital structure measures.

---

[25] We averaged balance sheet data and assume the market value of equity to equal its average book value.

[26] The case may be made that Apple's long-term debt in the latter years of the study was significant. Accounting for it as such did not alter the analysis.

Examine Dell's disclosure about the exercise of stock options at dell.com.

Cisco Systems, Inc., and some other technology firms allow their executives to invest in or receive stock options from clients. Do you think that creates a conflict of interest for the employee? Could it induce the employee to act unethically?

By 1999 over 50 percent of venture capital went to finance Internet companies. This was twenty percentage points higher than the previous year, when a greater proportion of venture capital was directed toward computer firms, microchip manufacturers, and biotechnology concerns.

NEW ECONOMY CAPITAL STRUCTURE

Chapter 13 characterizes the PC industry's asset composition. In it we note that firms invested a small proportion of their funds in long-term assets. Large expenditures for property, plant, and equipment were unnecessary given the needs of the industry: These firms produce knowledge-based products, and they create wealth by enhancing the information-processing capabilities of their products. Unlike many traditional manufacturers' products, the value of PCs increased inversely with their size. Moreover, companies purchased many PC components, rather than manufacturing them. In addition, they outsourced some of the actual manufacturing duties to other firms. This business environment produced balance sheets with substantial current assets and few long-term ones.

Debt composition mirrors asset structure. Companies did not require much long-term debt financing, due, in part, to their lack of fixed resources. However, significant current liabilities existed as claims against the firm's working capital assets. The entrepreneurial culture of the industry also contributed to lack of long-term debt financing requirements: Initially, PC companies were funded with venture capital, and stock options were an integral form of compensation. Many employees received a substantial portion of their pay in the form of company stock. This strategy reduced operating expenses, which enhanced earnings.

Companies that survived industry maturation produced healthy earnings and generated strong cash flows from operations. These firms retained those earnings, rather than paying cash dividends to investors. Retained earnings increased as a result, and that income provided a source of internal financing. Consequently, the PC industry's knowledge-based business structure, coupled with equity-related policies, reduced its need for long-term debt financing.

CAPITAL STRUCTURE MEASURES

The next two exhibits indicate the predominance of equity financing. Exhibit 14-7A presents debt and equity as a percentage of total assets. Data from the PC firms' balance sheets demonstrate the lack of long-term debt financing in the industry (Exhibit 14-7B).[27]

Exhibit 14-8A reports debt as a percentage of total assets. Debt load varied among firms. The reasons for the diverse results, however, differed for the companies examined. Apple and Compaq's operating performance significantly affected their debt to capital ratios. Data indicate that Apple Computer increased long-term debt financing in 1996 and maintained that level through 1998, which partially explains the company's increased debt to capital ratio. The company's large net losses in 1996 and 1997 also were a factor; they reduced the amount of earnings retained in the business. But Apple's increased debt load, to a certain extent, is illusory. The contraction of its shareholders' equity accounted for a substantial increase in the proportion of debt to assets. A similar situation affected Compaq Computer. Its 1998 net loss reduced equity, which in turn substantially increased the percentage of debt to total capital from the previous year.

Dell generated above-industry earnings, yet its debt increased as a proportion of assets. This result appears contradictory: Income should increase equity capital

---

[27] Long-term debt excludes long-term deferred tax liabilities.

Apple

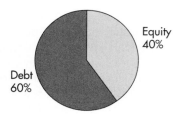

Compaq

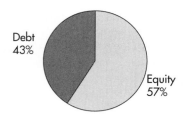

Dell

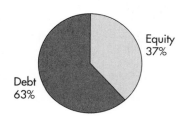

Gateway

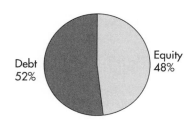

MICRO $\mathscr{A}$NALYSIS 12

*Some highly valued technology
firms began splitting stock 50 or
100 to 1. The strategy was to
reduce the stock's market price to
less than a dollar per share, so
that trading volume and market
price would increase.*

in the form of retained earnings, unless dividends are declared. But Dell paid few dividends from 1993 to 1998. The company did, however, contract equity. It purchased $1.5 billion of its stock in 1997 and 1998. That equity retrenchment, similar to Apple's retained earnings reduction, decreased Dell's equity as a percentage of total capitalization, thereby increasing its debt ratio.

Gateway's debt to equity ratio was relatively constant, with a slight increase in the last two years of the study. The company operated profitably and retained its income. Its current liabilities, however, increased faster than its equity. The company's experiment with its Gateway Country Stores concept in the later years of the analysis might partially account for the short-term debt acceleration.

Data in debt to equity ratios contain the same information as debt to asset ratios. Consider, for example, Apple Computer's 1998 financial leverage data. Exhibit 14-8A indicates that the company's debt to asset ratio was .667, which means each dollar invested in assets was financed with almost 67 cents of debt, or with slightly more than 33 cents (.333) of equity. The debt to equity ratio, shown in Exhibit 14-8B, expresses the relationship between the two components of asset financing. Apple's 1998 debt to equity ratio was 2.00 (.667 / .333); in other words,

EXHIBIT 14-7B

Personal Computer Industry Long-Term Debt as a Percentage of Total Assets (cumulative 1993–1998)

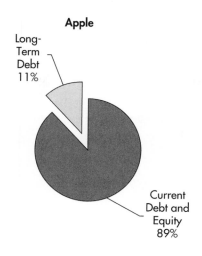

Apple

Long-Term Debt 11%

Current Debt and Equity 89%

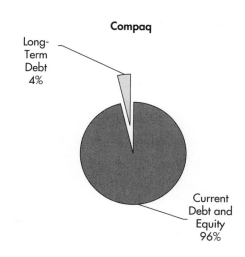

Compaq

Long-Term Debt 4%

Current Debt and Equity 96%

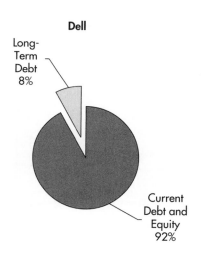

Dell

Long-Term Debt 8%

Current Debt and Equity 92%

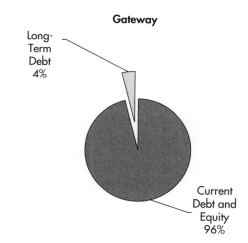

Gateway

Long-Term Debt 4%

Current Debt and Equity 96%

$2 of debt was used for every dollar owners invested in corporate resources. Note that the debt to equity line for each company in Exhibit 14-8B is parallel to its Exhibit 14-8A counterpart, except for the difference in scale. The analyst, therefore, can use either ratio to gauge the relationship between debt and equity.

Insignificant long-term debt financing reduced the need for computing either financial structure leverage ratios or financial leverage indexes. In most cases, the financial leverage index ratio provides a more accurate measure of financial leverage because the adjustment for financing charges alters the rate of ROE.[28] Interest expense, however, was immaterial for the PC firms analyzed; therefore,

---

[28] Refer to Exhibit 14-5 and the related discussion.

EXHIBIT 14-8A

Personal Computer Industry
Debt as a Percentage
of Total Assets
(1994–1998)

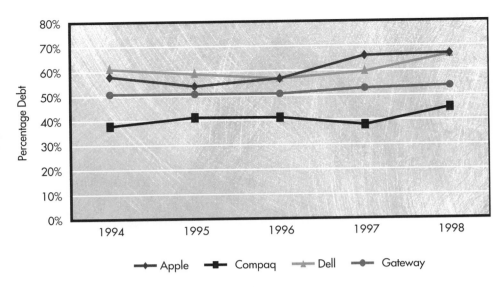

EXHIBIT 14-8B

Personal Computer Industry
Total Debt to Equity Ratio
(1994–1998)

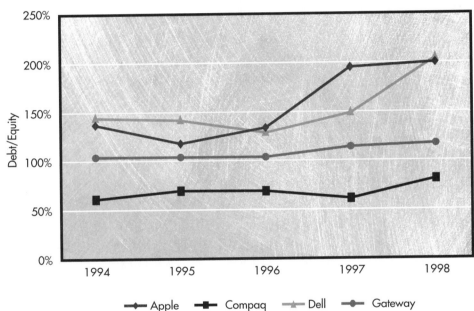

the financial leverage indexes equal the financial structure leverage ratios. Exhibit 14-9 presents each company's cumulative financial leverage or its financial structure leverage ratio. Note that Apple's financial leverage index is less favorable than its competitors'. Adjusting for the company's interest on borrowed funds would alter Apple's financial leverage index slightly, but that would not affect analysis.[29] The company's use of debt also produced an odd result. Apple's negative financial leverage index in Exhibit 14-9 seems to be a

---

[29] We would draw the same conclusion when Apple's ROE is adjusted for preferred dividends.

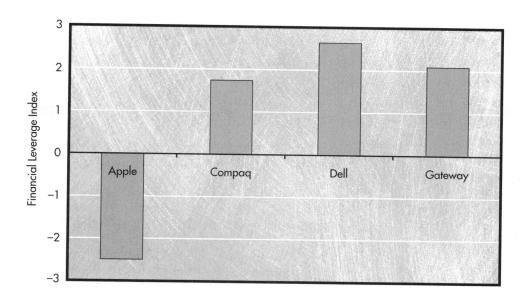

mathematical property violation; but we did this to present accurate information. The company's weighted average ROE was -7.88 percent and its ROA was -3.16 percent. The financial leverage index equals +2.49 (-7.88 percent / -3.16 percent) which implies positive leverage. To preserve the logic of the effect of leverage, we report the index as -2.49, rather than the mathematically correct +2.49.

APPLE'S PREFERRED STOCK FINANCING

Numerous financial problems affected Apple Computer by the end of fiscal 1997. Mounting operating losses, questionable recovery prospects, continual restructuring, and an inability to further reduce inventories threatened its cash flow. Apple needed financial assistance to support operations. What do you make of its deal with a rather unlikely source of cash?

Microsoft purchased $150 million in convertible preferred stock (150,000 shares at $1,000) from Apple in August 1997, convertible into common stock at $16.50 per common share. Each preferred share, therefore, equaled 60.6 shares of common ($1,000 / $16.50) for a total of 9,090,000 common shares (150,000 × 60.6) at the time of the transaction. It is worth noting that Apple's stock had not sold as low as $16.50 in over twenty years.

Apple's common stock traded at $30 per share when Microsoft provided the cash infusion; consequently, Microsoft would have had a $122.7 million gain if it had been able to convert (9,090,000 shares × $13.50 gain per share). However, the software giant could not make the conversion for three years. When Microsoft's option became exercisable, Apple's common stock was trading at $46 per share. Microsoft's gain was $268.2 million (9,090,000 × $29.50 unrealized gain per share) in early August 2000.[a] The gain was unrealized because Microsoft did not choose to convert to an equity investment in common stock.

Observations

Discuss why Microsoft was able to gain such favorable conditions in its deal with Apple? What was Apple's motivation for entering into the transaction? Why do you

think Microsoft did not choose to convert its preferred stock into common shares? Do you find it ironic that Microsoft provided equity financing to Apple Computer?

_____

ᵃ This analysis assumes the conversion of preferred stock would not affect the market price of Apple's common stock.

WEB EXERCISE 10

Go to apple.com and examine the company's most recent income statement. Was the company able to cover its interest costs?

Apple rivaled Dell as the most highly leveraged PC firm. The difference is that Dell's leveraged capital structure resulted from its strong operating performance. The company had the financial flexibility to repurchase stock. Apple's debt position, in contrast, was a consequence of the firm's inability to produce internal financing through profitable operations.

The analyst can infer that Apple's ability to cover its fixed costs lags the competition. The company had greater interest costs and fewer earnings before taxes and interest than Dell, Gateway, or Compaq did. A larger issue is whether Apple faced the possibility of bankruptcy due to its weak financial performance. Exhibit 14-10 plots the company's Z-scores to assess that potential.[30] According to these data, Apple had a low probability for bankruptcy in 1994, 1995, and 1998. The company's probability for bankruptcy increased in 1996 and 1997, but it could not be classified as high bankruptcy risk. (Recall that it would need a score of less than 1.81.) The company Z-scores in those years provides inconclusive evidence about the probability for bankruptcy. An analyst, however, could speculate on the bankruptcy implication if Apple had reported a net loss in 1998 instead of earning a profit. Analysts should also be concerned about the possibility of bankruptcy if Apple were to report net losses in subsequent years.

EXHIBIT 14-10

Apple Computer Z-Scores (1994–1998)

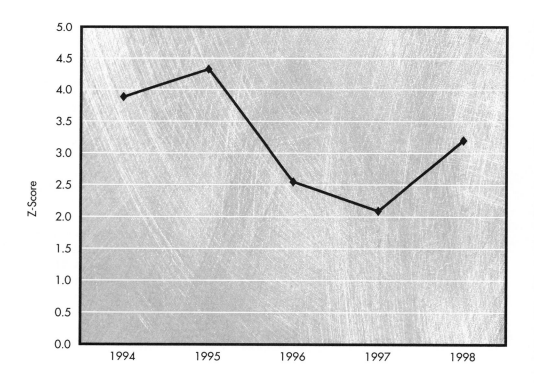

_____

[30] Apple's annual market values (the numerator in the final component of the Z-score) were based on an annual average of its high and low share prices.

SUMMARY

This chapter presents techniques for analyzing capital structure and applies them to the PC industry. The objective of this part of analysis is to determine if an entity has a combination of debt and equity that maximizes share value without unduly jeopardizing its ability to meet contractual obligations.

Understanding the concept of liability valuation as well as the difference between owner and creditor objectives gives the analyst the necessary background to appreciate the importance of financial leverage, risk analysis, and capital structure measures. Financial leverage, or the use of debt financing, increases the rates of return to shareholders, provided the ROA exceeds the cost of borrowing. If debt costs exceed asset returns, then financial leverage reduces ROE. The financial leverage index measures the effectiveness of debt financing by contrasting ROE with ROA.

Debt financing creates risk. The most severe outcome is corporate liquidation, which sometimes follows a bankruptcy petition to the courts. Numerous capital structure measures assist the analyst in assessing risk, including common size balance sheets, debt to equity ratios, and the earnings coverage ratio. Bankruptcy prediction models quantify the probability of financial distress.

Using capital structure analysis, we can determine that the PC industry was conservatively structured during the period analyzed. As a knowledge-based industry with strong entrepreneurial roots, PC companies primarily relied on equity financing. As with other aspects of analysis, data indicate that Apple Computer's capital structure was weaker than that of its competition.

KEY TERMS

Bankruptcy risk
Beta coefficient
Business risk
Capital structure
Capital structure analysis
Conservative capital structure
Credit risk
Earnings coverage ratio
Expected exit value
Financial distress
Financial leverage index
Financing risk

Historical proceeds
Long-term debt to total capital ratio
Long-term debt to total equity ratio
Long-term solvency
Present value of expected cash flows
Systematic (market) risk
Times interest earned ratio
Total debt to total capital ratio
Total debt to total equity ratio
Unsystematic risk
Z-score

NUMERICAL CASE

14-1

eXTREMESTUFF.com

Numerical case 3-2 at the end of Chapter 3 extends eSTUFF's financial statements through 2003. Use those data to compute the following measures for 2002 and 2003:

a. Financial leverage index
b. Total debt to capital (total assets)

c. Total debt to equity
d. Long-term debt to capital (total assets)
e. Long-term debt to equity
f. Earnings coverage ratio
g. Z-score

INDUSTRY CASES

Examine the industry information and corporate financial statements presented in the text's appendixes. Prepare a capital structure analysis from 1993 through 1998. Include leverage considerations and capital structure measures as necessary. Make technical adjustments for interest expense, preferred dividends, and deferred taxes if the data permit; otherwise, assume those adjustments are immaterial to the analysis. Construct graphs, as needed, to help you interpret the data.

14-1 *Personal Computers: Apple, Compaq, Dell, and Gateway*

14-2 *Airlines: American, Delta, and United*

14-3 *Athletic Footwear: Nike and Reebok*

14-4 *Discount Retailers: Kmart, Target, and Wal-Mart*

14-5 *Fast-Food Restaurants: McDonald's and Wendy's*

14-6 *Soft Drink Companies: Coca-Cola and PepsiCo.*

INDUSTRY INTERNET CASES

Extend your capital structure case analyses by incorporating financial statement disclosures from 1999 through the most recent year. (Financial statement disclosures may not be the same as those presented in the appendixes. Use your judgment to make the necessary modifications.)

14-1 *Personal Computers: Apple, Compaq, Dell, and Gateway*

14-2 *Airlines: American, Delta, and United*

14-3 *Athletic Footwear: Nike and Reebok*

14-4 *Discount Retailers: Kmart, Target, and Wal-Mart*

14-5 *Fast-Food Restaurants: McDonald's and Wendy's*

14-6 *Soft Drink Companies: Coca-Cola and PepsiCo.*

15 VALUATION AND FORECASTS

*C*HAPTER LEARNING OBJECTIVES

Upon completion of this chapter, you should be able to:

◆ *Understand the roles of valuation and forecasting in financial statement analysis.*

◆ *Describe and compute three measures related to corporate value.*

◆ *Discuss the advantages and disadvantages associated with statistical and judgmental forecasting techniques.*

◆ *Prepare pro forma financial statements based on your forecasts of future events.*

◆ *Identify the primary factors that affect financial statement forecasts of a company or industry.*

$\mathcal{A}$nalysts use information to make decisions and recommendations about how to allocate resources. These activities are part art and part science: Analysts rely on financial disclosures, other information, assorted techniques, logical thinking, creativity, and intuition to reach their conclusions. Financial statement analysts blend data about current and past events to project future occurrences. Nowhere does historical information play a larger role in the discipline than in the analysis of the financial statements themselves. Income statements, balance sheets, and cash flow statements summarize an entity's past activities. These backward-looking statements report previously completed corporate transactions. Even the method of disclosing those economic events, the historical system of financial reporting, reflects a retrospective orientation. The challenge is to leverage past corporate disclosures into knowledge about future ones.

Current company, industry, and economic data supplement corporate disclosures to produce robust analyses, enabling analysts to do their job. They must project future earnings, cash flows, and financial position. Analysts value economic resources for their ability to produce future returns, relative to the risk involved, and not for their historical performance. Past events are valuable only to the extent that they provide information about future results.

This chapter examines the linkages between historical events and projected activities. The first part defines two critical areas related to future performance: corporate value and financial statement forecasts. Next, this chapter describes three valuation techniques. Third, it looks at numerical and conceptual approaches to forecasting. The fourth section presents a method for constructing future financial statements, and the final section examines corporate valuation and financial forecasts of the personal computer (PC) industry.

VALUATION AND FORECAST OBJECTIVES

Economic theory states that an asset's value equals the present value of its future cash flows. The worth of a resource is affected by the mechanism that equates expected cash flows to their present value, called the **discount rate.** That interest rate adjusts differences in cash timing for their degree of risk. Financial economics also teaches us that markets are efficient. Investors consider all publicly available information in determining an entity's current value or price. Analysts use economic teachings as a starting point in valuing an enterprise. **Valuation** is the act of determining the price of something. The analyst should consider what market participants say about an entity when assessing its worth. A company's stock price expresses the market's collective wisdom about firm value.

Share price does not help analysts in every instance. Analysts may disagree with consensus opinion. Sometimes market values do not exist, as in the case of privately held concerns. At other times, people need to make decisions based on more specific data than a stock's price. A banker, for example, needs concrete information about the amount and timing of future cash flows. The market's valuation of a company's stock lacks such detail. Financial statement forecasts are the necessary complement to corporate value. **Pro forma** is defined as a matter of something's form. The analyst defines a company's future form in **pro forma financial statements**.[1]

---

[1] Pro forma financial statements are more inclusive than just financial statement forecasts. They also include the effects of alternative accounting treatments on historical disclosures. Those pro forma disclosures are contained in the notes and supplements to the financial statements.

These income statement, balance sheet, and cash flow projections quantify the analyst's expectations about a company's economic performance and financial position.

VALUATION METHODS

Analysts use current share price to begin assessing the public's perception of value. They must relate a stock's market price to another measure for it to be meaningful. It is, in a certain respect, similar to the approach used to interpret earnings. Analysts have a better understanding of the meaning of income disclosures when they are reported on a per-share basis.[2] Unlike earnings per share, which relates earnings to outstanding stock, however, analysts can compare stock prices with more than one measure. This section explores the three most popular comparative measures: price to earnings, price to cash flow, and price to book value.[3]

PRICE TO EARNINGS APPROACH

The **price to earnings ratio (P-E ratio)** reflects investors' expectations about the future performance of a company. A relatively high ratio means the market expects future earnings to increase, but a low P-E ratio means investors project a decrease in earnings. Price to earnings ratios vary among industries and are sensitive to economic conditions.[4] Comparisons are only valid within an industry and at a particular point in time.[5] The ratio is computed as follows:

$$\text{Price to earnings ratio} = \frac{\text{market price per share of stock}}{\text{earnings per share}}$$

All-inclusive income disclosures often report nonrecurring and unusual revenues and expenses. These items are unsustainable and influence earnings quality.[6] The analyst could substitute an alternative earnings per share (EPS) number (e.g., EPS before extraordinary items) for net earnings per share if he or she believes the alternative better measures the relationship between earnings and price.

Assume that eSTUFF's stock was priced at $6.30 per share at the end of 2001. The e-tailer's P-E ratio would be 15 for that year ($6.30 / $.42). In other words, the market values a dollar's worth of eSTUFF's earnings at $15.00, according to this measure. We could then benchmark that P-E ratio against competition to assess the market's perception about eSTUFF's future earnings and its relative ranking in the industry.

---

[2] Chapters 3 and 12 examine earnings per share.

[3] The discussion on valuation makes a simplifying assumption to convey the essence of market valuation. It uses reported income and cash flows as a surrogate for their discounted future amounts. As noted earlier in this chapter, markets value risk-adjusted expected cash flows and not past earnings or cash flow. This text uses financial statement data to illustrate how the alternative measures are computed. As a practical matter, many information sources report historical valuation measures, especially price to earnings ratios.

[4] Long-term interest rates and P-E ratios, for example, are inversely related.

[5] The P-E ratios of cyclical stocks are more difficult to trend over time than countercyclical issues because cyclical companies' earnings and prices are more sensitive to changes in economic activity than the less sensitive countercyclical issues.

[6] The discussion of operating performance analysis in Chapter 12 examines the earnings quality issue.

DO THE OLD MODELS WORK IN THE NEW ECONOMY?

Market capitalization for many Internet companies was quite high by the end of the twentieth century. What is your analysis of their worth?

Some investors questioned whether accepted methods for valuing stocks applied to firms in the new economy. The seemingly disproportionate share prices of many Internet firms challenged conventional wisdom. In fact, a standard ratio for measuring market perception of value, the P-E ratio, was replaced in many instances by the price to sales ratio (P-S ratio). The P-S ratio is computed by dividing stock market value by sales revenues. It became impossible to analyze share value in price to earnings multiples, because many firms lacked the "E" in the ratio: They had no earnings.

Market capitalization historically is usually no more than twice sales. Consider for a moment the P-S ratio for GoTo.com: 514 at the end of 1999. GoTo was not alone. Other companies, such as High Speed Access and Rhythms Net Connections, had similar P-S ratios.[a] These corporate values clearly did not fall within the range of historical ratios. They were even more surprising because these highly valued firms lacked any earnings history.

The bubble burst for many Internet companies by mid-2000. Share prices declined sharply for many Web-based firms. Some pundits referred to the formerly highly valued Internet firms as "dot-bombs."

Observations

What do the extremely large P-S ratios tell you about the market's views on historical and expected cash flows? Do you think investors expect to earn profits and produce cash flows in the future from companies with high P-S ratios? Do you think it would be more difficult to forecast financial statements for companies like GoTo.com or for more established companies in mature industries? How do you think traditional analysts reacted to the market declines for many Internet firms?

---

[a] R. McGough, "No Earnings? No Problem! Price-Sales Ratios Rise," *Wall Street Journal,* November 11, 1999, pp. C1 and C2.

WEB *Exercise 1*

Determine GoTo.com's most recent revenues by accessing its financial statements at goto.com. Has the company earned a profit?

PRICE TO CASH FLOW APPROACH

Alternative reporting methods, economic assumptions, and account measurement are less likely to affect cash flows than income. Income statements that report unsustainable economic activities also complicate corporate valuation. If an analyst is unsettled about earnings management or quality issues, he or she can use the **price to cash flow ratio** to supplement the P-E ratio. The price to cash flow ratio is computed as follows:

$$\text{Price to cash flow} = \frac{\text{market price per share of stock}}{\text{operating cash flows per share}}$$

Cash flows produced by operating activities represent ongoing business activities; therefore, they are a better point of comparison to market price than net cash flows. In eSTUFF's case, its cash flow to earnings ratio is −5 ($6.30 / −$1.26) for 2001. The operating cash flow per share (−$1.26) is computed by dividing −$63,000 of operating cash by 50,000 shares of common stock.

PRICE TO EQUITY APPROACH

Both the price and cash flow to earnings ratios compare an amount realized over time (income or operating cash flow) against the market's perception of value at a point in time (share price on a specific date). The **price to book value ratio** compares investors' assessment of a company's wealth at a particular moment with the firm's reported measure of corporate well-being at that same instant. This ratio is computed in the following manner:

$$\text{Price to book value ratio} = \frac{\text{market price per share of stock}}{\text{book value per share of stock}}$$

This ratio compares the financial reporting system's interpretation of corporate wealth (net assets at book value) with investors' perception of market value or capitalization. **Market capitalization**, or the total value of all of an entity's outstanding shares at a point in time, equals the value investors place on a company.[7] If the price to book value measure yields a ratio slightly in excess of one, then the reported costs of net assets (primarily on a historical cost basis) approximates the market's perception of the company's earnings power, according to investors. If, however, market price substantially exceeds book value, then the market thinks historical cost disclosures are irrelevant for projecting future rates of returns. A book value that exceeds market price (a ratio of less than one) means the market considers firm assets as impaired, although unrecognized by the financial reporting system. Investors, by pricing a company's stock low, are stating that they think the discounted value of expected cash flows is less than the balance sheet reports for net assets.

The 2001 price to book value ratio for eSTUFF is 1.38 times, based on the assumed P-E ratio of 15. Net asset book value, or shareholders' equity, equals $544,000. Given 50,000 shares of common stock outstanding, the book value per share is 10.9 ($544,000 / 50,000 shares). eSTUFF's price to book value ratio is 1.38 (15 / 10.9), which means the market values one dollar of the e-tailer's net assets at $1.38.

FORECASTING TECHNIQUES

Valuation measures provide information about the relationship between stock prices and specific financial statement disclosures, but they do not directly assist analysts in forecasting financial statements. This section examines forecasting methods—classified as either statistical or judgmental methods— that help analysts to project wealth creation, economic position, and cash flows.

THE SECURITIES AND EXCHANGE COMMISSION LEVELS THE PLAYING FIELD

The Securities and Exchange Commission (SEC) approved a rule in 2000 that changed how firms disclose information. What's your analysis of the new requirement?

The SEC's rule requires companies to disclose important information publicly. It ended the practice of "selective disclosure," whereby firms provided information to analysts and large investors before announcing it to the public. Companies must now

---

[7] Another way to compute market to book value is to divide market capitalization by book value of shareholders' equity

provide new information to everyone at the same time. Firms that violate the equal disclosure requirement, titled Regulation FD (for fair disclosure), are subject to injunctions and fines.

The SEC's Chairman, Arthur Levitt, was the leading advocate for eliminating selective disclosures. He felt that professional analysts and investors were given an unfair advantage over smaller scale, less powerful analysts and investors. Chairman Levitt stated, "Simply put, these practices (of selective disclosures) defy the principles of fairness and integrity."[a]

Company relationships with analysts began to change in the wake of FD. Executives became be more reluctant to comment on analysts' questions. Some companies also reduced the amount and type of information provided to investors at industry conferences.

Observations

Do you agree with Chairman Levitt's position that Regulation FD will make corporate disclosures fairer? Will markets become more efficient as a result of the ruling? Present an argument opposing Regulation FD.

---

[a] As reported by M. Schroeder and R. Smith, in "Disclosure Rule Cleared by the SEC," *Wall Street Journal*, August 11, 2000, p. C1.

STATISTICAL METHODS

Statistical forecasting methods are procedures that use a mathematical process to forecast financial statements. They consist of numerical expressions designed to capture the underlying behavior of reported data in order to project the future. Statistical forecasting methods range from relatively simple trend extensions to highly complex economic models. This section examines the most useful methods after presenting an overview of the most prevalent quantitative methods.

A **trend** is the general tendency or direction of events and conditions. **Trend analysis** or **time series analysis** is based on the assumption that successive observations in time are related. Past behavior, in other words, repeats itself. If, for example, revenues continually increased at 5 percent a year, then one would logically expect that pattern to continue into the foreseeable future, unless information to the contrary existed. Time series analysis mathematically expresses the observed relationship. This forecasting method works well when a discernible pattern exists and economic and industry conditions are stable over time.

However, a number of components influence economic activity, of which the aforementioned trend is only one. Others components include **cyclical behavior** (sensitivity to changes in the economy), **seasonality** (changes in activity levels within one reporting period), and **randomness** (unpredictable events). **Decomposition** statistically identifies and values how each component affected past performance. Analysts can derive a model from the component values and use it to predict the future.

Exponential smoothing uses past data to forecast future values, but unlike time series analysis, it places greater weight on more recent observations, though it does not totally discount older observations. Analysts need statistical packages to determine the optimal weights for past observations. They can also adjust exponential smoothing models to explicitly consider trend and seasonality in the data.

We now turn our attention to two methods of trend analysis that can assist in forecasting financial statements[8]: Linear regression and compound annual growth rates. Extended data for eSTUFF illustrate the value of these methods.

Linear regression statistically measures the relationship between two variables. One variable helps predict the other one. As it pertains financial statement forecasts, linear regression uses time to estimate a specific disclosure (such as revenues). Regression analysis fits a line to the observed data in a manner that minimizes the difference between the observations and the fitted line.[9] This method extends the estimate of historical amounts (i.e., the fitted line) to forecast a future financial statement value. We examine eSTUFF's revenues to illustrate regression analysis in the following series of exhibits. Exhibit 15-1A reports eSTUFF's sales revenues for 2000 and 2001, and presents two alternative assumptions about revenues in the next seven years. Revenues equal $16.5 million for both alternatives. The first alternative's sales, however, are more stable than those of the second alternative. Exhibits 15-1B and 15-1C fit regression lines to the two data sets.[10]

The analyst can confidently extend the trend line for Alternative 1's revenues (Exhibit 15-1B), due to the stable revenue history of that data set.[11] Sales disparities from year to year in the second data set (Exhibit 15-1C), in contrast, cast doubt about the validity of revenue projections for the next three years.

We can also use compound annual growth rates to project revenues. In addition to reporting the same total sales ($16.5 million), beginning (2000) and ending (2008) revenues are virtually identical for the two alternatives. Therefore, the two

EXHIBIT 15-1A

*eSTUFF.com
Alternative Revenue
Assumptions
2000–2008*

YEAR	REVENUES—ALTERNATIVE 1[a]	REVENUES—ALTERNATIVE 2
2000–actual	$1,000	$1,000
2001–actual	$1,200	$1,200
2002–assumed	$1,350	$880
2003–assumed	$1,590	$1,960
2004–assumed	$1,900	$1,290
2005–assumed	$2,110	$2,650
2006–assumed	$2,280	$1,480
2007–assumed	$2,420	$3,380
2008–assumed	$2,650	$2,660
Total	$16,500	$16,500

[a] Amounts in thousands of dollars.

---

[8] Statistical models all have assumptions that must be met to produce valid results. This discussion does not examine these assumptions, and they probably are not met, in the data presented. The intent of the book is to produce information for decisions, and these measures sometimes assist in that, despite their lack of mathematical rigor.

[9] Regression analysis technically minimizes the sum of the squared errors between the observations and regression line.

[10] We used Excel's trend function to graph and extend the regression lines.

[11] We made revenues forecasts arbitrarily for three years. The further one extrapolates, the less reliable forecasts become.

EXHIBIT 15-1B
eSTUFF.com
Revenue Trend (2000–2008)
Acceptable Three-Year
Projection
(in thousands of dollars)

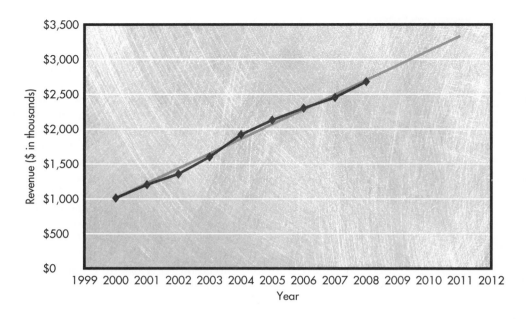

EXHIBIT 15-1C
eSTUFF.com
Revenue Trend (2000–2008)
Unacceptable Three-Year
Revenue Projections
2009–2011
(in thousands of dollars)

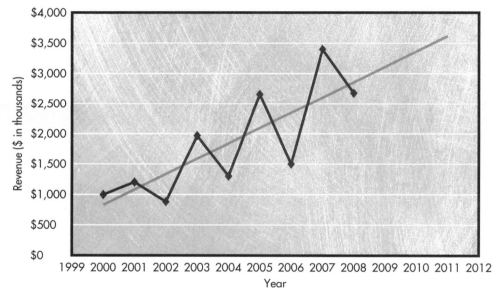

MICRO ANALYSIS 6

Past performances influence future ones and affect analysts' perceptions of companies. Procter & Gamble expected to meet EPS growth of 11–13 percent in 2000. Of course, it predicted a similar increase for the previous year but failed to meet it. Do you think low 1999 corporate earnings made it easier for the company to reach its 2000 goal? How would investors and analysts react if Procter & Gamble failed again to meet its forecast?

alternatives' compound growth rates are almost equal (12.96 percent for Alternative 1 and 13.01 percent for Alternative 2).[12] These growth rates are used to project the revenues from 2009 to 2011. Exhibit 15-1D presents the two alternatives' projected earnings as forecast by linear regression and compound annual growth. (Note that the data vary in the cells. We explain the disparity in the section "Judgmental Methods.")

Determining the investment level needed to generate earnings is an integral part of forecasting. Assume for the moment that eSTUFF.com demonstrated stable asset growth as well as earnings from 2000 to 2008 (Alternative 1 of Exhibit 15-1A

---

[12] Chapter 4 discusses compound annual growth rates.

EXHIBIT 15-1D
eSTUFF.com
Three-Year Revenue
Projections
2009–2011

ALTERNATIVE 1[a]	2009	2010	2011
Linear regression	$2,894	$3,106	$3,317
Compound annual growth	$2,994	$3,383	$3,821
ALTERNATIVE 2			
Linear regression	$3,089	$3,340	$3,592
Compound annual growth	$3,006	$3,389	$3,840

[a] Amounts in thousands of dollars.

EXHIBIT 15-2A
eSTUFF.com
Total and Net Assets

YEAR[a]	TOTAL ASSETS	NET ASSETS
2000–actual	$780	$445
2001–actual	$835	$544
2002–assumed	$930	$609
2003–assumed	$1,040	$686
2004–assumed	$1,152	$760
2005–assumed	$1,292	$838
2006–assumed	$1,432	$944
2007–assumed	$1,602	$1,046
2008–assumed	$1,770	$1,152
2009–projected	$1,830	$1,210
2010–projected	$1,955	$1,296
2011–projected	$2,081	$1,382

[a] Amounts in thousands of dollars.

EXHIBIT 15-2B
eSTUFF.com
Investment Forecasts
2009–2011

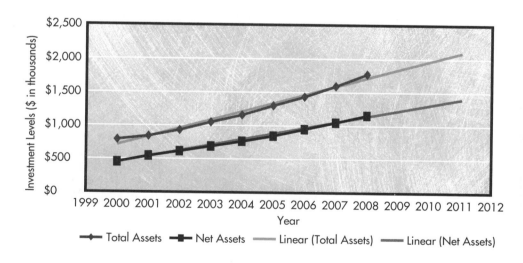

and Exhibit 15-1B). Continued revenue growth depends on similar increases in assets. eSTUFF, in other words, must have sufficient resources to produce revenues. Exhibits 15-2A and 15-2B report actual asset data for 2000 and 2001, assumed data for 2002–2008, and forecast resources from 2009 to 2011, based on linear regression calculations.

JUDGMENTAL METHODS

Exhibit 15-1D illustrates the problems associated with statistical forecast methods. Results depend on data and vary among methods for even a simple data set. First, linear regression's validity depends on the consistency of the historical observations. It generated adequate forecasts for Alternative 1 (Exhibit 15-1B) but not for Alternative 2 (Exhibit 15-1C). Therefore, it is not a valid predictor of those data's future revenues. A visual examination and logical extrapolation of the Alternative 1's revenues would have produced results similar to those contained in Exhibit 15-1B (and the first data row of Exhibit 15-1D). Neither logic nor linear regression would have assisted the analyst in predicting revenues for Alternative 2's revenues (Exhibit 15-1C and the third data row of Exhibit 15-1D). The data vary too much.

Second, linear regression and compound annual growth forecasts are both based on trends; yet, each method produced significantly different forecasts. Examine projected revenues for Alternative 1 in Exhibit 15-1D. The compound growth rates forecast more revenues than linear regression does. The flaw with compound growth is that this method determined annual changes by using only the first and last observations of the data set. Those two points may not be representative of the data over time. Recall how compound growth in Alternative 2 equaled that for Alternative 1 because 2000 and 2008 revenues were equal. The annual data from 2001 through 2007, however, were significantly different under the two assumptions. A relative advantage of linear regression is that all data are included in the model.

Informed opinion of future events is the basis for **judgmental forecasting method.** This approach uses relevant and reliable economic, industry, competitor, and corporate information to forecast financial statements. The analyst should use judgment unless he or she is thoroughly familiar with a quantitative method and the data fits that model. This is not to say that statistical techniques have no place in informing qualitative judgments, however. Regressing financial disclosures, such as revenues, over time helps the analyst to visualize data trends. Data stability lends itself to forecasting with compound growth rates. The analyst should also evaluate the elements of cyclicality, trend, and seasonality. Understanding an entity's sensitivity to business factors improves financial forecasts.

Forecasting financial statements is more of an art than a science. There is no single way to do it. Current information is the analyst's best tool for predicting financial statements. The analyst may want to construct various scenarios and produce multiple forecasts. One approach is to construct three sets of financial statements—one each for the best, worst, and most likely outcomes—to produce a range of financial statement expectations. That quantified span of expectations may be a more realistic expression of the future than the precise alternative offered by a single forecast.

Consensus opinion captures the essence of a range of forecasts. Compilations of quarterly EPS forecasts are the most notable example. Many financial services, such as First Call/Thompson Financial and Zacks Investment Research, produce consensus EPS forecasts, based on a compilation of analysts' forecasts, and Value Line, Moody's, and other investor services publish them. Although these quarterly consensus disclosures of EPS lack the detail of more complete financial statement forecasts, they do offer the opportunity to compare your earnings projections with those of other analysts.

Despite the inherent difficulties in forecasting, a specific format exists for producing pro forma financial statements, described in the next section.

PRO FORMA FINANCIAL STATEMENTS

The required order for constructing pro forma financial statements is the income statement, balance sheet, and statement of cash flows.[13] An analysts would initiate pro forma income statements and balance sheets by estimating total revenues and assets. Then he or she would determine individual accounts. The cash flow statement forecast is based on estimates of operating cash flows and the net change in cash.

WEB
EXERCISE 3

Visit the American Institute of Certified Public Accountants Web site at aicpa.org, examine its recommendations, and locate information about its "Guide for Prospective Financial Information" for the association's perspective on pro forma financial statement construction.

INCOME STATEMENT PROJECTION

Exhibit 15-3A presents eSTUFF's 2002 pro forma income statement along with its reported actual 2000 and 2001 income statements. The first assumption made is that revenues would continue to increase by 20 percent annually. Next, the proportion of cost of goods sold to sales is likely to remain at its 2001 level of 55 percent, rather than the higher percentage of the previous year. (Vendor costs should stabilize or become lower over time.) Selling and administrative costs are combined into a selling, general, and administrative category. They are estimated at 35 percent of sales, five percentage points less than the year before. The entity will establish better control of its operating costs under this assumption. The company's weak financial performance precludes additional long-term borrowing. eSTUFF's tax bracket is expected to remain at 40 percent and its EPS is based on 70,000 shares of outstanding stock ($74,000 / 70,000).

BALANCE SHEET PROJECTION

eSTUFF's 2002 balance sheet, shown in Exhibit 15-3B, incorporates income statement results and the expectations of additional resource requirements.

EXHIBIT 15-3A
eXTREMESTUFF.com, Inc.

INCOME STATEMENTS
FOR THE YEARS ENDED DECEMBER 31

	2002	2001	2000
Sales revenue	$1,440[a]	$1,200	$1,000
Cost of goods sold	792	660	600
Gross profit	648	540	400
Selling, general, and administrative expenses	504	485	335
Income from continuing operations	144	55	65
Financial expenses	20	20	10
Pretax income	124	35	55
Income tax expense	50	14	22
Net income	**$74**	**$21**	**$33**
Earnings per share	**$1.06**	**$.42**	**$.79**

[a] Amounts are in thousands of dollars, except per share amounts.

---

[13] The balance sheet reports the essence of the shareholders' equity statement in its equity section.

EXHIBIT 15-3B
eXTREMESTUFF.com, Inc.

BALANCE SHEETS
DECEMBER 31

	2002	2001	2000
Assets			
Current assets:			
Cash	$177[a]	$45	$30
Accounts receivable, net	168	140	120
Inventory	300	250	200
Prepaid expenses	0	5	10
Total current assets	645	440	360
Property, plant, and equipment:			
Equipment, net	460	380	400
Intangible Assets:	210	15	20
Total assets	**$1,315**	**$835**	**$780**
Liabilities and Shareholders' Equity			
Current liabilities:			
Accounts payable	$140	$50	$160
Accrued liabilities	37	21	50
Taxes payable	0	0	5
Total current liabilities	177	71	215
Long-term liabilities:			
Notes payable	220	220	120
Total liabilities	397	291	335
Shareholders' equity:			
Contributed capital:			
Common stock, $1 par value	70	50	42
Additional paid in capital	730	450	378
Total contributed capital	800	500	420
Retained earnings	118	44	25
Total shareholders' equity	918	544	445
Total liabilities and shareholders' equity	$1,315	$835	$780

[a] Dollar amounts are in thousands of dollars, except par value of stock.

The pro forma balance sheet begins with an assumption about the assets needed to produce earnings. The earnings per sales dollar are anticipated to increase substantially in 2002, due to increased sales and better cost controls. Therefore, we forecast a return on assets of 8 percent for that year. Net income, adjusted for net interest on borrowed funds, is $86,000 ($74,000 + $12,000). An average assets base of $1,075,000 is necessary to yield an 8 percent return ($86,000 / $1,075,000 = 8%). If beginning assets are $835,000, then ending assets must equal $1,315,000 to average $1,075,000 ([$835,000 + $1,315,000] / 2).

We forecast accounts receivable and inventory to increase at the same rate as revenues and cost of goods sold. We expect accounts payable to increase substantially, as the large pay down in the previous year was not a judicious use of cash. Corporate growth will require more fixed assets, costing $200,000. eSTUFF will spend an equivalent amount of cash to acquire intangible resources. We assume eSTUFF will purchase both the tangible and intangible assets at the end of 2002. A stock issue of $300,000 will fund the equipment acquisitions. The firm will issue 20,000 shares of stock at $15 per share to finance long-term asset growth. Equivalent amounts of equity and internal financing will pay for the intangible assets. eSTUFF will retain all earnings.

STATEMENT OF CASH FLOW PROJECTION

eSTUFF's pro forma cash flow statement reports a substantial increase in cash, resulting from increased profitability and better working capital management but partially offset by the $100,000 internal financing of intangible assets. eSTUFF's depreciation and amortization adjustment will not increase from 2001 because the 2002 capital expenditures will be placed in service at the end of the year. These

EXHIBIT 15-3C
eXTREMESTUFF.com, Inc.

STATEMENT OF CASH FLOWS
FOR THE YEARS ENDED DECEMBER 31

	2002	2001	2000
Cash, beginning of the year	$ 45[a]	$ 30	—
Cash flows from operating activities:			
Net income	$ 74	$ 21	$ 33
Depreciation and amortization expenses	125	125	105
Changes in current accounts:			
Accounts receivable	(28)	(20)	(120)
Inventory	(50)	(50)	(200)
Prepaid expenses	5	5	(10)
Accounts payable	90	(110)	160
Accrued liabilities	16	(29)	50
Taxes payable	0	(5)	5
Net cash provided (used) by operating activities	232	(63)	23
Cash flows from investing activities:			
Purchase of equipment	(200)	(100)	(500)
Acquisition of intangibles	(200)	0	(25)
Net cash provided (used) by investing activities	(400)	(100)	(525)
Cash flows from financing activities:			
Issue notes payable	0	100	120
Issue common stock	300	80	420
Pay cash dividend	0	(2)	(8)
Net cash provided (used) by financing activities	300	178	532
Net change in cash	$132	$ 15	$ 30
Cash, end of the year	$177	$ 45	$ 30

[a] Dollar amounts in thousands.

assets will start being depreciated in 2003. The $132,000 net increase in cash reconciles to the cash disclosures on the balance sheet, which report $177,000 at the end of 2002 and $45,000 at the beginning of the year.

We also forecast cash flows from operating activities are also forecast on a direct basis to provide greater clarity about expected cash receipts and disbursements:

EXHIBIT 15-3D
eXTREMESTUFF.com

CASH FLOWS FROM OPERATING ACTIVITIES—DIRECT BASIS

	2002	2001	2000
Sales revenue	$1,440	$1,200	$1,000
Change in accounts receivable	(28)	(20)	(120)
Cash received from customers	$1,412	$1,180	$880
Cost of goods sold	$792	$660	$600
Change in inventory	50	50	200
Change in accounts payable	(90)	110	(160)
Cash paid to suppliers	$752	$820	$640
Selling and administrative expenses	$504	$485	$335
Change in prepaid expenses	(5)	(5)	10
Change in accrued liabilities	(16)	29	(50)
Less: depreciation and amortization	(125)	(125)	(105)
Cash paid for operating expenses	$358	$384	$190
Tax expense	$50	$14	$22
Change in taxes payable	0	5	(5)
Cash paid for taxes	$50	$19	$17
Financial expense	$20	$20	$10
Change in interest expense	0	0	0
Cash paid for interest	$20	$20	$10

	2002	2001	2000
Cash flows from operating activities:			
Cash received from customers	$1,412	$1,180	$880
Cash paid:			
To suppliers	$752	$820	$640
For operations	358	384	190
For taxes	50	19	17
For interest	20	20	10
	1,180	1,243	857
Net cash provided by operating activities	$232	$(63)	$23

The direct method of reporting illustrates the anticipated increase in cash flow attributable to improved financial performance and better cash management.

The analyst can calculate projected short-term liquidity, cash flows, operating performance, asset utilization, and capital structure measures, once pro forma financial statements are constructed. For example, the analyst could compute pro forma ratios for eSTUFF based on his or her 2002 projections. Those expected financial measures could eventually be compared with eSTUFF's actual 2002 ratios.

VALUATION AND FORECAST OF THE PERSONAL COMPUTER INDUSTRY

The market valued Dell and Gateway more highly then it did Apple and Compaq by the end of the period examined as evidenced by market capitalization and P-E ratios. Every firm experienced an increase in market capitalization except Apple during the period analyzed. Dell's market capitalization was twice that of Compaq by 1998, and it dwarfed those for Gateway and Apple.

The direct computer sellers' P-E and price to equity ratios exceeded those for indirect sellers in 1998. These P-E ratios reinforce analysis presented in previous chapters indicating Dell and Gateway outperformed Apple and Compaq. Dell and Gateway more efficiently converted working capital into cash, generated greater operating cash flows and earnings, and earned higher rates of return than Apple and Compaq did. Data indicate future results will mirror the recent past. Dell and Gateway will lead the PC industry, and Apple and Compaq will lag it. This section examines some of the reasons why.

WHAT'S YOUR ANALYSIS

BE AN INFORMED PERSONAL COMPUTER INDUSTRY FORECASTER

Information drives financial statement analysis. Nowhere is this statement truer than in forecasting financial statements. How do you think the following information would improve your forecasts?

EXHIBIT 15-4A
Personal Computer Industry Market Capitalization 1994–1998

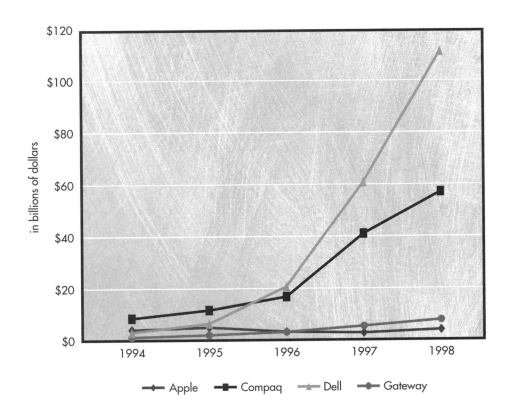

Businesses spend more for capital goods, including information technology, when economies are expanding. Consumer purchases of PCs are related to their confidence in the economy. Contracting economies reduce business and personal spending.

The Semiconductor Industry Association (SIA) measures and publicly reports global semiconductor chip orders and sales. The SIA also reports the book to bill ratio, which compares new orders for computer chips (bookings) with shipping of those products (billings).ᵃ Personal computer firms are the largest consumers of the semiconductor industry's products.

Business capital spending, consumer confidence, semiconductor sales forecasts, and book to bill ratios were all favorable toward the end of 1998. The U.S. economy was growing, and Asian economies appeared to be recovering. The SIA forecast continued growth in the semiconductor industry through 2002.

Observations

Discuss how the information presented here would affect your outlook for PC sales in 1999. How would it affect construction of pro forma financial statements? Do you think that information would affect all PC firms equally? List some online information sources that provide information about the economy and PC industry.

ᵃ The book to bill ratio is compiled for the U.S. market but not for foreign ones.

Learn more about the relationship between semiconductor and PC industries at semichips.org, the Internet address for the SIA.

Locate the current stock prices for Apple, Compaq, Dell, and Gateway at bigcharts.com.

Examine the stock prices reported by Apple on its Web site. What is Apple's source for those quotes?

Stock prices fluctuate over time. A company's P-E ratio depends on the specific stock price compared with periodic earnings. Exhibits 15-4B, 15-4C, and 15-4D present P-E ratios computed with the firms' high, low, and average stock prices.[14] The P-E ratios convey the same information about the firms' value, regardless of which stock price was used. The data graphed in the exhibits indicate a positive trend in the P-E ratios for Dell and Gateway. Compaq's 1998 multi-billion dollar loss altered its stable P-E ratio, which existed through 1997. Apple's P-E ratios were erratic but tended to decline over the time period examined. Exhibit 15-4E illustrates Apple's declining P-E ratio and demonstrates that P-E ratios reflect similar information, regardless of which market price is used to measure them.[15] In conclusion, the market anticipated superior cash flows from Dell and Gateway, according to the 1998 P-E data.

We used a derivative of the price to book equity valuation approach to provide additional evidence about the market's perceptions. We compared each PC firm's average market price with its book value per share of equity. Exhibit 15-5A presents the market to book value multiples for Apple, Compaq, and Gateway. We next examine the market's perception of Dell's superior value in Exhibit 15-5B. Notice the vast difference between Dell's annual market to book value of equity ratios when contrasted with those for Apple. Exhibits 15-5A and B contain information that supports the conclusions drawn from the analysis of P-E computations. Dell and Gateway's market value to book value multiples exceeded those of Apple and Compaq. This means that investors perceived more value in the net assets of Dell and Gateway than was reflected on their balance sheets. The lower multiples for Apple and Compaq means the market did not value the worth of these companies' net assets at substantially more than the amounts reported on

---

[14] Market prices were obtained from *Wall Street Journal* and *Standard and Poor's.*

[15] Negative P-E ratios are reported as zero. Negative ratios exist when a company reports a net loss, rather than net income. Reporting a negative P-E ratio implies the market places a negative value on the firm, a faulty connotation.

EXHIBIT 15-4B
*Personal Computer Industry
High Price Earnings Ratios
1994–1998*

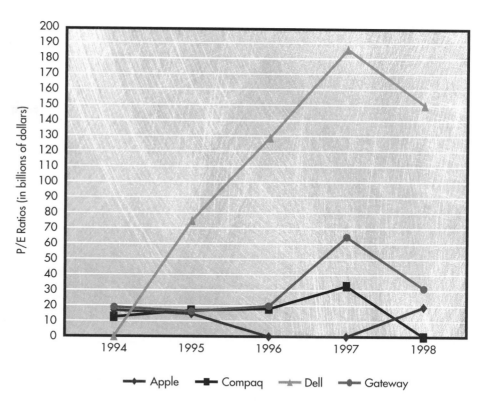

EXHIBIT 15-4C
*Personal Computer Industry
Low Price Earnings Ratio
1994–1998*

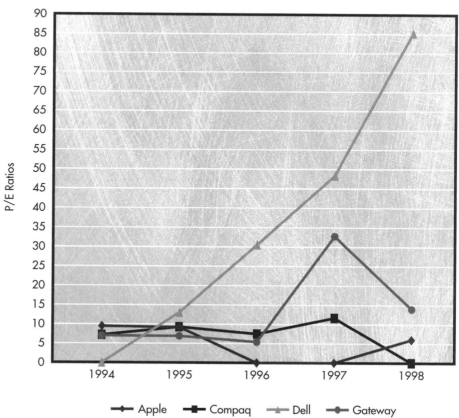

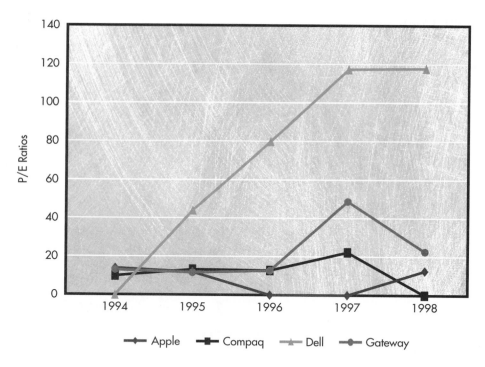

EXHIBIT 15-4E
*Apple Computer
P-E Ratio Range
1994–1998*

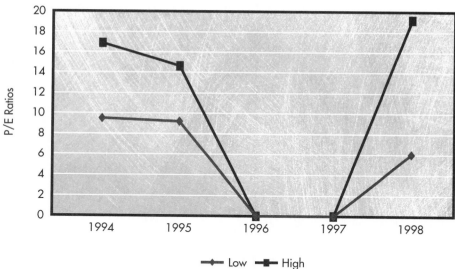

their balance sheets. The data indicate that investors increasingly believed Dell and Gateway's assets were capable of producing greater returns than those of Apple and Compaq.

We now turn our attention to critical areas affecting future financial performance and position. We discuss strengths and weaknesses for each firm[16] and present graphs to identify trends and assist in projecting the future.

---

[16] We do not present pro forma financial statements.

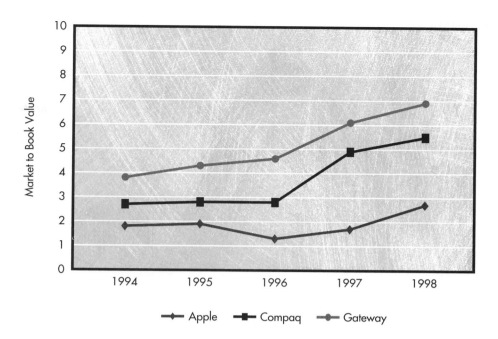

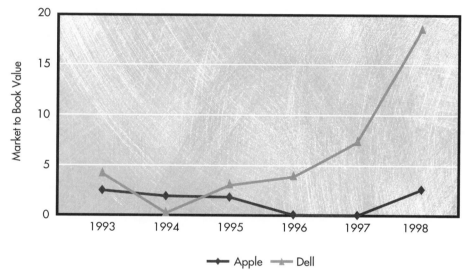

MICRO
△ *A*NALYSIS 8

Knowledge creation alone is not
sufficient to ensure a successful
future in the new economy.
Xerox's Palo Alto Research
Center (PARC) is renowned in
Silicon Valley for its high-tech
innovations. Many new economy
firms are indebted to PARC's
efforts, which they often applied
to their own product develop-
ments. Xerox, however, was
financially troubled in the early
part of the 21st century, despite
the success of PARC. The com-
pany had a poor track record of
converting its own knowledge
into saleable products.

Recall in Chapter 8 that we identified substantial inventory reductions throughout the industry. Holding large amounts of current assets became untenable as the industry matured. Companies increased their operating cycles as a result of faster inventory turnover. Efficient product manufacturing, sale, and distribution improved operating performance, cash flow, and returns on investment. Evidence indicates Dell and Gateway managed inventory better than the competition. These companies produced greater sales with relatively consistent inventory levels. Exhibit 15-6A demonstrates that inventory consistency and projects inventory levels for the next two years. An analyst would probably concur with the trend projection shown here. Dell and Gateway demonstrated sound inventory management in the past, and that trend should be reflected in stable dollar amounts (but decreasing percentages of total assets) of inventory in the near term. Both firms

EXHIBIT 15-6A
*Dell and Gateway
Inventory Trends*

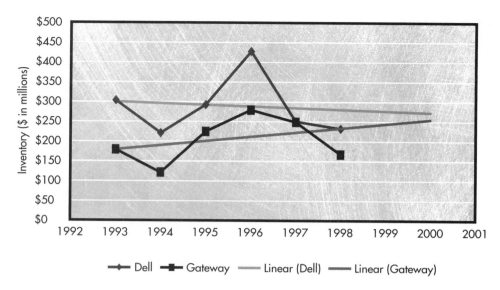

EXHIBIT 15-6B
*Apple and Compaq
Inventory Trends*

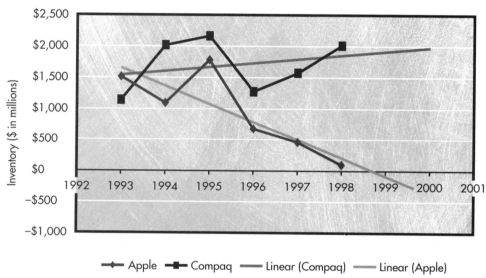

MICRO
*A*NALYSIS 9

*Dell's increase in share price was
among the highest of any publicly traded company from 1993
through 1998.*

should be able to increase returns on equity and assets with inventory investments
comparable to the quarter billion dollar amount projected in Exhibit 15-6A.

Exhibit 15-6B contains Apple and Compaq's inventory disclosures. Inventory
projections for these two firms reflect historical inventory management problems.
Compaq's inventory increased from 1996 to 1998, unlike that of the other three
firms. If the company was gaining market share, that increase would not be as
great a cause for concern. But by 1998, data indicate that Compaq was losing market share. Moreover, recall from Chapter 13 that the company's return on assets
(Exhibit 13-6) and return on equity (Exhibit 13-11A) were static, even if we ignore
the 1998 net loss. A significant explanatory variable for Compaq's relatively weak
returns on investment is its decreasing asset turnover (Exhibit 13-7B). Poor inventory control contributed to ineffective asset utilization. There is no evidence from
the data that Compaq will gain more control of inventory in the near term.

WEB EXERCISE 7

Compute an approximate price to book value ratio for Dell. Locate its current stock price, number of shares outstanding, and book value of net assets at dell.com.

MICRO ANALYSIS 10

Polaroid Corp. revived sagging sales by developing and marketing an inexpensive camera to teenagers. Polaroid's I-Zone Instant camera became the top-selling camera in 2000, a time when many people expected digital cameras to eliminate other types of photography. Do you think Polaroid's future earnings are sustainable if they are based on I-Zone sales?

MICRO ANALYSIS 11

Fueled by the success product innovations such as the iMAC, Apple exceeded analysts' earnings forecasts for seven straight quarters, beginning in the first quarter of 1999.

MICRO ANALYSIS 12

Apple's 2001 first quarter revenues were half of the same quarter's 2000 sales. Cost of goods sold exceeded revenues during the first quarter of 2001. The company reported a first quarter loss in 2001 of $195 million compared with a $183 million gain for the quarter a year earlier.

Apple Computer's inventory reductions produced most of its operating cash flows from 1993 to 1998. With inventory near zero, however, no future benefits will be wrought from inventory reductions. (Notice how inventory becomes negative in 1999 from linear regression. Negative inventory, obviously, is impossible.)[17] Apple's ability to produce acceptable rates of return in 1999 and beyond will depend on its ability to regain market share. The company's history of restructuring and retrenchment of research and development expenditures do not bode well for that to occur.

The fundamental issue is whether room will remain in the PC industry for a company whose products differ substantially from industry standards. The dominance of IBM clones and the Wintel duopoly showed no signs of slowing as the century came to a close. Apple's innovative technology has produced market successes. However, those successes were eventually matched or surpassed by the open architecture PC firms. Apple's recent history has been marked by periods of earnings followed by net losses. Unfortunately, this boom-and-bust cycle became decidedly more troubling by the late 1990s as Apple's downward slides became much more severe. The company's 1996 and 1997 losses substantially reduced retained earnings. Cash flows were propped up by inventory reductions, an opportunity that no longer exists.

An optimistic forecast for Apple would project 1998 earnings to continue in 1999 and 2000. If Apple continues to improve operating efficiencies and maintains its focus on PC innovation, the company could sustain those earnings well into the next century. Product innovation is a key to Apple's long-term financial health. The company's successful launch of the iMac computer, for example, spurred its return to profitability in 1998.

Three threats exist to Apple's success. The first is that a single-hit product boosts profits in the short term, but is unsustainable in the long run. Rapid technological changes and a decreasing price structure ensure short product life cycles. Success must be replicated. Apple's ability to produce one popular product is a short-term solution to a long-term problem. The second threat is that competitors rapidly replicate popular products. Moreover, the speed at which they can do so is contracting. Increased competition will reduce Apple's market share. In addition, the competition's more favorable cost structure and distribution channels will lead to lower prices, which will further erode Apple's profit margin and market share. The third troubling aspect for Apple is that products such as the iMac have limited revenue potential. Business accounts for 80 percent of PC sales, and that percentage is expected to remain the same.[18] iMacs are sold to home and educational users, which are minor market segments.

A more pessimistic forecast views Apple as becoming increasingly marginalized within the industry. With this forecast, investors will find future rates of return unacceptable, which could lead to a corporate takeover or filing for bankruptcy protection. A recent history of declining sales, poor earnings, illusory cash flows, higher financial leverage, continual restructuring, declining market share, and a failure to sell machines to businesses make acquisition or bankruptcy a possibility.

Pro forma financial statements begin with a forecast of revenues. Exhibits 15-7A and 15-7B present the linear regression estimates of Dell and Gateway and Apple and Compaq, respectively. Gateway's sales were consistently increased from 1993

---

[17] An inventory trend line that becomes negative also illustrates the problem of unduly relying on statistical forecasting measures.

[18] The exact percentage varies among sources, but the commercial segment dominates the PC market.

EXHIBIT 15-7A
*Dell and Gateway
Revenue Trends*

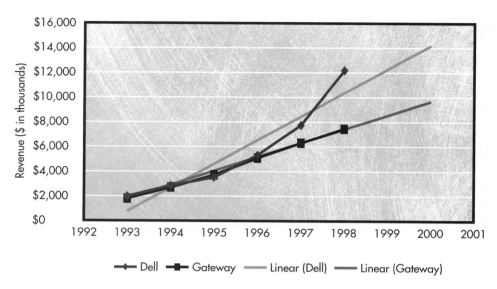

EXHIBIT 15-7B
*Apple and Compaq
Revenue Trends*

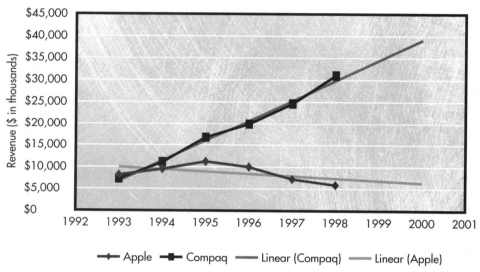

MICRO ANALYSIS 13

Dell was well positioned to claim market share leadership from Compaq by the end of 1998.

WEB EXERCISE 8

Examine Apple Computer's self-assessment by reading the management discussion and analysis section of its most recent Form 10-K.

through 1998, as can be seen in the fit of the trend line. Forecasting future sales extending the trend line seems reasonable in Gateway's case. The company also exhibited consistency in most of its financial disclosures. That stability bodes well for constructing a pro forma set of financial statements for Gateway.

Dell's revenues contained more variability than Gateway's did. Analysis in other chapters provides evidence that Dell's operations were not quite as stable as Gateway's.[19] Data also indicate Dell will experience larger sales and better earnings than Gateway in the foreseeable future. Constructing pro forma statements for Dell, therefore, would require greater judgment and be a more difficult exercise than doing so for Gateway.

Revenue forecasts for Compaq and Apple belie statistical trends. Compaq's revenue trend predicts a healthy increase in revenues. Moreover, the fitted regression

---

[19] Contrast the common size financial statements for Dell and Gateway in Appendix A.

WEB *E*XERCISE 9

Examine Apple's 1999 financial statements at sec.gov. Were their results better or worse than you expected?

line virtually matches historical revenues. But forecasters should not rely on the visual inspection of Compaq's data history and statistical projections to predict future revenues for a number of reasons. The company started losing market share in 1998, its Digital acquisition was a one-time boost to revenues, the firm incurred a substantial recent net loss, and its inventories and receivables are disproportionately high compared with sales. Apple's revenue trend is also misleading. A continued decline in sales would increase the probability of bankruptcy or acquisition. Either Apple's sales will increase, or the company will cease to be a going concern. Forecasting revenues and constructing pro forma financial statements for Apple and Compaq would be a challenging exercise.

MICRO *A*NALYSIS 14

Apple Computer's share price reflects the changing fortunes of the company.

SUMMARY

This chapter examines corporate valuation and financial statement forecasting. Stock prices provide analysts with an external source of corporate worth. These prices reflect investors' perceptions about the present value of an entity's risk-adjusted future cash flows. Analysts can benchmark their assessment of expected performance against that of the marketplace. Forecasting enables analysts to extend their evaluation of future corporate events beyond cash flows by quantifying operating performance and financial position in pro forma income statements, balance sheets, and cash flow statements.

This chapter presents three valuation techniques that compare share price to specific financial statement disclosures. The most prominent, the price to earnings ratio, reports share price per dollar of earnings. The other two valuation methods compare share price to a different measure: The price to cash flow substitutes operating cash flow per share for earnings per share, used when analysts judge earnings to be of low quality, and the price to book value ratio relates share price to a value at a point in time, book value of equity.

Forecasting methods are divided into statistical and judgmental categories. Judgment is the preferred forecasting technique, due to the mathematical complexities associated with statistical models. Trend analysis, however, does assist analysts in forming opinions about future corporate performance. Pro forma financial statements for eSTUFF illustrate the process of statement construction. The analyst quantifies expectations through an articulated set of financial statements, starting with the income statement and ending with the statement of cash flows.

We conclude with an analysis of the PC industry. Valuation measures indicate that the market placed a higher value on Dell and Gateway than it did on Apple and Compaq by 1998. Using evidence from inventory and revenues trends, we review some of the conclusions expressed in previous chapters and forecast results for Apple, Compaq, Dell, and Gateway. Dell and Gateway will outperform Apple and Compaq in the future, according to the analysis.

KEY TERMS

Cyclical behavior	Price to earnings ratio (P-E ratio)
Decomposition	Pro forma
Discount rate	Pro forma financial statements
Exponential smoothing	Randomness
Judgmental forecasting method	Seasonality
Linear regression	Statistical forecasting methods
Market capitalization	Trend
Price to book value ratio	Trend analysis (time series analysis)
Price to cash flow ratio	Valuation

NUMERICAL CASE

15-1

eXTREMESTUFF.com

Numerical case 3-2 at the end of Chapter 3 extends eSTUFF's financial statements through 2003. Use the 2003 data in conjunction with the assumptions made in Chapter 15 for the 2002 pro forma financial statements to construct pro forma financial statements for 2004. State any assumptions you had to make. Discuss whether you think the forecast would be reasonably accurate.

INDUSTRY CASES

Examine the industry information and corporate financial statements presented in the text's appendixes. In addition, identify key economic and industry issues that existed in 1998 that would have affected forecasts and pro forma financial construction. (It is not necessary to construct the statements.) Based on your information and analysis, rank-order the companies in terms of expected financial performance and wealth creation for future years. Determine the market's view by analyzing price to earnings ratios for 1998. Does the market concur with your assessment?

15-1   *Personal Computers: Apple, Compaq, Dell, and Gateway*

15-2   *Airlines: American, Delta, and United*

15-3   *Athletic Footwear: Nike and Reebok*

15-4   *Discount Retailers: Kmart, Target, and Wal-Mart*

15-5   *Fast-Food Restaurants: McDonald's and Wendy's*

15-6   *Soft Drink Companies: Coca-Cola and PepsiCo.*

INDUSTRY INTERNET CASES

Examine corporate financial statements from 1999 to the most recent year's disclosures. Do you think your firm rankings, which were made based on data through 1998, were accurate? What is the basis for your answer? Would you change the ranking of the firms' expected performance, based on data from 1999 to the present?

15-1   *Personal Computers: Apple, Compaq, Dell, and Gateway*

15-2   *Airlines: American, Delta, and United*

15-3   *Athletic Footwear: Nike and Reebok*

15-4   *Discount Retailers: Kmart, Target, and Wal-Mart*

15-5   *Fast-Food Restaurants: McDonald's and Wendy's*

15-6   *Soft Drink Companies: Coca-Cola and PepsiCo.*

A PERSONAL COMPUTER INDUSTRY

Apple Computer, Inc.
Income Statements
(in millions of dollars)

	1998	1997	1996	1995	1994	1993
Net sales	$5,941	$ 7,081	$9,833	$11,062	$9,188	$7,977
Cost of sales	4,462	5,713	8,865	8,204	6,844	5,248
Gross margin	1,479	1,368	968	2,858	2,344	2,729
Operating expenses:						
Research and development	303	485	604	614	564	664
Selling, general and administration	908	1,286	1,568	1,583	1,384	1,632
Restructuring costs	—	292	179	—	(126)	320
In–process research and development	7	375	—	—	—	—
Total operating expenses	1,218	2,438	2,351	2,197	1,822	2,616
Operating income	261	(1,070)	(1,383)	661	522	113
Other income and (expenses)	68	25	88	—	(21)	26
Income (loss) before taxes	329	(1,045)	(1,295)	661	501	139
Provision (benefit) for taxes	20	—	(479)	237	191	53
Net income (loss)	**$ 309**	**$(1,045)**	**$(816)**	**$ 424**	**$ 310**	**$ 86**
Basic EPS	$ 2.34	($8.29)	($6.59)	$ 3.50	$ 2.63	$ 0.73
Diluted EPS	$ 2.10			$ 3.45	$ 2.61	

Vertical Common Size

	1998	1997	1996	1995	1994	1993
Net sales	100.00%	100.00%	100.00%	100.00%	100.00%	100.00%
Cost of sales	75.11%	80.68%	90.16%	74.16%	74.49%	65.79%
Gross margin	24.89%	19.32%	9.84%	25.84%	25.51%	34.21%
Operating expenses:						
Research and development	5.10%	6.85%	6.14%	5.55%	6.14%	8.32%
Selling, general, and administrative	15.28%	18.16%	15.95%	14.31%	15.06%	20.46%
Restructuring costs	0.00%	4.12%	1.82%	0.00%	−1.37%	4.01%
Total operating expenses	20.50%	34.43%	23.91%	19.86%	19.83%	32.79%
Operating income	4.39%	−15.11%	−14.06%	5.98%	5.68%	1.42%
Other income and expenditures.	1.14%	0.35%	0.89%	0.00%	−0.23%	0.33%
Income (loss) before taxes	5.54%	−14.76%	−13.17%	5.98%	5.45%	1.74%
Provision (benefit) for taxes	0.34%	0.00%	−4.87%	2.14%	2.08%	0.66%
Net income (loss)	**5.20%**	**−14.76%**	**−8.30%**	**3.83%**	**3.37%**	**1.08%**

Horizontal Common Size—1993 Base

	1998	1997	1996	1995	1994	1993
Net sales	74.48%	88.77%	123.27%	138.67%	115.18%	100.00%
Cost of sales	85.02%	108.86%	168.92%	156.33%	130.41%	100.00%
Gross margin	54.20%	50.13%	35.47%	104.73%	85.89%	100.00%
Operating expenses:						
Research and development	45.63%	73.04%	90.96%	92.47%	84.94%	100.00%
Selling, general, and administrative	55.64%	78.80%	96.08%	97.00%	84.80%	100.00%
Restructuring costs	0.00%	91.25%	55.94%	0.00%	−39.38%	100.00%
Total operating expenses	46.56%	93.20%	89.87%	83.98%	69.65%	100.00%
Operating income	230.97%	−946.90%	−1223.89%	584.96%	461.95%	100.00%
Other income and expenditures.	261.54%	96.15%	338.46%	0.00%	−80.77%	100.00%
Income (loss) before taxes	236.69%	−751.80%	−931.65%	475.54%	360.43%	100.00%
Provision (benefit) for taxes	37.74%	0.00%	−903.77%	447.17%	360.38%	100.00%
Net income (loss)	359.30%	−1215.12%	−948.84%	493.02%	360.47%	100.00%

Horizontal Common Size—Rolling Forward

	1998	1997	1996	1995	1994	1993
Net sales	83.90%	72.01%	88.89%	120.40%	115.18%	100.00%
Cost of sales	78.10%	64.44%	108.06%	119.87%	130.41%	100.00%
Gross margin	108.11%	141.32%	33.87%	121.93%	85.89%	100.00%

Horizontal Common Size—Rolling Forward (continued)

	1998	1997	1996	1995	1994	1993
Operating expenses:						
Research and development	62.47%	80.30%	98.37%	108.87%	84.94%	100.00%
Selling, general, and administrative	70.61%	82.02%	99.05%	114.38%	84.80%	100.00%
Restructuring costs	0.00%	163.13%	0.00%	0.00%	−39.38%	100.00%
Total operating expenses	49.96%	103.70%	107.01%	120.58%	69.65%	100.00%
Operating income	−24.39%	77.37%	−209.23%	126.63%	461.95%	100.00%
Other income and expenditures	272.00%	28.41%	0.00%	0.00%	−80.77%	100.00%
Income (loss) before taxes	−31.48%	80.69%	−195.92%	131.94%	360.43%	100.00%
Provision (benefit) for taxes	0.00%	0.00%	−202.11%	124.08%	360.38%	100.00%
Net income (loss)	**−29.57%**	**128.06%**	**−192.45%**	**136.77%**	**360.47%**	**100.00%**

Compound Annual Growth 1993–1998

	1993	1994	1995	1996	1997	1998	Growth
Net sales	$(7,977)	0	0	0	0	$5,941	−5.7%
Cost of sales	$(5,248)	0	0	0	0	4,462	−3.2%
Gross margin	$(2,729)	0	0	0	0	1,479	−11.5%
Operating expenses:	$ —	0	0	0	0		
Research and development	$ (664)	0	0	0	0	303	−14.5%
Selling, general and administration	$(1,632)	0	0	0	0	908	−11.1%
Restructuring costs	$ (320)	0	0	0	0	—	
In–process research and development	$ —	0	0	0	0	7	
Total operating expenses	$(2,616)	0	0	0	0	1,218	−14.2%
Operating income	$ (113)	0	0	0	0	261	18.2%
Other income and (expenses)	$ (26)	0	0	0	0	68	21.2%
Income (loss) before taxes	$ (139)	0	0	0	0	329	18.8%
Provision (benefit) for taxes	$ (53)	0	0	0	0	20	−17.7%
Net income (loss)	$ (86)	0	0	0	0	$ 309	29.1%

Apple Computer, Inc.
Balance Sheets
(in millions of dollars)

	1998	1997	1996	1995	1994	1993
Assets						
Current Assets						
Cash and equivalents	$1,481	$1,230	$1,552	$ 756	$1,203	$ 676
Short-term investments	819	229	193	196	54	215
Accounts receivable, net	955	1,035	1,496	1,931	1,581	1,381
Inventories	78	437	662	1,775	1,088	1,506
Other current assets	365	493	612	566	550	560
Total current assets	3,698	3,424	4,515	5,224	4,476	4,338
Property, plant and equipment, net	348	486	598	711	667	659
Other assets	243	323	251	296	159	174
Total assets	**$4,289**	**$4,233**	**$5,364**	**$6,231**	**$5,302**	**$5,171**
Liabilities						
Current Liabilities						
Notes payable	$ —	$ 25	$ 186	$ 461	$ 292	$ 823
Accounts payable	719	685	791	1,165	881	742
Accrued expenses	801	1,108	1,026	699	771	943
Total current liabilities	1,520	1,818	2,003	2,325	1,944	2,508
Long-term debt	954	951	949	303	305	7
Deferred tax liabilities	173	264	354	702	670	629
Total liabilities	**$2,647**	**$3,033**	**$3,306**	**$3,330**	**$2,919**	**$3,144**
Shareholders' Equity						
Preferred stock	150	150	—	—	—	—
Common stock	633	498	439	398	297	203
Retained earnings	898	589	1,634	2,464	2,096	1,842
Other equity	(39)	(37)	(15)	39	(10)	(18)
Total shareholders' equity	1,642	1,200	2,058	2,901	2,383	2,027
Total liabilities and shareholders' equity	**$4,289**	**$4,233**	**$5,364**	**$6,231**	**$5,302**	**$5,171**

Vertical Common Size

	1998	1997	1996	1995	1994	1993
Assets						
Current assets						
Cash and equivalents	34.53%	29.06%	28.93%	12.13%	22.69%	13.07%
Short-term investments	19.10%	5.41%	3.60%	3.15%	1.02%	4.16%
Accounts receivable, net	22.27%	24.45%	27.89%	30.99%	29.82%	26.71%
Inventories	1.82%	10.32%	12.34%	28.49%	20.52%	29.12%
Other current assets	8.51%	11.65%	11.41%	9.08%	10.37%	10.83%
Total current assets	86.22%	80.89%	84.17%	83.84%	84.42%	83.89%
Property, plant and equipment, net	8.11%	11.48%	11.15%	11.41%	12.58%	12.74%
Other assets	5.67%	7.63%	4.68%	4.75%	3.00%	3.36%
Total assets	100.00%	100.00%	100.00%	100.00%	100.00%	100.00%

Vertical Common Size (continued)

	1998	1997	1996	1995	1994	1993
Liabilities						
Current liabilities						
Notes payable	0.00%	0.59%	3.47%	7.40%	5.51%	15.92%
Accounts payable	16.76%	16.18%	14.75%	18.70%	16.62%	14.35%
Accrued expenses	18.68%	26.18%	19.13%	11.22%	14.54%	18.24%
Total current liabilities	35.44%	42.95%	37.34%	37.31%	36.67%	48.50%
Long-term debt	22.24%	22.47%	17.69%	4.86%	5.75%	0.14%
Deferred tax liabilities	4.03%	6.24%	6.60%	11.27%	12.64%	12.16%
Total liabilities	61.72%	71.65%	61.63%	53.44%	55.05%	60.80%
Shareholders' Equity						
Preferred stock	3.50%	3.54%	0.00%	0.00%	0.00%	0.00%
Common stock	14.76%	11.76%	8.18%	6.39%	5.60%	3.93%
Retained earnings	20.94%	13.91%	30.46%	39.54%	39.53%	35.62%
Other equity	−0.91%	−0.87%	−0.28%	0.63%	−0.19%	−0.35%
Total shareholders' equity	38.28%	28.35%	38.37%	46.56%	44.95%	39.20%
Total liabilities and shareholders' equity	100.00%	100.00%	100.00%	100.00%	100.00%	100.00%

Horizontal Common Size—1993 Base Year

	1998	1997	1996	1995	1994	1993
Assets						
Current assets						
Cash and equivalents	219.08%	181.95%	229.59%	111.83%	177.96%	100.00%
Short-term investments	380.93%	106.51%	89.77%	91.16%	25.12%	100.00%
Accounts receivable, net	69.15%	74.95%	108.33%	139.83%	114.48%	100.00%
Inventories	5.18%	29.02%	43.96%	117.86%	72.24%	100.00%
Other current assets	65.18%	88.04%	109.29%	101.07%	98.21%	100.00%
Total current assets	85.25%	78.93%	104.08%	120.42%	103.18%	100.00%
Property, plant, and equipment, net	52.81%	73.75%	90.74%	107.89%	101.21%	100.00%
Other assets	139.66%	185.63%	144.25%	170.11%	91.38%	100.00%
Total assets	82.94%	81.86%	103.73%	120.50%	102.53%	100.00%
Liabilities						
Current liabilities						
Notes payable	0.00%	3.04%	22.60%	56.01%	35.48%	100.00%
Accounts payable	96.90%	92.32%	106.60%	157.01%	118.73%	100.00%
Accrued expenses	84.94%	117.50%	108.80%	74.13%	81.76%	100.00%
Total current liabilities	60.61%	72.49%	79.86%	92.70%	77.51%	100.00%
Long-term debt	13628.57%	13585.71%	13557.14%	4328.57%	4357.14%	100.00%
Deferred tax liabilities	27.50%	41.97%	56.28%	111.61%	106.52%	100.00%
Total liabilities	84.19%	96.47%	105.15%	105.92%	92.84%	100.00%

Horizontal Common Size—1993 Base Year (continued)

	1998	1997	1996	1995	1994	1993
Shareholders' Equity						
Preferred stock						
Common stock	311.82%	245.32%	216.26%	196.06%	146.31%	100.00%
Retained earnings	48.75%	31.98%	88.71%	133.77%	113.79%	100.00%
Other equity	216.67%	205.56%	83.33%	−216.67%	55.56%	100.00%
Total shareholders' equity	81.01%	59.20%	101.53%	143.12%	117.56%	100.00%
Total liabilities and shareholders' equity	82.94%	81.86%	103.73%	120.50%	102.53%	100.00%

Horizontal Common Size—Rolling Forward

	1998	1997	1996	1995	1994	1993
Assets						
Current assets						
Cash and equivalents	120.41%	79.25%	205.29%	62.84%	177.96%	100.00%
Short-term investments	357.64%	118.65%	98.47%	362.96%	25.12%	100.00%
Accounts receivable, net	92.27%	69.18%	77.47%	122.14%	114.48%	100.00%
Inventories	17.85%	66.01%	37.30%	163.14%	72.24%	100.00%
Other current assets	74.04%	80.56%	108.13%	102.91%	98.21%	100.00%
Total current assets	108.00%	75.84%	86.43%	116.71%	103.18%	100.00%
Property, plant and equipment, net	71.60%	81.27%	84.11%	106.60%	101.21%	100.00%
Other assets	75.23%	128.69%	84.80%	186.16%	91.38%	100.00%
Total assets	101.32%	78.91%	86.09%	117.52%	102.53%	100.00%
Liabilities						
Current liabilities						
Notes payable	0.00%	13.44%	40.35%	157.88%	35.48%	100.00%
Accounts payable	104.96%	86.60%	67.90%	132.24%	118.73%	100.00%
Accrued expenses	72.29%	107.99%	146.78%	90.66%	81.76%	100.00%
Total current liabilities	83.61%	90.76%	86.15%	119.60%	77.51%	100.00%
Long-term debt	100.32%	100.21%	313.20%	99.34%	4357.14%	100.00%
Deferred tax liabilities	65.53%	74.58%	50.43%	104.78%	106.52%	100.00%
Total liabilities	87.27%	91.74%	99.28%	114.08%	92.84%	100.00%
Shareholders' Equity						
Preferred stock	100.00%					
Common stock	127.11%	113.44%	110.30%	134.01%	146.31%	100.00%
Retained earnings	152.46%	36.05%	66.31%	117.56%	113.79%	100.00%
Other equity	105.41%	246.67%	−38.46%	−390.00%	55.56%	100.00%
Total shareholders' equity	136.83%	58.31%	70.94%	121.74%	117.56%	100.00%
Total liabilities and shareholders' equity	101.32%	78.91%	86.09%	117.52%	102.53%	100.00%

Compound Annual Growth 1993—1998

ASSETS	1993	1994	1995	1996	1997	1998	Growth
Cash and equivalents	$ (676)	0	0	0	0	$1,481	17.0%
Short-term investments	$ (215)	0	0	0	0	819	30.7%
Accounts receivable, net	$(1,381)	0	0	0	0	955	−7.1%
Inventories	$(1,506)	0	0	0	0	78	
Other current assets	$ (560)	0	0	0	0	365	−8.2%
Total current assets	$(4,338)	0	0	0	0	3,698	−3.1%
Property, plant and equipment, net	$ (659)	0	0	0	0	348	−12.0%
Other assets	$ (174)	0	0	0	0	243	6.9%
Total assets	$(5,171)	0	0	0	0	4,289	−3.7%
	$ —	0	0	0	0		
Liabilities	$ —	0	0	0	0		
Current liabilities	$ —	0	0	0	0		
Notes payable	$ (823)	0	0	0	0	$ —	
Accounts payable	$ (742)	0	0	0	0	719	−0.6%
Accrued expenses	$ (943)	0	0	0	0	801	−3.2%
Total current liabilities	$(2,508)	0	0	0	0	1,520	−9.5%
Long–term debt	$ (7)	0	0	0	0	954	167.2%
Deferred tax liabilities	$ (629)	0	0	0	0	173	
Total liabilities	$(3,144)	0	0	0	0	$2,647	−3.4%
		0	0	0	0		
Shareholders' Equity		0	0	0	0		
Preferred stock	—	0	0	0	0	150	
Common stock	(203)	0	0	0	0	633	25.5%
Retained earnings	(1,842)	0	0	0	0	898	−13.4%
Other equity	18	0	0	0	0	(39)	16.7%
Total shareholders' equity	(2,027)	0	0	0	0	1,642	−4.1%
Total liabilities and shareholders' equity	(5,171)	0	0	0	0	4,289	−3.7%

	1998	1997	1996	1995	1994	1993
Operating:						
Net income (loss)	$309	$(1,045)	$(816)	$ 424	$310	$ 87
Depreciation and amortization expense	111	118	116	127	168	166
Deferred income taxes	1	(50)	(437)			
In–process research and development	7	375				
Change in accounts receivable	72	469	435	(350)	(199)	(295)
Change in inventory	359	225	1,113	(687)	418	(927)
Change in accounts payable	34	(107)	(373)	283	139	316
Restructuring costs	(107)	109	124	(47)	(250)	203
Other	(11)	60	246	10	151	(201)
Cash generated by operating activities	$775	$ 154	$ 408	$(240)	$737	$(651)

*Apple Computer, Inc.
Consolidated Statements of
Cash Flows
(in millions of dollars)
(continued)*

	1998	1997	1996	1995	1994	1993
Investing:						
Purchase of short–term investments	$(2,313)	$(999)	$(437)	$(1,672)	$(312)	$(1,432)
Proceeds from sale of short-term investments	1,723	963	440	1,531	474	2,153
Proceeds from sale of property, plant, and equipment	89	47	47			
Purchase of property, plant, and equipment	(46)	(53)	(67)	(159)	(160)	(213)
Acquisition of technology	(10)	(384)				
Proceeds from sale of equity investment	24					
Other	(10)	(73)	9	(102)	(4)	(15)
Cash used for investing activities	$ (543)	$(499)	$ (8)	$ (402)	$ (2)	$ 493
Financing:						
Notes payable to bank	$ (25)	$(161)	$(275)	$ 169	$(531)	$ 590
Long-term borrowings	3		646	(2)	297	(10)
Proceeds from issuance of preferred stock		150				
Increase in common stock	41	34	39	86	82	(188)
Dividends			(14)	(58)	(56)	(56)
Cash generated by financing activities	$ 19	$ 23	$ 396	$ 195	$(208)	$ 336
Total cash generated (used)	$ 251	$(322)	$ 796	$ (447)	$ 527	$ 178
Cash and cash equivalents, beginning of year	$ 1,230	$1,552	$ 756	$ 1,203	$ 676	$ 498
Cash and cash equivalents, end of year	$ 1,481	$1,230	$1,552	$ 756	$1,203	$ 676

*Apple Computer, Inc.
Income Statements
(in millions of dollars)*

We initially presented these income statements (beginning with 1993) on p. 346. They are repeated here to facilitate analysis. We use the income statement data along with the "average" balance sheets, cash flow information, and market data (p. 354) as ratio inputs (pp. 355–356). We use this convention for the remaining companies in Appendixes A–F.

	1998	1997	1996	1995	1994
Net sales	$5,941	$ 7,081	$9,833	$11,062	$9,188
Cost of sales	4,462	5,713	8,865	8,204	6,844
Gross margin	1,479	1,368	968	2,858	2,344
Operating expenses:					
Research and development	303	485	604	614	564
Selling, general and administration	908	1,286	1,568	1,583	1,384
Restructuring costs	—	292	179	—	(126)
In–process research and development	7	375	—	—	—
Total operating expenses	1,218	2,438	2,351	2,197	1,822
Operating income	261	(1,070)	(1,383)	661	522
Other income and (expenses)	68	25	88	—	(21)
Income (loss) before taxes	329	(1,045)	(1,295)	661	501
Provision (benefit) for taxes	20	—	(479)	237	191
Net income (loss)	$ 309	$(1,045)	$(816)	$ 424	$ 310

	1998	1997	1996	1995	1994
Assets					
Current Assets					
Cash and equivalents	$1,355.50	$1,391.00	$1,154.00	$ 979.50	$ 939.50
Short–term investments	$ 524.00	$ 211.00	$ 194.50	$ 125.00	$ 134.50
Accounts receivable, net	$ 995.00	$1,265.50	$1,713.50	$1,756.00	$1,481.00
Inventories	$ 257.50	$ 549.50	$1,218.50	$1,431.50	$1,297.00
Other current assets	$ 429.00	$ 552.50	$ 589.00	$ 558.00	$ 555.00
Total current assets	$3,561.00	$3,969.50	$4,869.50	$4,850.00	$4,407.00
Property, plant and equipment, net	$ 417.00	$ 542.00	$ 654.50	$ 689.00	$ 663.00
Other assets	$ 283.00	$ 287.00	$ 273.50	$ 227.50	$ 166.50
Total assets	$4,261.00	$4,798.50	$5,797.50	$5,766.50	$5,236.50
Liabilities					
Current Liabilities					
Notes payable	$ 12.50	$ 105.50	$ 323.50	$ 376.50	$ 557.50
Accounts payable	$ 702.00	$ 738.00	$ 978.00	$1,023.00	$ 811.50
Accrued expenses	$ 954.50	$1,067.00	$ 862.50	$ 735.00	$ 857.00
Total current liabilities	$1,669.00	$1,910.50	$2,164.00	$2,134.50	$2,226.00
Long–term debt	$ 952.50	$ 950.00	$ 626.00	$ 304.00	$ 156.00
Deferred tax liabilities	$ 218.50	$ 309.00	$ 528.00	$ 686.00	$ 649.50
Total liabilities	$2,840.00	$3,169.50	$3,318.00	$3,124.50	$3,031.50
Shareholders' Equity					
Preferred stock	$ 150.00	$ 75.00	$ —	$ —	$ —
Common stock	$ 565.50	$ 468.50	$ 418.50	$ 347.50	$ 250.00
Retained earnings	$ 743.50	$1,111.50	$2,049.00	$2,280.00	$1,969.00
Other equity	$ (38.00)	$ (26.00)	$ 12.00	$ 14.50	$ (14.00)
Total shareholders' equity	$1,421.00	$1,629.00	$2,479.50	$2,642.00	$2,205.00
Total liabilities and shareholders' equity	$4,261.00	$4,798.50	$5,797.50	$5,766.50	$5,236.50

Cash Flow Data	1998	1997	1996	1995	1994
Cash flow from operations	$ 775	$ 154	$ 408	$ (240)	$ 737
Fixed asset purchases	46	53	67	159	160
Long–term debt repayment	25	161	275	2	531
Cash dividends				14	58	56
Depreciation and amortization	111	118	116	127	168

Market Data	1998	1997	1996	1995	1994
High market price	$ 21.90	$ 14.90	$ 17.80	$ 25.10	$ 21.90
Low market price	$ 6.80	$ 6.40	$ 8.00	$ 15.80	$ 12.30
Number of shares outstanding (millions)	270.39	255.90	248.99	245.84	239.09
Market capitalization	$3,880.10	$2,725.34	$3,211.97	$5,027.43	$4,088.44

Liquidity Ratios

	1998	1997	1996	1995	1994
Working capital	$1,892.0	$2,059.0	$2,705.5	$2,715.5	$2,181.0
Working capital ratio	2.13	2.08	2.25	2.27	1.98
Quick ratio	1.72	1.50	1.41	1.34	1.15
Inventory turnover	17.33	10.40	7.28	5.73	5.28
Days in inventory	21.06	35.11	50.17	63.69	69.17
Accounts receivable turnover	5.97	5.60	5.74	6.30	6.20
Days in accounts receivable	61.13	65.23	63.60	57.94	58.83
Inventory conversion cycle	82.19	100.34	113.77	121.63	128.00
Accounts payable turnover	6.36	7.74	9.06	8.02	8.43
Days in accounts payable	57.42	47.15	40.27	45.51	43.28
Net cash conversion cycle	24.77	53.19	73.51	76.12	84.73
Cash + short-term investments	1879.50	1602.00	1348.50	1104.50	1074.00
A/R*days in accounts receivable	60824.63	82551.04	108987.09	101743.87	87132.87
Inventory*days in inventory	5423.98	19291.41	61131.52	91169.57	89714.54
Product dollar days	68128.11	103444.46	171467.11	194017.94	177921.40
Current assets—other current assets	3132.00	3417.00	4280.50	4292.00	3852.00
Liquidity index	21.75	30.27	40.06	45.20	46.19

Cash Flow Ratios

	1998	1997	1996	1995	1994
Cash flow adequacy	10.92	0.72	1.15	(1.10)	0.99
Reinvestment ratio	0.06	0.34	0.16	(0.66)	0.22
Long–term debt repayment	0.03	1.05	0.67	(0.01)	0.72
Dividend payout	—	—	0.03	(0.24)	0.08
Free cash flow	729.00	101.00	327.00	(457.00)	521.00
Depreciation impact ratio	0.14	0.77	0.28	(0.53)	0.23
Recapitalization index	0.41	0.45	0.58	1.25	0.95
Cash flow return on assets	0.18	0.03	0.07	(0.04)	0.14
Cash flow return on sales	0.13	0.02	0.04	(0.02)	0.08
Operations index	2.97	(0.14)	(0.30)	(0.36)	1.41

Asset Utilization Ratios

	1998	1997	1996	1995	1994
Profit margin	5.201%	−14.758%	−8.299%	3.833%	3.374%
Asset turnover	1.394	1.476	1.696	1.918	1.755
Financial structure leverage	2.999	2.946	2.338	2.183	2.375
Return on assets	7.25%	−21.78%	−14.08%	7.35%	5.92%
Return on equity	21.75%	−64.15%	−32.91%	16.05%	14.06%

Capital Structure Ratios

	1998	1997	1996	1995	1994
Debt to capital	0.67	0.66	0.57	0.54	0.58
Debt to equity	2.00	1.95	1.34	1.18	1.37
Long–term debt to capital	0.22	0.20	0.11	0.05	0.03
Long–term debt to equity	0.67	0.58	0.25	0.12	0.07
Working capital/ total assets-Z1	0.53	0.51	0.56	0.57	0.50
Retained earnings/ total assets-Z2	0.24	0.32	0.49	0.55	0.53
EBIT/total assets–Z3	0.20	(0.74)	(0.79)	0.38	0.33
Sales/total assets–Z4	.82	.52	.58	.97	.81
Market to book–Z5	3.19	2.09	2.54	4.38	3.92
Z–Score	4.01	2.58	2.74	4.56	4.22

Market Ratio

	1998	1997	1996	1995	1994
Price to earnings	12.56	(2.61)	(3.94)	11.86	13.19

Compaq Income Statements
(in millions)

	1998	1997	1996	1995	1994	1993
Sales	$31,169	$24,584	$20,009	$16,675	$10,866	$7,191
Cost of goods sold	23,980	17,833	14,855	12,291	8,139	5,493
Gross profit	7,189	6,751	5,154	4,384	2,727	1,698
Selling, general, and administrative expenses	4,978	2,947	2,541	2,186	1,235	837
Research and development	1,353	817	695	552	110	169
Restructuring	393	52	52	158	265	—
Other expenses	(69)	21	(17)	(79)	(55)	76
In-process research and development	3,196	208		241		
Total expenses	9,851	4,003	3,271	3,058	1,555	1,082
Pretax income	(2,662)	2,748	1,883	1,326	1,172	616
Tax expense	81	903	565	433	305	154
Net income	$(2,743)	$ 1,845	$ 1,318	$ 893	$ 867	$ 462
Basic earnings per share	$ (1.71)	$ 1.23	$ 0.90	$ 0.62	$ 0.70	$ 0.01
Diluted earnings per share		$ 1.19	$ 0.87	$ 0.60	$ 0.68	

Vertical Common Size

	1998	1997	1996	1995	1994	1993
Sales	100.00%	100.00%	100.00%	100.00%	100.00%	100.00%
Cost of goods sold	76.94%	72.54%	74.24%	73.71%	74.90%	76.39%
Gross profit	23.06%	27.46%	25.76%	26.29%	25.10%	23.61%
Selling, general, and administrative expenses	15.97%	11.99%	12.70%	13.11%	11.37%	11.64%

Vertical Common Size (continued)

	1998	1997	1996	1995	1994	1993
Research and development	4.34%	3.32%	3.47%	3.31%	1.01%	2.35%
Restructuring	1.26%	0.21%	0.26%	0.95%	2.44%	0.00%
Other expenses	−0.22%	0.09%	−0.08%	−0.47%	−0.51%	1.06%
In-process research and development	10.25%	0.85%	0.00%	1.45%	0.00%	0.00%
Total expenses	31.61%	16.28%	16.35%	18.34%	14.31%	15.05%
Pretax income	−8.54%	11.18%	9.41%	7.95%	10.79%	8.57%
Tax expense	0.26%	3.67%	2.82%	2.60%	2.81%	2.14%
Net income	−8.80%	7.50%	6.59%	5.36%	7.98%	6.42%

Horizontal Common Size—1993 Base Year

	1998	1997	1996	1995	1994	1993
Sales	433.44%	341.87%	278.25%	231.89%	151.11%	100.00%
Cost of goods sold	436.56%	324.65%	270.44%	223.76%	148.17%	100.00%
Gross profit	423.38%	397.59%	303.53%	258.19%	160.60%	100.00%
Selling, general, and administrative expenses	594.74%	352.09%	303.58%	261.17%	147.55%	100.00%
Research and development	800.59%	483.43%	411.24%	326.63%	65.09%	100.00%
Restructuring						
Other expenses	−90.79%	27.63%	−22.37%	−103.95%	−72.37%	100.00%
In-process research and development						
Total expenses	910.44%	369.96%	302.31%	282.62%	143.72%	100.00%
Pretax income	−432.14%	446.10%	305.68%	215.26%	190.26%	100.00%
Tax expense	52.60%	586.36%	366.88%	281.17%	198.05%	100.00%
Net income	−593.72%	399.35%	285.28%	193.29%	187.66%	100.00%

Horizontal Common Size—Rolling Forward

	1998	1997	1996	1995	1994	1993
Sales	126.79%	122.86%	119.99%	153.46%	151.11%	100.00%
Cost of goods sold	134.47%	120.05%	120.86%	151.01%	148.17%	100.00%
Gross profit	106.49%	130.99%	117.56%	160.76%	160.60%	100.00%
Selling, general, and administrative expenses	168.92%	115.98%	116.24%	177.00%	147.55%	100.00%
Research and development	165.61%	117.55%	125.91%	501.82%	65.09%	100.00%
Restructuring	755.77%	100.00%	32.91%	59.62%		100.00%
Other expenses	−328.57%	−123.53%	21.52%	143.64%	−72.37%	100.00%
In-process research and development	1536.54%		0.00%			100.00%
Total expenses	246.09%	122.38%	106.97%	196.66%	143.72%	100.00%
Pretax income	−96.87%	145.94%	142.01%	113.14%	190.26%	100.00%

Horizontal Common Size—Rolling Forward (continued)

	1998	1997	1996	1995	1994	1993
Tax expense	8.97%	159.82%	130.48%	141.97%	198.05%	100.00%
Net income	−148.67%	139.98%	147.59%	103.00%	187.66%	100.00%

Compound Annual Growth

	1993	1994	1995	1996	1997	1998	Growth
Sales	$(7,191)	0	0	0	0	$ 31,169	34.1%
Cost of goods sold	$(5,493)	0	0	0	0	23,980	34.3%
Gross profit	$(1,698)	0	0	0	0	7,189	33.5%
Selling, general, and administrative expenses	$ (837)	0	0	0	0	4,978	42.8%
Research and development	$ (169)	0	0	0	0	1,353	51.6%
Restructuring	$ —	0	0	0	0	393	
Other expenses	$ (76)	0	0	0	0	(69)	
In-process research and development	$ —	0	0	0	0	3,196	
Total expenses	$(1,082)	0	0	0	0	9,851	55.5%
Pretax income	$ (616)	0	0	0	0	(2,662)	
Tax expense	$ (154)	0	0	0	0	81	−12.1%
Net income	$ (462)	0	0	0	0	$(2,743)	

	1998	1997	1996	1995	1994	1993
Cash	$ 4,091	$ 6,418	$ 3,008	$ 745	$ 471	$ 627
Short-term investments	—	344	1,073	—	—	—
Accounts receivable	6,998	2,891	3,718	3,141	2,287	1,377
Inventory	2,005	1,570	1,267	2,156	2,005	1,123
Deferred taxes	1,602	595	836	365	303	126
Other current assets	471	199	187	120	92	38
Total current assets	15,167	12,017	10,089	6,527	5,158	3,291
Property, plant, and equipment	2,902	1,985	1,753	1,110	944	779
Other assets	4,982	629	489	181	64	14
Total assets	$23,051	$14,631	$12,331	$7,818	$6,166	$4,084
Accounts payable	$ 4,237	$ 2,837	$ 2,098	$1,379	$ 888	$ 637
Taxes payable	282	195	533	190	246	69
Other current liabilities	6,214	2,170	2,110	1,111	879	538
Total current liabilities	10,733	5,202	4,741	2,680	2,013	1,244
Long-term debt	967	—	300	524	479	186
Total liabilities	11,700	5,202	5,041	3,204	2,492	1,430
Common stock	7,270	2,096	1,779	890	739	586
Retained earnings	4,081	7,333	5,511	3,724	2,935	2,068
Total shareholders' equity	11,351	9,429	7,290	4,614	3,674	2,654
Total liabilities and shareholders' equity	$23,051	$14,631	$12,331	$7,818	$6,166	$4,084

Vertical Common Size

	1998	1997	1996	1995	1994	1993
Cash	17.75%	43.87%	24.39%	9.53%	7.64%	15.35%
Short-term investments	0.00%	2.35%	8.70%	0.00%	0.00%	0.00%
Accounts receivable	30.36%	19.76%	30.15%	40.18%	37.09%	33.72%
Inventory	8.70%	10.73%	10.27%	27.58%	32.52%	27.50%
Deferred taxes	6.95%	4.07%	6.78%	4.67%	4.91%	3.09%
Other current assets	2.04%	1.36%	1.52%	1.53%	1.49%	0.93%
Total current assets	65.80%	82.13%	81.82%	83.49%	83.65%	80.58%
Property, plant, and equipment	12.59%	13.57%	14.22%	14.20%	15.31%	19.07%
Other assets	21.61%	4.30%	3.97%	2.32%	1.04%	0.34%
Total assets	100.00%	100.00%	100.00%	100.00%	100.00%	100.00%
Accounts payable	18.38%	19.39%	17.01%	17.64%	14.40%	15.60%
Taxes payable	1.22%	1.33%	4.32%	2.43%	3.99%	1.69%
Other current liabilities	26.96%	14.83%	17.11%	14.21%	14.26%	13.17%
Total current liabilities	46.56%	35.55%	38.45%	34.28%	32.65%	30.46%
Long-term debt	4.20%	0.00%	2.43%	6.70%	7.77%	4.55%
Total liabilities	50.76%	35.55%	40.88%	40.98%	40.42%	35.01%
Common stock	31.54%	14.33%	14.43%	11.38%	11.99%	14.35%
Retained earnings	17.70%	50.12%	44.69%	47.63%	47.60%	50.64%
Total shareholders' equity	49.24%	64.45%	59.12%	59.02%	59.58%	64.99%
Total liabilities and shareholders' equity	100.00%	100.00%	100.00%	100.00%	100.00%	100.00%

Horizontal Common Size—1993 Base Year

	1998	1997	1996	1995	1994	1993
Cash	652.47%	1023.60%	479.74%	118.82%	75.12%	100.00%
Short-term investments						
Accounts receivable	508.21%	209.95%	270.01%	228.10%	166.09%	100.00%
Inventory	178.54%	139.80%	112.82%	191.99%	178.54%	100.00%
Deferred taxes	1271.43%	472.22%	663.49%	289.68%	240.48%	100.00%
Other current assets	1239.47%	523.68%	492.11%	315.79%	242.11%	100.00%
Total current assets	460.86%	365.15%	306.56%	198.33%	156.73%	100.00%
Property, plant, and equipment	372.53%	254.81%	225.03%	142.49%	121.18%	100.00%
Other assets	35585.71%	4492.86%	3492.86%	1292.86%	457.14%	100.00%
Total assets	564.42%	358.25%	301.93%	191.43%	150.98%	100.00%
Accounts payable	665.15%	445.37%	329.36%	216.48%	139.40%	100.00%
Taxes payable	408.70%	282.61%	772.46%	275.36%	356.52%	100.00%
Other current liabilities	1155.02%	403.35%	392.19%	206.51%	163.38%	100.00%
Total current liabilities	862.78%	418.17%	381.11%	215.43%	161.82%	100.00%
Long-term debt	519.89%	0.00%	161.29%	281.72%	257.53%	100.00%
Total liabilities	818.18%	363.78%	352.52%	224.06%	174.27%	100.00%
Common stock	1240.61%	357.68%	303.58%	151.88%	126.11%	100.00%

Horizontal Common Size—1993 Base Year (continued)

	1998	1997	1996	1995	1994	1993
Retained earnings	197.34%	354.59%	266.49%	180.08%	141.92%	100.00%
Total shareholders' equity	427.69%	355.28%	274.68%	173.85%	138.43%	100.00%
Total liabilities and shareholders' equity	564.42%	358.25%	301.93%	191.43%	150.98%	100.00%

Horizontal Common Size—Rolling Forward

	1998	1997	1996	1995	1994	1993
Cash	63.74%	213.36%	403.76%	158.17%	75.12%	100.00%
Short-term investments						
Accounts receivable	242.06%	77.76%	118.37%	137.34%	166.09%	100.00%
Inventory	127.71%	123.91%	58.77%	107.53%	178.54%	100.00%
Deferred taxes	269.24%	71.17%	229.04%	120.46%	240.48%	100.00%
Other current assets	236.68%	106.42%	155.83%	130.43%	242.11%	100.00%
Total current assets	126.21%	119.11%	154.57%	126.54%	156.73%	100.00%
Property, plant, and equipment	146.20%	113.23%	157.93%	117.58%	121.18%	100.00%
Other assets	792.05%	128.63%	270.17%	282.81%	457.14%	100.00%
Total assets	157.55%	118.65%	157.73%	126.79%	150.98%	100.00%
Accounts payable	149.35%	135.22%	152.14%	155.29%	139.40%	100.00%
Taxes payable	144.62%	36.59%	280.53%	77.24%	356.52%	100.00%
Other current liabilities	286.36%	102.84%	189.92%	126.39%	163.38%	100.00%
Total current liabilities	206.32%	109.72%	176.90%	133.13%	161.82%	100.00%
Long-term debt		0.00%	57.25%	109.39%	257.53%	100.00%
Total liabilities	224.91%	103.19%	157.33%	128.57%	174.27%	100.00%
Common stock	346.85%	117.82%	199.89%	120.43%	126.11%	100.00%
Retained earnings	55.65%	133.06%	147.99%	126.88%	141.92%	100.00%
Total shareholders' equity	120.38%	129.34%	158.00%	125.59%	138.43%	100.00%
Total liabilities and shareholders' equity	157.55%	118.65%	157.73%	126.79%	150.98%	100.00%

Compound Annual Growth

	1993	1994	1995	1996	1997	1998	Growth
Cash	$ (627)	0	0	0	0	$ 4,091	45.5%
Short-term investments	$ —	0	0	0	0	—	
Accounts receivable	$(1,377)	0	0	0	0	6,998	38.4%
Inventory	$(1,123)	0	0	0	0	2,005	12.3%
Deferred taxes	$ (126)	0	0	0	0	1,602	66.3%
Other current assets	$ (38)	0	0	0	0	471	65.4%
Total current assets	$(3,291)	0	0	0	0	15,167	35.7%
Property, plant, and equipment	$ (779)	0	0	0	0	2,902	30.1%

*Compaq Balance Sheets
(in millions)
(continued)*

	1993	1994	1995	1996	1997	1998	Growth
Other assets	$ (14)	0	0	0	0	4,982	223.8%
Total assets	$(4,084)	0	0	0	0	$23,051	41.4%
	$ —	0	0	0	0		
Accounts payable	$ (637)	0	0	0	0	$ 4,237	46.1%
Taxes payable	$ (69)	0	0	0	0	282	32.5%
Other current liabilities	$ (538)	0	0	0	0	6,214	63.1%
Total current liabilities	$(1,244)	0	0	0	0	10,733	53.9%
Long-term debt	$ (186)	0	0	0	0	967	39.1%
Total liabilities	$(1,430)	0	0	0	0	11,700	52.3%
Common stock	$ (586)	0	0	0	0	7,270	65.5%
Retained earnings	$(2,068)	0	0	0	0	4,081	14.6%
Total shareholders' equity	$(2,654)	0	0	0	0	11,351	33.7%
Total liabilities and shareholders' equity	$(4,084)	0	0	0	0	$23,051	41.4%

*Compaq Computer, Inc.
Consolidated Statements of
Cash Flows
(in millions of dollars)*

	1998	1997	1996	1995	1994	1993
Operating:						
Net income (loss)	$(2,743)	$1,845	$ 1,318	$ 893	$ 867	$ 462
Depreciation and amortization expense	893	545	483	384	169	156
Purchased technology	3,196	208				
Deferred income taxes	(130)	202	(405)	(24)	(184)	(38)
Restructuring and asset impairment	393		52			
Change in accounts receivable	(1,736)	614	(228)	(910)	(926)	(484)
Change in inventory	857	(355)	1,014	(144)	(882)	(289)
Change in accounts payable	589	756	562	479	248	125
Other	(675)	(127)	770	355	607	308
Cash generated by operating activities	$ 644	$3,688	$ 3,566	$1,033	$(101)	$ 240
Investing:						
Purchase of property, plant, and equipment	$ (600)	$(729)	$ (484)	$(565)	$(357)	$(145)
Purchase of short-term investments	(77)	(2,405)	(1,401)			
Proceeds from sale of short-term investments	421	3,134	328			
Acquisition of technology	(1,413)	(268)	(22)	(318)		
Acquisition of lease portfolio	(361)					
Other	(437)	(31)	(75)	(29)	(51)	
Cash used for investing activities	$(2,467)	$(299)	$(1,654)	$(912)	$(408)	$(145)

Compaq Computer, Inc.
Consolidated Statements of
Cash Flows
(in millions of dollars)
(continued)

	1998	1997	1996	1995	1994	1993
Financing:						
Issue long-term debt					$ 300	
Repayment of long-term debt	(788)	(293)				
Purchase of treasury shares	(384)					
Issuance of common stock-stock options	407	188	131	123	100	142
Tax benefits of stock options	234	156	91	65		
Dividends	(95)					
Other	(18)	(37)				
Cash generated by financing activities	$ (644)	$ 14	$ 222	$188	$ 400	$142
Effect of exchange rate changes	140	7	21	–42	–47	33
Total cash generated (used)	$(2,327)	$3,410	$2,155	$267	$(156)	$270
Cash and cash equivalent, beginning of year	$ 6,418	$3,008	$ 853	$586	$ 627	$357
Cash and cash equivalents, end of year	$ 4,091	$6,418	$3,008	$853	$ 471	$627

Note: 1994 ending cash balance and 1995 beginning cash balance as reported.

Compaq Income Statements
(in millions)

	1998	1997	1996	1995	1994
Sales	$31,169	$24,584	$20,009	$16,675	$10,866
Cost of goods sold	23,980	17,833	14,855	12,291	8,139
Gross profit	7,189	6,751	5,154	4,384	2,727
Selling, general, and administrative expenses	4,978	2,947	2,541	2,186	1,235
Research and development	1,353	817	695	552	110
Restructuring	393	52	52	158	265
Other expenses	(69)	21	(17)	(79)	(55)
In-process research and development	3,196	208		241	
Total expenses	9,851	4,003	3,271	3,058	1,555
Pretax income	(2,662)	2,748	1,883	1,326	1,172
Tax expense	81	903	565	433	305
Net income	$(2,743)	$ 1,845	$ 1,318	$ 893	$ 867

Compaq AVERAGE Balance Sheets (in millions)

	1998	1997	1996	1995	1994
Cash	$ 5,254.50	$ 4,713.00	$ 1,876.50	$ 608.00	$ 549.00
Short–term investments	172.00	708.50	536.50	—	—
Accounts receivable	4,944.50	3,304.50	3,429.50	2,714.00	1,832.00
Inventory	1,787.50	1,418.50	1,711.50	2,080.50	1,564.00
Deferred taxes	1,098.50	715.50	600.50	334.00	214.50
Other current assets	335.00	193.00	153.50	106.00	65.00
Total current assets	13,592.00	11,053.00	8,308.00	5,842.50	4,224.50
Property, plant and equipment	2,443.50	1,869.00	1,431.50	1,027.00	861.50
Other assets	2,805.50	559.00	335.00	122.50	39.00
Total assets	$18,841.00	$13,481.00	$10,074.50	$6,992.00	$5,125.00
Accounts payable	$ 3,537.00	$ 2,467.50	$ 1,738.50	$1,133.50	$ 762.50
Taxes payable	238.50	364.00	361.50	218.00	157.50
Other current liabilities	4,192.00	2,140.00	1,610.50	995.00	708.50
Total current liabilities	7,967.50	4,971.50	3,710.50	2,346.50	1,628.50
Long–term debt	483.50	150.00	412.00	501.50	332.5
Total liabilities	8,451.00	5,121.50	4,122.50	2,848.00	1,961.00
Common stock	4,683.00	1,937.50	1,334.50	814.50	662.50
Retained earnings	5,707.00	6,422.00	4,617.50	3,329.50	2,501.50
Total shareholders' equity	10,390.00	8,359.50	5,952.00	4,144.00	3,164.00
Total liabilities and shareholders' equity	$18,841.00	$13,481.00	$10,074.50	$6,992.00	$5,125.00

Cash Flow Data

	1998	1997	1996	1995	1994
Cash flow from operations	$644	$3,688	$3,566	$1,033	($101)
Fixed asset purchases	600	729	484	565	357
Long-term debt repayment	788	293	—	—	—
Cash dividends	95	—	—	—	—
Depreciation and amortization	893	545	483	384	169

Market Data

	1998	1997	1996	1995	1994
High market price	$ 44.80	$ 39.80	$ 17.40	$ 11.40	$ 8.40
Low market price	$ 22.90	$ 14.20	$ 7.20	$ 6.20	$ 4.80
Number of shares outstanding (millions)	1,687	1,519	1,368	1,335	1,305
Market capitalization	$57,104.95	$41,013.00	$16,826.40	$11,748.00	$8,613.00

Liquidity Ratios

	1998	1997	1996	1995	1994
Working capital	$5,624.50	$6,081.50	$4,597.50	$3,496.00	$2,596.00
Working capital ratio	1.71	2.22	2.24	2.49	2.59
Quick ratio	1.30	1.76	1.57	1.42	1.46
Inventory turnover	13.42	12.57	8.68	5.91	5.20
Days in inventory	27.21	29.03	42.05	61.78	70.14
Accounts receivable turnover	6.30	7.44	5.83	6.14	5.93
Days in accounts receivable	57.90	49.06	62.56	59.41	61.54
Inventory conversion cycle	85.11	78.10	104.61	121.19	131.68
Accounts payable turnover	6.78	7.23	8.54	10.84	10.67
Days in accounts payable	53.84	50.50	42.72	33.66	34.19
Net cash conversion cycle	31.27	27.59	61.90	87.53	97.48
Cash + short-term investments	5,426.50	5,421.50	2,413.00	608.00	549.00
A/R*days in accounts receivable	286,295.66	162,125.69	214,550.28	161,230.32	112,738.98
Inventory*days in inventory	48,633.53	41,183.87	71,973.73	128,540.83	109,697.14
Product dollar days	340,355.68	208,731.06	288,937.02	290,379.14	222,985.12
Current assets–other current assets	13,257.00	10,860.00	8,154.50	5,736.50	4,159.50
Liquidity index	25.67	19.22	35.43	50.62	53.61

Cash Flow Ratios

	1998	1997	1996	1995	1994
Cash flow adequacy	0.43	3.61	7.37	1.83	(0.28)
Reinvestment ratio	0.93	0.20	0.14	0.55	(3.53)
Long-term debt repayment	1.22	0.08	—	—	—
Dividend payout	0.15	—	—	—	—
Free cash flow	(51.00)	2,959.00	3,082.00	468.00	(458.00)
Depreciation impact ratio	1.39	0.15	0.14	0.37	(1.67)
Recapitalization index	0.67	1.34	1.00	1.47	2.11
Cash flow return on assets	0.03	0.27	0.35	0.15	(0.02)
Cash flow return on sales	0.02	0.15	0.18	0.06	(0.01)
Operations index	(0.24)	1.34	1.89	0.78	(0.09)

Compaq Computer, Inc. Ratios (continued)

Asset Utilization Ratios

	1998	1997	1996	1995	1994
Profit margin	−8.80%	7.505%	6.587%	5.355%	7.979%
Asset turnover	1.654	1.824	1.986	2.385	2.120
Financial structure leverage	1.813	1.613	1.693	1.687	1.620
Return on assets	−14.56%	13.69%	13.08%	12.77%	16.92%
Return on equity	−26.40%	22.07%	22.14%	21.55%	27.40%

Capital Structure Ratios

	1998	1997	1996	1995	1994
Debt to capital	0.45	0.38	0.41	0.41	0.38
Debt to equity	0.81	0.61	0.69	0.69	0.62
Long-term debt to capital	0.03	0.01	0.04	0.07	0.06
Long-term debt to equity	0.05	0.02	0.07	0.12	0.11
Working capital/total assets-Z1	0.36	0.54	0.55	0.60	0.61
Retained earnings/total assets-Z2	0.42	0.67	0.64	0.67	0.68
EBIT/total assets-Z3	(0.47)	0.67	0.62	0.63	0.75
Sales/total assets-Z4	1.65	1.82	1.99	2.38	2.12
Market to book-Z5	4.05	4.80	2.45	2.48	2.64
Z-Score	6.02	8.51	6.24	6.75	6.80

Market Ratio

	1998	1997	1996	1995	1994
Price to earnings	(20.82)	22.23	12.77	13.16	9.93

Dell Income Statements (in millions)

	1998	1997	1996	1995	1994	1993
Sales revenues	$12,327	$7,759	$5,296	$3,475	$2,873	$2,013
Cost of goods sold	9,605	6,093	4,229	2,737	2,441	1,564
Gross profit	2,722	1,666	1,067	738	432	449
Selling, general and administrative expenses	1,202	826	595	424	422	267
Research and development expense	204	126	95	65	49	43
Total operating expenses	1,406	952	690	489	471	310
Operating income	1,316	714	377	249	(39)	139
Other gains and losses	52	33	6	(37)	(1)	4
Pretax income	1,368	747	383	212	(40)	143
Tax expense	424	216	111	63	3	42
Income before extraordinary items	944	531	272	148	(43)	101
Extraordinary items	—	13	12	—	—	—
Net income	$ 944	$ 518	$ 260	$ 148	$ (43)	$ 101
Basic EPS	$ 1.44	$ 0.75	$ 0.36	$ 0.23	$(0.07)	$ 0.65
Diluted EPS	$ 1.28	$ 0.68	$ 0.33	$ 0.19		

Vertical Common Size

	1998	1997	1996	1995	1994	1993
Sales revenues	100.00%	100.00%	100.00%	100.00%	100.00%	100.00%
Cost of goods sold	77.92%	78.53%	79.85%	78.76%	84.96%	77.69%
Gross profit	22.08%	21.47%	20.15%	21.24%	15.04%	22.31%
Selling, general, and administrative expenses	9.75%	10.65%	11.23%	12.20%	14.69%	13.26%
Research and development expense	1.65%	1.62%	1.79%	1.87%	1.71%	2.14%
Total operating expenses	11.41%	12.27%	13.03%	14.07%	16.39%	15.40%
Operating income	10.68%	9.20%	7.12%	7.17%	−1.36%	6.91%
Other gains and losses	0.42%	0.43%	0.11%	−1.06%	−0.03%	0.20%
Pretax income	11.10%	9.63%	7.23%	6.10%	−1.39%	7.10%
Tax expense	3.44%	2.78%	2.10%	1.81%	0.10%	2.09%
Income before extraordinary items	7.66%	6.84%	5.14%	4.26%	−1.50%	5.02%
Extraordinary items	0.00%	0.17%	0.23%	0.00%	0.00%	0.00%
Net income	7.66%	6.68%	4.91%	4.26%	−1.50%	5.02%

Horizontal Common Size—1993 Base Year

	1998	1997	1996	1995	1994	1993
Sales revenues	612.37%	385.44%	263.09%	172.63%	142.72%	100.00%
Cost of goods sold	614.13%	389.58%	270.40%	175.00%	156.07%	100.00%
Gross profit	606.24%	371.05%	237.64%	164.37%	96.21%	100.00%
Selling, general, and administrative expenses	450.19%	309.36%	222.85%	158.80%	158.05%	100.00%
Research and development expense	474.42%	293.02%	220.93%	151.16%	113.95%	100.00%
Total operating expenses	453.55%	307.10%	222.58%	157.74%	151.94%	100.00%
Operating income	946.76%	513.67%	271.22%	179.14%	−28.06%	100.00%
Other gains and losses	1300.00%	825.00%	150.00%	−925.00%	−25.00%	100.00%
Pretax income	956.64%	522.38%	267.83%	148.25%	−27.97%	100.00%
Tax expense	1009.52%	514.29%	264.29%	150.00%	7.14%	100.00%
Income before extraordinary items	934.65%	525.74%	269.31%	146.53%	−42.57%	100.00%
Extraordinary items						
Net income	934.65%	512.87%	257.43%	146.53%	−42.57%	100.00%

Dell Income Statements
(in millions)
(continued)

Horizontal Common Size—Rolling Forward

	1998	1997	1996	1995	1994	1993
Sales revenues	158.87%	146.51%	152.40%	120.95%	142.72%	100.00%
Cost of goods sold	157.64%	144.08%	154.51%	112.13%	156.07%	100.00%
Gross profit	163.39%	156.14%	144.58%	170.83%	96.21%	100.00%
Selling, general, and administrative expenses	145.52%	138.82%	140.33%	100.47%	158.05%	100.00%
Research and development expense	161.90%	132.63%	146.15%	132.65%	113.95%	100.00%
Total operating expenses	147.69%	137.97%	141.10%	103.82%	151.94%	100.00%
Operating income	184.31%	189.39%	151.41%	−638.46%	−28.06%	100.00%
Other gains and losses	157.58%	550.00%	−16.22%	3700.00%	−25.00%	100.00%
Pretax income	183.13%	195.04%	180.66%	−530.00%	−27.97%	100.00%
Tax expense	196.30%	194.59%	176.19%	2100.00%	7.14%	100.00%
Income before extraordinary items	177.78%	195.22%	183.78%	−344.19%	−42.57%	100.00%
Extraordinary items	0.00%	108.33%				
Net income	182.24%	199.23%	175.68%	−344.19%	−42.57%	100.00%

Compound Annual Growth

	1993	1994	1995	1996	1997	1998	Growth
Sales revenues	$(2,013)	0	0	0	0	$12,327	43.7%
Cost of goods sold	$(1,564)	0	0	0	0	9605	43.8%
Gross profit	$ (449)	0	0	0	0	2722	43.4%
Selling, general, and administrative expenses	$ (267)	0	0	0	0	1202	35.1%
Research and development expense	$ (43)	0	0	0	0	204	36.5%
Total operating expenses	$ (310)	0	0	0	0	1406	35.3%
Operating income	$ (139)	0	0	0	0	1316	56.8%
Other gains and losses	$ (4)	0	0	0	0	52	67.0%
Pretax income	$ (143)	0	0	0	0	1368	57.1%
Tax expense	$ (42)	0	0	0	0	424	58.8%
Income before extraordinary items	$ (101)	0	0	0	0	944	56.4%
Extraordinary items	$ —	0	0	0	0	0	
Net income	$ (101)	0	0	0	0	$ 944	56.4%

Dell Balance Sheets
(in millions)

	1998	1997	1996	1995	1994	1993
Cash	$ 320	$ 115	$ 55	$ 43	$ 3	$ 14
Short-term investments	1,524	1,237	591	484	334	80
Accounts receivable	1,486	903	726	538	410	374
Inventory	233	251	429	293	220	304
Other current assets	349	241	156	112	81	80
Total current assets	3,912	2,747	1,957	1,470	1,048	852
Property, plant, and equipment	342	235	179	117	86	71
Other assets	14	11	12	7	6	4
Total assets	$4,268	$2,993	$2,148	$1,594	$1,140	$927
Accounts payable	$1,643	$1,040	$ 466	$ 403	$ 282	$295
Accrued liabilities	1,054	618	473	349	255	198
Total current liabilities	2,697	1,658	939	752	537	493
Long-term debt	17	18	113	113	100	48
Warranty payable	225	219	116	68	32	—
Other liabilities	36	13	7	9	—	17
Total liabilities	2,975	1,908	1,175	942	669	558
Preferred stock	—	—	6	120	1	1
Common stock	747	474	430	242	320	177
Retained earnings	607	647	570	311	170	208
Other equity adjustments	(61)	(36)	(33)	(21)	(20)	(17)
Total shareholders' equity	1,293	1,085	973	652	471	369
Total liabilities and shareholders' equity	$4,268	$2,993	$2,148	$1,594	$1,140	$927

Vertical Common Sizing

	1998	1997	1996	1995	1994	1993
Cash	7.50%	3.84%	2.56%	2.70%	0.26%	1.51%
Short-term Investments	35.71%	41.33%	27.51%	30.36%	29.30%	8.63%
Accounts receivable	34.82%	30.17%	33.80%	33.75%	35.96%	40.35%
Inventory	5.46%	8.39%	19.97%	18.38%	19.30%	32.79%
Other current assets	8.18%	8.05%	7.26%	7.03%	7.11%	8.63%
Total current assets	91.66%	91.78%	91.11%	92.22%	91.93%	91.91%
Property, plant, and equipment	8.01%	7.85%	8.33%	7.34%	7.54%	7.66%
Other assets	0.33%	0.37%	0.56%	0.44%	0.53%	0.43%
Total assets	100.00%	100.00%	100.00%	100.00%	100.00%	100.00%
Accounts payable	38.50%	34.75%	21.69%	25.28%	24.74%	31.82%
Accrued liabilities	24.70%	20.65%	22.02%	21.89%	22.37%	21.36%
Total current liabilities	63.19%	55.40%	43.72%	47.18%	47.11%	53.18%

Vertical Common Sizing (continued)

	1998	1997	1996	1995	1994	1993
Long-term debt	0.40%	0.60%	5.26%	7.09%	8.77%	5.18%
Warranty payable	5.27%	7.32%	5.40%	4.27%	2.81%	0.00%
Other liabilities	0.84%	0.43%	0.33%	0.56%	0.00%	1.83%
Total liabilities	69.70%	63.75%	54.70%	59.10%	58.68%	60.19%
Preferred stock	0.00%	0.00%	0.28%	7.53%	0.09%	0.11%
Common stock	17.50%	15.84%	20.02%	15.18%	28.07%	19.09%
Retained earnings	14.22%	21.62%	26.54%	19.51%	14.91%	22.44%
Other equity adjustments	−1.43%	−1.20%	−1.54%	−1.32%	−1.75%	−1.83%
Total shareholders' equity	30.30%	36.25%	45.30%	40.90%	41.32%	39.81%
Total liabilities and shareholders' equity	100.00%	100.00%	100.00%	100.00%	100.00%	100.00%

Horizontal Common Size—1993 Base Year

	1998	1997	1996	1995	1994	1993
Cash	2285.71%	821.43%	392.86%	307.14%	21.43%	100.00%
Short-term Investments	1905.00%	1546.25%	738.75%	605.00%	417.50%	100.00%
Accounts receivable	397.33%	241.44%	194.12%	143.85%	109.63%	100.00%
Inventory	76.64%	82.57%	141.12%	96.38%	72.37%	100.00%
Other current assets	436.25%	301.25%	195.00%	140.00%	101.25%	100.00%
Total current assets	459.15%	322.42%	229.69%	172.54%	123.00%	100.00%
Property, plant, and equipment	481.69%	330.99%	252.11%	164.79%	121.13%	100.00%
Other assets	350.00%	275.00%	300.00%	175.00%	150.00%	100.00%
Total assets	460.41%	322.87%	231.72%	171.95%	122.98%	100.00%
Accounts payable	556.95%	352.54%	157.97%	136.61%	95.59%	100.00%
Accrued liabilities	532.32%	312.12%	238.89%	176.26%	128.79%	100.00%
Total current liabilities	547.06%	336.31%	190.47%	152.54%	108.92%	100.00%
Long-term debt Warranty payable	35.42%	37.50%	235.42%	235.42%	208.33%	100.00%
Other liabilities	211.76%	76.47%	41.18%	52.94%	0.00%	100.00%
Total liabilities	533.15%	341.94%	210.57%	168.82%	119.89%	100.00%
Preferred stock	0.00%	0.00%	600.00%	12000.00%	100.00%	100.00%
Common stock	422.03%	267.80%	242.94%	136.72%	180.79%	100.00%
Retained earnings	291.83%	311.06%	274.04%	149.52%	81.73%	100.00%
Other equity adjustments	358.82%	211.76%	194.12%	123.53%	117.65%	100.00%
Total shareholders' equity	350.41%	294.04%	263.69%	176.69%	127.64%	100.00%
Total liabilities and shareholders' equity	460.41%	322.87%	231.72%	171.95%	122.98%	100.00%

Horizontal Common Size—Rolling Forward

	1998	1997	1996	1995	1994	1993
Cash	278.26%	209.09%	127.91%	1433.33%	21.43%	100.00%
Short-term Investments	123.20%	209.31%	122.11%	144.91%	417.50%	100.00%
Accounts receivable	164.56%	124.38%	134.94%	131.22%	109.63%	100.00%
Inventory	92.83%	58.51%	146.42%	133.18%	72.37%	100.00%
Other current assets	144.81%	154.49%	139.29%	138.27%	101.25%	100.00%
Total current assets	142.41%	140.37%	133.13%	140.27%	123.00%	100.00%
Property, plant, and equipment	145.53%	131.28%	152.99%	136.05%	121.13%	100.00%
Other assets	127.27%	91.67%	171.43%	116.67%	150.00%	100.00%
Total assets	142.60%	139.34%	134.76%	139.82%	122.98%	100.00%
Accounts payable	157.98%	223.18%	115.63%	142.91%	95.59%	100.00%
Accrued liabilities	170.55%	130.66%	135.53%	136.86%	128.79%	100.00%
Total current liabilities	162.67%	176.57%	124.87%	140.04%	108.92%	100.00%
Long-term debt	94.44%	15.93%	100.00%	113.00%	208.33%	100.00%
Warranty payable	102.74%	188.79%	170.59%	212.50%		
Other liabilities	276.92%	185.71%	77.78%		0.00%	100.00%
Total liabilities	155.92%	162.38%	124.73%	140.81%	119.89%	100.00%
Preferred stock		0.00%	5.00%	12000.00%	100.00%	100.00%
Common stock	157.59%	110.23%	177.69%	75.63%	180.79%	100.00%
Retained earnings	93.82%	113.51%	183.28%	182.94%	81.73%	100.00%
Other equity adjustments	169.44%	109.09%	157.14%	105.00%	117.65%	100.00%
Total shareholders' equity	119.17%	111.51%	149.23%	138.43%	127.64%	100.00%
Total liabilities and shareholders' equity	142.60%	139.34%	134.76%	139.82%	122.98%	100.00%

Compound Annual Growth

	1993	1994	1995	1996	1997	1998	Growth
Cash	$ (14)	0	0	0	0	$ 320	87.0%
Short-term Investments	$ (80)	0	0	0	0	1,524	80.3%
Accounts receivable	$(374)	0	0	0	0	1,486	31.8%
Inventory	$(304)	0	0	0	0	233	−5.2%
Other current assets	$ (80)	0	0	0	0	349	34.3%
Total current assets	$(852)	0	0	0	0	3,912	35.6%
Property, plant, and equipment	$ (71)	0	0	0	0	342	36.9%
Other assets	$ (4)	0	0	0	0	14	28.5%
Total assets	$(927)	0	0	0	0	$4,268	35.7%
	$ —	0	0	0	0		
Accounts payable	$(295)	0	0	0	0	$1,643	41.0%
Accrued liabilities	$(198)	0	0	0	0	1,054	39.7%

Dell Balance Sheets
(continued)

	1993	1994	1995	1996	1997	1998	Growth
Total current liabilities	$(493)	0	0	0	0	2,697	40.5%
Long-term debt	$ (48)	0	0	0	0	17	−18.7%
Warranty payable	$ —	0	0	0	0	225	
Other liabilities	$ (17)	0	0	0	0	36	16.2%
Total liabilities	$(558)	0	0	0	0	2,975	39.8%
Preferred stock	$ (1)	0	0	0	0	—	
Common stock	$(177)	0	0	0	0	747	33.4%
Retained earnings	$(208)	0	0	0	0	607	23.9%
Other equity adjustments	$ 17	0	0	0	0	(61)	29.1%
Total shareholders' equity	$(369)	0	0	0	0	1,293	28.5%
Total liabilities and shareholders' equity	$(927)	0	0	0	0	$4,268	35.7%

Dell Computer, Inc.
Consolidated Statements of
Cash Flows
(in millions of dollars)

	1998	1997	1996	1995	1994	1993
Operating:						
Net income (loss)	$ 944	$ 518	$ 260	$ 148	$ (43)	$ 102
Depreciation and amortization expense	67	47	38	33	31	20
Other	24	29	22	24	4	
Changes in operating working capital	529	659	(195)	(3)	97	(163)
Noncurrent assets and liabilities	28	109	50	41	24	2
Cash generated by operating activities	$ 1,592	$ 1,362	$ 175	$ 243	$ 113	$ (39)
Investing:						
Securities purchases	$(12,305)	$(9,538)	$(4,545)	$(4,644)	$(2,588)	$(1,809)
Securities sales	12,017	8,891	4,442	4,463	2,335	1,828
Capital expenditures	(187)	(114)	(101)	(64)	(48)	(47)
Net cash used for investing activities	$ (475)	$ (761)	$ (204)	$ (245)	$ (301)	$ (28)
Financing:						
Purchase of common stock	(1,023)	(495)				
Issuance of debt				13	88	16
Repurchase of notes payable		(95)			(50)	(1)
Issuance of common stock	88	57	48			12
Issuance of preferred stock					120	
Sale of equity options	38			35	20	
Preferred stock dividends	(1)		(14)	(9)	(2)	
Net cash generated by financing activities	$ (898)	$ (533)	$ 34	$ 39	$ 176	$ 27
Foreign exchange effect on cash	(14)	(8)	7	3		

	1998	1997	1996	1995	1994	1993
Total cash generated (used)	**$205**	**$ 60**	**$12**	**$40**	**$(12)**	**$(40)**
Cash and cash equivalent, beginning of year	$115	$ 55	$43	$3	$ 15	$ 55
Cash and cash equivalents, end of year	$320	$115	$55	$43	$ 3	$ 15

*Dell Income Statements
(in millions)*

	1998	1997	1996	1995	1994
Sales revenues	$12,327	$7,759	$5,296	$3,475	$2,873
Cost of goods sold	9,605	6,093	4,229	2,737	2,441
Gross profit	2,722	1,666	1,067	738	432
Selling, general, and administrative expenses	1,202	826	595	424	422
Research and development expense	204	126	95	65	49
Total operating expenses	1,406	952	690	489	471
Operating income	1,316	714	377	249	(39)
Other gains and losses	52	33	6	(37)	(1)
Pretax income	1,368	747	383	212	(40)
Tax expense	424	216	111	63	3
Income before extraordinary items	944	531	272	148	(43)
Extraordinary items	—	13	12	—	—
Net income	$ 944	$ 518	$ 260	$ 148	$ (43)

*Dell AVERAGE Balance
Sheets
(in millions)*

	1998	1997	1996	1995	1994
Cash	$ 217.50	$ 85.00	$ 49.00	$ 23.00	$ 8.50
Short-term Investments	1,380.50	914.00	537.50	409.00	207.00
Accounts receivable	1,194.50	814.50	632.00	474.00	392.00
Inventory	242.00	340.00	361.00	256.50	262.00
Other current assets	295.00	198.50	134.00	96.50	80.50
Total current assets	3,329.50	2,352.00	1,713.50	1,259.00	950.00
Property, plant, and equipment	288.50	207.00	148.00	101.50	78.50
Other assets	12.50	11.50	9.50	6.50	5.00
Total assets	$3,630.50	$2,570.50	$1,871.00	$1,367.00	$1,033.50
Accounts Payable	$1,341.50	$ 753.00	$ 434.50	$ 342.50	$ 288.50
Accrued Liabilities	836.00	545.50	411.00	302.00	226.50
Total current liabilities	2,177.50	1,298.50	845.50	644.50	515.00
Long-term debt	17.50	65.50	113.00	106.50	74.00
Warranty payable	222.00	167.50	92.00	50.00	16.00
Other liabilities	24.50	10.00	8.00	4.50	8.50
Total liabilities	2,441.50	1,541.50	1,058.50	805.50	613.50

Dell AVERAGE *Balance Sheets (continued)*

	1998	1997	1996 ○	1995	1994
Preferred stock	—	3.00	63.00	60.50	1.00
Common stock	610.50	452.00	336.00	281.00	248.50
Retained earnings	627.00	608.50	440.50	240.50	189.00
Other equity adjustments	(48.50)	(34.50)	(27.00)	(20.50)	(18.50)
Total shareholders' equity	1,189.00	1,029.00	812.50	561.50	420.00
Total liabilities and shareholders' equity	$3,630.50	$2,570.50	$1,871.00	$1,367.00	$1,033.50

Cash Flow Data

	1998	1997	1996	1995	1994
Cash flow from operations	$1,592	$1,362	$175	$243	$113
Fixed asset purchases	187	114	101	64	48
Long-term debt repayment	—	95	—	—	50
Cash dividends	—	—	—	—	—
Depreciation and amortization	67	47	38	33	31

Market Data

	1998	1997	1996	1995	1994
High market price	$ 55.00	$ 37.90	$ 13.00	$ 4.00	$ 1.50
Low market price	$ 31.40	$ 9.90	$ 3.10	$ 0.70	$ 0.60
Number of shares outstanding (millions)	2,575.00	2,543.00	2,576.00	2,768.80	2,990.30
Market capitalization	$111,240.00	$60,777.70	$20,736.80	$6,506.68	$3,139.82

Dell Ratios

Liquidity Ratios

	1998	1997	1996	1995	1994
Working capital	$1,152.00	$1,053.50	$868.00	$614.50	$435.00
Working capital ratio	1.53	1.81	2.03	1.95	1.84
Quick ratio	1.28	1.40	1.44	1.41	1.18
Inventory turnover	39.69	17.92	11.71	10.67	9.32
Days in inventory	9.20	20.37	31.16	34.21	39.18
Accounts receivable turnover	10.32	9.53	8.38	7.33	7.33
Days in accounts receivable	35.37	38.32	43.56	49.79	49.80
Inventory conversion cycle	44.57	58.68	74.71	83.99	88.98
Accounts payable turnover	7.16	8.09	9.73	7.99	8.46
Days in accounts payable	50.98	45.11	37.50	45.68	43.14
Net cash conversion cycle	(6.41)	13.58	37.21	38.32	45.84
Cash + short-term investments	1,598.00	999.00	586.50	432.00	215.50
A/R*days in accounts receivable	42,248.16	31,208.24	27,528.28	23,599.06	19,522.23
Inventory*days in inventory	2,225.49	6,925.00	11,247.85	8,773.90	10,264.26

Liquidity Ratios (continued)

	1998	1997	1996	1995	1994
Product dollar days	46,071.65	39,132.24	39,362.63	32,804.96	30,001.99
Current assets-other current assets	3,034.50	2,153.50	1,579.50	1,162.50	869.50
Liquidity index	15.18	18.17	24.92	28.22	34.50

Cash Flow Ratios

	1998	1997	1996	1995	1994
Cash flow adequacy	8.51	6.52	1.73	3.80	1.15
Reinvestment ratio	0.12	0.08	0.58	0.26	0.42
Long-term debt repayment	—	0.07	—	—	0.44
Dividend payout	—	—	—	—	—
Free cash flow	1,405.00	1,248.00	74.00	179.00	65.00
Depreciation impact ratio	0.04	0.03	0.22	0.14	0.27
Recapitalization index	2.79	2.43	2.66	1.94	1.55
Cash flow return on assets	0.44	0.53	0.09	0.18	0.11
Cash flow return on sales	0.13	0.18	0.03	0.07	0.04
Operations index	1.21	1.91	0.46	0.98	(2.90)

Asset Utilization Ratios

	1998	1997	1996	1995	1994
Profit margin	7.658%	6.676%	4.909%	4.259%	−1.497%
Asset turnover	3.395	3.018	2.831	2.542	2.780
Financial structure leverage	3.053	2.498	2.303	2.435	2.461
Return on assets	26.00%	20.15%	13.90%	10.83%	−4.16%
Return on equity	79.39%	50.34%	32.00%	26.36%	−10.24%

Capital Structure Ratios

	1998	1997	1996	1995	1994
Debt to capital	0.67	0.60	0.57	0.59	0.59
Debt to equity	2.05	1.50	1.30	1.43	1.46
Long-term debt to capital	0.07	0.09	0.11	0.11	0.09
Long-term debt to equity	0.20	0.23	0.25	0.28	0.21
Working capital/total assets-Z1	0.38	0.49	0.56	0.54	0.51
Retained earnings/total assets-Z2	0.24	0.33	0.33	0.25	0.26
EBIT/total assets-Z3	1.20	0.92	0.66	0.60	−0.12
Sales/total assets-Z4	3.40	3.02	2.83	2.54	2.78
Market to book-Z5	27.34	23.66	11.75	4.85	3.07
Z-Score	32.55	28.41	16.14	8.78	6.49

Market Ratio

	1998	1997	1996	1995	1994
Price to earnings	117.84	117.33	79.76	43.96	(73.02)

Gateway Income Statements (in millions)

	1998	1997	1996	1995	1994	1993
Sales revenue	$7,467	$6,293	$5,035	$3,676	$2,701	$1,731
Cost of goods sold	5,921	5,217	4,099	3,070	2,343	1,460
Gross profit	1,546	1,076	936	606	358	271
Selling, general, and administrative expenses	1,052	900	580	357	218	121
Operating income	494	176	356	249	140	150
Other, net	46	27	26	13	5	4
Income before taxes	540	203	382	262	145	154
Provision for taxes	194	93	132	90	50	3
Net income	$ 346	$ 110	$ 250	$ 172	$ 95	$ 151

Vertical Common Size

	1998	1997	1996	1995	1994	1993
Sales revenue	100.00%	100.00%	100.00%	100.00%	100.00%	100.00%
Cost of goods sold	79.30%	82.90%	81.41%	83.51%	86.75%	84.34%
Gross profit	20.70%	17.10%	18.59%	16.49%	13.25%	15.66%
Selling, general, and administrative expenses	14.09%	14.30%	11.52%	9.71%	8.07%	6.99%
Operating income	6.62%	2.80%	7.07%	6.77%	5.18%	8.67%
Other, net	0.62%	0.43%	0.52%	0.35%	0.19%	0.23%
Income before taxes	7.23%	3.23%	7.59%	7.13%	5.37%	8.90%
Provision for taxes	2.60%	1.48%	2.62%	2.45%	1.85%	0.17%
Net income	4.63%	1.75%	4.97%	4.68%	3.52%	8.72%

Horizontal Common Size—1993 Base Year

	1998	1997	1996	1995	1994	1993
Sales revenue	431.37%	363.55%	290.87%	212.36%	156.04%	100.00%
Cost of goods sold	405.55%	357.33%	280.75%	210.27%	160.48%	100.00%
Gross profit	570.48%	397.05%	345.39%	223.62%	132.10%	100.00%
Selling, general, and administrative expenses	869.42%	743.80%	479.34%	295.04%	180.17%	100.00%
Operating income	329.33%	117.33%	237.33%	166.00%	93.33%	100.00%
Other, net	1150.00%	675.00%	650.00%	325.00%	125.00%	100.00%
Income before taxes	350.65%	131.82%	248.05%	170.13%	94.16%	100.00%
Provision for taxes	6466.67%	3100.00%	4400.00%	3000.00%	1666.67%	100.00%
Net income	229.14%	72.85%	165.56%	113.91%	62.91%	100.00%

Gateway Income Statements
(in millions)
(continued)

Horizontal Common Size—Rolling Forward

	1998	1997	1996	1995	1994	1993
Sales revenue	118.66%	124.99%	136.97%	136.10%	156.04%	100.00%
Cost of goods sold	113.49%	127.27%	133.52%	131.03%	160.48%	100.00%
Gross profit	143.68%	114.96%	154.46%	169.27%	132.10%	100.00%
Selling, general, and administrative expenses	116.89%	155.17%	162.46%	163.76%	180.17%	100.00%
Operating income	280.68%	49.44%	142.97%	177.86%	93.33%	100.00%
Other, net	170.37%	103.85%	200.00%	260.00%	125.00%	100.00%
Income before taxes	266.01%	53.14%	145.80%	180.69%	94.16%	100.00%
Provision for taxes	208.60%	70.45%	146.67%	180.00%	1666.67%	100.00%
Net income	314.55%	44.00%	145.35%	181.05%	62.91%	100.00%

Compound Annual Growth

	1993	1994	1995	1996	1997	1998	Growth
Sales revenue	$(1,731)	0	0	0	0	$7,467	34.0%
Cost of goods sold	$(1,460)	0	0	0	0	5,921	32.3%
Gross profit	$ (271)	0	0	0	0	1,546	41.7%
Selling, general, and administrative expenses	$ (121)	0	0	0	0	1,052	54.1%
Operating income	$ (150)	0	0	0	0	494	26.9%
Other, net	$ (4)	0	0	0	0	46	63.0%
Income before taxes	$ (154)	0	0	0	0	540	28.5%
Provision for taxes	$ (3)	0	0	0	0	194	130.2%
Net income	$ (151)	0	0	0	0	$ 346	18.0%

Gateway Balance Sheets
(in millions)

	1998	1997	1996	1995	1994	1993
Cash	$1,169	$ 593	$ 516	$ 166	$214	$113
Short-term investments	158	38	—	3	29	18
Accounts receivable	558	510	449	406	253	170
Inventory	167	249	278	224	120	177
Other current assets	176	154	75	67	33	22
Total current assets	2,228	1,544	1,318	866	649	500
Property, plant, and equipment	530	336	242	170	89	60
Intangible assets	65	121	77	59	27	3
Other assets	67	38	36	29	5	1
Total assets	$2,890	$2,039	$1,673	$1,124	$770	$564
Notes payable	$11	$13	$15	$13	$3	$5
Accounts payable	718	488	411	236	184	126
Accrued liabilities	415	271	190	110	57	24
Other current liabilities	285	231	183	166	104	99
Total current liabilities	1,429	1,003	799	525	348	254

Gateway Balance Sheets
(in millions)
(continued)

	1998	1997	1996	1995	1994	1993
Long-term liabilities	3	7	7	11	27	29
Warranty liability	113	99	51	32	19	—
Total Liabilities	1,545	1,109	857	568	394	283
Common stock	2	2	2	1	1	1
Additional paid-in-capital	365	299	288	280	274	275
Retained earnings	982	634	526	275	101	5
Other equity adjustments	(4)	(5)	—	—	—	—
Total shareholders' equity	1,345	930	816	556	376	281
Total liabilities and shareholders' equity	$2,890	$2,039	$1,673	$1,124	$770	$564

Vertical Common Size

	1998	1997	1996	1995	1994	1993
Cash	40.45%	29.08%	30.84%	14.77%	27.79%	20.04%
Short-term investments	5.47%	1.86%	0.00%	0.27%	3.77%	3.19%
Accounts receivable	19.31%	25.01%	26.84%	36.12%	32.86%	30.14%
Inventory	5.78%	12.21%	16.62%	19.93%	15.58%	31.38%
Other current assets	6.09%	7.55%	4.48%	5.96%	4.29%	3.90%
Total current assets	77.09%	75.72%	78.78%	77.05%	84.29%	88.65%
Property, plant, and equipment	18.34%	16.48%	14.47%	15.12%	11.56%	10.64%
Intangible assets	2.25%	5.93%	4.60%	5.25%	3.51%	0.53%
Other assets	2.32%	1.86%	2.15%	2.58%	0.65%	0.18%
Total assets	100.00%	100.00%	100.00%	100.00%	100.00%	100.00%
Notes payable	0.38%	0.64%	0.90%	1.16%	0.39%	0.89%
Accounts payable	24.84%	23.93%	24.57%	21.00%	23.90%	22.34%
Accrued liabilities	14.36%	13.29%	11.36%	9.79%	7.40%	4.26%
Other current liabilities	9.86%	11.33%	10.94%	14.77%	13.51%	17.55%
Total current liabilities	49.45%	49.19%	47.76%	46.71%	45.19%	45.04%
Long-term liabilities	0.10%	0.34%	0.42%	0.98%	3.51%	5.14%
Warranty liability	3.91%	4.86%	3.05%	2.85%	2.47%	0.00%
Total Liabilities	53.46%	54.39%	51.23%	50.53%	51.17%	50.18%
Common stock	0.07%	0.10%	0.12%	0.09%	0.13%	0.18%
Additional paid-in-capital	12.63%	14.66%	17.21%	24.91%	35.58%	48.76%
Retained earnings	33.98%	31.09%	31.44%	24.47%	13.12%	0.89%
Other equity adjustments	−0.14%	−0.25%	0.00%	0.00%	0.00%	0.00%
Total shareholders' equity	46.54%	45.61%	48.77%	49.47%	48.83%	49.82%
Total liabilities and shareholders' equity	100.00%	100.00%	100.00%	100.00%	100.00%	100.00%

Horizontal Common Size—1993 Base Year

	1998	1997	1996	1995	1994	1993
Cash	1034.51%	524.78%	456.64%	146.90%	189.38%	100.00%
Short-term investments	877.78%	211.11%	0.00%	16.67%	161.11%	100.00%
Accounts receivable	328.24%	300.00%	264.12%	238.82%	148.82%	100.00%
Inventory	94.35%	140.68%	157.06%	126.55%	67.80%	100.00%
Other current assets	800.00%	700.00%	340.91%	304.55%	150.00%	100.00%
Total current assets	445.60%	308.80%	263.60%	173.20%	129.80%	100.00%
Property, plant, and equipment	883.33%	560.00%	403.33%	283.33%	148.33%	100.00%
Intangible assets	2166.67%	4033.33%	2566.67%	1966.67%	900.00%	100.00%
Other assets	6700.00%	3800.00%	3600.00%	2900.00%	500.00%	100.00%
Total assets	512.41%	361.52%	296.63%	199.29%	136.52%	100.00%
Notes payable	220.00%	260.00%	300.00%	260.00%	60.00%	100.00%
Accounts payable	569.84%	387.30%	326.19%	187.30%	146.03%	100.00%
Accrued liabilities	1729.17%	1129.17%	791.67%	458.33%	237.50%	100.00%
Other current liabilities	287.88%	233.33%	184.85%	167.68%	105.05%	100.00%
Total current liabilities	562.60%	394.88%	314.57%	206.69%	137.01%	100.00%
Long-term liabilities	10.34%	24.14%	24.14%	37.93%	93.10%	100.00%
Warranty liability						
Total Liabilities	545.94%	391.87%	302.83%	200.71%	139.22%	100.00%
Common stock	200.00%	200.00%	200.00%	100.00%	100.00%	100.00%
Additional paid-in-capital	132.73%	108.73%	104.73%	101.82%	99.64%	100.00%
Retained earnings	19640.00%	12680.00%	10520.00%	5500.00%	2020.00%	100.00%
Other equity adjustments						
Total shareholders' equity	478.65%	330.96%	290.39%	197.86%	133.81%	100.00%
Total liabilities and shareholders' equity	512.41%	361.52%	296.63%	199.29%	136.52%	100.00%

Gateway Balance Sheets
(in millions)
(continued)

Horizontal Common Size—Rolling Forward

	1998	1997	1996	1995	1994	1993
Cash	197.13%	114.92%	310.84%	77.57%	189.38%	100.00%
Short-term investments	415.79%		0.00%	10.34%	161.11%	100.00%
Accounts receivable	109.41%	113.59%	110.59%	160.47%	148.82%	100.00%
Inventory	67.07%	89.57%	124.11%	186.67%	67.80%	100.00%
Other current assets	114.29%	205.33%	111.94%	203.03%	150.00%	100.00%
Total current assets	144.30%	117.15%	152.19%	133.44%	129.80%	100.00%
Property, plant and equipment	157.74%	138.84%	142.35%	191.01%	148.33%	100.00%
Intangible assets	53.72%	157.14%	130.51%	218.52%	900.00%	100.00%
Other assets	176.32%	105.56%	124.14%	580.00%	500.00%	100.00%
Total assets	141.74%	121.88%	148.84%	145.97%	136.52%	100.00%
Notes payable	84.62%	86.67%	115.38%	433.33%	60.00%	100.00%
Accounts payable	147.13%	118.73%	174.15%	128.26%	146.03%	100.00%
Accrued liabilities	153.14%	142.63%	172.73%	192.98%	237.50%	100.00%
Other current liabilities	123.38%	126.23%	110.24%	159.62%	105.05%	100.00%
Total current liabilities	142.47%	125.53%	152.19%	150.86%	137.01%	100.00%
Long-term liabilities	42.86%	100.00%	63.64%	40.74%	93.10%	100.00%
Warranty liability	114.14%	194.12%	159.38%	168.42%		
Total Liabilities	139.31%	129.40%	150.88%	144.16%	139.22%	100.00%
Common stock	100.00%	100.00%	200.00%	100.00%	100.00%	100.00%
Additional paid-in-capital	122.07%	103.82%	102.86%	102.19%	99.64%	100.00%
Retained earnings	154.89%	120.53%	191.27%	272.28%	2020.00%	100.00%
Other equity adjustments	80.00%					
Total shareholders' equity	144.62%	113.97%	146.76%	147.87%	133.81%	100.00%
Total liabilities and shareholders' equity	141.74%	121.88%	148.84%	145.97%	136.52%	100.00%

Gateway Balance Sheets
(in millions)
(continued)

	1993	1994	1995	1996	1997	1998	Growth
Cash	$(113)	0	0	0	0	$1,169	59.6%
Short-term investments	$ (18)	0	0	0	0	158	54.4%
Accounts receivable	$(170)	0	0	0	0	558	26.8%
Inventory	$(177)	0	0	0	0	167	–1.2%
Other current assets	$ (22)	0	0	0	0	176	51.6%
Total current assets	$(500)	0	0	0	0	2,228	34.8%
Property, plant, and equipment	$ (60)	0	0	0	0	530	54.6%
Intangible assets	$ (3)	0	0	0	0	65	85.0%
Other assets	$ (1)	0	0	0	0	67	131.9%
Total assets	$(564)	0	0	0	0	$2,890	38.7%
Notes payable	$ (5)	0	0	0	0	$ 11	17.1%
Accounts payable	$(126)	0	0	0	0	718	41.6%
Accrued liabilities	$ (24)	0	0	0	0	415	76.8%
Other current liabilities	$ (99)	0	0	0	0	285	23.5%
Total current liabilities	$(254)	0	0	0	0	1,429	41.3%
Long-term liabilities	$ (29)	0	0	0	0	3	
Warranty liability	$ —	0	0	0	0	113	
Total Liabilities	$(283)	0	0	0	0	1,545	40.4%
Common stock	$ (1)	0	0	0	0	2	14.9%
Additional paid-in-capital	$(275)	0	0	0	0	365	5.8%
Retained earnings	$ (5)	0	0	0	0	982	187.5%
Other equity adjustments	$ —	0	0	0	0	(4)	
Total shareholders' equity	$(281)	0	0	0	0	1,345	36.8%
Total liabilities and shareholders' equity	$(564)	0	0	0	0	$2,890	38.7%

Gateway, Inc.
Consolidated Statements of
Cash Flows
(in millions of dollars)

	1998	1997	1996	1995	1994	1993
Operating:						
Net income (loss)	$ 346	$ 110	$ 251	$ 173	$ 96	$ 151
Depreciation and amortization expense	106	87	62	38	18	8
Deferred income taxes	(58)	(63)	(13)	(24)	(1)	
Nonrecurring expenses		114				
Change in accounts receivable	(52)	(42)	(66)	(158)	(94)	(48)
Change in inventory	81	59	(54)	(121)	44	(84)
Change in accounts payable	229	66	177	52	57	63
Other	256	112	127	111	82	40
Cash generated by operating activities	$ 908	$ 443	$ 484	$ 71	$ 202	$ 130
Investing:						
Capital expenditures	$(235)	$(176)	$(144)	$(78)	$(29)	$(36)
Purchase of available-for-sale securities	(169)	(50)		(51)	(206)	(18)

	1998	1997	1996	1995	1994	1993
Proceeds from sale of available-for-sale securities	49	11	3	38	166	
Acquisition of technology		(142)		(4)		(3)
Other	(1)	(4)	3	(13)		
Cash used for investing activities	$(356)	$(361)	$(138)	$(108)	$(69)	$(57)
Financing:						
Proceeds from notes payable		$ 10	$ 10	$ 5		$ 18
Payments on long-term liabilities	(13)	(16)	(14)	(25)	(5)	(12)
Dividends					(28)	164
Stock options exercised	36	6	9	9		(145)
Cash generated by financing activities	$ 23	$ —	$ 5	$ (11)	$(33)	$ 25
Foreign exchange effect on cash	1	(5)	(1)			
Total cash generated (used)	$ 576	$ 77	$ 350	$ (48)	$ 100	$ 98
Cash and cash equivalent, beginning of year	$ 594	$ 517	$ 166	$ 214	$ 114	$ 16
Cash and cash equivalents, end of year	$1,170	$ 594	$ 516	$ 166	$ 214	$ 114

*Gateway Income Statements
(in millions)*

	1998	1997	1996	1995	1994
Sales revenue	$7,467	$6,293	$5,035	$3,676	$2,701
Cost of goods sold	5,921	5,217	4,099	3,070	2,343
Gross profit	1,546	1,076	936	606	358
Selling, general, and administrative expenses	1,052	900	580	357	218
Operating income	494	176	356	249	140
Other, net	46	27	26	13	5
Income before taxes	540	203	382	262	145
Provision for taxes	194	93	132	90	50
Net income	$ 346	$ 110	$ 250	$ 172	$ 95

*Gateway AVERAGE Balance
Sheets (in millions)*

	1998	1997	1996	1995	1994
Cash	$ 881.00	$ 554.50	$ 341.00	$190.00	$163.50
Short-term investments	98.00	19.00	1.50	16.00	23.50
Accounts receivable	534.00	479.50	427.50	329.50	211.50
Inventory	208.00	263.50	251.00	172.00	148.50
Other current assets	165.00	114.50	71.00	50.00	27.50
Total current assets	1,886.00	1,431.00	1,092.00	757.50	574.50

	1998	1997	1996	1995	1994
Property, plant, and equipment	433.00	289.00	206.00	129.50	74.50
Intangible assets	93.00	99.00	68.00	43.00	15.00
Other assets	52.50	37.00	32.50	17.00	3.00
Total assets	$2,464.50	$1,856.00	$1,398.50	$947.00	$667.00
Notes payable	$12.00	$14.00	$14.00	$8.00	$4.00
Accounts payable	603.00	449.50	323.50	210.00	155.00
Accrued liabilities	343.00	230.50	150.00	83.50	40.50
Other current liabilities	258.00	207.00	174.50	135.00	101.50
Total current liabilities	1,216.00	901.00	662.00	436.50	301.00
Long-term liabilities	5.00	7.00	9.00	19.00	28.00
Warranty liability	106.00	75.00	41.50	25.50	9.50
Total Liabilities	1,327.00	983.00	712.50	481.00	338.50
Common stock	2.00	2.00	1.50	1.00	1.00
Additional paid-in-capital	332.00	293.50	284.00	277.00	274.50
Retained earnings	808.00	580.00	400.50	188.00	53.00
Other equity adjustments	(4.50)	(2.50)	—	—	—
Total shareholders' equity	1,137.50	873.00	686.00	466.00	328.50
Total liabilities and shareholders' equity	$2,464.50	$1,856.00	$1,398.50	$947.00	$667.00

Cash Flow Data

	1998	1997	1996	1995	1994
Cash flow from operations	$908	$443	$484	$71	$202
Fixed asset purchases	235	176	144	78	29
Long-term debt repayment	13	16	14	25	5
Cash dividends	—	—	—	—	28
Depreciation and amortization	106	87	62	38	18

Market Data

	1998	1997	1996	1995	1994
High market price	$ 34.40	$ 23.10	$ 16.60	$ 9.40	$ 6.20
Low market price	$ 15.50	$ 11.80	$ 4.50	$ 4.00	$ 2.30
Number of shares outstanding (millions)	313.14	307.02	298.09	298.21	289.58
Market capitalization	$7,812.84	$5,357.50	$3,144.85	$1,998.01	$1,230.72

Liquidity Ratios

	1998	1997	1996	1995	1994
Working capital	$670.00	$530.00	$430.00	$321.00	$273.50
Working capital ratio	1.55	1.59	1.65	1.74	1.91
Quick ratio	1.24	1.17	1.16	1.23	1.32
Inventory turnover	28.47	19.80	16.33	17.85	15.78

Liquidity Ratios (continued)

	1998	1997	1996	1995	1994
Days in inventory	12.82	18.44	22.35	20.45	23.13
Accounts receivable turnover	13.98	13.12	11.78	11.16	12.77
Days in accounts receivable	26.10	27.81	30.99	32.72	28.58
Inventory conversion cycle	38.93	46.25	53.34	53.17	51.71
Accounts payable turnover	9.82	11.61	12.67	14.62	15.12
Days in accounts payable	37.17	31.45	28.81	24.97	24.15
Net cash conversion cycle	1.75	14.80	24.53	28.20	27.57
Cash + short-term investments	979.00	573.50	342.50	206.00	187.00
A/R*days in accounts receivable	13,938.92	13,335.59	13,248.47	10,780.23	6,044.90
Inventory*days in inventory	2,667.01	4,857.73	5,609.99	3,517.32	3,435.37
Product dollar days	17,584.93	18,766.82	19,200.96	14,503.55	9,667.27
Current assets-other current assets	1,721.00	1,316.50	1,021.00	707.50	547.00
Liquidity index	10.22	14.26	18.81	20.50	17.67

Cash Flow Ratios

	1998	1997	1996	1995	1994
Cash flow adequacy	3.66	2.31	3.06	0.69	3.26
Reinvestment ratio	0.26	0.40	0.30	1.10	0.14
Long-term debt repayment	0.01	0.04	0.03	0.35	0.02
Dividend payout	—	—	—	—	0.14
Free cash flow	660.00	251.00	326.00	(32.00)	168.00
Depreciation impact ratio	0.12	0.20	0.13	0.54	0.09
Recapitalization index	2.22	2.02	2.32	2.05	1.61
Cash flow return on assets	0.37	0.24	0.35	0.07	0.30
Cash flow return on sales	0.12	0.07	0.10	0.02	0.07
Operations index	1.84	2.52	1.36	0.29	1.44

Asset Utilization Ratios

	1998	1997	1996	1995	1994
Profit margin	4.634%	1.748%	4.965%	4.679%	3.517%
Asset turnover	3.030	3.391	3.600	3.882	4.049
Financial structure leverage	2.167	2.126	2.039	2.032	2.030
Return on assets	14.04%	5.93%	17.88%	18.16%	14.24%
Return on equity	30.42%	12.60%	36.44%	36.91%	28.92%

Gateway Ratios

Capital Structure Ratios

	1998	1997	1996	1995	1994
Debt to capital	0.54	0.53	0.51	0.51	0.51
Debt to equity	1.17	1.13	1.04	1.03	1.03
Long-term debt to capital	0.05	0.04	0.04	0.05	0.06
Long-term debt to equity	0.10	0.09	0.07	0.10	0.11
Working capital/total assets-Z1	0.33	0.34	0.37	0.41	0.49
Retained earnings/total assets-Z2	0.46	0.44	0.40	0.28	0.11
EBIT/total assets-Z3	0.66	0.31	0.84	0.87	0.69
Sales/total assets-Z4	3.03	3.39	3.60	3.88	4.05
Market to book-Z5	3.53	3.27	2.65	2.49	2.18
Z-Score	8.01	7.75	7.86	7.93	7.53

Market Data

	1998	1997	1996	1995	1994
Price to earnings	22.58	48.70	12.58	11.62	12.95

B AIRLINE INDUSTRY

$\mathscr{T}$he airline industry consists of companies that primarily derive revenues by transporting passengers from one location to another. Analysts often view this industry in three tiers: Major airlines realize annual revenues in excess of $1 billion; national carriers have sales ranging from $100 million to $1 billion; and regional air carriers generate less than $100 million of revenues. The assignments in this text and information in this appendix relate to the major airlines. Analysis concentrates on the three largest major airlines. As with the personal computer industry and other industries discussed in the following appendixes, we provide information for and analysis of the period beginning in 1993 and ending in 1998. (Internet Industry Case assignments at the end of many chapters offer you the opportunity to update analyses from 1999 to the present.)

American Airlines, Delta Air Lines, and United Airlines dominate the U.S. airline industry. These three air carriers control a majority of the market and have been referred to as *imperfect oligopoly*.[1] This domination can be attributed to survival of the fittest. This appendix discusses these factors with narrative, graphic, and financial accounts for the period analyzed.

---

[1] Airline Industry Survey, May 1999, *Standard & Poor's Industry Survey* (New York: McGraw-Hill, 1999).

REGULATORY BACKGROUND

The federal government regulated airfares until the late 1970s, when the Airline Deregulation Act of 1978 passed. Airfares fell rapidly during the 1980s as a result of competitive pricing. Air carriers' profit margins declined because they were no longer protected by governmental pricing policies. Industry consolidation took place during the 1980s to ease competitive pressure, resulting in increasingly larger air carriers. American, Delta, and United emerged as industry leaders after this consolidation frenzy subsided.

Exhibit B-1 presents major air carriers market share at the beginning and end of the period analyzed. Note the dominant position of United, Delta, and American during the 1990s.

EXHIBIT B-1
Market Share (based on revenue passenger miles) 1993 and 1998

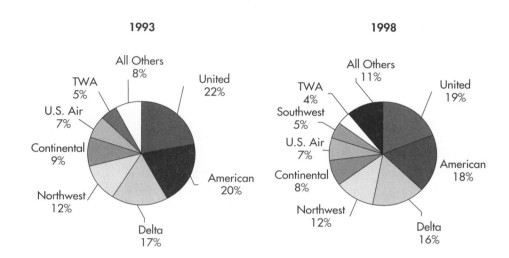

ASSET UTILIZATION

These three airlines, and other major carriers, operated *hub-and-spoke* networks. In this type of arrangement, airlines fly passengers from smaller spoke cities to a major hub airport. If necessary, passengers then transfer to their ultimate destination by boarding a flight to another spoke airport. Hub-and-spoke networks mean that each of three major airlines dominate traffic at certain airports. Exhibit B-2 presents the principal hub cities for each airline at the end of the period analyzed.[2]

---

[2] 1998 United States Department of Transportation.

CARRIER	HUB CITIES	MARKET SHARE AT AIRPORT
American	Dallas/Fort Worth	64.6%
	Miami	62.4%
	San Juan, Puerto Rico	53.1%
Delta	Atlanta	80.1%
	Cincinnati	77.5%
	Salt Lake City	72.7%
United	Denver	69.3%
	San Francisco	58.7%
	Washington (Dulles)	50.1
	Chicago (O'Hare)	47.6%

Hub-and-spoke systems evolved as a means of increasing aircraft productivity. They enable the airlines to increase their passenger load factor, or the number of occupants per flight.[3] In addition, the hub-and-spoke system virtually eliminated competition at certain airports (as evidenced by Exhibit B-2). Air carriers created an imperfect oligopoly, as noted earlier; their dominance virtually precluded start-up airlines from penetrating many desirable markets. In many instances, competitors could not secure gate space to serve their customers.

FINANCIAL STRUCTURE

The major airlines offered multiple pricing arrangement to the same destination on the same flight. In general, the closer passengers ordered tickets to the departure date, the more they paid. Sophisticated technological models emerged to predict the timing for flight demand. These software applications enabled major airlines to set prices to meet demand and maximize profits. Business travelers became especially lucrative clients for the airlines. These passengers were more likely to fly frequently, order tickets closer to departure, and travel first class than their leisure travel counterparts.

Airlines measure unit revenue on the basis of revenue (in cents) per passenger mile (RPM). These revenues are presented in Exhibit B-3A. The higher RPMs earned by American Airlines were somewhat offset by that firm's lower passenger load factor (Exhibit B-3B).[4]

---

[3] More specifically, load is determined by dividing RPMs by available seat miles. RPMs equal the total number of passengers times the average distance flown.

[4] 1998 United States Department of Transportation.

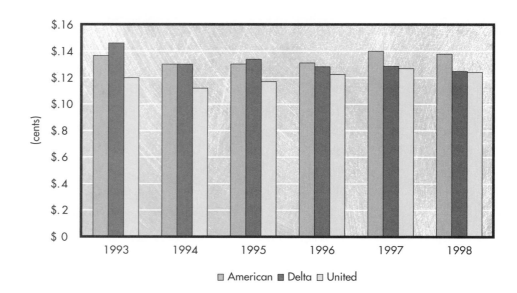

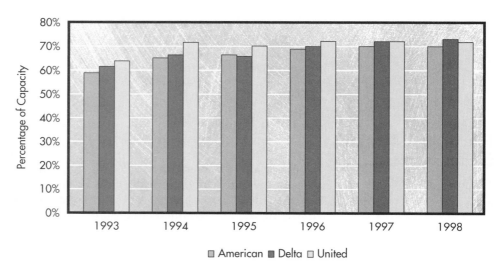

Exhibit B-4 indicates that three expenses dominated the cost of transporting passengers as a percentage of revenue from 1993 to 1998. Salaries, fuel costs (the volatility of jet fuel prices significantly affected annual profitability), and commissions.

Air carriers are service businesses with highly trained workforces. The government, as noted earlier, historically set airfares. There is also a strongly organized labor presence within the industry. These factors resulted in relatively high labor costs for the airlines. During the 1990s, air carriers began granting stock options as a means of reducing labor costs and relating compensation to corporate profits. United Airline, in fact, dramatically restructured its ownership base in the

---

[5] Data were derived from vertical common size income statements as disclosed by the airlines in their respective Form 10-Ks.

EXHIBIT B-4
Primary Operating Expenses
(as percentage of revenues)
1993 and 1998

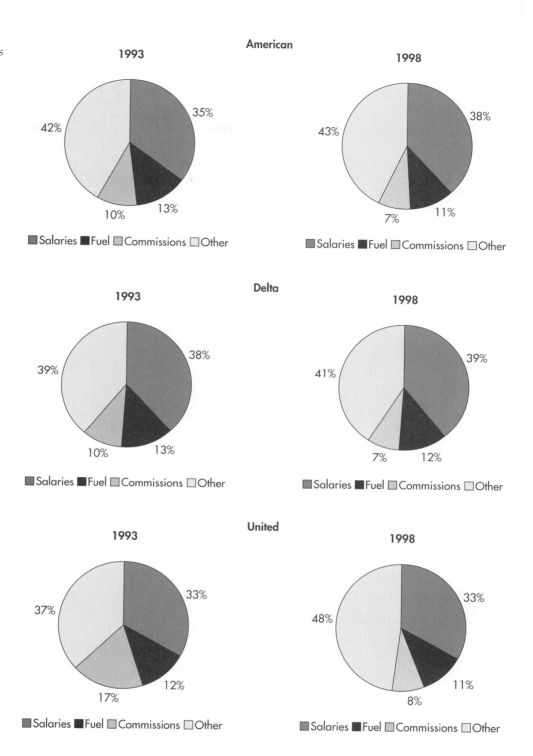

American

1993

35%
42%
10%
13%

■ Salaries ■ Fuel ■ Commissions □ Other

1998

38%
43%
7%
11%

■ Salaries ■ Fuel ■ Commissions □ Other

Delta

1993

38%
39%
10%
13%

■ Salaries ■ Fuel ■ Commissions □ Other

1998

39%
41%
7%
12%

■ Salaries ■ Fuel ■ Commissions □ Other

United

1993

33%
37%
17%
12%

■ Salaries ■ Fuel ■ Commissions □ Other

1998

33%
48%
8%
11%

■ Salaries ■ Fuel ■ Commissions □ Other

mid-1990s. It became the largest employee-owned company in the world after employees exchanged salaries and benefits for a 55 percent ownership stake in the company.

Variable fuel prices affected airline performance. Exhibit B-5 presents the average annual fuel price.[6] To some extent, companies offset variable jet fuel costs by entering into hedge agreements that locked in their fuel costs.

EXHIBIT B-5

Annual Average Fuel Costs (rounded to the nearest whole cent) 1993–1998

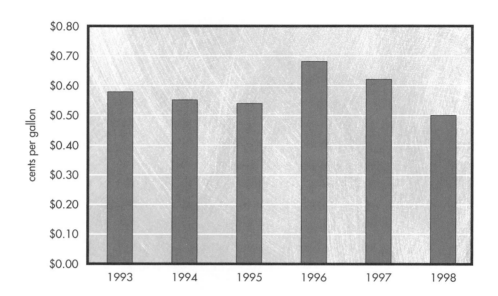

Airlines reduced commissions paid to travel agents during the period examined. Passengers increasingly purchased tickets directly from the companies, often over the Internet. Air carriers also began reducing the administrative costs of ticketing by issuing electronic tickets.

SIGNIFICANT EVENTS

1993

- ◆ Industry retrenches as all major airlines announce layoffs and reduce air fleets.
- ◆ Fifteen-member bipartisan federal commission is appointed to study ailing airline industry.
- ◆ American reports a loss of $1.2 billion on airline operations since 1990 but states its air services business was profitable during that period.
- ◆ Delta Airlines defers a $1 billion capital expansion plan.
- ◆ United Air Lines pilots and machinists consider purchasing a majority stake in the airline, but its flight attendants reject joining the employee buyout.

---

[6] Airline Industry Survey, May 1999, *Standard & Poor's Industry Survey* (New York: McGraw-Hill, 1999).

1994

◆ Industry layoffs continue; companies experiment with "ticketless travel" and reduce travel agent commissions; firms increase code sharing (the common marketing practices whereby two or more air carriers provide identical services).
◆ Southwest Airlines, the low-cost point-to-point carrier, announces plans to serve East Coast markets, a stronghold of the three major carriers.
◆ Delta announces "Project North America", a long-term restructuring program designed to improve profitability; the company eliminates 15,000 jobs.
◆ United's pilots and machinists purchase 55 percent of the company for $5 billion, making it the largest employee-owned company in the world.

1995

◆ Industry projects a profit after five years of losses.
◆ American reaches contract agreements with flight attendants and transport workers; company purchases a 25 percent interest in Japan Airlines.
◆ American and United consider acquiring US Air.
◆ United expands air fleet and hires more employees.

1996

◆ Governments negotiate "open sky" pacts, which would allow air carriers greater access to foreign airports.
◆ Air carriers expand fleets and hire more workers.
◆ Delta announces cost-cutting successes; the company launches Delta Express as a point-to-point carrier to compete with low-cost carriers.
◆ American's pilots and machinists reach tentative contract agreements, but its flight attendants do not agree to terms.

1997

◆ Passengers become increasingly dissatisfied with record flight delays.
◆ American forms an alliance with British Airways, the largest airline in the world.
◆ Delta's chief executive officer (CEO) Ronald Allen retires and is replaced by Leo Mullin, the first non-Delta employee appointed to the post.
◆ United expands its shuttle service to counter Southwest's growth; its flight attendants approve a ten-year contract.

1998

◆ Federal government investigates monopoly by large carriers at hub airports.
◆ Airlines continue to order new aircraft and recall furloughed workers.
◆ Delta and Northwest seek control of Continental Airlines.
◆ American's CEO Robert Crandell retires.
◆ Delta and United planned marketing alliance fails to materialize.

	1998	1997	1996	1995	1994	1993
Revenues:	$16,299	$15,856	$15,136	$14,503	$13,910	$14,737
Expenses:						
Salaries, wages, etc.	5,482	5,220	4,934	4,818	4,685	4,927
Aircraft fuel	1,551	1,860	1,866	1,565	1,556	1,818
Commissions	1,159	1,212	1,182	1,236	1,273	1,393
Depreciation and amortization	941	950	930	975	966	1,115
Rentals and landing fees	778	787	762	754	729	787
Services	671	672	667	675	663	693
Aircraft rentals	532	531	562	604	620	639
Maintenance, materials, and repairs	803	736	560	494	438	542
Other operating expenses	2,614	2,441	2,342	2,296	2,135	2,259
Restructuring	—	—	—	485	276	—
Total Operating Expenses	14,531	14,409	13,805	13,902	13,341	14,173
Operating Income	1,768	1,447	1,331	601	569	564
Other income (expenses)	(24)	(160)	(375)	(581)	(469)	(490)
Income (loss) before taxes	1,744	1,287	956	20	100	74
Income tax provision	681	507	387	31	46	51
Income before irregular items	1,063	780	569	(11)	54	23
Irregular items, net of tax	—	—	136	219	214	—
Net Income	$1,063	$780	$705	$208	$268	$23
Basic earnings per share	$7.78	$5.52	$11.63	$2.11	$4.51	$2.23
Diluted earnings per share	$7.42	$5.39	$11.19			

Vertical Common Size

	1998	1997	1996	1995	1994	1993
Revenues:	100.0%	100.0%	100.0%	100.0%	100.0%	100.0%
Expenses:						
Salaries, wages, etc.	33.6%	32.9%	32.6%	33.2%	33.7%	33.4%
Aircraft fuel	9.5%	11.7%	12.3%	10.8%	11.2%	12.3%
Commissions	7.1%	7.6%	7.8%	8.5%	9.2%	9.5%
Depreciation and amortization	5.8%	6.0%	6.1%	6.7%	6.9%	7.6%
Rentals and landing fees	4.8%	5.0%	5.0%	5.2%	5.2%	5.3%
Services	4.1%	4.2%	4.4%	4.7%	4.8%	4.7%
Aircraft rentals	3.3%	3.3%	3.7%	4.2%	4.5%	4.3%
Maintenance, materials and repairs	4.9%	4.6%	3.7%	3.4%	3.1%	3.7%
Other operating expenses	16.0%	15.4%	15.5%	15.8%	15.3%	15.3%
Restructuring	0.0%	0.0%	0.0%	3.3%	2.0%	0.0%
Total Operating Expenses	89.2%	90.9%	91.2%	95.9%	95.9%	96.2%
Operating Income	10.8%	9.1%	8.8%	4.1%	4.1%	3.8%
Other income (expenses)	–0.1%	–1.0%	–2.5%	–4.0%	–3.4%	–3.3%

Vertical Common Size (continued)

	1998	1997	1996	1995	1994	1993
Income (loss) before taxes	10.7%	8.1%	6.3%	0.1%	0.7%	0.5%
Income tax provision	4.2%	3.2%	2.6%	0.2%	0.3%	0.3%
Income before irregular items	6.5%	4.9%	3.8%	–0.1%	0.4%	0.2%
Irregular items, net of tax	0.0%	0.0%	0.9%	1.5%	1.5%	0.0%
Net Income	6.5%	4.9%	4.7%	1.4%	1.9%	0.2%

Horizontal Common Size—1993 Base Year

	1998	1997	1996	1995	1994	1993
Revenues:	110.6%	107.6%	102.7%	98.4%	94.4%	100.0%
Expenses:						
Salaries, wages, etc.	111.3%	105.9%	100.1%	97.8%	95.1%	100.0%
Aircraft fuel	85.3%	102.3%	102.6%	86.1%	85.6%	100.0%
Commissions	83.2%	87.0%	84.9%	88.7%	91.4%	100.0%
Depreciation and amortization	84.4%	85.2%	83.4%	87.4%	86.6%	100.0%
Rentals and landing fees	98.9%	100.0%	96.8%	95.8%	92.6%	100.0%
Services	96.8%	97.0%	96.2%	97.4%	95.7%	100.0%
Aircraft rentals	83.3%	83.1%	87.9%	94.5%	97.0%	100.0%
Maintenance, materials and repairs	148.2%	135.8%	103.3%	91.1%	80.8%	100.0%
Other operating expenses	115.7%	108.1%	103.7%	101.6%	94.5%	100.0%
Restructuring						
Total Operating Expenses	102.5%	101.7%	97.4%	98.1%	94.1%	100.0%
Operating Income	313.5%	256.6%	236.0%	106.6%	100.9%	100.0%
Other income (expenses)	4.9%	32.7%	76.5%	118.6%	95.7%	100.0%
Income (loss) before taxes	2356.8%	1739.2%	1291.9%	27.0%	135.1%	100.0%
Income tax provision	1335.3%	994.1%	758.8%	60.8%	90.2%	100.0%
Income before irregular items	4621.7%	3391.3%	2473.9%	–47.8%	234.8%	100.0%
Irregular items, net of tax						
Net Income	4621.7%	3391.3%	3065.2%	904.3%	1165.2%	100.0%

Horizontal Common Size—Rolling Forward

	1998	1997	1996	1995	1994	1993
Revenues:	102.8%	104.8%	104.4%	104.3%	94.4%	100.0%
Expenses:						
Salaries, wages, etc.	105.0%	105.8%	102.4%	102.8%	95.1%	100.0%
Aircraft fuel	83.4%	99.7%	119.2%	100.6%	85.6%	100.0%
Commissions	95.6%	102.5%	95.6%	97.1%	91.4%	100.0%
Depreciation and amortization	99.1%	102.2%	95.4%	100.9%	86.6%	100.0%
Rentals and landing fees	98.9%	103.3%	101.1%	103.4%	92.6%	100.0%

Horizontal Common Size—Rolling Forward (continued)

	1998	1997	1996	1995	1994	1993
Services	99.9%	100.7%	98.8%	101.8%	95.7%	100.0%
Aircraft rentals	100.2%	94.5%	93.0%	97.4%	97.0%	100.0%
Maintenance, materials and repairs	109.1%	131.4%	113.4%	112.8%	80.8%	100.0%
Other operating expenses	107.1%	104.2%	102.0%	107.5%	94.5%	100.0%
Restructuring			0.0%	175.7%		
Total Operating Expenses	100.8%	104.4%	99.3%	104.2%	94.1%	100.0%
Operating Income	122.2%	108.7%	221.5%	105.6%	100.9%	100.0%
Other income (expenses)	15.0%	42.7%	64.5%	123.9%	95.7%	100.0%
Income (loss) before taxes	135.5%	134.6%	4780.0%	20.0%	135.1%	100.0%
Income tax provision	134.3%	131.0%	1248.4%	67.4%	90.2%	100.0%
Income before irregular items	136.3%	137.1%	–5172.7%	–20.4%	234.8%	100.0%
Irregular items, net of tax		0.0%	62.1%	102.3%		
Net Income	136.3%	110.6%	338.9%	77.6%	1165.2%	100.0%

Compound Annual Growth Rate

	1993	1994	1995	1996	1997	1998	Growth
Revenues:	$(14,737)	0	0	0	0	$16,299	2.0%
Expenses:							
Salaries, wages, etc.	(4,927)	0	0	0	0	5,482	2.2%
Aircraft fuel	(1,818)	0	0	0	0	1,551	-3.1%
Commissions	(1,393)	0	0	0	0	1,159	-3.6%
Depreciation and amortization	(1,115)	0	0	0	0	941	-3.3%
Rentals and landing fees	(787)	0	0	0	0	778	-0.2%
Services	(693)	0	0	0	0	671	-0.6%
Aircraft rentals	(639)	0	0	0	0	532	-3.6%
Maintenance, materials and repairs	(542)	0	0	0	0	803	8.2%
Other operating expenses	(2,259)	0	0	0	0	2,614	3.0%
Restructuring							
Total Operating Expenses	(14,173)	0	0	0	0	14,531	0.5%
Operating Income	(564)	0	0	0	0	1,768	25.7%
Other income (expenses)	490	0	0	0	0	(24)	
Income (loss) before taxes	(74)	0	0	0	0	1,744	88.1%
Income tax provision	(51)	0	0	0	0	681	67.9%
Income before irregular items	(23)	0	0	0	0	1,063	115.3%
Irregular items, net of tax							
Net Income	(23)	0	0	0	0	1,063	115.3%

American Airlines,
Incorporated
Balance Sheets
(in millions of dollars)

	1998	1997	1996	1995	1994	1993
Assets						
Current Assets:						
Cash	$85	$47	$37	$70	$13	$55
Short-term investments	1,398	1,762	1,312	816	744	514
Receivables	2,036	1,057	1,087	1,013	1,370	954
Inventories	520	555	559	516	590	606
Deferred income taxes	426	360	328	310	270	269
Other current assets	167	201	221	128	115	130
Total current assets	4,632	3,982	3,544	2,853	3,102	2,528
Property, plant, and equipment	12,353	11,461	11,601	12,350	12,645	12,829
Other assets	2,239	2,310	2,417	2,426	2,069	2,392
Total Assets	**$19,224**	**$17,753**	**$17,562**	**$17,629**	**$17,816**	**$17,749**
Liabilities and Stockholders' Equity						
Current Liabilities:						
Accounts payable	$940	$855	$914	$742	$831	$857
Payables to affiliates	—	595	1,410	907	759	479
Accrued salaries and wages	892	805	733	651	581	467
Accrued liabilities	1,178	915	1,005	1,138	853	814
Air traffic liability	2,163	2,044	1,889	1,467	1,473	1,461
Current maturities of long-term debt	23	21	22	242	49	70
Current obligations under capital leases	129	112	109	101	110	92
Total current liabilities	5,325	5,347	6,082	5,248	4,656	4,240
Noncurrent liabilities:						
Long-term debt	920	937	1,101	2,994	4,714	5,498
Obligations under capital leases	1,542	1,382	1,520	1,777	1,964	1,792
Other liabilities and deferred credits	5,009	4,733	4,331	3,964	3,249	3,051
Total noncurrent liabilities	7,471	7,052	6,952	8,735	9,927	10,341
Stockholders' Equity:						
Common stock	—	—	—	—	—	—
Additional paid-in-capital	1,743	1,732	1,717	1,699	1,699	1,699
Retained earnings	4,688	3,625	2,833	1,948	1,733	1,469
Other comprehensive income	(3)	(3)	(22)	(1)	(199)	—
Total stockholders' equity	**6,428**	**5,354**	**4,528**	**3,646**	**3,233**	**3,168**
Total Liabilities and Stockholders' Equity	**$19,224**	**$17,753**	**$17,562**	**$17,629**	**$17,816**	**$17,749**

Vertical Common Size

	1998	1997	1996	1995	1994	1993
Assets						
Current Assets:						
Cash	0.4%	0.3%	0.2%	0.4%	0.1%	0.3%
Short-term investments	7.3%	9.9%	7.5%	4.6%	4.2%	2.9%
Receivables	10.6%	6.0%	6.2%	5.7%	7.7%	5.4%
Inventories	2.7%	3.1%	3.2%	2.9%	3.3%	3.4%
Deferred income taxes	2.2%	2.0%	1.9%	1.8%	1.5%	1.5%
Other current assets	0.9%	1.1%	1.3%	0.7%	0.6%	0.7%
Total current assets	24.1%	22.4%	20.2%	16.2%	17.4%	14.2%
Property, plant, and equipment	64.3%	64.6%	66.1%	70.1%	71.0%	72.3%
Other assets	11.6%	13.0%	13.8%	13.8%	11.6%	13.5%
Total Assets	100.0%	100.0%	100.0%	100.0%	100.0%	100.0%
Liabilities and Stockholders' Equity						
Current Liabilities:						
Accounts payable	4.9%	4.8%	5.2%	4.2%	4.7%	4.8%
Payables to affiliates	0.0%	3.4%	8.0%	5.1%	4.3%	2.7%
Accrued salaries and wages	4.6%	4.5%	4.2%	3.7%	3.3%	2.6%
Accrued liabilities	6.1%	5.2%	5.7%	6.5%	4.8%	4.6%
Air traffic liability	11.3%	11.5%	10.8%	8.3%	8.3%	8.2%
Current maturities of long-term debt	0.1%	0.1%	0.1%	1.4%	0.3%	0.4%
Current obligations under capital leases	0.7%	0.6%	0.6%	0.6%	0.6%	0.5%
Total current liabilities	27.7%	30.1%	34.6%	29.8%	26.1%	23.9%
Noncurrent liabilities:						
Long-term debt	4.8%	5.3%	6.3%	17.0%	26.5%	31.0%
Obligations under capital leases	8.0%	7.8%	8.7%	10.1%	11.0%	10.1%
Other liabilities and deferred credits	26.1%	26.7%	24.7%	22.5%	18.2%	17.2%
Total noncurrent liabilities	38.9%	39.7%	39.6%	49.5%	55.7%	58.3%
Stockholders' Equity:						
Common stock	0.0%	0.0%	0.0%	0.0%	0.0%	0.0%
Additional paid-in-capital	9.1%	9.8%	9.8%	9.6%	9.5%	9.6%
Retained earnings	24.4%	20.4%	16.1%	11.0%	9.7%	8.3%
Other comprehensive income	0.0%	0.0%	–0.1%	0.0%	–1.1%	0.0%
Total stockholders' equity	33.4%	30.2%	25.8%	20.7%	18.1%	17.8%
Total Liabilities and Stockholders' Equity	100.0%	100.0%	100.0%	100.0%	100.0%	100.0%

American Airlines,
Incorporated
Balance Sheets
(in millions of dollars)

Horizontal Common Size—1993 Base Year

	1998	1997	1996	1995	1994	1993
Assets						
Current Assets:						
Cash	154.5%	85.5%	67.3%	127.3%	23.6%	100.0%
Short-term investments	272.0%	342.8%	255.3%	158.8%	144.7%	100.0%
Receivables	213.4%	110.8%	113.9%	106.2%	143.6%	100.0%
Inventories	85.8%	91.6%	92.2%	85.1%	97.4%	100.0%
Deferred income taxes	158.4%	133.8%	121.9%	115.2%	100.4%	100.0%
Other current assets	128.5%	154.6%	170.0%	98.5%	88.5%	100.0%
Total current assets	183.2%	157.5%	140.2%	112.9%	122.7%	100.0%
Property, plant, and equipment	96.3%	89.3%	90.4%	96.3%	98.6%	100.0%
Other assets	93.6%	96.6%	101.0%	101.4%	86.5%	100.0%
Total Assets	108.3%	100.0%	98.9%	99.3%	100.4%	100.0%
Liabilities and Stockholders' Equity						
Current Liabilities:						
Accounts payable	109.7%	99.8%	106.7%	86.6%	97.0%	100.0%
Payables to affiliates	0.0%	124.2%	294.4%	189.4%	158.5%	100.0%
Accrued salaries and wages	191.0%	172.4%	157.0%	139.4%	124.4%	100.0%
Accrued liabilities	144.7%	112.4%	123.5%	139.8%	104.8%	100.0%
Air traffic liability	148.0%	139.9%	129.3%	100.4%	100.8%	100.0%
Current maturities of long-term debt	32.9%	30.0%	31.4%	345.7%	70.0%	100.0%
Current obligations under capital leases	140.2%	121.7%	118.5%	109.8%	119.6%	100.0%
Total current liabilities	125.6%	126.1%	143.4%	123.8%	109.8%	100.0%
Noncurrent liabilities:						
Long-term debt	16.7%	17.0%	20.0%	54.5%	85.7%	100.0%
Obligations under capital leases	86.0%	77.1%	84.8%	99.2%	109.6%	100.0%
Other liabilities and deferred credits	164.2%	155.1%	142.0%	129.9%	106.5%	100.0%
Total noncurrent liabilities	72.2%	68.2%	67.2%	84.5%	96.0%	100.0%
Stockholders' Equity:						
Common stock						
Additional paid-in-capital	102.6%	101.9%	101.1%	100.0%	100.0%	100.0%
Retained earnings	319.1%	246.8%	192.9%	132.6%	118.0%	100.0%
Other comprehensive income						
Total stockholders' equity	202.9%	169.0%	142.9%	115.1%	102.1%	100.0%
Total Liabilities and Stockholders' Equity	108.3%	100.0%	98.9%	99.3%	100.4%	100.0%

Horizontal Common Size—Rolling Forward

	1998	1997	1996	1995	1994	1993
Assets						
Current Assets:						
Cash	180.9%	127.0%	52.9%	538.5%	23.6%	100.0%
Short-term investments	79.3%	134.3%	160.8%	109.7%	144.7%	100.0%
Receivables	192.6%	97.2%	107.3%	73.9%	143.6%	100.0%
Inventories	93.7%	99.3%	108.3%	87.5%	97.4%	100.0%
Deferred income taxes	118.3%	109.8%	105.8%	114.8%	100.4%	100.0%
Other current assets	83.1%	91.0%	172.7%	111.3%	88.5%	100.0%
Total current assets	116.3%	112.4%	124.2%	92.0%	122.7%	100.0%
Property, plant, and equipment	107.8%	98.8%	93.9%	97.7%	98.6%	100.0%
Other assets	96.9%	95.6%	99.6%	117.3%	86.5%	100.0%
Total Assets	108.3%	101.1%	99.6%	99.0%	100.4%	100.0%
Liabilities and Stockholders' Equity						
Current Liabilities:						
Accounts payable	109.9%	93.5%	123.2%	89.3%	97.0%	100.0%
Payables to affiliates	0.0%	42.2%	155.5%	119.5%	158.5%	100.0%
Accrued salaries and wages	110.8%	109.8%	112.6%	112.0%	124.4%	100.0%
Accrued liabilities	128.7%	91.0%	88.3%	133.4%	104.8%	100.0%
Air traffic liability	105.8%	108.2%	128.8%	99.6%	100.8%	100.0%
Current maturities of long-term debt	109.5%	95.5%	9.1%	493.9%	70.0%	100.0%
Current obligations under capital leases	115.2%	102.8%	107.9%	91.8%	119.6%	100.0%
Total current liabilities	99.6%	87.9%	115.9%	112.7%	109.8%	100.0%
Noncurrent liabilities:						
Long-term debt	98.2%	85.1%	36.8%	63.5%	85.7%	100.0%
Obligations under capital leases	111.6%	90.9%	85.5%	90.5%	109.6%	100.0%
Other liabilities and deferred credits	105.8%	109.3%	109.3%	122.0%	106.5%	100.0%
Total noncurrent liabilities	105.9%	101.4%	79.6%	88.0%	96.0%	100.0%
Stockholders' Equity:						
Common stock						
Additional paid-in-capital	100.6%	100.9%	101.1%	100.0%	100.0%	100.0%
Retained earnings	129.3%	128.0%	145.4%	112.4%	118.0%	100.0%
Other comprehensive income	100.0%	13.6%	2200.0%	0.5%		
Total stockholders' equity	120.1%	118.2%	124.2%	112.8%	102.1%	100.0%
Total Liabilities and Stockholders' Equity	108.3%	101.1%	99.6%	99.0%	100.4%	100.0%

American Airlines,
Incorporated
Balance Sheets
(in millions of dollars)

Compound Annual Growth Rate

	1993	1994	1995	1996	1997	1998	Growth
Assets							
Current Assets:							
Cash	$(55)	—	—	—	—	$85	9.1%
Short-term investments	(514)	—	—	—	—	1,398	22.2%
Receivables	(954)	—	—	—	—	2,036	16.4%
Inventories	(606)	—	—	—	—	520	–3.0%
Deferred income taxes	(269)	—	—	—	—	426	9.6%
Other current assets	(130)	—	—	—	—	167	5.1%
Total current assets	(2,528)	—	—	—	—	4,632	12.9%
Property, plant, and equipment	(12,829)	—	—	—	—	12,353	–0.8%
Other assets	(2,392)	—	—	—	—	2,239	–1.3%
Total Assets	(17,749)	—	—	—	—	19,224	1.6%
Liabilities and Stockholders' Equity							
Current Liabilities:							
Accounts payable	(857)	—	—	—	—	940	1.9%
Payables to affiliates	(479)	—	—	—	—	—	
Accrued salaries and wages	(467)	—	—	—	—	892	13.8%
Accrued liabilities	(814)	—	—	—	—	1,178	7.7%
Air traffic liability	(1,461)	—	—	—	—	2,163	8.2%
Current maturities of long-term debt	(70)	—	—	—	—	23	–20.0%
Current obligations under capital leases	(92)	—	—	—	—	129	7.0%
Total current liabilities	(4,240)	—	—	—	—	5,325	4.7%
Noncurrent liabilities:							
Long-term debt	(5,498)	—	—	—	—	920	
Obligations under capital leases	(1,792)	—	—	—	—	1,542	–3.0%
Other liabilities and deferred credits	(3,051)	—	—	—	—	5,009	10.4%
Total noncurrent liabilities	(10,341)	—	—	—	—	7,471	–6.3%
Stockholders' Equity:							
Common stock	—	—	—	—	—	—	
Additional paid-in-capital	(1,699)	—	—	—	—	1,743	0.5%
Retained earnings	(1,469)	—	—	—	—	4,688	26.1%
Other comprehensive income	—	—	—	—	—	(3)	
Total stockholders' equity	(3,168)	—	—	—	—	6,428	15.2%
Total Liabilities and Stockholders' Equity	(17,749)	—	—	—	—	19,224	1.6%

American Airlines
Condensed Statements of Cash
Flows (in millions of dollars)

	1998	1997	1996	1995	1994
Net income	$1,063	$780	$705	$208	$268
Depreciation expense	941	950	930	975	966
Other adjustments to operations	839	512	504	813	457
Cash flows from operating activities	2,843	2,242	2,139	1,996	1,691
Purchase of property, plant, and equipment	(2,342)	(1,139)	(547)	(928)	(1114)
Other adjustments to investing activities	879	(2)	(90)	(73)	(13)
Cash flows from investing activities	(1,463)	(1,141)	(637)	(855)	(1,101)
Dividends	—	—	—	—	(68)
Other adjustments to financing activities	(1,342)	(1,091)	(1,535)	(1,084)	(564)
Cash flows from financing activities	(1,342)	(1,091)	(1,535)	(1,084)	(632)
Net change in cash	**$38**	**$10**	**$ (33)**	**$57**	**$ (42)**

American Airlines,
Incorporated
Income Statements
(in millions of dollars)

	1998	1997	1996	1995	1994
Revenues:	$16,299	$15,856	$15,136	$14,503	$13,910
Expenses:					
Salaries, wages, etc.	5,482	5,220	4,934	4,818	4,685
Aircraft fuel	1,551	1,860	1,866	1,565	1,556
Commissions	1,159	1,212	1,182	1,236	1,273
Depreciation and amortization	941	950	930	975	966
Rentals and landing fees	778	787	762	754	729
Services	671	672	667	675	663
Aircraft rentals	532	531	562	604	620
Maintenance, materials and repairs	803	736	560	494	438
Other operating expenses	2,614	2,441	2,342	2,296	2,135
Restructuring	—	—	—	485	276
Total Operating Expenses	14,531	14,409	13,805	13,902	13,341
Operating Income	1,768	1,447	1,331	601	569
Other income (expenses)	−24	−160	−375	−581	−469
Income (loss) before taxes	1,744	1,287	956	20	100
Income tax provision	681	507	387	31	46
Income before irregular items	1,063	780	569	−11	54
Irregular items, net of tax	—	—	136	219	214
Net Income	**$1,063**	**$780**	**$705**	**$208**	**$268**

American Airlines, Incorporated
AVERAGE Balance Sheets
(in millions)

	1998	1997	1996	1995	1994
Assets					
Current Assets:					
Cash	$66.00	$42.00	$53.50	$41.50	$34.00
Short-term investments	1,580.00	1,537.00	1,064.00	780.00	629.00
Receivables	1,546.50	1,072.00	1,050.00	1,191.50	1,162.00
Inventories	537.50	557.00	537.50	553.00	598.00
Deferred income taxes	393.00	344.00	319.00	290.00	269.50
Other current assets	184.00	211.00	174.50	121.50	122.50
Total current assets	4,307.00	3,763.00	3,198.50	2,977.50	2,815.00
Property, plant, and equipment	11,907.00	11,531.00	11,975.50	12,497.50	12,737.00
Other assets	2,274.50	2,363.50	2,421.50	2,247.50	2,230.50
Total Assets	$18,488.50	$17,657.50	$17,595.50	$17,722.50	$17,782.50
Liabilities and Stockholders' Equity					
Current Liabilities:					
Accounts payable	$897.50	$884.50	$828.00	$786.50	$844.00
Payables to affiliates	297.50	1,002.50	1,158.50	833.00	619.00
Accrued salaries and wages	848.50	769.00	692.00	616.00	524.00
Accrued liabilities	1,046.50	960.00	1,071.50	995.50	833.50
Air traffic liability	2,103.50	1,966.50	1,678.00	1,470.00	1,467.00
Current maturities of long-term debt	22.00	21.50	132.00	145.50	59.50
Current obligations under capital leases	120.50	110.50	105.00	105.50	101.00
Total current liabilities	5,336.00	5,714.50	5,665.00	4,952.00	4,448.00
Noncurrent liabilities:					
Long-term debt	928.50	1,019.00	2,047.50	3,854.00	5,106.00
Obligations under capital leases	1,462.00	1,451.00	1,648.50	1,870.50	1,878.00
Other liabilities and deferred credits	4,871.00	4,532.00	4,147.50	3,606.50	3,150.00
Total noncurrent liabilities	7,261.50	7,002.00	7,843.50	9,331.00	10,134.00
Stockholders' Equity:					
Common stock	—	—	—	—	—
Additional paid-in-capital	1,737.50	1,724.50	1,708.00	1,699.00	1,699.00
Retained earnings	4,156.50	3,229.00	2,390.50	1,840.50	1,601.00
Other comprehensive income	−3.00	−12.50	−11.50	−100.00	−99.50
Total stockholders' equity	5,891.00	4,941.00	4,087.00	3,439.50	3,200.50
Total Liabilities and Stockholders' Equity	$18,488.50	$17,657.50	$17,595.50	$17,722.50	$17,782.50
Cash Flow Data					
Cash flow from operations	$2,843	$2,242	$2,139	$1,996	$1,691
Fixed asset purchases	2,342	1,139	547	928	1,114
Cash dividends	—	—	—	—	66
Depreciation and amortization	941	950	950	975	966
Market Data					
High market price	$89.90	$66.30	$48.80	$40.10	$36.40
Low market price	$45.60	$39.10	$34.00	$26.70	$24.10
Number of shares outstanding (millions)	161.35	173.2	182	152.8	151.8
Market capitalization	$10,931.46	$9,127.64	$7,534.80	$5,103.52	$4,591.95

Liquidity Ratios

	1998	1997	1996	1995	1994
Working capital	–$1,029.00	–$1,951.50	–$2,466.50	–$1,974.50	–$1,633.00
Working capital ratio	0.81	0.66	0.56	0.60	0.63
Quick ratio	0.60	0.46	0.38	0.41	0.41
Inventory turnover	NA	NA	NA	NA	NA
Days in inventory	NA	NA	NA	NA	NA
Accounts receivable turnover	10.54	14.79	14.42	12.17	11.97
Days in accounts receivable	34.63	24.68	25.32	29.99	30.49
Inventory conversion cycle	34.63	24.68	25.32	29.99	30.49
Accounts payable turnover	NA	NA	NA	NA	NA
Days in accounts payable	NA	NA	NA	NA	NA
Net cash conversion cycle	NA	NA	NA	NA	NA
Cash + short-term investments	1,646.00	1,579.00	1,117.50	821.50	663.00
A/R*days in accounts receivable	53,558.91	26,453.84	26,586.45	35,729.19	35,430.56
Inventory*days in inventory	537.50	557.00	537.50	553.00	598.00
Product dollar days	55,742.41	28,589.84	28,241.45	37,103.69	36,691.56
Current assets-other current assets	3,730.00	3,208.00	2,705.00	2,566.00	2,423.00
Liquidity index	14.94	8.91	10.44	14.46	15.14

Cash Flow Ratios

	1998	1997	1996	1995	1994
Cash flow adequacy	1.21	1.97	3.91	2.15	1.43
Reinvestment ratio	0.82	0.51	0.26	0.46	0.66
Dividend payout	—	—	—	—	0.04
Free cash flow	$501	$1,103	$1,592	$1,068	$511
Depreciation impact ratio	0.33	0.42	0.43	0.49	0.57
Recapitalization index	2.49	1.20	0.59	0.95	1.15
Cash flow return on assets	0.15	0.13	0.12	0.11	0.10
Cash flow return on sales	0.17	0.14	0.14	0.14	0.12
Operations index	1.61	1.55	1.61	3.32	2.97

Asset Utilization Ratios

	1998	1997	1996	1995	1994
Profit margin	6.52%	4.92%	4.66%	1.43%	1.93%
Asset turnover	0.88	0.90	0.86	0.82	0.78
Financial structure leverage	3.14	3.57	4.31	5.15	5.56
Return on assets	5.75%	4.42%	4.01%	1.17%	1.51%
Return on equity	18.04%	15.79%	17.25%	6.05%	8.37%

Capital Structure Ratios

	1998	1997	1996	1995	1994
Debt to capital	0.68	0.72	0.77	0.81	0.82
Debt to equity	2.14	2.57	3.31	4.15	4.56
Long-term debt to capital	0.39	0.40	0.45	0.53	0.57
Long-term debt to equity	1.23	1.42	1.92	2.71	3.17
Working capital/total assets-Z1	−0.07	−0.13	−0.17	−0.13	−0.11
Retained earnings/total assets-Z2	0.31	0.26	0.19	0.15	0.13
EBIT/total assets-Z3	0.32	0.27	0.25	0.11	0.11
Sales/total assets-Z4	0.88	0.90	0.86	0.82	0.78
Market to book-Z5	0.52	0.43	0.33	0.21	0.19
Z-Score	1.97	1.72	1.47	1.16	1.09

Market Ratio

	1998	1997	1996	1995	1994
Price to earnings	10.28	11.70	10.69	24.54	17.13

Delta Airlines, Incorporated
Income Statements
(in millions of dollars)

	1998	1997	1996	1995	1994	1993
Revenues:	$14,138	$13,594	$12,455	$12,194	$12,359	$11,997
Expenses:						
Salaries, wages, etc.	4,850	4,534	4,206	4,354	4,589	4,798
Aircraft fuel	1,507	1,722	1,464	1,370	1,411	1,592
Commissions	980	1,017	1,042	1,195	1,318	1,250
Depreciation and amortization	860	710	634	622	678	735
Rentals and landing fees	649	649	627	702	641	618
Services	1,144	1,019	1,072	999	530	549
Aircraft rentals	552	547	555	671	732	729
Maintenance, materials, and repairs	495	434	376	430	418	465
Restructuring	—	52	829	—	526	82
Other operating expenses	1,407	1,379	1,187	1,190	1,963	1,754
Total Operating Expenses	12,444	12,063	11,992	11,533	12,806	12,572
Operating Income	1,694	1,531	463	661	−447	−575
Other income (expenses)	−46	−116	−187	−167	−213	−76
Income (loss) before taxes	1,648	1,415	276	494	−660	−651
Income tax provision	-647	-561	-120	-200	251	236
Income before irregular items	1,001	854	156	294	-409	-415
Irregular items, net of tax	—	—	—	114	—	−587
Net Income	$1,001	$854	$156	$408	($409)	($1,002)
Basic earnings per share	$6.64	$5.70	$1.42	$6.32	($10.32)	($22.32)
Diluted earnings per share	$6.34	$5.52		$5.43		

Delta Airlines, Incorporated
Income Statements
(in millions of dollars)
(continued)

Vertical Common Size

	1998	1997	1996	1995	1994	1993
Revenues:	100.0%	100.0%	100.0%	100.0%	100.0%	100.0%
Expenses:						
Salaries, wages, etc.	34.3%	33.4%	33.8%	35.7%	37.1%	40.0%
Aircraft fuel	10.7%	12.7%	11.8%	11.2%	11.4%	13.30%
Commissions	6.9%	7.5%	8.4%	9.8%	10.7%	10.4%
Depreciation and amortization	6.1%	5.2%	5.1%	5.1%	5.5%	6.1%
Rentals and landing fees	4.6%	4.8%	5.0%	5.8%	5.2%	5.2%
Services	8.1%	7.5%	8.6%	8.2%	4.3%	4.6%
Aircraft rentals	3.9%	4.0%	4.5%	5.5%	5.9%	6.1%
Maintenance, materials, and repairs	3.5%	3.2%	3.0%	3.5%	3.4%	3.9%
Restructuring	0.0%	0.4%	6.7%	0.0%	4.3%	0.7%
Other operating expenses	10.0%	10.1%	9.5%	9.8%	15.9%	14.6%
Total Operating Expenses	88.0%	88.7%	96.3%	94.6%	103.6%	104.8%
Operating Income	12.0%	11.3%	3.7%	5.4%	−3.60	−4.8%
Other income (expenses)	−0.3%	−0.9%	−1.5%	−1.4%	−1.7%	−0.6%
Income (loss) before taxes	11.7%	10.4%	2.2%	4.1%	−5.3%	−5.4%
Income tax provision	−4.6%	−4.1%	−1.0%	−1.6%	2.0%	2.0%
Income before irregular items	7.1%	6.3%	1.3%	2.4%	−3.3%	−3.5%
Irregular items, net of tax	0.0%	0.0%	0.0%	0.9%	0.0%	−4.9%
Net Income	7.1%	6.3%	1.3%	3.3%	−3.3%	−8.4%

Horizontal Common Size—1993 Base Year

	1998	1997	1996	1995	1994	1993
Revenues:	117.8%	113.3%	103.8%	101.6%	103.0%	100.0%
Expenses:						
Salaries, wages, etc.	101.1%	94.5%	87.7%	90.7%	95.6%	100.0%
Aircraft fuel	94.7%	108.2%	92.0%	86.1%	88.6%	100.0%
Commissions	78.4%	81.4%	83.4%	95.6%	105.4%	100.0%
Depreciation and amortization	117.0%	96.6%	86.3%	84.6%	92.2%	100.0%
Rentals and landing fees	105.0%	105.0%	101.5%	113.6%	103.7%	100.0%
Services	208.4%	185.6%	195.3%	182.0%	96.5%	100.0%
Aircraft rentals	75.7%	75.0%	76.1%	92.0%	100.4%	100.0%
Maintenance, materials, and repairs	106.5%	93.3%	80.9%	92.5%	89.9%	100.0%
Restructuring	0.0%	63.4%	1011.0%	0.0%	641.5%	100.0%
Other operating expenses	80.2%	78.6%	67.7%	67.8%	111.9%	100.0%
Total Operating Expenses	99.0%	96.0%	95.4%	91.7%	101.9%	100.0%
Operating Income	−294.6%	−266.3%	−80.5%	−115.0%	77.7%	100.0%
Other income (expenses)	60.5%	152.6%	246.1%	219.7%	280.3%	100.0%
Income (loss) before taxes	−253.1%	−217.4%	−42.4%	−75.9%	101.4%	100.0%

Horizontal Common Size-1993 Base Year (continued)

	1998	1997	1996	1995	1994	1993
Income tax provision	−274.2%	−237.7%	−50.8%	−84.7%	106.4%	100.0%
Income before irregular items	−241.2%	−205.8%	−37.6%	−70.8%	98.6%	100.0%
Irregular items, net of tax	0.0%	0.0%	0.0%	−19.4%	0.0%	100.0%
Net Income	−99.9%	−85.2%	−15.6%	−40.7%	40.8%	100.0%

Horizontal Common Size-Rolling Forward

	1998	1997	1996	1995	1994	1993
Revenues:	104.0%	109.1%	102.1%	98.7%	103.0%	100.0%
Expenses:						
Salaries, wages, etc.	107.0%	107.8%	96.6%	94.9%	95.6%	100.0%
Aircraft fuel	87.5%	117.6%	106.9%	97.1%	88.6%	100.0%
Commissions	96.4%	97.6%	87.2%	90.7%	105.4%	100.0%
Depreciation and amortization	121.1%	112.0%	101.9%	91.7%	92.2%	100.0%
Rentals and landing fees	100.0%	103.5%	89.3%	109.5%	103.7%	100.0%
Services	112.3%	95.1%	107.3%	188.5%	96.5%	100.0%
Aircraft rentals	100.9%	98.6%	82.7%	91.7%	100.4%	100.0%
Maintenance, materials, and repairs	114.1%	115.4%	87.4%	102.9%	89.9%	100.0%
Restructuring	0.0%	6.3%		0.0%	641.5%	100.0%
Other operating expenses	102.0%	116.2%	99.7%	60.6%	111.9%	100.0%
Total Operating Expenses	103.2%	100.6%	104.0%	90.1%	101.9%	100.0%
Operating Income	110.6%	330.7%	70.0%	-147.9%	77.7%	100.0%
Other income (expenses)	39.7%	62.0%	112.0%	78.4%	280.3%	100.0%
Income (loss) before taxes	116.5%	512.7%	55.9%	-74.8%	101.4%	100.0%
Income tax provision	115.3%	467.5%	60.0%	−79.7%	106.4%	100.0%
Income before irregular items	117.2%	547.4%	53.1%	−71.9%	98.6%	100.0%
Irregular items, net of tax			0.0%		0.0%	100.0%
Net Income	117.2%	547.4%	38.2%	-99.8%	40.8%	100.0%

Compound Annual Growth Rate

	1993	1994	1995	1996	1997	1993	Growth
Revenues:	($11,997)	$—	$—	$—	$—	$14,138	3.3%
Expenses:							
Salaries, wages, etc.	−4,798	0	0	0	0	4,850	0.2%
Aircraft fuel	−1,592	0	0	0	0	1,507	−1.1%
Commissions	−1,250	0	0	0	0	980	−4.8%
Depreciation and amortization	−735	0	0	0	0	860	3.2%
Rentals and landing fees	−618	0	0	0	0	649	1.0%
Services	−549	0	0	0	0	1,144	15.8%
Aircraft rentals	−729	0	0	0	0	552	−5.4%

Delta Airlines, Incorporated
Income Statements
(in millions of dollars)
(continued)

	1993	1994	1995	1996	1997	1998	Growth
Maintenance, materials, and repairs	−465	0	0	0	0	495	1.3%
Restructuring	−82	0	0	0	0	—	
Other operating expenses	−1,754	0	0	0	0	1,407	−4.3%
Total Operating Expenses	−12,572	0	0	0	0	12,444	−0.2%
Operating Income	575	0	0	0	0	1,694	
Other income (expenses)	76	0	0	0	0	−46	−9.6%
Income (loss) before taxes	651	0	0	0	0	1,648	
Income tax provision	−236	0	0	0	0	−647	
Income before irregular items	415	0	0	0	0	1,001	
Irregular items, net of tax	587	0	0	0	0	—	
Net Income	1,002	0	0	0	0	1,001	

Delta Airlines, Incorporated
Balance Sheets
(in millions of dollars)

	1998	1997	1996	1995	1994	1993
Assets						
Current Assets:						
Cash	$1,077	$662	$1,145	$1,233	$1,302	$1,180
Short-term investments	557	508	507	529	408	—
Receivables	938	943	968	755	886	1,055
Deferred income taxes	464	413	352	234	336	173
Prepaid expenses and other current assets	326	341	310	263	291	414
Total current assets	3,362	2,867	3,282	3,014	3,223	2,822
Property, plant, and equipment	9,321	8,042	6,795	6,936	6,603	7,141
Other assets	1,920	1,832	2,149	2,193	2,070	1,908
Total Assets	$14,603	$12,74	$12,226	$12,143	$11,896	$11,871
Liabilities and Stockholders' Equity						
Current Liabilities:						
Current maturities of long-term debt	$67	$236	$40	$151	$227	$35
Current obligations under capital leases	63	62	58	61	11	12
Accounts payable and miscellaneous accrued liabilities	2,025	1,691	1,540	1,473	1,660	1,387
Air traffic liability	1,667	1,418	1,414	1,143	1,247	1,190
Accrued salaries and vacation	553	463	385	378	196	194
Accrued aircraft rent	202	213	201	235	195	201
Total current liabilities	4,577	4,083	3,638	3,441	3,536	3,019

Delta Airlines, Incorporated
Balance Sheets
(in millions of dollars)
(continued)

Balance Sheet (continued)

	1998	1997	1996	1995	1994	1993
Noncurrent liabilities:						
Long-term debt	1,533	1,475	1,799	2,683	3,142	3,619
Obligations under capital leases	249	322	376	438	86	97
Deferrals	1,011	851	898	969	986	1,096
Accruals	651	602	616	556	541	440
Other noncurrent liabilities	2,384	2,245	2,221	2,109	2,036	1,604
Total noncurrent liabilities	5,828	5,495	5,910	6,755	6,791	6,856
Stockholders' Equity:						
Preferred stock	175	156	138	120	102	83
Common stock	265	251	217	164	163	163
Additional paid-in-capital	3,034	2,645	2,627	2,016	2,013	2,012
Retained earnings	1,687	711	–119	–184	–490	36
Other comprehensive income	89	101	126	83	—	—
Treasury stock	–1,052	–701	–311	–252	–272	–297
Other stockholders' equity	—	—	—	—	53	–1
Total stockholders' equity	4,198	3,163	2,678	1,947	1,569	1,996
Total Liabilities and Stockholders' Equity	$14,603	$12,741	$12,226	$12,143	$11,896	$11,871

Vertical Common Size

	1998	1997	1996	1995	1994	1993
Assets						
Current Assets:						
Cash	7.4%	5.2%	9.4%	10.2%	10.9%	9.9%
Short-term investments	3.8%	4.0%	4.1%	4.4%	3.4%	0.0%
Receivables	6.4%	7.4%	7.9%	6.2%	7.4%	8.9%
Deferred income taxes	3.2%	3.2%	2.9%	1.9%	2.8%	1.5%
Prepaid expenses and other current assets	2.2%	2.7%	2.5%	2.2%	2.4%	3.5%
Total current assets	23.0%	22.5%	26.8%	24.8%	27.1%	23.8%
Property, plant, and equipment	63.8%	63.1%	55.6%	57.1%	55.5%	60.2%
Other assets	13.1%	14.4%	17.6%	18.1%	17.4%	16.1%
Total Assets	100.0%	100.0%	100.0%	100.0%	100.0%	100.0%
Liabilities and Stockholders' Equity						
Current Liabilities:						
Current maturities of long-term debt	0.5%	1.9%	0.3%	1.2%	1.9%	0.3%
Current obligations under capital leases	0.4%	0.5%	0.5%	0.5%	0.1%	0.1%
Accounts payable and miscellaneous accrued liabilities	0.0%	0.0%	0.0%	0.0%	0.0%	0.0%
	13.9%	13.3%	12.6%	12.1%	14.0%	11.7%

Vertical Common Size (continued)

	1998	1997	1996	1995	1994	1993
Air traffic liability	11.4%	11.1%	11.6%	9.4%	10.5%	10.0%
Accrued salaries and vacation	3.8%	3.6%	3.1%	3.1%	1.6%	1.6%
Accrued aircraft rent	1.4%	1.7%	1.6%	1.9%	1.6%	1.7%
Total current liabilities	31.3%	32.0%	29.8%	28.3%	29.7%	25.4%
Noncurrent liabilities:						
Long-term debt	10.5%	11.6%	14.7%	22.1%	26.4%	30.5%
Obligations under capital leases	1.7%	2.5%	3.1%	3.6%	0.7%	0.8%
Deferrals	6.9%	6.7%	7.3%	8.0%	8.3%	9.2%
Accruals	4.5%	4.7%	5.0%	4.6%	4.5%	3.7%
Other noncurrent liabilities	16.3%	17.6%	18.2%	17.4%	17.1%	13.5%
Total noncurrent liabilities	39.9%	43.1%	48.3%	55.6%	57.1%	57.8%
Stockholders' Equity:	0.0%	0.0%	0.0%	0.0%	0.0%	0.0%
Preferred stock	1.2%	1.2%	1.1%	1.0%	0.9%	0.7%
Common stock	1.8%	2.0%	1.8%	1.4%	1.4%	1.4%
Additional paid-in-capital	20.8%	20.8%	21.5%	16.6%	16.9%	16.9%
Retained earnings	11.6%	5.6%	–1.0%	–1.5%	–4.1%	0.3%
Other comprehensive income	0.6%	0.8%	1.0%	0.7%	0.0%	0.0%
Treasury stock	–7.2%	–5.5%	–2.5%	–2.1%	–2.3%	–2.5%
Other stockholders' equity	0.0%	0.0%	0.0%	0.0%	0.4%	0.0%
Total stockholders' equity	28.7%	24.8%	21.9%	16.0%	13.2%	16.8%
Total Liabilities and Stockholders' Equity	100.0%	100.0%	100.0%	100.0%	100.0%	100.0%

Horizontal Common Size—1993 Base Year

	1998	1997	1996	1995	1994	1993
Assets						
Current Assets:						
Cash	91.3%	56.1%	97.0%	104.5%	110.3%	100.0%
Short-term investments						
Receivables	88.9%	89.4%	91.8%	71.6%	84.0%	100.0%
Deferred income taxes	268.2%	238.7%	203.5%	135.3%	194.2%	100.0%
Prepaid expenses and other current assets	78.7%	82.4%	74.9%	63.5%	70.3%	100.0%
Total current assets	119.1%	101.6%	116.3%	106.8%	114.2%	100.0%
Property, plant, and equipment	130.5%	112.6%	95.2%	97.1%	92.5%	100.0%
Other assets	100.6%	96.0%	112.6%	114.9%	108.5%	100.0%
Total Assets	123.0%	107.3%	103.0%	102.3%	100.2%	100.0%
Liabilities and Stockholders' Equity						
Current Liabilities:						
Current maturities of long-term debt	191.4%	674.3%	114.3%	431.4%	648.6%	100.0%
Current obligations under capital leases	525.0%	516.7%	483.3%	508.3%	91.7%	100.0%

Delta Airlines, Incorporated
Balance Sheets
(in millions of dollars)
(continued)

Horizontal Common Size—1993 Base Year (continued)

	1998	1997	1996	1995	1994	1993
Accounts payable and miscellaneous accrued liabilities	146.0%	121.9%	111.0%	106.2%	119.7%	100.0%
Air traffic liability	140.1%	119.2%	118.8%	96.1%	104.8%	100.0%
Accrued salaries and vacation	285.1%	238.7%	198.5%	194.8%	101.0%	100.0%
Accrued aircraft rent	100.5%	106.0%	100.0%	116.9%	97.0%	100.0%
Total current liabilities	151.6%	135.2%	120.5%	114.0%	117.1%	100.0%
Noncurrent liabilities:						
Long-term debt	42.4%	40.8%	49.7%	74.1%	86.8%	100.0%
Obligations under capital leases	256.7%	332.0%	387.6%	451.5%	88.7%	100.0%
Deferrals	92.2%	77.6%	81.9%	88.4%	90.0%	100.0%
Accruals	148.0%	136.8%	140.0%	126.4%	123.0%	100.0%
Other noncurrent liabilities	148.6%	140.0%	138.5%	131.5%	126.9%	100.0%
Total noncurrent liabilities	85.0%	80.1%	86.2%	98.5%	99.1%	100.0%
Stockholders' Equity:						
Preferred stock	210.8%	188.0%	166.3%	144.6%	122.9%	100.0%
Common stock	162.6%	154.0%	133.1%	100.6%	100.0%	100.0%
Additional paid-in-capital	150.8%	131.5%	130.6%	100.2%	100.0%	100.0%
Retained earnings	4686.1%	1975.0%	−330.6%	−511.1%	-1361.1%	100.0%
Other comprehensive income:						
Treasury stock	354.2%	236.0%	104.7%	84.8%	91.6%	100.0%
Other stockholders' equity	0.0%	0.0%	0.0%	0.0%	−5300.0%	100.0%
Total stockholders' equity	210.3%	158.5%	134.2%	97.5%	78.6%	100.0%
Total Liabilities and Stockholders' Equity	123.0%	107.3%	103.0%	102.3%	100.2%	100.0%

Horizontal Common Size—Rolling Forward

	1998	1997	1996	1995	1994	1993
Assets						
Current Assets:						
Cash	162.7%	57.8%	92.9%	94.7%	110.3%	100.0%
Short-term investments	109.6%	100.2%	95.8%	129.7%		
Receivables	99.5%	97.4%	128.2%	85.2%	84.0%	100.0%
Deferred income taxes	112.3%	117.3%	150.4%	69.6%	194.2%	100.0%
Prepaid expenses and other current assets	95.6%	110.0%	117.9%	90.4%	70.3%	100.0%
Total current assets	117.3%	87.4%	108.9%	93.5%	114.2%	100.0%
Property, plant, and equipment	115.9%	118.4%	98.0%	105.0%	92.5%	100.0%
Other assets	104.8%	85.2%	98.0%	105.9%	108.5%	100.0%
Total Assets	114.6%	104.2%	100.7%	102.1%	100.2%	100.0%

Horizontal Common Size—Rolling Forward (continued)

	1998	1997	1996	1995	1994	1993
Liabilities and Stockholders' Equity						
Current Liabilities:						
Current maturities of long-term debt	28.4%	590.0%	26.5%	66.5%	648.6%	100.0%
Current obligations under capital leases	101.6%	106.9%	95.1%	554.5%	91.7%	100.0%
Accounts payable and miscellaneous accrued liabilities	119.8%	109.8%	104.5%	88.7%	119.7%	100.0%
Air traffic liability	117.6%	100.3%	123.7%	91.7%	104.8%	100.0%
Accrued salaries and vacation	119.4%	120.3%	101.9%	192.9%	101.0%	100.0%
Accrued aircraft rent	94.8%	106.0%	85.5%	120.5%	97.0%	100.0%
Total current liabilities	112.1%	112.2%	105.7%	97.3%	117.1%	100.0%
Noncurrent liabilities:						
Long-term debt	103.9%	82.0%	67.1%	85.4%	86.8%	100.0%
Obligations under capital leases	77.3%	85.6%	85.8%	509.3%	88.7%	100.0%
Deferrals	118.8%	94.8%	92.7%	98.3%	90.0%	100.0%
Accruals	108.1%	97.7%	110.8%	102.8%	123.0%	100.0%
Other noncurrent liabilities	106.2%	101.1%	105.3%	103.6%	126.9%	100.0%
Total noncurrent liabilities	106.1%	93.0%	87.5%	99.5%	99.1%	100.0%
Stockholders' Equity:						
Preferred stock	112.2%	113.0%	115.0%	117.6%	122.9%	100.0%
Common stock	105.6%	115.7%	132.3%	100.6%	100.0%	100.0%
Additional paid-in-capital	114.7%	100.7%	130.3%	100.1%	100.0%	100.0%
Retained earnings	237.3%	−597.5%	64.7%	37.6%	−1361.1%	100.0%
Other comprehensive income	88.1%	80.2%	151.8%			
Treasury stock	150.1%	225.4%	123.4%	92.6%	91.6%	100.0%
Other stockholders' equity				0.0%	−5300.0%	100.0%
Total stockholders' equity	132.7%	118.1%	137.5%	124.1%	78.6%	100.0%
Total Liabilities and Stockholders' Equity	114.6%	104.2%	100.7%	102.1%	100.2%	100.0%

Compound Annual Growth Rate

	1993	1994	1995	1996	1997	1998	Growth
Assets							
Current Assets:	−$1,180	0	0	0	0	$1,077	−1.8%
Cash	—	0	0	0	0	557	
Short-term investments	−1,055	0	0	0	0	938	−2.3%
Receivables	−173	0	0	0	0	464	21.8%
Deferred income taxes	−414	0	0	0	0	326	−4.7%
Prepaid expenses and other current assets	−2,822	0	0	0	0	3,362	3.6%

Delta Airlines, Incorporated
Balance Sheets
(in millions of dollars)
(continued)

Compound Annual Growth Rate (continued)

	1993	1994	1995	1996	1997	1998	Growth
Total current assets	−7,141	0	0	0	0	9,321	5.5%
Property, plant, and equipment	−1,908	0	0	0	0	1,920	0.1%
Other assets	−11,871	0	0	0	0	14,603	4.2
Total Assets							
Liabilities and Stockholders' Equity							
Current Liabilities:							
Current maturities of long-term debt	−35	0	0	0	0	67	13.9
Current obligations under capital leases	−12	0	0	0	0	63	39.3
Accounts payable and miscellaneous accrued liabilities	— −1,387	0	0	0	0	2,025	7.9
Air traffic liability	−1,190	0	0	0	0	1,667	7.0
Accrued salaries and vacation	194	0	0	0	0	553	—
Accrued aircraft rent	−201	0	0	0	0	202	0.1
Total current liabilities	−3,019	0	0	0	0	4,577	8.7
Noncurrent liabilities:	—	0	0	0	0		
Long-term debt	−3,619	0	0	0	0	1,533	−15.8
Obligations under capital leases	−97	0	0	0	0	249	20.7
Deferrals	−1,096	0	0	0	0	1,011	−1.6
Accruals	−440	0	0	0	0	651	8.1
Other noncurrent liabilities	−1,604	0	0	0	0	2,384	8.2
Total noncurrent liabilities	−6,856	0	0	0	0	5,828	−3.2
Stockholders' Equity:							
Preferred stock	−83	0	0	0	0	175	16.1
Common stock	−163	0	0	0	0	265	10.2
Additional paid-in-capital	−2,012	0	0	0	0	3,034	8.6
Retained earnings	−36	0	0	0	0	1,687	115.9
Other comprehensive income	—	0	0	0	0	89	
Treasury stock	297	0	0	0	0	−1,052	28.8
Other stockholders' equity	1	0	0	0	0	—	
Total stockholders' equity	−1,996	0	0	0	0	4,198	16.0
Total Liabilities and Stockholders' Equity	−11,871	0	0	0	0	14,603	4.2

	1998	1997	1996	1995	1994
Net income	$1,001	$854	$156	$408	$–409
Depreciation expense	960	710	634	622	678
Other adjustments to operations	1,055	475	601	84	1,055
Cash flows from operating activities	2,916	2,039	1,391	1,114	1,324
Purchase of property, plant, and equipment	–2,291	–1,948	–936	–626	–1,205
Other adjustments to investing activities	–33	7	48	131	–305
Cash flow from investing activities	–2,324	–1,941	–888	–495	–1,510
Dividends	–43	–44	–120	–120	–120
Other adjustments to financing activities	–134	–537	–471	–568	428
Cash flows from financing activities	–177	–581	–591	–688	308
Net change in cash	$415	$483	$88	$69	$122

	1998	1997	1996	1995	1994
Revenues:	$14,138	$13,594	$12,455	$12,194	$12,359
Expenses:					
Salaries, wages, etc.	4,850	4,534	4,206	4,354	4,589
Aircraft fuel	1,507	1,722	1,464	1,370	1,411
Commissions	980	1,017	1,042	1,195	1,318
Depreciation and amortization	860	710	634	622	678
Rentals and landing fees	649	649	627	702	641
Services	1,144	1,019	1,072	999	530
Aircraft rentals	552	547	555	671	732
Maintenance, materials and repairs	495	434	376	430	418
Restructuring	—	52	829	—	526
Other operating expenses	1,407	1,379	1,187	1,190	1,963
Total Operating Expenses	12,444	12,063	11,992	11,533	12,806
Operating Income	1,694	1,531	463	661	–447
Other income (expenses)	–46	–116	–187	–167	–213
Income (loss) before taxes	1,648	1,415	276	494	–660
Income tax provision	–647	-561	–120	–200	251
Income before irregular items	1,001	854	156	294	–409
Irregular items, net of tax	—	—	—	114	—
Net Income	$1,001	$854	$156	$408	($409)

Delta Airlines, Incorporated
AVERAGE *Balance Sheets*
(in millions)

	1998	1997	1996	1995	1994
Assets					
Current Assets:					
Cash	$869.50	$903.50	$1,189.00	$1,267.50	$1,241.00
Short-term investments	532.50	507.50	518.00	468.50	204.00
Receivables	940.50	955.50	861.50	820.50	970.50
Deferred income taxes	438.50	382.50	293.00	285.00	254.50
Prepaid expenses and other current assets	333.50	325.50	286.50	277.00	352.50
Total current assets	3,114.50	3,074.50	3,148.00	3,118.50	3,022.50
Property, plant, and equipment	8,681.50	7,418.50	6,865.50	6,769.50	6,872.00
Other assets	1,876.00	1,990.50	2,171.00	2,131.50	1,989.00
Total Assets	$13,672.00	$12,483.50	$12,184.50	$12,019.50	$11,883.50
Liabilities and Stockholders' Equity					
Current Liabilities:					
Current maturities of long-term debt	$151.50	$138.00	$95.50	$189.00	$131.00
Current obligations under capital leases	62.50	60.00	59.50	36.00	11.50
Accounts payable and miscellaneous accrued liabilities	1,858.00	1,615.50	1,506.50	1,566.50	1,523.50
Air traffic liability	1,542.50	1,416.00	1,278.50	1,195.00	1,218.50
Accrued salaries and vacation	508.00	424.00	381.50	287.00	195.00
Accrued aircraft rent	207.50	207.00	218.00	215.00	198.00
Total current liabilities	4,330.00	3,860.50	3,539.50	3,488.50	3,277.50
Noncurrent liabilities:					
Long-term debt	1,504.00	1,637.00	2,241.00	2,912.50	3,380.50
Obligations under capital leases	285.50	349.00	407.00	262.00	91.50
Deferrals	931.00	874.50	933.50	977.50	1,041.00
Accruals	626.50	609.00	586.00	548.50	490.50
Other noncurrent liabilities	2,314.50	2,233.00	2,165.00	2,072.50	1,820.00
Total noncurrent liabilities	5,661.50	5,702.50	6,332.50	6,773.00	6,823.50
Stockholders' Equity:					
Preferred stock	165.50	147.00	129.00	111.00	92.50
Common stock	258.00	234.00	190.50	163.50	163.00
Additional paid-in-capital	2,839.50	2,636.00	2,321.50	2,014.50	2,012.50
Retained earnings	1,199.00	296.00	−151.50	−337.00	−227.00
Other comprehensive income	95.00	113.50	104.50	41.50	—
Treasury stock	−876.50	−506.00	−281.50	−262.00	−284.50
Other stockholders' equity	—	—	—	26.50	26.00
Total stockholders' equity	3,680.50	2,920.50	2,312.50	1,758.00	1,782.50
Total Liabilities and Stockholders' Equity	$13,672.00	$12,483.50	$12,184.50	$12,019.50	$11,883.50

Cash Flow Data

	1998	1997	1996	1995	1994
Cash flow from operations	$2,916	$2,039	$1,391	$1,114	$1,324
Fixed asset purchases	2,291	1,948	936	626	1,205
Cash dividends	43	44	120	120	120
Depreciation and amortization	860	710	634	622	678

Market Data

	1998	1997	1996	1995	1994
High market price	$71.80	$60.30	$43.50	$40.60	$28.90
Low market price	$40.90	$34.60	$33.40	$25.10	$19.80
Number of shares outstanding (millions)	150.45	147.39	135.56	101.4	100.91
Market capitalization	$8,477.86	$6,993.66	$5,212.28	$3,330.99	$2,457.16

Delta Airlines Ratios

Liquidity Ratios

	1998	1997	1996	1995	1994
Working capital	−$1,215.50	−$786.00	−$391.50	−$370.00	−$255.00
Working capital ratio	0.72	0.8	0.89	0.89	0.92
Quick ratio	0.54	0.61	0.73	0.73	0.74
Inventory turnover	NA	NA	NA	NA	NA
Days in inventory	NA	NA	NA	NA	NA
Accounts receivable turnover	15.03	14.23	14.46	14.86	12.73
Days in accounts receivable	24.28	25.66	25.25	24.56	28.66
Inventory conversion cycle	24.28	25.66	25.25	24.56	28.66
Accounts payable turnover	NA	NA	NA	NA	NA
Days in accounts payable	NA	NA	NA	NA	NA
Net cash conversion cycle	NA	NA	NA	NA	NA
Cash + short-term investments	1,402.00	1,411.00	1,707.00	1,736.00	1,445.00
A/R*days in accounts receivable	22,836.13	24,513.59	21,750.02	20,151.34	27,816.38
Inventory*days in inventory	—	—	—	—	—
Product dollar days	24,238.13	25,924.59	23,457.02	21,887.34	29,261.38
Current assets-other current assets	2,342.50	2,366.50	2,568.50	2,556.50	2,415.50
Liquidity index	10.35	10.95	9.13	8.56	12.11

Cash Flow Ratios

	1998	1997	1996	1995	1994
Cash flow adequacy	1.25	1.02	1.32	1.49	1.00
Reinvestment ratio	0.79	0.96	0.67	0.56	0.91
Dividend payout	0.01	0.02	0.09	0.11	0.09
Free cash flow	582.00	47.00	335	368	−1.00
Depreciation impact ratio	0.29	0.35	0.46	0.56	0.51
Recapitalization index	2.66	2.74	1.48	1.01	1.78
Cash flow return on assets	0.21	0.16	0.11	0.09	0.11
Cash flow return on sales	0.21	0.15	0.11	0.09	0.11
Operations index	1.72	1.33	3.00	1.69	−2.96

Asset Utilization Ratios

	1998	1997	1996	1995	1994
Profit margin	7.08%	6.28%	1.25%	3.35%	−3.31%
Asset turnover	1.034	1.089	1.022	1.015	1.04
Financial structure leverage	3.715	4.274	5.269	6.837	6.667
Return on assets	7.32%	6.84%	1.28%	3.39%	−3.44%
Return on equity	27.20%	29.24%	6.75%	23.21%	−22.95%

Capital Structure Ratios

	1998	1997	1996	1995	1994
Debt to capital	0.73	0.77	0.81	0.85	0.85
Debt to equity	2.71	3.27	4.27	5.84	5.67
Long-term debt to capital	0.41	0.46	0.52	0.56	0.57
Long-term debt to equity	1.54	1.95	2.74	3.85	3.83
Working capital/total assets-Z1	−0.11	−0.08	−0.04	−0.04	−0.03
Retained earnings/total assets-Z2	0.12	0.03	−0.02	−0.04	−0.03
EBIT/total assets-Z3	0.41	0.4	0.13	0.18	−0.12
Sales/total assets-Z4	1.03	1.09	1.02	1.01	1.04
Market to book-Z5	0.51	0.44	0.32	0.19	0.15
Z-Score	1.97	1.89	1.41	1.31	1.01

Market Ratio

	1998	1997	1996	1995	1994
Price to earnings	8.47	8.19	33.41	8.16	−6.01

United Airlines, Incorporated
Income Statements
(in million of dollars)

	1998	1997	1996	1995	1994	1993
Revenues:	$17,561	$17,378	$16,362	$14,943	$13,950	$14,354
Expenses:						
Salaries, wages, etc.	5,341	5,018	4,719	4,526	4,679	4,695
Aircraft fuel	1,788	2,061	2,082	1,680	1,585	1,718
Commissions	1,325	1,508	1,466	1,471	1,426	2,500
Depreciation and amortization	793	724	759	724	725	722
Rentals and landing fees	881	863	846	803	1,555	1,466
Services	1,505	1,285	1,187	1,062	1,426	1,291
Aircraft rentals	893	942	952	1,009	—	—
Maintenance, materials, and repairs	624	603	449	407	410	366
Other operating expenses	2,933	3,115	2,779	2,432	1,623	1,301
Total Operating Expenses	16,083	16,119	15,239	14,114	13,429	14,059
Operating Income	1,478	1,259	1,123	829	521	295
Other income (expenses)	−222	265	−153	−208	−350	−321
Income (loss) before taxes	1,256	1,524	970	621	171	−26
Income tax provision	429	561	370	243	94	−9
Income before irregular items	827	963	600	378	77	−17
Irregular items, net of tax	−6	−14	−67	−29	−26	−19
Net Income	$821	$949	$533	$349	$51	$ −36
Basic earnings per share	$12.71	$14.98	$5.16	$5.00	$ −0.15	$ −3.40
Diluted earnings per share	$6.83	$8.95	$5.04	$4.78		

Vertical Common Size

	1998	1997	1996	1995	1994	1993
Revenues:	100.0%	100.0%	100.0%	100.0%	100.0%	100.0%
Expenses:	0.0%	0.0%	0.0%	0.0%	0.0%	0.0%
Salaries, wages, etc.	30.4%	28.9%	28.8%	30.3%	33.5%	32.7%
Aircraft fuel	10.2%	11.9%	12.7%	11.2%	11.4%	12.0%
Commissions	7.5%	8.7%	9.0%	9.8%	10.2%	17.4%
Depreciation and amortization	4.5%	4.2%	4.6%	4.8%	5.2%	5.0%
Rentals and landing fees	5.0%	5.0%	5.2%	5.4%	11.1%	10.2%
Services	8.6%	7.4%	7.3%	7.1%	10.2%	9.0%
Aircraft rentals	5.1%	5.4%	5.8%	6.8%	0.0%	0.0%
Maintenance, materials and repairs	3.6%	3.5%	2.7%	2.7%	2.9%	2.5%
Other operating expenses	16.7%	17.9%	17.0%	16.3%	11.6%	9.1%
Total Operating Expenses	91.6%	92.8%	93.1%	94.5%	96.3%	97.9%
Operating income	8.4%	7.2%	6.9%	5.5%	3.7%	2.1%
Other income (expenses)	−1.3%	1.5%	−0.9%	−1.4%	-2.5%	−2.2%
Income (loss) before taxes	7.2%	8.8%	5.9%	4.2%	1.2%	−0.2%
Income tax provision	2.4%	3.2%	2.3%	1.6%	0.7%	−0.1%
Income before irregular items	4.7%	5.5%	3.7%	2.5%	0.6%	−0.1%
Irregular items, net of tax	0.0%	−0.1%	−0.4%	−0.2%	−0.2%	−0.1%
Net Income	4.7%	5.5%	3.3%	2.3%	0.4%	−0.3%

Horizontal Common Size—1993 Base Year

	1998	1997	1996	1995	1994	1993
Revenues:	122.3%	121.1%	114.0%	104.1%	97.2%	100.0%
Expenses:						
Salaries, wages, etc.	113.8%	106.9%	100.5%	96.4%	99.7%	100.0%
Aircraft fuel	104.1%	120.0%	121.2%	97.8%	92.3%	100.0%
Commissions	53.0%	60.3%	58.6%	58.8%	57.0%	100.0%
Depreciation and amortization	109.8%	100.3%	105.1%	100.3%	100.4%	100.0%
Rentals and landing fees	60.1%	58.9%	57.7%	54.8%	106.1%	100.0%
Services	116.6%	99.5%	91.9%	82.3%	110.5%	100.0%
Aircraft rentals						
Maintenance, materials, and repairs	170.5%	164.8%	122.7%	111.2%	112.0%	100.0%
Other operating expenses	225.4%	239.4%	213.6%	186.9%	124.8%	100.0%
Total operating expenses	114.4%	114.7%	108.4%	100.4%	95.5%	100.0%
Operating income	501.0%	426.8%	380.7%	281.0%	176.6%	100.0%
Other income (expenses)	69.2%	-82.6%	47.7%	64.8%	109.0%	100.0%
Income (loss) before taxes	-4830.8%	-5861.5%	-3730.8%	-2388.5%	-657.7%	100.0%
Income tax provision	-4766.7%	-6233.3%	-4111.1%	-2700.0%	-1044.4%	100.0%
Income before irregular items	-4864.7%	-5664.7%	-3529.4%	-2223.5%	-452.9%	100.0%
Irregular items, net of tax	31.6%	73.7%	352.6%	152.6%	136.8%	100.0%
Net Income	-2280.6%	-2636.1%	-1480.6%	-969.4%	-141.7%	100.0%

Horizontal Common Size—Rolling Forward Method

	1998	1997	1996	1995	1994	1993
Revenues:	101.1%	106.2%	109.5%	107.1%	97.2%	100.0%
Expenses:						
Salaries, wages, etc.	106.4%	106.3%	104.3%	96.7%	99.7%	100.0%
Aircraft fuel	86.8%	99.0%	123.9%	106.0%	92.3%	100.0%
Commissions	87.9%	102.9%	99.7%	103.2%	57.0%	100.0%
Depreciation and amortization	109.5%	95.4%	104.8%	99.9%	100.4%	100.0%
Rentals and landing fees	102.1%	102.0%	105.4%	51.6%	106.1%	100.0%
Services	117.1%	108.3%	111.8%	74.5%	110.5%	100.0%
Aircraft rentals	94.8%	98.9%	94.4%			
Maintenance, materials, and repairs	103.5%	134.3%	110.3%	99.3%	112.0%	100.0%
Other operating expenses	94.2%	112.1%	114.3%	149.8%	124.8%	100.0%
Total operating expenses	99.8%	105.8%	108.0%	105.1%	95.5%	100.0%
Operating income	117.4%	112.1%	135.5%	159.1%	176.6%	100.0%
Other income (expenses)	-83.8%	-173.2%	73.6%	59.4%	109.0%	100.0%
Income (loss) before taxes	82.4%	157.1%	156.2%	363.2%	-657.7%	100.0%
Income tax provision	76.5%	151.6%	152.3%	258.5%	-1044.4%	100.0%
Income before irregular items	85.9%	160.5%	158.7%	490.9%	-452.9%	100.0%
Irregular items, net of tax	42.9%	20.9%	231.0%	111.5%	136.8%	100.0%
Net Income	86.5%	178.0%	152.7%	684.3%	-141.7%	100.0%

United Airlines, Incorporated
Income Statements
(in million of dollars)
(continued)

Compound Annual Growth Rate

	1993	1994	1995	1996	1997	1998	Growth
Revenues:	$(14,354)	$ —	$ —	$ —	$ —	$17,561	4.1%
Expenses:							
Salaries, wages, etc.	(4,695)	0	0	0	0	5,341	2.6%
Aircraft fuel	(1,718)	0	0	0	0	1,788	0.8%
Commissions	(2,500)	0	0	0	0	1,325	−11.9%
Depreciation and amortization	(722)	0	0	0	0	793	1.9%
Rentals and landing fees	(1,466)	0	0	0	0	881	−9.7%
Services	(1,291)	0	0	0	0	1,505	3.1%
Aircraft rentals	—	0	0	0	0	893	
Maintenance, materials and repairs	(366)	0	0	0	0	624	11.3%
Other operating expenses	(1,301)	0	0	0	0	2,933	17.7%
Total operating expenses	(14,059)	0	0	0	0	16,083	2.7%
Operating income	(295)	0	0	0	0	1,478	38.0%
Other income (expenses)	321	0	0	0	0	(222)	−7.1%
Income (loss) before taxes	26	0	0	0	0	1,256	
Income tax provision	9	0	0	0	0	429	
Income before irregular items	17	0	0	0	0	827	
Irregular items, net of tax	19	0	0	0	0	(6)	−20.6%
Net Income	36	0	0	0	0	821	

United Airlines, Incorporated
Balance Sheets
(in millions of dollars)

	1998	1997	1996	1995	1994	1993
Assets						
Current Assets:						
Cash	$390	$295	$229	$194	$500	$285
Short-term investments	425	550	468	949	1,032	681
Receivables	1,138	1,051	962	951	889	1,489
Inventories	384	355	369	298	285	277
Deferred income taxes	256	244	227	236	151	127
Prepaid expenses	315	453	427	415	335	408
Total current assets	2,908	2,948	2,682	3,043	3,192	3,267
Property, plant, and equipment	13,054	10,774	8,243	7,021	6,723	7,204
Other assets	2,597	1,742	1,752	1,577	1,849	1,682
Total assets	$18,559	$15,464	$12,677	$11,641	$11,764	$12,153
Liabilities and Stockholders' Equity						
Current Liabilities:						
Short-term borrowings and notes payable	$184	$ —	$ —	$ —	$269	$315
Current maturity of long-term debt	98	235	165	90	384	125

United Airlines, Incorporated
Balance Sheets
(in millions of dollars)
(continued)

Balance Sheet (continued)

	1998	1997	1996	1995	1994	1993
Current obligations under capital leases	176	171	132	99	76	62
Accounts payable	1,151	1,030	994	696	651	632
Accrued salaries and wages	952	869	906	870	843	941
Accrued aircraft rent	793	830	800	771	825	886
Other current liabilities and accruals	2,314	2,113	2,006	1,907	1,858	1,914
Total current liabilities	5,668	5,248	5,003	4,433	4,906	4,875
Noncurrent liabilities:						
Long-term debt	2,858	2,092	1,661	2,919	2,887	2,603
Obligations under capital leases	2,113	1,679	1,325	994	730	824
Other liabilities and deferred credits	3,816	3,493	3,395	3,415	3,508	3,142
Total noncurrent liabilities	8,787	7,264	6,381	7,328	7,125	6,569
Minority interest income and other obligations	823	615	298	119	49	35
Stockholders' Equity:						
Preferred stock	—	—	—	—	—	—
Common stock	1	1	1	—	—	—
Additional paid-in-capital	3,517	2,876	2,160	1,353	1,287	839
Retained earnings	1,028	309	—	—	(1,335)	(95)
Other comprehensive income	(2)	(2)	—	—	—	—
Treasury stock	(1,140)	(663)	(385)	(282)	(161)	—
Other stockholders' equity	(123)	(184)	(781)	(1,310)	(107)	(70)
Total stockholders' equity	3,281	2,337	995	(239)	(316)	674
Total liabilities and stockholders' equity	$18,559	$15,464	$12,677	$11,641	$11,764	$12,153

Vertical Common Size

	1998	1997	1996	1995	1994	1993
Assets						
Current Assets:						
Cash	2.1%	1.9%	1.8%	1.7%	4.3%	2.3%
Short-term investments	2.3%	3.6%	3.7%	8.2%	8.8%	5.6%
Receivables	6.1%	6.8%	7.6%	8.2%	7.6%	12.3%
Inventories	2.1%	2.3%	2.9%	2.6%	2.4%	2.3%
Deferred income taxes	1.4%	1.6%	1.8%	2.0%	1.3%	1.0%
Prepaid expenses	1.7%	2.9%	3.4%	3.6%	2.8%	3.4%
Total current assets	15.7%	19.1%	21.2%	26.1%	27.1%	26.9%
Property, plant, and equipment	70.3%	69.7%	65.0%	60.3%	57.1%	59.3%
Other assets	14.0%	11.3%	13.8%	13.5%	15.7%	13.8%
Total assets	100.0%	100.0%	100.0%	100.0%	100.0%	100.0%
Liabilities and Stockholders' Equity						
Current Liabilities:						
Short-term borrowings and notes payable	1.0%	0.0%	0.0%	0.0%	2.3%	2.6%

United Airlines, Incorporated
Balance Sheets
(in millions of dollars)
(continued)

Vertical Common Size (continued)

	1998	1997	1996	1995	1994	1993
Current maturity of long-term debt	0.5%	1.5%	1.3%	0.8%	3.3%	1.0%
Current obligations under capital leases	0.9%	1.1%	1.0%	0.9%	0.6%	0.5%
Accounts payable	6.2%	6.7%	7.8%	6.0%	5.5%	5.2%
Accrued salaries and wages	5.1%	5.6%	7.1%	7.5%	7.2%	7.7%
Accrued aircraft rent	4.3%	5.4%	6.3%	6.6%	7.0%	7.3%
Other current liabilities and accruals	12.5%	13.7%	15.8%	16.4%	15.8%	15.7%
Total current liabilities	30.5%	33.9%	39.5%	38.1%	41.7%	40.1%
Noncurrent liabilities:	0.0%	0.0%	0.0%	0.0%	0.0%	0.0%
Long-term debt	15.4%	13.5%	13.1%	25.1%	24.5%	21.4%
Obligations under capital leases	11.4%	10.9%	10.5%	8.5%	6.2%	6.8%
Other liabilities and deferred credits	20.6%	22.6%	26.8%	29.3%	29.8%	25.9%
Total noncurrent liabilities	47.3%	47.0%	50.3%	62.9%	60.6%	54.1%
Minority interest income and other obligations	4.4%	4.0%	2.4%	1.0%	0.4%	0.3%
Stockholders' Equity: Preferred stock						
Common stock	0.0%	0.0%	0.0%	0.0%	0.0%	0.0%
Additional paid-in-capital	19.0%	18.6%	17.0%	11.6%	10.9%	6.9%
Retained earnings	5.5%	2.0%	0.0%	0.0%	–11.3%	–0.8%
Other comprehensive income	0.0%	0.0%	0.0%	0.0%	0.0%	0.0%
Treasury stock	–6.1%	–4.3%	–3.0%	–2.4%	–1.4%	0.0%
Other stockholders' equity	–0.7%	–1.2%	–6.2%	–11.3%	–0.9%	–0.6%
Total stockholders' equity	17.7%	15.1%	7.8%	–2.1%	–2.7%	5.5%
Total liabilities and stockholders' equity	100.0%	100.0%	100.0%	100.0%	100.0%	100.0%

Horizontal Common Size—1993 Base Year

	1998	1997	1996	1995	1994	1993
Assets						
Current Assets:						
Cash	136.8%	103.5%	80.4%	68.1%	175.4%	100.0%
Short-term investments	62.4%	80.8%	68.7%	139.4%	151.5%	100.0%
Receivables	76.4%	70.6%	64.6%	63.9%	59.7%	100.0%
Inventories	138.6%	128.2%	133.2%	107.6%	102.9%	100.0%
Deferred income taxes	201.6%	192.1%	178.7%	185.8%	118.9%	100.0%
Prepaid expenses	77.2%	111.0%	104.7%	101.7%	82.1%	100.0%
Total current assets	89.0%	90.2%	82.1%	93.1%	97.7%	100.0%
Property, plant, and equipment	181.2%	149.6%	114.4%	97.5%	93.3%	100.0%

Horizontal Common Size—1993 Base Year (continued)

	1998	1997	1996	1995	1994	1993
Other assets	154.4%	103.6%	104.2%	93.8%	109.9%	100.0%
Total Assets	152.7%	127.2%	104.3%	95.8%	96.8%	100.0%
Liabilities and Stockholders' Equity						
Current Liabilities:						
Short-term borrowings and notes payable	58.4%	0.0%	0.0%	0.0%	85.4%	100.0%
Current maturity of long-term debt	78.4%	188.0%	132.0%	72.0%	307.2%	100.0%
Current obligations under capital leases	283.9%	275.8%	212.9%	159.7%	122.6%	100.0%
Accounts payable	182.1%	163.0%	157.3%	110.1%	103.0%	100.0%
Accrued salaries and wages	101.2%	92.3%	96.3%	92.5%	89.6%	100.0%
Accrued aircraft rent	89.5%	93.7%	90.3%	87.0%	93.1%	100.0%
Other current liabilities and accruals	120.9%	110.4%	104.8%	99.6%	97.1%	100.0%
Total current liabilities	116.3%	107.7%	102.6%	90.9%	100.6%	100.0%
Noncurrent liabilities:						
Long-term debt	109.8%	80.4%	63.8%	112.1%	110.9%	100.0%
Obligations under capital leases	256.4%	203.8%	160.8%	120.6%	88.6%	100.0%
Other liabilities and deferred credits	121.5%	111.2%	108.1%	108.7%	111.6%	100.0%
Total noncurrent liabilities	133.8%	110.6%	97.1%	111.6%	108.5%	100.0%
Minority interest income and other obligations	2351.4%	1757.1%	851.4%	340.0%	140.0%	100.0%
Stockholders' Equity:						
Preferred stock						
Common stock						
Additional paid-in-capital	419.2%	342.8%	257.4%	161.3%	153.4%	100.0%
Retained earnings	−1082.1%	-325.3%	0.0%	0.0%	1405.3%	100.0%
Other comprehensive income						
Treasury stock						
Other stockholders' equity	175.7%	262.9%	1115.7%	1871.4%	152.9%	100.0%
Total stockholders' equity	486.8%	346.7%	147.6%	−35.5%	−46.9%	100.0%
Total liabilities and stockholders' equity	152.7%	127.2%	104.3%	95.8%	96.8%	100.0%

Horizontal Common Size—Rolling Forward

	1998	1997	1996	1995	1994	1993
Assets						
Current Assets:						
Cash	132.2%	128.8%	118.0%	38.8%	175.4%	100.0%
Short-term investments	77.3%	117.5%	49.3%	92.0%	151.5%	100.0%
Receivables	108.3%	109.3%	101.2%	107.0%	59.7%	100.0%
Inventories	108.2%	96.2%	123.8%	104.6%	102.9%	100.0%
Deferred income taxes	104.9%	107.5%	96.2%	156.3%	118.9%	100.0%
Prepaid expenses	69.5%	106.1%	102.9%	123.9%	82.1%	100.0%
Total current assets	98.6%	109.9%	88.1%	95.3%	97.7%	100.0%
Property, plant, and equipment	121.2%	130.7%	117.4%	104.4%	93.3%	100.0%
Other assets	149.1%	99.4%	111.1%	85.3%	109.9%	100.0%
Total Assets	120.0%	122.0%	108.9%	99.0%	96.8%	100.0%
Liabilities and Stockholders' Equity						
Current Liabilities:						
Short-term borrowings and notes payable				0.0%	85.4%	100.0%
Current maturity of long-term debt	41.7%	142.4%	183.3%	23.4%	307.2%	100.0%
Current obligations under capital leases	102.9%	129.5%	133.3%	130.3%	122.6%	100.0%
Accounts payable	111.7%	103.6%	142.8%	106.9%	103.0%	100.0%
Accrued salaries and wages	109.6%	95.9%	104.1%	103.2%	89.6%	100.0%
Accrued aircraft rent	95.5%	103.8%	103.8%	93.5%	93.1%	100.0%
Other current liabilities and accruals	109.5%	105.3%	105.2%	102.6%	97.1%	100.0%
Total current liabilities	108.0%	104.9%	112.9%	90.4%	100.6%	100.0%
Noncurrent liabilities:						
Long-term debt	136.6%	125.9%	56.9%	101.1%	110.9%	100.0%
Obligations under capital leases	125.8%	126.7%	133.3%	136.2%	88.6%	100.0%
Other liabilities and deferred credits	109.2%	102.9%	99.4%	97.3%	111.6%	100.0%
Total noncurrent liabilities	121.0%	113.8%	87.1%	102.8%	108.5%	100.0%
Minority interest income and other obligations	133.8%	206.4%	250.4%	242.9%	140.0%	100.0%
Stockholders' Equity:						
Preferred stock						
Common stock	100.0%	100.0%				
Additional paid-in-capital	122.3%	133.1%	159.6%	105.1%	153.4%	100.0%
Retained earnings	332.7%			0.0%	1405.3%	100.0%
Other comprehensive income	100.0%					
Treasury stock	171.9%	172.2%	136.5%	175.2%		
Other stockholders' equity	66.8%	23.6%	59.6%	1224.3%	152.9%	100.0%

Horizontal Common Size—Rolling Forward (continued)

	1998	1997	1996	1995	1994	1993
Total stockholders' equity	140.4%	234.9%	−416.3%	75.6%	−46.9%	100.0%
Total Liabilities and Stockholders' Equity	120.0%	122.0%	108.9%	99.0%	96.8%	100.0%

Compound Annual Growth Rate

	1993	1994	1995	1996	1997	1998	Growth
Assets							
Current Assets:							
Cash	$(285)	$—	$—	$—	$—	$390	6.5%
Short-term investments	(681)	0	0	0	0	425	−9.0%
Receivables	(1,489)	0	0	0	0	1,138	−5.2%
Inventories	(277)	0	0	0	0	384	6.8%
Deferred income taxes	(127)	0	0	0	0	256	15.1%
Prepaid expenses	(408)	0	0	0	0	315	−5.0%
Total current assets	(3,267)	0	0	0	0	2,908	−2.3%
Property, plant, and equipment	(7,204)	0	0	0	0	13,054	12.6%
Other assets	(1,682)	0	0	0	0	2,597	9.1%
Total Assets	(12,153)	0	0	0	0	18,559	8.8%
Liabilities and Stockholders' Equity							
Current Liabilities:							
Short-term borrowings and notes payable	(315)	0	0	0	0	184	−10.2%
Current maturity of long-term debt	(125)	0	0	0	0	98	−4.8%
Current obligations under capital leases	(62)	0	0	0	0	176	23.2%
Accounts payable	(632)	0	0	0	0	1,151	12.7%
Accrued salaries and wages	(941)	0	0	0	0	952	0.2%
Accrued aircraft rent	(886)	0	0	0	0	793	−2.2%
Other current liabilities and accruals	(1,914)	0	0	0	0	2,314	3.9%
Total current liabilities	(4,875)	0	0	0	0	5,668	3.1%
Noncurrent liabilities:	—	0	0	0	0		
Long-term debt	(2,603)	0	0	0	0	2,858	1.9%
Obligations under capital leases	(824)	0	0	0	0	2,113	20.7%
Other liabilities and deferred credits	(3,142)	0	0	0	0	3,816	4.0%
Total noncurrent liabilities	(6,569)	0	0	0	0	8,787	6.0%
Minority interest income and other obligations	(35)	0	0	0	0	823	88.0%
Stockholders' Equity:							
Preferred stock							
Common stock	—	0	0	0	0	1	

United Airlines, Incorporated Balance Sheets (in millions of dollars) (continued)

Compound Annual Growth Rate (continued)

	1993	1994	1995	1996	1997	1998	Growth
Additional paid-in-capital	(839)	0	0	0	0	3,517	33.2%
Retained earnings	95	0	0	0	0	1,028	
Other comprehensive income	—	0	0	0	0	(2)	
Treasury stock	—	0	0	0	0	(1,140)	
Other stockholders' equity	70	0	0	0	0	(123)	11.9%
Total stockholders' equity	(674)	0	0	0	0	3,281	37.2%
Total Liabilities and Stockholders' Equity	(12,153)	0	0	0	0	18,559	8.8%

United Airlines Condensed Statements of Cash Flows (in millions of dollars)

	1998	1997	1996	1995	1994
Net income	$821	$949	$533	$349	$ 51
Depreciation expense	793	724	759	664	725
Other adjustments to operations	1,501	889	1,105	574	417
Cash flows from operating activities	3,115	2,562	2,397	1,587	1,193
Purchase of property, plant, and equipment	(2,832)	(2,812)	(1,538)	(1,111)	(636)
Other adjustments to investing activities	515	472	183	1,038	296
Cash flow from investing activities	(2,317)	(2,340)	(1,355)	(73)	(340)
Dividends	(10)	(10)	(22)	(49)	(53)
Other adjustments to financing activities	(693)	(147)	(985)	(1,767)	(641)
Cash flows from financing activities	(740)	(15)	(1,007)	(1,816)	(694)
Net change in cash	$95	$65	$35	$–302	$159

United Airlines
Income Statements
(in millions of dollars)

	1998	1997	1996	1995	1994
Revenues:	$17,561	$17,378	$16,362	$14,943	$13,950
Expenses:					
Salaries, wages, etc.	5,341	5,018	4,719	4,526	4,679
Aircraft fuel	1,788	2,061	2,082	1,680	1,585
Commissions	1,325	1,508	1,466	1,471	1,426
Depreciation & amortization	793	724	759	724	725
Rentals & landing fees	881	863	846	803	1,555
Services	1,505	1,285	1,187	1,062	1,426
Aircraft rentals	893	942	952	1,009	—
Maintenance, materials & repairs	624	603	449	407	410
Other operating expenses	2,933	3,115	2,779	2,432	1,623
Total Operating Expenses	16,083	16,119	15,239	14,114	13,429
Operating Income	1,478	1,259	1,123	829	521
Other income (expenses)	(222)	265	(153)	(208)	(350)
Income (loss) before taxes	1,256	1,524	970	621	171
Income tax provision	429	561	370	243	94
Income before irregular items	827	963	600	378	77
Irregular items, net of tax	(6)	(14)	(67)	(29)	(26)
Net Income	$821	$949	$533	$349	$51

United Airlines AVERAGE
Balance Sheets
(in millions)

	1998	1997	1996	1995	1994
Assets					
Current Assets:					
Cash	$342.50	$262.00	$211.50	$347.00	$392.50
Short-term investments	487.50	509.00	708.50	990.50	856.50
Receivables	1,094.50	1,006.50	956.50	920.00	1,189.00
Inventories	369.50	362.00	333.50	291.50	281.00
Deferred income taxes	250.00	235.50	231.50	193.50	139.00
Prepaid expenses	384.00	440.00	421.00	375.00	371.50
Total current assets	2,928.00	2,815.00	2,862.50	3,117.50	3,229.50
Property, plant, and equipment	11,914.00	9,508.50	7,632.00	6,872.00	6,963.50
Other assets	2,169.50	1,747.00	1,664.50	1,713.00	1,765.50
Total Assets	$17,011.50	$14,070.50	$12,159.00	$11,702.50	$11,958.50
Liabilities and Stockholders' Equity					
Current Liabilities:					
Short-term borrowings and notes payable	$92.00	$ —	$ —	$134.50	$292.00
Current maturity of long-term debt	166.50	200.00	127.50	237.00	254.50
Current obligations under capital leases	173.50	151.50	115.50	87.50	69.00
Accounts payable	1,090.50	1,012.00	845.00	673.50	641.50
Accrued salaries and wages	910.50	887.50	888.00	856.50	892.00

United Airlines AVERAGE
Balance Sheets
(in millions)

	1998	1997	1996	1995	1994
Accrued aircraft rent	811.50	815.00	785.50	798.00	855.50
Other current liabilities and accruals	2,213.50	2,059.50	1,956.50	1,882.50	1,886.00
Total current liabilities	5,458.00	5,125.50	4,718.00	4,669.50	4,890.50
Noncurrent liabilities:	—	—	—	—	—
Long-term debt	2,475.00	1,876.50	2,290.00	2,903.00	2,745.00
Obligations under capital leases	1,896.00	1,502.00	1,159.50	862.00	777.00
Other liabilities and deferred credits	3,654.50	3,444.00	3,405.00	3,461.50	3,325.00
Total noncurrent liabilities	8,025.50	6,822.50	6,854.50	7,226.50	6,847.00
Minority interest income and other obligations	719.00	456.50	208.50	84.00	42.00
Stockholders' Equity:					
Preferred stock					
Common stock	1.00	1.00	0.50	—	—
Additional paid-in-capital	3,196.50	2,518.00	1,756.50	1,320.00	1,063.00
Retained earnings	668.50	154.50	—	(667.50)	(715.00)
Other comprehensive income	(2.00)	(1.00)	—	—	—
Treasury stock	(901.50)	(524.00)	(333.50)	(221.50)	(80.50)
Other stockholders' equity	(153.50)	(482.50)	(1,045.50)	(708.50)	(88.50)
Total stockholders' equity	2,809.00	1,666.00	378.00	(277.50)	179.00
Total Liabilities and Stockholders' Equity	$17,011.50	$14,070.50	$12,159.00	$11,702.50	$11,958.50

Cash Flow Data

	1998	1997	1996	1995	1994
Cash flow from operations	$3,115	$2,562	$2,397	$1,587	$1,193
Fixed asset purchases	2,832	2,812	1,538	1,111	636
Cash dividends	10	10	22	49	53
Depreciation and amortization	793	724	759	664	725

Market Data

	1998	1997	1996	1995	1994
High market price	$97.50	$101.80	$64.80	$53.00	$37.50
Low market price	$55.30	$55.40	$38.60	$21.90	$20.80
Number of shares outstanding (millions)	51.80	57.32	58.82	50.72	49.76
Market capitalization	$3,957.52	$4,505.35	$3,040.99	$1,899.46	$1,450.50

Liquidity Ratios

	1998	1997	1996	1995	1994
Working capital	$(2,530.0)	$(2,310.5)	$(1,855.5)	$(1,552.0)	$(1,661.0)
Working capital ratio	0.54	0.55	0.61	0.67	0.66
Quick ratio	0.35	0.35	0.40	0.48	0.50
Inventory turnover	NA	NA	NA	NA	NA
Days in inventory	NA	NA	NA	NA	NA
Accounts receivable turnover	16.04	17.27	17.11	16.24	11.73
Days in accounts receivable	22.75	21.14	21.34	22.47	31.11
Inventory conversion cycle	22.75	21.14	21.34	22.47	31.11
Accounts payable turnover	NA	NA	NA	NA	NA
Days in accounts payable	NA	NA	NA	NA	NA
Net cash conversion cycle	NA	NA	NA	NA	NA
Cash + short-term investments	830.00	771.00	920.00	1,337.50	1,249.00
A/R*days in accounts receivable	24,898.61	21,277.50	20,409.22	20,674.30	36,989.83
Inventory*days in inventory	369.50	362.00	333.50	291.50	281.00
Product dollar days	26,098.11	22,410.50	21,662.72	22,303.30	38,519.83
Current assets-other current assets	2,294.00	2,139.50	2,210.00	2,549.00	2,719.00
Liquidity index	11.38	10.47	9.80	8.75	14.17

Cash Flow Ratios

	1998	1997	1996	1995	1994
Cash flow adequacy	1.10	0.91	1.54	1.37	1.73
Reinvestment ratio	0.91	1.10	0.64	0.70	0.53
Dividend payout	0.00	0.00	0.01	0.03	0.04
Free cash flow	273.00	(260.00)	837.00	427.00	504.00
Depreciation impact ratio	0.25	0.28	0.32	0.42	0.61
Recapitalization index	3.57	3.88	2.03	1.67	0.88
Cash flow return on assets	0.18	0.18	0.20	0.14	0.10
Cash flow return on sales	0.18	0.15	0.15	0.11	0.09
Operations index	2.11	2.03	2.13	1.91	2.29

Asset Utilization Ratios

	1998	1997	1996	1995	1994
Profit margin	4.675%	5.461%	3.258%	2.336%	0.366%
Asset turnover	1.032	1.235	1.346	1.277	1.167
Financial structure leverage	6.056	8.446	32.167	−42.171	66.807
Return on assets	4.83%	6.74%	4.38%	2.98%	0.43%
Return on equity	29.23%	56.96%	141.01%	−125.77%	28.49%

Capital Structure Ratios

	1998	1997	1996	1995	1994
Debt to capital	0.79	0.85	0.95	1.02	0.98
Debt to equity	4.80	7.17	30.62	(42.87)	65.57
Long-term debt to capital	0.47	0.48	0.56	0.62	0.57
Long-term debt to equity	2.86	4.10	18.13	(26.04)	38.25
Working capital/total assets-Z1	(0.18)	(0.20)	(0.18)	(0.16)	(0.17)
Retained earnings/ total assets-Z2	0.06	0.02	—	(0.08)	(0.08)
EBIT/total assets-Z3	0.29	0.30	0.30	0.23	0.14
Sales/total assets-Z4	1.03	1.24	1.35	1.28	1.17
Market to book-Z5	0.18	0.23	0.16	0.10	0.07
Z-Score	1.37	1.57	1.62	1.37	1.13

Market Ratio

	1998	1997	1996	1995	1994
Price to earnings	4.82	4.75	5.71	5.44	28.44

C
ATHLETIC FOOTWEAR AND APPAREL

$\mathcal{T}$he athletic shoe and apparel industry is part of the more comprehensive apparel and footwear economic sector. The emergence of athletic shoe and clothing manufacturers as a significant portion of the overall sector is a relatively recent phenomenon. These companies evolved to meet increased consumer demand for high-quality, stylish active wear. The dominant companies in this industry originated as athletic shoe manufacturers and subsequently extended their product lines to sports-related clothing and gear.

This appendix presents an overview of the athletic shoe and apparel industry from 1993 to 1998. It focuses on Nike and Reebok, the two largest companies in the industry. This material provides information to be used in conjunction with the two firms' financial statements, which appear at the conclusion of the appendix.

Makers of athletic shoes grew rapidly during the 1980s and 1990s. These sophisticated successors to sneaker makers tapped into pent-up consumer demand for high-quality, stylish athletic footwear. Companies such as Nike, Inc. and Reebok International, Ltd. created an industry in which athletic shoes became part of people's wardrobe, rather than just exercise equipment. The distribution outlets of athletic shoes attest to its appeal to a more general audience than just athletes. Exhibit C-1 presents the percentage of athletic shoes sold by various retailers.[1]

EXHIBIT C-1
Retail Athletic Shoe Sales

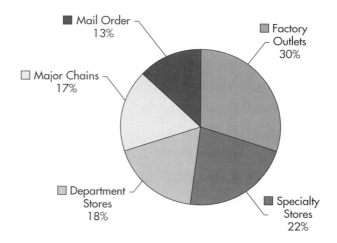

Exhibit C-2 indicates that Nike was the industry leader during the period examined. The company was an early market entrant and a conscientious builder of image. The firm committed significant resources to maintaining and enhancing the Nike brand name.[2] Nike's competitors followed its lead by carefully crafting their own brand names. Companies aligned themselves with athletes, professional and collegiate teams, and sporting events in fostering their images. These promotional activities supplemented more traditional forms of advertising.

EXHIBIT C-2
United States Athletic Shoe Market Share 1998

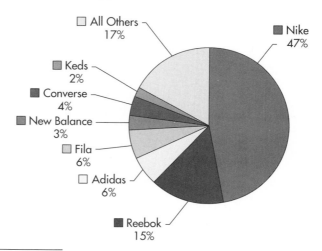

---

[1] Apparel & Footwear Industry Survey, *Standard & Poor's*, September, 1999 (New York: McGraw-Hill).
[2] Apparel & Footwear Industry Survey, *Standard & Poor's*, September, 1999 (New York: McGraw-Hill)

PRODUCT EXTENSION

Nike, Reebok, and other athletic shoemakers extended product lines to athletic apparel. For example, Exhibit C-3 shows that sales of sports-related clothing and gear became a more significant portion of Nike's sales.[3] However, the rapid increase in apparel sales was accompanied by decreased demand for athletic shoes in the 1997 and 1998. Casual dress shoes and hiking boots became fashionable alternatives to athletic shoes. Nike, Reebok, and others had limited product lines in these areas, but they faced formidable competition outside of the athletic sector in the selling of what are known as *brown shoes*.

EXHIBIT C-3

Nike, Inc.

Shoes and Apparel as a Percentage of Sales 1993–1998

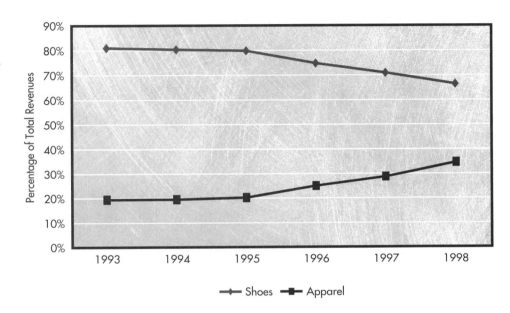

INTERNATIONAL BUSINESS

Athletic shoe and apparel companies increased their global presence during the period analyzed in two ways: they continued to move manufacturing operations overseas, and they increasingly developed foreign markets. The rationale behind relocating shoe-making operations was partly to contain costs, but it also reflected a reorientation of corporate strategy. Manufacturers began regarding themselves as designers, marketers, and distributors of athletic attire, rather than as makers of shoes and clothes. Thus, increasingly they outsourced production of goods to contract manufacturers.

A maturing U.S. market motivated companies to develop foreign markets for their products. Sales of shoes and clothing increased faster overseas than they did in the United States during the 1990s. Exhibit C-4 discloses Nike's domestic and foreign revenues as a percentage of total sales, indicating its globalization tactics.[4]

---

[3] Nike, Inc., 1994–1998 Form 10-K.
[4] Nike, Inc., 1995–1998 Form 10-K.

EXHIBIT C-4

*Nike's Domestic and Foreign
Sales (as a percentage of total
revenues) 1993–1998*

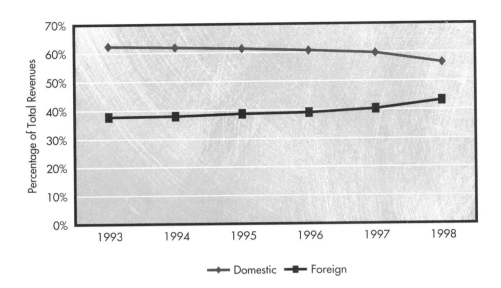

SIGNIFICANT EVENTS

1993

◆ Industry expands contract manufacturing with Indonesian and Chinese companies.
◆ Companies increasingly use endorsements by sports stars as a marketing vehicle.
◆ Global markets emerging: American firms increase European market share, and Adidas (Germany) increases its American market share.
◆ Reebok announces a $200 million stock repurchase plan and sells its boat division.

1994

◆ Industry sales level off as athletic shoe market weakens.
◆ Media exposure about working conditions in foreign factories causes public relations problems.
◆ Doc Martens, Timberland, and Deckers Outdoor cut into athletic shoe sales as boots and outdoor shoes become increasingly popular.
◆ Nike and Reebok shift strategy to meet the "brown shoe" challenge.
◆ Nike purchases Canstar, the largest manufacturer of ice hockey skates and equipment, for $395 million.

1995

◆ Companies increasingly seek exclusive affiliation with professional sports leagues and teams.
◆ Devalued peso spurs Nike to increase Mexican manufacturing operations.
◆ Nike increases its retail market share at outlets such as Foot Locker, often at the expense of Reebok.
◆ Reebok concedes the high end of the athletic shoe market to Nike.

- Key employees resign Reebok positions, and chief executive officer (CEO) Paul Fireman is pressured by institutional investors to improve corporate performance.

1996

- Nike expands sales efforts in emerging markets and announces a department to monitor factory conditions overseas.
- Reebok recognizes a loss on its Avia subsidiary, has its debt downgraded by Moody's Investor Services and Standard & Poor's Corp., and is given two years by its board to improve performance.
- Reebok purchases $612 million of its stock to improve shareholder value.

1997

- Nike experiences labor unrest in Asian factories.
- Institutional investors rate Reebok among the worst performing companies.
- Reebok introduces "Air Pockets" shoe technology in bid to reverse its declining fortunes.

1998

- Industry moves away from athletic star endorsements.
- Nike reports first decrease in annual earnings in 13 years, reduces its temporary workforce, and fails to make gains in the sports equipment market.
- Reebok reduces payroll by 10 percent and appoints Carl Yankowski as CEO of its branded unit.

Nike Income Statements (in millions)

	1998	1997	1996	1995	1994	1993
Revenues	$9,554	$9,186	$6,471	$4,761	$3,789	$3,931
Cost of sales	6,066	5,503	3,907	2,865	2,301	2,387
Selling, general, and administrative expenses	2,624	2,304	1,589	1,210	974	922
Interest expense	60	52	39	24	15	26
Other revenues and expenses	21	32	37	12	8	1
Restructuring charge	130	—	—	—	—	—
Income before taxes	653	1,295	899	650	491	595
Income taxes	253	499	346	250	192	230
Net income	$400	$796	$553	$400	$299	$365
Basic earnings per share	$2.76	$1.93	$1.38	$1.00	$1.20	$1.48
Diluted earnings per share	$2.68	$1.88	$1.36	$0.99	$1.18	

Vertical Common Size

	1998	1997	1996	1995	1994	1993
Revenues	100.0%	100.0%	100.0%	100.0%	100.0%	100.0%
Cost of sales	63.5%	59.9%	60.4%	60.2%	60.7%	60.7%
Selling, general, and administrative expenses	27.5%	25.1%	24.6%	25.4%	25.7%	23.5%
Interest expense	0.6%	0.6%	0.6%	0.5%	0.4%	0.7%
Other revenues and expenses	0.2%	0.3%	0.6%	0.3%	0.2%	0.0%
Restructuring charge	1.4%	0.0%	0.0%	0.0%	0.0%	0.0%
Income before taxes	6.8%	14.1%	13.9%	13.7%	13.0%	15.1%
Income taxes	2.6%	5.4%	5.3%	5.3%	5.1%	5.9%
Net income	4.2%	8.7%	8.5%	8.4%	7.9%	9.3%

Horizontal Common Size — 1993 Base Year

	1998	1997	1996	1995	1994	1993
Revenues	243.0%	233.7%	164.6%	121.1%	96.4%	100.0%
Cost of sales	254.1%	230.5%	163.7%	120.0%	96.4%	100.0%
Selling, general, and administrative expenses	284.6%	249.9%	172.3%	131.2%	105.6%	100.0%
Interest expense	230.8%	200.0%	150.0%	92.3%	57.7%	100.0%
Other revenues and expenses	2100.0%	3200.0%	3700.0%	1200.0%	800.0%	100.0%
Restructuring charge						
Income before taxes	109.7%	217.6%	151.1%	109.2%	82.5%	100.0%
Income taxes	110.0%	217.0%	150.4%	108.7%	83.5%	100.0%
Net income	109.6%	218.1%	151.5%	109.6%	81.9%	100.0%

Nike Income Statements
(in millions)
(continued)

Horizontal Common Size—Rolling Forward

	1998	1997	1996	1995	1994	1993
Revenues	104.0%	142.0%	135.9%	125.7%	96.4%	100.0%
Cost of sales	110.2%	140.8%	136.4%	124.5%	96.4%	100.0%
Selling, general, and administrative expenses	113.9%	145.0%	131.3%	124.2%	105.6%	100.0%
Interest expense	115.4%	133.3%	162.5%	160.0%	57.7%	100.0%
Other revenues and expenses	65.6%	86.5%	308.3%	150.0%	800.0%	100.0%
Restructuring charge						
Income before taxes	50.4%	144.0%	138.3%	132.4%	82.5%	100.0%
Income taxes	50.7%	144.2%	138.4%	130.2%	83.5%	100.0%
Net income	50.3%	143.9%	138.3%	133.8%	81.9%	100.0%

Compound Annual Growth Rate

	1993	1994	1995	1996	1997	1998	Growth
Revenues	($3,931)	0	0	0	0	$9,554	19.4%
Cost of sales	($2,387)	0	0	0	0	6066	20.5%
Selling, general, and administrative expenses	($922)	0	0	0	0	2624	23.3%
Interest expense	($26)	0	0	0	0	60	18.2%
Other revenues and expenses	($1)	0	0	0	0	21	83.8%
Restructuring charge	—	0	0	0	0	130	
Income before taxes	($595)	0	0	0	0	653	1.9%
Income taxes	($230)	0	0	0	0	253	1.9%
Net income	($365)	0	0	0	0	$400	1.8%

Nike Balance Sheets
(in millions)

	1998	1997	1996	1995	1994	1993
Assets						
Cash	$108	$445	$262	$216	$519	$291
Accounts receivable, net	1,674	1,754	1,346	1,053	704	668
Inventory	1,397	1,339	931	630	470	594
Other current assets	353	293	187	147	77	68
Total current assets	3,532	3,831	2,726	2,046	1,770	1,621
Property, plant, and equipment, net	1,153	922	644	555	406	378
Intangible assets	436	464	475	496	163	158
Other long-term assets	276	144	106	46	34	30
Total long-term assets	1,865	1,530	1,225	1,097	603	566
Total assets	$5,397	$5,361	$3,951	$3,143	$2,373	$2,187
Liabilities and shareholders' equity						
Current portion of long-term debt	$2	$2	$7	$32	$4	$53
Notes payable	480	553	445	397	127	108
Accounts payable	585	687	455	297	211	136
Other current liabilities	637	625	559	381	220	156
Total current liabilities	1,704	1,867	1,466	1,107	562	453
Long-term debt	379	296	10	11	12	15
Other long-term liabilities	53	42	44	60	58	73
Total long-term liabilities	432	338	54	71	70	88
Total liabilities	2,136	2,205	1,520	1,178	632	541
Shareholders' equity						
Common stock	$3	$3	$3	$3	$3	$3
Additional paid-in-capital	262	210	154	122	108	108
Foreign currency translation adjust	(47)	(31)	(16)	2	(15)	(7)
Retained earnings	3,043	2,974	2,290	1,838	1,645	1,542
Total shareholders' equity	3,261	3,156	2,431	1,965	1,741	1,646
Total liabilities and shareholders' equity	$5,397	$5,361	$3,951	$3,143	$2,373	$2,187

Vertical Common Size

	1998	1997	1996	1995	1994	1993
Assets						
Cash	2.0%	8.3%	6.6%	6.9%	21.9%	13.3%
Accounts receivable, net	31.0%	32.7%	34.1%	33.5%	29.7%	30.5%
Inventory	25.9%	25.0%	23.6%	20.0%	19.8%	27.2%
Other current assets	6.5%	5.5%	4.7%	4.7%	3.2%	3.1%
Total current assets	65.4%	71.5%	69.0%	65.1%	74.6%	74.1%
Property, plant, and equipment, net	21.4%	17.2%	16.3%	17.7%	17.1%	17.3%
Intangible assets	8.1%	8.7%	12.0%	15.8%	6.9%	7.2%
Other long-term assets	5.1%	2.7%	2.7%	1.5%	1.4%	1.4%
Total long-term assets	34.6%	28.5%	31.0%	34.9%	25.4%	25.9%
Total assets	100.%	100.0%	100.0%	100.0%	100.0%	100.0%

*Nike Balance Sheets
(in millions)
(continued)*

Vertical Common Size (continued)

	1998	1997	1996	1995	1994	1993
Liabilities and shareholders' equity						
Current portion of long-term debt	0.0%	0.0%	0.2%	1.0%	0.2%	2.4%
Notes payable	8.9%	10.3%	11.3%	12.6%	5.4%	4.9%
Accounts payable	10.8%	12.8%	11.5%	9.4%	8.9%	6.2%
Other current liabilities	11.8%	11.7%	14.1%	12.1%	9.3%	7.1%
Total current liabilities	31.6%	34.8%	37.1%	35.2%	23.7%	20.7%
Long-term debt	7.0%	5.5%	0.3%	0.3%	0.5%	0.7%
Other long-term liabilities	1.0%	0.8%	1.1%	1.9%	2.4%	3.3%
Total long-term liabilities	8.0%	6.3%	1.4%	2.3%	2.9%	4.0%
Total liabilities	39.6%	41.1%	38.5%	37.5%	26.6%	24.7%
Shareholders' equity						
Common stock	0.1%	0.1%	0.1%	0.1%	0.1%	0.1%
Additional paid-in-capital	4.9%	3.9%	3.9%	3.9%	4.6%	4.9%
Foreign currency translation adjust	−0.9%	−0.6%	−0.4%	0.1%	−0.6%	−0.3%
Retained earnings	56.4%	55.5%	58.0%	58.5%	69.3%	70.5%
Total shareholders' equity	60.4%	58.9%	61.5%	62.5%	73.4%	75.3%
Total liabilities and shareholders' equity	100.0%	100.0%	100.0%	100.0%	100.0%	100.0

Horizontal Common Size—1993 Base Year

	1998	1997	1996	1995	1994	1993
Assets						
Cash	37.1%	152.9%	90.0%	74.2%	178.40%	100.0%
Accounts receivable, net	250.6%	262.6%	201.5%	157.6%	105.4%	100.0%
Inventory	235.2%	225.4%	156.7%	106.1%	79.1%	100.0%
Other current assets	519.1%	430.9%	275.0%	216.2%	113.2%	100.0%
Total current assets	217.9%	236.3%	168.2%	126.2%	109.2%	100.0%
Property, plant, and equipment, net	305.0%	243.9%	170.4%	146.8%	107.4%	100.0%
Intangible assets	275.9%	293.7%	300.6%	313.9%	103.2%	100.0%
Other long-term assets	920.0%	480.0%	353.3%	153.3%	113.3%	100.0%
Total long-term assets	329.5%	270.3%	216.4%	193.8%	106.5%	100.0%
Total assets	246.8%	245.1%	180.7%	143.7%	108.5%	100.0%
Liabilities and shareholders' equity						
Current portion of long-term debt						
Notes payable	444.4%	512.0%	412.0%	367.6%	117.6%	100.0%
Accounts payable	430.1%	505.1%	334.6%	218.4%	155.1%	100.0%
Other current liabilities	408.3%	400.6%	358.3%	244.2%	141.0%	100.0%
Total current liabilities	376.2%	412.1%	323.6%	244.4%	124.1%	100.0%
Long-term debt	2526.7%	1973.3%	66.7%	73.3%	80.0%	100.0%
Other long-term liabilities	72.6%	57.5%	60.3%	82.2%	79.5%	100.0%
Total long-term liabilities	490.9%	384.1%	61.4%	80.7%	79.5%	100.0%
Total liabilities	394.8%	407.6%	281.0%	217.7%	116.8%	100.0%

Horizontal Common Size—1993 Base Year (continued)

	1998	1997	1996	1995	1994	1993
Shareholders' equity						
Common stock	100.0%	100.0%	100.0%	100.0%	100.0%	100.0%
Additional paid-in-capital	242.6%	194.4%	142.6%	113.0%	100.0%	100.0%
Foreign currency translation adjust	671.4%	442.9%	228.6%	−28.6%	214.3%	100.0%
Retained earnings	197.3%	192.9%	148.5%	119.2%	106.7%	100.0%
Total shareholders' equity	198.1%	191.7%	147.7%	119.4%	105.8%	100.0%
Total liabilities and shareholders' equity	246.8%	245.1%	180.7%	143.7%	108.5%	100.0%

Horizontal Common Size—Rolling Forward Method

	1998	1997	1996	1995	1994	1993
Assets						
Cash	24.3%	169.8%	121.3%	41.6%	178.4%	100.0%
Accounts receivable, net	95.4%	130.3%	127.8%	149.6%	105.4%	100.0%
Inventory	104.3%	143.8%	147.8%	134.0%	79.1%	100.0%
Other current assets	120.5%	156.7%	127.2%	190.9%	113.2%	100.0%
Total current assets	92.2%	140.5%	133.2%	115.6%	109.2%	100.0%
Property, plant, and equipment, net	125.1%	143.2%	116.0%	136.7%	107.4%	100.0%
Intangible assets	94.0%	97.7%	95.8%	304.3%	103.2%	100.0%
Other long-term assets	191.7%	135.8%	230.4%	135.3%	113.3%	100.0%
Total long-term assets	121.9%	124.9%	111.7%	181.9%	106.5%	100.0%
Total assets	100.7%	135.7%	125.7%	132.4%	108.5%	100.0%
Liabilities and shareholders' equity						
Current portion of long-term debt	100.0%	28.6%	21.9%	800.0%	7.5%	100.0%
Notes payable	86.8%	124.3%	112.1%	312.6%	117.6%	100.0%
Accounts payable	85.2%	151.0%	153.2%	140.8%	155.1%	100.0%
Other current liabilities	101.9%	111.8%	146.7%	173.2%	141.0%	100.0%
Total current liabilities	91.3%	127.4%	132.4%	197.0%	124.1%	100.0%
Long-term debt	128.0%	2960.0%	90.9%	91.7%	80.0%	100.0%
Other long-term liabilities	126.2%	95.5%	73.3%	103.4%	79.5%	100.0%
Total long-term liabilities	127.8%	625.9%	76.1%	101.4%	79.5%	100.0%
Total liabilities	96.9%	145.1%	129.0%	186.4%	116.8%	100.0%
Shareholders' equity						
Common stock	100.0%	100.0%	100.0%	100.0%	100.0%	100.0%
Additional paid-in-capital	124.8%	136.4%	126.2%	113.0%	100.0%	100.0%
Foreign currency translation adjust	151.6%	193.8%	-800.0%	−13.3%	214.3%	100.0%
Retained earnings	102.3%	129.9%	124.6%	111.7%	106.7%	100.0%
Total shareholders' equity	103.3%	129.8%	123.7%	112.9%	105.8%	100.0%
Total liabilities and shareholders' equity	100.7%	135.7%	125.7%	132.4%	108.5%	100.0%

Compound Annual Growth Rate

	1993	1994	1995	1996	1997	1998	Growth
Assets							
Cash	($291)	0	0	0	0	$108	–18.0%
Accounts receivable, net	($668)	0	0	0	0	1,674	20.2%
Inventory	($594)	0	0	0	0	1,397	18.7%
Other current assets	($68)	0	0	0	0	353	39.0%
Total current assets	($1,621)	0	0	0	0	3,532	16.9%
Property, plant, and equipment, net	($378)	0	0	0	0	1,153	25.0%
Intangible assets	($158)	0	0	0	0	436	22.5%
Other long-term assets	($30)	0	0	0	0	276	55.9%
Total long-term assets	($566)	0	0	0	0	1,865	26.9%
Total assets	($2,187)	0	0	0	0	$5,397	19.8%
Liabilities and shareholders' equity							
Current portion of long-term debt	($53)	0	0	0	0	$2	
Notes payable	($108)	0	0	0	0	480	34.8%
Accounts payable	($136)	0	0	0	0	585	33.9%
Other current liabilities	($156)	0	0	0	0	637	32.5%
Total current liabilities	($453)	0	0	0	0	1,704	30.3%
Long-term debt	($15)	0	0	0	0	379	90.8%
Other long-term liabilities	($73)	0	0	0	0	53	–6.20%
Total long-term liabilities	($88)	0	0	0	0	432	37.5%
Total liabilities	($541)	0	0	0	0	2,136	31.6%
Shareholders' equity							
Common stock	($3)	0	0	0	0	$3	0.0%
Additional paid-in-capital	($108)	0	0	0	0	262	19.4%
Foreign currency translation adjust	$7	0	0	0	0	(47)	46.4%
Retained earnings	($1,542)	0	0	0	0	3,043	14.6%
Total shareholders' equity	($1,646)	0	0	0	0	3,261	14.7%
Total liabilities and shareholders' equity	($2,187)	0	0	0	0	$5,397	19.8%

Nike, Inc.
Condensed Statements of Cash Flows (in millions of dollars)

	1998	1997	1996	1995	1994
Net income	$400	$796	$553	$400	$299
Depreciation expense	185	138	97	71	65
Other adjustments to operations	(67)	(611)	(310)	(216)	212
Cash flows from operating activities	518	323	340	255	576
Purchase of property, plant, and equipment	−506	−466	−216	−154	−95
Other adjustments to investing activities	−89	−30	−14	−428	3
Cash flows from investing activities	−595	−496	−230	−582	−92
Dividends	−127	−101	−79	−65	−60
Other adjustments to financing activities	−144	414	25	89	−190
Cash flows from financing activities	−271	313	−54	24	−250
Other adjustments to cash	11	43	—	−1	−6
Net change in cash	$−337	$183	$ 46	$−304	$228

Nike Income Statements (in millions)

	1998	1997	1996	1995	1994
Revenues	$9,554	$9,186	$6,471	$4,761	$3,789
Cost of sales	6,066	5,503	3,907	2,865	2,301
Selling, general, and administrative expenses	2,624	2,304	1,589	1,210	974
Interest expense	60	52	39	24	15
Other revenues and expenses	21	32	37	12	8
Restructuring charge	130	—	—	—	—
Income before taxes	653	1,295	899	650	491
Income taxes	253	499	346	250	192
Net income	$400	$796	$553	$400	$299

Nike AVERAGE Balance Sheets (in millions)

	1998	1997	1996	1995	1994
Assets					
Cash	$276.50	$353.50	$239.00	$367.50	$405.00
Accounts receivable, net	$1,714.00	$1,550.00	$1,199.50	$878.50	$686.00
Inventory	$1,368.00	$1,135.00	$780.50	$550.00	$532.00
Other current assets	$323.00	$240.00	$167.00	$112.00	$72.50
Total current assets	$3,681.50	$3,278.50	$2,386.00	$1,908.00	$1,695.50
Property, plant, and equipment, net	$1,037.50	$783.00	$599.50	$480.50	$392.00
Intangible assets	$450.00	$469.50	$485.50	$329.50	$160.50
Other long-term assets	$210.00	$125.00	$76.00	$40.00	$32.00
Total long-term assets	$1,697.50	$1,377.50	$1,161.00	$850.00	$584.50
Total assets	$5,379.00	$4,656.00	$3,547.00	$2,758.00	$2,280.00

Continued

Liabilities and shareholders' equity	1998	1997	1996	1995	1994
Current portion of long-term debt	$2.00	$4.50	$19.50	$18.00	$28.50
Notes payable	$516.50	$499.00	$421.00	$262.00	$117.50
Accounts payable	$636.00	$571.00	$376.00	$254.00	$173.50
Other current liabilities	$631.00	$592.00	$470.00	$300.50	$188.00
Total current liabilities	$1,785.50	$1,666.50	$1,286.50	$834.50	$507.50
Long-term debt	$337.50	$153.00	$10.50	$11.50	$13.50
Other long-term liabilities	$47.50	$43.00	$52.00	$59.00	$65.50
Total long-term liabilities	$385.00	$196.00	$62.50	$70.50	$79.00
Total liabilities	$2,170.50	$1,862.50	$1,349.00	$905.00	$586.50
Shareholders' equity					
Common stock	$3.00	$3.00	$3.00	$3.00	$3.00
Additional paid-in-capital	$236.00	$182.00	$138.00	$115.00	$108.00
Foreign currency translation adjust	($39.00)	($23.50)	($7.00)	($6.50)	($11.00)
Retained earnings	$3,008.50	$2,632.00	$2,064.00	$1,741.50	$1,593.50
Total shareholders' equity	$3,208.50	$2,793.50	$2,198.00	$1,853.00	$1,693.50
Total liabilities and shareholders' equity	$5,379.00	$4,656.00	$3,547.00	$2,758.00	$2,280.00

Cash Flow Data

	1998	1997	1996	1995	1994
Cash flows from operations	$518	$323	$340	$255	$576
Fixed assets purchased	506	466	216	154	95
Dividends	127	101	79	65	60
Depreciation	185	138	97	71	65

Market Data

	1998	1997	1996	1995	1994
High market price	$52.70	$76.40	$64.00	$35.20	$19.10
Low market price	$31.00	$37.80	$31.80	$17.20	$11.60
Number of shares outstanding (millions)	287	289.27	287.26	285.78	304.8
Market capitalization	$12,010.95	$16,517.32	$13,759.75	$7,487.44	$4,678.68

Nike, Inc. Ratios

Liquidity Ratios

	1998	1997	1996	1995	1994
Working capital	$1,896.00	$1,612.00	$1,099.50	$1,073.50	$1,188.00
Working capital ratio	2.06	1.97	1.85	2.29	3.34
Quick ratio	1.11	1.14	1.12	1.49	2.15
Inventory turnover	4.43	4.85	5.01	5.21	4.33
Days in inventory	82.31	75.28	72.92	70.07	84.39
Accounts receivable turnover	5.57	5.93	5.39	5.42	5.52
Days in accounts receivable	65.48	61.59	67.66	67.35	66.08
Inventory conversion cycle	147.8	136.87	140.57	137.42	150.47
Accounts payable turnover	9.54	9.64	10.39	11.28	13.26
Days in accounts payable	38.27	37.87	35.13	32.36	27.52
Net cash conversion cycle	109.53	99	105.45	105.06	122.95
Cash + short-term investments	276.5	353.5	239	367.5	405
A/R*days in accounts receivable	112,235.25	95,461.84	81,156.25	59,166.82	45,333.21
Inventory*days in inventory	112,606.29	85,444.69	56,910.88	38,538.39	44,895.16
Product dollar days	225,118.04	181,260.03	138,306.13	98,072.71	90,633.37
Current assets-other current assets	3,358.50	3,038.50	2,219.00	1,796.00	1,623.00
Liquidity index	67.03	59.65	62.33	54.61	55.84

Cash Flow Ratios

	1998	1997	1996	1995	1994
Cash flow adequacy	0.82	0.57	1.15	1.16	3.72
Reinvestment ratio	0.98	1.44	0.64	0.60	0.16
Dividend payout	0.25	0.31	0.23	0.25	0.10
Free cash flow	($115)	($244)	$45	$36	$421
Depreciation impact ratio	0.36	0.43	0.29	0.28	0.11
Recapitalization index	2.74	3.38	2.23	2.17	1.46
Cash flow return on assets	0.10	0.07	0.10	0.09	0.25
Cash flow return on sales	0.05	0.04	0.05	0.05	0.15
Operations index	0.79	0.25	0.38	0.39	1.17

Asset Utilization Ratios

	1998	1997	1996	1995	1994
Profit margin	4.187%	8.665%	8.546%	8.402%	7.891%
Asset turnover	1.776	1.973	1.824	1.726	1.662
Financial structure leverage	1.676	1.667	1.614	1.488	1.346
Return on assets	7.44%	17.10%	15.59%	14.50%	13.11%
Return on equity	12.47%	28.49%	25.16%	21.59%	17.66%

Nike, Inc. Ratios
(continued)

Capital Structure Ratios

	1998	1997	1996	1995	1994
Debt to capital	0.40	0.40	0.38	0.33	0.26
Debt to equity	0.68	0.67	0.61	0.49	0.35
Long-term debt to capital	0.06	0.03	0.00	0.00	0.01
Long-term debt to equity	0.11	0.05	0.00	0.01	0.01
Working capital/total assets-Z1	0.42	0.42	0.37	0.47	0.63
Retained earnings/total assets-Z2	0.78	0.79	0.81	0.88	0.98
EBIT/total assets-Z3	0.44	0.95	0.87	0.81	0.73
Sales/total assets-Z4	1.78	1.97	1.82	1.73	1.66
Market to book-Z5	3.32	5.32	6.12	4.96	4.79
Z-Score	6.74	9.46	10.00	8.85	8.78

Market Ratio

	1998	1997	1996	1995	1994
Price to earnings	30.03	20.75	24.88	18.72	15.65

Reebok Income Statements
(in millions)

	1998	1997	1996	1995	1994	1993
Revenues	$3,205	$3,636	$3,482	$3,484	$3,287	$2,893
Cost of sales	2,037	2,294	2,144	2,114	1,966	1,720
Selling, general, and administrative expenses	1,081	1,131	1,069	1,075	894	788
Interest expense	61	64	42	26	16	25
Interest income	−11	−11	−11	−7	−6	−11
Minority interest	1	10	15	11	9	8
Income before taxes	36	148	223	265	408	363
Income taxes	12	12	84	100	154	140
Net income	$24	$136	$139	$165	$254	$223
Basic earnings per share	$0.42	$2.41	$2.06	$2.10	$3.02	$2.53
Diluted earnings per share		$2.32	$2.03			

Vertical Common Size

	1998	1997	1996	1995	1994	1993
Revenues	100.0%	100.0%	100.0%	100.0%	100.0%	100.0%
Cost of sales	63.6%	63.1%	61.6%	60.7%	59.8%	59.5%
Selling, general, and administrative expenses	33.7%	31.1%	30.7%	30.9%	27.2%	27.2%
Interest expense	1.9%	1.8%	1.2%	0.7%	0.5%	0.9%
Interest income	−0.3%	−0.3%	−0.3%	−0.2%	−0.2%	−0.4%
Minority interest	0.0%	0.3%	0.4%	0.3%	0.3%	0.3%
Income before taxes	1.1%	4.1%	6.4%	7.6%	12.4%	12.5%
Income taxes	0.4%	0.3%	2.4%	2.9%	4.7%	4.8%
Net income	0.7%	3.7%	4.0%	4.7%	7.7%	7.7%

Horizontal Common Size—1993 Base Year

	1998	1997	1996	1995	1994	1993
Revenues	110.8%	125.7%	120.4%	120.4%	113.6%	100.0%
Cost of sales	118.4%	133.4%	124.7%	122.9%	114.3%	100.0%
Selling, general, and administrative expenses	137.2%	143.5%	135.7%	136.4%	113.5%	100.0%
Interest expense	244.0%	256.0%	168.0%	104.0%	64.0%	100.0%
Interest income	100.0%	100.0%	100.0%	63.6%	54.5%	100.0%
Minority interest	12.5%	125.0%	187.5%	137.5%	112.5%	100.0%
Income before taxes	9.9%	40.8%	61.4%	73.0%	112.4%	100.0%
Income taxes	8.6%	8.6%	60.0%	71.4%	110.0%	100.0%
Net income	10.8%	61.0%	62.3%	74.0%	113.9%	100.0%

Horizontal Common Size—Rolling Forward Method

	1998	1997	1996	1995	1994	1993
Revenues	88.1%	104.4%	99.9%	106.0%	113.6%	100.0%
Cost of sales	88.8%	107.0%	101.4%	107.5%	114.3%	100.0%
Selling, general, and administrative expenses	95.6%	105.8%	99.4%	120.2%	113.5%	100.0%
Interest expense	95.3%	152.4%	161.5%	162.5%	64.0%	100.0%
Interest income	100.0%	100.0%	157.1%	116.7%	54.5%	100.0%
Minority interest	10.0%	66.7%	136.4%	122.2%	112.5%	100.0%
Income before taxes	24.3%	66.4%	84.2%	65.0%	112.4%	100.0%
Income taxes	100.0%	14.3%	84.0%	64.9%	110.0%	100.0%
Net income	17.6%	97.8%	84.2%	65.0%	113.9%	100.0%

Compound Annual Growth Rate

	1993	1994	1995	1996	1997	1998	Growth
Revenues	($2,893)	0	0	0	0	$3,205	2.1%
Cost of sales	($1,720)	0	0	0	0	2,037	3.4%
Selling, general, and administrative expenses	($788)	0	0	0	0	1,081	6.5%
Interest expense	($25)	0	0	0	0	61	19.5%
Interest income	$11	0	0	0	0	−11	0.0%
Minority interest	($8)	0	0	0	0	1	
Income before taxes	($363)	0	0	0	0	36	
Income taxes	($140)	0	0	0	0	12	
Net income	($223)	0	0	0	0	24	

Reebok Balance Sheets
(in millions)

	1998	1997	1996	1995	1994	1993
Assets						
Cash	$180	$210	$233	$81	$84	$79
Accounts receivable, net	518	562	591	506	532	457
Inventory	535	564	544	635	625	514
Other current assets	128	129	95	121	96	77
Total current assets	1,361	1,465	1,463	1,343	1,337	1,127
Property, plant, and equipment, net	173	157	185	192	165	131
Intangible assets	69	66	70	64	96	94
Other long-term assets	136	68	68	57	51	39
Total long-term assets	378	291	323	313	312	264
Total assets	$1,739	$1,756	$1,786	$1,656	$1,649	$1,391
Liabilities and shareholders' equity						
Current portion of long-term debt	$87	$121	$53	$1	$5	$3
Notes payable	48	41	33	67	64	24
Accounts payable	203	192	196	166	171	138
Other current liabilities	274	224	235	198	265	231
Total current liabilities	612	578	517	432	505	396
Long-term debt	554	639	854	254	132	134
Other long-term liabilities	—	—	—	5	—	—
Total long-term liabilities	554	639	854	259	132	134
Total liabilities	1,166	1,217	1,371	691	637	530
Minority interest	32	32	34	31	22	14
Outstanding redemption value—equity put options	17	—	—	39	—	—
Shareholders' equity						
Common stock	1	1	1	1	1	1
Additional paid-in-capital	—	—	—	—	167	267
Retained earnings	1,157	1,145	993	1,487	1,428	1,198
Treasury stock	−618	−618	−618	−603	−603	−603
Other shareholders' equity	−16	−21	5	10	−3	−16
Total shareholders' equity	524	507	381	895	990	847
Total liabilities and shareholders' equity	$1,739	$1,756	$1,786	$1,656	$1,649	$1,391

Reebok Balance Sheets
(in millions)
(continued)

Vertical Common Size

	1998	1997	1996	1995	1994	1993
Assets						
Cash	10.4%	12.0%	13.0%	4.9%	5.1%	5.7%
Accounts receivable, net	29.8%	32.0%	33.1%	30.6%	32.3%	32.9%
Inventory	30.8%	32.1%	30.5%	38.3%	37.9%	37.0%
Other current assets	7.4%	7.3%	5.3%	7.3%	5.8%	5.5%
Total current assets	78.3%	83.4%	81.9%	81.1%	81.1%	81.0%
Property, plant, and equipment, net	9.9%	8.9%	10.4%	11.6%	10.0%	9.4%
Intangible assets	4.0%	3.8%	3.9%	3.9%	5.8%	6.8%
Other long-term assets	7.8%	3.9%	3.8%	3.4%	3.1%	2.8%
Total long-term assets	21.7%	16.6%	18.1%	18.9%	18.9%	19.0%
Total assets	100.0%	100.0%	100.0%	100.0%	100.0%	100.0%
Liabilities and shareholders' equity	0.0%	0.0%	0.0%	0.0%	0.0%	0.0%
Current portion of long-term debt	5.0%	6.9%	3.0%	0.1%	0.3%	0.2%
Notes payable	2.8%	2.3%	1.8%	4.0%	3.9%	1.7%
Accounts payable	11.7%	10.9%	11.0%	10.0%	10.4%	9.9%
Other current liabilities	15.8%	12.8%	13.2%	12.0%	16.1%	16.6%
Total current liabilities	35.2%	32.9%	28.9%	26.1%	30.6%	28.5%
Long-term debt	31.9%	36.4%	47.8%	15.3%	8.0%	9.6%
Other long-term liabilities	0.0%	0.0%	0.0%	0.3%	0.0%	0.0%
Total long-term liabilities	31.9%	36.4%	47.8%	15.6%	8.0%	9.6%
Total liabilities	67.1%	69.3%	76.8%	41.7%	38.6%	38.1%
Minority interest	1.8%	1.8%	1.9%	1.9%	1.3%	1.0%
Outstanding redemption value-equity put options	1.0%	0.0%	0.0%	2.4%	0.0%	0.0%
Shareholders' equity						
Common stock	0.1%	0.1%	0.1%	0.1%	0.1%	0.1%
Additional paid-in-capital	0.0%	0.0%	0.0%	0.0%	10.1%	19.2%
Retained earnings	66.5%	65.2%	55.6%	89.8%	86.6%	86.1%
Treasury stock	−35.5%	−35.2%	−34.6%	−36.4%	−36.6%	−43.4%
Other shareholders' equity	−0.9%	−1.2%	0.3%	0.6%	−0.2%	−1.2%
Total shareholders' equity	30.1%	28.9%	21.3%	54.0%	60.0%	60.9%
Total liabilities and shareholders' equity	100.0%	100.0%	100.0%	100.0%	100.0%	100.0%

Reebok Balance Sheets
(in millions)
(continued)

Horizontal Common Size—1993 Base Year

	1998	1997	1996	1995	1994	1993
Assets						
Cash	227.8%	265.8%	294.9%	102.5%	106.3%	100.0%
Accounts receivable, net	113.3%	123.0%	129.3%	110.7%	116.4%	100.0%
Inventory	104.1%	109.7%	105.8%	123.5%	121.6%	100.0%
Other current assets	166.2%	167.5%	123.4%	157.1%	124.7%	100.0%
Total current assets	120.8%	130.0%	129.8%	119.2%	118.6%	100.0%
Property, plant, and equipment, net	132.1%	119.8%	141.2%	146.6%	126.0%	100.0%
Intangible assets	73.4%	70.2%	74.5%	68.1%	102.1%	100.0%
Other long-term assets	348.7%	174.4%	174.4%	146.2%	130.8%	100.0%
Total long-term assets	143.2%	110.2%	122.3%	118.6%	118.2%	100.0%
Total assets	125.0%	126.2%	128.4%	119.1%	118.5%	100.0%
Liabilities and shareholders' equity						
Current portion of long-term debt	2900.0%	4033.3%	1766.7%	33.3%	166.7%	100.0%
Notes payable	200.0%	170.8%	137.5%	279.2%	266.70%	100.0%
Accounts payable	147.1%	139.1%	142.0%	120.3%	123.90%	100.0%
Other current liabilities	118.6%	97.0%	101.7%	85.7%	114.70%	100.0%
Total current liabilities	154.5%	146.0%	130.6%	109.1%	127.50%	100.0%
Long-term debt	413.4%	476.9%	637.3%	189.6%	98.50%	100.0%
Other long-term liabilities						
Total long-term liabilities	413.4%	476.9%	637.3%	193.3%	98.5%	100.0%
Total liabilities	220.0%	229.6%	258.7%	130.4%	120.2%	100.0%
Minority interest	228.6%	228.6%	242.9%	221.4%	157.1%	100.0%
Outstanding redemption value—equity put options						
Shareholders' equity						
Common stock	100.0%	100.0%	100.0%	100.0%	100.0%	100.0%
Additional paid-in-capital	0.0%	0.0%	0.0%	0.0%	62.5%	100.0%
Retained earnings	96.6%	95.6%	82.9%	124.1%	119.2%	100.0%
Treasury stock	102.5%	102.5%	102.5%	100.0%	100.0%	100.0%
Other shareholders' equity	100.0%	131.3%	−31.3%	−62.5%	18.8%	100.0%
Total shareholders' equity	61.9%	59.9%	45.0%	105.7%	116.9%	100.0%
Total liabilities and shareholders' equity	125.0%	126.2%	128.4%	119.1%	118.5%	100.0%

Horizontal Common Size—Rolling Forward

	1998	1997	1996	1995	1994	1993
Assets						
Cash	85.7%	90.1%	287.7%	96.4%	106.3%	100.0%
Accounts receivable, net	92.2%	95.1%	116.8%	95.1%	116.4%	100.0%
Inventory	94.9%	103.7%	85.7%	101.6%	121.6%	100.0%
Other current assets	99.2%	135.8%	78.5%	126.0%	124.7%	100.0%
Total current assets	92.9%	100.1%	108.9%	100.4%	118.6%	100.0%
Property, plant, and equipment, net	110.2%	84.9%	96.4%	116.4%	126.0%	100.0%
Intangible assets	104.5%	94.3%	109.4%	66.7%	102.1%	100.0%
Other long-term assets	200.0%	100.0%	119.3%	111.8%	130.8%	100.0%
Total long-term assets	129.9%	90.1%	103.2%	100.3%	118.2%	100.0%
Total assets	99.0%	98.3%	107.9%	100.4%	118.5%	100.0%
Liabilities and shareholders' equity						
Current portion of long-term debt	71.9%	228.3%	5300.0%	20.0%	166.7%	100.0%
Notes payable	117.1%	124.2%	49.3%	104.7%	266.7%	100.0%
Accounts payable	105.7%	98.0%	118.1%	97.1%	123.9%	100.0%
Other current liabilities	122.3%	95.3%	118.7%	74.7%	114.7%	100.0%
Total current liabilities	105.9%	111.8%	119.7%	85.5%	127.5%	100.0%
Long-term debt	86.7%	74.8%	336.2%	192.4%	98.5%	100.0%
Other long-term liabilities						
Total long-term liabilities	86.7%	74.8%	329.7%	196.2%	98.5%	100.0%
Total liabilities	95.8%	88.8%	198.4%	108.5%	120.2%	100.0%
Minority interest	100.0%	94.1%	109.7%	140.9%	157.1%	100.0%
Outstanding redemption value—equity put options						
Shareholders' equity						
Common stock	100.0%	100.0%	100.0%	100.0%	100.0%	100.0%
Additional paid-in-capital	—	—	—	0.0%	62.5%	100.0%
Retained earnings	101.0%	115.3%	66.8%	104.1%	119.2%	100.0%
Treasury stock	100.0%	100.0%	102.5%	100.0%	100.0%	100.0%
Other shareholders' equity	76.2%	−420.0%	50.0%	−333.3%	18.8%	100.0%
Total shareholders' equity	103.4%	133.1%	42.6%	90.4%	116.9%	100.0%
Total liabilities and shareholders' equity	99.0%	98.3%	107.9%	100.4%	118.5%	100.0%

Compound Annual Growth Rate

	1993	1994	1995	1996	1997	1998	Growth
Assets							
Cash	($79)	0	0	0	0	180	17.9%
Accounts receivable, net	($457)	0	0	0	0	518	2.5%
Inventory	($514)	0	0	0	0	535	0.8%
Other current assets	($77)	0	0	0	0	128	10.7%
Total current assets	($1,127)	0	0	0	0	1,361	3.8%
Property, plant, and equipment, net	($131)	0	0	0	0	173	–5.7%
Intangible assets	($94)	0	0	0	0	69	–6.0%
Other long-term assets	($39)	0	0	0	0	136	28.4%
Total long-term assets	($264)	0	0	0	0	378	7.4%
Total assets	($1,391)	0	0	0	0	1,739	4.6%
Liabilities and shareholders' equity							
Current portion of long-term debt	($3)	0	0	0	0	$87	96.1%
Notes payable	($24)	0	0	0	0	48	14.9%
Accounts payable	($138)	0	0	0	0	203	8.0%
Other current liabilities	($231)	0	0	0	0	274	3.5%
Total current liabilities	($396)	0	0	0	0	612	9.1%
Long-term debt	($134)	0	0	0	0	554	32.8%
Other long-term liabilities							
Total long-term liabilities	($134)	0	0	0	0	554	32.8%
Total liabilities	($530)	0	0	0	0	$1,166	17.1%
Minority interest	($14)	0	0	0	0	32	18.0%
Outstanding redemption value—equity put options	$—	0	0	0	0	17	
Shareholders' equity							
Common stock	($1)	0	0	0	0	$1	0.0%
Additional paid-in-capital	($267)	0	0	0	0	—	
Retained earnings	($1,198)	0	0	0	0	1,157	–0.7%
Treasury stock	$603	0	0	0	0	–618	0.5%
Other shareholders' equity	$16	0	0	0	0	–16	0.0%
Total shareholders' equity	($847)	0	0	0	0	524	–9.2%
Total liabilities and shareholders' equity	($1,391)	0	0	0	0	1,739	4.6%

Reebok International Condensed Statements of Cash Flows (in millions of dollars)

	1998	1997	1996	1995	1994
Net income	$ 24	$136	$139	$165	$254
Depreciation expense	48	47	43	35	32
Other adjustments to operations	80	−56	98	−31	−113
Cash flows from operating activities	152	127	280	169	173
Purchase of property, plant, and equipment	−54	−24	−30	−64	−62
Other adjustments to investing activities	1	—	7	1	−4
Cash flows from investing activities	−53	−24	−23	−63	−66
Dividends	—	—	−7	−24	−25
Other adjustments to financing activities	−137	−116	−99	−91	−64
Cash flows from financing activities	−137	−116	−106	−115	−89
Other adjustments to cash	−6	−9	1	6	−13
Net change in cash	$ −44	$ −22	$152	$ −3	$ 5

Reebok Income Statements (in millions)

	1998	1997	1996	1995	1994
Revenues	$3,205	$3,636	$3,482	$3,484	$3,287
Cost of sales	2,037	2,294	2,144	2,114	1,966
Selling, general and administrative expenses	1,081	1,131	1,069	1,075	894
Interest expense	61	64	42	26	16
Interest income	−11	−11	−11	−7	−6
Minority interest	1	10	15	11	9
Income before taxes	36	148	223	265	408
Income taxes	12	12	84	100	154
Net income	$24	$136	$139	$165	$254

Reebok AVERAGE *Balance Sheets (in millions)*

	1998	1997	1996	1995	1994
Assets					
Cash	$195.00	$221.50	$157.00	$82.50	$81.50
Accounts receivable, net	$540.00	$576.50	$548.50	$519.00	$494.50
Inventory	$549.50	$554.00	$589.50	$630.00	$569.50
Other current assets	$128.50	$112.00	$108.00	$108.50	$86.50
Total current assets	$1,413.00	$1,464.00	$1,403.00	$1,340.00	$1,232.00
Property, plant, and equipment, net	$165.00	$171.00	$188.50	$178.50	$148.00
Intangible assets	$67.50	$68.00	$67.00	$80.00	$95.00
Other long-term assets	$102.00	$68.00	$62.50	$54.00	$45.00
Total long-term assets	$334.50	$307.00	$318.00	$312.50	$288.00
Total assets	$1,747.50	$1,771.00	$1,721.00	$1,652.50	$1,520.00
Liabilities and shareholders' equity					
Current portion of long-term debt	$104.00	$87.00	$27.00	$3.00	$4.00
Notes payable	$44.50	$37.00	$50.00	$65.50	$44.00
Accounts payable	$197.50	$194.00	$181.00	$168.50	$154.50
Other current liabilities	$249.00	$229.50	$216.50	$231.50	$248.00
Total current liabilities	$595.00	$547.50	$474.50	$468.50	$450.50
Long-term debt	$596.50	$746.50	$554.00	$193.00	$133.00
Other long-term liabilities	—	—	$2.50	$2.50	—
Total long-term liabilities	$596.50	$746.50	$556.50	$195.50	$133.00
Total liabilities	$1,191.50	$1,294.00	$1,031.00	$664.00	$583.50
Minority interest	$32.00	$33.00	$32.50	$26.50	$18.00
Outstanding redemption value—equity put options	$8.50	—	$19.50	$19.50	—
Shareholders' equity					
Common stock	$1.00	$1.00	$1.00	$1.00	$1.00
Additional paid-in-capital	—	—	—	$83.50	$217.00
Retained earnings	$1,151.00	$1,069.00	$1,240.00	$1,457.50	$1,313.00
Treasury stock	($618.00)	($618.00)	($610.50)	($603.00)	($603.00)
Other shareholders' equity	($18.50)	($8.00)	$7.50	$3.50	($9.50)
Total shareholders' equity	$515.50	$444.00	$638.00	$942.50	$918.50
Total liabilities and shareholders' equity	$1,747.50	$1,771.00	$1,721.00	$1,652.50	$1,520.00

Cash Flow Data

	1998	1997	1996	1995	1994
Cash flow from operations	$152	$127	$280	$169	$173
Fixed asset purchases	54	24	30	64	62
Cash dividends	—	—	7	24	25
Depreciation and amortization	48	47	43	35	32

Reebok AVERAGE *Balance Sheets (in millions) (continued)*

Market Data

	1998	1997	1996	1995	1994
High market price	$33.20	$52.90	$45.30	$39.60	$40.10
Low market price	$12.60	$27.60	$25.40	$24.10	$28.40
Number of shares outstanding (millions)	56.59	56.40	55.84	74.80	80.94
Market capitalization	$1,295.91	$2,270.10	$1,973.94	$2,382.38	$2,772.20

Reebok International Ratios

Liquidity Ratios

	1998	1997	1996	1995	1994
Working capital	$818.00	$916.50	$928.50	$871.50	$781.50
Working capital ratio	2.37	2.67	2.96	2.86	2.73
Quick ratio	1.24	1.46	1.49	1.28	1.28
Inventory turnover	3.71	4.14	3.64	3.36	3.45
Days in inventory	98.46	88.15	100.36	108.77	105.73
Accounts receivable turnover	5.94	6.31	6.35	6.71	6.65
Days in accounts receivable	61.50	57.87	57.50	54.37	54.91
Inventory conversion cycle	159.96	146.02	157.85	163.15	160.64
Accounts payable turnover	10.31	11.82	11.85	12.55	12.72
Days in accounts payable	35.39	30.87	30.81	29.09	28.68
Net cash conversion cycle	124.57	115.15	127.04	134.05	131.96
Cash + short-term investments	195.00	221.50	157.00	82.50	81.50
A/R*days in accounts receivable	33,208.74	33,363.19	31,536.78	28,219.51	27,153.50
Inventory*days in inventory	54,104.98	48,833.63	59,161.03	68,528.15	60,213.91
Product dollar days	87,508.71	82,418.32	90,854.81	96,830.15	87,448.90
Current assets-other current assets	1,284.50	1,352.00	1,295.00	1,231.50	1,145.50
Liquidity index	68.13	60.96	70.16	78.63	76.34

Cash Flow Ratios

	1998	1997	1996	1995	1994
Cash flow adequacy	2.815	5.292	7.568	1.92	1.989
Reinvestment ratio	0.355	0.189	0.107	0.379	0.358
Dividend payout	-	-	0.025	0.142	0.145
Free cash flow	$98	$103	$243	$81	$86
Depreciation impact ratio	0.316	0.370	0.154	0.207	0.185
Recapitalization index	1.125	0.511	0.698	1.829	1.938
Cash flow return on assets	0.087	0.072	0.163	0.102	0.114
Cash flow return on sales	0.047	0.035	0.080	0.049	0.053
Operations index	4.222	0.858	1.256	0.638	0.424

Reebok International Ratios
(continued)

Asset Utilization Ratios

	1998	1997	1996	1995	1994
Profit margin	0.75%	3.74%	3.99%	4.74%	7.73%
Asset turnover	1.83	2.05	2.02	2.11	2.16
Financial structure leverage	3.39	3.99	2.70	1.75	1.65
Return on assets	1.37%	7.68%	8.08%	9.98%	16.71%
Return on equity	4.66%	30.63%	21.79%	17.51%	27.65%

Capital Structure Ratios

	1998	1997	1996	1995	1994
Debt to capital	0.68	0.73	0.60	0.40	0.38
Debt to equity	2.31	2.91	1.62	0.70	0.64
Long-term debt to capital	0.34	0.42	0.32	0.12	0.09
Long-term debt to equity	1.16	1.68	0.87	0.21	0.14
Working capital/total assets-Z1	0.56	0.62	0.65	0.63	0.62
Retained earnings/total assets-Z2	0.92	0.85	1.01	1.23	1.21
EBIT/total assets-Z3	0.18	0.40	0.51	0.58	0.92
Sales/total assets-Z4	1.83	2.05	2.02	2.11	2.16
Market to book-Z5	0.65	1.05	1.15	2.15	2.85
Z-Score	4.15	4.97	5.34	6.71	7.76

Market Ratio

	1998	1997	1996	1995	1994
Price to earnings	54.00	16.69	14.20	14.44	10.91

DISCOUNT RETAILER INDUSTRY

$\mathcal{D}$iscount merchants are a cross between general merchandising concerns and the department store industry, operating within the retailing sector of the economy. These companies are characterized by high-volume and rapid turnover of diverse product lines. Wal-Mart, Kmart, and Target were the three largest discount mass merchants from 1993 to 1998. This appendix presents an overview of the discount retailing industry and its three largest companies during that time period. It provides material to be used in conjunction with the three firms' financial statements, which appear at the conclusion of this appendix.[1]

---

[1] Appendix D yearly disclosures precede the fiscal year end by one month: 1998 disclosures represent the fiscal period ending January 31, 1999 and so on.

BACKGROUND

Mass merchant discounters surpassed department stores as the leading retail outlets in the last two decades of the 20th century. Discounters grew by offering shoppers value and convenience. By improving their image, discounters reduced the stigma often attached to discount shopping.

Wal-Mart Stores was the country's largest retailer during the period examined. It surpassed Kmart in the 1980s as the industry leader and increased its industry leadership position during the 1990s. Exhibit D-1 depicts Wal-Mart's number of discount, supercenter, and Sam's Club stores.[2]

EXHIBIT D-1

Wal-Mart Stores, Inc.
Number of Stores
1993–1998

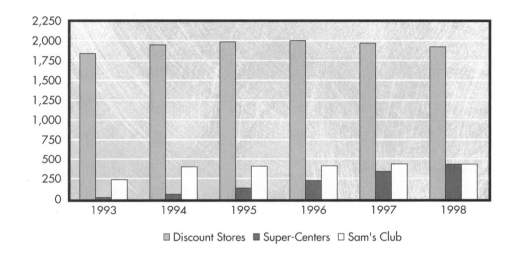

■ Discount Stores ■ Super-Centers □ Sam's Club

The Target stores segment of the Dayton-Hudson Corp. expanded by positioning itself as an upscale discounter.[3] Dayton-Hudson's discount and full service stores' revenues demonstrate the growth of the discount-retailing segment. Exhibit D-2 contrasts sales per square foot for the parent company's Department Store Division (DSD) and Target outlets.[4]

---

[2] Wal-Mart Stores 1998 Form 10-K.
[3] Numerous analysts have pointed out the seeming oxymoron in being an *upscale* discounter.
[4] Dayton-Hudson Corp.'s 1995–1998 Form 10-Ks.

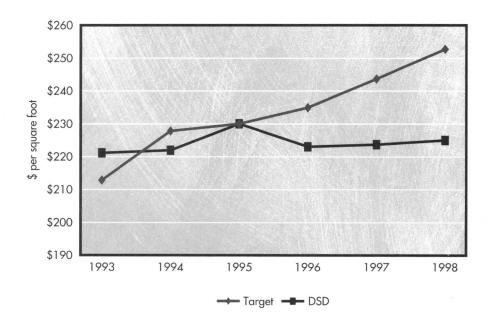

PRODUCTS AND MARKETS

Discount retailers generate revenues by offering wide product variety. Exhibit D-3 illustrates this diversity by presenting Wal-Mart's 1998 product line percentage revenues.[5]

EXHIBIT D-3
Wal-Mart Stores, Inc.
1998 Product Line Revenues
(in percent)

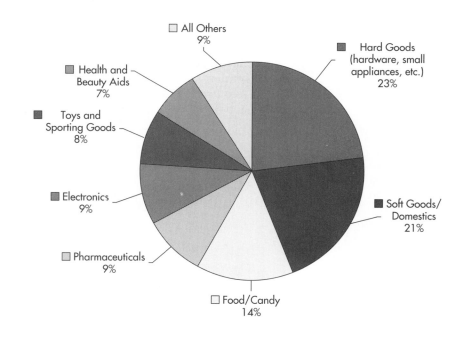

---

[5] Wal-Mart Stores 1998 Form 10-K.

Discounters appeal to less affluent consumers. The median family income for Wal-Mart and Kmart shoppers was $25,000 in 1998, and Target's customers averaged $43,000 of income that year. Discount shoppers tend to favor low, everyday prices as opposed to periodic sales. They are also sensitive to economic conditions. Discounters sell more during economic prosperity, when their customers have more disposable income.

GROWTH STRATEGIES

Discounters operated primarily within the United States during the early years analyzed. Increased competition among industry leaders and revamped business strategies from other categories of retailers spurred foreign investment. Wal-Mart led in store openings beyond the Unite States' borders. Exhibit D-4 presents the growth in the industry leader's foreign operations.[6]

EXHIBIT D-4
Wal-Mart Stores, Inc.
Foreign Stores

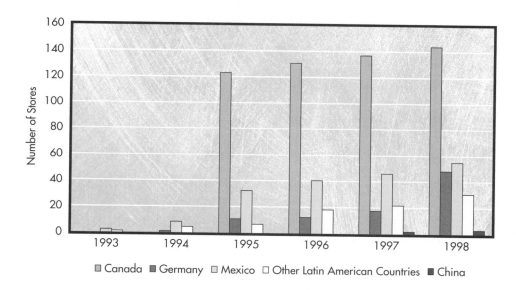

Number of Stores

□ Canada ■ Germany □ Mexico ☐ Other Latin American Countries ■ China

TECHNOLOGY

Discounters invested heavily in improving their information systems throughout the period analyzed. Those technological innovations greatly affected the discount business during the 1990s. Point-of-sale scanners, bar-coded merchandise, and computerized warehouses became accepted business practices in the early 1990s. Discounters used these and other technologies to improve inventory management. Companies enhanced operating cycles by reducing inventory, order time, and stock-outs. Technology also enabled discounters to develop greater

---

[6] Wal-Mart Stores 1998 Form 10-K. The numbers in the graph combine discount, supercenter, and Sam's Club stores. It includes stores resulting from consolidations with Wertkauf (Germany), and McLane's (Canada) but excludes those from Cifra (Mexico).

insights into its customers' shopping habits and preferences. This knowledge resulted in more appealing product placement, mix, and pricing. Discount merchants also developed or were creating Web-based operations by the end of the period analyzed. They were not, however, leaders in electronic retailing. Management of all three discounters wrestled with how to combine e-commerce with their traditional storefront operations.

SIGNIFICANT EVENTS

1993

- Industry tries to increase profitability by selling more private label merchandise; it attempts to force toy companies to sell products on a consignment basis, thereby shifting inventory holding cost to the manufacturers.
- Wal-Mart purchases over 100 Pace Membership stores from Kmart; splits stock two for one.
- Kmart sells PayLess drugstore unit for $1 billion; Standard & Poor's and Moody's Investor Service downgrades its debt rating.

1994

- Retailers expanding store hours to meet market demand.
- Wal-Mart establishes joint ventures in Brazil and Hong Kong.
- Kmart considers issuing stock tied to the earnings of its specialty stores—Sports Authority, Borders, OfficeMax, and Builders Square; institutional investors oppose plan; the company closes 110 Kmart stores.
- Robert J. Ulrich succeeds Kenneth A. Macke as Target's chief executive officer (CEO); company issues its own credit card.

1995

- Wal-Mart announces stock repurchase plan; delays Mexican expansion.
- Kmart eliminates dividend, sells OfficeMax and Sports Authority, closes 72 Kmart stores, has its debt downgraded, fires Joseph E. Antonini as chairman, CEO, and president, and appoints Floyd Hall, formerly of Target stores, as Antonini's successor.
- Target's Mervyn's unit performs poorly.

1996

- Wal-Mart expands store openings and joint ventures in Latin America.
- Kmart's debt is reduced to junk bond status; the company considers issuing $870 million in convertible preferred stock as an initial restructuring step; and it communicates to concerned vendors that the majority of its financial problems are over.
- Target splits stock three for one and sells its Marshall Fields stores in Texas.

1997

◆ Wal-Mart is added to the list of companies composing Dow Industrial Average, which measures stock price movements; the company acquires an interest in Mexican and German retailers and buys out its Brazilian partner; announces stock buyback.
◆ Kmart's debt is upgraded; the company sells its Builders Square unit.
◆ Target's board closes 35 Mervyn's stores.

1998

◆ Both Wal-Mart and Kmart expand their grocery operations.
◆ Wal-Mart names Lee Scott as president; establishes a presence in South Korea and expands its German operations; ends its experiment with McDonald's by closing the "mini-McDonald's" restaurants in its stores.
◆ Target announces a two for one stock split; the company's board of directors gives management 18 months to improve business at its Mervyn's unit. (information disclosed because companies have a January 31 fiscal year-end)

1999

◆ Wal-Mart revamps its international operations in an effort to decrease costs; penetrates the United Kingdom market with the announced acquisition of the Asda Group; management seeks to improve its Web business, which lags those of other retailers.
◆ Kmart's credit rating is upgraded by Standard and Poor's; the company announces a $1 billion stock repurchase program; $230 million is charged against revenues for lease commitments made on behalf of its Builders Square and Hechinger units; announces a Web alliance with Yahoo!
◆ Target announces that its Target Stores division is responsible for corporate profitability.

	1998	1997	1996	1995	1994	1993
Sales	$33,674	$32,183	$31,437	$31,713	$29,563	$33,295
Cost of sales, buying, and occupancy	26,319	25,152	24,390	24,675	22,331	24,950
Gross margin	7,355	7,031	7,047	7,038	7,232	8,345
Selling, general, and administrative expenses	6,245	6,136	6,274	6,876	6,651	7,477
Voluntary early retirement programs	19	114	—	—	—	—
Other gains, net	—	—	–10	41	—	1,348
Continuing income before other activities	1,091	781	783	121	581	-480
Interest expense, net	293	363	453	434	479	302
Income tax provision	230	120	68	–83	6	192
Dividends securities of subsidiary	50	49	31	—	—	—
Net income before discontinued operations and extraordinary item	518	249	231	-230	96	-974
Discontinued operations, net	—	—	–5	–260	83	-77
Loss (gain) on discount operations, net of tax	—	—	446	30	–117	521
Extraordinary item, net	—	—	—	–51	—	–10
Net income (loss)	$518	$249	($220)	($571)	$296	($1,582)
Basic earnings per share	$1.05	$0.51	($0.45)	($1.25)	$0.63	$2.15

Vertical Common Size

	1998	1997	1996	1995	1994	1993
Sales	100.0%	100.0%	100.0%	100.0%	100.0%	100.0%
Cost of sales, buying, and occupancy	78.2%	78.2%	77.6%	77.8%	75.5%	74.9%
Gross margin	21.8%	21.8%	22.4%	22.2%	24.5%	25.1%
Selling, general, and administrative expenses	18.5%	19.1%	20.0%	21.7%	22.5%	22.5%
Voluntary early retirement programs	0.1%	0.4%	0.0%	0.0%	0.0%	0.0%
Other gains, net	0.0%	0.0%	0.0%	0.1%	0.0%	4.0%
Continuing income before other activities	3.2%	2.4%	2.5%	0.4%	2.0%	–1.4%
Interest expense, net	0.9%	1.1%	1.4%	1.4%	1.6%	0.9%
Income tax provision	0.7%	0.4%	0.2%	–0.3%	0.0%	0.6%
Dividends securities of subsidiary	0.1%	0.2%	0.1%	0.0%	0.0%	0.0%
Net income before discontinued operations and extra. Item	1.5%	0.8%	0.7%	–0.7%	0.3%	–2.9%
Discontinued operations, net	0.0%	0.0%	0.0%	–0.8%	0.3%	–0.2%

Vertical Common Size (continued)

	1998	1997	1996	1995	1994	1993
Loss (gain) on discount operations, net of tax	0.0%	0.0%	1.4%	0.1%	−0.4%	1.6%
Extraordinary item, net	0.0%	0.0%	0.0%	−0.2%	0.0%	0.0%
Net income (loss)	1.5%	0.8%	−0.7%	−1.8%	1.0%	−4.8%

Horizontal Common Size-1993 Base Year

	1998	1997	1996	1995	1994	1993
Sales	101.1%	96.7%	94.4%	95.2%	88.8%	100.0%
Cost of sales, buying, and occupancy	105.5%	100.8%	97.8%	98.9%	89.5%	100.0%
Gross margin	88.1%	84.3%	84.4%	84.3%	86.7%	100.0%
Selling, general, and administrative expenses	83.5%	82.1%	83.9%	92.0%	89.0%	100.0%
Voluntary early retirement programs						
Other gains, net	0.0%	0.0%	−0.7%	3.0%	0.0%	100.0%
Continuing income before other activities	−227.3%	−162.7%	−163.1%	−25.2%	−121.0%	100.0%
Interest expense, net	97.0%	120.2%	150.0%	143.7%	158.6%	100.0%
Income tax provision	119.8%	62.5%	35.4%	−43.2%	3.1%	100.0%
Dividends securities of subsidiary						
Net income before discontinued operations and extra. Item	−53.2%	−25.6%	−23.7%	23.6%	−9.9%	100.0%
Discontinued operations, net	0.0%	0.0%	6.5%	337.7%	−107.8%	100.0%
Loss (gain) on discount operations, net of tax	0.0%	0.0%	85.6%	5.8%	−22.5%	100.0%
Extraordinary item, net	0.0%	0.0%	0.0%	510.0%	0.0%	100.0%
Net income (loss)	−32.7%	−15.7%	13.9%	36.1%	−18.7%	100.0%

Horizontal Common Size-Rolling Forward

	1998	1997	1996	1995	1994	1993
Sales	104.6%	102.4%	99.1%	107.3%	88.8%	100.0%
Cost of sales, buying, and occupancy	104.6%	103.1%	98.8%	110.5%	89.5%	100.0%
Gross margin	104.6%	99.8%	100.1%	97.3%	86.7%	100.0%
Selling, general, and administrative expenses	101.8%	97.8%	91.2%	103.4%	89.0%	100.0%
Voluntary early retirement programs	16.7%					
Other gains, net		0.0%	−24.4%		0.0%	100.0%
Continuing income before other activities	139.7%	99.7%	647.1%	20.8%	−121.0%	100.0%
Interest expense, net	80.7%	80.1%	104.4%	90.6%	158.6%	100.0%

Horizontal Common Size-Rolling Forward (continued)

	1998	1997	1996	1995	1994	1993
Income tax provision	191.7%	176.5%	−81.9%	−1383.3%	3.1%	100.0%
Dividends securities of subsidiary	102.0%	158.1%				
Net income before discontinued operations and extra. Item	208.0%	107.8%	−100.4%	−239.6%	−9.9%	100.0%
Discontinued operations, net		0.0%	1.9%	−313.3%	−107.8%	100.0%
Loss (gain) on discount operations, net of tax		0.0%	1486.7%	−25.6%	−22.5%	100.0%
Extraordinary item, net			0.0%		0.0%	100.0%
Net income (loss)	208.0%	−113.2%	38.5%	−192.9%	−18.7%	100.0%

Compound Annual Growth Rate

	1993	1994	1995	1996	1997	1998	Growth
Sales	($33,295)	$—	$—	$—	$—	$33,674	0.2%
Cost of sales, buying, and occupancy	($24,950)	$—	$—	$—	$—	26,319	1.1%
Gross margin	($8,345)	$—	$—	$—	$—	7,355	−2.5%
Selling, general, and administrative expenses	($7,477)	$—	$—	$—	$—	6,245	−3.5%
Voluntary early retirement programs	$—	$—	$—	$—	$—	19	
Other gains, net	($1,348)	$—	$—	$—	$—	—	
Continuing income before other activities	$480	$—	$—	$—	$—	1,091	
Interest expense, net	($302)	$—	$—	$—	$—	293	−0.6%
Income tax provision	($192)	$—	$—	$—	$—	230	3.7%
Dividends securities of subsidiary	$—	$—	$—	$—	$—	50	
Net income before discontinued operations and extra. Item	$974	$—	$—	$—	$—	518	
Discontinued operations, net	$77	$—	$—	$—	$—	—	
Loss (gain) on discount operations, net of tax	($521)	$—	$—	$—	$—	—	
Extraordinary item, net	$10	$—	$—	$—	$—	—	
Net income (loss)	$1,582	$—	$—	$—	$—	$518	

Kmart
Balance Sheets
(in millions of dollars)

	1998	1997	1996	1995	1994	1993
Assets						
Current assets						
Cash and cash equivalents	$710	$498	$406	$1,083	$480	$449
Merchandise inventories	6,536	6,367	6,354	6,022	7,382	7,252
Other current assets	584	611	973	894	1,325	1,816
Discontinued operations	—	—	—	554	—	—
Total current assets	7,830	7,476	7,733	8,553	9,187	9,517
Property and equipment, net	5,914	5,472	5,740	5,365	6,280	5,886
Property held for sale or financing	—	—	200	434	—	—
Other assets and deferred charges	422	610	613	526	1,278	1,405
Discontinued operations	—	—	—	155	284	696
Total assets	$14,166	$13,558	$14,286	$15,033	$17,029	$17,504
Liabilities and Stockholders' Equity						
Current liabilities						
Long-term debt due within one year	$77	$78	$156	$7	$236	$390
Trade accounts payable	2,047	1,923	2,009	1,793	3,548	3,681
Accrued payroll and other liabilities	1,359	1,064	1,298	1,019	1,313	1,347
Taxes other than income taxes	208	209	139	176	529	306
Total current liabilities	3,691	3,274	3,602	2,995	5,626	5,724
Long-term debt and notes payable	1,538	1,725	2,121	3,922	2,011	2,227
Capital lease obligations	1,091	1,179	1,478	1,586	1,777	1,720
Other long-term liabilities	883	965	1,013	1,250	1,583	1,740
Total liabilities	7,203	7,143	8,214	9,753	10,997	11,411
Stockholders' equity						
Convertible preferred stock	984	981	980	—	132	1,140
Common stock	493	489	486	486	465	417
Capital in excess of par value	1,667	1,605	1,608	1,624	1,505	538
Retained earnings	3,819	3,340	3,105	3,326	4,074	4,237
Treasury shares and restricted stock	—	—	−37	−92	−86	−109
Foreign currency translation adjustment	—	—	−70	−64	−58	−130
Total shareholders' equity	6,963	6,415	6,072	5,280	6,032	6,093
Total liabilities and shareholders' equity	$14,166	$13,558	$14,286	$15,033	$17,029	$17,504

Kmart
Balance Sheets
(in millions of dollars)
(continued)

Vertical Common Size

	1998	1997	1996	1995	1994	1993
Assets						
Current assets						
Cash and cash equivalents	5.0%	3.7%	2.8%	7.2%	2.8%	2.6%
Merchandise inventories	46.1%	47.0%	44.5%	40.1%	43.3%	41.4%
Other current assets	4.1%	4.5%	6.8%	5.9%	7.8%	10.4%
Discontinued operations	0.0%	0.0%	0.0%	3.7%	0.0%	0.0%
Total current assets	55.3%	55.1%	54.1%	56.9%	53.9%	54.4%
Property and equipment, net	41.7%	40.4%	40.2%	35.7%	36.9%	33.6%
Property held for sale or financing	0.0%	0.0%	1.4%	2.9%	0.0%	0.0%
Other assets and deferred charges	3.0%	4.5%	4.3%	3.5%	7.5%	8.0%
Discontinued operations	0.0%	0.0%	0.0%	1.0%	1.7%	4.0%
Total assets	100.0%	100.0%	100.0%	100.0%	100.0%	100.0%
Liabilities and Stockholders' Equity						
Current liabilities						
Long-term debt due within one year	0.5%	0.6%	1.1%	0.0%	1.4%	2.2%
Trade accounts payable	14.5%	14.2%	14.1%	11.9%	20.8%	21.0%
Accrued payroll and other liabilities	9.6%	7.8%	9.1%	6.8%	7.7%	7.7%
Taxes other than income taxes	1.5%	1.5%	1.0%	1.2%	3.1%	1.7%
Total current liabilities	26.1%	24.1%	25.2%	19.9%	33.0%	32.7%
Long-term debt and notes payable	10.9%	12.7%	14.8%	26.1%	11.8%	12.7%
Capital lease obligations	7.7%	8.7%	10.3%	10.6%	10.4%	9.8%
Other long-term liabilities	6.2%	7.1%	7.1%	8.3%	9.3%	9.9%
Total liabilities	50.8%	52.7%	57.5%	64.9%	64.6%	65.2%
Stockholders' equity						
Convertible preferred stock	6.9%	7.2%	6.9%	0.0%	0.8%	6.5%
Common stock	3.5%	3.6%	3.4%	3.2%	2.7%	2.4%
Capital in excess of par value	11.8%	11.8%	11.3%	10.8%	8.8%	3.1%
Retained earnings	27.0%	24.6%	21.7%	22.1%	23.9%	24.2%
Treasury shares and restricted stock	0.0%	0.0%	−0.3%	−0.6%	−0.5%	−0.6%
Foreign currency translation adjustment	0.0%	0.0%	−0.5%	−0.4%	−0.3%	−0.7%
Total shareholders' equity	49.2%	47.3%	42.5%	35.1%	35.4%	34.8%
Total liabilities and shareholders' equity	100.0%	100.0%	100.0%	100.0%	100.0%	100.0%

Horizontal Common Size—1993 Base Year

	1998	1997	1996	1995	1994	1993
Assets						
Current assets						
Cash and cash equivalents	158.1%	110.9%	90.4%	241.2%	106.9%	100.0%
Merchandise inventories	90.1%	87.8%	87.6%	83.0%	101.8%	100.0%
Other current assets	32.2%	33.6%	53.6%	49.2%	73.0%	100.0%
Discontinued operations						
Total current assets	82.3%	78.6%	81.3%	89.9%	96.5%	100.0%
Property and equipment, net	100.5%	93.0%	97.5%	91.1%	106.7%	100.0%
Property held for sale or financing						
Other assets and deferred charges	30.0%	43.4%	43.6%	37.4%	91.0%	100.0%
Discontinued operations	0.0%	0.0%	0.0%	22.3%	40.8%	100.0%
Total assets	80.9%	77.5%	81.6%	85.9%	97.3%	100.0%
Liabilities and Stockholders' Equity						
Current liabilities						
Long-term debt due within one year	19.7%	20.0%	40.0%	1.8%	60.5%	100.0%
Trade accounts payable	55.6%	52.2%	54.6%	48.7%	96.4%	100.0%
Accrued payroll and other liabilities	100.9%	79.0%	96.4%	75.6%	97.5%	100.0%
Taxes other than income taxes	68.0%	68.3%	45.4%	57.5%	172.9%	100.0%
Total current liabilities	64.5%	57.2%	62.9%	52.3%	98.3%	100.0%
Long-term debt and notes payable	69.1%	77.5%	95.2%	176.1%	90.3%	100.0%
Capital lease obligations	63.4%	68.5%	85.9%	92.2%	103.3%	100.0%
Other long-term liabilities	50.7%	55.5%	58.2%	71.8%	91.0%	100.0%
Total liabilities	63.1%	62.6%	72.0%	85.5%	96.4%	100.0%
Stockholders' equity						
Convertible preferred stock	86.3%	86.1%	86.0%	0.0%	11.6%	100.0%
Common stock	118.2%	117.3%	116.5%	116.5%	111.5%	100.0%
Capital in excess of par value	309.9%	298.3%	298.9%	301.9%	279.7%	100.0%
Retained earnings	90.1%	78.8%	73.3%	78.5%	96.2%	100.0%
Treasury shares and restricted stock	0.0%	0.0%	33.9%	84.4%	78.9%	100.0%
Foreign currency translation adjustment	0.0%	0.0%	53.8%	49.2%	44.6%	100.0%
Total shareholders' equity	114.3%	105.3%	99.7%	86.7%	99.0%	100.0%
Total liabilities and shareholders' equity	80.9%	77.5%	81.6%	85.9%	97.3%	100.0%

Kmart
Balance Sheets
(in millions of dollars)
(continued)

	1998	1997	1996	1995	1994	1993
Assets						
Current assets						
Cash and cash equivalents	142.6%	122.7%	37.5%	225.6%	106.9%	100.0%
Merchandise inventories	102.7%	100.2%	105.5%	81.6%	101.8%	100.0%
Other current assets	95.6%	62.8%	108.8%	67.5%	73.0%	100.0%
Discontinued operations						
Total current assets	104.7%	96.7%	90.4%	93.1%	96.5%	100.0%
Property and equipment, net	108.1%	95.3%	107.0%	85.4%	106.7%	100.0%
Property held for sale or financing		0.0%	46.1%			
Other assets and deferred charges	69.2%	99.5%	116.5%	41.2%	91.0%	100.0%
Discontinued operations			0.0%	54.6%	40.8%	100.0%
Total assets	104.5%	94.9%	95.0%	88.3%	97.3%	100.0%
Liabilities and Stockholders' Equity						
Current liabilities						
Long-term debt due within one year	98.7%	50.0%	2228.6%	3.0%	60.5%	100.0%
Trade accounts payable	106.4%	95.7%	112.0%	50.5%	96.4%	100.0%
Accrued payroll and other liabilities	127.7%	82.0%	127.4%	77.6%	97.5%	100.0%
Taxes other than income taxes	99.5%	150.4%	79.0%	33.3%	172.9%	100.0%
Total current liabilities	112.7%	90.9%	120.3%	53.2%	98.3%	100.0%
Long-term debt and notes payable	89.2%	81.3%	54.1%	195.0%	90.3%	100.0%
Capital lease obligations	92.5%	79.8%	93.2%	89.3%	103.3%	100.0%
Other long-term liabilities	91.5%	95.3%	81.0%	79.0%	91.0%	100.0%
Total liabilities	100.8%	87.0%	84.2%	88.7%	96.4%	100.0%
Stockholders' equity						
Convertible preferred stock	100.3%	100.1%		0.0%	11.6%	100.0%
Common stock	100.8%	100.6%	100.0%	104.5%	111.5%	100.0%
Capital in excess of par value	103.9%	99.8%	99.0%	107.9%	279.7%	100.0%
Retained earnings	114.3%	107.6%	93.4%	81.6%	96.2%	100.0%
Treasury shares and restricted stock		0.0%	40.2%	107.0%	78.9%	100.0%
Foreign currency translation adjustment		0.0%	109.4%	110.3%	44.6%	100.0%
Total shareholders' equity	108.5%	105.6%	115.0%	87.5%	99.0%	100.0%
Total liabilities and shareholders' equity	104.5%	94.9%	95.0%	88.3%	97.3%	100.0%

Compound Annual Growth Rate

	1993	1994	1995	1996	1997	1998	Growth
Assets							
Current assets							
Cash and cash equivalents	($449)	—	—	—	—	$710	9.6%
Merchandise inventories	(7,252)	—	—	—	—	6,536	–2.1%
Other current assets	(1,816)	—	—	—	—	584	–20.3%
Discontinued operations	—	—	—	—	—		
Total current assets	(9,517)	—	—	—	—	7,830	–3.8%
Property and equipment, net	(5,886)	—	—	—	—	5,914	0.1%
Property held for sale or financing	—					—	
Other assets and deferred charges	(1,405)	—	—	—	—	422	–21.4%
Discontinued operations	(696)	—	—	—	—	—	
Total assets	(17,504)	—	—	—	—	14,166	–4.1%
Liabilities and Stockholders' Equity							
Current liabilities							
Long-term debt due within one year	(390)	—	—	—	—	77	
Trade accounts payable	(3,681)	—	—	—	—	2,047	–11.1%
Accrued payroll and other liabilities	(1,347)	—	—	—	—	1,359	0.2%
Taxes other than income taxes	(306)	—	—	—	—	208	–7.4%
Total current liabilities	(5,724)	—	—	—	—	3,691	–8.4%
Long-term debt and notes payable	(2,227)	—	—	—	—	1,538	–7.1%
Capital lease obligations	(1,720)	—	—	—	—	1,091	–8.7%
Other long-term liabilities	(1,740)	—	—	—	—	883	–12.7%
Total liabilities	(11,411)	—	—	—	—	7,203	–8.8%
Stockholders' equity							
Convertible preferred stock	(1,140)	—	—	—	—	984	–2.9%
Common stock	(417)	—	—	—	—	493	3.4%
Capital in excess of par value	(538)	—	—	—	—	1,667	25.4%
Retained earnings	(4,237)	—	—	—	—	3,819	–2.1%
Treasury shares and restricted stock	109	—	—	—	—	—	
Foreign currency translation adjustment	130	—	—	—	—	—	
Total shareholders' equity	(6,093)	—	—	—	—	6,963	2.7%
Total liabilities and shareholders' equity	(17,504)	—	—	—	—	14,166	–4.1%

Kmart
Condensed Statements of Cash Flows (in millions of dollars)

	1998	1997	1996	1995	1994
Net income	$518	$249	($220)	($571)	$296
Depreciation expense	671	660	654	685	639
Other adjustments to operations	48	(68)	334	(303)	(1,066)
Cash flows from operating activities	1,237	841	768	(189)	(131)
Purchase of property, plant, and equipment	(981)	(678)	(343)	(540)	(1,021)
Other adjustments to investing activities	186	493	(128)	940	2,151
Cash flows from investing activities	(795)	(185)	(471)	400	1,130
Dividends	—	—	—	(283)	(474)
Other adjustments to financing activities	(230)	(564)	(974)	675	(543)
Cash flows from financing activities	(230)	(564)	(974)	392	(1,017)
Net change in cash	$212	$92	($677)	$603	($18)

Kmart
Income Statements (in millions of dollars)

	1998	1997	1996	1995	1994
Sales	$33,674	$32,183	$31,437	$31,713	$29,563
Cost of sales, buying, and occupancy	26,319	25,152	24,390	24,675	22,331
Gross margin	7,355	7,031	7,047	7,038	7,232
Selling, general, and administrative expenses	6,245	6,136	6,274	6,876	6,651
Voluntary early retirement programs	19	114	—	—	—
Other gains, net	—	—	(10)	41	—
Continuing income before other activities	1,091	781	783	121	581
Interest expense, net	293	363	453	434	479
Income tax provision	230	120	68	(83)	6
Dividends securities of subsidiary	50	49	31	—	—
Net income before discontinued operations and extraordinary item	518	249	231	(230)	96
Discontinued operations, net	—	—	(5)	(260)	83
Loss (gain) on discount operations, net of tax	—	—	446	30	(117)
Extraordinary item, net	—	—	—	(51)	—
Net income (loss)	$518	$249	($220)	($571)	$296

Kmart AVERAGE *Balance Sheets (in millions of dollars)*

	1998	1997	1996	1995	1994
Assets					
Current assets					
Cash and cash equivalents	$604.00	$452.00	$744.50	$781.50	$464.50
Merchandise inventories	6,451.50	6,360.50	6,188.00	6,702.00	7,317.00
Other current assets	597.50	792.00	933.50	1,109.50	1,570.50
Discontinued operations	—	—	277	277	—
Total current assets	7,653.00	7,604.50	8,143.00	8,870.00	9,352.00
Property and equipment, net	5,693.00	5,606.00	5,552.50	5,822.50	6,083.00
Property held for sale or financing	—	100.00	317.00	217.00	—
Other assets and deferred charges	516.00	611.50	569.50	902.00	1,341.50
Discontinued operations	—	—	77.5	219.5	490
Total assets	$13,862.00	$13,922.00	$14,659.50	$16,031.00	$17,266.50
Liabilities and Stockholders' Equity					
Current liabilities					
Long-term debt due within one year	77.50	117.00	81.50	121.50	313.00
Trade accounts payable	1,985.00	1,966.00	1,901.00	2,670.50	3,614.50
Accrued payroll and other liabilities	1,211.50	1,181.00	1,158.50	1,166.00	1,330.00
Taxes other than income taxes	208.50	174.00	157.50	352.50	417.50
Total current liabilities	3,482.50	3,438.00	3,298.50	4,310.50	5,675.00
Long-term debt and notes payable	1,631.50	1,923.00	3,021.50	2,966.50	2,119.00
Capital lease obligations	1,135.00	1,328.50	1,532.00	1,681.50	1,748.50
Other long-term liabilities	924.00	989.00	1,131.50	1,416.50	1,661.50
Total liabilities	7,173.00	7,678.50	8,983.50	10,375.00	11,204.00
Stockholders' equity					
Convertible preferred stock	982.50	980.50	490.00	66.00	636.00
Common stock	491.00	487.50	486.00	475.50	441.00
Capital in excess of par value	1,636.00	1,606.50	1,616.00	1,564.50	1,021.50
Retained earnings	3,579.50	3,222.50	3,215.50	3,700.00	4,155.50
Treasury shares and restricted stock	—	−18.50	−64.50	−89.00	−97.50
Foreign currency translation adjustment	—	−35.00	−67.00	−61.00	−94.00
Total shareholders' equity	6,689.00	6,243.50	5,676.00	5,656.00	6,062.50
Total liabilities and shareholders' equity	$13,862.00	$13,922.00	$14,659.50	$16,031.00	$17,266.50

Cash Flow Data

	1998	1997	1996	1995	1994
Cash flow from operations	1,237	841	768	−189	−131
Fixed asset purchases	981	678	343	540	1021
Cash dividends	0	0	0	283	474
Depreciation and amortization	671	660	654	685	639

Market Data

	1998	1997	1996	1995	1994
High market price	$18.60	$20.90	$15.30	$14.30	$16.30
Low market price	$9.10	$10.50	$10.10	$5.80	$5.90
Number of shares outstanding (millions)	481.38	493.36	488.81	487	486.51
Market capitalization	$6,667.11	$7,745.75	$6,207.89	$4,894.35	$5,400.26

Kmart Ratios

Liquidity Ratios

	1998	1997	1996	1995	1994
Working capital	$4,171	$4,167	$4,845	$4,560	$3,677
Working capital ratio	2.2	2.21	2.47	2.06	1.65
Quick ratio	0.17	0.13	0.23	0.18	0.08
Inventory turnover	4.08	3.95	3.94	3.68	3.05
Days in inventory	89.47	92.3	92.6	99.14	119.6
Accounts receivable turnover	N/A	N/A	N/A	N/A	N/A
Days in accounts receivable	N/A	N/A	N/A	N/A	N/A
Inventory conversion cycle	89.47	92.30	92.60	99.14	119.60
Accounts payable turnover	13.26	12.79	12.83	9.24	6.18
Days in accounts payable	27.53	28.53	28.45	39.50	59.08
Net cash conversion cycle	61.94	63.77	64.16	59.64	60.52
Cash + short-term investments	604.00	452.00	744.50	781.50	464.50
A/R*days in accounts receivable	—	—	—	—	—
Inventory*days in inventory	577,224.67	587,087.53	573,035.69	664,422.84	875,086.14
Product dollar days	577,828.67	587,539.53	573,780.19	665,204.34	875,550.64
Current assets-other current assets	7,055.50	6,812.50	6,932.50	7,483.50	7,781.50
Liquidity index	81.90	86.24	82.77	88.89	112.52

Cash Flow Ratios

	1998	1997	1996	1995	1994
Cash flow adequacy	1.26	1.24	2.24	(0.23)	(0.09)
Reinvestment ratio	0.79	0.81	0.45	(2.86)	(7.79)
Dividend payout	—	—	—	(1.50)	(3.62)
Free cash flow	256.00	163.00	425.00	(1,012.00)	(1,626.00)
Depreciation impact ratio	0.54	0.78	0.85	(3.62)	(4.88)
Recapitalization index	1.46	1.03	0.52	0.79	1.60
Cash flow return on assets	0.09	0.06	0.05	(0.01)	(0.01)
Cash flow return on sales	0.04	0.03	0.02	(0.01)	—
Operations index	1.13	1.08	0.98	(1.56)	(0.23)

Asset Utilization Ratios

	1998	1997	1996	1995	1994
Profit margin	1.54%	0.77%	–0.70%	–1.80%	1.00%
Asset turnover	2.43	2.31	2.14	1.98	1.71
Financial structure leverage	2.07	2.23	2.58	2.83	2.85
Return on assets	3.74%	1.79%	–1.50%	–3.56%	1.71%
Return on equity	7.74%	3.99%	–3.88%	–10.10%	4.88%

Capital Structure Ratios

	1998	1997	1996	1995	1994
Debt to capital	0.52	0.55	0.61	0.65	0.65
Debt to equity	1.07	1.23	1.58	1.83	1.85
Long-term debt to capital	0.27	0.30	0.39	0.38	0.32
Long-term debt to equity	0.55	0.68	1.00	1.07	0.91
Working capital/total assets-Z1	0.36	0.36	0.40	0.34	0.26
Retained earnings/total assets-Z2	0.36	0.32	0.31	0.32	0.34
EBIT/total assets-Z3	0.26	0.19	0.18	0.02	0.11
Sales/total assets-Z4	2.43	2.31	2.14	1.98	1.71
Market to book-Z5	0.56	0.61	0.41	0.28	0.29
Z-Score	3.97	3.79	3.44	2.95	2.70

Market Ratio

	1998	1997	1996	1995	1994
Price to earnings	12.87	31.11	(28.22)	(8.57)	18.24

	1998	1997	1996	1995	1994	1993
Revenues	$30,951	$27,757	$25,371	$23,516	$21,311	$19,233
Cost of sales, buying, and occupancy	22,634	20,320	18,628	17,527	15,636	14,164
Selling, publicity and administration	5,077	4,532	4,289	4,043	3,614	3,158
Depreciation and amortization	780	693	650	594	548	515
Interest expense, net	446	449	442	442	426	446
Taxes other than income	458	437	445	409	373	343
Real estate repositioning	—	—	134	—	—	—
Total costs and expenses	29,395	26,431	24,588	23,015	20,597	18,626
Earnings before taxes	1,556	1,326	783	501	714	607
Provision for taxes	594	524	309	190	280	232
Net earnings before extraordinary expenses	962	802	474	311	434	375
Extraordinary expenses	27	51	11	—	—	—
Net Earnings	$935	$751	$463	$311	$434	$375
Basic earnings per share	$2.08	$1.68	$1.02	$0.67	$0.96	$0.83
Diluted earnings per share	$1.98	$1.59	$0.97	$0.64	$0.92	$0.79

Vertical Common Size

	1998	1997	1996	1995	1994	1993
Revenues	100.0%	100.0%	100.0%	100.0%	100.0%	100.0%
Cost of sales, buying, and occupancy	73.1%	73.2%	73.4%	74.5%	73.4%	73.6%
Selling, publicity and administration	16.4%	16.3%	16.9%	17.2%	17.0%	16.4%
Depreciation and amortization	2.5%	2.5%	2.6%	2.5%	2.6%	2.7%
Interest expense, net	1.4%	1.6%	1.7%	1.9%	2.0%	2.3%
Taxes other than income	1.5%	1.6%	1.8%	1.7%	1.8%	1.8%
Real estate repositioning	0.0%	0.0%	0.5%	0.0%	0.0%	0.0%
Total costs and expenses	95.0%	95.2%	96.9%	97.9%	96.6%	96.8%
Earnings before taxes	5.0%	4.8%	3.1%	2.1%	3.4%	3.2%
Provision for taxes	1.9%	1.9%	1.2%	0.8%	1.3%	1.2%
Net earnings before extraordinary expenses	3.1%	2.9%	1.9%	1.3%	2.0%	1.9%
Extraordinary expenses	0.1%	0.2%	0.0%	0.0%	0.0%	0.0%
Net Earnings	3.0%	2.7%	1.8%	1.3%	2.0%	1.9%

Horizontal Common Size—1993 Base Year

	1998	1997	1996	1995	1994	1993
Revenues	160.9%	144.3%	131.9%	122.3%	110.8%	100.0%
Cost of sales, buying, and occupancy	159.8%	143.5%	131.5%	123.7%	110.4%	100.0%
Selling, publicity and administration	160.8%	143.5%	135.8%	128.0%	114.4%	100.0%
Depreciation and amortization	151.5%	134.6%	126.2%	115.3%	106.4%	100.0%
Interest expense, net	100.0%	100.7%	99.1%	99.1%	95.5%	100.0%
Taxes other than income	133.5%	127.4%	129.7%	119.2%	108.7%	100.0%
Real estate repositioning						
Total costs and expenses	157.8%	141.9%	132.0%	123.6%	110.6%	100.0%
Earnings before taxes	256.3%	218.5%	129.0%	82.5%	117.6%	100.0%
Provision for taxes	256.0%	225.9%	133.2%	81.9%	120.7%	100.0%
Net earnings before extraordinary expenses	256.5%	213.9%	126.4%	82.9%	115.7%	100.0%
Extraordinary expenses						
Net Earnings	249.3%	200.3%	123.5%	82.9%	115.7%	100.0%

Horizontal Common Size—Rolling Forward

	1998	1997	1996	1995	1994	1993
Revenues	111.5%	109.4%	107.9%	110.3%	110.8%	100.0%
Cost of sales, buying, and occupancy	111.4%	109.1%	106.3%	112.1%	110.4%	100.0%
Selling, publicity and administration	112.0%	105.7%	106.1%	111.9%	114.4%	100.0%
Depreciation and amortization	112.6%	106.6%	109.4%	108.4%	106.4%	100.0%
Interest expense, net	99.3%	101.6%	100.0%	103.8%	95.5%	100.0%
Taxes other than income	104.8%	98.2%	108.8%	109.7%	108.7%	100.0%
Real estate repositioning						
Total costs and expenses	111.2%	107.5%	106.8%	111.7%	110.6%	100.0%
Earnings before taxes	117.3%	169.3%	156.3%	70.2%	117.6%	100.0%
Provision for taxes	113.4%	169.6%	162.6%	67.9%	120.7%	100.0%
Net earnings before extraordinary	120.0%	169.2%	152.4%	71.7%	115.7%	100.0%
Extraordinary expenses	52.9%	463.6%				
Net Earnings	124.5%	162.2%	148.9%	71.7%	115.7%	100.0%

*Target Corporation
(Dayton-Hudson)
Income Statements
(in millions of dollars)
(continued)*

	1993	1994	1995	1996	1997	1998	Growth
Revenues	−$19,233	—	—	—	—	$30,951	10.0%
Cost of sales, buying, and occupancy	−14,164	—	—	—	—	22,634	9.8%
Selling, publicity and administration	−3,158	—	—	—	—	5,077	10.0%
Depreciation and amortization	−515	—	—	—	—	780	8.7%
Interest expense, net	−446	—	—	—	—	446	0.0%
Taxes other than income	−343	—	—	—	—	458	6.0%
Real estate repositioning	—	—	—	—	—	—	
Total costs and expenses	−18,626	—	—	—	—	29,395	9.6%
Earnings before taxes	−607	—	—	—	—	1,556	20.7%
Provision for taxes	−232	—	—	—	—	594	20.7%
Net earnings before extraordinary expenses	−375	—	—	—	—	962	20.7%
Extraordinary expenses	—	—	—	—	—	27	
Net Earnings	−375	—	—	—	—	935	20.0%

*Target Corporation
(Dayton-Hudson)
Balance Sheets
(in millions of dollars)*

	1998	1997	1996	1995	1994	1993
Assets						
Current assets:						
Cash and cash equivalent	$255	$211	$201	$175	$147	$321
Receivables	1,656	1,555	1,720	1,510	1,810	1,536
Inventories at LIFO cost	3,475	3,251	3,031	3,018	2,777	2,497
Other current assets	619	544	488	252	225	157
Total current assets	6,005	5,561	5,440	4,955	4,959	4,511
Property, plant, and equipment, at cost:						
Land	1,868	1,712	1,557	1,496	1,251	1,120
Building and improvements	7,217	6,497	5,943	5,812	5,208	4,753
Fixtures and equipment	3,274	2,915	2,652	2,482	2,257	2,162
Construction in process	378	389	317	434	293	248
Total property, plant, and equipment	12,737	11,513	10,469	10,224	9,009	8,283
Less: accumulated depreciation	−3,768	−3,388	−3,002	−2,930	−2,624	−2,336
Net property, plant, and equipment	8,969	8,125	7,467	7,294	6,385	5,947
Other assets	692	505	482	321	353	320
Total assets	$15,666	$14,191	$13,389	$12,570	$11,697	$10,778
Liabilities and Shareholders' Equity						
Current liabilities:						
Commercial paper	$—	$—	$—	$—	$—	$—
Accounts payable	3,150	2,727	2,528	2,247	1,961	1,654
Accrued liabilities	1,444	1,346	1,168	957	1,045	903

*Target Corporation
(Dayton-Hudson)
Balance Sheets
 (in millions of dollars)
(continued)*

	1998	1997	1996	1995	1994	1993
Accrued income taxes	207	210	182	137	175	145
Long-term debt due within one year	256	273	233	182	209	373
Total current liabilities	5,057	4,556	4,111	3,523	3,390	3,075
Long-term debt	4,452	4,425	4,808	4,959	4,488	4,279
Deferred income taxes and other	822	720	630	623	582	536
Convertible preferred stock	24	30	50	62	44	368
Total long term liabilities	5,298	5,175	5,488	5,644	5,114	5,183
Total liabilities	10,355	9,731	9,599	9,167	8,504	8,258
Shareholders' Equity						
Convertible preferred stock	268	280	271	257	277	—
Preferred stock	—	—	—	—	—	—
Common stock	74	73	72	72	72	72
Capital in excess of par value	286	196	146	110	89	73
Retained earnings	4,683	3,930	3,348	3,044	2,882	2,592
Loans to ESOP	—	–19	–47	–80	–127	–217
Total shareholders' equity shareholders' equity	5,311	4,460	3,790	3,403	3,193	2,520
Total liabilities and shareholders' equity	$15,666	$14,191	$13,389	$12,570	$11,697	$10,778

Vertical Common Size

	1998	1997	1996	1995	1994	1993
Assets						
Current assets:						
Cash and cash equivalent	1.6%	1.5%	1.5%	1.4%	1.3%	3.0%
Receivables	10.6%	11.0%	12.8%	12.0%	15.5%	14.3%
Inventories at LIFO cost	22.2%	22.9%	22.6%	24.0%	23.7%	23.2%
Other current assets	4.0%	3.8%	3.6%	2.0%	1.9%	1.5%
Total current assets	38.3%	39.2%	40.6%	39.4%	42.4%	41.9%
Property, plant, and equipment, at cost:						
Land	11.9%	12.1%	11.6%	11.9%	10.7%	10.4%
Building and improvements	46.1%	45.8%	44.4%	46.2%	44.5%	44.1%
Fixtures and equipment	20.9%	20.5%	19.8%	19.7%	19.3%	20.1%
Construction in process	2.4%	2.7%	2.4%	3.5%	2.5%	2.3%
Total property, plant, and equipment	81.3%	81.1%	78.2%	81.3%	77.0%	76.9%
Less: accumulated depreciation	–24.1%	–23.9%	–22.4%	–23.3%	–22.4%	–21.7%
Net property, plant, and equipment	57.3%	57.3%	55.8%	58.0%	54.6%	55.2%
Other assets	4.4%	3.6%	3.6%	2.6%	3.0%	3.0%
Total assets	100.0%	100.0%	100.0%	100.0%	100.0%	100.0%
Liabilities and Shareholders' Equity						
Current liabilities:						
Commercial paper	0.0%	0.0%	0.0%	0.0%	0.0%	0.0%

Vertical Common Size (continued)

	1998	1997	1996	1995	1994	1993
Accounts payable	20.1%	19.2%	18.9%	17.9%	16.8%	15.3%
Accrued liabilities	9.2%	9.5%	8.7%	7.6%	8.9%	8.4%
Accrued income taxes	1.3%	1.5%	1.4%	1.1%	1.5%	1.3%
Long-term debt due within one year	1.6%	1.9%	1.7%	1.4%	1.8%	3.5%
Total current liabilities	32.3%	32.1%	30.7%	28.0%	29.0%	28.5%
Long-term debt	28.4%	31.2%	35.9%	39.5%	38.4%	39.7%
Deferred income taxes and other	5.2%	5.1%	4.7%	5.0%	5.0%	5.0%
Convertible preferred stock	0.2%	0.2%	0.4%	0.5%	0.4%	3.4%
Total long-term liabilities	33.8%	36.5%	41.0%	44.9%	43.7%	48.1%
Total liabilities	66.1%	68.6%	71.7%	72.9%	72.7%	76.6%
Shareholders' Equity						
Convertible preferred stock	1.7%	2.0%	2.0%	2.0%	2.4%	0.0%
Preferred stock	0.0%	0.0%	0.0%	0.0%	0.0%	0.0%
Common stock	0.5%	0.5%	0.5%	0.6%	0.6%	0.7%
Capital in excess of par value	1.8%	1.4%	1.1%	0.9%	0.8%	0.7%
Retained earnings	29.9%	27.7%	25.0%	24.2%	24.6%	24.0%
Loans to ESOP	0.0%	−0.1%	−0.4%	−0.6%	−1.1%	−2.0%
Total shareholders' equity	33.9%	31.4%	28.3%	27.1%	27.3%	23.4%
Total liabilities and shareholders' equity	100.0%	100.0%	100.0%	100.0%	100.0%	100.0%

Horizontal Common Size—1993 Base Year

	1998	1997	1996	1995	1994	1993
Assets						
Current assets:						
Cash and cash equivalent	79.4%	65.7%	62.6%	54.5%	45.8%	100.0%
Receivables	107.8%	101.2%	112.0%	98.3%	117.8%	100.0%
Inventories at LIFO cost	139.2%	130.2%	121.4%	120.9%	111.2%	100.0%
Other current assets	394.3%	346.5%	310.8%	160.5%	143.3%	100.0%
Total current assets	133.1%	123.3%	120.6%	109.8%	109.9%	100.0%
Property, plant, and equipment, at cost:						
Land	166.8%	152.9%	139.0%	133.6%	111.7%	100.0%
Building and improvements	151.8%	136.7%	125.0%	122.3%	109.6%	100.0%
Fixtures and equipment	151.4%	134.8%	122.7%	114.8%	104.4%	100.0%
Construction in process	152.4%	156.9%	127.8%	175.0%	118.1%	100.0%
Total property, plant, and equipment	153.8%	139.0%	126.4%	123.4%	108.8%	100.0%
Less: accumulated depreciation	161.3%	145.0%	128.5%	125.4%	112.3%	100.0%
Net property, plant, and equipment	150.8%	136.6%	125.6%	122.7%	107.4%	100.0%
Other assets	216.3%	157.8%	150.6%	100.3%	110.3%	100.0%
Total assets	145.4%	131.7%	124.2%	116.6%	108.5%	100.0%

Horizontal Common Size—1993 Base Year (continued)

	1998	1997	1996	1995	1994	1993
Liabilities and Shareholders' Equity						
Current liabilities:						
Commercial paper						
Accounts payable	190.4%	164.9%	152.8%	135.9%	118.6%	100.0%
Accrued liabilities	159.9%	149.1%	129.3%	106.0%	115.7%	100.0%
Accrued income taxes	142.8%	144.8%	125.5%	94.5%	120.7%	100.0%
Long-term debt due within one year	68.6%	73.2%	62.5%	48.8%	56.0%	100.0%
Total current liabilities	164.5%	148.2%	133.7%	114.6%	110.2%	100.0%
Long-term debt	104.0%	103.4%	112.4%	115.9%	104.9%	100.0%
Deferred income taxes and other	153.4%	134.3%	117.5%	116.2%	108.6%	100.0%
Convertible preferred stock	6.5%	8.2%	13.6%	16.8%	12.0%	100.0%
Total long term liabilities	102.2%	99.8%	105.9%	108.9%	98.7%	100.0%
Total liabilities	125.4%	117.8%	116.2%	111.0%	103.0%	100.0%
Shareholders' Equity						
Convertible preferred stock						
Preferred stock						
Common stock	102.8%	101.4%	100.0%	100.0%	100.0%	100.0%
Capital in excess of par value	391.8%	268.5%	200.0%	150.7%	121.9%	100.0%
Retained earnings	180.7%	151.6%	129.2%	117.4%	111.2%	100.0%
Loans to ESOP	0.0%	8.8%	21.7%	36.9%	58.5%	100.0%
Total shareholders' equity	210.8%	177.0%	150.4%	135.0%	126.7%	100.0%
Total liabilities and shareholders' equity	145.4%	131.7%	124.2%	116.6%	108.5%	100.0%

Horizontal Common Size—Rolling Forward

	1998	1997	1996	1995	1994	1993
Assets						
Current assets:						
Cash and cash equivalent	120.9%	105.0%	114.9%	119.0%	45.8%	100.0%
Receivables	106.5%	90.4%	113.9%	83.4%	117.8%	100.0%
Inventories at LIFO cost	106.9%	107.3%	100.4%	108.7%	111.2%	100.0%
Other current assets	113.8%	111.5%	193.7%	112.0%	143.3%	100.0%
Total current assets	108.0%	102.2%	109.8%	99.9%	109.9%	100.0%
Property, plant, and equipment, at cost:						
Land	109.1%	110.0%	104.1%	119.6%	111.7%	100.0%
Building and improvements	111.1%	109.3%	102.3%	111.6%	109.6%	100.0%
Fixtures and equipment	112.3%	109.9%	106.8%	110.0%	104.4%	100.0%
Construction in process	97.2%	122.7%	73.0%	148.1%	118.1%	100.0%
Total property, plant, and equipment	110.6%	110.0%	102.4%	113.5%	108.8%	100.0%
Less: accumulated depreciation	111.2%	112.9%	102.5%	111.7%	112.3%	100.0%

Horizontal Common Size—Rolling Forward (continued)

	1998	1997	1996	1995	1994	1993
Net property, plant, and equipment	110.4%	108.8%	102.4%	114.2%	107.4%	100.0%
Other assets	137.0%	104.8%	150.2%	90.9%	110.3%	100.0%
Total assets	110.4%	106.0%	106.5%	107.5%	108.5%	100.0%
Liabilities and Shareholders' Equity						
Current liabilities:						
Commercial paper						
Accounts payable	115.5%	107.9%	112.5%	114.6%	118.6%	100.0%
Accrued liabilities	107.3%	115.2%	122.0%	91.6%	115.7%	100.0%
Accrued income taxes	98.6%	115.4%	132.8%	78.3%	120.7%	100.0%
Long-term debt due within one year	93.8%	117.2%	128.0%	87.1%	56.0%	100.0%
Total current liabilities	111.0%	110.8%	116.7%	103.9%	110.2%	100.0%
Long-term debt	100.6%	92.0%	97.0%	110.5%	104.9%	100.0%
Deferred income taxes and other	114.2%	114.3%	101.1%	107.0%	108.6%	100.0%
Convertible preferred stock	80.0%	60.0%	80.6%	140.9%	12.0%	100.0%
Total long term liabilities	102.4%	94.3%	97.2%	110.4%	98.7%	100.0%
Total liabilities	106.4%	101.4%	104.7%	107.8%	103.0%	100.0%
Shareholders' Equity						
Convertible preferred stock	95.7%	103.3%	105.4%	92.8%		
Preferred stock						
Common stock	101.4%	101.4%	100.0%	100.0%	100.0%	100.0%
Capital in excess of par value	145.9%	134.2%	132.7%	123.6%	121.9%	100.0%
Retained earnings	119.2%	117.4%	110.0%	105.6%	111.2%	100.0%
Loans to ESOP	0.0%	40.4%	58.8%	63.0%	58.5%	100.0%
Total shareholders' equity	119.1%	117.7%	111.4%	106.6%	126.7%	100.0%
Total liabilities and shareholders' equity	110.4%	106.0%	106.5%	107.5%	108.5%	100.0%

	1993	1994	1995	1996	1997	1998	Growth
Assets							
Current assets:							
Cash and cash equivalent	–$321	—	—	—	—	$255	–4.5%
Receivables	–1,536	—	—	—	—	1,656	1.5%
Inventories at LIFO cost	–2,497	—	—	—	—	3,475	6.8%
Other current assets	–157	—	—	—	—	619	31.6%
Total current assets	–4,511	—	—	—	—	6,005	5.9%
Property, plant, and equipment, at cost:							
Land	–1,120	—	—	—	—	1,868	10.8%
Building and improvements	–4,753	—	—	—	—	7,217	8.7%
Fixtures and equipment	–2,162	—	—	—	—	3,274	8.7%
Construction in process	–248	—	—	—	—	378	8.8%
Total property, plant, and equipment	–8,283	—	—	—	—	12,737	9.0%
Less: accumulated depreciation	2,336	—	—	—	—	–3,768	10.0%
Net property, plant, and equipment	–5,947	—	—	—	—	8,969	8.6%
Other assets	–320	—	—	—	—	692	16.7%
Total assets	–10,778	—	—	—	—	15,666	7.8%
Liabilities and Shareholders' Equity							
Current liabilities:							
Commercial paper							
Accounts payable	–1,654	—	—	—	—	3,150	13.8%
Accrued liabilities	–903	—	—	—	—	1,444	9.8%
Accrued income taxes	–145	—	—	—	—	207	7.4%
Long-term debt due within one year	–373	—	—	—	—	256	–7.3%
Total current liabilities	–3,075	—	—	—	—	5,057	10.5%
Long-term debt	–4,279	—	—	—	—	4,452	0.8%
Deferred income taxes and other	–536	—	—	—	—	822	8.9%
Convertible preferred stock	–368	—	—	—	—	24	
Total long term liabilities	–5,183	—	—	—	—	5,298	0.4%
Total liabilities	–8,258	—	—	—	—	10,355	4.6%
Shareholders' Equity							
Convertible preferred stock	—	—	—	—	—	268	
Preferred stock	—	—	—	—	—	—	
Common stock	–72	—	—	—	—	74	0.5%
Capital in excess of par value	–73	—	—	—	—	286	31.4%
Retained earnings	–2,592	—	—	—	—	4,683	12.6%
Loans to ESOP	217	—	—	—	—	—	
Total shareholders' equity	–2,520	—	—	—	—	5,311	16.1%
Total liabilities and shareholders' equity	–10,778	—	—	—	—	15,666	7.8%

Target, Inc.
Condensed Statements of Cash
Flows (in millions of dollars)

	1998	1997	1996	1995	1994
Net income	$935	$751	$463	$311	$434
Depreciation expense	780	693	650	594	531
Other adjustments to operations	147	351	345	256	−73
Cash flows from operating activities	1,862	1,795	1,458	1161	892
Purchase of property, plant and equipment	−1,657	−1,354	−1,301	−1,522	−1,095
Other adjustments to investing activities	2	123	103	17	89
Cash flows from investing activities	−1,655	−1,231	−1,198	−1,505	−1,006
Dividends	−178	−165	−155	−148	−144
Other adjustments to financing activities	15	−389	−79	520	84
Cash flows from financing activities	−163	−554	−234	372	−60
Net change in cash	$ 44	$ 10	$ 26	$ 28	$−174

Target Corporation
(Dayton-Hudson)
Income Statements
(in millions of dollars)

	1998	1997	1996	1995	1994
Revenues	$30,951	$27,757	$25,371	$23,516	$21,311
Cost of sales, buying, and occupancy	22,634	20,320	18,628	17,527	15,636
Selling, publicity and administration	5,077	4,532	4,289	4,043	3,614
Depreciation and amortization	780	693	650	594	548
Interest expense, net	446	449	442	442	426
Taxes other than income	458	437	445	409	373
Real estate repositioning	—	—	134	—	—
Total costs and expenses	29,395	26,431	24,588	23,015	20,597
Earnings before taxes	1,556	1,326	783	501	714
Provision for taxes	594	524	309	190	280
Net earnings before extraordinary expenses	962	802	474	311	434
Extraordinary expenses	27	51	11	—	—
Net Earnings	$935	$751	$463	$311	$434

Target Corporation
(Dayton-Hudson)
AVERAGE *Balance Sheets*
(in millions of dollars)

	1998	1997	1996	1995	1994
Assets					
Current assets:					
Cash and cash equivalent	$233.00	$206.00	$188.00	$161.00	$234.00
Receivables	1,605.50	1,637.50	1,615.00	1,660.00	1,673.00
Inventories at LIFO cost	3,363.00	3,141.00	3,024.50	2,897.50	2,637.00
Other current assets	581.50	516.00	370.00	238.50	191.00
Total current assets	5,783.00	5,500.50	5,197.50	4,957.00	4,735.00
Property, plant, and equipment, at cost:					
Land	1,790.00	1,634.50	1,526.50	1,373.50	1,185.50
Building and improvements	6,857.00	6,220.00	5,877.50	5,510.00	4,980.50
Fixtures and equipment	3,094.50	2,783.50	2,567.00	2,369.50	2,209.50
Construction in process	383.50	353.00	375.50	363.50	270.50
Total property, plant, and equipment	12,125.00	10,991.00	10,346.50	9,616.50	8,646.00
Less: accumulated depreciation	–3,578.00	–3,195.00	–2,966.00	–2,777.00	–2,480.00
Net property, plant, and equipment	8,547.00	7,796.00	7,380.50	6,839.50	6,166.00
Other assets	598.50	493.50	401.50	337.00	336.50
Total assets	$14,928.50	$13,790.00	$12,979.50	$12,133.50	$11,237.50
Liabilities and Shareholders' Equity					
Current liabilities:					
Commercial paper					
Accounts payable	$2,938.50	$2,627.50	$2,387.50	$2,104.00	$1,807.50
Accrued liabilities	1,395.00	1,257.00	1,062.50	1,001.00	974.00
Accrued income taxes	208.50	196.00	159.50	156.00	160.00
Long-term debt due within one year	264.50	253.00	207.50	195.50	291.00
Total current liabilities	4,806.50	4,333.50	3,817.00	3,456.50	3,232.50
Long-term debt	4,438.50	4,616.50	4,883.50	4,723.50	4,383.50
Deferred income taxes and other	771.00	675.00	626.50	602.50	559.00
Convertible preferred stock	27.00	40.00	56.00	53.00	206.00
Total long term liabilities	5,236.50	5,331.50	5,566.00	5,379.00	5,148.50
Total liabilities	10,043.00	9,665.00	9,383.00	8,835.50	8,381.00
Shareholders' Equity					
Convertible preferred stock	274.00	275.50	264.00	267.00	138.50
Preferred stock	—	—	—	—	—
Common stock	73.50	72.5	72.00	72.00	72.00
Capital in excess of par value	241.00	171.00	128.00	99.50	81.00
Retained earnings	4,306.50	3,639.00	3,196.00	2,963.00	2,737.00
Loans to ESOP	-9.50	-33.00	-63.50	-103.50	-172.00
Total shareholders' equity	4,885.50	4,125.00	3,596.50	3,298.00	2,856.50
Total liabilities and shareholders' equity	$14,928.50	$13,790.00	$12,979.50	$12,133.50	$11,237.50

Cash Flow Data

	1998	1997	1996	1995	1994
Cash flow from operations	$1,862	$1,795	$1,458	$1,161	$892
Fixed asset purchases	1,657	1,354	1,301	1,522	1,095
Cash dividends	178	165	155	148	144
Depreciation and amortization	780	693	650	594	531

Market Data

	1998	1997	1996	1995	1994
High market price	$38.50	$27.10	$18.50	$10.20	$6.70
Low market price	$25.00	$15.70	$9.00	$5.80	$5.30
Number of shares outstanding (millions)	911.68	883.62	875.67	868.82	863.58
Market capitalization	$28,945.84	$18,909.47	$12,040.46	$6,950.56	$5,181.48

Target Corporation (Dayton-Hudson) Ratios

Liquidity Ratios

	1998	1997	1996	1995	1994
Working capital	$976.50	$1,167.00	$1,380.50	$1,500.50	$1,502.50
Working capital ratio	1.20	1.27	1.36	1.43	1.46
Quick ratio	0.38	0.43	0.47	0.53	0.59
Inventory turnover	6.73	6.47	6.16	6.05	5.93
Days in inventory	54.23	56.42	59.26	60.34	61.56
Accounts receivable turnover	19.28	16.95	15.71	14.17	12.74
Days in accounts receivable	18.93	21.53	23.23	25.77	28.65
Inventory conversion cycle	73.17	77.95	82.5	86.11	90.21
Accounts payable turnover	7.70	7.73	7.80	8.33	8.65
Days in accounts payable	47.39	47.20	46.78	43.82	42.19
Net cash conversion cycle	25.78	30.76	35.72	42.29	48.02
Cash + short-term investments	233	206	188	161	234
A/R*days in accounts receivable	30,397.57	35,260.05	37,523.24	42,770.62	47,938.11
Inventory*days in inventory	182,383.39	177,216.86	179,239.54	174,836.53	162,325.77
Product dollar days	213,013.96	212,682.91	216,950.78	217,768.15	210,497.88
Current assets-other current assets	5,201.50	4,984.50	4,827.50	4,718.50	4,544.00
Liquidity index	40.95	42.67	44.94	46.15	46.32

*Target Corporation
(Dayton-Hudson) Ratios
(continued)*

Cash Flow Ratios

	1998	1997	1996	1995	1994
Cash flow adequacy	1.01	1.18	1.00	0.70	0.72
Reinvestment ratio	0.89	0.75	0.89	1.31	1.23
Dividend payout	0.10	0.09	0.11	0.13	0.16
Free cash flow	$27	$276	$ 2	($509)	($347)
Depreciation impact ratio	0.42	0.39	0.45	0.51	0.60
Recapitalization index	2.12	1.95	2.00	2.56	2.06
Cash flow return on assets	0.12	0.13	0.11	0.10	0.08
Cash flow return on sales	0.06	0.06	0.06	0.05	0.04
Operations index	1.20	1.35	1.86	2.32	1.25

Asset Utilization Ratios

	1998	1997	1996	1995	1994
Profit margin	3.021%	2.706%	1.825%	1.323%	2.037%
Asset turnover	2.073	2.013	1.955	1.938	1.896
Financial structure leverage	3.056	3.343	3.609	3.679	3.934
Return on assets	6.263%	5.446%	3.567%	2.563%	3.862%
Return on equity	19.138%	18.206%	12.874%	9.430%	15.193%

Capital Structure Ratios

	1998	1997	1996	1995	1994
Debt to capital	0.67	0.70	0.72	0.73	0.75
Debt to equity	2.06	2.34	2.61	2.68	2.93
Long-term debt to capital	0.30	0.34	0.38	0.39	0.41
Long-term debt to equity	0.91	1.13	1.37	1.45	1.61
Working capital/total assets-Z1	0.08	0.10	0.13	0.15	0.16
Retained earnings/total assets-Z2	0.40	0.37	0.34	0.34	0.34
EBIT/total assets-Z3	0.34	0.32	0.20	0.14	0.21
Sales/total assets-Z4	2.07	2.01	1.95	1.94	1.90
Market to book-Z5	1.73	1.17	0.77	0.47	0.37
Z-Score	4.63	3.98	3.40	3.04	2.98

Market Ratio

	1998	1997	1996	1995	1994
Price to earnings	30.96	25.18	26.01	22.35	11.94

Wal-Mart Stores
Income Statements
(in millions of dollars)

	1998	1997	1996	1995	1994	1993
Revenues:						
Net sales	$137,634	$117,958	$104,859	$93,627	$82,494	$67,344
Other income-net	1,574	1,341	1,319	1,122	918	641
Total	139,208	119,299	106,178	94,749	83,412	67,985
Costs and expenses:						
Costs of sales	108,725	93,438	83,510	74,564	65,586	53,444
Operating, selling, general and administrative expenses	22,363	19,358	16,946	14,951	12,858	10,333
Interest costs:						
Debt	529	555	629	692	520	331
Capital leases	268	229	216	196	186	186
Total costs and expenses	131,885	113,580	101,301	90,403	79,150	64,294
Income before income taxes	7,323	5,719	4,877	4,346	4,262	3,691
Provision for income taxes:						
Current	3,380	2,095	1,974	1,530	1,572	1,325
Deferred	(640)	20	(180)	76	9	33
Total income tax	2,740	2,115	1,794	1,606	1,581	1,358
Income before minority interest	4,583	3,604	3,083	2,740	2,681	2,333
Minority interest	(153)	(78)	(27)	—	—	—
Net income	$4,430	$3,526	$3,056	$2,740	$2,681	$2,333
Basic EPS	$0.99	$0.78	$0.67	$0.60	$0.59	$0.51

Vertical Common Size

	1998	1997	1996	1995	1994	1993
Revenues:						
Net sales	98.9%	98.9%	98.8%	98.8%	98.9%	99.1%
Other income-net	1.1%	1.1%	1.2%	1.2%	1.1%	0.9%
Total	100.0%	100.0%	100.0%	100.0%	100.0%	100.0%
Costs and expenses:						
Costs of sales	78.1%	78.3%	78.7%	78.7%	78.6%	78.6%
Operating, selling, general and administrative expenses	16.1%	16.2%	16.0%	15.8%	15.4%	15.2%
Interest costs:						
Debt	0.4%	0.5%	0.6%	0.7%	0.6%	0.5%
Capital leases	0.2%	0.2%	0.2%	0.2%	0.2%	0.3%
Total costs and expenses	94.7%	95.2%	95.4%	95.4%	94.9%	94.6%
Income before income taxes	5.3%	4.8%	4.6%	4.6%	5.1%	5.4%
Provision for income taxes:						
Current	2.4%	1.8%	1.9%	1.6%	1.9%	1.9%
Deferred	−0.5%	0.0%	−0.2%	0.1%	0.0%	0.0%
Total income tax	2.0%	1.8%	1.7%	1.7%	1.9%	2.0%
Income before minority interest	3.3%	3.0%	2.9%	2.9%	3.2%	3.4%
Minority interest	−0.1%	−0.1%	0.0%	0.0%	0.0%	0.0%
Net income	3.2%	3.0%	2.9%	2.9%	3.2%	3.4%

Wal-Mart Stores
Income Statements
(in millions of dollars)
(continued)

Horizontal Common Size—1993 Base Year

	1998	1997	1996	1995	1994	1993
Revenues:						
Net sales	204.4%	175.2%	155.7%	139.0%	122.5%	100.0%
Other income-net	245.6%	209.2%	205.8%	175.0%	143.2%	100.0%
Total	204.8%	175.5%	156.2%	139.4%	122.7%	100.0%
Costs and expenses:						
Costs of sales	203.4%	174.8%	156.3%	139.5%	122.7%	100.0%
Operating, selling, general and administrative expenses	216.4%	187.3%	164.0%	144.7%	124.4%	100.0%
Interest costs:						
Debt	159.8%	167.7%	190.0%	209.1%	157.1%	100.0%
Capital leases	144.1%	123.1%	116.1%	105.4%	100.0%	100.0%
Total costs and expenses	205.1%	176.7%	157.6%	140.6%	123.1%	100.0%
Income before income taxes,	198.4%	154.9%	132.1%	117.7%	115.5%	100.0%
Provision for income taxes:						
Current	255.1%	158.1%	149.0%	115.5%	118.6%	100.0%
Deferred	−1,939.4%	60.6%	−545.5%	230.3%	27.3%	100.0%
Total income tax	201.8%	155.7%	132.1%	118.3%	116.4%	100.0%
Income before minority interest	196.4%	154.5%	132.1%	117.4%	114.9%	100.0%
Minority interest						
Net income	189.9%	151.1%	131.0%	117.4%	114.9%	100.0%

Horizontal Common Size—Rolling Forward

	1998	1997	1996	1995	1994	1993
Revenues:						
Net sales	116.7%	112.5%	112.0%	113.5%	122.5%	100.0%
Other income-net	117.4%	101.7%	117.6%	122.2%	143.2%	100.0%
Total	116.7%	112.4%	112.1%	113.6%	122.7%	100.0%
Costs and expenses:						
Costs of sales	116.4%	111.9%	112.0%	113.7%	122.7%	100.0%
Operating, selling, general and administrative expenses	115.5%	114.2%	113.3%	116.3%	124.4%	100.0%
Interest costs:						
Debt	95.3%	88.2%	90.9%	133.1%	157.1%	100.0%
Capital leases	117.0%	106.0%	110.2%	105.4%	100.0%	100.0%
Total costs and expenses	116.1%	112.1%	112.1%	114.2%	123.1%	100.0%
Income before income taxes,	128.0%	117.3%	112.2%	102.0%	115.5%	100.0%
Provision for income taxes:						
Current	161.3%	106.1%	129.0%	97.3%	118.6%	100.0%
Deferred	−3,200.0%	−11.1%	−236.8%	844.4%	27.3%	100.0%
Total income tax	129.6%	117.9%	111.7%	101.6%	116.4%	100.0%
Income before minority interest	127.2%	116.9%	112.5%	102.2%	114.9%	100.0%
Minority interest						
Net income	125.6%	115.4%	111.5%	102.2%	114.9%	100.0%

Wal-Mart Stores
Income Statements
(in millions of dollars)
(continued)

Compound Annual Growth Rate

	1993	1994	1995	1996	1997	1998	Growth
Revenues:							
Net sales	$(67,344)	—	—	—	—	$137,634	15.4%
Other income-net	(641)	—	—	—	—	1,574	19.7%
Total	(67,985)	—	—	—	—	139,208	15.4%
Costs and expenses:							
Costs of sales	(53,444)	—	—	—	—	108,725	15.3%
Operating, selling, general and administrative expenses	(10,333)	—	—	—	—	22,363	16.7%
Interest costs:							
Debt	(331)	—	—	—	—	529	9.8%
Capital leases	(186)	—	—	—	—	268	7.6%
Total costs and expenses	(64,294)	—	—	—	—	131,885	15.5%
Income before income taxes	(3,691)	—	—	—	—	7,323	14.7%
Provision for income taxes:							
Current	(1,325)	—	—	—	—	3,380	20.6%
Deferred	(33)	—	—	—	—	(640)	
Total income tax	(1,358)	—	—	—	—	2,740	15.1%
Income before minority interest	(2,333)	—	—	—	—	4,583	14.5%
Minority interest	—	—	—	—	—	(153)	
Net income	(2,333)	—	—	—	—	$4,430	13.7%

Wal-Mart Stores
Balance Sheets
(in millions of dollars)

	1998	1997	1996	1995	1994	1993
Assets						
Current assets:						
Cash and cash equivalent	$1,879	$1,447	$883	$83	$45	$20
Receivables	1,118	976	845	853	900	898
Inventories at LIFO cost	17,076	16,497	15,897	15,989	14,064	11,014
Prepaid expenses and other	1,059	432	368	406	329	182
Total current assets	21,132	19,352	17,993	17,331	15,338	12,114
Property, plant, and equipment, at cost:						
Land	5,219	4,691	3,689	3,559	3,036	2,741
Building and improvements	16,061	14,646	12,724	11,290	8,973	6,818
Fixtures and equipment	9,296	7,636	6,390	5,665	4,768	3,981
Transportation equipment	553	403	379	336	313	260
Total property, plant, and equipment	31,129	27,376	23,182	20,850	17,090	13,800
Less: accumulated depreciation	−7,455	−5,907	−4,849	−3,752	−2,782	−2,713
Net property, plant, and equipment	23,674	21,469	18,333	17,098	14,308	11,087
Property under capital lease:						
Property under capital lease	3,335	3,040	2,782	2,476	2,147	2,059

	1998	1997	1996	1995	1994	1993
Less: accumulated amortization	−1,036	−903	−791	−680	−581	−510
Net property under capital leases	2,299	2,137	1,991	1,796	1,566	1,549
Other assets and deferred charges	2,891	2,426	1,287	1,316	1,607	1,151
Total assets	$49,996	$45,384	$39,604	$37,541	$32,819	$25,901
Liabilities and Shareholders' Equity						
Current liabilities:						
Commercial paper	$—	$—	$—	$2,458	$1,795	$1,575
Accounts payable	10,257	9,126	7,628	6,442	5,907	4,104
Accrued liabilities	4,998	3,628	2,413	2,091	1,819	1,473
Accrued income taxes	501	565	298	123	365	183
Long-term debt due within one year	900	1,039	523	271	23	20
Obligations under capital leases due within one year	106	102	95	69	64	51
Total current liabilities	16,762	14,460	10,957	11,454	9,973	7,406
Long-term debt	6,908	7,191	7,709	8,508	7,871	6,156
Long-term obligations under capital leases	2,699	2,483	2,307	2,092	1,838	1,804
Deferred income taxes and other	716	809	463	400	411	322
Minority interest	1,799	1,938	1,025	331	—	—
Total long-term liabilities	12,122	12,421	11,504	11,331	10,120	8,282
Shareholders' Equity						
Preferred stock	—	—	—	—	—	—
Common stock	445	224	228	229	230	230
Capital in excess of par value	435	585	547	545	539	536
Retained earnings	20,741	18,167	16,768	14,394	12,213	9,987
Other accumulated comprehensive income	−509	−473	−400	−412	−256	−540
Total shareholders' equity	21,112	18,503	17,143	14,756	12,726	10,213
Total liabilities and shareholders' equity	$49,996	$45,384	$39,604	$37,541	$32,819	$25,901

Vertical Common Size

	1998	1997	1996	1995	1994	1993
Assets						
Current assets:						
Cash and cash equivalent	3.8%	3.2%	2.2%	0.2%	0.1%	0.1%
Receivables	2.2%	2.2%	2.1%	2.3%	2.7%	3.5%
Inventories at LIFO cost	34.2%	36.3%	40.1%	42.6%	42.9%	42.5%
Prepaid expenses and other	2.1%	1.0%	0.9%	1.1%	1.0%	0.7%
Total current assets	42.3%	42.6%	45.4%	46.2%	46.7%	46.8%
Property, plant, and equipment, at cost:						
Land	10.4%	10.3%	9.3%	9.5%	9.3%	10.6%
Building and improvements	32.1%	32.3%	32.1%	30.1%	27.3%	26.3%
Fixtures and equipment	18.6%	16.8%	16.1%	15.1%	14.5%	15.4%
Transportation equipment	1.1%	0.9%	1.0%	0.9%	1.0%	1.0%
Total property, plant, and equipment	62.3%	60.3%	58.5%	55.5%	52.1%	53.3%
Less: accumulated depreciation	−14.9%	−13.0%	−12.2%	−10.0%	−8.5%	−10.5%
Net property, plant, and equipment	47.4%	47.3%	46.3%	45.5%	43.6%	42.8%
Property under capital lease:						
Property under capital lease	6.7%	6.7%	7.0%	6.6%	6.5%	7.9%
Less: accumulated amortization	−2.1%	−2.0%	−2.0%	−1.8%	−1.8%	−2.0%
Net property under capital leases	4.6%	4.7%	5.0%	4.8%	4.8%	6.0%
Other assets and deferred charges	5.8%	5.3%	3.2%	3.5%	4.9%	4.4%
Total assets	100.0%	100.0%	100.0%	100.0%	100.0%	100.0%
Liabilities and Shareholders' Equity						
Current liabilities:	0.0%	0.0%	0.0%	0.0%	0.0%	0.0%
Commercial paper	0.0%	0.0%	0.0%	6.5%	5.5%	6.1%
Accounts payable	20.5%	20.1%	19.3%	17.2%	18.0%	15.8%
Accrued liabilities	10.0%	8.0%	6.1%	5.6%	5.5%	5.7%
Accrued income taxes	1.0%	1.2%	0.8%	0.3%	1.1%	0.7%
Long-term debt due within one year	1.8%	2.3%	1.3%	0.7%	0.1%	0.1%
Obligations under capital leases due within one year	0.2%	0.2%	0.2%	0.2%	0.2%	0.2%
Total current liabilities	33.5%	31.9%	27.7%	30.5%	30.4%	28.6%
Long-term debt	13.8%	15.8%	19.5%	22.7%	24.0%	23.8%
Long-term obligations under capital leases	5.4%	5.5%	5.8%	5.6%	5.6%	7.0%
Deferred income taxes and other	1.4%	1.8%	1.2%	1.1%	1.3%	1.2%
Minority interest	3.6%	4.3%	2.6%	0.9%	0.0%	0.0%
Total long-term liabilities	24.2%	27.4%	29.0%	30.2%	30.8%	32.0%

Vertical Common Size (continued)

	1998	1997	1996	1995	1994	1993
Shareholders' Equity						
Preferred stock						
Common stock	0.9%	0.5%	0.6%	0.6%	0.7%	0.9%
Capital in excess of par value	0.9%	1.3%	1.4%	1.5%	1.6%	2.1%
Retained earnings	41.5%	40.0%	42.3%	38.3%	37.2%	38.6%
Other accumulated comprehensive income	−1.0%	−1.0%	−1.0%	−1.1%	−0.8%	−2.1%
Total shareholders' equity	42.2%	40.8%	43.3%	39.3%	38.8%	39.4%
Total liabilities and shareholders' equity	100.0%	100.0%	100.0%	100.0%	100.0%	100.0%

Horizontal Common Size—1993 Base Year

	1998	1997	1996	1995	1994	1993
Assets						
Current assets:						
Cash and cash equivalent	9,395.0%	7,235.0%	4,415.0%	415.0%	225.0%	100.0%
Receivables	124.5%	108.7%	94.1%	95.0%	100.2%	100.0%
Inventories at LIFO cost	155.0%	149.8%	144.3%	145.2%	127.7%	100.0%
Prepaid expenses and other	581.9%	237.4%	202.2%	223.1%	180.8%	100.0%
Total current assets	174.4%	159.7%	148.5%	143.1%	126.6%	100.0%
Property, plant, and equipment, at cost:						
Land	190.4%	171.1%	134.6%	129.8%	110.8%	100.0%
Building and improvements	235.6%	214.8%	186.6%	165.6%	131.6%	100.0%
Fixtures and equipment	233.5%	191.8%	160.5%	142.3%	119.8%	100.0%
Transportation equipment	212.7%	155.0%	145.8%	129.2%	120.4%	100.0%
Total property, plant, and equipment	225.6%	198.4%	168.0%	151.1%	123.8%	100.0%
Less: accumulated depreciation	274.8%	217.7%	178.7%	138.3%	102.5%	100.0%
Net property, plant, and equipment	213.5%	193.6%	165.4%	154.2%	129.1%	100.0%
Property under capital lease:						
Property under capital lease	162.0%	147.6%	135.1%	120.3%	104.3%	100.0%
Less: accumulated amortization	203.1%	177.1%	155.1%	133.3%	113.9%	100.0%
Net property under capital leases	148.4%	138.0%	128.5%	115.9%	101.1%	100.0%
Other assets and deferred charges	251.2%	210.8%	111.8%	114.3%	139.6%	100.0%
Total assets	193.0%	175.2%	152.9%	144.9%	126.7%	100.0%

Horizontal Common Size—1993 Base Year (continued)

	1998	1997	1996	1995	1994	1993
Liabilities and Shareholders' Equity						
Current liabilities:						
Commercial paper	0.0%	0.0%	0.0%	156.1%	114.0%	100.0%
Accounts payable	249.9%	222.4%	185.9%	157.0%	143.9%	100.0%
Accrued liabilities	339.3%	246.3%	163.8%	142.0%	123.5%	100.0%
Accrued income taxes	273.8%	308.7%	162.8%	67.2%	199.5%	100.0%
Long-term debt due within one year	4,500.0%	5,195.0%	2,615.0%	1,355.0%	115.0%	100.0%
Obligations under capital leases due within one year	207.8%	200.0%	186.3%	135.3%	125.5%	100.0%
Total current liabilities	226.3%	195.2%	147.9%	154.7%	134.7%	100.0%
Long-term debt	112.2%	116.8%	125.2%	138.2%	127.9%	100.0%
Long-term obligations under capital leases	149.6%	137.6%	127.9%	116.0%	101.9%	100.0%
Deferred income taxes and other	222.4%	251.2%	143.8%	124.2%	127.6%	100.0%
Minority interest						
Total long-term liabilities	146.4%	150.0%	138.9%	136.8%	122.2%	100.0%
Shareholders' Equity						
Preferred stock						
Common stock	193.5%	97.4%	99.1%	99.6%	100.0%	100.0%
Capital in excess of par value	81.2%	109.1%	102.1%	101.7%	100.6%	100.0%
Retained earnings	207.7%	181.9%	167.9%	144.1%	122.3%	100.0%
Other accumulated comprehensive income	94.3%	87.6%	74.1%	76.3%	47.4%	100.0%
Total shareholders' equity	206.7%	181.2%	167.9%	144.5%	124.6%	100.0%
Total liabilities and shareholders' equity	193.0%	175.2%	152.9%	144.9%	126.7%	100.0%

Horizontal Common Size—Rolling Forward

	1998	1997	1996	1995	1994	1993
Assets						
Current assets:						
Cash and cash equivalent	129.9%	163.9%	1,063.9%	184.4%	225.0%	100.0%
Receivables	114.5%	115.5%	99.1%	94.8%	100.2%	100.0%
Inventories at LIFO cost	103.5%	103.8%	99.4%	113.7%	127.7%	100.0%
Prepaid expenses and other	245.1%	117.4%	90.6%	123.4%	180.8%	100.0%
Total current assets	109.2%	107.6%	103.8%	113.0%	126.6%	100.0%
Property, plant, and equipment, at cost:						
Land	111.3%	127.2%	103.7%	117.2%	110.8%	100.0%
Building and improvements	109.7%	115.1%	112.7%	125.8%	131.6%	100.0%

Horizontal Common Size—Rolling Forward (continued)

	1998	1997	1996	1995	1994	1993
Fixtures and equipment	121.7%	119.5%	112.8%	118.8%	119.8%	100.0%
Transportation equipment	137.2%	106.3%	112.8%	107.3%	120.4%	100.0%
Total property, plant, and equipment	113.7%	118.1%	111.2%	122.0%	123.8%	100.0%
Less: accumulated depreciation	126.2%	121.8%	129.2%	134.9%	102.5%	100.0%
Net property, plant, and equipment	110.3%	117.1%	107.2%	119.5%	129.1%	100.0%
Property under capital lease:						
Property under capital lease	109.7%	109.3%	112.4%	115.3%	104.3%	100.0%
Less: accumulated amortization	114.7%	114.2%	116.3%	117.0%	113.9%	100.0%
Net property under capital leases	107.6%	107.3%	110.9%	114.7%	101.1%	100.0%
Other assets and deferred charges	119.2%	188.5%	97.8%	81.9%	139.6%	100.0%
Total assets	110.2%	114.6%	105.5%	114.4%	126.7%	100.0%
Liabilities and Shareholders' Equity:						
Current liabilities:						
Commercial paper			0.0%	136.9%	114.0%	100.0%
Accounts payable	112.4%	119.6%	118.4%	109.1%	143.9%	100.0%
Accrued liabilities	137.8%	150.4%	115.4%	115.0%	123.5%	100.0%
Accrued income taxes	88.7%	189.6%	242.3%	33.7%	199.5%	100.0%
Long-term debt due within one year	86.6%	198.7%	193.0%	1,178.3%	115.0%	100.0%
Obligations under capital leases due within one year	103.9%	107.4%	137.7%	107.8%	125.5%	100.0%
Total current liabilities	115.9%	132.0%	95.7%	114.9%	134.7%	100.0%
Long-term debt	96.1%	93.3%	90.6%	108.1%	127.9%	100.0%
Long-term obligations under capital leases	108.7%	107.6%	110.3%	113.8%	101.9%	100.0%
Deferred income taxes and other	88.5%	174.7%	115.8%	97.3%	127.6%	100.0%
Minority interest						
Total long-term liabilities	97.6%	108.0%	101.5%	112.0%	122.2%	100.0%
Shareholders' Equity						
Preferred stock						
Common stock	198.7%	98.2%	99.6%	99.6%	100.0%	100.0%
Capital in excess of par value	74.4%	106.9%	100.4%	101.1%	100.6%	100.0%
Retained earnings	114.2%	108.3%	116.5%	117.9%	122.3%	100.0%
Other accumulated comprehensive income	107.6%	118.3%	97.1%	160.9%	47.4%	100.0%
Total shareholders' equity	114.1%	107.9%	116.2%	116.0%	124.6%	100.0%
Total liabilities and shareholders' equity	110.2%	114.6%	105.5%	114.4%	126.7%	100.0%

Compound Annual Growth Rate

	1998	1997	1996	1995	1994	1993
Assets						
Current assets:						
Cash and cash equivalent	($20)	0	0	0	0	$1,879	148.1%
Receivables	–898	0	0	0	0	1,118	4.5%
Inventories at LIFO cost	–11,014	0	0	0	0	17,076	9.2%
Prepaid expenses and other	–182	0	0	0	0	1,059	42.2%
Total current assets	–12,114	0	0	0	0	21,132	11.8%
Property, plant, and equipment, at cost:						
Land	–2,741	0	0	0	0	5,219	13.7%
Building and improvements	–6,818	0	0	0	0	16,061	18.7%
Fixtures and equipment	–3,981	0	0	0	0	9,296	18.5%
Transportation equipment	–260	0	0	0	0	553	16.3%
Total property, plant, and equipment	–13,800	0	0	0	0	31,129	17.7%
Less: accumulated depreciation	2,713	0	0	0	0	–7,455	22.4%
Net property, plant, and equipment	–11,087	0	0	0	0	23,674	16.4%
Property under capital lease:						
Property under capital lease	–2,059	0	0	0	0	3,335	10.1%
Less: accumulated amortization	510	0	0	0	0	–1,036	15.2%
Net property under capital leases	–1,549	0	0	0	0	2,299	8.2%
Other assets and deferred charges	–1,151	0	0	0	0	2,891	20.2%
Total assets	–25,901	0	0	0	0	$49,996	14.1%
Liabilities and Shareholders' Equity						
Current liabilities:						
Commercial paper	–1,575	0	0	0	0	$—	
Accounts payable	–4,104	0	0	0	0	10,257	20.1%
Accrued liabilities	–1,473	0	0	0	0	4,998	27.7%
Accrued income taxes	–183	0	0	0	0	501	22.3%
Long-term debt due within one year	–20	0	0	0	0	900	114.1%
Obligations under capital leases due within one year	–51	0	0	0	0	106	15.8%
Total current liabilities	–7,406	0	0	0	0	16,762	17.7%
Long-term debt	–6,156	0	0	0	0	6,908	2.3%
Long-term obligations under capital leases	–1,804	0	0	0	0	2,699	8.4%
Deferred income taxes and other	–322	0	0	0	0	716	17.3%
Minority interest	—	0	0	0	0	1,799	
Total long-term liabilities	–8,282	0	0	0	0	12,122	7.9%
Shareholders' Equity	—	0	0	0	0		
Preferred stock	—	0	0	0	0	—	

Wal-Mart Stores
Balance Sheets
(in millions of dollars)
(continued)

Compound Annual Growth Rate (continued)

	1998	1997	1996	1995	1994	1993
Common stock	−230	0	0	0	0	445	14.1%
Capital in excess of par value	−536	0	0	0	0	435	−4.1%
Retained earnings	−9,987	0	0	0	0	20,741	15.7%
Other accumulated comprehensive income	540	0	0	0	0	−509	−1.2%
Total shareholders' equity	−10,213	0	0	0	0	21,112	15.6%
Total liabilities and shareholders' equity	−25,901	0	0	0	0	$49,996	14.1%

Wal-Mart Stores
Condensed Statements of Cash
Flows (in millions of dollars)

	1998	1997	1996	1995	1994
Net income	$4,430	$3,526	$3,056	$2,740	$2,681
Depreciation expense	1,872	1,634	1,463	1,304	1,070
Other adjustments to operations	1,278	1,963	1,411	−1,661	−845
Cash flows from operating activities	7,580	7,123	5,930	2,383	2,906
Purchase of property, plant and equipment	−3,734	−2,636	−2,643	−3,566	−3,734
Other adjustments to investing activities	−684	−1,785	575	234	−58
Cash flows from investing activities	−4,418	−4,421	−2,068	−3,332	−3,792
Dividends	−693	−611	−481	−458	−391
Other adjustments to financing activities	−2,037	−1,527	−2,581	1,445	1,302
Cash flows from financing activities	−2,730	−2,138	−3,062	987	911
Net change in cash	$432	$564	$800	$ 38	$ 25

Wal-Mart Stores
Income Statement
(in millions of dollars)

	1998	1997	1996	1995	1994
Revenues:					
Net sales	$137,634	$117,958	$104,859	$93,627	$82,494
Other income-net	1,574	1,341	1,319	1,122	918
Total	139,208	19,299	106,178	94,749	83,412
Costs and expenses:					
Costs of sales	108,725	93,438	83,510	74,564	65,586
Operating, selling, general and administrative expenses	22,363	9,358	16,946	14,951	12,858
Interest costs:					
Debt	529	555	629	692	520
Capital leases	268	229	216	196	186
Total costs and expenses	131,885	113,580	101,301	90,403	79,150
Income before income taxes,	$7,323	$5,719	$4,877	$4,346	$4,262
Provision for income taxes:					
Current	3,380	2,095	1,974	1,530	1,572
Deferred	−640	20	−180	76	9
Total income tax	2,740	2,115	1,794	1,606	1,581
Income before minority interest	$4,583	$3,604	$3,083	$2,740	$2,681
Minority interest	−153	−78	−27	—	—
Net income	$4,430	$3,526	$3,056	$2,740	$2,681

Wal-Mart Stores AVERAGE
Balance Sheets
(in millions)

	1998	1997	1996	1995	1994
Assets					
Current assets:					
Cash and cash equivalent	$1,663.00	$1,165.00	$483.00	$64.00	$32.50
Receivables	1,047.00	910.50	849.00	876.50	899.00
Inventories at LIFO cost	16,786.50	16,197.00	15,943.00	15,026.50	12,539.00
Prepaid expenses and other	745.00	400.00	387.00	367.50	255.50
Total current assets	20,242.00	18,672.50	17,662.00	16,334.50	13,726.00
Property, plant, and equipment, at cost:					
Land	4,955.00	4,190.00	3,624.00	3,297.50	2,888.50
Building and improvements	15,353.50	13,685.00	12,007.00	10,131.50	7,895.50
Fixtures and equipment	8,466.00	7,013.00	6,027.50	5,216.50	4,374.50
Transportation equipment	478.00	391.00	357.50	324.50	286.50
Total property, plant, and equipment	29,252.50	25,279.00	22,016.00	18,970.00	15,445.00
Less: accumulated depreciation	−6,681.00	−5,378.00	−4,300.50	−3,267.00	−2,747.50
Net property, plant, and equipment	22,571.50	19,901.00	17,715.50	15,703.00	12,697.50
Property under capital lease:	—	—	—	—	—
Property under capital lease	3,187.50	2,911.00	2,629.00	2,311.50	2,103.00
Less: accumulated amortization	−969.50	−847.00	−735.50	−630.50	−545.50
Net property under capital leases	2,218.00	2,064.00	1,893.50	1,681.00	1,557.50
Other assets and deferred charges	2,658.50	1,856.50	1,301.50	1,461.50	1,379.00
Total assets	47,690.00	42,494.00	38,572.50	35,180.00	29,360.00

	1998	1997	1996	1995	1994
Liabilities and Shareholders' Equity					
Current liabilities:					
Commercial paper	$—	$—	$1,229.00	$2,126.50	$1,685.00
Accounts payable	9,691.50	8,377.00	7,035.00	6,174.50	5,005.50
Accrued liabilities	4,313.00	3,020.50	2,252.00	1,955.00	1,646.00
Accrued income taxes	533.00	431.50	210.50	244.00	274.00
Long-term debt due within one year	969.50	781.00	3970	147.00	21.50
Obligations under capital leases due within one year	104.00	98.50	82.00	66.50	57.50
Total current liabilities	15,611.00	12,708.50	11,205.50	10,713.50	8,689.50
Long-term debt	7,049.50	7,450.00	8,108.50	8,189.50	7,013.50
Long-term obligations under capital leases	2,591.00	2,395.00	2,199.50	1,965.00	1,821.00
Deferred income taxes and other	762.50	636.00	431.50	405.50	366.50
Minority interest	1,868.50	1,481.50	678.00	165.50	—
Total long-term liabilities	12,271.50	11,962.50	11,417.50	10,725.50	9,201.00
Shareholders' Equity	—	—	—	—	—
Preferred stock	—	—	—	—	—
Common stock	334.50	226.00	228.50	229.50	230.00
Capital in excess of par value	510.00	566.00	546.00	542.00	537.50
Retained earnings	19,454.00	17,467.50	15,581.00	13,303.50	11,100.00
Other accumulated comprehensive income	−491.00	−436.50	−406.00	−334.00	−398.00
Total shareholders' equity	19,807.50	17,823.00	15,949.50	13,741.00	11,469.50
Total liabilities and shareholders' equity	$47,690.00	$42,494.00	$38,572.50	$35,180.00	$29,360.00

Cash Flow Data

	1998	1997	1996	1995	1994
Cash flow from operations	$7,580	$7,123	$5,930	$2,383	$2,906
Fixed asset purchases	3,734	2,636	2,643	3,566	3,734
Cash dividends	693	611	481	458	391
Depreciation and amortization	1,872	1,634	1,463	1,304	1,070

Market Data

	1998	1997	1996	1995	1994
High market price	$70.30	$41.40	$21.00	$14.10	$13.80
Low market price	$38.70	$18.80	$11.00	$9.50	$10.30
Number of shares outstanding (millions)	4,457.00	4,482.00	4,482.00	4,586.00	4,586.00
Market capitalization	$242,906.50	$134,908.20	$71,712.00	$54,114.80	$55,261.30

Liquidity Ratios

	1998	1997	1996	1995	1994
Working capital	$4,631	$5,964	$6,457	$5,621	$5,037
Working capital ratio	1.30	1.47	1.58	1.52	1.58
Quick ratio	0.17	0.16	0.12	0.09	0.11
Inventory turnover	6.48	5.77	5.24	4.96	5.23
Days in inventory	56.35	63.27	69.68	73.56	69.78
Accounts receivable turnover	131.46	129.55	123.51	106.82	91.76
Days in accounts receivable	2.78	2.82	2.96	3.42	3.98
Inventory conversion cycle	59.13	66.09	72.64	76.97	73.76
Accounts payable turnover	11.22	11.15	11.87	12.08	13.10
Days in accounts payable	32.54	32.72	30.75	30.22	27.86
Net cash conversion cycle	26.60	33.36	41.89	46.75	45.90
Cash + short-term investments	1,663.00	1,165.00	483.00	64.00	32.50
A/R*days in accounts receivable	2,907.10	2,565.22	2,509.01	2,994.99	3,575.94
Inventory*days in inventory	945,983.93	1,024,798.53	1,110,949.90	1,105,297.88	874,998.94
Product dollar days	950,554.03	1,028,528.76	1,113,941.91	1,108,356.87	878,607.37
Current assets— other current assets	19,496.50	18,272.50	17,275.00	15,967.00	13,470.50
Liquidity index	48.76	56.29	64.48	69.42	65.22

Cash Flow Ratios

	1998	1997	1996	1995	1994
Cash flow adequacy	1.71	2.19	1.90	0.59	0.70
Reinvestment ratio	0.49	0.37	0.45	1.50	1.28
Dividend payout	0.09	0.09	0.08	0.19	0.13
Free cash flow	$3,153	$3,876	$2,806	($1,641)	($1,219)
Depreciation impact ratio	0.25	0.23	0.25	0.55	0.37
Recapitalization index	1.99	1.61	1.81	2.73	3.49
Cash flow return on assets	0.16	0.17	0.15	0.07	0.10
Cash flow return on sales	0.06	0.06	0.06	0.03	0.04
Operations index	1.04	1.25	1.22	0.55	0.68

Asset Utilization Ratios

	1998	1997	1996	1995	1994
Profit margin	3.182%	2.956%	2.878%	2.892%	3.214%
Asset turnover	2.919	2.807	2.753	2.693	2.841
Financial structure leverage	2.408	2.384	2.418	2.560	2.560
Return on assets	9.29%	8.30%	7.92%	7.79%	9.13%
Return on equity	22.37%	19.78%	19.16%	19.94%	23.38%

Capital Structure Ratios

	1998	1997	1996	1995	1994
Debt to capital	0.58	0.58	0.59	0.61	0.61
Debt to equity	1.41	1.38	1.42	1.56	1.56
Long-term debt to capital	0.20	0.23	0.27	0.29	0.30
Long-term debt to equity	0.49	0.55	0.65	0.74	0.77
Working capital/total assets-Z1	0.12	0.17	0.20	0.19	0.21
Retained earnings/total assets-Z2	0.57	0.58	0.57	0.53	0.53
EBIT/total assets-Z3	0.51	0.44	0.42	0.41	0.48
Sales/total assets-Z4	2.89	2.78	2.72	2.66	2.81
Market to book-Z5	5.23	3.28	1.90	1.51	1.85
Z-Score	9.31	7.24	5.80	5.30	5.88

Market Ratio

	1998	1997	1996	1995	1994
Price to earnings	54.83	38.26	23.47	19.75	20.61

E

FAST-FOOD RESTAURANTS

*T*he commercial eating and drinking establishment industry consists of five sectors: full-service restaurants, limited-service restaurants, cafeterias, ice cream/yogurt shops, and bars/taverns. Full-service restaurants historically dominated the industry, but rapid growth of fast-food restaurants fueled the ascension of the limited-service sector. Changing demographics contributed to the increased revenues of sandwich, pizza, and chicken stores, the three dominant types of fast-food establishments. This appendix presents an overview of the eating and drinking industry in order to provide background for the analysis of McDonald's Corp. and Wendy's International, Inc. from 1993 to 1998. These two restaurants' financial statements are disclosed at the end of this appendix.

DEMOGRAPHIC CHANGES

An increase in dual income households, disposable income, time demands, and societal mobility all contributed to the growth in the fast food industry during the last quarter of the 20th century. Fast-food restaurant sales increased from 15 percent of industry sales in 1970 to 46 percent by 1998.[1] Sales made by limited-service restaurants virtually equaled the estimated $104 billion of revenues earned by full-service establishments in 1997.

Fast-food restaurants saturated the market during the 1990s. Consumers became more price conscious during that time, exhibiting less loyalty to brand name establishments. The industry responded by value pricing items, offering meal combinations, increasing promotional efforts, and improving customer service. These strategies met with mixed results.

MARKET SHARE

The food and beverage industry remained fragmented from 1993 to 1998. Combined sales of the top 20 restaurant chains accounted for less than 30 percent of the industry's revenues.[2] Fast-food restaurant chains were the largest organizations within the restaurant industry. They commanded the top ten market share positions. McDonald's was the largest restaurant chain in the world during the period analyzed. Burger King, a unit of British conglomerate D:2-geo, PLC, was a distant second. Wendy's International exhibited strong growth in the mid-1990s. Exhibit E-1 presents the relative market shares of the five largest fast-food restaurants in 1993 and 1998, listed as a percentage of the combined revenues for that year's five largest restaurant chains.[3]

EXHIBIT E-1

Relative Market Share Among the Top Five Restaurants

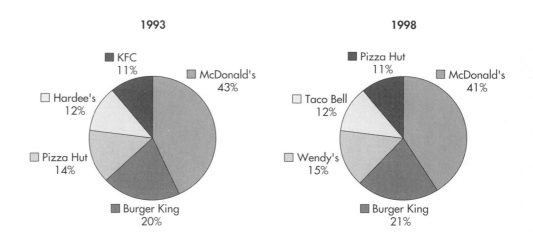

1993

1998

---

[1] Restaurant Industry Surveys, *Standard & Poor's Industry Surveys*, March 1994 and June 1998 (New York: McGraw-Hill).

[2] *Nation's Restaurant News*, Annual Reports 1993 and 1998. (Web site address listed in the text's supplement).

[3] Restaurant Industry Surveys, *Standard & Poor's Industry Surveys*, March 1994 and June 1998 (New York: McGraw-Hill).

BUSINESS MODEL

The franchising concept spurred the growth of fast-food restaurants. A branded concept, such as McDonald's, owns some of its restaurants, but others are independently owned and operated. Franchisees make payments to franchisors in exchange for various services from the parent company under this arrangement. The franchisee pays to use the company's name, employ its business concept, benefit from large-scale advertising campaigns, and receive technical support and training. Approximately 70 percent of fast-food restaurants were owned by franchisees in 1998.[4] Both McDonald's and Wendy's restaurant ownership arrangements approximated the industry's average.[5]

Systemwide sales for each restaurant chain exceeded parent company revenues as a result of the franchising arrangement. Wendy's, for example, recognized $2.04 billion in total 1997 revenues, $1.65 billion from company-owned stores and $.39 billion from franchise royalties. The company generated $6 billion of sales systemwide in that year.[6] (Market share data are based on systemwide revenues.)

OPERATING STRUCTURE

The franchising model gained popularity among fast-food companies because of the industry's structure. Franchisees needed significant real estate commitments to establish outlets. Moreover, individual units generated low profit margins. Adequate returns on investment, therefore, were determined by large volume sales, significant cost control, and efficient asset utilization. Motivated owner–operators, trained by the parent firm, were well positioned to ensure that individual units achieved those results.

The healthy economy of the 1990s was a two-edged sword for fast-food operations. Low inflation rates stabilized food costs, but healthy employment rates put an upward pressure on labor costs. Exhibit E-2 depicts the importance of these two operating costs to a fast-food restaurateur.[7]

---

[4] Restaurant Industry Surveys, *Standard & Poor's Industry Surveys,* June 1998 (New York: McGraw-Hill).

[5] Corporate disclosures made by McDonald's and Wendy's on their respective home pages and Form 10-Ks.

[6] *Nation's Restaurant News,* 1998 Annual Report.

[7] Income statement information provided by the National Restaurant Association.

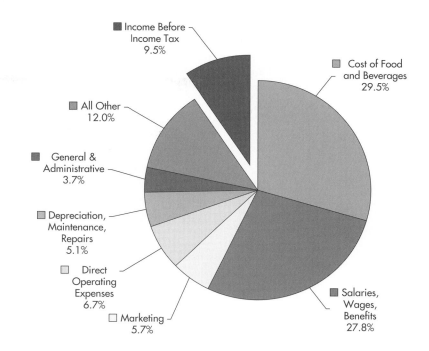

Income Before
Income Tax
9.5%

Cost of Food
and Beverages
29.5%

All Other
12.0%

General &
Administrative
3.7%

Depreciation,
Maintenance,
Repairs
5.1%

Direct
Operating
Expenses
6.7%

Marketing
5.7%

Salaries,
Wages,
Benefits
27.8%

INDUSTRY CHALLENGES

Fast-food restaurants saturated the United States in the 1990s. There was one lim-ited-service store for every 1,373 people in 1996, as opposed to one restaurant for every 1,672 consumers a decade earlier. In addition, informal full-service restau-rants (e.g., Applebee's, Chili's, Red Lobster, Olive Garden) rivaled limited-service venues, capitalizing on an aging population with broader menu selections, more nutritious food, and a more comfortable dining experience.

Consumer willingness to spend more on dining out offset some of those trends. Exhibit E-3 compares the amount spent on restaurant meals per dollar spent in food stores at three points in time.[8]

EXHIBIT E-3

*Restaurant Spending Per Food
Store Dollar*

$.34 $.54 $.65

1976   1986   1996

[8] Estimated by the National Restaurant Association.

Same-store sales provide insight as to the relative success of fast-food restaurants. Additional store openings often masked flat or declining sales per store. McDonald's same-store revenues were essentially the same from 1993 to 1998.[9] Wendy's increased market share was attributable to its increase in per store sales. Exhibit E-4 contrasts the same-store sales for the two companies.

EXHIBIT E-4
*Same-Store Sales
1993 and 1997*

McDonald's

$1.44 million — 1993

$1.47 million — 1998

Wendy's

$.92 million — 1993

$1.38 million — 1998

Fast-food restaurants capitalized on two opportunities to improve performance during the period analyzed. First, they increasingly looked overseas to expand. Foreign countries offered greater growth opportunities than the increasingly saturated domestic market, but they offered many challenges as well. Second, limited service chains invested heavily in technology to reduce costs. Technological innovations improved such areas as employee staffing, inventory management, cooking efficiency, drive-through service, and customer wait time.

SIGNIFICANT EVENTS

1993

◆ Industry considers marketing products at gas stations and other unconventional outlets; consumption trends toward tasty high-fat products, despite health concerns.
◆ McDonald's increases its dividend.

---

[9] Restaurant Industry Surveys, *Standard & Poor's Industry Surveys*, March 1994 and June 1998 (New York: McGraw-Hill).

1994

◆ Industry increases drive-through sales, contemplates how to improve efficiency, extends promotional tie-ins to movies and other entertainment sources, and eliminates smoking in stores.

◆ McDonald's announces a $1 billion, three-year stock repurchase program; the company also doubles its initial franchise fee.

1995

◆ Companies increase menus, despite concern that too many products blur brand image and decrease revenues; the industry reduces selling prices on many of its projects.

◆ Wendy's acquires Canada's second largest fast-food company, Tim Horton's, for $400 million; the firm markets the "create your own combo" concept.

◆ McDonald's eliminates plans for its Hearth Express restaurant concept.

1996

◆ Price wars continue as companies vie for market share.

◆ McDonald's requires franchisees to comply with stricter rules, increases hamburger quality and quantity, purchases 183 Roy Rogers restaurants, and rolls out its Arch Deluxe sandwich.

◆ Wendy's purchases 40 Roy Rogers restaurants; Dave Thomas, Wendy's founder and spokesperson, has heart bypass surgery.

1997

◆ Price discounts continue throughout the industry.

◆ McDonald's sells its interest in Discovery Zone.

◆ Wendy's names Gordon Teter as chair, expands Japanese operations by opening 152 stores, and eliminates self-serve salad bars.

1998

◆ Industry hampered by high labor costs.

◆ McDonald's records a one-time expense as it overhauls kitchen and administrative operations, announces its first ever layoffs, and replaces Michael Quinlan with Jack M. Greenberg as chief executive officer.

◆ Wendy's decreases its number of new store openings, begins exclusively serving Coca-Cola soft-drinks, and exits the Korean market.

	1998	1997	1996	1995	1994	1993
Revenues						
Sales by company-operated restaurants	$8,895	$8,138	$7,572	$6,863	$5,793	$5,158
Revenues from franchised and affiliated restaurants	3,527	3,272	3,116	2,931	2,528	2,251
Total Revenues	12,422	11,410	10,688	9,794	8,321	7,409
Operating Costs and Expenses						
Company-operated restaurants						
Food and packaging	2,997	2,773	2,547	2,319	1,934	1,735
Payroll and employee benefits	2,220	2,025	1,910	1,731	1,459	1,291
Occupancy and other operating expenses	2,044	1,852	1,707	1,497	1,252	1,138
	7,261	6,650	6,164	5,547	4,645	4,164
Franchised restaurants—occupancy expenses	678	614	570	515	436	381
Selling, general, and administrative expenses	1,459	1,451	1,366	1,236	1,083	941
Made For You costs	162	—	—	—	—	—
Special charges, net of other operating (income) expenses	100	–114	–46	–105	–84	–62
Total Operating Expenses	9,660	8,601	8,054	7,193	6,080	5,424
Operating Income	2,762	2,809	2,634	2,601	2,241	1,985
Interest expense, net	414	364	343	340	306	316
Nonoperating (income) expense	41	37	39	92	49	-7
Income before provision for income taxes	2,307	2,408	2,252	2,169	1,886	1,676
Provision for income taxes	757	765	679	742	662	593
Net Income	$1,550	$1,643	$1,573	$1,427	$1,224	$1,083
Basic earnings per share	$1.14	$2.35	$2.21	$1.97	$1.68	$1.45
Diluted earnings per share	$1.10	$2.29	$2.16	$1.93		

Vertical Common Size

	1998	1997	1996	1995	1994	1993
Revenues						
Sales by company-operated restaurants	71.6%	71.3%	70.8%	70.1%	69.6%	69.6%
Revenues from franchised and affiliated restaurants	28.4%	28.7%	29.2%	29.9%	30.4%	30.4%
Total Revenues	100.0%	100.0%	100.0%	100.0%	100.0%	100.0%
Operating Costs and Expenses						
Company-operated restaurants						
Food and packaging	24.1%	24.3%	23.8%	23.7%	23.2%	23.4%

Vertical Common Size (continued)

	1998	1997	1996	1995	1994	1993
Payroll and employee benefits	17.9%	17.7%	17.9%	17.7%	17.5%	17.4%
Occupancy and other	16.5%	16.2%	16.0%	15.3%	15.0%	15.4%
operating expenses	58.5%	58.3%	57.7%	56.6%	55.8%	56.2%
Franchised restaurants— occupancy expenses	5.5%	5.4%	5.3%	5.3%	5.2%	5.1%
Selling, general and administrative expenses	11.7%	12.7%	12.8%	12.6%	13.0%	12.7%
Made For You costs	1.3%	0.0%	0.0%	0.0%	0.0%	0.0%
Special charges, net of other operating (income) expenses	0.8%	−1.0%	−0.4%	−1.1%	−1.0%	−0.8%
Total Operating Expenses	77.8%	75.4%	75.4%	73.4%	73.1%	73.2%
Operating Income	22.2%	24.6%	24.6%	26.6%	26.9%	26.8%
Interest expense, net	3.3%	3.2%	3.2%	3.5%	3.7%	4.3%
Nonoperating (income) expense	0.3%	0.3%	0.4%	0.9%	0.6%	−0.1%
Income before provision for income taxes	18.6%	21.1%	21.1%	22.1%	22.7%	22.6%
Provision for income taxes	6.1%	6.7%	6.4%	7.6%	8.0%	8.0%
Net Income	12.5%	14.4%	14.7%	14.6%	14.7%	14.6%

Horizontal Common Size—1993 Base Year

	1998	1997	1996	1995	1994	1993
Revenues						
Sales by company-operated restaurants	172.5%	157.8%	146.8%	133.1%	112.3%	100.0%
Revenues from franchised and affiliated restaurants	156.7%	145.4%	138.4%	130.2%	112.3%	100.0%
Total Revenues	167.7%	154.0%	144.3%	132.2%	112.3%	100.0%
Operating Costs and Expenses						
Company-operated restaurants						
Food and packaging	172.7%	159.8%	146.8%	133.7%	111.5%	100.0%
Payroll and employee benefits	172.0%	156.9%	147.9%	134.1%	113.0%	100.0%
Occupancy and other	179.6%	162.7%	150.0%	131.5%	110.0%	100.0%
operating expenses	174.4%	159.7%	148.0%	133.2%	111.6%	100.0%
Franchised restaurants— occupancy expenses	178.0%	161.2%	149.6%	135.2%	114.4%	100.0%
Selling, general, and administrative expenses	155.0%	154.2%	145.2%	131.3%	115.1%	100.0%
Made For You costs						
Special charges, net of other operating (income) expenses	−161.3%	183.9%	73.9%	169.4%	135.5%	100.0%

Horizontal Common Size—1993 Base Year (continued)

	1998	1997	1996	1995	1994	1993
Total operating expenses	178.1%	158.6%	148.5%	132.6%	112.1%	100.0%
Operating income	139.1%	141.5%	132.7%	131.0%	112.9%	100.0%
Interest expense, net	131.0%	115.2%	108.5%	107.6%	96.8%	100.0%
Nonoperating (income) expense	−585.7%	−528.6%	−557.1%	−1314.3%	−700.0%	100.0%
Income before provision for income taxes	137.6%	143.7%	134.4%	129.4%	112.5%	100.0%
Provision for income taxes	127.7%	129.0%	114.5%	125.1%	111.6%	100.0%
Net Income	143.1%	151.7%	145.2%	131.8%	113.0%	100.0%

Horizontal Common Size—Rolling Forward Method

	1998	1997	1996	1995	1994	1993
Revenues						
Sales by company-operated restaurants	109.3%	107.5%	110.3%	118.5%	112.3%	100.0%
Revenues from franchised and affiliated restaurants	107.8%	105.0%	106.3%	115.9%	112.3%	100.0%
Total Revenues	108.9%	106.8%	109.1%	117.7%	112.3%	100.0%
Operating Costs and Expenses						
Company-operated restaurants						
Food and packaging	108.1%	108.9%	109.8%	119.9%	111.5%	100.0%
Payroll and employee benefits	109.6%	106.0%	110.3%	118.6%	113.0%	100.0%
Occupancy and other operating expenses	110.4%	108.5%	114.0%	119.6%	110.0%	100.0%
	109.2%	107.9%	111.1%	119.4%	111.6%	100.0%
Franchised restaurants—occupancy expenses	110.4%	107.7%	110.7%	118.1%	114.4%	100.0%
Selling, general, and administrative expenses	100.6%	106.2%	110.5%	114.1%	115.1%	100.0%
Made For You costs						
Special charges, net of other operating (income) expenses	−87.7%	248.9%	43.6%	125.0%	135.5%	100.0%
Total Operating Expenses	112.3%	106.8%	112.0%	118.3%	112.1%	100.0%
Operating Income	98.3%	106.7%	101.3%	116.1%	112.9%	100.0%
Interest expense, net	113.7%	106.1%	100.9%	111.1%	96.8%	100.0%
Nonoperating (income) expense	110.8%	94.9%	42.4%	187.8%	−700.0%	100.0%
Income before provision for income taxes	95.8%	106.9%	103.8%	115.0%	112.5%	100.0%
Provision for income taxes	99.0%	112.7%	91.5%	112.1%	111.6%	100.0%
Net Income	94.3%	104.5%	110.2%	116.6%	113.0%	100.0%

Compound Annual Growth Rate

	1993	1994	1995	1996	1997	1998	Growth
Revenues							
Sales by company-operated restaurants	($5,158)	0	0	0	0	$8,895	11.5%
Revenues from franchised and affiliated restaurants	($2,251)	0	0	0	0	3,527	9.4%
Total Revenues	($7,409)	0	0	0	0	12,422	10.9%
Operating Costs and Expenses							
Company-operated restaurants							
Food and packaging	($1,735)	0	0	0	0	2,997	11.6%
Payroll and employee benefits	($1,291)	0	0	0	0	2,220	11.5%
Occupancy and other	($1,138)	0	0	0	0	2,044	12.4%
operating expenses	($4,164)	0	0	0	0	7,261	11.8%
Franchised restaurants—occupancy expenses	($381)	0	0	0	0	678	12.2%
Selling, general, and administrative expenses	($941)	0	0	0	0	1,459	9.2%
Made For You costs	$—	0	0	0	0	162	
Special charges, net of other operating (income) expenses	$62	0	0	0	0	100	
Total Operating Expenses	($5,424)	0	0	0	0	9,660	12.2%
Operating Income	($1,985)	0	0	0	0	2,762	6.8%
Interest expense, net	($316)	0	0	0	0	414	5.6%
Nonoperating (income) expense	$7	0	0	0	0	41	
Income before provision for income taxes	($1,676)	0	0	0	0	2,307	6.6%
Provision for income taxes	($593)	0	0	0	0	757	5.0%
Net Income	($1,083)	0	0	0	0	$1,550	7.4%

	1998	1997	1996	1995	1994	1993
Cash	$299	$341	$330	$335	$180	$186
Accounts receivable	609	484	495	413	379	314
Inventory	77	71	70	58	51	44
Prepaid and other current assets	324	247	208	149	131	119
Total current assets	1,309	1,143	1,103	955	741	663
Property, plant, and equipment	16,042	14,961	14,352	12,811	11,328	10,081
Other long-term assets	2,433	2,138	1,931	1,648	1,523	1,291
Total assets	$19,784	$18,242	$17,386	$15,414	$13,592	$12,035

	1998	1997	1996	1995	1994	1993
Accounts payable	$1,308	$1,945	$1,236	$977	$1,556	$589
Taxes payable	238	200	160	182	127	146
Other current liabilities	951	839	739	635	768	367
Total current liabilities	2,497	2,984	2,135	1,794	2,451	1,102
Long-term debt	6,189	4,834	4,830	4,258	2,935	3,490
Other long-term liabilities and minority interests	493	428	727	665	423	334
Deferred income taxes	1,082	1,064	976	836	841	835
Common equity put options	59	80	—	—	56	—
Total liabilities	10,320	9,390	8,668	7,553	6,706	5,761
Preferred stock	—	—	358	358	674	677
Common stock	17	17	8	92	92	46
Additional paid-in capital	989	691	574	387	286	303
Guarantee of ESOP notes	−149	−171	−193	−214	−234	−254
Retained earnings	13,880	12,569	11,173	9,831	8,626	7,613
Accumulated other comprehensive income	−523	−471	—	—	—	—
Common stock in treasury, at cost	−4,750	−3,783	−3,027	−2,506	−2,443	−1,919
Foreign currency translation adjustment	—	—	−175	−87	−115	−192
Total shareholders' equity	9,464	8,852	8,718	7,861	6,886	6,274
Total liabilities and shareholders' equity	$19,784	$18,242	$17,386	$15,414	$13,592	$12,035

Vertical Common Size

	1998	1997	1996	1995	1994	1993
Cash	1.5%	1.9%	1.9%	2.2%	1.3%	1.5%
Accounts receivable	3.1%	2.7%	2.8%	2.7%	2.8%	2.6%
Inventory	0.4%	0.4%	0.4%	0.4%	0.4%	0.4%
Prepaid and other current assets	1.6%	1.4%	1.2%	1.0%	1.0%	1.0%
Total current assets	6.6%	6.3%	6.3%	6.2%	5.5%	5.5%
Property, plant, and equipment	81.1%	82.0%	82.5%	83.1%	83.3%	83.8%
Other long-term assets	12.3%	11.7%	11.1%	10.7%	11.2%	10.7%
Total assets	100.0%	100.0%	100.0%	100.0%	100.0%	100.0%
Accounts payable	6.6%	10.7%	7.1%	6.3%	11.4%	4.9%
Taxes payable	1.2%	1.1%	0.9%	1.2%	0.9%	1.2%
Other current liabilities	4.8%	4.6%	4.3%	4.1%	5.7%	3.0%
Total current liabilities	12.6%	16.4%	12.3%	11.6%	18.0%	9.2%
Long-term debt	31.3%	26.5%	27.8%	27.6%	21.6%	29.0%
Other long-term liabilities and minority interests	2.5%	2.3%	4.2%	4.3%	3.1%	2.8%
Deferred income taxes	5.5%	5.8%	5.6%	5.4%	6.2%	6.9%
Common equity put options	0.3%	0.4%	0.0%	0.0%	0.4%	0.0%
Total liabilities	52.2%	51.5%	49.9%	49.0%	49.3%	47.9%

Vertical Common Size (continued)

	1998	1997	1996	1995	1994	1993
Preferred stock	0.0%	0.0%	2.1%	2.3%	5.0%	5.6%
Common stock	0.1%	0.1%	0.0%	0.6%	0.7%	0.4%
Additional paid-in capital	5.0%	3.8%	3.3%	2.5%	2.1%	2.5%
Guarantee of ESOP notes	−0.8%	−0.9%	−1.1%	−1.4%	−1.7%	−2.1%
Retained earnings	70.2%	68.9%	64.3%	63.8%	63.5%	63.3%
Accumulated other comprehensive income	−2.6%	−2.6%	0.0%	0.0%	0.0%	0.0%
Common stock in treasury, at cost	−24.0%	−20.7%	−17.4%	−16.3%	−18.0%	−15.9%
Foreign currency translation adjustment	0.0%	0.0%	−1.0%	−0.6%	−0.8%	−1.6%
Total shareholders' equity	47.8%	48.5%	50.1%	51.0%	50.7%	52.1%
Total liabilities and shareholders' equity	100.0%	100.0%	100.0%	100.0%	100.0%	100.0%

Horizontal Common Size—1993 Base Year

	1998	1997	1996	1995	1994	1993
Cash	160.8%	183.3%	177.4%	180.1%	96.8%	100.0%
Accounts receivable	193.9%	154.1%	157.6%	131.5%	120.7%	100.0%
Inventory	175.0%	161.4%	159.1%	131.8%	115.9%	100.0%
Prepaid and other current assets	272.3%	207.6%	174.8%	125.2%	110.1%	100.0%
Total current assets	197.4%	172.4%	166.4%	144.0%	111.8%	100.0%
Property, plant, and equipment	159.1%	148.4%	142.4%	127.1%	112.4%	100.0%
Other long-term assets	188.5%	165.6%	149.6%	127.7%	118.0%	100.0%
Total assets	164.4%	151.6%	144.5%	128.1%	112.9%	100.0%
Accounts payable	222.1%	330.2%	209.8%	165.9%	264.2%	100.0%
Taxes payable	163.0%	137.0%	109.6%	124.7%	87.0%	100.0%
Other current liabilities	259.1%	228.6%	201.4%	173.0%	209.3%	100.0%
Total current liabilities	226.6%	270.8%	193.7%	162.8%	222.4%	100.0%
Long-term debt	177.3%	138.5%	138.4%	122.0%	84.1%	100.0%
Other long-term liabilities and minority interests	147.6%	128.1%	217.7%	199.1%	126.6%	100.0%
Deferred income taxes	129.6%	127.4%	116.9%	100.1%	100.7%	100.0%
Common equity put options						
Total liabilities	179.1%	163.0%	150.5%	131.1%	116.4%	100.0%
Preferred stock	0.0%	0.0%	52.9%	52.9%	99.6%	100.0%
Common stock	37.0%	37.0%	17.4%	200.0%	200.0%	100.0%
Additional paid-in capital	326.4%	228.1%	189.4%	127.7%	94.4%	100.0%
Guarantee of ESOP notes	58.7%	67.3%	76.0%	84.3%	92.1%	100.0%
Retained earnings	182.3%	165.1%	146.8%	129.1%	113.3%	100.0%
Accumulated other comprehensive income						
Common stock in treasury, at cost	247.5%	197.1%	157.7%	130.6%	127.3%	100.0%

Horizontal Common Size—1993 Base Year (continued)

	1998	1997	1996	1995	1994	1993
Foreign currency translation adjustment	0.0%	0.0%	91.1%	45.4%	59.9%	100.0%
Total shareholders' equity	150.8%	141.1%	139.0%	125.3%	109.8%	100.0%
Total liabilities and shareholders' equity	164.4%	151.6%	144.5%	128.1%	112.9%	100.0%

Horizontal Common Size—Rolling Forward Method

	1998	1997	1996	1995	1994	1993
Cash	87.7%	103.3%	98.5%	186.1%	96.8%	100.0%
Accounts receivable	125.8%	97.8%	119.9%	109.0%	120.7%	100.0%
Inventory	108.5%	101.4%	120.7%	113.7%	115.9%	100.0%
Prepaid and other current assets	131.2%	118.8%	139.6%	113.7%	110.1%	100.0%
Total current assets	114.5%	103.6%	115.5%	128.9%	111.8%	100.0%
Property, plant, and equipment	107.2%	104.2%	112.0%	113.1%	112.4%	100.0%
Other long-term assets	113.8%	110.7%	117.2%	108.2%	118.0%	100.0%
Total assets	108.5%	104.9%	112.8%	113.4%	112.9%	100.0%
Accounts payable	67.2%	157.4%	126.5%	62.8%	264.2%	100.0%
Taxes payable	119.0%	125.0%	87.9%	143.3%	87.0%	100.0%
Other current liabilities	113.3%	113.5%	116.4%	82.7%	209.3%	100.0%
Total current liabilities	83.7%	139.8%	119.0%	73.2%	222.4%	100.0%
Long-term debt	128.0%	100.1%	113.4%	145.1%	84.1%	100.0%
Other long-term liabilities and minority interests	115.2%	58.9%	109.3%	157.2%	126.6%	100.0%
Deferred income taxes	101.7%	109.0%	116.7%	99.4%	100.7%	100.0%
Common equity put options	73.8%					
Total liabilities	109.9%	108.3%	114.8%	112.6%	116.4%	100.0%
Preferred stock		0.0%	100.0%	53.1%	99.6%	100.0%
Common stock	100.0%	212.5%	8.7%	100.0%	200.0%	100.0%
Additional paid-in capital	143.1%	120.4%	148.3%	135.3%	94.4%	100.0%
Guarantee of ESOP notes	87.1%	88.6%	90.2%	91.5%	92.1%	100.0%
Retained earnings	110.4%	112.5%	113.7%	114.0%	113.3%	100.0%
Accumulated other comprehensive income	111.0%					
Common stock in treasury, at cost	125.6%	125.0%	120.8%	102.6%	127.3%	100.0%
Foreign currency translation adjustment		0.0%	200.9%	75.7%	59.9%	100.0%
Total shareholders' equity	106.9%	101.5%	110.9%	114.2%	109.8%	100.0%
Total liabilities and shareholders' equity	108.5%	104.9%	112.8%	113.4%	112.9%	100.0%

McDonald's Balance Sheets (in millions) (continued)

Compound Annual Growth Rate

	1993	1994	1995	1996	1997	1998	Growth
Cash	($186)	0	0	0	0	$299	10.0%
Accounts receivable	($314)	0	0	0	0	609	14.2%
Inventory	($44)	0	0	0	0	77	11.8%
Prepaid and other current assets	($119)	0	0	0	0	324	22.2%
Total current assets	($663)	0	0	0	0	1,309	14.6%
Property, plant and equipment	($10,081)	0	0	0	0	16,042	9.7%
Other long-term assets	($1,291)	0	0	0	0	2,433	13.5%
Total assets	($12,035)	0	0	0	0	19,784	10.5%
Accounts payable	($589)	0	0	0	0	1,308	17.3%
Taxes payable	($146)	0	0	0	0	238	10.3%
Other current liabilities	($367)	0	0	0	0	951	21.0%
Total current liabilities	($1,102)	0	0	0	0	2,497	17.8%
Long-term debt	($3,490)	0	0	0	0	6,189	12.1%
Other long-term liabilities and minority interests	($334)	0	0	0	0	493	8.1%
Deferred income taxes	($835)	0	0	0	0	1,082	5.3%
Common equity put options	$—	0	0	0	0	59	
Total liabilities	($5,761)	0	0	0	0	10,320	12.4%
Preferred stock	($677)	0	0	0	0	—	
Common stock	($46)	0	0	0	0	17	–18.1%
Additional paid-in capital	($303)	0	0	0	0	989	26.7%
Guarantee of ESOP notes	$254	0	0	0	0	–149	–10.1%
Retained earnings	($7,613)	0	0	0	0	13,880	12.8%
Accumulated other comprehensive income	$—	0	0	0	0	–523	
Common stock in treasury, at cost	$1,919	0	0	0	0	–4,750	19.9%
Foreign currency translation adjustment	$192	0	0	0	0	—	
Total shareholders' equity	($6,274)	0	0	0	0	9,464	8.6%
Total liabilities and shareholders' equity	($12,035)	0	0	0	0	$19,784	10.5%

McDonald's. Inc.
Condensed Statements of Cash
Flows (in millions of dollars)

	1998	1997	1996	1995	1994
Net income	$1,550	$1,643	$1,573	$1.427	$1,224
Depreciation expense	881	794	743	709	629
Other adjustments to operations	335	5	145	160	73
Cash flows from operating activities	2,766	2,442	2,461	2,296	1,926
Purchase of property, plant, and equipment	−1,879	−2,111	−2,375	−2,064	−1,539
Other adjustments to investing activities	−69	−106	−195	−45	33
Cash flows from investing activities	−1,948	−2,217	−2,570	−2,109	−1,506
Dividends	−240	−248	−232	−227	−216
Other adjustments to financing activities	−620	34	336	195	−210
Cash flows from financing activities	−860	−214	104	−32	−426
Net change in cash	$ −42	$ 11	$ −5	$155	$ −6

McDonald's Income
Statements (in millions)

	1998	1997	1996	1995	1994
Revenues					
Sales by company-operated restaurants	$8,895	$8,138	$7,572	$6,863	$5,793
Revenues from franchised and affiliated restaurants	3,527	3,272	3,116	2,931	2,528
Total Revenues	12,422	11,410	10,688	9,794	8,321
Operating Costs and Expenses					
Company-operated restaurants					
Food and packaging	2,997	2,773	2,547	2,319	1,934
Payroll and employee benefits	2,220	2,025	1,910	1,731	1,459
Occupancy and other operating expenses	2,044	1,852	1,707	1,497	1,252
	7,261	6,650	6,164	5,547	4,645
Franchised restaurants- occupancy expenses	678	614	570	515	436
Selling, general, and administrative expenses	1,459	1,451	1,366	1,236	1,083
Made For You costs	162	—	—	—	—
Special charges, net of other operating (income) expenses	100	−114	−46	−105	−84
Total Operating Expenses	9,660	8,601	8,054	7,193	6,080
Operating Income	2,762	2,809	2,634	2,601	2,241
Interest expense, net	414	364	343	340	306
Nonoperating (income) expense	41	37	39	92	49
Income before provision for income taxes	2,307	2,408	2,252	2,169	1,886
Provision for income taxes	757	765	679	742	662
Net Income	$1,550	$1,643	$1,573	$1,427	$1,224

	1998	1997	1996	1995	1994
Cash	$320.00	$335.50	$332.50	$257.50	$183.00
Accounts receivable	546.50	489.50	454.00	396.00	346.50
Inventory	74.00	70.50	64.00	54.50	47.50
Prepaid and other current assets	285.50	227.50	178.50	140.00	125.00
Total current assets	1,226.00	1,123.00	1,029.00	848.00	702.00
Property, plant, and equipment	15,501.50	14,656.50	13,581.50	12,069.50	10,704.50
Other long-term assets	2,285.50	2,034.50	1,789.50	1,585.50	1,407.00
Total assets	$19,013.00	$17,814.00	$16,400.00	$14,503.00	$12,813.50
Accounts payable	$1,626.50	$1,590.50	$1,106.50	$1,266.50	$1,072.50
Taxes payable	219.00	180.00	171.00	154.50	136.50
Other current liabilities	895.00	789.00	687.00	701.50	567.50
Total current liabilities	2,740.50	2,559.50	1,964.50	2,122.50	1,776.50
Long-term debt	5,511.50	4,832.00	4,544.00	3,596.50	3,212.50
Other long-term liabilities and minority interests	460.50	577.50	696.00	544.00	378.50
Deferred income taxes	1,073.00	1,020.00	906.00	838.50	838.00
Common equity put options	69.50	40.00	—	28.00	28.00
Total liabilities	9,855.00	9,029.00	8,110.50	7,129.50	6,233.50
Preferred stock	—	179.00	358.00	516.00	675.50
Common stock	17.00	12.50	50.00	92.00	69.00
Additional paid-in capital	840.00	632.50	480.50	336.50	294.50
Guarantee of ESOP notes	−160.00	−182.00	−203.50	−224.00	−244.00
Retained earnings	13,224.50	11,871.00	10,502.00	9,228.50	8,119.50
Accumulated other comprehensive income	−497.00	−235.50	—	—	—
Common stock in treasury, at cost	−4,266.50	−3,405.00	−2,766.50	−2,474.50	−2,181.00
Foreign currency translation adjustment	—	−87.50	−131.05	−101.05	−153.50
Total shareholders' equity	9,158.00	8,785.00	8,289.50	7,373.50	6,580.00
Total liabilities and shareholders' equity	$19,013.00	$17,814.00	$16,400.00	$14,503.00	$12,813.50

Cash Flow Data

	1998	1997	1996	1995	1994
Cash flow from operations	$2,766	$2,442	$2,461	$2,296	$1,926
Fixed asset purchases	1,879	2,111	2,375	2,064	1,539
Cash dividends	240	248	232	227	216
Depreciation and amortization	881	794	743	709	629

Market Data

	1998	1997	1996	1995	1994
High market price	$39.8	$27.4	$27.1	$ 24	$15.8
Low market price	$22.3	$21.1	$20.5	$14.3	$12.8
Number of shares outstanding (millions)	1,356.2	1,371.4	1,389.2	1,399.4	1,387.4
Market capitalization	$42,110.01	$33,256.45	$33,062.96	$26,798.51	$19,839.82

McDonald's Ratios

Liquidity Ratios

	1998	1997	1996	1995	1994
Working capital	($1,514.50)	($1,436.50)	($935.50)	($1,274.50)	($1,074.50)
Working capital ratio	0.45	0.44	0.52	0.40	0.40
Quick ratio	0.32	0.32	0.40	0.31	0.30
Inventory turnover	40.50	39.33	39.80	42.55	40.72
Days in inventory	9.01	9.28	9.17	8.58	8.96
Accounts receivable turnover	22.73	23.31	23.54	24.73	24.01
Days in accounts receivable	16.06	15.66	15.50	14.76	15.20
Inventory conversion cycle	25.07	24.94	24.68	23.34	24.16
Accounts payable turnover	1.84	1.74	2.30	1.83	1.80
Days in accounts payable	198.09	209.35	158.57	199.34	202.41
Net cash conversion cycle	−173.02	−184.41	−133.89	−176.01	−178.25
Cash + short-term investments	320.00	335.50	332.50	257.50	183.00
A/R*days in accounts receivable	8,775.70	7,665.01	7,038.95	5,844.17	5,266.52
Inventory*days in inventory	666.91	654.22	586.98	467.50	425.82
Product dollar days	9,762.61	8,654.72	7,958.43	6,569.18	5,875.34
Current assets-other current assets	940.50	895.50	850.50	708.00	577.00
Liquidity index	10.38	9.66	9.36	9.28	10.18

Cash Flow Ratios

	1998	1997	1996	1995	1994
Cash flow adequacy	1.31	1.04	0.94	1.00	1.10
Reinvestment ratio	0.68	0.86	0.97	0.90	0.80
Dividend payout	0.09	0.10	0.09	0.10	0.11
Free cash flow	647.00	83.00	−146.00	5.00	171.00
Depreciation impact ratio	0.32	0.33	0.30	0.31	0.33
Recapitalization index	2.13	2.66	3.20	2.91	2.45
Cash flow return on assets	0.15	0.14	0.15	0.16	0.15
Cash flow return on sales	0.22	0.21	0.23	0.23	0.23
Operations index	1.00	0.87	0.93	0.88	0.86

Asset Utilization Ratios

	1998	1997	1996	1995	1994
Profit margin	12.478%	14.400%	14.716%	14.570%	14.710%
Asset turnover	0.653	0.641	0.652	0.675	0.649
Financial structure leverage	2.076	2.028	1.978	1.967	1.947
Return on assets	8.15%	9.22%	9.59%	9.84%	9.55%
Return on equity	16.93%	18.70%	18.97%	19.35%	18.60%

Capital Structure Ratios

	1998	1997	1996	1995	1994
Debt to capital	0.52	0.51	0.49	0.49	0.49
Debt to equity	1.08	1.03	0.98	0.97	0.95
Long-term debt to capital	0.29	0.27	0.28	0.25	0.25
Long-term debt to equity	0.60	0.55	0.55	0.49	0.49
Working capital/total assets-Z1	−0.10	−0.10	−0.07	−0.11	−0.10
Retained earnings/total assets-Z2	0.97	0.93	0.90	0.89	0.89
EBIT/total assets-Z3	0.48	0.52	0.53	0.59	0.58
Sales/total assets-Z4	0.65	0.64	0.65	0.68	0.65
Market to book-Z5	2.56	2.21	2.45	2.26	1.91
Z-Score	4.57	4.21	4.46	4.31	3.92

Market Ratio

	1998	1997	1996	1995	1994
Price to earnings	27.17	20.24	21.02	18.78	16.21

Wendy's International
Income Statements
(in millions)

	1998	1997	1996	1995	1994	1993
Revenues						
Retail sales	$1,586	$1,652	$1,567	$1,462	$1,366	$1,199
Royalties and other	362	386	330	284	226	121
Total Revenues	1,948	2,037	1,897	1,746	1,592	1,320
Operating Costs and Expenses						
Company-operated restaurants	360	390	379	351	333	319
Cost of sales	996	1,026	977	890	818	706
Interest, net	2	4	7	10	13	12
Depreciation of property and equipment	95	96	89	81	75	66
Selling, general, and administrative expenses	287	303	190	249	203	101
Total Operating Expenses	1,741	1,818	1,642	1,581	1,441	1,204
Income before provision for income taxes	207	219	255	165	150	116
Provision for income taxes	84	89	99	55	53	36
Net Income	$123	$130	$156	$110	$97	$79
Basic earnings per share	0.96	0.99	1.23	0.93	0.83	0.70
Diluted earnings per share	0.95	0.97	1.19	0.88	0.79	0.67

Vertical Common Size

	1998	1997	1996	1995	1994	1993
Revenues						
Retail sales	81.4%	81.1%	82.6%	83.7%	85.8%	90.8%
Royalties and other	18.6%	18.9%	17.4%	16.3%	14.2%	9.2%
Total Revenues	100.0%	100.0%	100.0%	100.0%	100.0%	100.0%
Operating Costs and Expenses						
Company-operated restaurants	18.5%	19.1%	20.0%	20.1%	20.9%	24.2%
Cost of sales	51.1%	50.4%	51.5%	51.0%	51.4%	53.5%
Interest, net	0.1%	0.2%	0.4%	0.6%	0.8%	0.9%
Depreciation of property and equipment	4.9%	4.7%	4.7%	4.6%	4.7%	5.0%
Selling, general, and administrative expenses	14.7%	14.9%	10.0%	14.3%	12.8%	7.7%
Total Operating Expenses	89.3%	89.2%	86.6%	90.5%	90.6%	91.2%
	0.00%	0.0%	0.0%	0.0%	0.0%	0.0%
Income before provision for income taxes	10.7%	10.8%	13.4%	9.5%	9.4%	8.8%
Provision for income taxes	4.3%	4.4%	5.2%	3.2%	3.3%	2.7%
Net Income	6.3%	6.4%	8.2%	6.3%	6.1%	6.0%

Horizontal Common Size—1933 Base Year

	1998	1997	1996	1995	1994	1993
Revenues						
Retail sales	132.3%	137.8%	130.7%	121.9%	113.9%	100.0%
Royalties and other	298.5%	317.9%	272.2%	234.4%	186.2%	100.0%
Total Revenues	147.6%	154.3%	143.7%	132.3%	120.6%	100.0%
Operating Costs and Expenses						
Company-operated restaurants	112.7%	122.0%	118.8%	109.9%	104.2%	100.0%
Cost of sales	141.1%	145.4%	138.4%	126.2%	115.8%	100.0%
Interest, net	17.4%	30.8%	58.2%	87.4%	112.5%	100.0%
Depreciation of property and equipment	145.3%	145.7%	135.5%	122.70%	113.5%	100.0%
Selling, general, and administrative expenses	281.3%	296.6%	186.5%	243.6%	198.9%	100.0%
Total Operating Expenses	144.5%	150.9%	136.3%	131.3%	119.7%	100.0%
Income before provision for income taxes	179.7%	190.0%	220.6%	142.9%	130.1%	100.0%
Provision for income taxes	232.4%	245.3%	272.6%	151.9%	145.8%	100.0%
Net Income	155.6%	164.6%	196.7%	138.9%	122.9%	100.0%

Horizontal Common Size—Rolling Forward

	1998	1997	1996	1995	1994	1993
Revenues						
Retail sales	96.0%	105.4%	107.2%	107.0%	113.9%	100.0%
Royalties and other	93.9%	116.8%	116.1%	125.9%	186.2%	100.0%
Total Revenues	95.6%	107.4%	108.6%	109.7%	120.6%	100.0%
Operating Costs and Expenses						
Company-operated restaurants	92.4%	102.7%	108.1%	105.5%	104.2%	100.0%
Cost of sales	97.1%	105.1%	109.7%	108.9%	115.8%	100.0%
Interest, net	56.6%	52.9%	66.6%	77.7%	112.5%	100.0%
Depreciation of property and equipment	99.7%	107.5%	110.4%	108.1%	113.5%	100.0%
Selling, general, and administrative expenses	94.8%	159.1%	76.5%	122.5%	198.9%	100.0%
Total Operating Expenses	95.7%	110.7%	103.9%	109.7%	119.7%	100.0%
Income before provision for income taxes	94.6%	86.1%	154.3%	109.9%	130.1%	100.0%
Provision for income taxes	94.8%	90.0%	179.5%	104.2%	145.8%	100.0%
Net Income	94.5%	83.7%	141.7%	113.0%	122.9%	100.0%

Compound Annual Growth Rate

	1993	1994	1995	1996	1997	1998	Growth
Revenues							
Retail sales	($1,199)	0	0	0	0	$1,586	5.8%
Royalties and other	–121	0	0	0	0	362	24.4%
Total Revenues	–1,320	0	0	0	0	1,948	8.1%
Operating Costs and Expenses							
Company-operated restaurants	–319	0	0	0	0	360	2.4%
Cost of sales	–706	0	0	0	0	996	7.1%
Interest, net	–12	0	0	0	0	2	
Depreciation of property and equipment	–66	0	0	0	0	95	7.7%
Selling, general, and administrative expenses	–102	0	0	0	0	287	22.9%
Total Operating Expenses	–1,205	0	0	0	0	1,741	7.6%
Income before provision for income taxes	–116	0	0	0	0	208	12.5%
Provision for income taxes	–36	0	0	0	0	84	18.3%
Net Income	–79	0	0	0	0	$123	9.2%

	1998	1997	1996	1995	1994	1993
Cash	$161	$234	$219	$206	$120	$72
Accounts receivable	95	81	64	62	52	33
Inventory	35	36	33	27	27	21
Deferred income taxes	23	31	16	18	11	12
Other current assets	—	—	5	8	23	41
Total current assets	314	382	337	321	233	179
Property, plant and equipment	1,281	1,266	1,208	939	802	643
Other long-term assets	243	295	237	249	181	175
Total assets	$1,838	$1,942	$1,781	$1,509	$1,215	$996
Accounts payable	$136	$191	$182	$206	$187	$132
Taxes payable	31	—	—	–3	2	3
Other current liabilities	82	22	26	93	98	8
Total current liabilities	249	213	208	296	286	143
Long-term debt	205	206	198	297	105	157
Other long-term liab. and minority interests	54	58	56	50	82	55
Deferred income taxes	61	81	63	48	40	41
Total liabilities	570	557	525	690	513	396
Preferred stock	200	200	200	—	—	—
Common stock	12	12	11	10	10	10
Additional paid-in capital	370	353	313	200	172	161

	1998	1997	1996	1995	1994	1993
Retained earnings	932	839	740	615	529	431
Accumulated other comprehensive income			−1	−2	−1	—
Common stock in treasury, at cost	-212	-2	-2	-2	−2	0
Pension liability adjustment	—	—	—	—	−3	−3
Foreign currency translation adjustment	−33	−18	−5	−3	−4	1
Total shareholders' equity	1,268	1,384	1,257	819	702	601
Total liabilities and shareholders' equity	$1,838	$1,942	$1,781	$1,509	$1,215	$996

Vertical Common Size

	1998	1997	1996	1995	1994	1993
Cash	8.7%	12.1%	12.3%	13.7%	9.8%	7.2%
Accounts receivable	5.2%	4.2%	3.6%	4.1%	4.3%	3.3%
Inventory	1.9%	1.8%	1.9%	1.8%	2.2%	2.2%
Deferred income taxes	1.3%	1.6%	0.9%	1.2%	0.9%	1.2%
Other current assets	0.0%	0.0%	0.3%	0.5%	1.9%	4.1%
Total current assets	17.1%	19.7%	18.9%	21.3%	19.2%	17.9%
Property, plant, and equipment	69.7%	65.2%	67.8%	62.2%	66.0%	64.5%
Other long-term assets	13.2%	15.2%	13.3%	16.5%	14.9%	17.5%
Total assets	100.0%	100.0%	100.0%	100.0%	100.0%	100.0%
Accounts payable	7.4%	9.8%	10.2%	13.6%	15.4%	13.3%
Taxes payable	1.7%	0.0%	0.0%	-0.2%	0.1%	0.3%
Other current liabilities	4.5%	1.1%	1.4%	6.1%	8.0%	0.8%
Total current liabilities	13.6%	11.0%	11.7%	19.6%	23.6%	14.4%
Long-term debt	11.2%	10.6%	11.1%	19.7%	8.6%	15.7%
Other long-term liab. and minority interests	3.0%	3.0%	3.2%	3.3%	6.8%	5.5%
Deferred income taxes	3.3%	4.2%	3.5%	3.2%	3.3%	4.1%
Total liabilities	31.0%	28.7%	29.5%	45.7%	42.2%	39.7%
Preferred stock	10.9%	10.3%	11.2%	0.0%	0.0%	0.0%
Common stock	0.6%	0.6%	0.6%	0.7%	0.8%	1.0%
Additional paid-in capital	20.1%	18.2%	17.5%	13.2%	14.1%	16.2%
Retained earnings	50.7%	43.2%	41.6%	40.7%	43.6%	43.2%
Accumulated other comprehensive income	0.0%	0.0%	−0.1%	−0.1%	−0.1%	0.0%
Common stock in treasury, at cost	−11.5%	−0.1%	−0.1%	−0.1%	−0.1%	0.0%
Pension liability adjustment	0.0%	0.0%	0.0%	0.0%	−0.3%	-0.3%
Foreign currency translation adjustment	−1.8%	−0.9%	−0.3%	−0.2%	−0.3%	0.1%
Total shareholders' equity	69.0%	71.3%	70.5%	54.3%	57.8%	60.3%
Total liabilities and shareholders' equity	100.0%	100.0%	100.0%	100.0%	100.0%	100.0%

Horizontal Common Size—1993 Base Year

	1998	1997	1996	1995	1994	1993
Cash	224.2%	326.7%	305.4%	287.5%	166.9%	100.0%
Accounts receivable	290.1%	247.1%	196.9%	189.4%	159.4%	100.0%
Inventory	163.4%	165.9%	154.6%	126.9%	125.4%	100.0%
Deferred income taxes	189.3%	253.2%	128.7%	150.2%	88.3%	100.0%
Other current assets	0.0%	0.0%	11.8%	18.9%	57.2%	100.0%
Total current assets	175.5%	213.5%	188.6%	179.8%	130.2%	100.0%
Property, plant and equipment	199.1%	196.8%	187.8%	146.1%	124.6%	100.0%
Other long-term assets	139.4%	168.7%	135.4%	142.3%	103.4%	100.0%
Total assets	184.4%	194.9%	178.8%	151.4%	121.9%	100.0%
Accounts payable	102.7%	144.2%	137.6%	155.3%	141.0%	100.0%
Taxes payable	1,074.1%	0.0%	0.0%	-86.9%	58.1%	100.0%
Other current liabilities	1,040.0%	272.6%	323.1%	1,171.8%	1,234.7%	100.0%
Total current liabilities	174.1%	148.4%	145.0%	206.5%	199.7%	100.0%
Long-term debt	131.0%	131.3%	126.1%	189.5%	66.9%	100.0%
Other long-term liab. and minority interests	99.2%	105.7%	102.7%	90.5%	149.8%	100.0%
Deferred income taxes	148.6%	198.3%	154.1%	117.1%	97.4%	100.0%
Total liabilities	144.0%	140.9%	132.6%	174.5%	129.6%	100.0%
Preferred stock						
Common stock	117.0%	115.0%	112.2%	103.1%	101.0%	100.0%
Additional paid-in capital	229.7%	219.1%	193.9%	123.9%	106.6%	100.0%
Retained earnings	216.2%	194.8%	171.8%	142.7%	122.8%	100.0%
Accumulated other comprehensive income						
Common stock in treasury, at cost	127,870.5%	1,031.3%	1,031.3%	1,031.3%	1,031.3%	100.0%
Pension liability adjustment	0.0%	0.0%	0.0%	0.0%	124.9%	100.0%
Foreign currency translation adjustment	–2,476.2%	–1,350.5%	–352.1%	–223.2%	–281.1%	100.0%
Total shareholders' equity	211.1%	230.4%	209.2%	136.3%	116.8%	100.0%
Total liabilities and shareholders' equity	184.4%	194.9%	178.8%	151.4%	121.9%	100.0%

Horizontal Common Size—Rolling Forward Method

	1998	1997	1996	1995	1994	1993
Cash	68.6%	107.0%	106.2%	172.3%	166.9%	100.0%
Accounts receivable	117.4%	125.5%	103.9%	118.8%	159.4%	100.0%
Inventory	98.5%	107.3%	121.8%	101.2%	125.4%	100.0%
Deferred income taxes	74.7%	196.7%	85.7%	170.2%	88.3%	100.0%
Other current assets		0.0%	62.4%	33.1%	57.2%	100.0%
Total current assets	82.2%	113.2%	104.9%	138.1%	130.2%	100.0%
Property, plant, and equipment	101.2%	104.8%	128.6%	117.2%	124.6%	100.0%

Horizontal Common Size—Rolling Forward Method (continued)

	1998	1997	1996	1995	1994	1993
Other long-term assets	82.6%	124.6%	95.2%	137.7%	103.4%	100.0%
Total assets	94.7%	109.0%	118.0%	124.2%	121.9%	100.0%
Accounts payable	71.2%	104.9%	88.6%	110.1%	141.0%	100.0%
Taxes payable			0.0%	−149.5%	58.1%	100.0%
Other current liabilities	381.4%	84.4%	27.6%	94.9%	1,234.7%	100.0%
Total current liabilities	117.3%	102.3%	70.2%	103.4%	199.7%	100.0%
Long-term debt	99.8%	104.2%	66.5%	283.3%	66.9%	100.0%
Other long-term liabilities and minority interests	93.9%	102.9%	113.5%	60.4%	149.8%	100.0%
Deferred income taxes	74.9%	128.7%	131.6%	120.2%	97.4%	100.0%
Total liabilities	102.2%	106.2%	76.0%	134.6%	129.6%	100.0%
Preferred stock	100.0%	100.0%				
Common stock	101.7%	102.5%	108.8%	102.2%	101.0%	100.0%
Additional paid-in capital	104.8%	113.0%	156.4%	116.2%	106.6%	100.0%
Retained earnings	111.0%	113.4%	120.4%	116.2%	122.8%	100.0%
Accumulated other comprehensive income		0.0%	64.4%	208.0%		
Common stock in treasury, at cost	12,398.7%	100.0%	100.0%	100.0%	1,031.3%	100.0%
Pension liability adjustment				0.0%	124.9%	100.0%
Foreign currency translation adjustment	183.4%	383.5%	157.7%	79.4%	−281.1%	100.0%
Total shareholders' equity	91.6%	110.1%	153.5%	116.6%	116.8%	100.0%
Total liabilities and shareholders' equity	94.7%	109.0%	118.0%	124.2%	121.9%	100.0%

Compound Annual Growth Rate

	1993	1994	1995	1996	1997	1998	Growth
Cash	−72	0	0	0	0	161	17.5%
Accounts receivable	−33	0	0	0	0	95	23.5%
Inventory	−21	0	0	0	0	35	10.8%
Deferred income taxes	−12	0	0	0	0	23	13.9%
Other current assets	−41	0	0	0	0	0	
Total current assets	−179	0	0	0	0	314	11.9%
Property, plant, and equipment	−643	0	0	0	0	1,281	14.8%
Other long-term assets	−175	0	0	0	0	243	6.8%
Total assets	−996	0	0	0	0	1,838	13.0%
Accounts payable	−132	0	0	0	0	136	0.6%
Taxes payable	−3	0	0	0	0	31	59.5%
Other current liabilities	−8	0	0	0	0	82	59.3%
Total current liabilities	−143	0	0	0	0	249	11.7%
Long-term debt	−157	0	0	0	0	205	5.5%
Other long-term liabilities and minority interests	−55	0	0	0	0	54	−0.4%
Deferred income taxes	−41	0	0	0	0	61	8.3%
Total liabilities	−396	0	0	0	0	570	7.6%

Wendy's International Balance Sheets (in millions) (continued)

	1998	1997	1996	1995	1994	1993	
Preferred stock	0	0	0	0	0	200	
Common stock	−10	0	0	0	0	12	3.7%
Additional paid-in capital	−161	0	0	0	0	370	18.1%
Retained earnings	−431	0	0	0	0	932	16.7%
Accumulated other comprehensive income	0	0	0	0	0	0	
Common stock in treasury, at cost	0	0	0	0	0	−212	
Pension liability adjustment	−3	0	0	0	0	0	
Foreign currency translation adjustment	−1	0	0	0	0	−33	
Total shareholders' equity	−601	0	0	0	0	1,268	16.1%
Total liabilities and shareholders' equity	−996	0	0	0	0	1,838	13.0%

Wendy's International Condensed Statements of Cash Flows (in millions of dollars)

	1998	1997	1996	1995	1994
Net income	$123	$130	$156	$110	$97
Depreciation expense	95	96	89	84	80
Other adjustments to operations	16	−3	−55	−29	−9
Cash flows from operating activities	234	223	190	165	168
Purchase of property, plant, and equipment	−242	−295	−307	−218	−172
Other adjustments to investing activities	168	94	45	31	45
Cash flows from investing activities	−74	−201	−262	−187	−127
Dividends	−31	−32	−30	−25	−25
Other adjustments to financing activities	−202	25	114	134	32
Cash flows from financing activities	−233	−7	84	109	7
Net change in cash	$ −73	$ 15	$ 12	$ 87	$ 48

Wendy's International Income Statements (in millions)

	1998	1997	1996	1995	1994
Revenues					
Retail sales	$1,586	$1,652	$1,567	$1,462	$1,366
Royalties and other	362	386	330	284	226
Total Revenues	1,948	2,037	1,897	1,746	1,592
Operating Costs and Expenses					
Company-operated restaurants	360	390	379	351	333
Cost of sales	996	1,026	977	890	818
Interest, net	2	4	7	10	13
Depreciation of property and equipment	95	96	89	81	75
Selling, general, and administrative expenses	287	303	190	249	203
Total Operating Expenses	1,741	1,818	1,642	1,581	1,442
Income before provision for income taxes	207	219	255	165	150
Provision for income taxes	84	89	99	55	53
Net Income	$123	$130	$156	$110	$97

Wendy's International AVERAGE Balance Sheets (in millions)

	1998	1997	1996	1995	1994
Cash	$198	$227	$213	$163	$96
Accounts receivable	88	72	63	57	42
Inventory	35	34	30	27	24
Deferred income taxes	27	24	17	15	12
Other current assets	—	2	6	15	32
Total current assets	348	359	329	277	206
Property, plant, and equipment	1,273	1,237	1,074	870	722
Other long-term assets	269	266	242	215	178
Total assets	$1,890	$1,862	$1,645	$1,362	$1,106
Accounts payable	$164	$187	$194	$196	$160
Taxes payable	16	—	–1	0	2
Other current liabilities	51	23	59	95	53
Total current liabilities	231	210	252	291	215
Long-term debt	206	202	247	201	131
Other long-term liab. and minority interests	56	57	53	66	68
Deferred income taxes	71	72	55	44	40
Total liabilities	564	541	607	602	454
Preferred stock	200	200	100	—	—
Common stock	12	11	11	10	10
Additional paid-in capital	362	333	256	186	167
Retained earnings	885	790	678	572	480
Accumulated other comprehensive income			–1	–1	0
Common stock in treasury, at cost	–107	–2	–2	–2	–1
Pension liability adjustment	—	—	—	–2	–3

	1998	1997	1996	1995	1994
Foreign currency translation adjustment	–26	–11	–4	–3	–1
Total shareholders' equity	$1,326	$1,321	$1,038	$760	$652
Total liabilities and shareholders' equity	$1,890	$1,862	$1,645	$1,362	$1,106

Cash Flow Data

	1998	1997	1996	1995	1994
Cash flow from operations	$234	$223	$190	$165	$168
Fixed asset purchases	242	295	307	218	172
Cash dividends	31	32	30	25	25
Depreciation and amortization	95	96	89	84	80

Market Data

	1998	1997	1996	1995	1994
High market price	$25.20	$27.90	$23.00	$22.80	$18.40
Low market price	$18.10	$19.60	$16.80	$14.40	$13.40
Number of shares outstanding (millions)	108.56	115.82	113.02	103.86	101.76
Market capitalization	$2,350.32	$2,750.73	$2,249.10	$1,931.80	$1,617.98

Wendy's International Ratios

Liquidity Ratios

	1998	1997	1996	1995	1994
Working capital	$117	$149	$77	($14)	($9)
Working capital ratio	1.50	1.71	1.31	0.95	0.96
Quick ratio	1.23	1.42	1.09	0.76	0.64
Inventory turnover	28.17	29.81	32.31	32.86	33.77
Days in inventory	12.96	12.24	11.3	11.11	10.81
Accounts receivable turnover	22.22	28.12	30.09	30.68	37.6
Days in accounts receivable	16.42	12.98	12.13	11.9	9.71
Inventory conversion cycle	29.38	25.22	23.42	23.01	20.52
Accounts payable turnover	6.09	5.50	5.04	4.54	5.12
Days in accounts payable	59.94	66.39	72.48	80.44	71.26
Net cash conversion cycle	–30.55	–41.17	–49.06	–57.44	–50.75
Cash + short-term investments	197.50	226.61	212.54	162.88	95.67
A/R*days in accounts receivable	1,439.98	940.46	764.58	677.33	410.97
Inventory*days in inventory	458.19	421.36	341.45	301.01	261.68
Product dollar days	2,095.68	1,588.43	1,318.57	1,141.23	768.32
Current assets-other current assets	320.53	333.48	305.81	246.91	162.21
Liquidity index	6.54	4.76	4.31	4.62	4.74

Cash Flow Ratios

	1998	1997	1996	1995	1994
Cash flow adequacy	0.86	0.68	0.56	0.68	0.85
Reinvestment ratio	1.03	1.32	1.62	1.32	1.02
Dividend payout	0.13	0.14	0.16	0.15	0.15
Free cash flow	−39.00	−104.00	−147.00	−78.00	−29.00
Depreciation impact ratio	0.41	0.43	0.47	0.51	0.48
Recapitalization index	2.55	3.07	3.45	2.6	2.15
Cash flow return on assets	0.12	0.12	0.12	0.12	0.15
Cash flow return on sales	0.12	0.11	0.10	0.09	0.11
Operations index	1.13	1.02	0.75	1.00	1.12

Asset Utilization Ratios

	1998	1997	1996	1995	1994
Profit margin	6.33%	6.41%	8.22%	6.30%	6.12%
Asset turnover	1.03	1.09	1.15	1.28	1.44
Financial structure leverage	1.43	1.41	1.59	1.79	1.7
Return on assets	6.53%	7.01%	9.48%	8.08%	8.81%
Return on equity	9.30%	9.88%	15.03%	14.48%	14.96%

Capital Structure Ratios

	1998	1997	1996	1995	1994
Debt to capital	0.30	0.29	0.37	0.44	0.41
Debt to equity	0.43	0.41	0.59	0.79	0.70
Long-term debt to capital	0.14	0.14	0.18	0.20	0.18
Long-term debt to equity	0.20	0.20	0.29	0.35	0.31
Working capital/total assets-Z1	0.07	0.10	0.06	-0.01	-0.01
Retained earnings/total assets-Z2	0.66	0.59	0.58	0.59	0.61
EBIT/total assets-Z3	0.36	0.39	0.51	0.4	0.45
Sales/total assets-Z4	1.03	1.09	1.15	1.28	1.44
Market to book-Z5	2.50	3.05	2.22	1.93	2.14
Z-Score	4.63	5.22	4.52	4.18	4.62

Market Ratio

	1998	1997	1996	1995	1994
Price to earnings	19.05	21.08	14.42	17.55	16.61

F

SOFT DRINK INDUSTRY

$\mathcal{T}$he Coca-Cola Company and PepsiCo dominated the soft drink industry from 1993 to 1998. Consumer demand increased for their products during the period analyzed, and much of that growth came from emerging markets. The companies also broadened their product offerings as consumer preferences evolved. The growing trend among analysts in the 1990s was to refer to Coke and Pepsi as creators, producers, and distributors of brand-name nonalcoholic beverages, as opposed to soft drink manufacturers. Coca-Cola focused its efforts in this direction, but PepsiCo remained a more diversified company. This appendix presents an overview of the soft drink industry. It provides material to be used in conjunction with the two firms' financial statements, which appear at the conclusion of this appendix.

PRODUCTS

The Coca-Cola Company and PepsiCo make and distribute syrup-based, flavor concentrates to bottlers. The bottlers then package the syrups in cans and bottles and sell them to retail establishments. The soft drink firms controlled some of the bottlers with whom they trade and have equity interests in others. These investments are disclosed on their balance sheets. Other bottling companies operated independently of Coke and Pepsi. This industry analysis focuses on the soft drink *concentrate* industry, as opposed to the soft drink *bottling* industry.

Coke and Pepsi adapted to consumer preferences by adding noncarbonated beverages to their product lines during the period analyzed. Percentage growth of bottled water, sports drinks, and fruit beverages exceeded that of carbonated beverages; Coke and Pepsi introduced numerous products to capitalize on those markets.

Coca-Cola's operations centered on nonalcoholic beverage concentrates. PepsiCo's operations, however, were more diverse. The company consisted of three business segments through 1997. In addition to its soft drink business, PepsiCo owned snack food maker Frito-Lay and a restaurant division consisting of Pizza Hut, Taco Bell, and KFC. The company sold the restaurants in 1997, citing the incompatibility of retail stores with packaged drink and food products.

MARKETS

Exhibit F-1 discloses Coke and Pepsi's soft drink market shares from the beginning to the end of the period analyzed.[1] Coke increased market share at the expense of smaller competitors, whereas Pepsi maintained market share from 1993 to 1998.

EXHIBIT F-1
Global Market Share

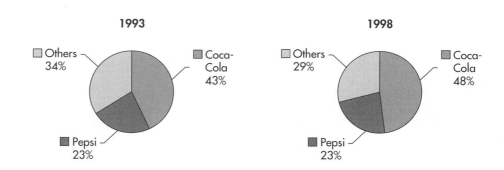

Coke's foreign sales increased as a percentage of total sales, but Pepsi's U.S. sales declined slightly. Exhibit F-2 presents the percentage of cases sold domestically and internationally. (Corresponding percentages for Pepsi-Cola were unavailable in 1993 and 1994.)[2]

---

[1] Food and Nonalcoholic Beverage Industry Surveys, *Standard & Poor's Industry Surveys,* August 1994 and November 1998, (New York: McGraw-Hill).

[2] Food and Nonalcoholic Beverage Industry Surveys, *Standard & Poor's Industry Surveys,* November 1998, (New York: McGraw-Hill), and *Soft-Drink Industry,* Merrill Lynch Industry Report, 1997.

	1993	1994	1995	1996	1997	1998
Coke-Foreign	68.2%	69.9%	70.3%	70.8%	71.3%	72.0%
Coke-Domestic	31.8%	30.1%	29.7%	29.2%	28.7%	28.0%
Pepsi-Foreign	—	—	52.3%	50.5%	50.2%	49.5%
Pepsi-Domestic	—	—	47.7%	49.5%	49.8%	50.5%

Emerging markets accounted for much of Coke's sales growth. They company benefited by the rise of market-based economies in many parts of the world. It penetrated previously closed markets, such as Russia and the People's Republic of China. Exhibit F-3 is an example of the difference between growth in an established and emerging market. It reports the annual percentage growth in Coke's case volume sales in the United States and China from 1993 (base year) to 1998.[3]

EXHIBIT F-3
*The Coca-Cola Company
U.S. and China Case Volume
Growth (from the previous
year)*

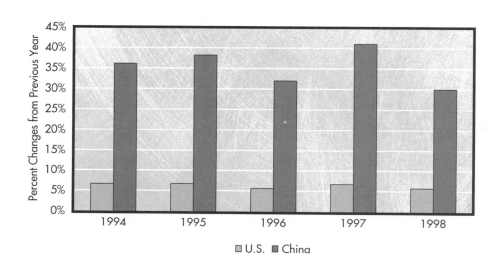

BUSINESS FOCUS

Soft drink companies placed a premium on product placement. The two industry giants employed strategies that squeezed smaller competitors' products off grocers' shelves and reached exclusive contracts with restaurants, schools, and athletic organizations. The companies increased the number of soft drink vending machines and in-store soda fountains during the 1990s. These efforts presented high barriers to market entry and strengthened brand loyalty among customers.

Coke and Pepsi's brand name development continued from 1993 to 1998. The ubiquitous appearance of the soft drink giants' products reflected the drive to monopolize the industry. Significant promotional and advertising expenditures were made to strengthen trade names and consumer identity. Unlike manufacturers in other industries, Coke and Pepsi had relatively small investments in plant and equipment. Consequently, the firms carried little long-term debt.

---

[3] *Soft-Drink Industry,* Merrill Lynch Industry Report, 1998.

Coca-Cola focused on improving its market lead in the nonalcoholic beverage industry during the period analyzed. PepsiCo restructured but remained more diverse than Coke. In addition, Pepsi decided to spin off its restaurants, thus demonstrating its commitment to soft drinks and snack foods. The capital-intensive, low-profit margin profile of the limited-service restaurant sector did not jibe with the firm's strategic vision of a high-margin, packaged goods producer. The Frito-Lay Company, in contrast, exceeded Pepsi-Cola's operating profits. Exhibit F-4 presents the operating income for PepsiCo's two remaining business segments.[4]

EXHIBIT F-4
Pepsi-Cola and Frito-Lay Operating Income (in millions) 1993–1998

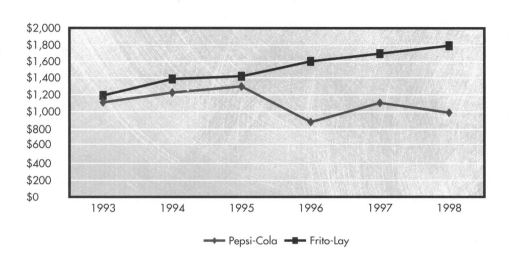

SIGNIFICANT EVENTS

1993

◆ Industry penetrates Eastern European markets, realizes its greatest growth in noncola soft drinks, and experiences heightened competition in the orange juice market.
◆ Coca-Cola purchases Indian brands from Parle Exports, reenters the Saudi Arabian market, and experiments with 20-ounce plastic bottle.
◆ Pepsi introduces a one-calorie product, invests heavily in Mexico, and stems a product tampering crises.

1994

◆ New logos and corporate images appear throughout the industry; companies aggressively seek exclusive contracts with managers of sports stadiums and

---

[4] PepsiCo, Inc. 1995–1999 Form 10-K.

other entertainment venues; sports drinks are the hottest segment of the industry.

◆ Coca-Cola announces Roberto Goizueta will stay on after reaching the mandatory retirement age, names Douglas Ivester as his apparent successor, forms an iced tea joint venture with Nestlé, and expands the Fruitopia line.

◆ PepsiCo has declining sales in its restaurants, reduces the number of soft drink personnel, positions Doritos as a global brand, and reenters the South African market.

1995

◆ Industry increases cross-promotional activities and maintains aggressive growth in Eastern Europe.

◆ Coca-Cola acquires Barq's Root Beer, an interest in Vital S.A. of Chile; company continues to dominate throughout the world and experiences strong growth in overseas markets.

◆ Pepsi's restaurants remain poor performers while its Frito-Lay division increases market share and profit.

1996

◆ Industry experiences slowing of foreign sales; orange juice businesses falter.

◆ Coca-Cola introduces Surge, attains a 90 percent market share in Japan, and gains a foothold in Venezuela by acquiring Cisneros Bottling, a former Pepsi bottler.

◆ Pepsi's accounting change results in a significant loss; chief executive officer (CEO) Wayne Calloway retires and is succeeded by Roger Enrico; the company begins "Project Blue", a restructuring of foreign operations; and it recognizes a $.5 billion loss from restructuring.

1997

◆ Soft drink sales weaken in some markets and price reductions result.

◆ Douglas Ivester succeeds Roberto Goizueta as Coca-Cola chair and CEO.

◆ Pepsi spins off its restaurant division as Tricon Global; company focuses on packaged goods; the firm reorganizes its remaining U.S. operations.

1998

◆ Companies seek to stem weakening markets; aggressively pursue overseas growth.

◆ Coca-Cola's sales and earnings slump; the company buys some of Cadbury's brands and explores selling bottled water products.

◆ Pepsi considers realigning bottling system, purchases Tropicana for $3.3 billion, and sues Coca-Cola for antitrust violations.

The Coca-Cola Co.
Consolidated Statements
of Income
(in millions of dollars)

	1998	1997	1996	1995	1994	1993
Net operating revenues	$18,813	$18,868	$18,546	$18,018	$16,172	$13,957
Cost of goods sold	5,562	6,015	6,738	6,940	6,167	5,160
Gross profit	13,251	12,853	11,808	11,078	10,005	8,797
Selling, general, and administrative expenses	8,284	7,852	7,893	7,052	6,297	5,695
Other operating charges	—	—	—	—	—	—
Operating income (loss)	4,967	5,001	3,915	4,026	3,708	3,102
Interest income	219	211	238	245	181	144
Interest expense	−277	−258	−286	−272	−199	−168
Equity income (loss)	32	155	211	169	134	91
Other income (deductions) —net	230	583	87	86	-96	4
Gains on issues of stock by equity investees	27	363	431	74		12
Income before income taxes	5,198	6,055	4,596	4,328	3,728	3,185
Income taxes	1,665	1,926	1,104	1,342	1,174	997
Net income (loss)	$3,533	$4,129	$3,492	$2,986	$2,554	$2,188
Basic earnings per share	$1.78	$1.82	$1.74	$1.13	$1.98	$1.68
Diluted earnings per share	$1.75	$1.79	$1.73			

Vertical Common Size

	1998	1997	1996	1995	1994	1993
Net operating revenues	100.0%	100.0%	100.0%	100.0%	100.0%	100.0%
Cost of goods sold	29.6%	31.9%	36.3%	38.5%	38.1%	37.0%
Gross profit	70.4%	68.1%	63.7%	61.5%	61.9%	63.0%
Selling, general, and administrative expenses	44.0%	41.6%	42.6%	39.1%	38.9%	40.8%
Other operating charges	0.0%	0.0%	0.0%	0.0%	0.0%	0.0%
Operating income (loss)	26.4%	26.5%	21.1%	22.3%	22.9%	22.2%
Interest income	1.2%	1.1%	1.3%	1.4%	1.1%	1.0%
Interest expense	−1.5%	−1.4%	−1.5%	−1.5%	−1.2%	−1.2%
Equity income (loss)	0.2%	0.8%	1.1%	0.9%	0.8%	0.7%
Other income (deductions) —net	1.2%	3.1%	0.5%	0.5%	−0.6%	0.0%
Gains on issues of stock by equity investees	0.1%	1.9%	2.3%	0.4%	0.0%	0.1%
Income before income taxes	27.6%	32.1%	24.8%	24.0%	23.1%	22.8%
Income taxes	8.9%	10.2%	6.0%	7.4%	7.3%	7.1%
Net income (loss)	18.8%	21.9%	18.8%	16.6%	15.8%	15.7%

Horizontal Common Size—1993 Base Year

	1998	1997	1996	1995	1994	1993
Net operating revenues	134.8%	135.2%	132.9%	129.1%	115.9%	100.0%
Cost of goods sold	107.8%	116.6%	130.6%	134.5%	119.5%	100.0%
Gross profit	150.6%	146.1%	134.2%	125.9%	113.7%	100.0%
Selling, general, and administrative expenses	145.5%	137.9%	138.6%	123.8%	110.6%	100.0%
Other operating charges						
Operating income (loss)	160.1%	161.2%	126.2%	129.8%	119.5%	100.0%
Interest income	152.1%	146.5%	165.3%	170.1%	125.7%	100.0%
Interest expense	164.9%	153.6%	170.2%	161.9%	118.5%	100.0%
Equity income (loss)	35.2%	170.3%	231.9%	185.7%	147.3%	100.0%
Other income (deductions)—net	5750.0%	14575.0%	2175.0%	2150.0%	−2400.0%	100.0%
Gains on issues of stock by equity investees	225.0%	3025.0%	3591.7%	616.7%	0.0%	100.0%
Income before income taxes	163.2%	190.1%	144.3%	135	117.0%	100.0%
Income taxes	167.0%	193.2%	110.7%	134.6%	117.8%	100.0%
Net income (loss)	161.5%	188.7%	159.6%	136.5%	116.7%	100.0%

Horizontal Common Size—Rolling Forward Method

	1998	1997	1996	1995	1994	1993
Net operating revenues	99.7%	101.7%	102.9%	111.4%	115.9%	100.0%
Cost of goods sold	92.5%	89.3%	97.1%	112.5%	119.5%	100.0%
Gross profit	103.1%	108.8%	106.6%	110.7%	113.7%	100.0%
Selling, general, and administrative expenses	105.5%	99.5%	111.9%	112.0%	110.6%	100.0%
Other operating charges						
Operating income (loss)	99.3%	127.7%	97.2%	108.6%	119.5%	100.0%
Interest income	103.8%	88.7%	97.1%	135.4%	125.7%	100.0%
Interest expense	107.4%	90.2%	105.1%	136.7%	118.5%	100.0%
Equity income (loss)	20.6%	73.5%	124.9%	126.1%	147.3%	100.0%
Other income (deductions)—net	39.5%	670.1%	101.2%	−89.6%	−2400.0%	100.0%
Gains on issues of stock by equity investees	7.4%	84.2%	582.4%	—	0.0%	100.0%
Income before income taxes	85.8%	131.7%	106.2%	116.1%	117.0%	100.0%
Income taxes	86.4%	174.5%	82.3%	114.3%	117.8%	100.0%
Net income (loss)	85.6%	118.2%	116.9%	116.9%	116.7%	100.0%

The Coca-Cola Co.
Consolidated Statements
of Income
(in millions of dollars)
(continued)

Compound Annual Growth Rate

	1993	1994	1995	1996	1997	1998	Growth
Net operating revenues	–$13,957	0	0	0	0	$18,813	6.2%
Cost of goods sold	–5,160	0	0	0	0	5,562	1.5%
Gross profit	–8,797	0	0	0	0	13,251	8.5%
Selling, general, and administrative expenses	–5,695	0	0	0	0	8,284	7.8%
Other operating charges	—					—	
Operating income (loss)	–3,102	0	0	0	0	4,967	9.9%
Interest income	–144	0	0	0	0	219	8.7%
Interest expense	168	0	0	0	0	–277	10.5%
Equity income (loss)	–91	0	0	0	0	32	–18.9%
Other income (deductions) —net	–4	0	0	0	0	230	124.9%
Gains on issues of stock by equity investees	–12	0	0	0	0	27	17.6%
Income before income taxes	–3,185	0	0	0	0	5,198	10.3%
Income taxes	–997	0	0	0	0	1,665	10.8%
Net income (loss)	–2,188	0	0	0	0	3,533	10.1%

The Coca-Cola Co.
Consolidated Balance Sheets
(in millions of dollars)

	1998	1997	1996	1995	1994	1993
Assets						
Current						
Cash and cash equivalents	$1,648	$1,737	$1,433	$1,167	$1,386	$998
Marketable securities	159	106	255	148	145	80
Total cash and securities	1,807	1,843	1,688	1,315	1,531	1,078
Trade accounts receivable, net	1,666	1,639	1,641	1,695	1,470	1,243
Inventories	890	959	952	1,117	1,047	1,049
Prepaid expenses and other assets	2,017	1,528	1,659	1,323	1,102	1,064
Total current assets	6,380	5,969	5,940	5,450	5,150	4,434
Investment and other assets						
Investments						
Coca-Cola Enterprises Inc (CCE)	584	184	547	556	524	498
Coca-Cola Amatil Limited	1,255	1,204	881	682	694	592
Coca-Cola Beverages Co.	879	—	—	—	—	—
Other, principally bottling cos.	3,573	3,049	2,004	1,157	1,114	1,125
Cost method invest, principally bottling companies	395	457	737	319	178	226
Marketable securities and other assets	1,863	1,607	1,779	1,597	1,163	868

	1998	1997	1996	1995	1994	1993
Total investments and other assets	8,549	6,501	5,948	4,311	3,673	3,309
Property, plant, and equipment						
Land	199	183	204	233	221	197
Building and improvements	1,507	1,535	1,528	1,944	1,814	1,616
Machinery and equipment	3,855	3,896	3,649	4,135	3,776	3,380
Containers	124	157	200	345	346	403
Total property, plant, and equipment, gross	5,685	5,771	5,581	6,657	6,157	5,596
Less allowances for depreciation	2,016	2,028	2,031	2,321	2,077	1,867
Total property, plant, and equipment, net	3,669	3,743	3,550	4,336	4,080	3,729
Goodwill and other intangible assets	547	727	753	944	660	549
Total assets	$19,145	$16,940	$16,191	$15,041	$13,563	$12,021
Liabilities						
Current						
Accounts payable and accrued expenses	$3,141	$3,249	$2,972	$3,103	$2,564	$2,217
Loans and notes payable	4,459	2,677	3,388	2,371	1,757	1,409
Current maturities of long-term debt	3	397	9	552	35	264
Accrued income taxes	1,037	1,056	1,037	1,322	1,530	1,282
Total current liabilities	8,640	7,379	7,406	7,348	5,886	5,172
Long-term debt	687	801	1,116	1,141	1,426	1,428
Postretirement benefit liability	—	—	—	—	252	—
Other liabilities	991	1,001	1,182	966	603	725
Deferred income taxes	424	448	301	194	180	113
Total liabilities	10,742	9,629	10,005	9,649	8,347	7,438
Share-Owners' Equity						
Common stock	865	861	858	856	427	426
Capital surplus	2,195	1,527	1,058	863	1,173	1,086
Reinvested earnings	17,054	15,025	13,711	11,898	10,295	9,287
Unearned compensation-outstanding restricted stock	1,434	50	61	68	74	85
Foreign current currency translation adjustment	—	1,372	662	424	272	–420
Unrealized gain on securities for sale	—	58	156	82	48	—
Total share-owners' equity before treasury stock	21,548	18,893	16,506	14,191	12,289	10,464
Less treasury stock, at cost	13,145	11,582	10,320	8,799	7,073	5,881
Total share-owners' equity	8,403	7,311	6,186	5,392	5,216	4,583
Total liabilities and share-owners' equity	$19,145	$16,940	$16,191	$15,041	$13,563	$12,021

Vertical Common Size

	1998	1997	1996	1995	1994	1993
Assets						
Current						
Cash and cash equivalents	8.6%	10.3%	8.9%	7.8%	10.2%	8.3%
Marketable securities	0.8%	0.6%	1.6%	1.0%	1.1%	0.7%
Total cash and securities	9.4%	10.9%	10.4%	8.7%	11.3%	9.0%
Trade accounts receivable, net	8.7%	9.7%	10.1%	11.3%	10.8%	10.3%
Inventories	4.6%	5.7%	5.9%	7.4%	7.7%	8.7%
Prepaid expenses and other assets	10.5%	9.0%	10.2%	8.8%	8.1%	8.9%
Total current assets	33.3%	35.2%	36.7%	36.2%	38.0%	36.9%
Investment and other assets						
Investments						
Coca-Cola Enterprises Inc (CCE)	3.1%	1.1%	3.4%	3.7%	3.9%	4.1%
Coca-Cola Amatil Limited	6.6%	7.1%	5.4%	4.5%	5.1%	4.9%
Coca-Cola Beverages Co.	4.6%	0.0%	0.0%	0.0%	0.0%	0.0%
Other, principally bottling cos.	18.7%	18.0%	12.4%	7.7%	8.2%	9.4%
Cost method invest, principally bottling companies	2.1%	2.7%	4.6%	2.1%	1.3%	1.9%
Marketable securities and other assets	9.7%	9.5%	11.0%	10.6%	8.6%	7.2%
Total investments and other assets	44.7%	38.4%	36.7%	28.7%	27.1%	27.5%
Property, plant and equipment						
Land	1.0%	1.1%	1.3%	1.5%	1.6%	1.6%
Building and improvements	7.9%	9.1%	9.4%	12.9%	13.4%	13.4%
Machinery and equipment	20.1%	23.0%	22.5%	27.5%	27.8%	28.1%
Containers	0.6%	0.9%	1.2%	2.3%	2.6%	3.4%
Total property, plant, and equipment, gross	29.7%	34.1%	34.5%	44.3%	45.4%	46.6%
Less allowances for depreciation	10.5%	12.0%	12.5%	15.4%	15.3%	15.5%
Total property, plant, and equipment, net	19.2%	22.1%	21.9%	28.8%	30.1%	31.0%
Goodwill and other intangible assets	2.9%	4.3%	4.7%	6.3%	4.9%	4.6%
Total Assets	100.0%	100.0%	100.0%	100.0%	100.0%	100.0%
Liabilities						
Current						
Accounts payable and accrued expenses	16.4%	19.2%	18.4%	20.6%	18.9%	18.4%
Loans and notes payable	23.3%	15.8%	20.9%	15.8%	13.0%	11.7%
Current maturities of long-term debt	0.0%	2.3%	0.1%	3.7%	0.3%	2.2%
Accrued income taxes	5.4%	6.2%	6.4%	8.8%	11.3%	10.7%
Total current liabilities	45.1%	43.6%	45.7%	48.9%	43.4%	43.0%
Long-term debt	3.6%	4.7%	6.9%	7.6%	10.5%	11.9%

Vertical Common Size (continued)

	1998	1997	1996	1995	1994	1993
Postretirement benefit liability	0.0%	0.0%	0.0%	0.0%	1.9%	0.0%
Other liabilities	5.2%	5.9%	7.3%	6.4%	4.4%	6.0%
Deferred income taxes	2.2%	2.6%	1.9%	1.3%	1.3%	0.9%
Total liabilities	56.1%	56.8%	61.8%	64.2%	61.5%	61.9%
Share-Owners' Equity						
Common stock	4.5%	5.1%	5.3%	5.7%	3.1%	3.5%
Capital surplus	11.5%	9.0%	6.5%	5.7%	8.6%	9.0%
Reinvested earnings	89.1%	88.7%	84.7%	79.1%	75.9%	77.3%
Unearned compensation— outstanding restricted stock	7.5%	0.3%	0.4%	0.5%	0.5%	0.7%
Foreign current currency translation adjustment	0.0%	8.1%	4.1%	2.8%	2.0%	–3.5%
Unrealized gain on securities for sale	0.0%	0.3%	1.0%	0.5%	0.4%	0.0%
Total share-owners' equity before treasury stock	112.6%	111.5%	101.9%	94.3%	90.6%	87.0%
Less treasury stock, at cost	68.7%	68.4%	63.7%	58.5%	52.1%	48.9%
Total share-owners' equity	43.9%	43.2%	38.2%	35.8%	38.5%	38.1%
Total liabilities and share-owners' equity	100.0%	100.0%	100.0%	100.0%	100.0%	100.0%

Horizontal Common Size—1993 Base Year

	1998	1997	1996	1995	1994	1993
Assets						
Current						
Cash and cash equivalents	165.1%	174.0%	143.6%	116.9%	138.9%	100.0%
Marketable securities	198.8%	132.5%	318.8%	185.0%	181.3%	100.0%
Total cash and securities	167.6%	171.0%	156.6%	122.0%	142.0%	100.0%
Trade accounts receivable, net	34.0%	131.9%	132.0%	136.4%	118.3%	100.0%
Inventories	84.8%	91.4%	90.8%	106.5%	99.8%	100.0%
Prepaid expenses and other assets	189.6%	143.6%	155.9%	124.3%	103.6%	100.0%
Total current assets	143.9%	134.6%	134.0%	122.9%	116.1%	100.0%
Investment and other assets						
Investments						
Coca-Cola Enterprises Inc (CCE)	117.3%	36.9%	109.8%	111.6%	105.2%	100.0%
Coca-Cola Amatil Limited Coca-Cola Beverages Co.	212.0%	203.4%	148.8%	115.2%	117.2%	100.0%
Other, principally bottling cos.	317.6%	271.0%	178.1%	102.8%	99.0%	100.0%
Cost method invest, principally bottling companies	174.8%	202.2%	326.1%	141.2%	78.8%	100.0%

The Coca-Cola Co.
Consolidated Balance Sheets
(in millions of dollars)
(continued)

Horizontal Common Size—1993 Base Year (continued)

	1998	1997	1996	1995	1994	1993
Marketable securities and other assets	214.6%	185.1%	205.0%	184.0%	134.0%	100.0%
Total investments and other assets	258.4%	196.5%	179.8%	130.3%	111.0%	100.0%
Property, plant, and equipment						
Land	101.0%	92.9%	103.6%	118.3%	112.2%	100.0%
Building and improvements	93.3%	95.0%	94.6%	120.3%	112.3%	100.0%
Machinery and equipment	114.1%	115.3%	108.0%	122.3%	111.7%	100.0%
Containers	30.8%	39.0%	49.6%	85.6%	85.9%	100.0%
Total property, plant, and equipment, gross	101.6%	103.1%	99.7%	119.0%	110.0%	100.0%
Less allowances for depreciation	108.0%	108.6%	108.8%	124.3%	111.2%	100.0%
Total property, plant, and equipment, net	98.4%	100.4%	95.2%	116.3%	109.4%	100.0%
Goodwill and other intangible assets	99.6%	132.4%	137.2%	171.9%	120.2%	100.0%
Total Assets	159.3%	140.9%	134.7%	125.1%	112.8%	100.0%
Liabilities						
Current						
Accounts payable and accrued expenses	141.7%	146.5%	134.1%	140.0%	115.7%	100.0%
Loans and notes payable	316.5%	190.0%	240.5%	168.3%	124.7%	100.0%
Current maturities of long-term debt	1.1%	150.4%	3.4%	209.1%	13.3%	100.0%
Accrued income taxes	80.9%	82.4%	80.9%	103.1%	119.3%	100.0%
Total current liabilities	167.1%	142.7%	143.2%	142.1%	113.8%	100.0%
Long-term debt	48.1%	56.1%	78.2%	79.9%	99.9%	100.0%
Postretirement benefit liability						
Other liabilities	136.7%	138.1%	163.0%	133.2%	83.2%	100.0%
Deferred income taxes	375.2%	396.5%	266.4%	171.7%	159.3%	100.0%
Total liabilities	144.4%	129.5%	134.5%	129.7%	112.2%	100.0%
Share-Owners' Equity						
Common stock	203.1%	202.1%	201.4%	200.9%	100.2%	100.0%
Capital surplus	202.1%	140.6%	97.4%	79.5%	108.0%	100.0%
Reinvested earnings	183.6%	161.8%	147.6%	128.1%	110.9%	100.0%
Unearned compensation —outstanding restricted stock	1687.1%	58.8%	71.8%	80.0%	87.1%	100.0%
Foreign current currency translation adjustment	0.0%	−326.7%	−157.6%	−101.0%	−64.8%	100.0%
Unrealized gain on securities for sale						
Total share-owners' equity before treasury stock	205.9%	180.6%	157.7%	135.6%	117.4%	100.0%
Less treasury stock, at cost	223.5%	196.9%	175.5%	149.6%	120.3%	100.0%
Total share-owners' equity	183.4%	159.5%	135.0%	117.7%	113.8%	100.0%
Total liabilities and share-owners' equity	159.3%	140.9%	134.7%	125.1%	112.8%	100.0%

Horizontal Common Size—Rolling Forward

	1998	1997	1996	1995	1994	1993
Assets						
Current						
Cash and cash equivalents	94.9%	121.2%	122.8%	84.2%	138.9%	100.0%
Marketable securities	150.0%	41.6%	172.3%	102.1%	181.3%	100.0%
Total cash and securities	98.0%	109.2%	128.4%	85.9%	142.0%	100.0%
Trade accounts receivable, net	101.6%	99.9%	96.8%	115.3%	118.3%	100.0%
Inventories	92.8%	100.7%	85.2%	106.7%	99.8%	100.0%
Prepaid expenses and other assets	132.0%	92.1%	125.4%	120.1%	103.6%	100.0%
Total current assets	106.9%	100.5%	109.0%	105.8%	116.1%	100.0%
Investment and other assets						
Investments						
Coca-Cola Enterprises Inc (CCE)	317.4%	33.6%	98.4%	106.1%	105.2%	100.0%
Coca-Cola Amatil Limited	104.2%	136.7%	129.2%	98.3%	117.2%	100.0%
Coca-Cola Beverages Co.						
Other, principally bottling cos.	117.2%	152.1%	173.2%	103.9%	99.0%	100.0%
Cost method invest, principally bottling companies	86.4%	62.0%	231.0%	179.2%	78.8%	100.0%
Marketable securities and other assets	115.9%	90.3%	111.4%	137.3%	134.0%	100.0%
Total investments and other assets	131.5%	109.3%	138.0%	117.4%	111.0%	100.0%
Property, plant, and equipment						
Land	108.7%	89.7%	87.6%	105.4%	112.2%	100.0%
Building and improvements	98.2%	100.5%	78.6%	107.2%	112.3%	100.0%
Machinery and equipment	98.9%	106.8%	88.2%	109.5%	111.7%	100.0%
Containers	79.0%	78.50%	58.0%	99.7%	85.9%	100.0%
Total property, plant, and equipment, gross	98.50%	103.4%	83.8%	108.1%	110.0%	100.0%
Less allowances for depreciation	99.4%	99.9%	87.5%	111.7%	111.2%	100.0%
Total property, plant, and equipment, net	98.0%	105.4%	81.9%	106.3%	109.4%	100.0%
Goodwill and other intangible assets	75.2%	96.5%	79.8%	143.0%	120.2%	100.0%
Total Assets	113.0%	104.6%	107.6%	110.9%	112.8%	100.0%
Liabilities						
Current						
Accounts payable and accrued expenses	96.7%	109.3%	95.8%	121.0%	115.7%	100.0%
Loans and notes payable	166.6%	79.0%	142.9%	134.9%	124.7%	100.0%
Current maturities of long-term debt	0.8%	4411.1%	1.6%	1577.1%	13.3%	100.0%
Accrued income taxes	98.2%	101.8%	78.4%	86.4%	119.3%	100.0%
Total current liabilities	117.1%	99.6%	100.8%	124.8%	113.8%	100.0%

Horizontal Common Size—Rolling Forward (continued)

	1998	1997	1996	1995	1994	1993
Long-term debt	85.8%	71.8%	97.8%	80.0%	99.9%	100.0%
Postretirement benefit liability						
Other liabilities	99.0%	84.7%	122.4%	160.2%	83.2%	100.0%
Deferred income taxes	94.6%	148.8%	155.2%	107.8%	159.3%	100.0%
Total liabilities	111.6%	96.2%	103.7%	115.6%	112.2%	100.0%
Share-Owners' Equity						
Common stock	100.5%	100.3%	100.2%	200.5%	100.2%	100.0%
Capital surplus	143.7%	144.3%	122.6%	73.6%	108.0%	100.0%
Reinvested earnings	113.5%	109.6%	115.2%	115.6%	110.9%	100.0%
Unearned compensation-outstanding restricted stock	2868.0%	82.0%	89.7%	91.9%	87.1%	100.0%
Foreign current currency translation adjustment	0.0%	207.3%	156.1%	155.9%	−64.8%	100.0%
Unrealized gain on securities for sale	0.0%	37.2%	190.2%	170.8%	—	—
Total share-owners' equity before treasury stock	114.1%	114.5%	116.3%	115.5%	117.4%	100.0%
Less treasury stock, at cost	113.5%	112.2%	117.3%	124.4%	120.3%	100.0%
Total share-owners' equity	114.9%	118.2%	114.7%	103.4%	113.8%	100.0%
Total liabilities and share-owners' equity	113.0%	104.6%	107.6%	110.9%	112.8%	100.0%

Compound Annual Growth

	1993	1994	1995	1996	1997	1998	Growth
Assets							
Current							
Cash and cash equivalents	($998)	0	0	0	0	$1,648	10.6%
Marketable securities	−80	0	0	0	0	159	14.7%
Total cash and securities	−1,078	0	0	0	0	1,807	10.9%
Trade accounts receivable, net	−1,243	0	0	0	0	1,666	6.0%
Inventories	−1,049	0	0	0	0	890	−3.2%
Prepaid expenses and other assets	−1,064	0	0	0	0	2,017	13.6%
Total current assets	−4,434	0	0	0	0	6,380	7.50%
Investment and other assets							
Investments							
Coca-Cola Enterprises Inc (CCE)	−498	0	0	0	0	584	3.2%
Coca-Cola Amatil Limited	−592	0	0	0	0	1,255	16.2%
Coca-Cola Beverages Co.	—	0	0	0	0	879	
Other, principally bottling cos.	−1,125	0	0	0	0	3,573	26.0%
Cost method invest, principally bottling ompanies	−226	0	0	0	0	395	11.8%

Compound Annual Growth (continued)

	1993	1994	1995	1996	1997	1998	Growth
Marketable securities and other assets	−868	0	0	0	0	1,863	16.5%
Total investments and other assets	−3,309	0	0	0	0	8,549	20.9%
Property, plant, and equipment							
Land	−197	0	0	0	0	199	0.2%
Building and improvements	−1,616	0	0	0	0	1,507	−1.4%
Machinery and equipment	−3,380	0	0	0	0	3,855	2.7%
Containers	−403	0	0	0	0	124	−21.0%
Total property, plant, and equipment, gross	−5,596	0	0	0	0	5,685	0.3%
Less allowances for depreciation	−1,867	0	0	0	0	2,016	1.5%
Total property, plant, and equipment, net	−3,729	0	0	0	0	3,669	−0.3%
Goodwill and other intangible assets	−549	0	0	0	0	547	−0.1%
Total Assets	−12,021	0	0	0	0	19,145	9.8%
Liabilities							
Current							
Accounts payable and accrued expenses	−2,217	0	0	0	0	3,141	7.2%
Loans and notes payable	−1,409	0	0	0	0	4,459	25.9%
Current maturities of long-term debt	−264	0	0	0	0	3	
Accrued income taxes	−1,282	0	0	0	0	1,037	−4.2%
Total current liabilities	−5,172	0	0	0	0	8,640	10.8%
Long-term debt	−1,428	0	0	0	0	687	−13.6%
Postretirement benefit liability	—	0	0	0	0	—	
Other liabilities	−725	0	0	0	0	991	6.5%
Deferred income taxes	−113	0	0	0	0	424	30.3%
Total liabilities	−7,438	0	0	0	0	10,742	7.6%
Share-Owners' Equity							
Common stock	−426	0	0	0	0	865	15.2%
Capital surplus	−1,086	0	0	0	0	2,195	15.1%
Reinvested earnings	−9,287	0	0	0	0	17,054	12.9%
Unearned compensation- outstanding restricted stock	−85	0	0	0	0	1,434	76.0%
Foreign current currency translation adjustment	420	0	0	0	0	—	
Unrealized gain on securities for sale							
Total share-owners' equity before treasury stock	−10,464	0	0	0	0	21,548	15.5%
Less treasury stock, at cost	−5,881	0	0	0	0	13,145	17.5%
Total share-owners' equity	−4,583	0	0	0	0	8,403	12.9%
Total liabilities and share-owners' equity	−12,021	0	0	0	0	19,145	9.8%

The Coca-Cola Co.
Condensed Statements of Cash
Flows (in millions of dollars)

	1998	1997	1996	1995	1994
Net income	$3,533	$4,129	$3,492	$2,986	$2,554
Depreciation expense	645	626	633	562	411
Other adjustments to operations	−745	−722	−662	−220	218
Cash flows from operating activities	3,433	4,033	3,463	3,328	3,183
Purchase of property, plant, and equipment	−863	−1,093	−990	−937	−682
Other adjustments to investing activities	−1,298	593	−60	−289	−355
Cash flows from investing activities	−2,161	−500	−1,050	−1,226	−1,037
Dividends	−1,480	−1,387	−1,247	−1,110	−550
Other adjustments to financing activities	147	−1,708	−855	−1,168	−1,242
Cash flows from financing activities	−1,333	−3,095	−2,102	−2,278	−1,792
Other adjustments to cash	−28	−134	−45	−43	34
Net change in cash	$−89	$304	$ 266	$−219	$388

The Coca-Cola Co.
Consolidated Statement
of Income
(in millions of dollars)

	1998	1997	1996	1995	1994
Net operating revenues	$18,813	$18,868	$18,546	$18,018	$16,172
Cost of goods sold	5,562	6,015	6,738	6,940	6,167
Gross profit	13,251	12,853	11,808	11,078	10,005
Selling, general, and administrative expenses	8,284	7,852	7,893	7,052	6,297
Other operating charges	—	—	—	—	—
Operating income (loss)	4,967	5,001	3,915	4,026	3,708
Interest income	219	211	238	245	181
Interest expense	−277	−258	−286	−272	−199
Equity income (loss)	32	155	211	169	134
Other income (deductions)-net	230	583	87	86	−96
Gains on issues of stock by equity investees	27	363	431	74	
Income before income taxes	5,198	6,055	4,596	4,328	3,728
Income taxes	1,665	1,926	1,104	1,342	1,174
Net income (loss)	$3,533	$4,129	$3,492	$2,986	$2,554

	1998	1997	1996	1995	1994
Assets					
Current					
Cash and cash equivalents	$1,692.50	$1,585.00	$1,300.00	$1,276.50	$1,192.00
Marketable securities	132.50	180.50	201.50	146.50	112.50
Total cash and securities	1,825.00	1,765.50	1,501.50	1,423.00	1,304.50
Trade accounts receivable, net	1,652.50	1,640.00	1,668.00	1,582.50	1,356.50
Inventories	924.50	955.50	1,034.50	1,082.00	1,048.00
Prepaid expenses and other assets	1,772.50	1,593.50	1,491.00	1,212.50	1,083.00
Total current assets	6,174.50	5,954.50	5,695.00	5,300.00	4,792.00
Investment and other assets					
Investments					
Coca-Cola Enterprises Inc (CCE)	384.00	365.50	551.50	540.00	511.00
Coca-Cola Amatil Limited	1,229.50	1,042.50	781.50	688.00	643.00
Coca-Cola Beverages Co.	439.50	—	—	—	—
Other, principally bottling cos.	3,311.00	2,526.50	1,580.50	1,135.50	1,119.50
Cost method invest, principally bottling companies	426.00	597.00	528.00	248.50	202.00
Marketable securities and other assets	1,735.00	1,693.00	1,688.00	1,380.00	1,015.50
Total investments and other assets	7,525.00	6,224.50	5,129.50	3,992.00	3,491.00
Property, plant, and equipment					
Land	191.00	193.50	218.50	227.00	209.00
Building and improvements	1,521.00	1,531.50	1,736.00	1,879.00	1,715.00
Machinery and equipment	3,875.50	3,772.50	3,892.00	3,955.50	3,578.00
Containers	140.50	178.50	272.50	345.50	374.50
Total property, plant, and equipment, gross	5,728.00	5,676.00	6,119.00	6,407.00	5,876.50
Less allowances for depreciation	2,022.00	2,029.50	2,176.00	2,199.00	1,972.00
Total property, plant, and equipment, net	3,706.00	3,646.50	3,943.00	4,208.00	3,904.50
Goodwill and other intangible assets	637.00	740.00	848.50	802.00	604.50
Total Assets	$18,042.50	$16,565.50	$15,616.00	$14,302.00	$12,792.00
Liabilities					
Current					
Accounts payable and accrued expenses	$3,195.00	$3,110.50	$3,037.50	$2,833.50	$2,390.50
Loans and notes payable	3,568.00	3,032.50	2,879.50	2,064.00	1,583.00
Current maturities of long-term debt	200.00	203.00	280.50	293.00	149.50
Accrued income taxes	1,046.50	1,046.50	1,179.50	1,426.00	1,406.00
Total current liabilities	8,009.50	7,392.50	7,377.00	6,617.00	5,529.00
Long-term debt	744.00	958.50	1,128.50	1,283.50	1,427.00
Postretirement benefit liability	—	—	—	126.00	126.00
Other liabilities	996.00	1,091.50	1,074.00	784.50	664.00
Deferred income taxes	436.00	374.50	247.50	187.00	146.50
Total liabilities	$10,185.50	$9,817.00	$9,827.00	$8,998.00	$7,892.50

	1998	1997	1996	1995	1994
Share-Owners' Equity					
Common stock	$863.00	$859.50	$857.00	$641.50	$426.50
Capital surplus	1,861.00	1,292.50	960.50	1,018.00	1,129.50
Reinvested earnings	16,039.50	14,368.00	12,804.50	11,096.50	9,791.00
Unearned compensation-outstanding restricted stock	742.00	55.50	64.50	71.00	79.50
Foreign current currency translation adjustment	686.00	1,017.00	543.00	348.00	–74.00
Unrealized gain on securities for sale	29.00	107.00	119.00	65.00	24.00
Total share-owners' equity before treasury stock	20,220.50	17,699.50	15,348.50	13,240.00	11,376.50
Less treasury stock, at cost	12,363.50	10,951.00	9,559.50	7,936.00	6,477.00
Total share-owners' equity	7,857.00	6,748.50	5,789.00	5,304.00	4,899.50
Total liabilities and share-owners' equity	$18,042.50	$16,565.50	$15,616.00	$14,302.00	$12,792.00

Cash Flow Data

	1998	1997	1996	1995	1994
Cash flow from operations	$3,433	$4,033	$3,463	$3,328	$3,183
Fixed asset purchases	863	1,093	990	937	682
Cash dividends	1,480	1,387	1,247	1,110	550
Depreciation and amortization	645	626	633	562	411

Market Data

	1998	1997	1996	1995	1994
High market price	$88.90	$72.60	$54.30	$40.20	$26.70
Low market price	$53.60	$50.00	$36.10	$24.40	$19.40
Number of shares outstanding (millions)	2,465.50	2,470.50	2,481.00	2,504.60	2,551.90
Market capitalization	$175,666.88	$151,441.65	$112,141.20	$80,898.58	$58,821.30

Liquidity Ratios

	1998	1997	1996	1995	1994
Working capital	($1,835.00)	($1,438.00)	($1,682.00)	($1,317.00)	($737.00)
Working capital ratio	0.77	0.81	0.77	0.80	0.87
Quick ratio	0.43	0.46	0.43	0.45	0.48
Inventory turnover	6.02	6.30	6.51	6.41	5.88
Days in inventory	60.67	57.98	56.04	56.91	62.03
Accounts receivable turnover	11.38	11.50	11.12	11.39	11.92
Days in accounts receivable	32.06	31.73	32.83	32.06	30.62
Inventory conversion cycle	92.73	89.71	88.87	88.96	92.64
Accounts payable turnover	1.74	1.93	2.22	2.45	2.58
Days in accounts payable	209.67	188.75	164.54	149.02	141.48
Net cash conversion cycle	−116.94	−99.04	−75.68	−60.06	−48.84
Cash + short-term investments	1825.00	1765.50	1501.50	1423.00	1304.50
A/R*days in accounts receivable	52980.71	52030.10	54756.38	50731.03	41530.65
Inventory*days in inventory	56088.74	55401.13	57972.61	61572.66	65004.21
Product dollar days	110894.45	109196.73	114230.49	113726.69	107839.36
Current assets-other current assets	4402.00	4361.00	4204.00	4087.50	3709.00
Liquidity index	25.19	25.04	27.17	27.82	29.08

Cash Flow Ratios

	1998	1997	1996	1995	1994
Cash flow adequacy	1.47	1.63	1.55	1.63	2.58
Reinvestment ratio	0.25	0.27	0.29	0.28	0.21
Dividend payout	0.43	0.34	0.36	0.33	0.17
Free cash flow	$1,090.00	$1,553.00	$1,226.00	$1,281.00	$1,951.00
Depreciation impact ratio	0.19	0.16	0.18	0.17	0.13
Recapitalization index	1.34	1.75	1.56	1.67	1.66
Cash flow return on assets	0.19	0.24	0.22	0.23	0.25
Cash flow return on sales	0.18	0.21	0.19	0.18	0.2
Operations index	0.69	0.81	0.88	0.83	0.86

Asset Utilization Ratios

	1998	1997	1996	1995	1994
Profit margin	18.780%	21.884%	18.829%	16.572%	15.793%
Asset turnover	1.043	1.139	1.188	1.260	1.264
Financial structure leverage	2.296	2.455	2.698	2.696	2.611
Return on assets	19.58%	24.93%	22.36%	20.88%	19.97%
Return on equity	44.97%	61.18%	60.32%	56.30%	52.13%

The Coca-Cola Co. Ratios (continued)

Capital Structure Ratios

	1998	1997	1996	1995	1994
Debt to capital	0.56	0.59	0.63	0.63	0.62
Debt to equity	1.30	1.45	1.70	1.70	1.61
Long-term debt to capital	0.10	0.12	0.14	0.15	0.17
Long-term debt to equity	0.22	0.30	0.38	0.41	0.45
Working capital/total assets-Z1	−0.12	−0.10	−0.13	−0.11	−0.07
Retained earnings/total assets-Z2	1.24	1.21	1.15	1.09	1.07
EBIT/total assets-Z3	0.91	1.00	0.83	0.93	0.96
Sales/total assets-Z4	1.04	1.14	1.19	1.26	1.26
Market to book-Z5	10.35	9.26	6.85	5.39	4.47
Z-Score	13.42	12.50	9.88	8.56	7.69

Market Ratio

	1998	1997	1996	1995	1994
Price to earnings	49.72	36.68	32.11	27.09	23.03

PepsiCo, Inc
Consolidated Statements of Income
(in millions of dollars)

	1998	1997	1996	1995	1994	1993
Net sales	$22,348	$20,917	$20,337	$30,421	$28,472	$25,020
Cost and expenses, net						
Cost of sales	9,329	8,525	8,452	15,406	13,715	11,946
Selling, general, and administrative expenses	9,925	9,241	9,063	11,712	11,244	9,864
Amortization of intangible assets	510	489	782	316	312	303
Operating profit	2,584	2,662	2,040	2,987	3,201	2,907
Interest expense	−395	−478	−565	−682	−581	−573
Interest income	74	125	91	127	90	89
Income before income taxes	2,263	2,309	1,566	2,432	2,710	2,423
Previsions for income tax	−270	−818	−624	-826	−880	−835
Post employment benefits					−55	
Pension assets					−23	
Income from continuing operation	1,993	1,491	942	1,606	1,752	1,588
Income from discontinuing operations, net of tax	—	651	207	—	—	—
Net income (loss)	$1,993	$2,142	$1,149	$1,606	$1,752	$1,588
Basic earnings per share	$1.35	$1.40	$0.73	$1.24	$1.10	$1.00

Vertical Common Size

	1998	1997	1996	1995	1994	1993
Net sales	100.0%	100.0%	100.0%	100.0%	100.0%	100.0%
Cost and expenses, net						
Cost of sales	41.7%	40.8%	41.6%	50.6%	48.2%	47.7%
Selling, general, and administrative expenses	44.4%	44.2%	44.6%	38.5%	39.5%	39.4%
Amortization of intangible assets	2.3%	2.3%	3.8%	1.0%	1.1%	1.2%
Operating profit	11.6%	12.7%	10.0%	9.8%	11.2%	11.6%
Interest expense	−1.8%	−2.3%	−2.8%	−2.2%	−2.0%	−2.3%
Interest income	0.3%	0.6%	0.4%	0.4%	0.3%	0.4%
Income before income taxes	10.1%	11.0%	7.7%	8.0%	9.5%	9.7%
Previsions for income tax	−1.2%	−3.9%	−3.1%	−2.7%	−3.1%	−3.3%
Post employment benefits	0.0%	0.0%	0.0%	0.0%	−0.2%	0.0%
Pension assets	0.0%	0.0%	0.0%	0.0%	−0.1%	0.0%
Income from continuing operation	8.9%	7.1%	4.6%	5.3%	6.2%	6.3%
Income from discontinuing operations, net of tax	0.0%	3.1%	1.0%	0.0%	0.0%	0.0%
Net income (loss)	8.9%	10.2%	5.6%	5.3%	6.2%	6.3%

Horizontal Common Size—1993 Base Year

	1998	1997	1996	1995	1994	1993
Net sales	89.3%	83.6%	81.3%	121.6%	113.8%	100.0%
Cost and expenses, net						
Cost of sales	78.1%	71.4%	70.8%	129.0%	114.8%	100.0%
Selling, general, and administrative expenses	100.6%	93.7%	91.9%	118.7%	114.0%	100.0%
Amortization of intangible assets	168.3%	161.4%	258.1%	104.3%	103.0%	100.0%
Operating profit	88.9%	91.6%	70.2%	102.8%	110.1%	100.0%
Interest expense	68.9%	83.4%	98.6%	119.0%	101.4%	100.0%
Interest income	83.1%	140.4%	102.2%	142.7%	101.1%	100.0%
Income before income taxes	93.4%	95.3%	64.6%	100.4%	111.8%	100.0%
Previsions for income tax	32.3%	98.0%	74.7%	98.9%	105.4%	100.0%
Post employment benefits						
Pension assets						
Income from continuing operation	125.5%	93.9%	59.3%	101.1%	110.3%	100.0%
Income from discontinuing operations, net of tax						
Net income (loss)	125.5%	134.9%	72.4%	101.1%	110.3%	100.0%

Horizontal Common Size—Rolling Forward

	1998	1997	1996	1995	1994	1993
Net sales	106.8%	102.9%	66.9%	106.8%	113.8%	100.0%
Cost and expenses, net						
Cost of sales	109.4%	100.9%	54.9%	112.3%	114.8%	100.0%
Selling, general, and administrative expenses	107.4%	102.0%	77.4%	104.2%	114.0%	100.0%
Amortization of intangible assets	104.3%	62.5%	247.5%	101.3%	103.0%	100.0%
Operating profit	97.1%	130.5%	68.3%	93.3%	110.1%	100.0%
Interest expense	82.6%	84.6%	82.8%	117.4%	101.4%	100.0%
Interest income	59.2%	137.4%	71.7%	141.1%	101.1%	100.0%
Income before income taxes	98.0%	147.4%	64.4%	89.7%	111.8%	100.0%
Previsions for income tax	33.0%	131.1%	75.5%	93.9%	105.4%	100.0%
Post employment benefits						
Pension assets						
Income from continuing operation	133.7%	158.3%	58.7%	91.7%	110.3%	100.0%
Income from discontinuing operations, net of tax						
Net income (loss)	93.0%	186.4%	71.5%	91.7%	110.3%	100.0%

Compound Annual Growth Rate

	1993	1994	1995	1996	1997	1998	Growth
Net sales	($25,020)	0	0	0	0	$22,348	−2.2%
Cost and expenses, net							
Cost of sales	−11,946	0	0	0	0	9,329	−4.8%
Selling, general, and administrative expenses	−9,864	0	0	0	0	9,925	0.1%
Amortization of intangible assets	−303	0	0	0	0	510	11.0%
Operating profit	−2,907	0	0	0	0	2,584	−2.3%
Interest expense	573	0	0	0	0	−395	−7.2%
Interest income	−89	0	0	0	0	74	−3.6%
Income before income taxes	−2,423	0	0	0	0	2,263	−1.4%
Previsions for income tax	835	0	0	0	0	−270	−20.2%
Post employment benefits	—	0	0	0	0		
Pension assets	—	0	0	0	0		
Income from continuing operation	−1,588	0	0	0	0	1,993	4.6%
Income from discontinuing operations, net of tax	—	0	0	0	0	—	
Net income (loss)	−1,588	0	0	0	0	1,993	4.6%

PepsiCo, Inc.
Consolidated Balance Sheets
(in millions of dollars)

	1998	1997	1996	1995	1994	1993
Assets						
Current						
Cash and cash equivalents	$311	$1,928	$447	$382	$331	$227
Short-term investments, at cost	83	955	339	1,116	1,157	1,629
Total cash and securities	394	2,883	786	1,498	1,488	1,856
Trade accounts receivable, net	2,453	2,150	2,516	2,407	2,051	1,883
Inventories	1,016	732	1,038	1,051	970	925
Prepaid expenses and other assets	499	486	799	590	563	500
Total current assets	4,362	6,251	5,139	5,546	5,072	5,164
Property, plant, and equipment						
Total property, plant, and equipment, net	7,318	6,261	10,191	9,870	9,883	8,855
Intangible assets	8,996	5,855	7,136	7,584	7,842	7,929
Investments in unconsolidated affiliates	1,396	1,201	1,375	1,635	1,295	1,756
Other assets	588	533	671	797	700	
Total assets	$22,660	$20,101	$24,512	$25,432	$24,792	$23,704
Liabilities and Share-Owners' Equity						
Current						
Short term borrowings	$3,921	$—	$26	$706	$678	$2,191
Accounts payable and accrued expenses	3,870	3,617	4,626	4,137	3,920	3,559
Income taxes payable	123	640	487	387	672	823
Total current liabilities	7,914	4,257	5,139	5,230	5,270	6,573
Long-term debt	4,028	4,946	8,439	8,509	8,840	7,443
Other liabilities	2,314	2,265	2,533	2,495	912	1,342
Deferred income taxes	2,003	1,697	1,778	1,885	1,973	2,007
Total long-term liabilities	8,345	8,908	12,750	12,889	11,725	10,792
Total liabilities	$16,259	$13,165	$17,889	$18,119	$16,995	$17,365
Share-Owners' Equity						
Capital stock	29	29	29	14	14	14
Capital in excess of par	1,166	1,314	1,201	1,060	934	879
Retained earnings	11,741	10,579	8,416	7,922	8,210	6,358
Total share-owners' equity before treasury stock	12,936	11,922	9,646	8,996	9,158	7,251
Less treasury stock, at cost	6,535	4,986	3,023	1,683	1,361	912
Total share-owners' equity	6,401	6,936	6,623	7,313	7,797	6,339
Total liabilities and share-owners' equity	$22,660	$20,101	$24,512	$25,432	$24,792	$23,704

PepsiCo, Inc.
Consolidated Balance Sheets
(in millions of dollars)
(continued)

Vertical Common Size

	1998	1997	1996	1995	1994	1993
Assets						
Current						
Cash and cash equivalents	1.4%	9.6%	1.8%	1.5%	1.3%	1.0%
Short-term investments, at cost	0.4%	4.8%	1.4%	4.4%	4.7%	6.9%
Total cash and securities	1.7%	14.3%	3.2%	5.9%	6.0%	7.8%
Trade accounts receivable, net	10.8%	10.7%	10.3%	9.5%	8.3%	7.9%
Inventories	4.5%	3.6%	4.2%	4.1%	3.9%	3.9%
Prepaid expenses and other assets	2.2%	2.4%	3.3%	2.3%	2.3%	2.1%
Total current assets	19.2%	31.1%	21.0%	21.8%	20.5%	21.8%
Property, plant, and equipment						
Total property, plant, and equipment, net	32.3%	31.1%	41.6%	38.8%	39.9%	37.4%
Intangible assets	39.7%	29.1%	29.1%	29.8%	31.6%	33.5%
Investments in unconsolidated affiliates	6.2%	6.0%	5.6%	6.4%	5.2%	7.4%
Other assets	2.6%	2.7%	2.7%	3.1%	2.8%	0.0%
Total assets	100.0%	100.0%	100.0%	100.0%	100.0%	100.0%
Liabilities and Share-Owners' Equity						
Current						
Short term borrowings	17.3%	0.0%	0.1%	2.8%	2.7%	9.2%
Accounts payable and accrued expenses	17.1%	18.0%	18.9%	16.3%	15.8%	15.0%
Income taxes payable	0.5%	3.2%	2.0%	1.5%	2.7%	3.5%
Total current liabilities	34.9%	21.2%	21.0%	20.6%	21.3%	27.7%
Long-term debt	17.8%	24.6%	34.4%	33.5%	35.7%	31.4%
Other liabilities	10.2%	11.3%	10.3%	9.8%	3.7%	5.7%
Deferred income taxes	8.8%	8.4%	7.3%	7.4%	8.0%	8.5%
Total long-term liabilities	36.8%	44.3%	52.0%	50.7%	47.3%	45.5%
Total liabilities	71.8%	65.5%	73.0%	71.2%	68.6%	73.3%
Share-owners' equity						
Capital stock	0.1%	0.1%	0.1%	0.1%	0.1%	0.1%
Capital in excess of par	5.1%	6.5%	4.9%	4.2%	3.8%	3.7%
Retained earnings	51.8%	52.6%	34.3%	31.1%	33.1%	26.8%
Total share-owners' equity before treasury stock	57.1%	59.3%	39.4%	35.4%	36.9%	30.6%
Less treasury stock, at cost	28.8%	24.8%	12.3%	6.6%	5.5%	3.8%
Total share-owners' equity	28.2%	34.5%	27.0%	28.8%	31.4%	26.7%
Total liabilities and share-owners' equity	100.0%	100.0%	100.0%	100.0%	100.0%	100.0%

Horizontal Common Size—1993 Base Year

	1998	1997	1996	1995	1994	1993
Assets						
Current						
Cash and cash equivalents	137.0%	849.3%	196.9%	168.3%	145.8%	100.0%
Short-term investments, at cost	5.1%	58.6%	20.8%	68.5%	71.0%	100.0%
Total cash and securities	21.2%	155.3%	42.3%	80.7%	80.2%	100.0%
Trade accounts receivable, net	130.3%	114.2%	133.6%	127.8%	108.9%	100.0%
Inventories	109.8%	79.1%	112.2%	113.6%	104.9%	100.0%
Prepaid expenses and other assets	99.8%	97.2%	159.8%	118.0%	112.6%	100.0%
Total current assets	84.5%	121.0%	99.5%	107.4%	98.2%	100.0%
Property, plant, and equipment						
Total property, plant, and equipment, net	82.6%	70.7%	115.1%	111.5%	111.6%	100.0%
Intangible assets	113.5%	73.8%	90.0%	95.6%	98.9%	100.0%
Investments in unconsolidated affiliates	79.5%	68.4%	78.3%	93.1%	73.7%	100.0%
Other assets						
Total assets	95.6%	84.8%	103.4%	107.3%	104.6%	100.0%
Liabilities and Share-Owners' Equity						
Current						
Short term borrowings	179.0%	0.0%	1.2%	32.2%	30.9%	100.0%
Accounts payable and accrued expenses	108.7%	101.6%	130.0%	116.2%	110.1%	100.0%
Income taxes payable	14.9%	77.8%	59.2%	47.0%	81.7%	100.0%
Total current liabilities	120.4%	64.8%	78.2%	79.6%	80.2%	100.0%
Long-term debt	54.1%	66.5%	113.4%	114.3%	118.8%	100.0%
Other liabilities	172.4%	168.8%	188.7%	185.9%	68.0%	100.0%
Deferred income taxes	99.8%	84.6%	88.6%	93.9%	98.3%	100.0%
Total long-term liabilities	77.3%	82.5%	118.1%	119.4%	108.6%	100.0%
Total liabilities	93.6%	75.8%	103.0%	104.3%	97.9%	100.0%
Share-Owners' Equity						
Capital stock	207.1%	207.1%	207.1%	100.0%	100.0%	100.0%
Capital in excess of par	132.7%	149.5%	136.6%	120.6%	106.3%	100.0%
Retained earnings	184.7%	166.4%	132.4%	124.6%	129.1%	100.0%
Total share-owners' equity before treasury stock	178.4%	164.4%	133.0%	124.1%	126.3%	100.0%
Less treasury stock, at cost	716.6%	546.7%	331.5%	184.5%	149.2%	100.0%
Total share-owners' equity	101.0%	109.4%	104.5%	115.4%	123.0%	100.0%
Total liabilities and share-owners' equity	95.6%	84.8%	103.4%	107.3%	104.6%	100.0%

Horizontal Common Size—Rolling Forward

	1998	1997	1996	1995	1994	1993
Assets						
Current						
Cash and cash equivalents	16.1%	431.3%	117.0%	115.4%	145.8%	100.0%
Short-term investments, at cost	8.7%	281.7%	30.4%	96.5%	71.0%	100.0%
Total cash and securities	13.7%	366.8%	52.5%	100.7%	80.2%	100.0%
Trade accounts Receivable, net	114.1%	85.5%	104.5%	117.4%	108.9%	100.0%
Inventories	138.8%	70.5%	98.8%	108.4%	104.9%	100.0%
Prepaid expenses and other assets	102.7%	60.8%	135.4%	104.8%	112.6%	100.0%
Total current assets	69.8%	121.6%	92.7%	109.3%	98.2%	100.0%
Property, plant, and equipment						
Total property, plant and equipment, net	116.9%	61.4%	103.3%	99.9%	111.6%	100.0%
Intangible assets	153.6%	82.0%	94.1%	96.7%	98.9%	100.0%
Investments in unconsolidated affiliates	116.2%	87.3%	84.1%	126.3%	73.7%	100.0%
Other assets						
Total assets	112.7%	82.0%	96.4%	102.6%	104.6%	100.0%
Liabilities and Share-Owners' Equity						
Current						
Short term borrowings		0.0%	3.7%	104.1%	30.9%	100.0%
Accounts payable and accrued expenses	107.0%	78.2%	111.8%	105.5%	110.1%	100.0%
Income taxes payable	19.2%	131.4%	125.8%	57.6%	81.7%	100.0%
Total current liabilities	185.9%	82.8%	98.3%	99.2%	80.2%	100.0%
Long-term debt	81.4%	58.6%	99.2%	96.3%	118.8%	100.0%
Other liabilities	102.2%	89.4%	101.5%	273.6%	68.0%	100.0%
Deferred income taxes	118.0%	95.4%	94.3%	95.5%	98.3%	100.0%
Total long-term liabilities	93.7%	69.9%	98.9%	109.9%	108.6%	100.0%
Total liabilities	123.5%	73.6%	98.7%	106.6%	97.9%	100.0%
Share-Owners' Equity						
Capital stock	100.0%	100.0%	207.1%	100.0%	100.0%	100.0%
Capital in excess of par	88.7%	109.4%	113.3%	113.5%	106.3%	100.0%
Retained earnings	111.0%	125.7%	106.2%	96.5%	129.1%	100.0%
Total share-owners' equity before treasury stock	108.5%	123.6%	107.2%	98.2%	126.3%	100.0%
Less treasury stock, at cost	131.1%	164.9%	179.6%	123.7%	149.2%	100.0%
Total share-owners' equity	92.3%	104.7%	90.6%	93.8%	123.0%	100.0%
Total liabilities and share-owners' equity	112.7%	82.0%	96.4%	102.6%	104.6%	100.0%

Compound Annual Growth Rate

	1993	1994	1995	1996	1997	1998	Growth
Assets							
Current							
Cash and cash equivalents	–$227	—	—	—	—	$311	6.5%
Short-term investments, at cost	–1,629	—	—	—	—	83	
Total cash and securities	–1,856	—	—	—	—	394	
Trade accounts receivable, net	–1,883	—	—	—	—	2,453	5.4%
Inventories	-925	—	—	—	—	1,016	1.9%
Prepaid expenses and other assets	-500	—	—	—	—	499	0.0%
Total current assets	–5,164	—	—	—	—	4,362	–3.3%
Property, plant, and equipment							
Total property, plant, and equipment, net	–8,855	—	—	—	—	7,318	–3.7%
Intangible assets	–7,929	—	—	—	—	8,996	2.6%
Investments in unconsolidated affiliates	–1,756	—	—	—	—	1,396	–4.5%
Other assets	—	—	—	—	—	588	
Total assets	–23,704	—	—	—	—	22,660	–0.9%
Liabilities and Share-Owners' Equity							
Current							
Short term borrowings	–2,191	—	—	—	—	3,921	12.3%
Accounts payable and accrued expenses	–3,559	—	—	—	—	3,870	1.7%
Income taxes payable	–823	—	—	—	—	123	
Total current liabilities	–6,573	—	—	—	—	7,914	3.8%
Long-term debt	–7,443	—	—	—	—	4,028	–11.6%
Other liabilities	–1,342	—	—	—	—	2,314	11.5%
Deferred income taxes	–2,007	—	—	—	—	2,003	0.0%
Total long-term liabilities	–10,792	—	—	—	—	8,345	–5.0%
Total liabilities	–17,365	—	—	—	—	16,259	–1.3%
Share-owners' equity	—	—	—	—	—		
Capital stock	–14	—	—	—	—	29	15.7%
Capital in excess of par	–879	—	—	—	—	1,166	5.8%
Retained earnings	–6,358	—	—	—	—	11,741	13.1%
Total share-owners' equity before treasury stock	–7,251	—	—	—	—	12,936	12.3%
Less treasury stock, at cost	–912	—	—	—	—	6,535	48.3%
Total share-owners' equity	–6,339	—	—	—	—	6,401	0.2%
Total liabilities and share-owners' equity	–23,704	—	—	—	—	22,660	–0.9%

PepsiCo
Condensed Statements of Cash
Flows (in millions of dollars)

	1998	1997	1996	1995	1994
Net income	$1,993	$2,142	$1,149	$1,606	$1,752
Depreciation expense	1,234	1,106	1,073	1,046	1,566
Other adjustments to operations	−16	171	970	1,090	398
Cash flows from operating activities	3,211	3,419	3,192	3,742	3,716
Purchase of property, plant, and equipment	−1,405	−1,506	−1,630	−1,365	−2,253
Other adjustments to investing activities	−3,614	−564	576	−1,085	−108
Cash flows from investing activities	−5,019	−2,070	−1,054	−2,450	−2,361
Dividends	−751	−731	−675	−599	−540
Other adjustments to financing activities	941	−5,231	−2,041	−634	700
Cash flows from financing activities	190	−5,962	−2,716	−1,233	−1,240
Discontinued operations adjustment	1	6,094	643	−8	−11
Net change in cash	$−1,617	$1,481	$ 65	$ 51	$104

PepsiCo, Inc
Consolidated Statements
of Income
(in millions of dollars)

	1998	1997	1996	1995	1994
Net sales	$22,348	$20,917	$20,337	$30,421	$28,472
Cost and expenses, net					
Cost of sales	9,329	8,525	8,452	15,406	13,715
Selling, general, and administrative expenses	9,925	9,241	9,063	11,712	11,244
Amortization of intangible assets	510	489	782	316	312
Operating profit	2,584	2,662	2,040	2,987	3,201
Interest expense	−395	−478	−565	−682	−581
Interest income	74	125	91	127	90
Income before income taxes	2,263	2,309	1,566	2,432	2,710
Previsions for income tax	−270	-818	−624	−826	−880
Post employment benefits					−55
Pension assets					−23
Income from continuing operation	1,993	1,491	942	1,606	1,752
Income from discontinuing operations, net of tax	—	651	207	—	—
Net income (loss)	$1,993	$2,142	$1,149	$1,606	$1,752

	1998	1997	1996	1995	1994
Assets					
Current					
Cash and cash equivalents	$1,119.50	$1,187.50	$414.50	$356.50	$279.00
Short-term investments, at cost	519.00	647.00	727.50	1,136.50	1,393.00
Total cash and securities	1,638.50	1,834.50	1,142.00	1,493.00	1,672.00
Trade accounts receivable, net	2,301.50	2,333.00	2,461.50	2,229.00	1,967.00
Inventories	874.00	885.00	1,044.50	1,010.50	947.50
Prepaid expenses and other assets	492.50	642.50	694.50	576.50	531.50
Total current assets	5,306.50	5,695.00	5,342.50	5,309.00	5,118.00
Property, plant, and equipment					
Total property, plant, and equipment, net	6,789.50	8,226.00	10,030.50	9,876.50	9,369.00
Intangible assets	7,425.50	6,495.50	7,360.00	7,713.00	7,885.50
Investments in unconsolidated affiliates	1,298.50	1,288.00	1,505.00	1,465.00	1,525.50
Other assets	560.50	602.00	734.00	748.50	350.00
Total assets	$21,380.50	$22,306.50	$24,972.00	$25,112.00	$24,248.00
Liabilities and Share-Owners' Equity					
Current					
Short term borrowings	$1,960.50	$13.00	$366.00	$692.00	$1,434.50
Accounts payable and accrued expenses	3,743.50	4,121.50	4,381.50	4,028.50	3,739.50
Income taxes payable	381.50	563.50	437.00	529.50	747.50
Total current liabilities	6,085.50	4,698.00	5,184.50	5,250.00	5,921.50
Long-term debt	4,487.00	6,692.50	8,474.00	8,674.50	8,141.50
Other liabilities	2,289.50	2,399.00	2,514.00	1,703.50	1,127.00
Deferred income taxes	1,850.00	1,737.50	1,831.50	1,929.00	1,990.00
Total long-term liabilities	8,626.50	10,829.00	12,819.50	12,307.00	11,258.50
Total liabilities	14,712.00	15,527.00	18,004.00	17,557.00	17,180.00
Share-owners' equity					
Capital stock	29.00	29.00	21.50	14.00	14.00
Capital in excess of par	1,240.00	1,257.50	1,130.50	997.00	906.50
Retained earnings	11,160.00	9,497.50	8,169.00	8,066.00	7,284.00
Total share-owners' equity before treasury stock	12,429.00	10,784.00	9,321.00	9,077.00	8,204.50
Less treasury stock, at cost	5,760.50	4,004.50	2,353.00	1,522.00	1,136.50
Total share-owners' equity	6,668.50	6,779.50	6,968.00	7,555.00	7,068.00
Total liabilities and share-owners' equity	$21,380.50	$22,306.50	$24,972.00	$25,112.00	$24,248.00

Cash Flow Data

	1998	1997	1996	1995	1994
Cash flow from operations	$3,211	$3,419	$3,192	$3,742	$3,716
Fixed asset purchases	1,405	1,506	1,630	1,365	2,253
Cash dividends	751	731	675	599	540
Depreciation and amortization	1,234	1,106	1,073	1,046	1,566

Market Data

	1998	1997	1996	1995	1994
High market price	$44.80	$41.30	$35.90	$29.40	$20.60
Low market price	$27.60	$28.30	$27.30	$16.90	$14.60
Number of shares outstanding (millions)	1,471.00	1,502.00	1,545.00	1,576.00	1,579.80
Market capitalization	$53,250.20	$52,269.60	$48,822.00	$36,484.40	$27,804.48

PepsiCo, Inc Ratios

PepsiCo Liquidity Ratios

	1998	1997	1996	1995	1994
Working capital	($779.00)	$997.00	$158.00	$59.00	($803.50)
Working capital ratio	0.87	1.21	1.03	1.01	0.86
Quick ratio	0.65	0.89	0.70	0.71	0.61
Inventory turnover	10.67	9.63	8.09	15.25	14.47
Days in inventory	34.20	37.89	45.11	23.94	25.22
Accounts receivable turnover	9.71	8.97	8.26	13.65	14.47
Days in accounts receivable	37.59	40.71	44.18	26.74	25.22
Inventory conversion cycle	71.78	78.60	89.28	50.69	50.43
Accounts payable turnover	2.49	2.07	1.93	3.82	3.67
Days in accounts payable	146.47	176.46	189.22	95.44	99.52
Net cash conversion cycle	−74.68	−97.86	−99.93	−44.76	−49.09
Cash + short-term investments	1638.50	1834.50	1142.00	1493.00	1672.00
A/R*days in accounts receivable	86511.96	94977.98	108744.09	59612.8	49600.22
Inventory*days in inventory	29886.88	33533.97	47114.03	24192.21	23892.16
Product dollar days	118037.35	130346.46	157000.12	85298.01	75164.38
Current assets-other current assets	4814.00	5052.50	4648.00	4732.50	4586.50
Liquidity index	24.52	25.80	33.78	18.02	16.39

Cash Flow Ratios

	1998	1997	1996	1995	1994
Cash flow adequacy	1.49	1.53	1.38	1.91	1.33
Reinvestment ratio	0.44	0.44	0.51	0.36	0.61
Dividend payout	0.23	0.21	0.21	0.16	0.15
Free cash flow	$1,055	$1,182	887	$1,778	923
Depreciation impact ratio	0.38	0.32	0.34	0.28	0.42
Recapitalization index	1.14	1.36	1.52	1.30	1.44
Cash flow return on assets	0.15	0.15	0.13	0.15	0.15
Cash flow return on sales	0.14	0.16	0.16	0.12	0.13
Operations index	1.24	1.28	1.56	1.25	1.16

Asset Utilization Ratios

	1998	1997	1996	1995	1994
Profit margin	8.918%	10.240%	5.650%	5.279%	6.153%
Asset turnover	1.045	0.938	0.814	1.211	1.174
Financial structure leverage	3.206	3.29	3.584	3.324	3.431
Return on assets	9.32%	9.60%	4.60%	6.40%	7.23%
Return on equity	29.89%	31.60%	16.49%	21.26%	24.79%

Capital Structure Ratios

	1998	1997	1996	1995	1994
Debt to capital	0.69	0.70	0.72	0.70	0.71
Debt to equity	2.21	2.29	2.58	2.32	2.43
Long-term debt to capital	0.32	0.41	0.44	0.41	0.38
Long-term debt to equity	1.02	1.34	1.58	1.37	1.31
Working capital/total assets-Z1	−0.04	0.05	0.01	0.00	−0.04
Retained earnings/total assets-Z2	0.73	0.60	0.46	0.45	0.42
EBIT/total assets-Z3	0.40	0.39	0.27	0.39	0.44
Sales/total assets-Z4	1.05	0.94	0.81	1.21	1.17
Market to book-Z5	2.17	2.02	1.63	1.25	0.97
Z-Score	4.30	4.00	3.18	3.30	2.96

Market Ratio

	1998	1997	1996	1995	1994
Price to earnings	26.72	24.40	42.49	22.72	15.87

COMPENDIUM OF FINANCIAL ANALYSIS MEASURES

SHORT-TERM LIQUIDITY ANALYSIS MEASURES

Working capital = average current assets − average current liabilities

$$\text{Current (working capital) ratio} = \frac{\text{average current assets}}{\text{average current liabilities}}$$

$$\text{Quick (acid-test) ratio} = \frac{\text{average cash + average short-term investments + average accounts receivable}}{\text{average current liabilities}}$$

$$\text{Inventory turnover} = \frac{\text{cost of goods sold}}{\text{average inventory}}$$

$$\text{Number of days in inventory} = \frac{365 \text{ days}}{\text{inventory turnover}}$$

$$\text{Accounts receivable turnover} = \frac{\text{credit revenues}}{\text{average net accounts receivable}}$$

$$\text{Number of days in accounts receivable} = \frac{365 \text{ days}}{\text{accounts receivable turnover}}$$

Inventory conversion cycle = number of days in inventory + number of days in accounts receivable

$$\text{Accounts payable turnover} = \frac{\text{cost of goods sold}}{\text{average accounts payable}}$$

$$\text{Number of days in accounts payable} = \frac{365 \text{ days}}{\text{accounts payable turnover}}$$

Net cash conversion cycle = number of days in inventory + number of days in accounts receivable − number of days in accounts payable

$$\text{Liquidity index} = \frac{\text{total product dollar days}}{\text{current assets} - (\text{prepaid expenses} + \text{other non-cash current assets})}$$

where:

Product dollar days = current asset * number of days removed from cash

$$\text{Accrued liability turnover} = \frac{\text{operating expenses} - \text{depreciation expense}}{\text{average accrued liabilities}}$$

$$\text{Number of days in accrued liabilities} = \frac{365 \text{ days}}{\text{accrued liability turnover}}$$

CASH FLOW ANALYSIS MEASURES

$$\text{Cash flow adequacy} = \frac{\text{cash flow from operation}}{\text{fixed assets purchased} + \text{long-term debt paid} + \text{dividends paid}}$$

$$\text{Reinvestment ratio} = \frac{\text{fixed assets purchased}}{\text{cash flow from operations}}$$

$$\text{Long-term debt repayment ratio} = \frac{\text{long-term debt paid}}{\text{cash flow from operations}}$$

$$\text{Dividend payout ratio} = \frac{\text{cash dividends paid}}{\text{cash flow from operations}}$$

Free cash flows = cash flow from operations − (fixed assets purchased + dividends paid)

$$\text{Depreciation impact ratio} = \frac{\text{depreciation} + \text{amortization expense}}{\text{cash flow from operations}}$$

$$\text{Recapitalization index} = \frac{\text{reinvestment ratio}}{\text{depreciation impact ratio}}$$

$$\text{Cash flow return on assets} = \frac{\text{cash flow from operations}}{\text{average total assets}}$$

$$\text{Cash flow return on sales} = \frac{\text{cash flow from operations}}{\text{revenues}}$$

$$\text{Operations index} = \frac{\text{cash flow from operations}}{\text{income from continuing operations}}$$

OPERATING PERFORMANCE ANALYSIS MEASURES

$$\text{Profit margin} = \frac{\text{income}}{\text{revenues}}$$

$$\text{Gross profit margin} = \frac{\text{gross profit}}{\text{revenues}}$$

$$\text{Operating profit margin} = \frac{\text{income from continuing operations}}{\text{revenues}}$$

$$\text{Net profit margin} = \frac{\text{net income}}{\text{revenues}}$$

$$\text{Basic earnings per share} = \frac{\text{net income} - \text{preferred dividends}}{\text{weighted average number of common shares outstanding}}$$

Diluted earnings per share = basic earnings per share – impact of dilutive securities

ASSET UTILIZATION ANALYSIS

$$\text{Asset turnover} = \frac{\text{revenues}}{\text{average total assets}}$$

$$\text{Return on assets (unadjusted)} = \frac{\text{net income}}{\text{average total assets}}$$

Components of return on assets (unadjusted) = net profit margin * asset turnover

Return on assets (adjusted) = $\dfrac{\text{net income} + [\text{interest expense} * (1 - \text{tax rate})]}{\text{average total assets}}$

Components of return on assets (adjusted) = adjusted net profit margin * asset turnover where:

Adjusted profit margin = $\dfrac{\text{net income} + [\text{interest expense} * (1 - \text{tax rate})]}{\text{revenues}}$

Financial structure leverage ratio = $\dfrac{\text{average total assets}}{\text{average common shareholders' equity}}$

Return on equity (unadjusted) = $\dfrac{\text{net income}}{\text{average common shareholders' equity}}$

Components of return on equity (unadjusted) = profit margin * asset turnover * financial structure leverage ratio

Return on equity (adjusted) = $\dfrac{\text{net income} - \text{current preferred dividends}}{\text{average common shareholders' equity} - \text{preferred dividends in arrears}}$

Components of return on equity (adjusted) = adjusted profit margin * asset turnover * adjusted financial structure leverage ratio where:

Adjusted profit margin = $\dfrac{\text{net income} - \text{preferred dividends}}{\text{revenues}}$

Adjusted financial structure leverage ratio = $\dfrac{\text{average total assets}}{\text{average common shareholders' equity} - \text{preferred dividends in arrears}}$

Fixed asset turnover = $\dfrac{\text{revenues}}{\text{average fixed assets}}$

CAPITAL STRUCTURE ANALYSIS MEASURES

Financial leverage index = $\dfrac{\text{adjusted return on equity}}{\text{adjusted return on assets}}$

Total debt to total capital ratio = $\dfrac{\text{average total liabilities}}{\text{average total assets}}$

Total debt to total equity ratio = $\dfrac{\text{average total liabilities}}{\text{average total shareholders' equity}}$

Long-term debt to total capital ratio = $\dfrac{\text{average long-term liabilities}}{\text{average total assets}}$

Long-term debt to total equity ratio = $\dfrac{\text{average long-term liabilities}}{\text{average total shareholders' equity}}$

Earnings coverage (times interest earned) ratio = $\dfrac{\text{income before interest and taxes}}{\text{interest expense}}$

Z-score = 1.2 (net working capital / total assets) + 1.4 (retained earnings / total assets) + 3.3 (earnings before interest and taxes / total assets) + 1.0 (sales / total assets) + .6 (market value of equity / book value of liabilities)

MARKET VALUE MEASURES

Market capitalization = number of common shares outstanding * market price per share

Price to earnings ratio = $\dfrac{\text{market price per share of stock}}{\text{earnings per share}}$

Price to cash flow ratio = $\dfrac{\text{market price per share of stock}}{\text{operating cash flows per share}}$

Price to book value ratio = $\dfrac{\text{market price per share of stock}}{\text{book value per share}}$

or:

Market to book value ratio = $\dfrac{\text{market capitalization}}{\text{common shareholders' equity}}$

TWO ALTERNATIVE MEANS FOR CONDUCTING ANALYSIS AND CLASSIFYING MEASURES (INCLUDING EXAMPLES)

Alternative 1:	Alternative 2:
Profitability measures—return on assets and return on equity	Profitability measures—return on assets and return on equity
Liquidity measures—current ratio, quick ratio	Asset utilization measures—accounts receivable and inventory turnover
Activity measures—inventory and receivable turnover	Short-term liquidity risk measures—number of days in receivable and inventory
Coverage measures—debt to capital and earnings coverage ratios	Long-term solvency risk measures—debt to capital and earnings coverage ratios

GLOSSARY

accounts payable turnover   Measures the number of times accounts payable are liquidated annually. It is computed as follows: cost of goods sold / average accounts payable. —*See* number of days in accounts payable.

accounts receivable turnover   Measures the number of times accounts receivables are collected annually. This ratio is computed as follows: net credit sales / average net accounts receivable. —*See* number of days in accounts receivables.

accrual accounting   Financial reporting basis that recognizes revenues when earned and expenses when incurred, as opposed to when cash is received and paid. —*See* revenue realization and matching principles.

accrued liability turnover   Measure of the number of times a selling, general, and administrative expense is paid annually. This ratio is computed as follows: operating expenses / average accrued liabilities. —*See* number of days in accrued liabilities.

active investment   Security investment in which an equity investor significantly influences the investee's operations. —*Compare* passive investment.

active minority ownership   Equity investment in another firm where the investor significantly influences but does not control investee operations. —*Compare* majority ownership.

activity ratio   Measures the number of times a current account is liquidated in the normal course of business. —*Also called* turnover ratio.

additional paid in capital   Difference between issue price of stock and its par value. —*Also called* contributed capital in excess of par.

all-inclusive income basis   Disclosure of all revenues, gains, expenses and losses in the income statement, irrespective of how they occurred. —*See* comprehensive income and other comprehensive income.

amount of future cash flows   One of the primary financial statement objectives, according to the Financial Accounting Standards Board. —*See* timing and uncertainty of future cash flows.

annual shareholders report   Annual corporate report sent to shareholders containing financial information and other information. Less objective and comprehensive than Form 10-K. —*Compare* Form 10-K.

articulation   Processes by which financial statements and their accounts relate to one another.

asset   Economic resource controlled by an entity as a result of a past transaction. —*Also called* economic resource or a resource.

asset impairment   Condition where a resource's expected future cash flow is less than its reported book value. The income statement reports losses on impaired assets.

asset turnover   Ratio that measure reports the amount of sales produced by each dollar of assets. Asset turnover is a component of return on assets and return on equity. It is computed as follows: sales revenues / average total assets. —*Also called* asset turn.

asset utilization analysis   Aspect of financial statement analysis that links earnings to invested capital. —*See* capital.

available-for-sale securities   Category of debt security investments that are not classified as either trading or held-to-maturity securities. Management might sell these debt instruments in the short-term or retain them beyond the next reporting period.

back-end loading of an expense   Management's deliberate deferral of an expense, which is undertaken to enhance current income. It is a violation of GAAP's intent and sometimes its standards. —*See* front-end loading revenues.

bad debt   Credit sale that is not collected in cash.

balance sheet   Financial statement that reports the assets, liabilities, and shareholders' equity of an enterprise at a specific date. —*Also called* the statement of financial position. —*See* financial statements.

bankruptcy protection   Legal arrangement in which creditor claims are suspended while a court appointed trustee reorganizes the bankrupt firm. —*Also called* reorganization and Chapter 11 bankruptcy.

bankruptcy risk   Probability that an entity's obligations will exceed its assets and force bankruptcy protection or liquidation. —*See* bankruptcy protection.

basic earnings per share   Earnings per share disclosure for a firm with a simple capital structure. It is computed as follows: (Net income – preferred stock dividends) / Weighted number of outstanding shares of common stock. —*Also called* basic EPS. —*See* simple capital structure. —*Compare* diluted earnings per share.

benchmark   Comparison of corporate disclosures with similar observations from other companies or industry data. Analysts use benchmarking to establish performance rank in an industry.

beta coefficient   Measures the sensitivity of an asset's return to market movements. It is a mathematical measure of the systematic risk of a security. —*Also called* beta. —*See* systematic risk.

book value   Monetary amount of an account reported on a financial statement, often an adjusted historical cost amount. —*See* historical cost.

breakeven point   Level of sales where revenues equal expenses; consequently no profit is earned or loss incurred.

business acquisition   Establishment of economic control by one independent entity over a previously independent enterprise. —*Also called* business consolidation or combination.

business cycle   1. Irregularly recurring cycles of economic expansion, prosperity, contraction, and recession. 2. In forecasting financial statements, the expected sensitivity to changes in the economy. —*Also called* cyclical behavior. —*See* business life cycle, trend, and seasonality.

business life cycle   Organizational phases of existence from inception to demise. —*See* life cycle.

business risk   Fluctuations in earnings and operating cash flows attributable to overall economic and industry-specific conditions that affect all companies.

capital   Any form of wealth used to produce additional wealth, such as total assets or shareholders' equity.

capital expenditure   Expenditure that contributes to revenues in future reporting periods as well as the current one. Costs are initially reported on the balance sheet and expensed on a systematic basis. —*Also called* asset expenditure. —*Compare* revenue expenditure.

capital intensive   Activities, companies, and industries that are dominated by non-human means of production. —*See* fixed cost. —*Compare* labor intensive.

capital maintenance concepts   Alternative theories about what amount of investment must be recovered through revenues before income is earned. Financial statements are based on a specific capital maintenance concept. —*See* nominal dollar concept of capital maintenance.

capital structure   Amount, types, and proportion of an entity's liabilities and shareholders' equity. Current liabilities are often excluded from capital structure considerations.

capital structure analysis   Aspect of financial statement analysis that determines if an entity's combination of debt and equity enables wealth creation without unduly jeopardizing its long-term solvency or financial flexibility. —*See* long-term solvency and financial flexibility.

cash flow adequacy ratio   Primary cash sufficiency ratio, which measures an entity's ability to replenish its productive base, pay long-term debt, and make distributions to owners. This ratio is computed as: cash flow from operations / fixed assets purchased + long-term debt paid + cash dividends distributed. —*See* reinvestment, long-term debt repayment, and dividend payout ratios.

cash flow analysis   Aspect of financial statement analysis that evaluates past events and present conditions to forecast the amount, timing, and probability of future cash receipts and disbursements.

cash flow return on assets ratio   Cash efficiency ratio that measures the amount of operating cash produced per invested dollar. It is computed as follows: operating cash flows / average total assets. —*See* cash flow return on sales ratio.

cash flow return on sales ratio   Cash efficiency ratio that measures the amount of operating cash produced per invested dollar. It is computed as follows: operating cash flows / sales revenues. —*See* cash flow return on assets ratio.

cash flows from financing activities   Section of the statement of cash flows that reports sources, uses, and net cash provided (used) from financing an entity. —*Also called* cash flows from financing, CFFs, financing cash flows, or FCFs.

cash flows from investing activities   Section of the statement of cash flows that reports sources, uses, and net cash provided (used) from productive resource acquisitions and disposals. —*Also called* cash flows from investing, CFIs, investing cash flows, or ICFs.

cash flows from operating activities   Section of the statement of cash flows that reports sources, uses, and net cash provided (used) from central, recurring business activities. —*Also called* cash flows from operations, CFOs, operating cash flows, or OCFs.

cash sufficiency measures   Measures of cash flows that enumerate an entity's ability to compensate investors and maintain productive resources. —*See* cash flow adequacy ratio.

change in accounting principle   switch from one generally accepted accounting principle to another. Gains and losses are separately reported as an irregular item on the income statement. —*See* irregular items.

commercial paper   Unsecured promissory notes exchanged for cash. These obligations are payable within nine months.

common size financial statements   Financial statement disclosures reported as a percentage of another account or as a proportion of that account's previous balance. —*Also called* percentage statements.

common stock   Class of stock representing active business ownership as evidenced by its voting rights. Common stock has no priority claim to earnings or asset distributions. —*Also called* capital stock. —*Compare* preferred stock.

comparability   Financial reporting characteristic in which companies in the same industry use the same accounting methods. —*Compare* consistency.

complex capital structure   capital structure that has potentially dilutive securities such as convertible debt, preferred stock, and options. —*Compare* simple capital structure.

compound annual growth rate   Horizontal common size financial statement method that measures an account's average rate of change over a specified time period as opposed to the base year or rolling forward approaches to horizontal common sizing.

comprehensive income   All wealth changes occurring during a period of time, even those unreported on the income statement. —*See* other comprehensive income.

conservative capital structure   Entity that has a disproportionately small amount of debt financing, which means it is less of a credit risk than a more highly leveraged firm. —*See* credit risk.

consistency   Financial reporting characteristic in which a company uses the same accounting methods from one period to the next. —*Compare* comparability.

consolidated financial statements   Combined financial statements of legally separate corporations that are economically controlled by a single entity. —*Compare* segment disclosures.

consumer price index   Percentage change in average family's cost of living. —*Also called* CPI.

contributed capital   Owners' investment in a business, usually in the form of cash.

controllable cost   Cost that can be controlled or heavily influenced by managerial decisions. —*Also called* discretionary cost. —*Compare* uncontrollable cost.

convertible securities   Debt and equity securities that can be converted into common stock. —*See* complex capital structure.

corporate restructuring   Major realignment of corporate goals that usually results in reported losses on the income statement.

cost   Economic sacrifice made to acquire something of value.

cost of goods sold   The acquisition or manufacturing cost of inventory sold in a reporting period. —*Also called* cost of sales.

credit risk   1. Possibility that a firm will not be able to make interest and principal payments of borrowed funds on time. 2. Pertaining to risk management, gross exposure to an accounting loss if the counter party in a transaction fails to perform according to the agreement.

current asset   Resource that will be converted into cash or consumed within the longer of one year or one operating cycle. Cash, short-term security investments, accounts receivable, inventory, and prepaid expenses are the most prominent current assets. —*Also called* short-term asset. —*Compare* long-term asset.

current liability   Obligation requiring settlement within the longer of one year or one operating cycle. Accounts payable and accrued liabilities are the most prominent current liabilities. —*Also called* short-term liability. —*Compare* long-term liability.

current rate method   Financial reporting method that translates a foreign subsidiary's financial statements at the current exchange rates. —*Compare* temporal method

current ratio   Measure that determines the amount of current assets for each dollar of current liabilities. It is computed as follows: average current assets / average current liabilities. —*Also called* the working capital ratio. —*See* working capital.

debt security   Instrument that indicates a creditor relationship with a firm or governmental agency. Entities purchase debt securities to earn interest income and realize gains on their sale. —*Compare* equity security.

decline   Final stage of the business life cycle. —*See* emergence, growth, and maturity.

decomposition   Mathematical model that statistically values past cyclical, trend, and seasonal behavior to predict future behavior. This information can be used in forecasting financial statements. —*See* statistical forecasting methods.

deferred compensation arrangement   Agreement to provide employees with future benefits for services rendered in the current reporting period.

deferred tax   Financial implication of alternative income views held by GAAP and tax agencies.

deferred tax liability   Increase in future periods' taxes payable resulting from the taxable temporary difference existing at the end of the current period. —*Compare* deferred tax asset.

deferred tax asset   Increase in tax savings or refunds resulting from the deductible temporary difference existing at the end of the current period. —*Compare* deferred tax liability.

defined benefit arrangement   Deferred employee compensation agreement in which a company provides vested employees with specific benefits, regardless of the financial performance of the invested funds. —*See* deferred compensation arrangement. —*Compare* defined contribution arrangement.

defined contribution arrangement   Deferred compensation arrangement in which a company contributes to a pension fund and recognizes an expense based on a predetermined formula, usually a percentage of employees' current earnings. Employee benefits are a function of the fund's performance. —*See* deferred compensation arrangement. —*Compare* defined benefit arrangement.

depreciation impact ratio   Measures the percentage of operating cash flows derived from the periodic cost allocation of long-term assets. It is computed as follows: (depreciation + amortization expenses) / cash from operations. —*See* recapitalization index.

derivative Financial instrument whose value stems from the worth of the another asset to which it is related.

diluted earnings per share Second earnings per share amount that is reported when an entity has securities that could reduce basic earnings per share if those securities were converted into common stock. —*Also called* diluted EPS. —*See* basic earnings per share and dual earnings per share.

direct method of operating cash flows Method of disclosing cash flows from operating activities that reports cash collected from (paid for) various categories of revenues (expenses). —*Also called* the income statement approach.

direct selling Product distribution method involving only a manufacturer and end user, often facilitated by technological advances such as the Internet. For example, personal computer companies increasing sold directly to businesses and home users during the 1990s. —*Compare* indirect selling.

service-based economy Economy in which services increase add value and increase wealth to a greater extent than physical goods do. —*See* new economy.

discontinued operation Cessation and disposal of a significant business segment. Gains and losses are separately reported on the income statement as an irregular item. —*See* irregular items.

discount rate Mathematical mechanism that equates expected cash flows produced by a resource to its present value.

discretionary cash flow Incremental cash flow produced by ongoing business activities. —*See* free cash flows.

disruptive technology Product or process that displaces entrenched ways of conducting business and creating value. For example, the personal computer was a disruptive technology in the 1980s and the Internet became one in the 1990s.

dividend payout ratio Component of cash flow adequacy ratio that measures the proportion of operating cash flows distributed to shareholders. It is computed as follows: dividends paid / cash from operations. —*See* reinvestment and long-term debt repayment ratios.

dividend Income distributed to shareholder, usually in the form of cash. —*Compare* retained earnings.

dividend in arrears Preferred dividend unpaid in previous years. An adjustment is made to common shareholders' equity for it to gain precision in computing return on equity.

dual earnings per share Income statement disclosure of two earnings per share numbers. —*Also called* dual EPS. —*See* basic and diluted earnings per share.

earnings coverage ratio Measures the extent to which operating income is able to meet the fixed charges on borrowed funds. It is computed as follows: operating income before interest and taxes / fixed charges. —*Compare* times interest earned ratio.

earnings management   Disclosure practices designed to present financial results in the most favorable light as opposed to the most economically valid ones.

earnings measurement   Policies and procedures used by an entity to determine income and asset value.

earnings per share   Amount of income earned per share of common stock. —*Also called* EPS. —*See also* basic, diluted, and dual earnings per share.

earnings quality   Analytic assessment of the extent to which reported income disclosures are sustainable and sufficient. —*See* earnings sustainability and sufficiency.

earnings sufficiency   Analytical assessment of the level of operating earnings required to produce acceptable returns on investment. A necessary condition for earnings quality. —*See* earnings quality.

earnings sustainability   Capacity of an enterprise to produce income on a recurring basis. —*See* earnings quality.

economic entity assumption   Financial reporting assumption that discloses the economic activities of an entity, which are separate and distinct entity from those of its owners.

economic sector   Significant portion of economic activity composed of related industries. —*See* industry.

electronic data gathering, analysis, and retrieval system   System of automated collection, validation, indexing, acceptance, and forwarding of submissions by companies who are required by law to file forms with the Securities and Exchange Commission. —*Also called* EDGAR.

emergence   First stage of the business life cycle. —*See* growth, maturity, and decline.

equity investor   Corporate owner who supplies risk capital to an enterprise. One whose wealth increases and decreases as a result of corporate performance. —*Also called* owner, stockholder, shareholder, and shareowner.

equity security   Instrument that demonstrates ownership interest in a company. Entities purchase equity securities in other companies to employ otherwise idle cash, significantly influence an entity's operations, or to acquire control of it. —*Compare* debt security.

European Union   Voluntary union of European countries dedicated to eliminating economic, legal, and tax rule differences among member nations. —*Also called* the EU.

expected exit value   Nondiscounted cash flows expected from the disposal of an asset or settlement of a liability. —*Compare* present value of expected cash flows.

expense   Portion of cost incurred in generating revenues. Viewed another way: Asset decrease or liability increase that occurs from revenue recognition.

exponential smoothing   Mathematical model that uses weighted average of past observations to predict future ones. This information can be used in forecasting financial statements. —*See* statistical forecasting methods.

external financing   Financing provided by owners and creditors to launch and sustain a business. —*Compare* internal financing.

extraordinary item   Unusual and infrequently occurring business event. Gains and losses are separately reported as an irregular item on the income statement. —*See* irregular items.

fiduciary duty   Management's obligation to protect the interests of equity investors. Accomplished by productively and prudently acquiring, controlling, and utilizing economic resources.

Financial Accounting Standards Board   Private sector organization that works in partnership with the Securities and Exchange Commission to establish and improve financial reporting standards in the United States. —*Also called* FASB.

financial distress   Uncertainty about an entity's ability to pay obligations or maintain long-term solvency. —*See* long-term solvency.

financial flexibility   Ability of an organization to take advantage of unexpected opportunities and meet unforeseen obligations because it has available cash or access to it.

financial leverage   Substitution of fixed charged financing (debt and preferred stock) for common equity financing.

financial leverage index   Measure that contrasts the technically adjusted return on equity to that for the return on assets. It is computed as follows: adjusted return on equity / adjusted return on assets. —*Compare* financial structure leverage ratio.

financial revenue   Revenue earned from investing in debt and equity securities of other entities.

financial statement analysis   Art and science of examining corporate financial disclosures and related information in order to make economic decisions. —*Also called* FSA.

financial statement analysis decision model   Systematic method of using financial information to make economic decisions.

financial statement inconsistencies   Of, or related to, differences in financial statement wording, formatting, and disclosures from one reporting period to another or from one company to another.

financial statements   Corporate reports and related notational disclosures that summarize economic activities. —*See* balance sheet, income statement, statement of shareholders' equity, and statement of cash flows.

financial structure leverage ratio Ratio that measures the degree to which asset financing is provided by common shareholders. This ratio is a return on equity component and is computed as follows: average total assets / average common shareholders' equity. —*Compare* financial leverage index.

financing decision Corporate choice pertaining to the amount, timing, and types of debt and equity financing used to obtain resources. —*Compare* investment decision.

financing risk Additional burden that shareholders bear when debt is substituted for equity financing.

first-in, first-out Inventory costing method that assumes the first inventory units available for sale are sold first. —*Also called* FIFO. —*See* last-in, still-here. —*Compare* last-in, first-out.

first-in, still-here Complement of last-in, first-out inventory costing method. Assumes the earliest inventory purchases compose ending inventory. —*Also called* FISH. —*See* last-in, first-out. —*Compare* last-in, still-here.

fixed asset turnover Subset of total asset turnover ratio that measures the productivity of property, plant, equipment, and sometimes intangible assets. It is computed as follows: revenues / average property, plant, equipment, and intangible assets. —*See* asset turnover.

fixed cost Cost that remains constant in the short run regardless of an activity's level, such as sales revenues. —*Compare* variable costs.

foreign direct investments Investment strategy in which a company acquires control of an existing foreign company or establishes a subsidiary in a foreign country to secure raw materials, penetrate new markets, or lower production costs. —*Also called* FDI.

Form 10-K Annual corporate form filed with the Securities and Exchange Commission by publicly traded companies. It contains audited financial statements, notes to the financial statements, and other financial, operational, managerial, and legal information. —*Compare* shareholders' annual report.

Form 10-Q Quarterly corporate form filed with the Securities and Exchange Commission, similar to Form 10-K but less detailed and unaudited.

Form 8-K Form filed with the Securities and Exchange Commission disclosing material corporate events affecting financial condition.

Form S-1 Form filed with the Securities and Exchange Commission listing securities to be traded on a national stock market as well as information about the business.

Form S-4 Form filed with the Securities and Exchange Commission that registers securities used to effect a business combination.

free cash flows Measures net operating cash available to a company after it has maintained its productive capacity and met its obligations to shareholders. It is computed as follows: cash flows from operations – (capital expenditures for capital maintenance + dividends). —*See* cash flow adequacy ratio and discretionary cash flow.

front-end loading of revenue   Management's premature realization of revenue, which is undertaken to enhance current income. It is a violation of GAAP's intent and sometimes their standards. —*See* back-end loading of an expense.

full consolidation   Consolidated financial statement disclosures summarizing all of the economic events of a parent company and its subsidiaries.

functional currency   Currency in which a foreign subsidiary conducts business. The functional currency determines which method is used to translate a foreign subsidiary's financial statements into the parent company's reporting currency. —*See* current rate and temporal methods.

generally accepted accounting principles   Common standards and procedures that govern financial reporting. Determined by authoritative pronouncements and universal acceptance of accounting practices. —*Also called* GAAP.

general-purpose external financial reports   Alternative definition of the financial statements that captures the intent of corporate disclosures to meet the needs of a broad group of interested parties including investors, creditors, and regulators. —*See* financial statements.

going concern   Financial reporting assumption that assumes an entity will continue normal business operations indefinitely into the future.

goodwill   Difference between the cost of an acquired company and the fair market value of its identifiable assets. —*See* purchase method of accounting.

gross domestic product   Output of goods and services produced by an economy, usually reported on an annual basis. —*Also called* GDP.

gross profit   Difference between revenues realized and the cost of goods sold. —*Also called* gross margin or gross profit margin.

gross profit margin   Ratio of gross profit to revenues. —*See* gross profit and profit margin.

growth   Second stage of the business life cycle. —*See* emergence, maturity, and decline.

held-to-maturity debt security   Debt security that a company intends to hold until it matures.

historical cost   Financial reporting principle that requires measurement and disclosure of most assets and liabilities at their historical exchange price. —*See* book value.

historical proceeds   Amount of cash or cash equivalent received at the date of an economic transaction.

horizontal common size financial statements Expression of each financial statement account as a percentage of its previous amount. —*See* compound annual growth rate.

income Extent to which an entity can consume products over time and be as well off at the end of the period as it was at the beginning. —*See* wealth changes.

income from continuing operations before tax Disclosed difference between operating revenues and expenses that sometimes includes aspects of non-operating items, such as interest expense. —*Compare* net income.

income statement Financial statement that reports the results of a company's wealth-seeking activities during a reporting period. —*Also called* profit and loss statement, P&L statement, statement of income, statement of earnings, and the statement of financial performance. —*See* financial statements.

indirect method of operating cash flows Method of disclosing cash flows from operating activities that reports operating cash flows on an income-adjusted basis. —*Also called* the reconciliation approach.

indirect selling Product distribution method employing entities in addition to a manufacturer and end user. For example, personal computer companies originally sold computers to retailers who sold them to the end-users. —*Compare* direct selling.

industry Specific portion or branch of economic activity in which companies offer similar products and pursue common markets. —*See* economic sector.

information overload Amount of data that unnecessarily complicates analysis.

information pyramid Research method that classifies information into economic, industry, and corporate categories.

internal financing Financing provided from cash generated from business operations. —*Compare* external financing.

International Accounting Standards Committee Private sector organization represented by national accountancy bodies that establishes global financial reporting standards and harmonizes accounting standards among countries. —*Also called* IASC.

interperiod Of, or related to, more than one reporting period. —*See* horizontal common size financial statements.

intraperiod Of, or related to, one reporting period. —*See* vertical common size financial statements.

inventory conversion cycle Length of time between inventory acquisition and collection on its sale. This cycle is computed as follows: number of days in inventory + number of days in accounts receivable. —*See* net cash conversion cycle.

inventory turnover   Measures the number of times inventory is sold annually. This ratio is computed as follows: cost of goods sold / average inventory. —*See* number of days in inventory.

investment decision   Managerial choice of an asset acquisition acquired with available funds. —*Compare* financing decision

irregular item   Unusual or infrequently occurring economic event that has a material impact on net income. An irregular item must be reported separately from operating income and on an after tax basis. —*See* discontinued operation, extraordinary item, and change in accounting principle.

judgment   Human decisions about the value information and its implication for analysis.

judgmental forecasting method   Use of informed opinions about relevant and reliable economic, industry, competitor, and corporate information to forecast financial statements. —*Compare* statistical forecasting methods.

labor intensive   Activities, companies, and industries that are dominated by human effort. —*See* variable cost. —*Compare* capital intensive.

last-in, first-out   Inventory costing method that assumes the last units available for sale are sold first. —*Also called* LIFO. —*See* first-in, still-here. —*Compare* first-in, first-out.

last-in, still-here   Complement of first-in, first-out inventory costing method. Assumes the most recent inventory purchases comprise ending inventory. —*Also called* LISH. —*See* first-in, first-out. —*Compare* first-in, still-here.

lease   Contractual arrangement whereby one party, the lessee, pays for the right to use an asset, which is legally controlled by another party, called the lessor.

liability   Future economic sacrifice arising from present obligation as the result of past transaction. —*Also called* economic obligation or an obligation.

life cycle   Progression of a product, company, or industry from inception, through growth, to maturity, and into decline. —*See* business life cycle.

LIFO liquidation   Inventory reductions that match significant amounts of inventory costs from previous periods against current revenues. LIFO liquidation complicates analysis by producing income numbers that are neither representationally faithful nor sustainable.

LIFO reserve   Difference between the last-in, first-out and first-in, first-out inventory costing methods when last-in, first-out is used to report inventory.

line of credit   Prearranged loan from a financial institution, guaranteeing a specified maximum amount of short-term financing.

linear regression   Mathematical model that statistically measures the previous relationship between a dependent variable and one or more independent ones. This information can be used in forecasting financial statements. —*See* statistical forecasting methods.

liquidity   Of, or relating to, the time required for cash conversion.

liquidity index   Measure of an entity's overall degree of current asset liquidity. This ratio is computed as follows: total product dollar days / (current assets – prepaid expenses). —*See* product dollar days.

long-term asset   Resource that will not be converted into cash or consumed within the longer of one year or one operating cycle. Security investments held to maturity, property, plant, equipment, and intangible assets are the most prominent long-term assets. —*Compare* current asset.

long-term creditor   Supplier of funds to an entity, usually for the acquisition of long-term assets. These creditors will have their funds returned sometime after the next year. —*Compare* short-term creditors.

long-term debt payment ratio   Component of cash flow adequacy that measures the percentage of cash used to pay long-term debt maturities. It is computed as follows: long-term debt paid / cash from operations. —*See* reinvestment and dividend payout ratios.

long-term debt to equity   Ratio of long-term liabilities to shareholders' equity. It is computed as follows: average long-term liabilities / average shareholders' equity. —*Compare* total debt to equity.

long-term debt to total capital   Comprehensive measure of capital structure that excludes short-term liquidity factors. It is computed as follows: average long-term liabilities / average total assets. —*Compare* total debt to capital.

long-term liability   Obligation requiring settlement beyond the longer of one year or one operating cycle. Bonds payable and notes payable are the most prominent long-term liabilities. —*Also called* noncurrent liability. —*See* long-term creditor. —*Compare* current liability.

long-term solvency   Analytical assessment as to whether a company can generate sufficient cash flows to pay all of its obligations in the future. —*Compare* to short-term liquidity.

majority ownership   Equity investment in which the investor runs investee operations through its control of a voting majority. —*Compare* active minority ownership.

management approach   Managerially determined processes of defining business segments, which are then reported as segment disclosures. —*See* segment disclosures.

manager   Business professional who attempts to maximize shareholders' wealth in exchange for financial consideration.

manufacturers for hire   Subcontracting manufacturing specialists who make components or assembly products for brand name companies.

market capitalization   Total value of an entity's outstanding shares at a point in time, which reflects the value investors place on a company. It is computed by multiplying the number of common shares outstanding by the share price.

matching principle   Financial reporting principle that requires subtracting the costs incurred in producing revenues in the period those revenues are realized. —*See* accrual accounting.

maturity   Third stage of the business life cycle. —*See* emergence, growth, and decline.

merger and acquisition specialist   Individual who attempts to increase shareholder value through corporate realignment. —*Also called* M&A specialist.

minority interest   Noncontrolling shareholders of a subsidiary company.

multinational enterprise   Entity engaged in significant transnational business activities. —*Also called* MNE, transnational company, or global company.

multiple restructurings   Numerous restructurings reported in a brief period of time, which may indicate poor management decisions or an attempt to conceal recurring expenses as part of corporate realignments.

net cash conversion cycle   Difference between the inventory conversion cycle and the number of days in accounts payable. This cycle is computed as follows: (number of days in inventory + number of days in accounts receivable) – number of days in accounts payable. —*Also called* net merchandising cycle. —*See* inventory conversion cycle.

net income   Disclosed difference between all revenues (gains) and expenses (losses) as reported on the income statement.

net interest expense   Actual cost of borrowed funds. Explicitly considers the tax deductibility feature of interest. Net income is adjusted for net interest expense to gain precision in computing the return on assets. Net interest expense is computed by multiplying interest expense by one minus the tax rate.

net operating loss   Result when tax-deductible expenses exceed taxable revenues.

net profit margin   Ratio of net income to revenues, often used in computing return on investment. —*See* profit margin.

new economy   Economy in which information, knowledge, and technology are the primary means of adding value and creating wealth. —*Compare* old economy.

nominal dollar concept of capital maintenance   Theory that recognizes income when a company recovers more dollars from revenues than it originally invested in the asset sold. This capital maintenance concept underlies the financial reporting system in the United States and throughout most of the world. —*See* capital maintenance concepts.

nonoperating section   Section of the income statement that reports secondary economic events such as gains and losses that changed wealth. —*Compare* operating section.

notes to the financial statements   Disclosures that amplify and clarify the numbers presented in the financial statements. These disclosures consist of words, numbers, and tables that provide additional information about the data contained in the statements themselves. —*Also called* footnotes or notes.

number of days in accounts payable   Measures the average number of days an entity takes to make vendor payment. It is computed as follows: 365 days / accounts payable turnover. —*See* accounts payable turnover.

number of days in accounts receivables   Measures the average length of time required to collect credit sales and is computed as follows: 365 days / accounts receivable turnover. —*See* accounts receivable turnover.

number of days in accrued liabilities   Measures the average length of time an entity takes to pay its accrued obligations. It is computed as follows: 365 days / accrued liability turnover. —*See* accrued liability turnover.

number of days in inventory   Measures the average number of days required to sell inventory and is computed as follows: 365 days / inventory turnover. —*See* inventory turnover.

numerical rounding   Elimination of insignificant numbers from the result of mathematical operation.

observations   Number of data points needed for a valid analysis. Too few observations fail to reveal trends and too many cause information overload.

old economy   Economy in which the manufacture and distribution of tangible goods were the primary creators of value and wealth. —*Also called* industrial economy. —*Compare* new economy.

operating cycle   Length of time needed to convert goods or services into cash through revenue producing activities.

operating cycle efficiency   Favorable cash flow resulting from an advantageous balance sheet account change when compared to the change in its corresponding income statement account. —*Compare* operating cycle inefficiency.

operating cycle inefficiency   Unfavorable cash flow resulting from a disadvantageous balance sheet account change when compared to the change in its corresponding income statement account. —*Compare* operating cycle efficiency.

operating cycle stability   Neutral cash flow when a balance sheet account and its corresponding income statement item change to the same extent. —*See* also operating cycle efficiency and inefficiency.

operating expense Recurring business cost matched to revenue during a reporting period. —*Also called* a selling and administrative expense; selling, general and administrative expense; or S,G&A expense.

operating performance analysis Aspect of financial statement analysis that evaluates the sufficiency and sustainability of an entity's earnings.

operating section Section of the income statement reports the difference between a company's primary sources of revenues and the costs required to produce them. —*Compare* nonoperating section and irregular items.

operations index Cash flow efficiency measure that relates cash from operations to income from continuing operations. It is computed as follows: cash from operations / income from continuing operations. This index provides evidence of earnings quality.

order of liquidity Balance sheet sequence of current asset disclosure based on the accounts' nearness to cash.

other comprehensive income Disclosure of wealth changes that are excluded from net income determination. These economic events are reported as equity changes in the statement of shareholders' equity. —*See* comprehensive income.

over- (under-) funded deferred compensation arrangements Extent to which assets (liabilities) exceed liabilities (assets) in a defined benefit arrangement.

par value Legally mandated minimum selling price of a share of stock. —*Also called* legal capital.

parent company Entity that economically controls another legal entity by controlling a voting majority. —*Compare* subsidiary company.

passive investment Security investment in which the investor does not significantly influence the investee's operations. —*Compare* active investment.

pension trustee Entity that administers a pension plan on behalf of the obligated firm.

period cost Cost treated as an expense in a reporting period as opposed to being matched against the sale of a product. —*Compare* product costs.

preferred stock Class of stock representing passive business ownership as evidenced by lack of voting rights. Preferred stock has a priority claim to earnings and asset distributions over common stock. —*Compare* common stock.

present value of expected exit values Discounted value of cash flows expected from the disposal of an asset or settlement of a liability. —*Compare* expected exit value.

price changes Differences in the cost of goods and services between two reporting periods. —*See* business life cycle, business cycle, and trend.

price to book value ratio Measure that compares investors' assessment of corporate wealth at a particular moment to the firm's reported measure of corporate well being. This ratio is computed as follows: aggregate stock market price / aggregate book value of common equity. —*Compare* price to earnings ratio.

price to cash flow ratio Alternative to the price to earnings ratio. Used when earnings management or quality issues exist. This ratio is computed as follows: market price per share of stock / operating cash flows per share. —*Compare* price to earnings ratio.

price to earnings ratio Measure that reflects investors' expectations about the future performance of a company. It is computed as follows: market price per share of stock / earnings per share. —*Also called* P-E ratio. —*Compare* price to cash flow and price to book value ratios.

pro forma Something's form. —*See* pro forma financial statements.

pro forma financial statements Logically derived forecast of corporate financial statements quantifying an analyst's expectations about operating performance, financial position, and cash flows.

producer price index Percentage change in wholesale prices. —*Also called* PPI.

product cost Inventory-related cost that becomes an expense, called cost of goods sold, when the product is sold. —*Compare* period costs.

product duration Elapsed time in which a product is economically viable. For example, product duration is short in the personal computer industry. —*See* life cycle.

product-dollar days Product of a current asset's account balance multiplied by the number of days required to convert it into cash. —*See* liquidity index.

profit margin Measure of income, however defined, as a percentage of reported revenues. —*See* gross and net profit margins.

proxy statement Corporate report required by the Securities and Exchange Commission accompanying a proxy solicitation, which is the written authority to act on behalf of another individual. It lists the items that a corporation will vote on at its annual meeting including candidates for the Board of Directors, salaries for officers, and the hiring (retention) of an independent auditor.

purchase method of accounting Business acquisition in which one entity acquires control of another in exchange for cash, stock, or debt. This method measures the net assets acquired at the fair value of the consideration given to acquire them. —*See* goodwill.

quick ratio Conservative measure of working capital. This ratio modifies the current ratio by eliminating inventory and prepaid expenses from its numerator and is computed as follows: (cash + short-term investments + accounts receivable) / current liabilities. —*Also called* the acid-test ratio.

randomness   Unpredictable events that cannot be explicitly accounted for or forecast. —*Compare* business cycle, trend, and seasonality.

ratio   Quotient resulting from dividing one financial statement amount by another account's balance.

realized gain (loss)   Gain (loss) reported as a component of net income from non operating business transactions, such as the sale of debt and equity securities. —*Compare* unrealized gain (loss).

realtime   Availability of information as it occurs, often conveyed by a technologically advanced medium.

recapitalization index   Measure of an entity's ability to maintain productivity. It is computed as follows: reinvestment ratio / depreciation impact ratio. —*See* reinvestment and depreciation impact ratios.

reinvestment ratio   Component of cash flow adequacy that measures the amount of operating cash used to replenish productive assets. It is computed as fixed assets purchased / cash from operations. —*See* long-term debt repayment and dividend payout ratios.

relevant information   Qualitative financial reporting characteristic that provides analysts with information about past financial results and helps them forecast future ones. —*Compare* reliable information.

reliable information   Qualitative financial reporting characteristic that contains unbiased and verifiable data. —*Compare* relevant information.

representationally faithful   Financial reporting characteristic in which information disclosures equal economic reality, to the extent possible under GAAP.

retained earnings   Cumulative amount of undistributed income. —*Compare* dividends.

return on assets   Measure that reports the percentage of income earned for each dollar invested in an entity's resources. It is computed as follows: net income / average total assets. This ratio is often analyzed by its components. —*Also called* return on total assets, ROA, and ROTA. —*See* profit margin and asset turnover. —*Compare* return on equity.

return on equity   Measure that reports the percentage of income earned for each dollar invested by an entity's owners. It is computed as follows: net income / average common shareholders' equity. This ratio is often analyzed by its components. —*Also called* return on common equity, return on common shareholders' equity, ROE, ROCE, and ROCSE. —*See* profit margin, asset turnover, and financial leverage structure ratio. —*Compare* return on assets.

return on investment Measures of wealth creation from a given level and type of capital. —*Also called* ROI. —*See* return on assets and equity.

revenue Asset increase or liability decrease during a reporting period resulting from the sale of goods, rendering of services, or other central operating activities.

revenue expenditure Expenditure that produces measurable revenue in the current reporting. It is reported as an expense on the current income statement. —*Compare* capital expenditure.

revenue realization principle Financial reporting principle that recognizes revenues when realized or realizable and earned. Revenues are realized when goods and services are exchanged for cash or claims to cash. They are realizable when assets can be converted into cash in active markets at determinable prices. Revenues are earned when an entity has completed its obligations and is entitled to the benefits represented by the revenues. —*See* accrual accounting.

risk management Strategies and tactics used to reduce the financial exposure of risky transactions. —*See* credit risk.

scaling Disclosure of monetary amounts as a multiple of another number to facilitate comprehension. In the case of financial statements, amounts are usually reported in thousands or millions of dollars.

seasonality 1. Differences in economic activity within a reporting period attributable to time. 2. In financial forecasting, recognition of and compensation for changes in activity levels within one reporting period. —*See* business life cycle, business cycle, and trend.

Securities and Exchange Commission Independent quasi-judicial branch of the federal government empowered by the 1934 Securities Exchange Act to regulate the United States' securities markets. Maintains legal authority to set financial reporting rules and regulations. —*Also called* SEC.

segment disclosures Disaggregated asset, revenue, and income information about diversified companies. Disclosed to provide more information about the business segments that compose total operations of consolidated enterprises. —*Compare* consolidated financial statements.

shareholder wealth maximization Commercial endeavors designed increase share price. The primary objective of every for-profit enterprise.

shareholders' annual report Glossary covered yearly sent to shareholders containing financial statements and corporate information. Less comprehensive and objective than forms filed with the Securities and Exchange Commission. —*Compare* Form 10-K.

shareholders' equity Owners' interest in a business enterprise. It is the residual interest in assets after subtracting liabilities. —*Also called* stockholders' equity or owners' equity.

short-term creditor   Supplier of goods, services, or cash to an enterprise in the normal course of business. These creditors expect payment in the near term, usually within one year. —*Compare* long-term creditor.

short-term liquidity analysis   Aspect of financial statement analysis that measures a firm's ability to pay current obligations with cash generated from current assets.

simple capital structure   Capital structure composed of common stock and, possibly, preferred stock. —*Compare* complex capital structure.

source and information matrix   Table summarizing the contents of information sources.

Standard & Poor's (S&P) 500   Index that measures equity market movements by compiling a weighted average stock price performance of 500 large companies.

statement of cash flows   Financial statement that reports amounts and types of sources, uses, and net change in cash during a reporting period. —*See* financial statements.

statement of shareholders' equity   Financial statement that reports changes in the owners' interest in a business. —*Also called* statement of stockholders' equity, statement of owners' equity, and statement of retained earnings. —*See* financial statements.

statistical forecasting methods   Mathematical procedures used to forecast financial statements. —*See* decomposition, exponential smoothing, and linear regression. —*Compare* judgmental forecasting method.

stock options   Corporate warrants granting certain employees the right to purchase stock at predetermined prices during prescribed time periods.

subsidiary company   Entity economically controlled by another company, despite its independent legal status. —*Compare* parent company.

supplementary information   Additional disclosures that appear in financial statement presentations. This information is not directly part of the financial statements, but it is affected by authoritative financial reporting standards.

systematic risk   Market risk that affects all firms to some degree. This risk cannot be eliminated through diversification. —*Also called* market or nondiversifiable risk. —*See* beta coefficient. —*Compare* unsystematic risk

temporal method   Financial reporting method that remeasures a foreign subsidiary's accounts at either the current exchange rate or an historical one, depending on account classification. —*Compare* current rate method.

temporary difference   Disparity between the book value of an asset or liability as determined by GAAP and its tax basis. —*See* deferred tax liability and asset.

times interest earned ratio   Simplified version of the earnings coverage ratio that substitutes interest expense for fixed charges in the calculation of earnings coverage. This ratio is referred to as the times interest earned ratio because it reports operating earnings as a multiple of interest expense. The times interest earned ratio is computed as follows: operating income before interest and taxes / interest expense. —*Compare* earnings coverage ratio

timing of future cash flows   One of the primary financial statement objectives, according to the Financial Accounting Standards Board. —*See* amount and uncertainty of future cash flows.

total debt to equity   Ratio of liabilities to shareholders' equity. It is computed as follows: average total liabilities / average shareholders' equity. —*Compare* long-term debt to equity.

total debt to total capital   Comprehensive measure of capital structure. It is computed as follows: average total liabilities / average total assets. —*Compare* long-term debt to total capital.

trading security   Debt or equity investment that will be sold in the near future. —*Compare* available-for-sale security.

transaction approach   Basis for income statement disclosures, which summarizes revenue and expense activities that produce wealth changes during a reporting period. —*See* income statement.

trend   1. Economic movement in a specific direction over multiple reporting periods. 2. In time series analysis, the assumption that successive observations time are related. —*See* business life cycle, business cycle, and seasonality.

uncertainty of future cash flows   One of the primary financial statement objectives, according to the Financial Accounting Standards Board. —*See* amount and timing of future cash flows.

uncontrollable cost   Cost that is beyond the control of or cannot be significantly influenced by management in the short run. —*Compare* controllable cost.

unemployment rate   Percentage of employable people who were without jobs during a reporting period.

unrealized gain (loss)   Difference between fair value and previously reported value of a security. These gains and losses are either included as part of net income or as a component of other comprehensive income, depending on applicable GAAP. —*Compare* realized gain (loss).

unsystematic risk   Investment risk that can be eliminated through diversification. —*Also called* diversifiable risk. —*Compare* systematic risk.

valuation   Determination of the cost or price of something for disclosure purposes. —*See* price to earnings ratio.

value Business activities that produce revenues in excess of costs, which cause share prices to increase. —*See* income and wealth.

value gap Difference between a firm's optimal worth and actual value.

variable cost Total cost that changes as activity changes. —*Compare* fixed cost.

venture capital Funding by investment firms that specialize in financing unproven, but potentially very profitable, businesses.

vertical common size financial statement Expression of each financial statement account as a percentage of that statement's largest account balance (revenues in the case of vertical common size income statements and assets for balance sheets).

vetting Process of investigating, evaluating, and examining a subject in a thorough and expert manner.

wealth Amount of goods and services that an entity can consume at a given point in time. —*See* wealth changes.

wealth changes Extent to which the ability to consume goods and services changes over a period of time. —*See* wealth and income.

wintel duopoly Expression for the market domination of Microsoft's Windows operating system and Intel's Pentium microprocessors in the personal computer industry.

working capital Difference between a company's current assets and its current liabilities. —*See* current ratio.

Z-score Statistically derived combination of weighted ratios to predict the likelihood of bankruptcy. It is computed as follows: 1.2 (net working capital / total assets) + 1.4 (retained earnings / total assets) + 3.3 (earnings before interest and taxes / total assets) + 1.0 (sales / total assets) + .6 (market value of equity / book value of liabilities)

INDEX